AutoCAD 2024 A Project-Based Tutorial

Tutorial Books

For Technical Support, contact us at:
online.books999@gmail.com

Table of Contents

Scope of this Book

The AutoCAD 2024 A Project-Based Tutorial book helps users to discover the essential tools and features necessary to use Autodesk AutoCAD in a project-based approach. As the flagship product of Autodesk, AutoCAD is a powerful design and drafting tool used in the CAD industry. Its yearly releases include enhanced features, bug fixes, and new commands, making it an ever-evolving software. With 2D drafting, 3D modeling, drawing management and collaboration tools, 3D rendering capabilities, and cloud-based features, AutoCAD is much more than just a drafting tool. Create 2D drawings, 3D models, and photorealistic renderings with ease.

Explore the tools and commands of Autodesk AutoCAD with this book, using AutoCAD 2024 as our version. However, this guide is applicable to users of all versions of AutoCAD, whether newer or older. Along with the essential commands and toolsets, we also cover the new features of AutoCAD 2024.

The topics covered in this book are as follows:

- Part 1, "Creating 2D Architectural Drawings", helps you to create architectural floor plans and elevations. Also, you learn to add dimensions and annotations, and then print drawings
- Part 2, "Creating 3D Architectural Models", teaches you to create three-dimensional models using the 2D drawings.
- Part 3, "Rendering," teaches you to locate the model on the live map, add materials to the objects, add lights and camera, and then generate photorealistic images. You also learn to prepare the 3D model for 3D printing.

Getting Started with AutoCAD

This chapter covers understanding the user interface, navigating in AutoCAD. To ensure the smooth functioning of Autodesk AutoCAD software, ensure your system meets the minimum hardware requirements for AutoCAD 2024, as recommended by Autodesk. Download the lesson files used in this book by sending us an email to online.books999@gmail.com

AutoCAD's Interface Explained

AutoCAD 2024 has a ribbon at the top with different tabs and panels, just like older versions. You can start the software by clicking on its icon on your computer's desktop or by finding the AutoCAD 2024 - English folder in the Start menu. When you open it, you'll see the Start Screen with some information displayed.

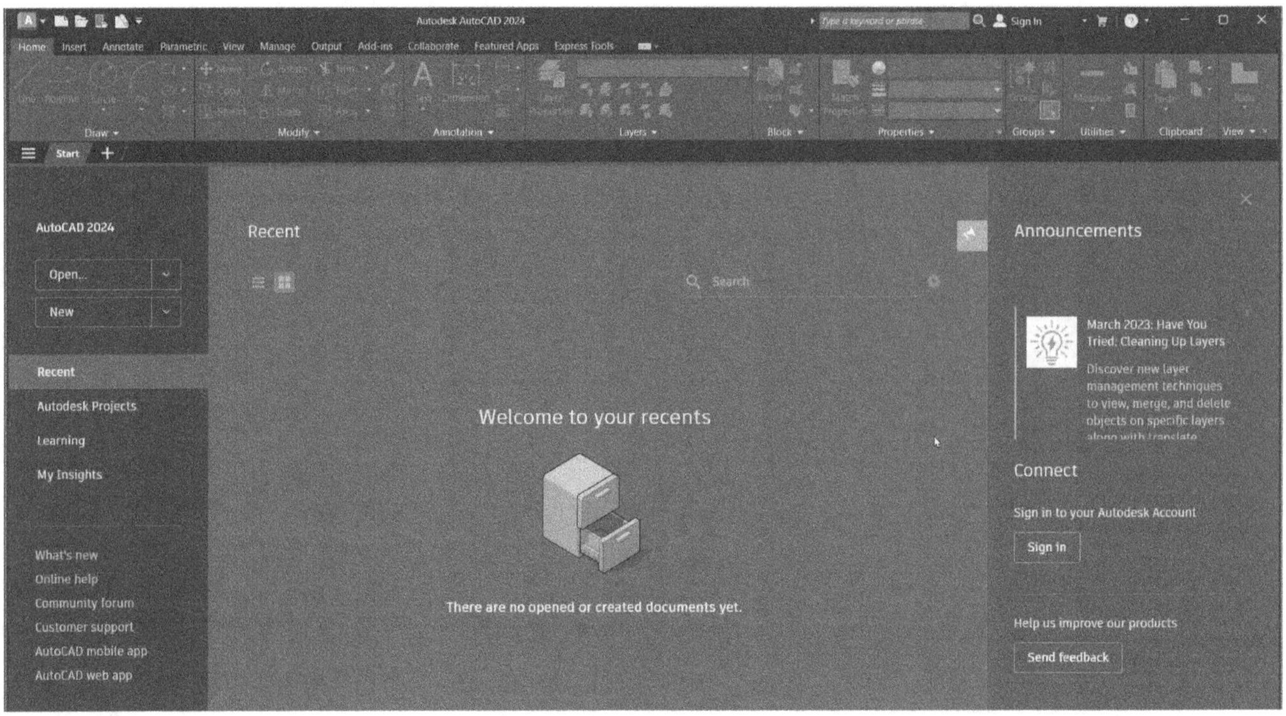

When you start AutoCAD 2024, you will see the Start screen, which is split into two primary sections. The left-side panel displays commonly used tools to access a new file or template, while the central section presents a roster of all your previous drawings.

Accessing an old file is simple: just click on its preview image, and it will open. You can also click the Open button under AutoCAD 2024 to open a previous drawing; the **Select File** dialog appears. Browse to the directory of the previous drawing and double-tap on it.

To generate a new blank drawing, click on the New button under AutoCAD 2024. This will launch a fresh empty drawing using the most recent template.

To view the most recent template, click the pointer next to the New button. A drop-down will appear, and the most recent template will be at the top. The default templates for AutoCAD 2024 are usually acad.dwt or acadiso.dwt, but your template may differ.

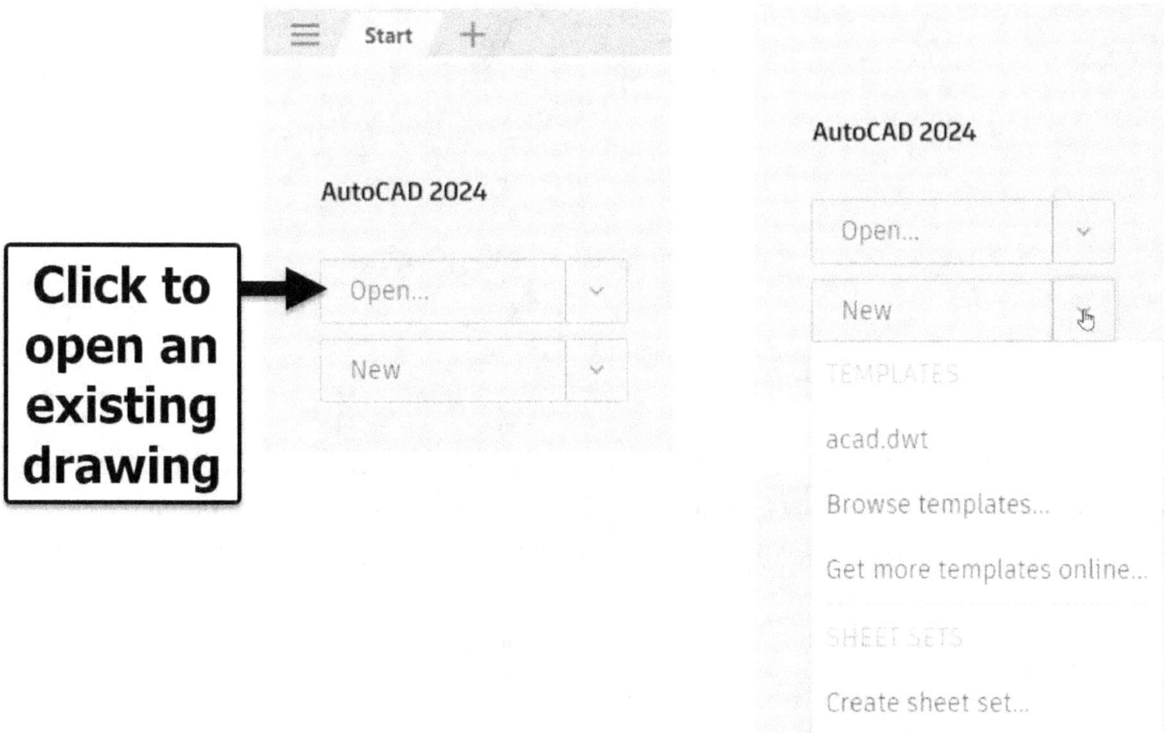

If you want to use other templates, you can choose Browse Templates from the **New** drop-down. This will allow you to view through all the pre-designed CAD software templates available. It is worth noting that these templates come with predefined configurations for units, boundaries, and accuracy.

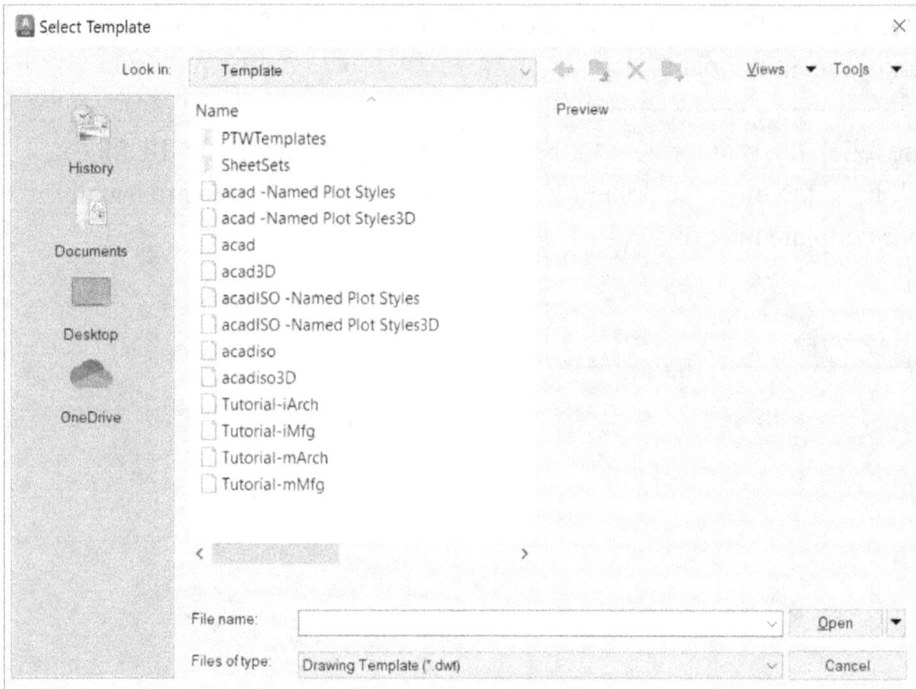

When you start a fresh drawing in AutoCAD 2024, the workspace appears empty, featuring a functional ribbon at the top and several supplementary components. Subsequent sections will explore into a comprehensive exploration and discussion of all the constituents comprising the AutoCAD workspace

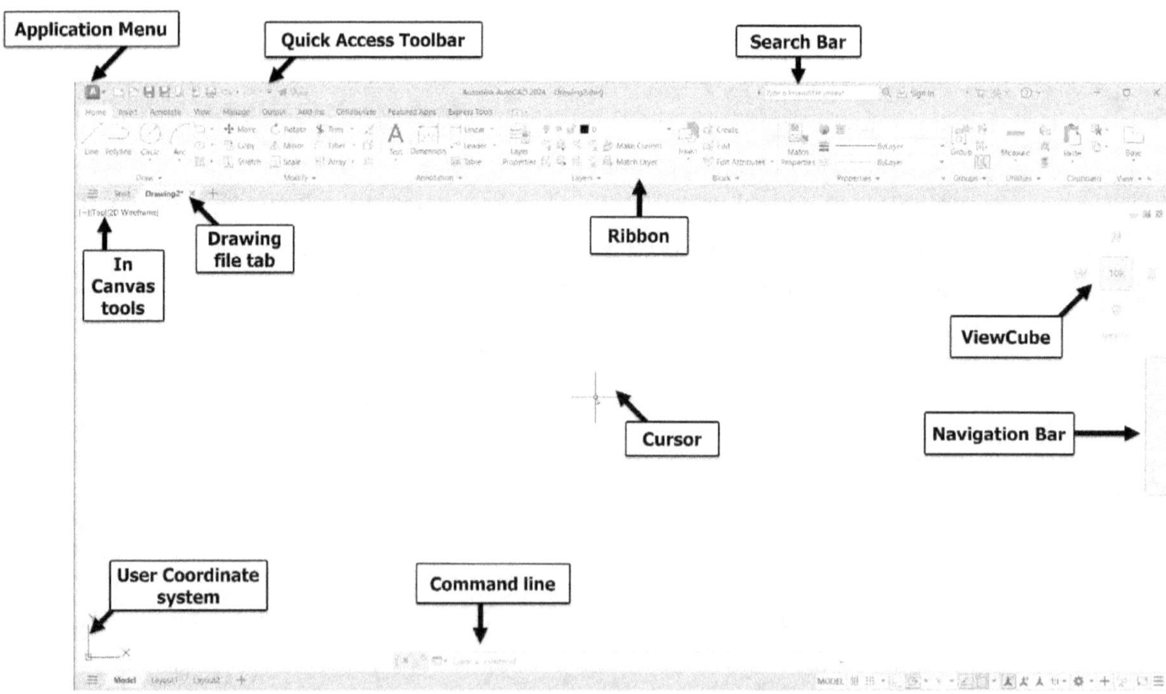

The Application menu

The Application menu, a crucial component of AutoCAD's user interface, is typically positioned in the top-left corner of the software's window. It is distinguished by its box-like shape containing the

AutoCAD logo at the center. By selecting the application button, you can conveniently access important functions such as file operations (open and save), printing, and software configuration. Moreover, the application button grants access to program options, allowing users to personalize settings based on their preferences.

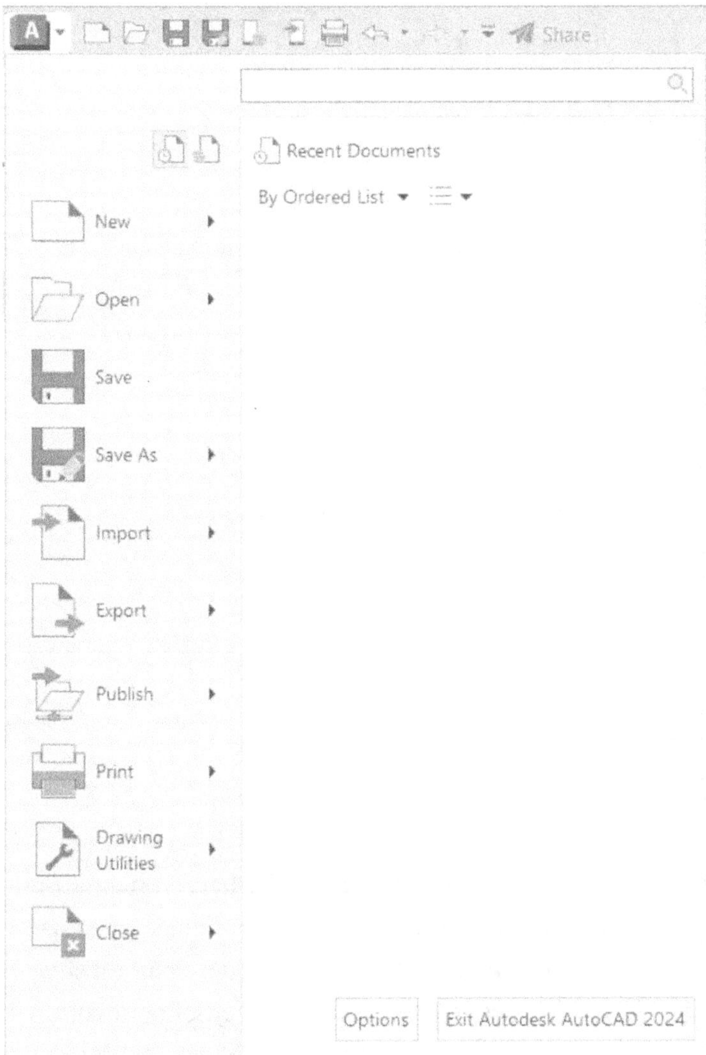

The Quick Access toolbar

The Quick Access Toolbar, positioned above the ribbon in AutoCAD 2024, provides a powerful and efficient way to access frequently used tools and commands like Save, Undo, Redo, and more. Initially, it contains a limited set of tools, but customization options are available to tailor it to your requirements.

To personalize the Quick Access Toolbar, simply click the toolbar's dropdown arrow and select "Customize Quick Access Toolbar." This enables you to add or remove tools and commands, creating a customized workflow. Additionally, you have the flexibility to reposition the Quick Access Toolbar above or below the ribbon based on your preferences.

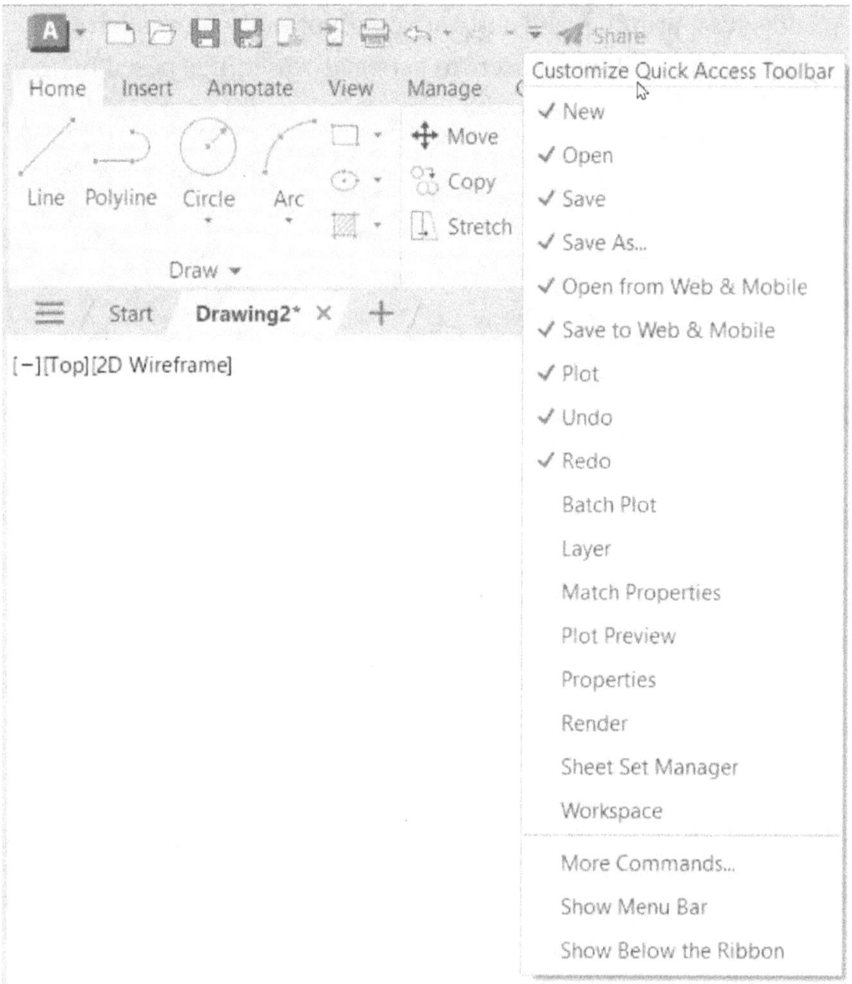

The Search bar

The Search bar in AutoCAD, situated at the top of the window, contains a text field where you can input keywords or phrases. This useful functionality enables you to search for particular commands or tools within the software. By entering the name of the command or tool and pressing Enter, you can retrieve comprehensive information from the associated help file. It is necessary to have an internet connection to utilize this feature. Furthermore, the Search bar grants access to your sign-in account, the Autodesk app store, and other valuable resources available in the Help options

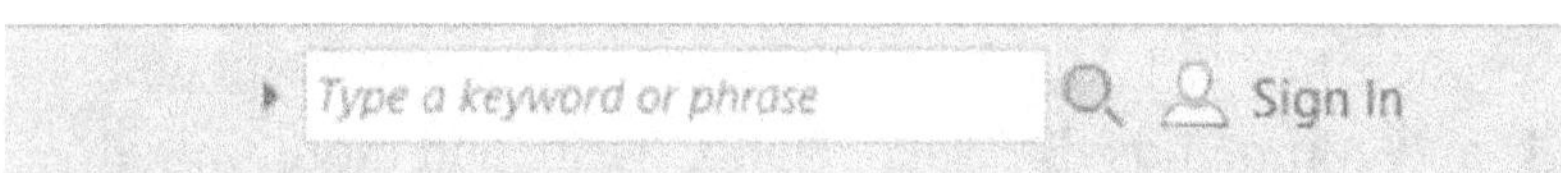

Ribbon

The ribbon in AutoCAD is an essential component that allows users to conveniently access various tools and commands. Positioned below the Application menu, it comprises several panels and tabs categorized based on tasks and functionalities.

These panels within the ribbon are thoughtfully arranged, containing relevant commands and tools. Switching between panels is effortless by clicking on the corresponding tabs.

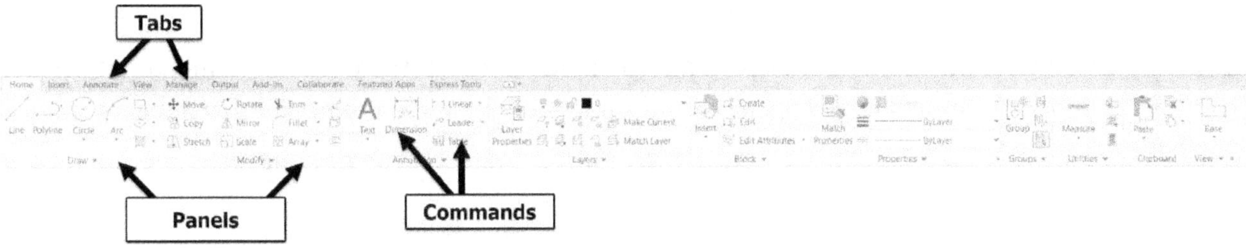

To personalize your workflow in AutoCAD, you have the flexibility to customize the ribbon. This involves adding or removing tabs, panels, and commands that you frequently use. To display a specific tab, simply right-click on any panel and choose "Show Tabs." You can then select the desired tab you want to see. If you wish to hide a tab, repeat the process and uncheck it from the context menu on the right side. Managing panels within a tab is also easy. Right-click on the desired tab and select "Show Panels" to display or hide specific panels by checking or unchecking them.

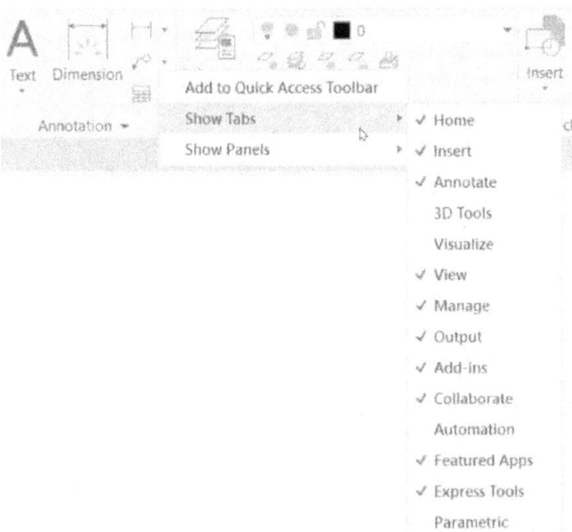

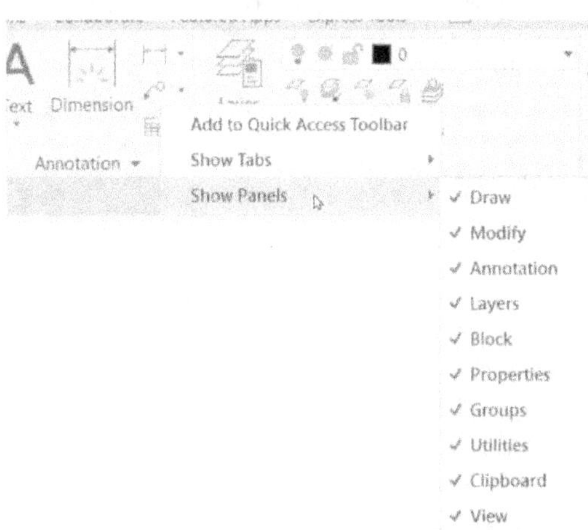

The ribbon in AutoCAD also includes contextual tabs that become visible when specific objects are selected or certain actions are performed. These tabs consist of specialized commands and tools that are specifically applicable to the chosen object or action, enabling you to accomplish your tasks with speed and efficiency.

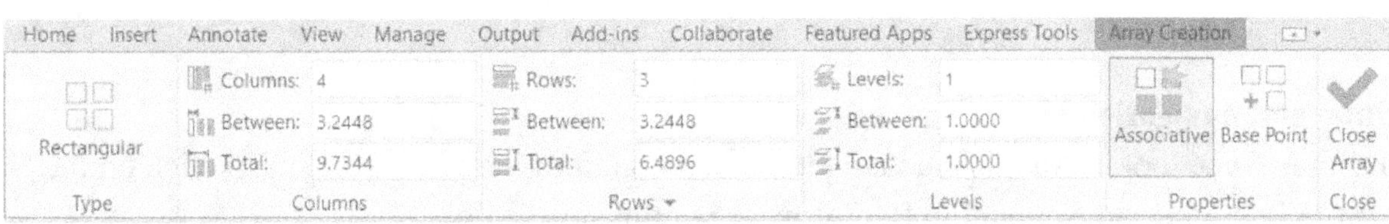

Overall, the ribbon is a powerful and versatile tool that helps you work more efficiently in AutoCAD.

Drawing File tabs

The file tabs in AutoCAD show all the currently open drawing files. You can have multiple tabs open and easily open a new blank drawing by clicking the plus (+) icon next to the last tab.

If a file is in read-only mode, its tab will display a padlock icon. You can preview a thumbnail of the file by hovering your cursor over its tab. To open the file, simply click on the thumbnail that appears.

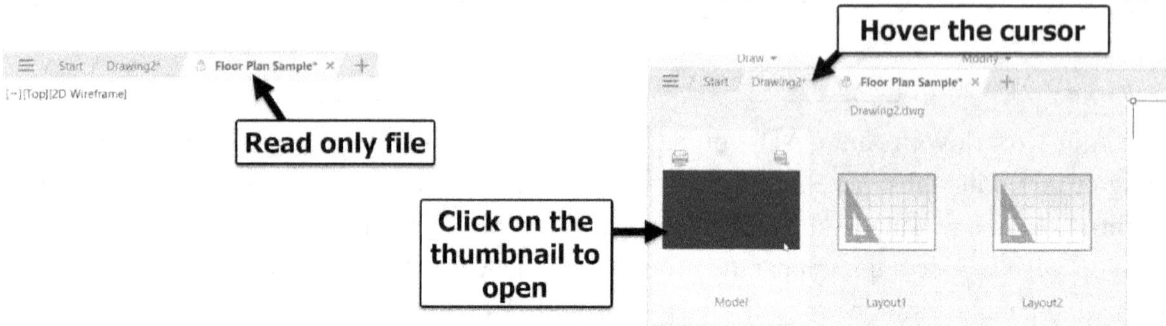

You can use the **Options** button located on the left side of the Drawing File tabs to switch between the file tabs, open, save, or close a drawing file tab.

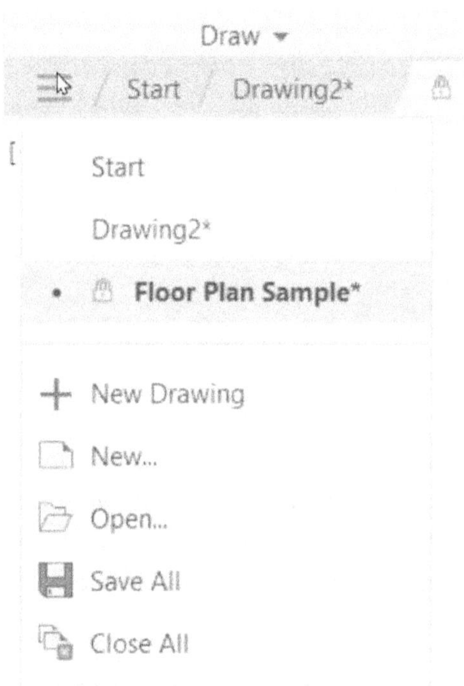

The ViewCube and navigation bar

To access the ViewCube tool in AutoCAD, navigate to the top left of the display area and click on the "-" sign. Choose "ViewCube and Navigation Bar" from the options presented.

The ViewCube is a helpful tool for navigating in a 3D space. It appears as a cube-shaped icon that can be clicked and dragged to rotate the view of your drawing. Each face of the cube represents a different orientation, and clicking on a face instantly adjusts your view accordingly.

Aside from navigation, the ViewCube offers options for controlling perspective, adjusting camera angles, and saving custom viewpoints. Right-clicking on the ViewCube provides access to these features.

The Navigation Bar, located on the right side of the AutoCAD window below the ViewCube, provides convenient access to common navigation tools. It includes buttons for zooming, panning, and orbiting your model. The Zoom button enables zooming in or out, the Pan button allows movement in different directions, and the Orbit button enables rotation in 3D space.

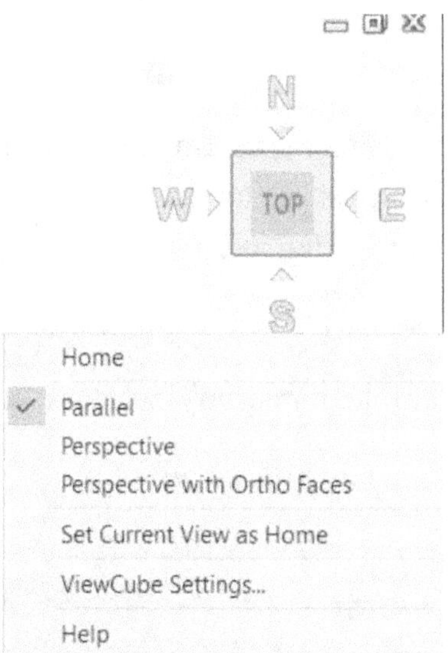

The Selection Cursor
The default cursor in AutoCAD is the selection cursor, which looks like two intersecting lines with a small cube at the center. Depending on the selection mode, the cursor's appearance and icons may vary. AutoCAD has different types of cursors: the standard cursor, the Point Selection cursor, the Object Selection cursor, and the Cursor with a badge.

The standard cursor is used when the program is waiting for user input. It consists of two intersecting lines with a small cube in the middle. It allows users to edit objects using grips, which are squares, rectangles, or arrowheads that appear when objects are selected.

The Point Selection cursor is a simple cursor with two intersecting lines at a central point. It appears when point input is required, such as when using drawing commands like Line, Polyline, Circle, and Arc. It may also appear with a rubber-banding line.

The Object Selection cursor, also known as the Pickbox, is a simple box that appears when selecting objects. It indicates that you need to click on objects or use object-selection options to select them.

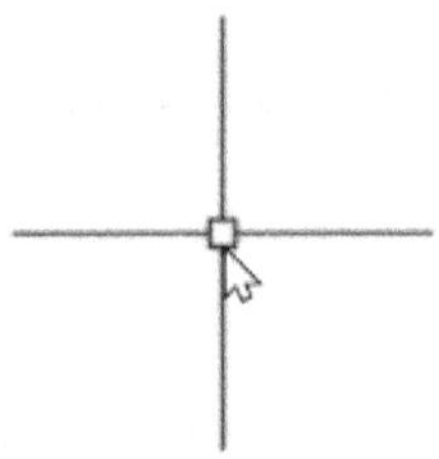

Standard Cursor

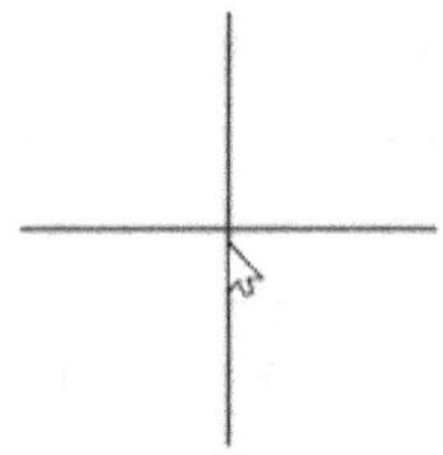

Point Selection Cursor

Object Selection Cursor

The Object Snap marker appears when you turn on Object Snap mode. It helps you select specific points on objects precisely, like endpoints or midpoints.

When using Polar Tracking or Object Snap Tracking, you will see tracelines. Polar Tracking helps you draw perpendicular lines, while Object Snap Tracking aligns points based on existing object geometry. This feature works with Object Snap. More details on Object Snaps, Polar Tracking, and Object Snap Tracking will be covered later.

The cursor with a badge shows an icon similar to the selected tool. For example, a magnifying glass badge allows you to define the zoom area by dragging it.

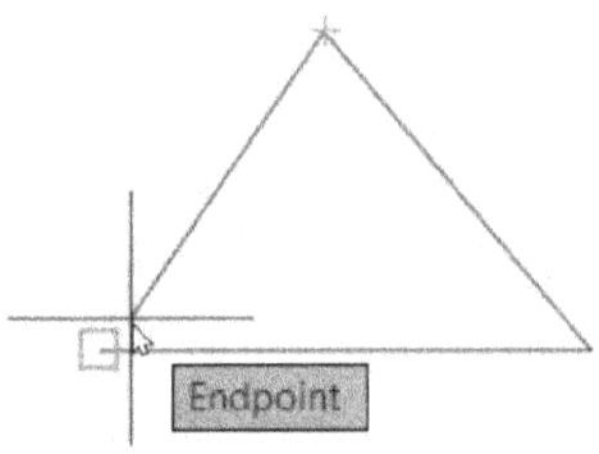

Object Snap marker displayed alongside the Point Selection cursor

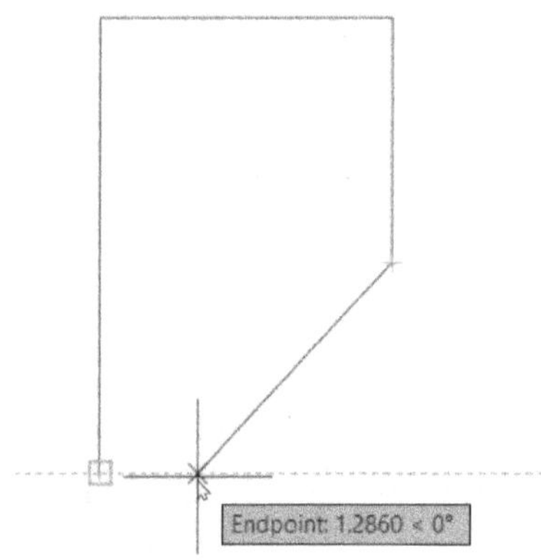

Tracelines displayed along with the Point Selection Cursor

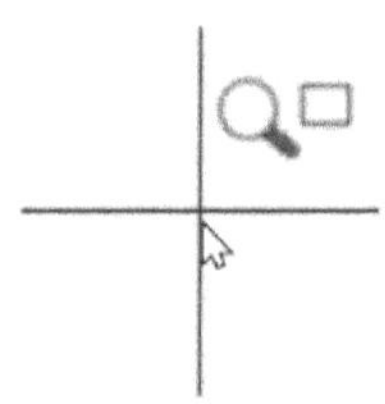

Cursor with badge

UCS

The User Coordinate System (UCS), displayed as an L-shaped line, can be found in the bottom-left corner of the drawing area. It consists of three axes: X, Y, and Z. The X and Y axes are denoted by the letters X and Y on the icon, while the Z-axis is represented by Z. The Z-axis is perpendicular to the screen and is not visible. The point where the X and Y coordinates intersect in the UCS is known as the origin or 0,0 point.

The UCS helps determine the orientation of the drawing. Further details about the UCS will be covered in later sections of this book.

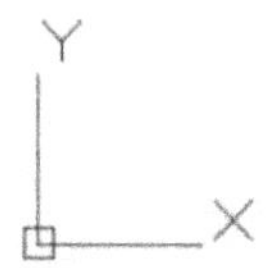

Command line

The Command line, positioned at the bottom of the screen, is a small horizontal window that prompts you to "Type a command." It signifies that AutoCAD is ready to receive your command input. You can directly enter commands without the need to click on it. The Command line is also helpful in suggesting commands by displaying a list when you type the first letter. It presents a single line of text that shows the current responses and command options as you enter a command. As you continue with the command, additional responses appear while earlier ones fade away by scrolling upward.

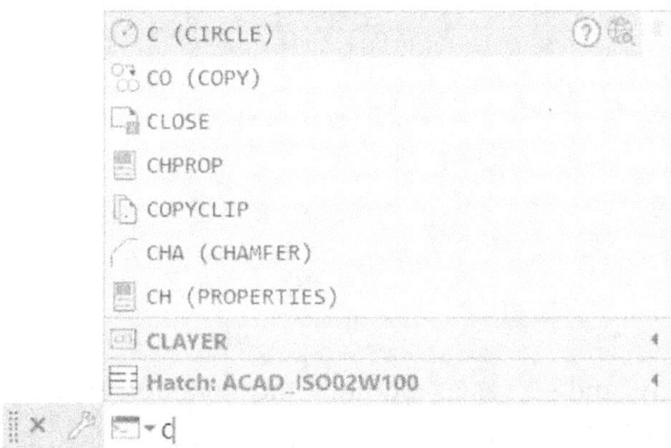

To reveal the command line if it's currently hidden, just press Ctrl + 9 on your keyboard. To hide it again, press the same keys once more. The command line can be adjusted in size and position within the drawing area according to your liking. By pressing the F2 function key, you can also access a list of previously utilized commands in the command line.

Model and Layout tabs

At the bottom-left corner, below the drawing area, you'll see three tabs: Model and two Layout tabs. These tabs allow you to switch between different views.

The **Model** tab is the default tab when you start a new drawing. It's where you create and modify your 2D or 3D models using various drawing and editing tools. Think of it as your workspace.

The **Layout** tabs work like sheets in a drawing, letting you arrange different views and plot multiple sheets. For example, if you're designing a product, you can use layout tabs to create separate sheets for top, front, and side views, as well as detailed drawings of specific parts. This makes it easy to present and share your design without constantly switching between different views in the model space.

You can use the **Options** button located on the left side of the **Model** tab to create a new layout, define the page settings of the model tab or layouts, select all layouts, publish the selected layouts, and dock the model and layout tabs above the status bar or inline with it.

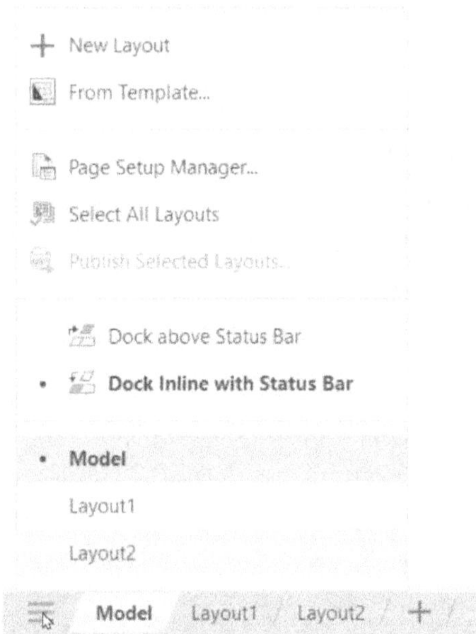

Status bar

The status bar is positioned at the bottom of the window and serves as a crucial tool in a designer's workflow. It offers toggles for various functions like Grid Display, Ortho Mode, and Polar Tracking, enabling easy adjustment of settings and activation or deactivation of features while working on designs. By utilizing the status bar, designers can streamline their drafting process and concentrate on producing exceptional designs.

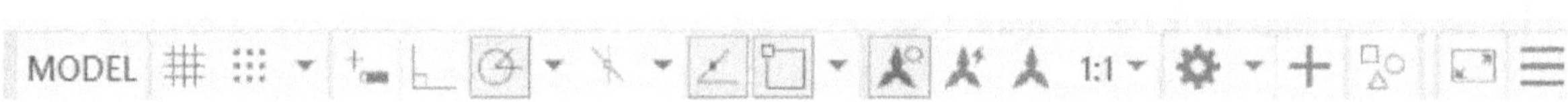

The **Grid Display** option controls whether the grid is shown or hidden in AutoCAD.

Ortho Mode restricts cursor movement to right angles only, making it easier to draw straight lines.

Polar Tracking enables or disables the tracking of cursor movement along specific angles.

Snap Mode determines whether the cursor snaps to predefined points on the grid.

Object Snap enables or disables the ability to snap to specific points on objects.

Dynamic Input controls the display of a command line near the cursor for entering commands and values.

Annotation Scale allows you to change the scale of text, dimensions, and other annotations.

Linetype Scale adjusts the scale of linetypes used in your drawing.

Please note that the Status bar displays only a limited number of options. To make more icons visible, click the **Customization** button situated at the right corner and select the options you wish to appear on the status bar.

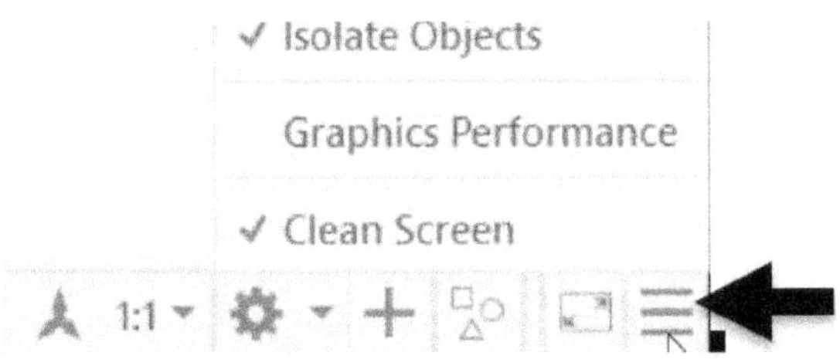

AutoCAD Navigation using the Mouse

In AutoCAD, you have the option to navigate using a mouse. Alternatively, you can use the touchpad on your laptop, although there are limitations to its functionality. Here are the functions of each mouse button:

- Left mouse button: Used for selecting objects or executing commands by clicking on toolbar icons.
- Middle mouse button: Activates the **Pan** command, allowing you to move the drawing area. It can also rotate the view when used in conjunction with the Shift key.
- Right mouse button: Displays shortcut menus or enters the **Repeat Last Command** mode when clicked in an empty space.

Part 1: Creating 2D Architectural Drawings

In this chapter, you learn to do the following:

- **Starting AutoCAD 2024**
- **Inserting Hand Sketches**
- **Creating Layers**
- **Creating Grid Lines**
- **Creating Walls**
- **Doors Windows, and Stairs**
- **Kitchen and Bathroom fixtures**
- **Blocks and Hatch Patterns**
- **Adding Text**
- **Creating Elevations**
- **Adding Dimensions**
- **Layouts and Title Block**
- **Printing Drawings**

In this chapter, you learn to create architectural drawings shown below.

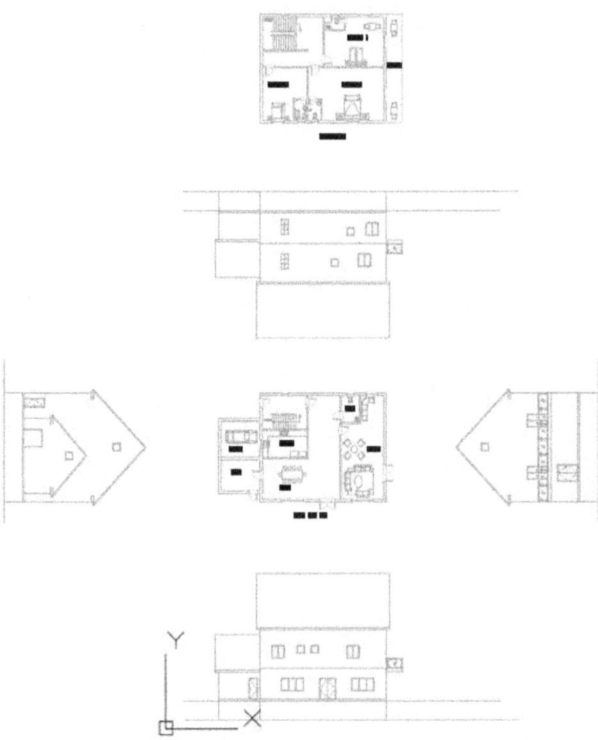

Tutorial 1: Starting AutoCAD 2024

- Click **Start > AutoCAD 2024 – English** > **AutoCAD 2024** icon on the taskbar. If you are working in Windows 7, click **Start > All Programs > Autodesk > AutoCAD 2024 > AutoCAD 2024**.
- To start a new document, click **Quick Access Toolbar > New** .

- On the **Select Template** dialog, select **acad** and click **Open** to open the drawing file. The drawing units are inches.
- On the Status bar, click **Workspace Switching > Drafting & Annotation**.

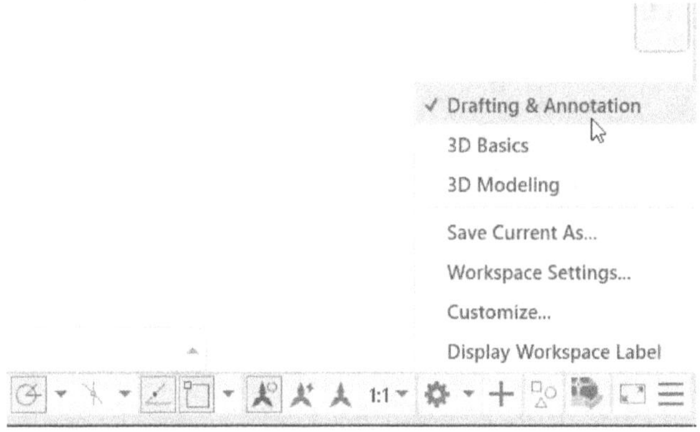

- On the Status bar, click the **GRIDMODE** icon to turn off the grid.

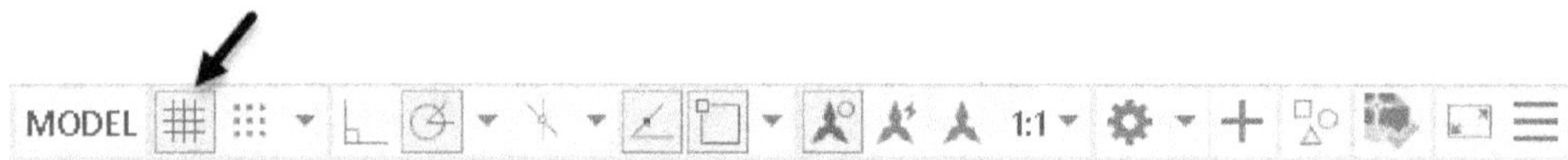

Now, you need to specify the display units of the drawing.

- Type **UN** in the command line and press Enter (or) click **Application Menu > Drawing Utilities > Units**.

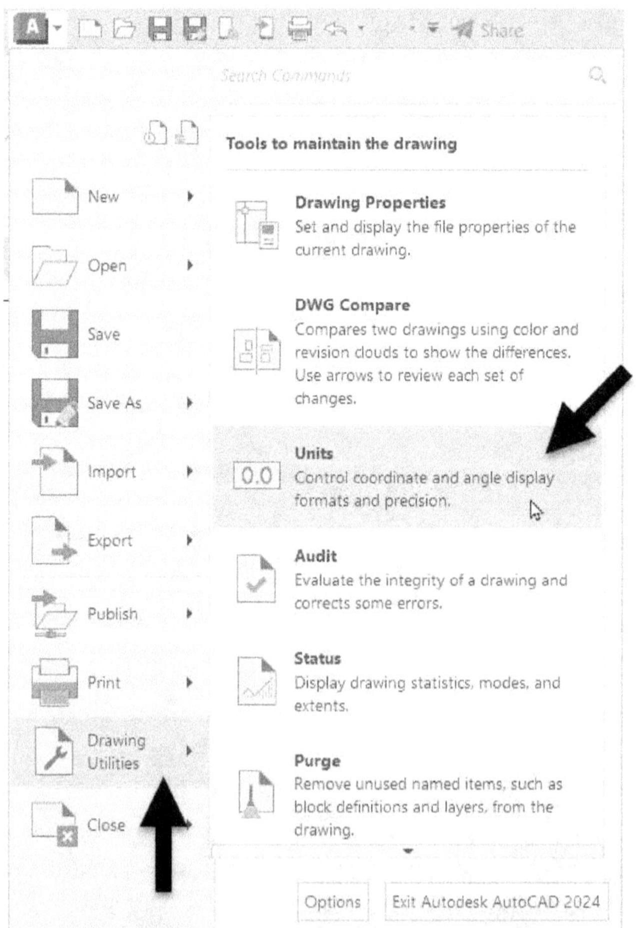

- On the **Drawing Units** dialog, select **Type > Architectural**. Select **Precision > 0'-0 1/16"**. Set the **Insertion Scale** to

Inches, and click **OK**.

- Right-click and select **Options** from the shortcut menu; the **Options** dialog appears on the screen, and it allows you to change the settings of the user interface and various functionalities.
- On the **Options** dialog, click the **Selection** tab, and set the **Pickbox size**, as shown.

- Click **OK** to close the **Options** dialog.

Tutorial 2: Creating Layers

Layers are essential for grouping objects in a drawing. They are like a group of transparent sheets that are combined into a complete drawing. The figure below displays a drawing consisting of object lines and dimension lines. In this example, the object lines are created on the 'Object' layer, and dimensions are created on the layer called 'Dimension.' You can easily turn-off the 'Dimension' layer for a more unobstructed view of the object lines.

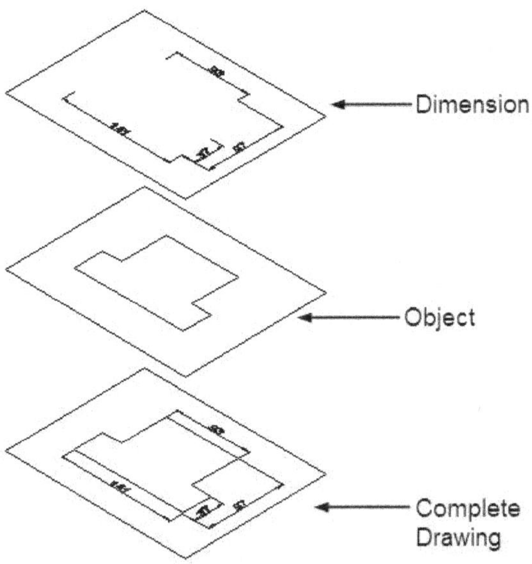

You can assign properties such as name, color, line weight (thickness), and linetype to a layer. The features can vary for each layer.

- On the ribbon, click **Home** tab > **Layers** panel > **Layer Properties** .
- On the Layer Properties Manager, click **New Layer** icon located at the top left corner. Type A-WALL in the **Name** box, and press Enter.

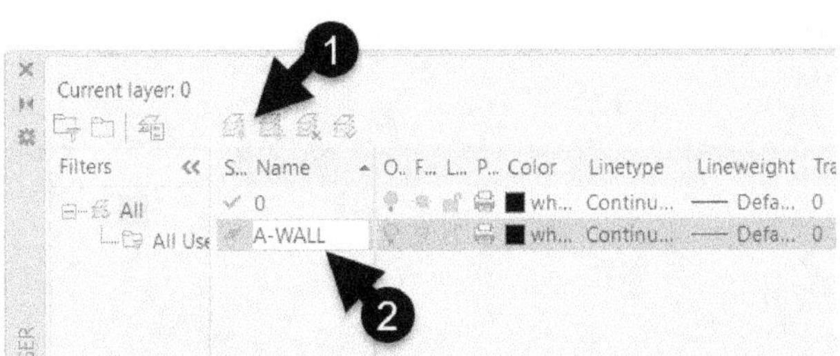

The naming framework for layers, according to United States National CAD standards, is shown below.

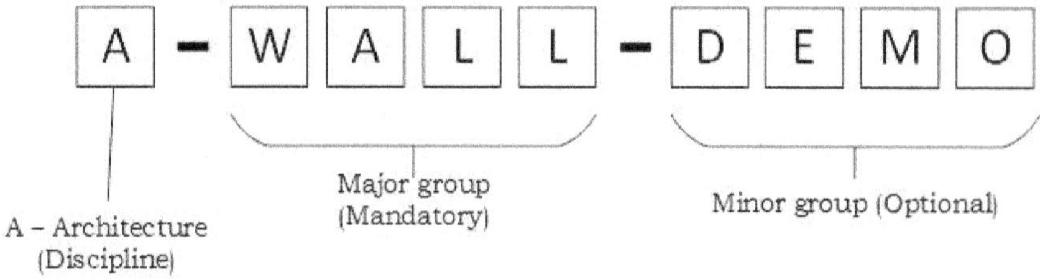

- On the **Layer Properties Manager**, click the square in the **Color** column of the **A-WALL** row.

- On the **Select Color** dialog, select the **Cyan (4)** color from the **Index color** section. Click **OK**.

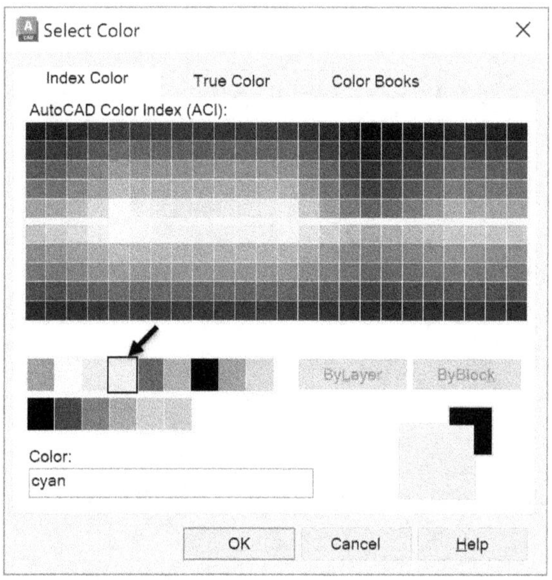

The color assigned to a layer determines the lineweight (line thickness) of the object when you print the drawing. This condition is valid only when you use a color-dependent plot style. However, you can define your lineweight separately if you use a Named plot style. You can set lineweights for each color in a Color dependent plot style. The lineweights for different colors in this example are given below.

Color	Lineweight
Color 9	0.05 mm
Color 8	0.09 mm
Red	0.1 mm
Yellow	0.2 mm
Green	0.4 mm

Cyan	0.5 mm
Blue	0.7 mm
Magenta	1.0 mm

- Create a new layer called **A-GRID** and assign the Index color 9 to it.
- On the **Layer Properties Manager**, click in the **Linetype** column of the **A-GRID** row.

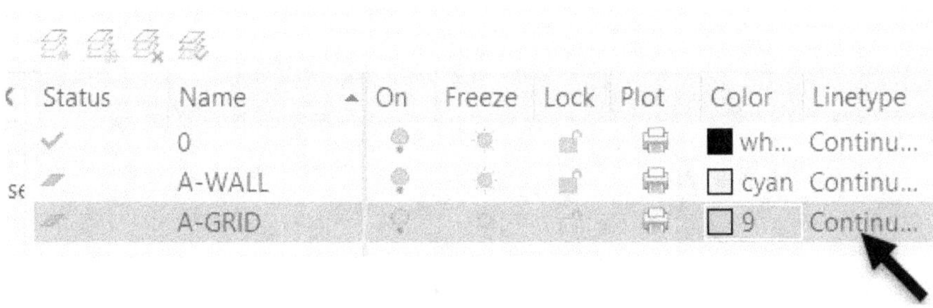

- Click the **Load** button on the **Select Linetype** dialog. On the **Load or Reload Linetypes** dialog, select the **DASHED** linetype from the **Available Linetypes** list. Click **OK.**
- Select the **DASHED** linetype from the **Loaded Linetypes** list and click **OK.**

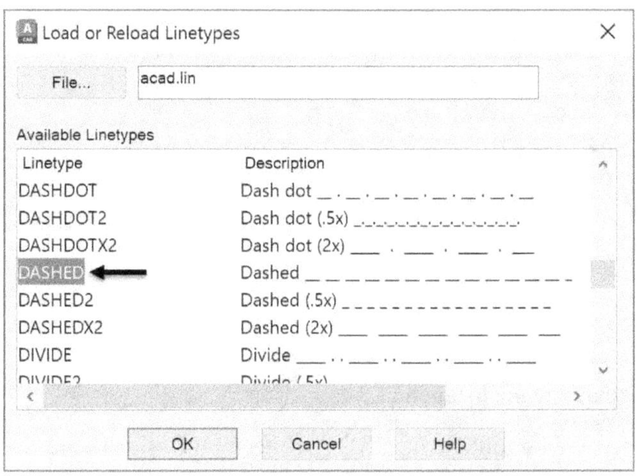

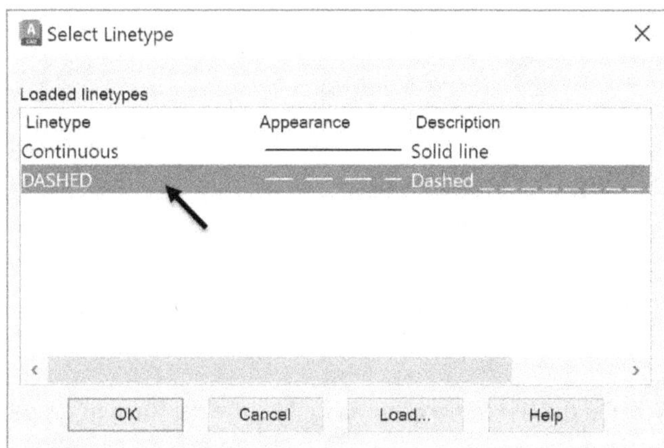

- Create other layers and assign colors, as shown. Close the **Layer Properties Manager** by clicking the **X** symbol on the top left/right corner.

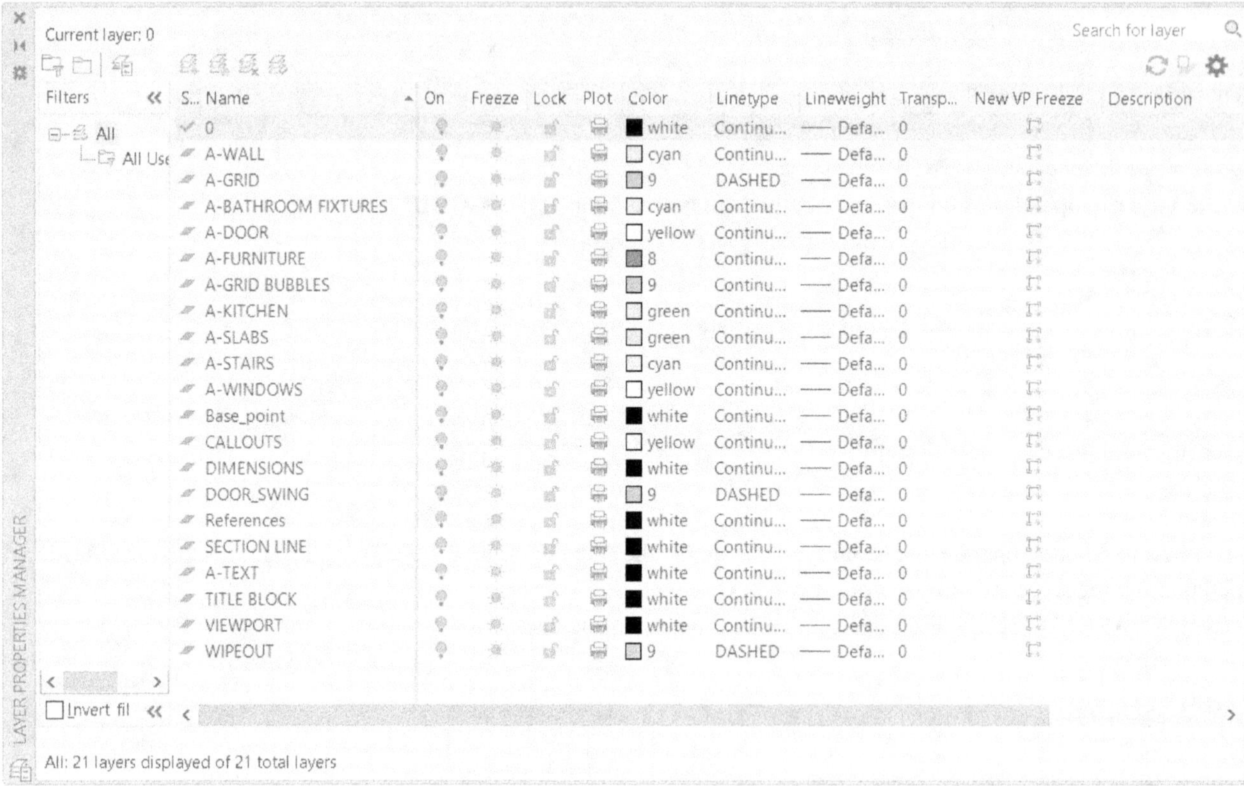

Saving the Document

- Click the **Save** icon on the **Quick Access Toolbar**.

- On the **Save Drawing As** dialog, use the **Save in** drop-down to define the location of the drawing.
- Click the **Create New Folder** icon on the **Save Drawing As** dialog. Enter AutoCAD Architectural Design as the folder. Next, double click on the folder.
- Type **Tutorial 1** in the **File name** box, and click **Save**.

Saving a new drawing to Web & Mobile

You can save a drawing to AutoCAD Web & Mobile using the Save to AutoCAD Web & Mobile application. This application helps you view and make changes to the drawing from the AutoCAD Web and AutoCAD Mobile application. The drawings edited in AutoCAD Web and AutoCAD Mobile can be opened in AutoCAD.

- Click the **Save to Web & Mobile** icon on the Quick Access Toolbar.

- On the **Save in AutoCAD Web & Mobile** dialog, type in the **File name** box and then click the **Save** button.

To open the file saved in AutoCAD Web and Mobiles applications, click the **Open from Web & Mobile** icon on the Quick Access Toolbar. Next, select the files from the **Open from AutoCAD Web & Mobile** dialog, and then click **Open**.

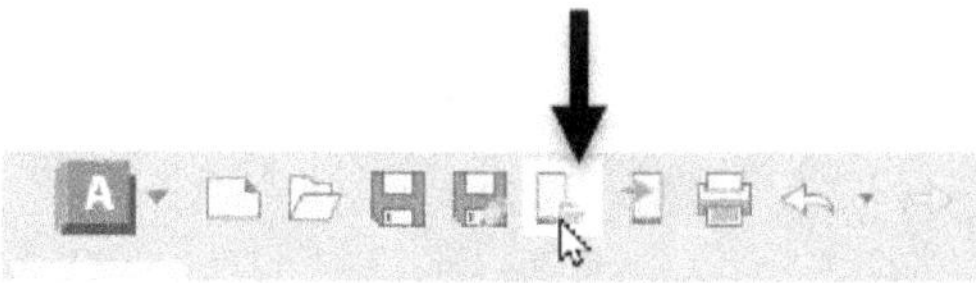

Tutorial 3: Creating Grid Lines

Creating grid lines is a good starting point for architectural design. They help you to create components of the architectural drawing quickly and accurately. Now, you create gridlines on the A-GRID layer.

- On the ribbon, click **Home** tab > **Layers** panel > **Layer** drop-down > **A-GRID**.
- Activate the **ORTHOMODE (F8)** icon on the status bar.
- On the ribbon, click **Home** tab > **Draw** panel > **Line**.
- Click at the lower portion of the graphics window.
- Move the vertically upward, type **640**, and press **Enter**. Next, press **Esc** to deactivate the Line command.
- On the **Navigation bar**, click the **Zoom** drop-down > **Zoom Extents** .
- Click the inclined arrow on the **Properties** panel; the **Properties** palette appears. On the **Properties** palette, click in the **Linetype scale** box, type **2**, and then press **Enter**; the linetype scale is changed to **2**.

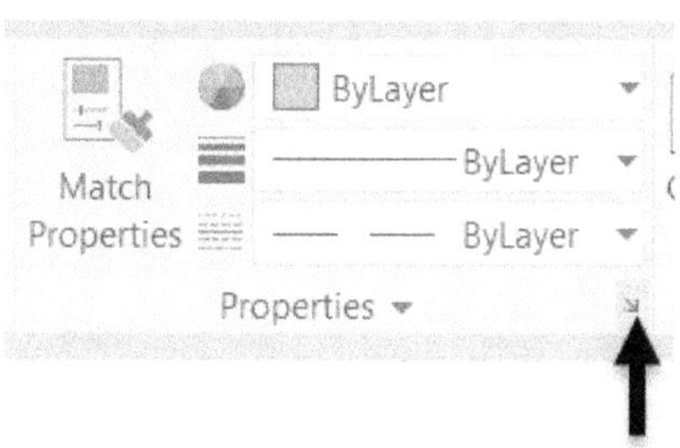

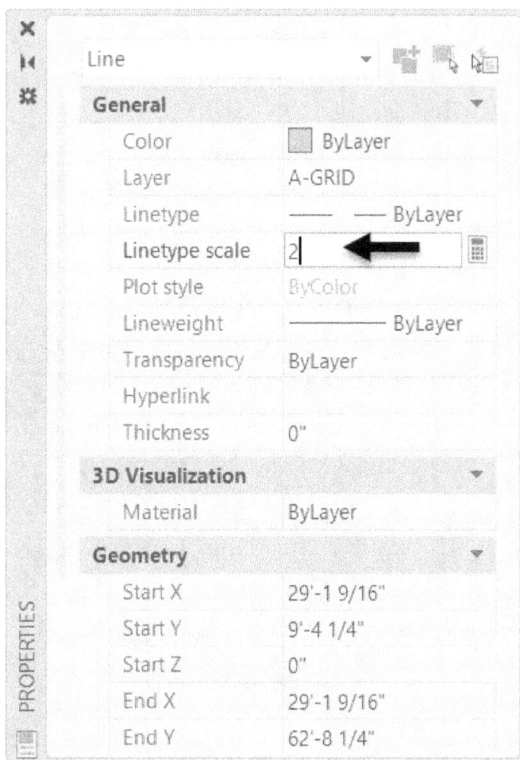

- On the ribbon, click **Home** tab > **Modify** panel > **Offset** . Type **220** and press **Enter** to define the offset distance. Select the first grid line, move the pointer toward the right and click. Select **Exit** from the command line.

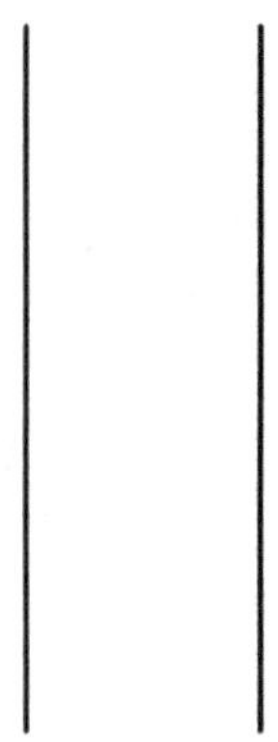

- Likewise, create other grid lines by offsetting the first one.

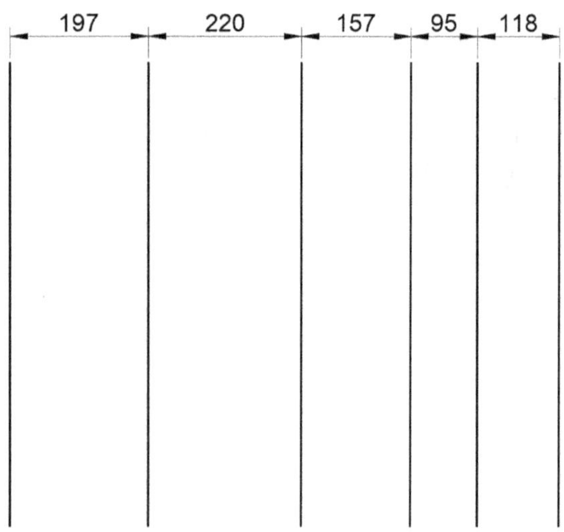

- Select the second grid line from the right-hand side. Click the lower endpoint grip and move the pointer upward. The length of the line is reduced.
- Likewise, drag down the upper-end point grip to shorten the grid line, as shown.

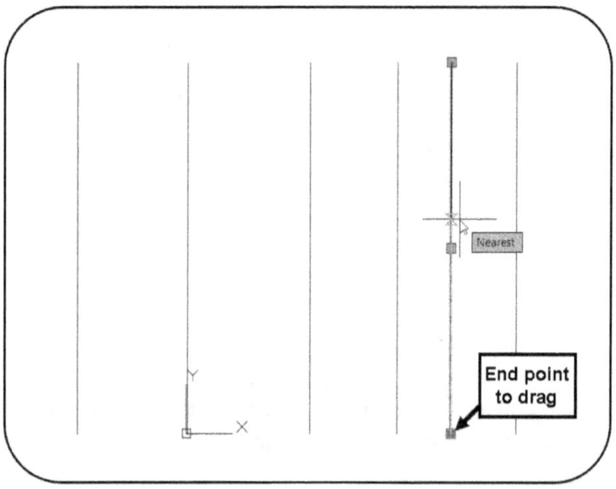

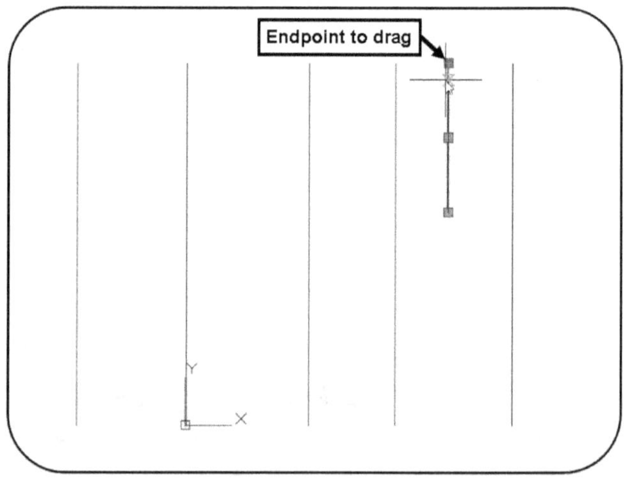

- Click the **Line** tool on the **Draw** panel of the **Home** ribbon tab.
- Specify the first point of the line at the top left corner, as shown in the figure.

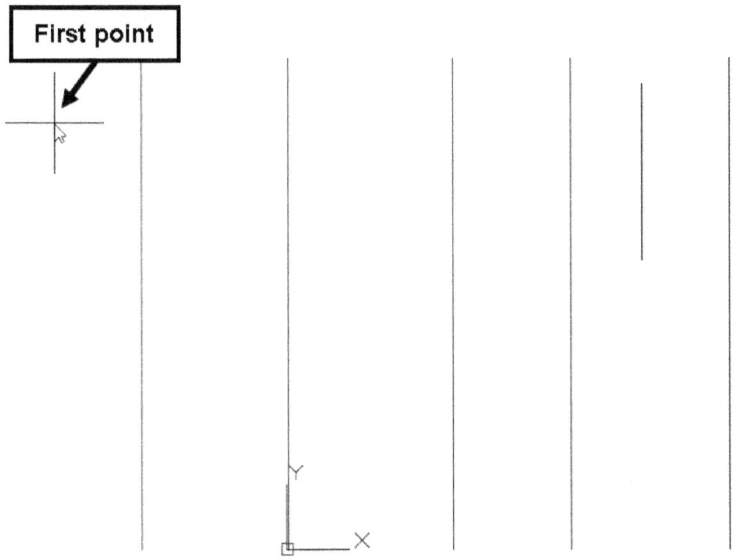

- Move the pointer horizontally toward the right and specify the endpoint of the line, as shown. Next, press **Esc**.

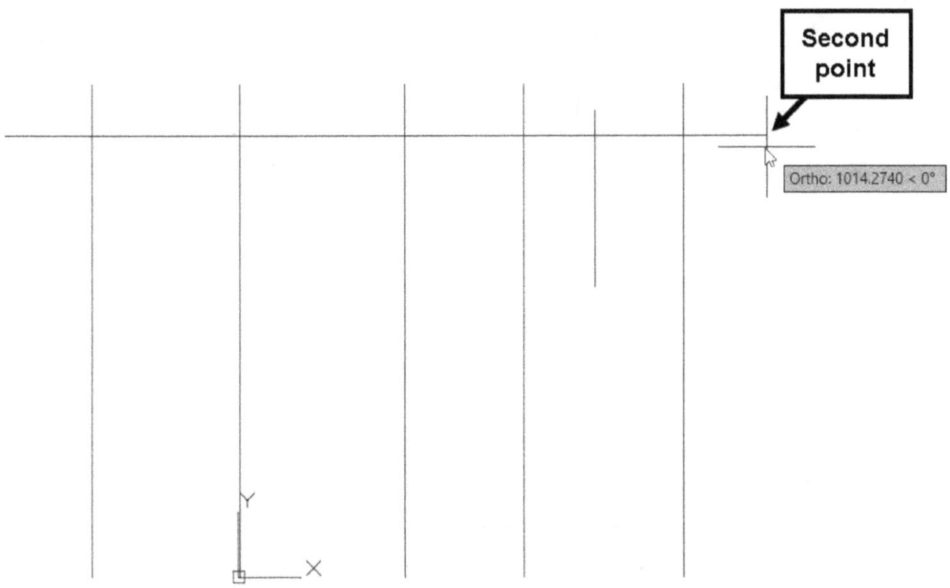

- Activate the **Offset** command, type **490** in the command line, and press **Enter**. Next, click on the horizontal line, as shown. Move the pointer downward and click to create an offset line.

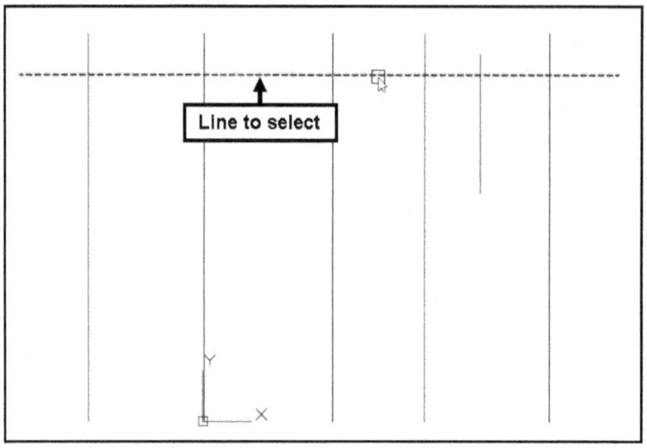

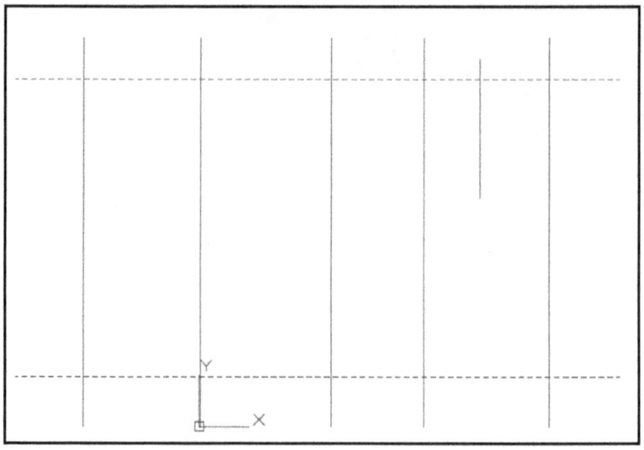

- Create other horizontal grid lines by using the **Offset** tool.

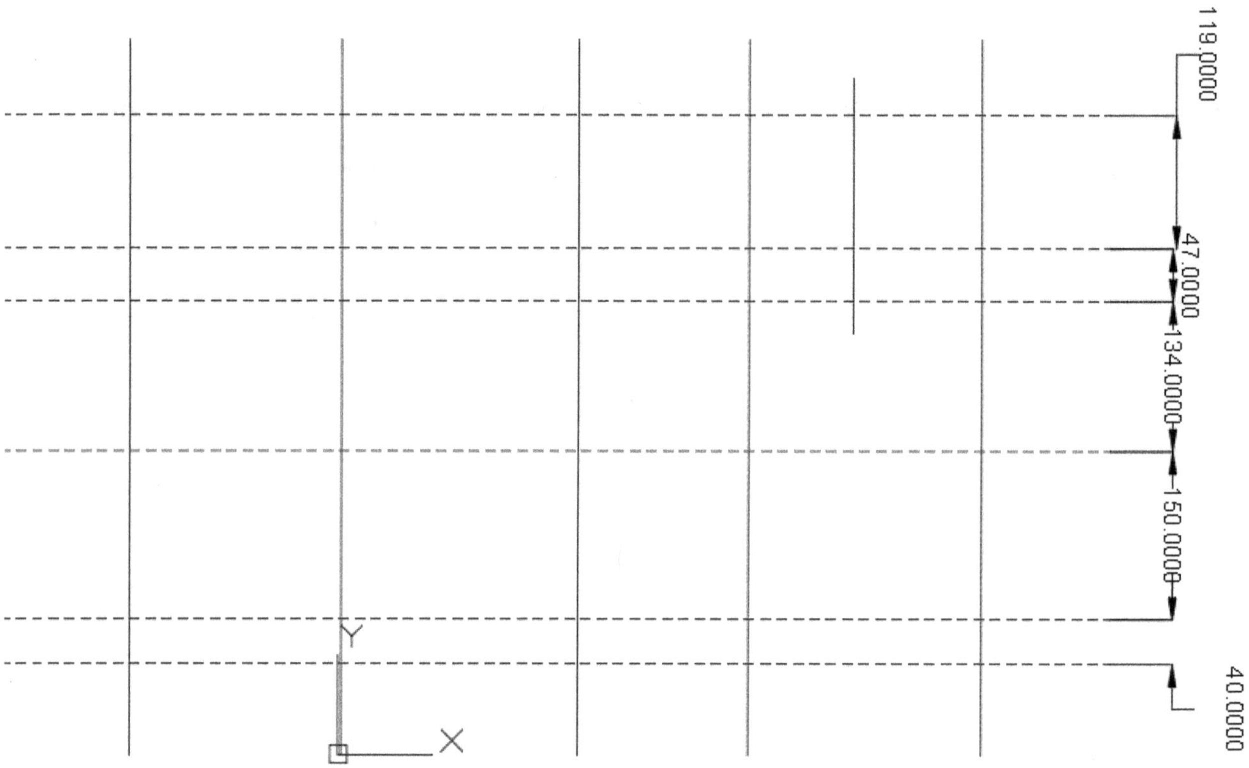

- Modify the grid lines by using the line grips.

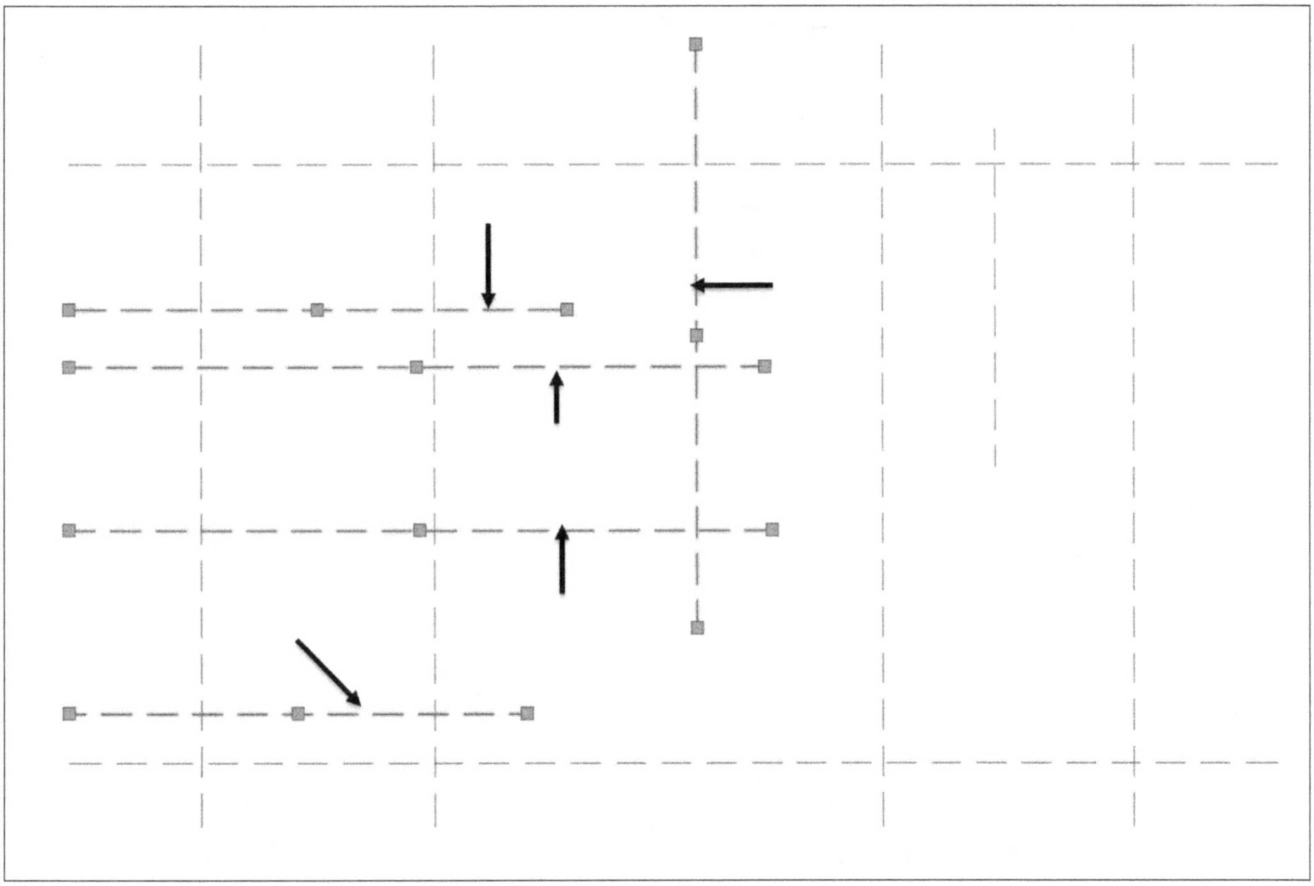

- Create another offset line and reduce its length using grips, as shown.

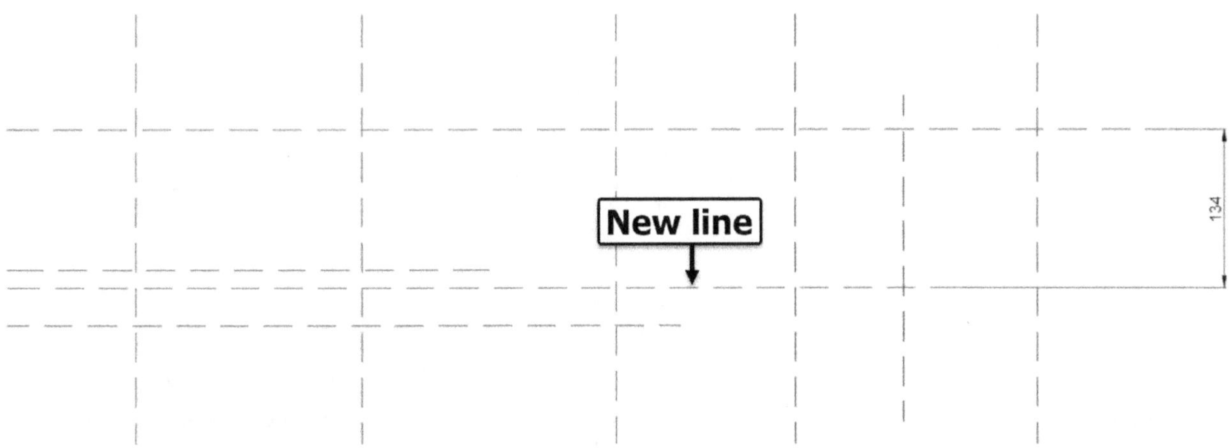

Tutorial 4: Creating Walls

AutoCAD offers many tools to create walls. Now, you learn to create walls using various tools.

- On the ribbon, click **Home** tab > **Layers** panel > **Layer** drop-down > **A-WALL.**
- On the ribbon, click **Home** tab > **Modify** panel > **Offset**. Select the **Layer** option from the command line. Select the **Current** option from the command line. Type **6** in the command line and press **Enter.**
- Select the topmost grid line, as shown. Move the pointer downwards and click to create an offset line in the current layer.

Again, select the same grid line, move the pointer upward, and click to create another offset line.

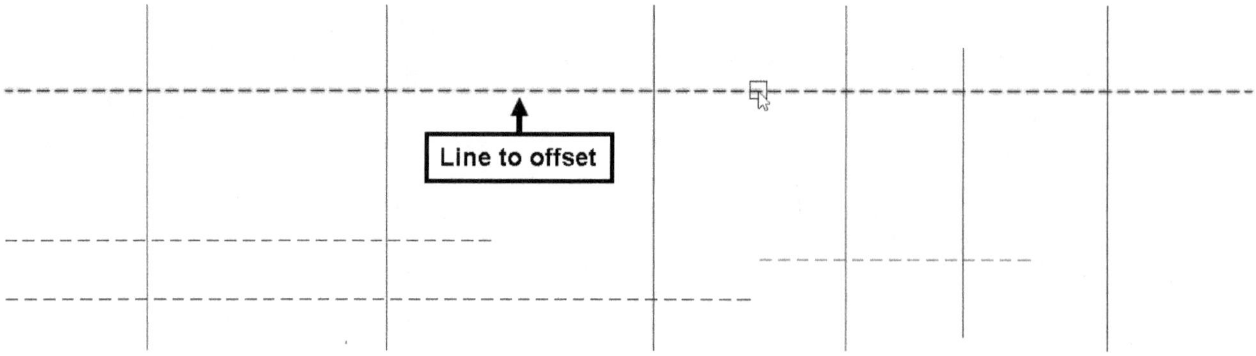

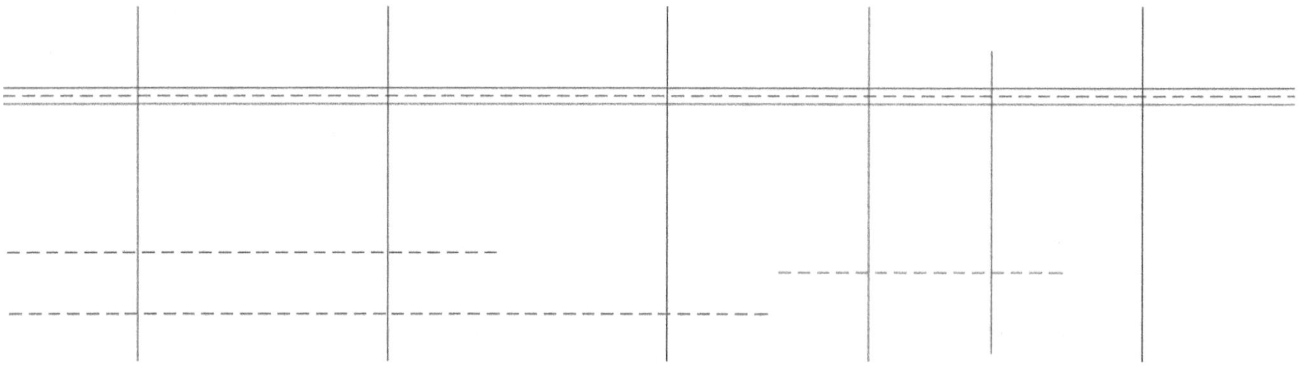

- Likewise, create other offset lines, as shown.

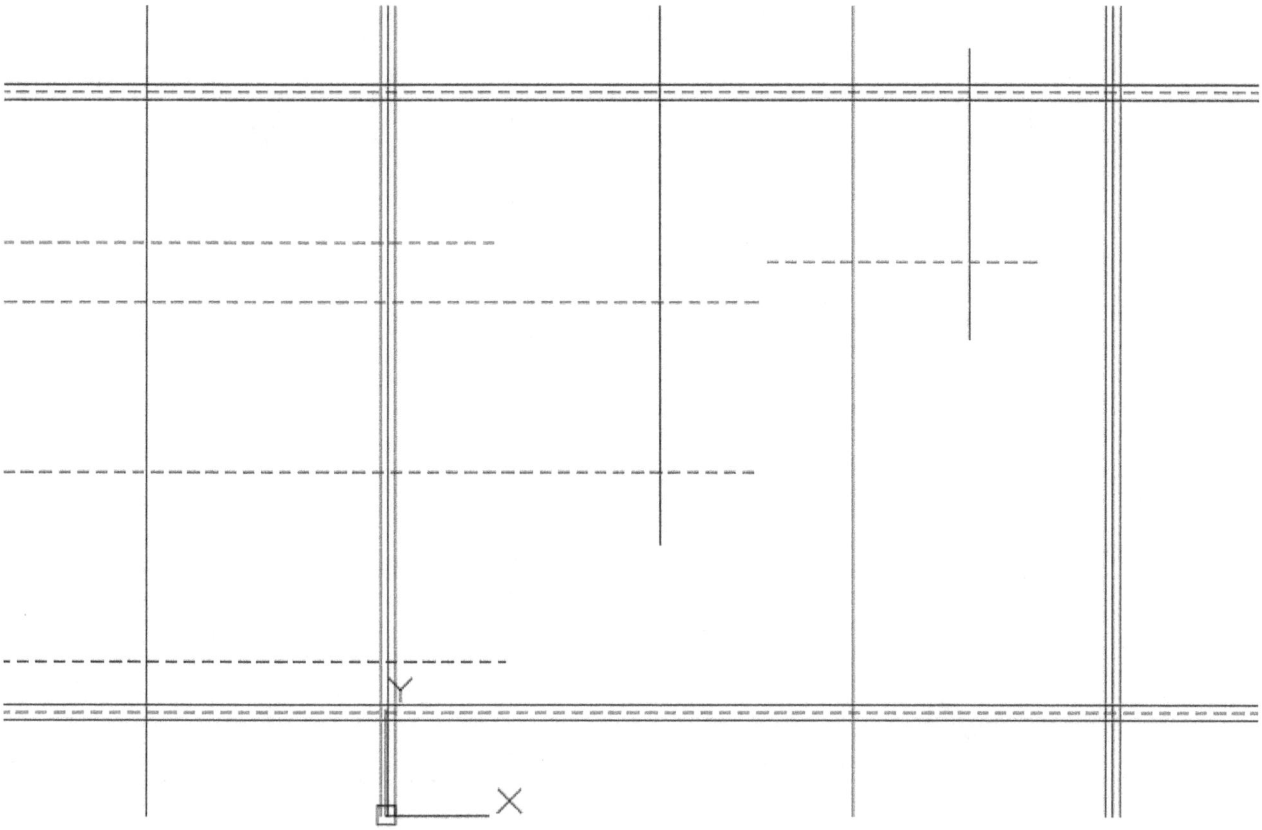

- On the ribbon, click **Home** tab > **Modify** panel > **Fillet** . Select Radius from the command line. Next, type 0 in the command line and press ENTER.
- Select the offset lines forming a corner, as shown. Note that you need to click on the portions of the lines forming the inside corner.

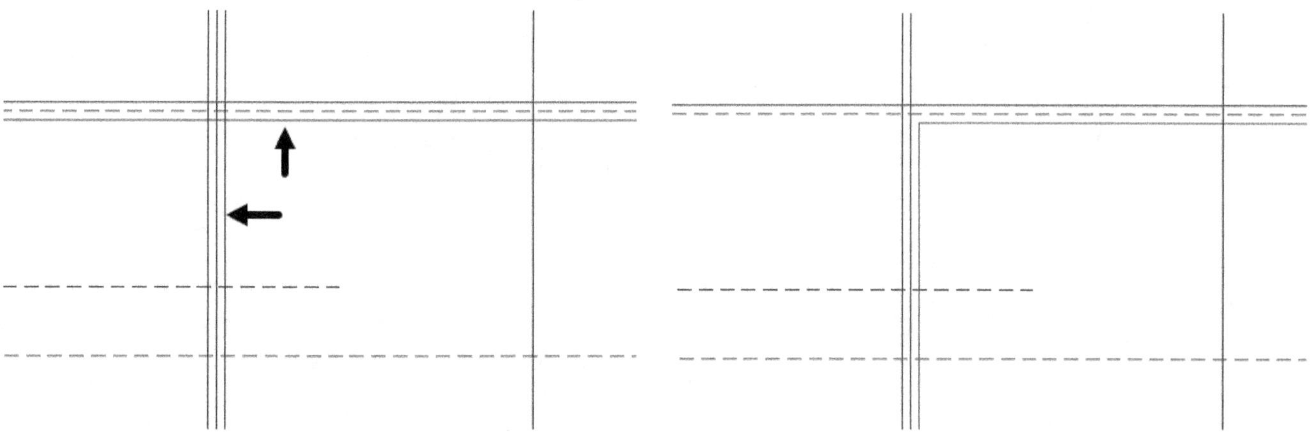

- Likewise, fillet the other corners, as shown.

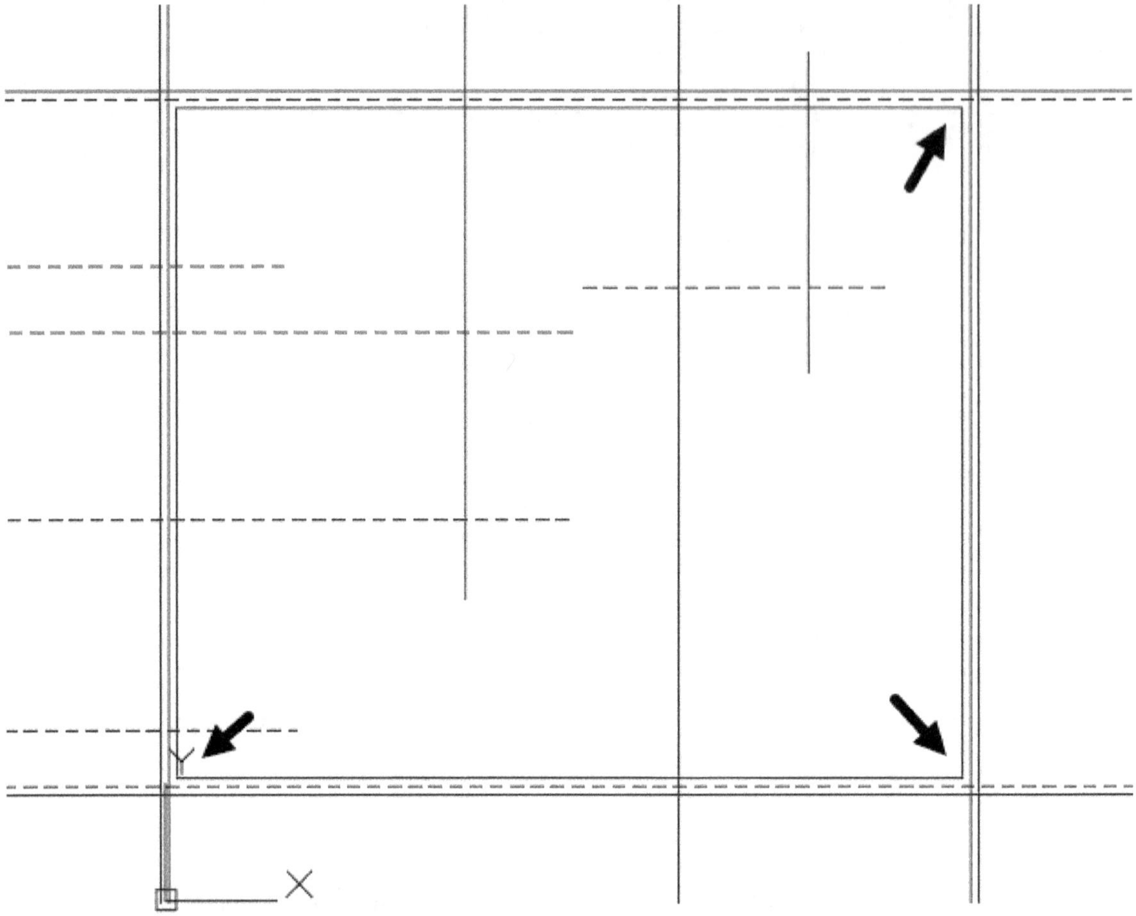

- Create corners on the outside edges using the **Fillet** command.

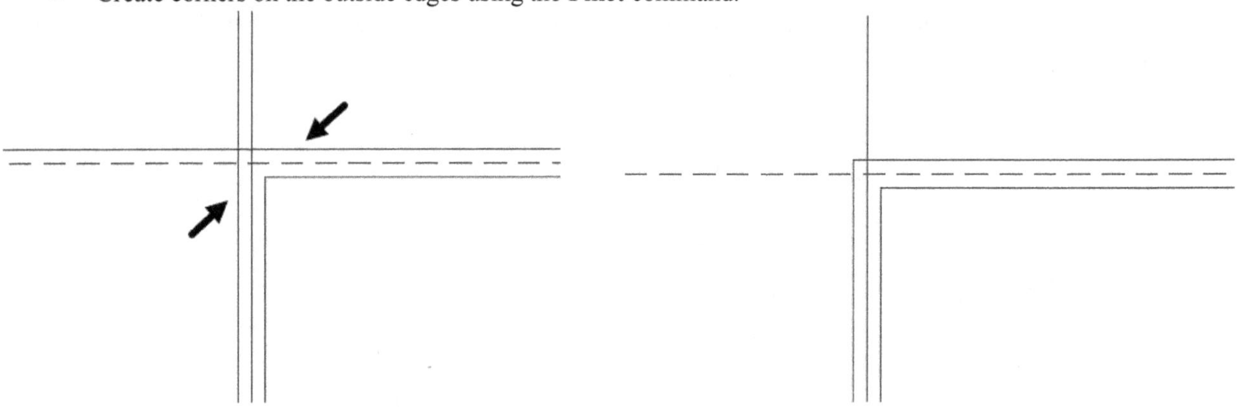

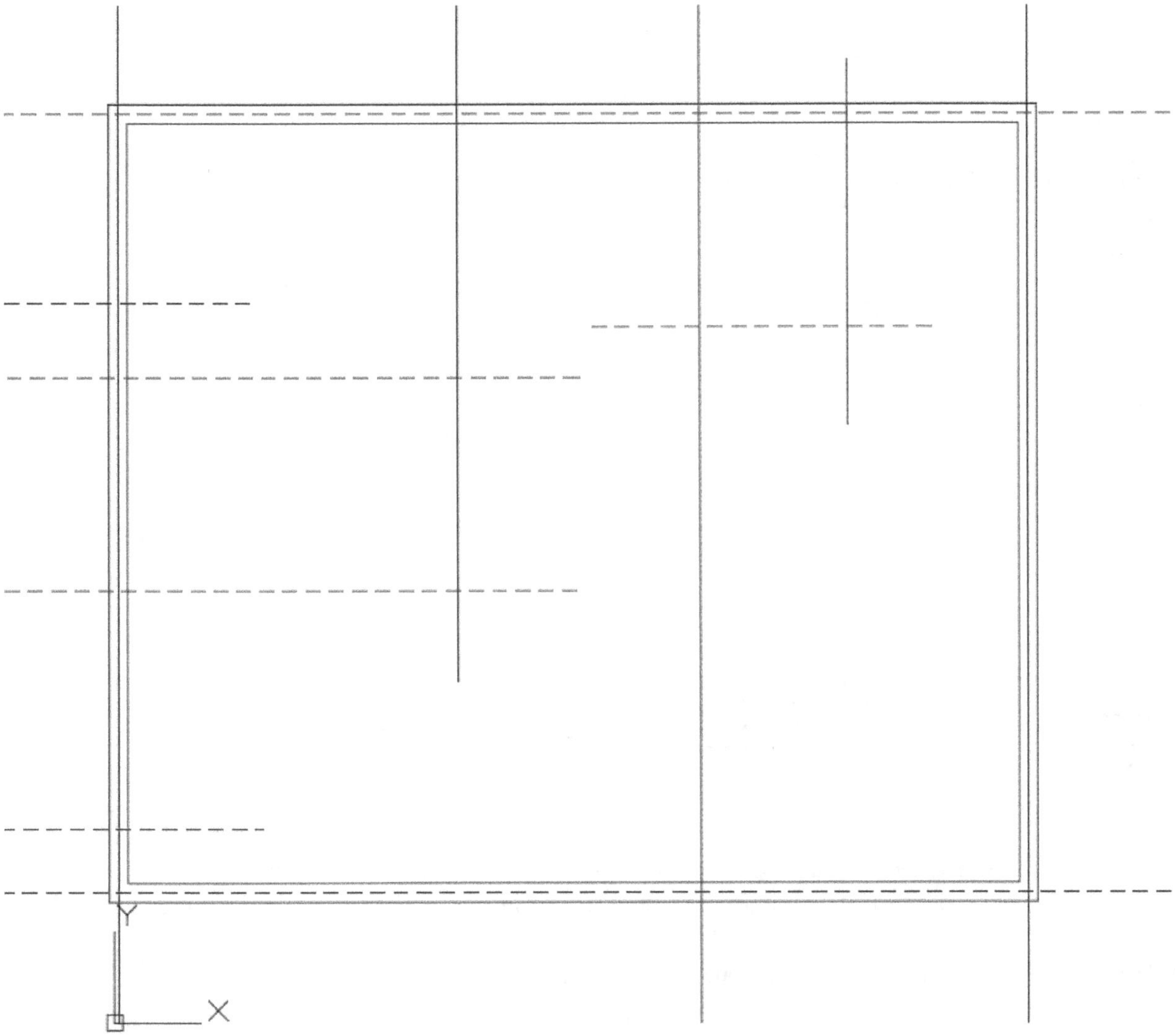

- On the status bar, click the down arrow next to the **Object Snap** icon and make sure that the **Intersection** option is selected.
- On the ribbon, click **Home** tab > **Draw** panel > **Polyline** . Zoom to the left-hand side of the drawing and select the intersection point between the grid lines, as shown in the figure. Select the other intersection points, as shown. Next, deactivate the **Polyline** command by pressing the **Esc** key.

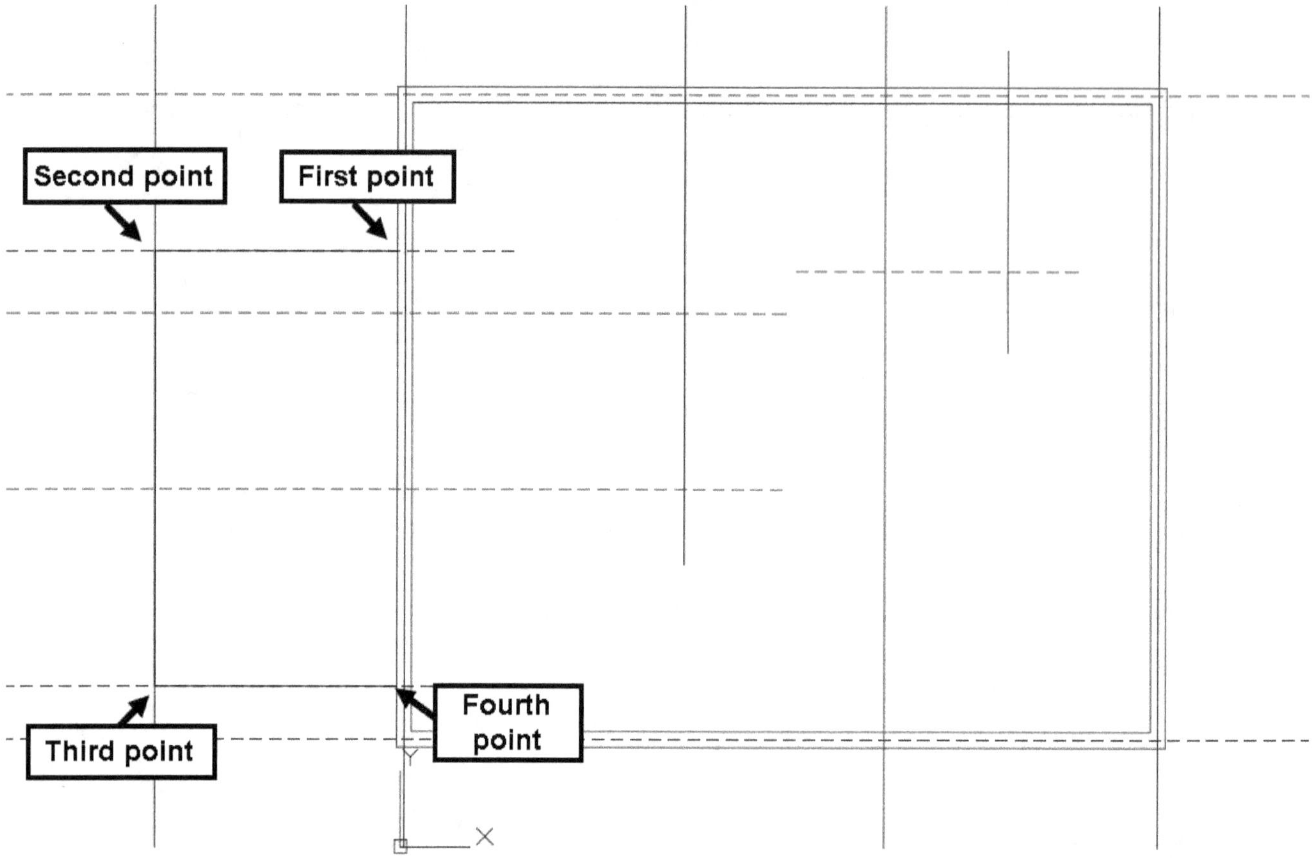

- Type **O** and press **Enter**. Type **6** and press **Enter** to define the offset distance. Select the polyline, move the pointer up and click. Again, select the polyline, move the pointer downward, and click. Press **Esc** to deactivate the **Offset** tool.
- Select the polyline coinciding with the grid line and press **Delete**.

- Use the **Offset** tool to create a wall, as shown. The offset distance is **6**.

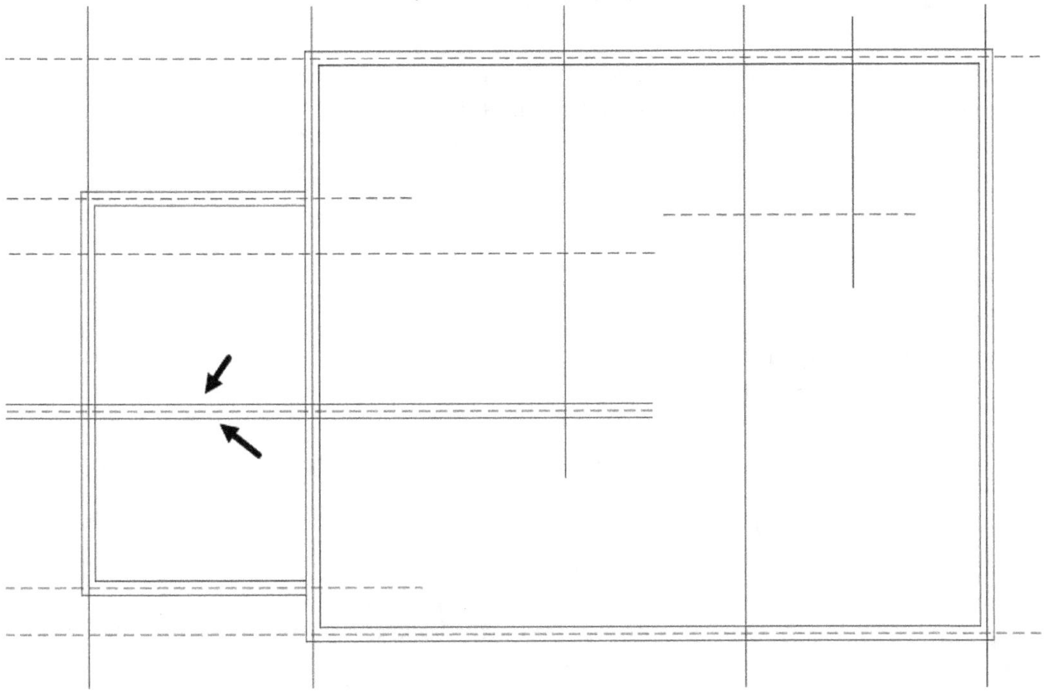

- On the ribbon, click **Home** tab > **Modify** panel > **Trim** . Next, select the **cuTting edges** option from the command line. Select the two polylines, as shown. Press **Enter** to accept the selected entities as trimming boundaries. Select the portions to be trimmed, as shown. Press **Esc** to deactivate the **Trim** command.

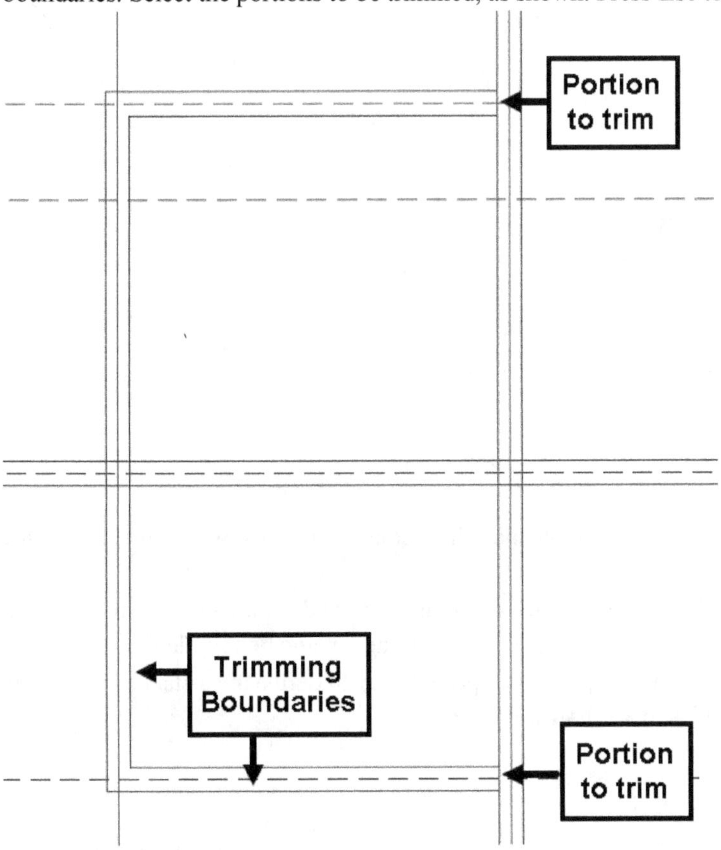

- On the ribbon, click **Home** tab > **Modify** panel > **Trim** . Next, select the **cuTting edges** option from the command line.
- Select the inner edges of the walls, as shown. Press **Enter** to accept the selected entities as trimming boundaries. Select the portions to trim, as shown. Press **Esc** to deactivate the **Trim** command.

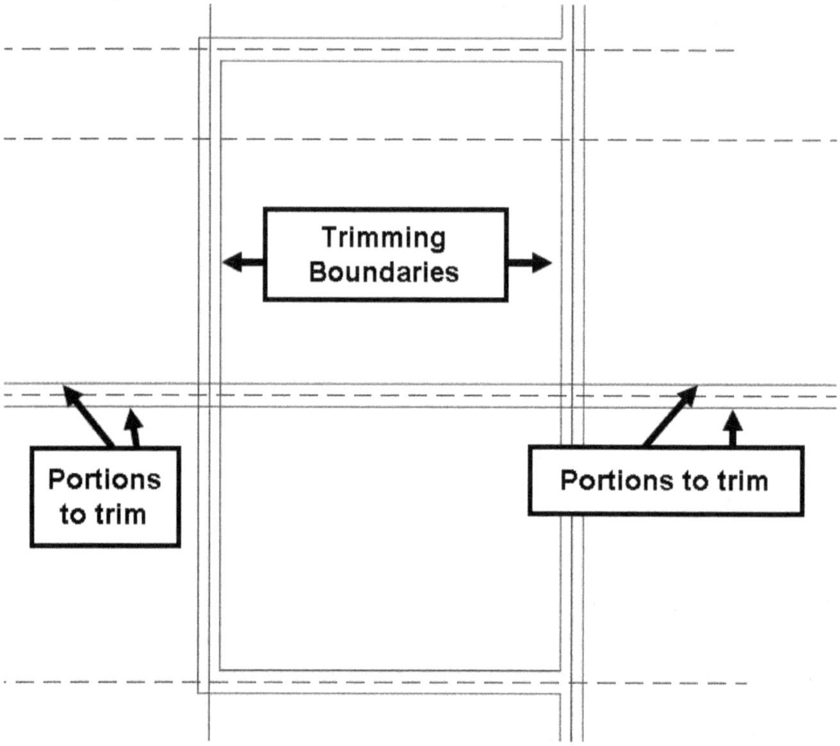

- Type **TR** and press **Enter**. Next, select the **cuTting edges** option from the command line. Select the edges of the horizontal wall, and press **Enter**. Select the portions of the wall edges, as shown. Press **Esc** to deactivate the **Trim** tool.

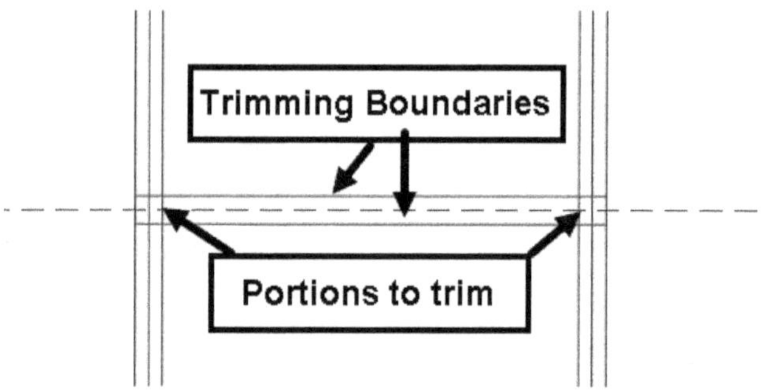

- Type **ML** and press **Enter** to activate the **MLINE** command. This command creates two parallel lines when you specify points in the graphics window.
- Select **Justification** from the command line. Select the **Zero** option to create the multi-lines on both sides of the origin point. The **Top** and **Bottom** options align the origin point with the top and bottom lines, respectively.
- Select the **Scale** option from the command line. Type **5.9** and press **Enter** to define the distance between the lines. Select the start and endpoints of the multi-line, as shown. Press **Esc**.

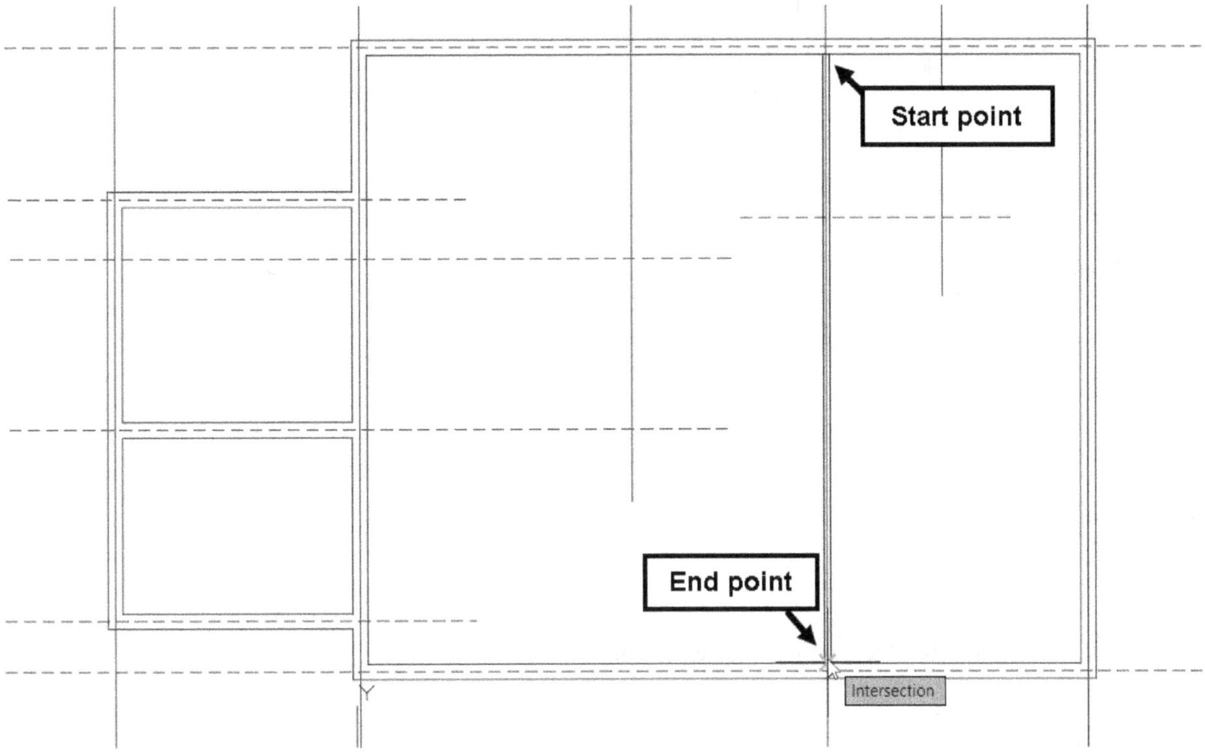

- Activate the MLINE command and create the bathroom wall, as shown.

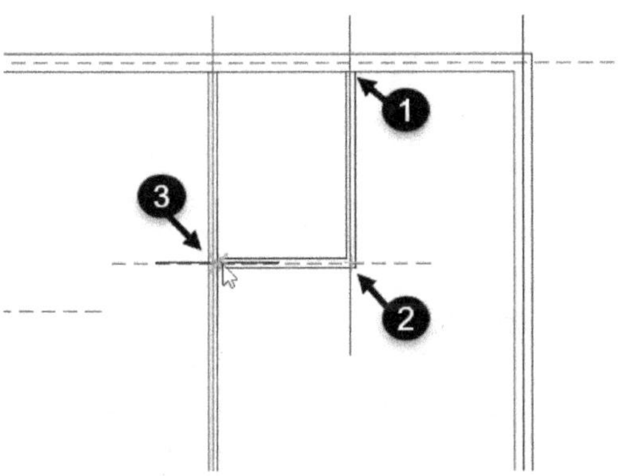

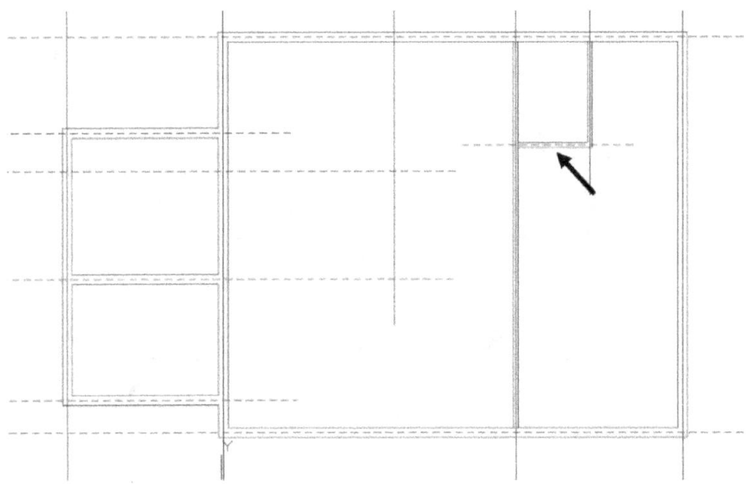

- Type **MLEDIT** in the command line and press **Enter**. Select **Open Tree** from the **Multiline Edit Tools** dialog. Select the two multi-lines in the order, as shown. The open tree is created at the intersection. Press **Esc** to deactivate the **MLEDIT** command.

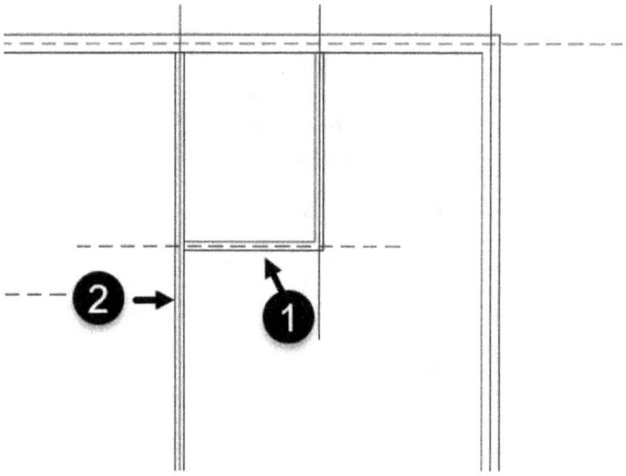

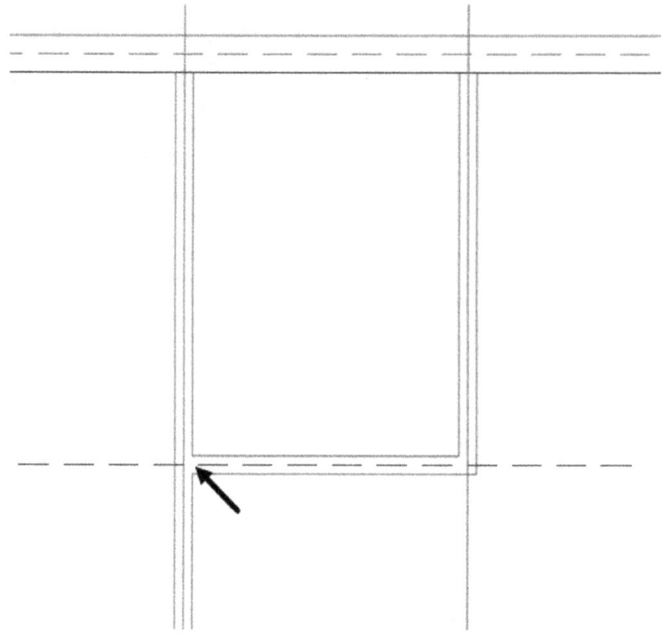

- Likewise, create the other walls using the MLINE command, as shown.

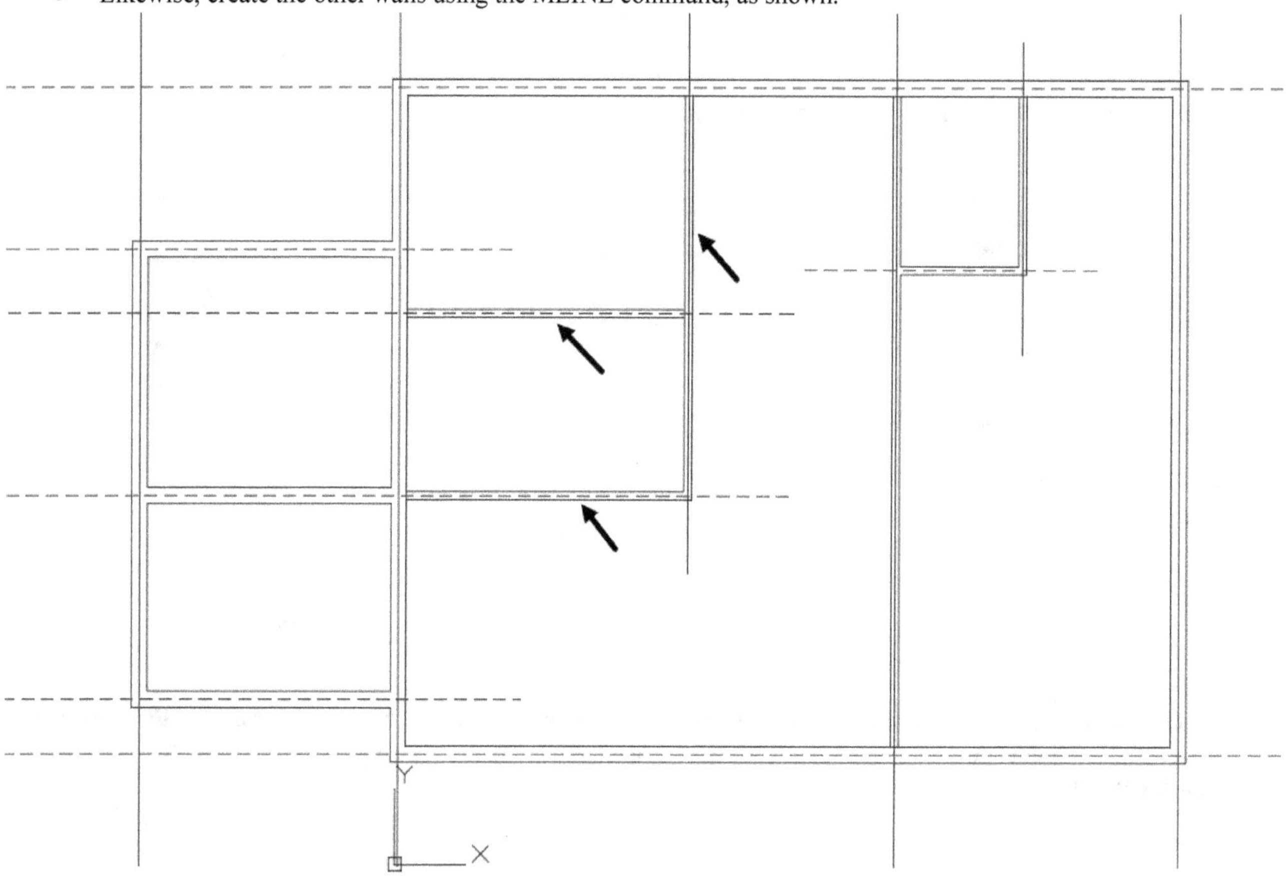

- Use the **Trim** command, and then trim the unwanted portions at the intersections, as shown.

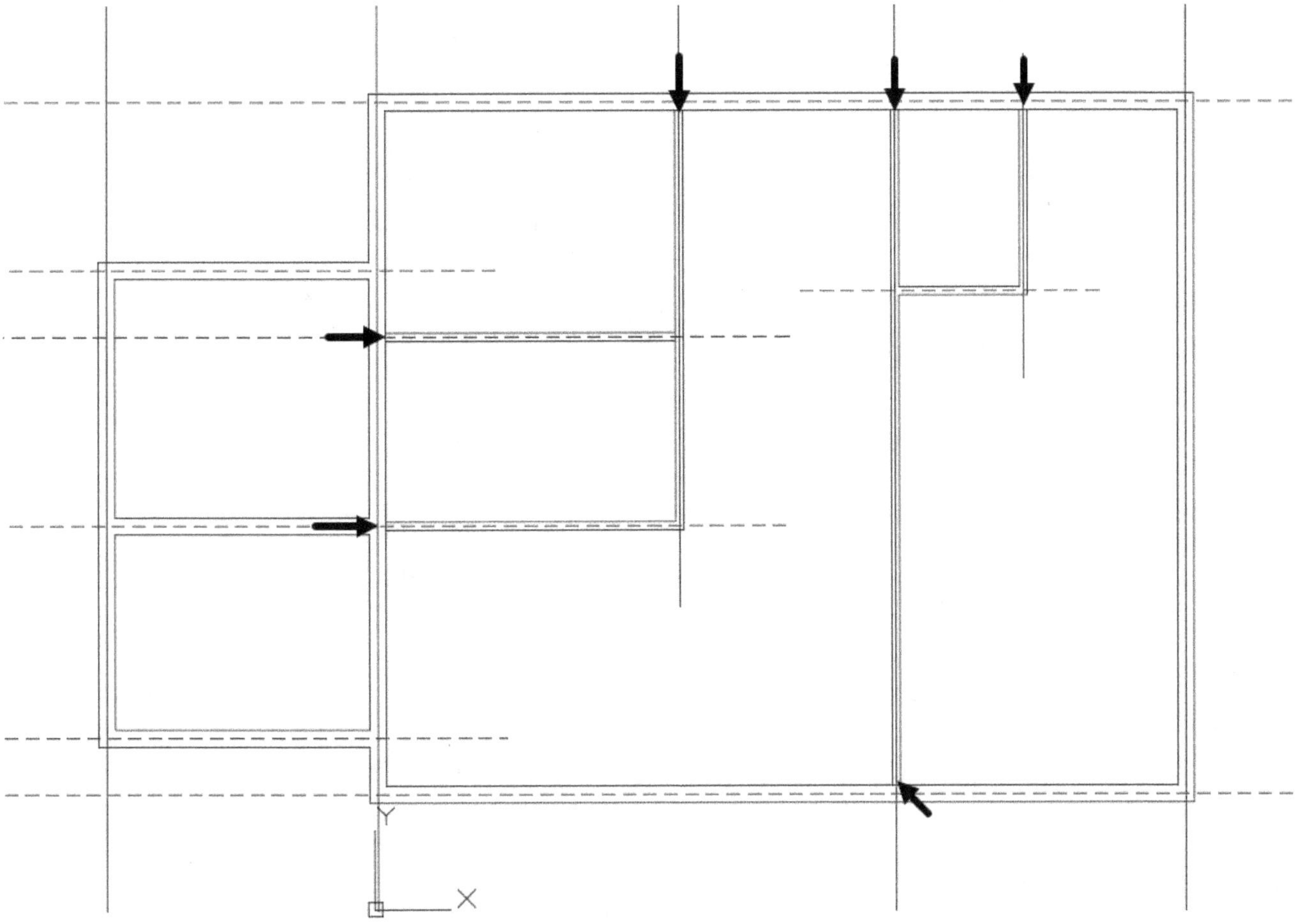

- Use the **MLEDIT** command to create an **Open Tree** at the intersection of two walls, as shown.

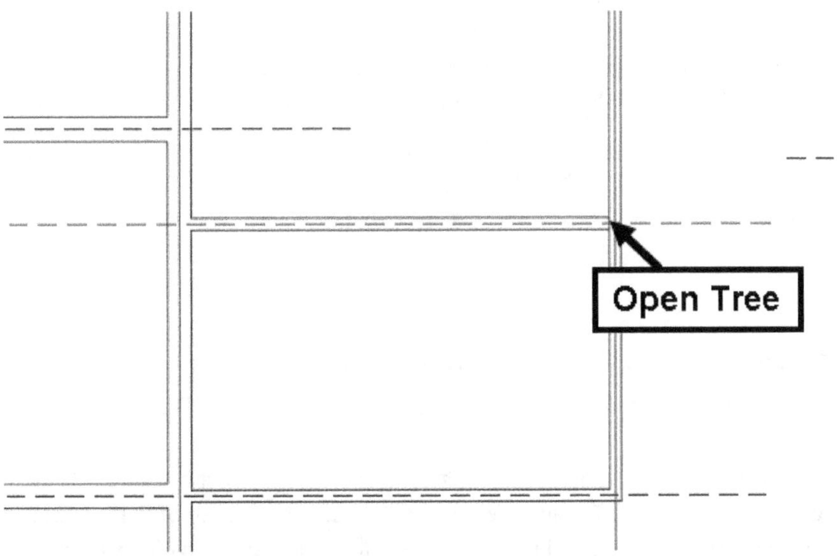

- On the ribbon, click **Home** tab > **Modify** panel > **Explode**  . Select the multi-lines and press **Enter**. The multi-lines are exploded into individual lines.

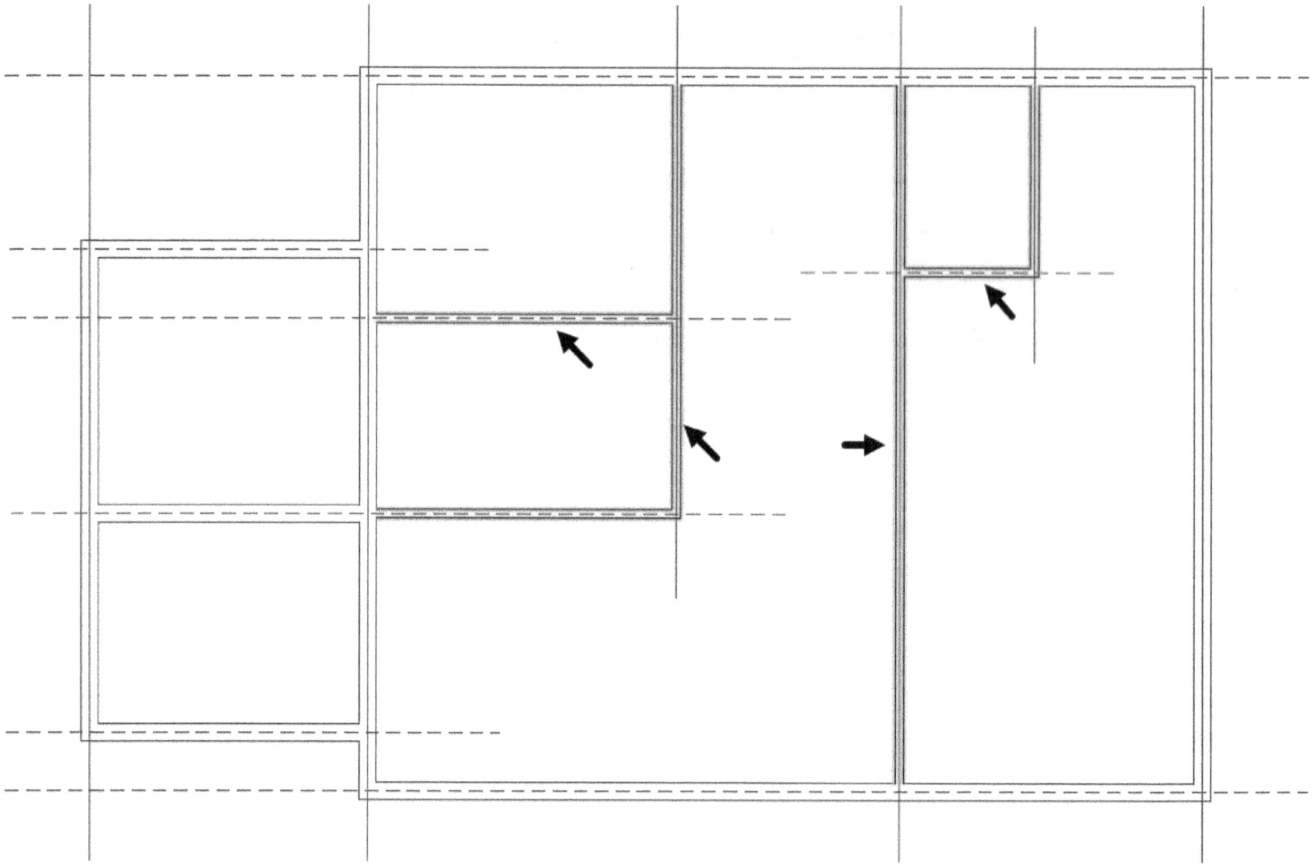

Tutorial 5: Creating Doors and Windows

- On the ribbon, click **Home** tab > **Layers** panel > **Layer** drop-down > **A-DOOR**.
- On the ribbon, click **Home** tab > **Draw** panel > **Rectangle** . Define the first corner of the rectangle by selecting an arbitrary point in the space.
- Select **Dimensions** from the command line. Type **2.5** and press **Enter** to define the length of the rectangle. Type **4** and press **Enter** to define the width of the rectangle. Move the pointer up and click to create the rectangle.

- To **Zoom** into the rectangle, type **Z** in the command line, and then select **Object**.
- Create a window in the area in which the rectangle was created; the rectangle is selected. Press **Enter** to zoom in to the rectangle.
- Type **REC** and press **Enter**. Select the top right corner of the rectangle to define the first corner of the rectangle. Select **Dimensions** from the command line. Type **1.2** and press **Enter** to define the length of the rectangle. Type **23.5** and press **Enter** to define the width of the rectangle. Move the pointer up and click to create the rectangle.

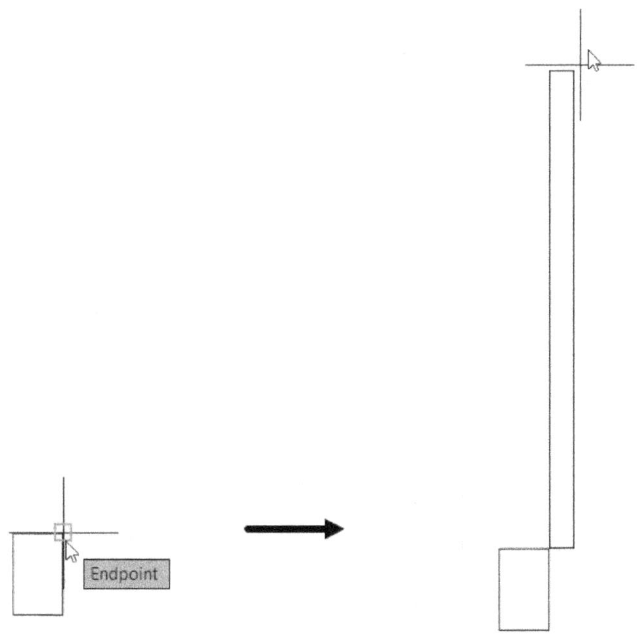

- Activate the **ORTHOMODE** icon on the status bar.
- Select the small rectangle and click **Home** tab > **Modify** panel > **Copy** on the ribbon. Make sure that the **Endpoint** option is checked on the **Object Snap** menu of the status bar.
- Select the bottom left corner of the rectangle to define the base point. Move the pointer toward the right, type **26**, and press **Enter**. Click **Exit** in the command line.

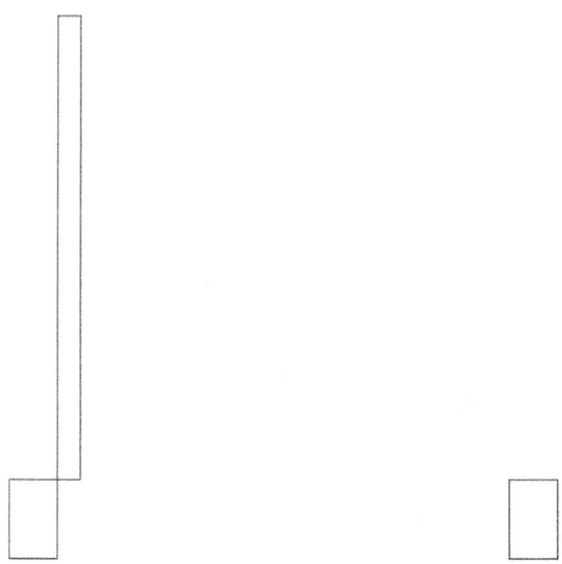

- On the ribbon, click **Home** tab > **Layers** panel > **Layer** drop-down > **DOOR_SWING**.
- On the ribbon, click **Home** tab > **Draw** panel > **Arc** drop-down > **Start, Center, End** . Specify the start, center, and endpoints of the arc, as shown.

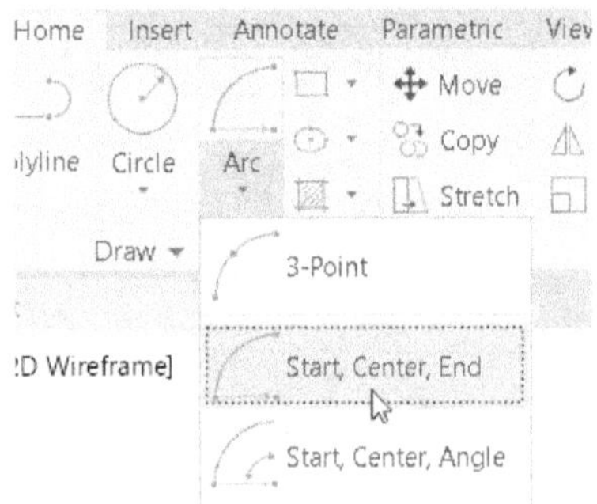

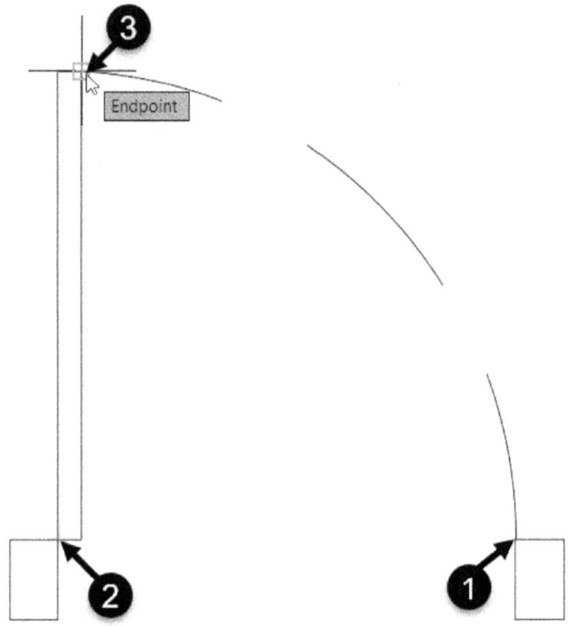

- On the ribbon, click **Home** tab > **Layers** panel > **Layer** drop-down > **A-WALL**. Create two vertical lines of **12** inches long, as shown.

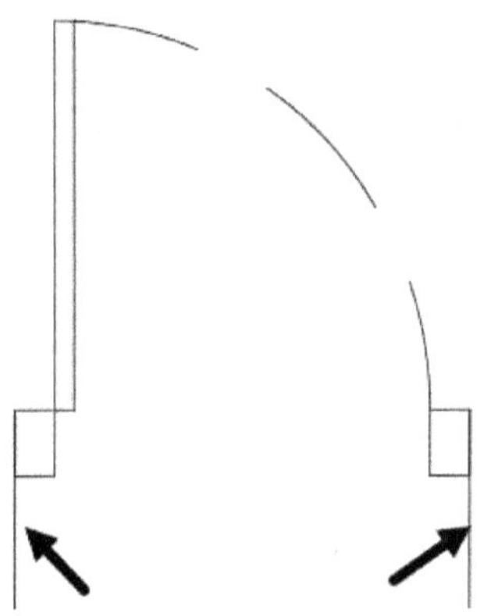

Now, you need to use the **Wipeout** tool to hide the wall edges at the door openings.

- On the ribbon, click **Home** tab > **Layers** panel > **Layer** drop-down > **WIPEOUT**. On the **Home** tab of the ribbon, expand the **Draw** panel and click the **Wipeout** icon. Select the endpoints of the vertical lines in the order, as shown. Select **Close** from the command line.

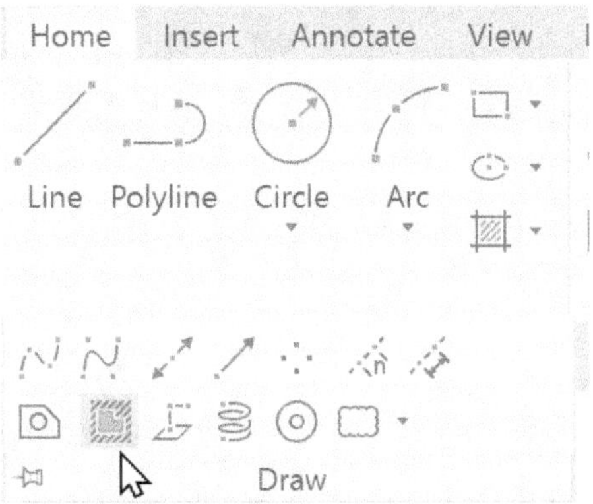

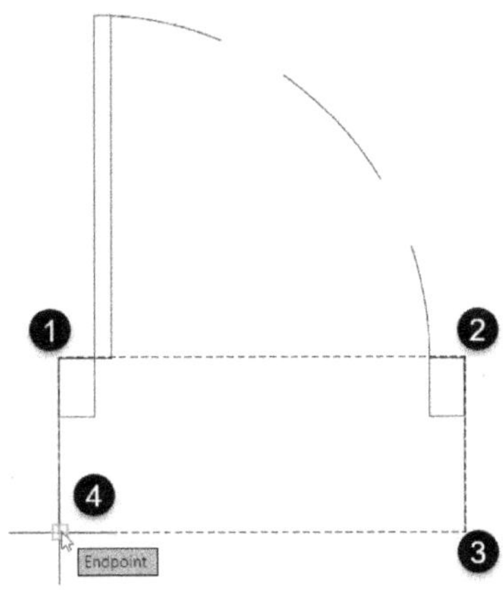

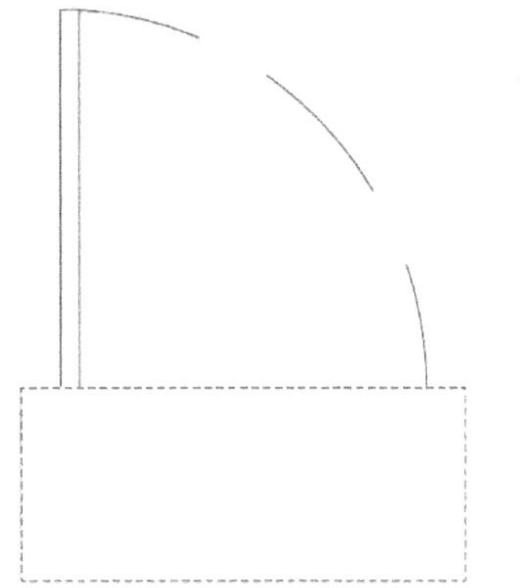

- Select the wipeout frame, right-click, and select **Draw Order > Send to Back**. The wipeout is sent back, and the wall edges and door frames are displayed.

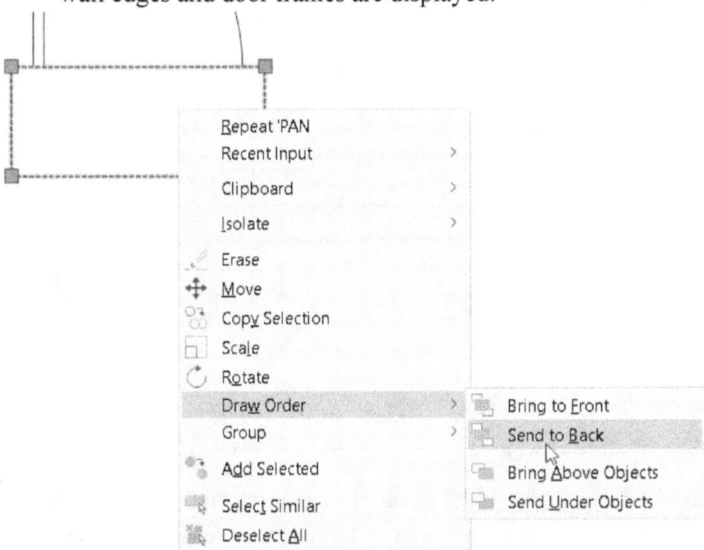

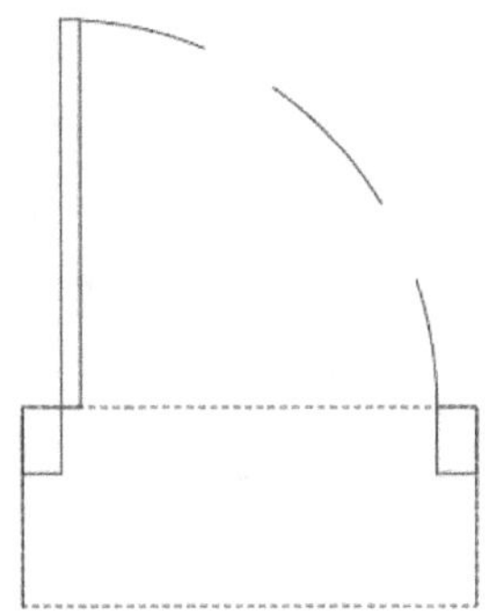

You need to make sure that the wipeout thickness is more than the wall thickness.

- Select the wipeout to highlight its grips at the corners. Select the top right corner grip of the wipeout and move the pointer vertically upward. Type **0.4** and press **Enter**. Likewise, extend the top left corner grip by **0.4** inches upwards.

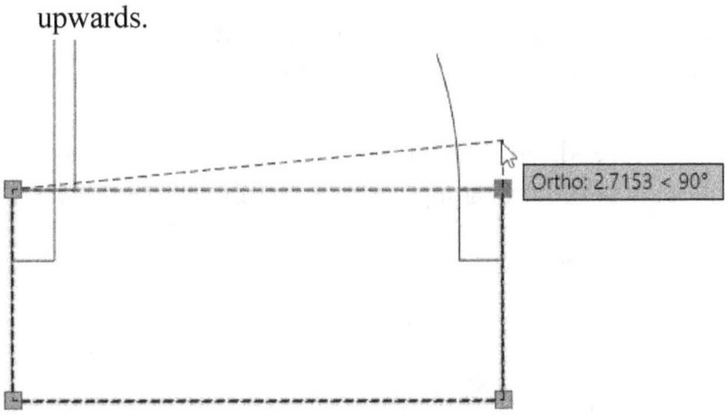

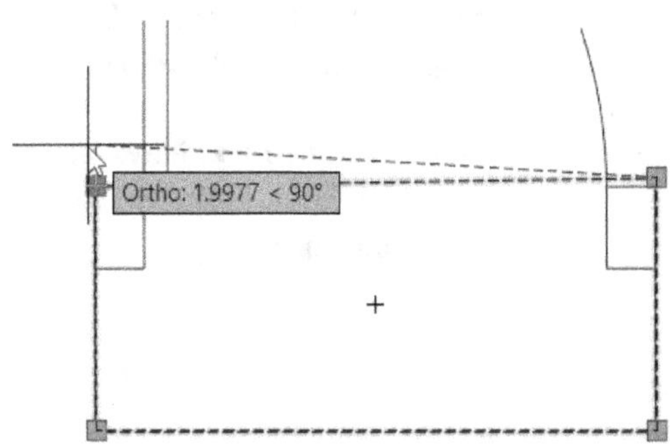

- Likewise, extend the wipeout in the opposite direction.

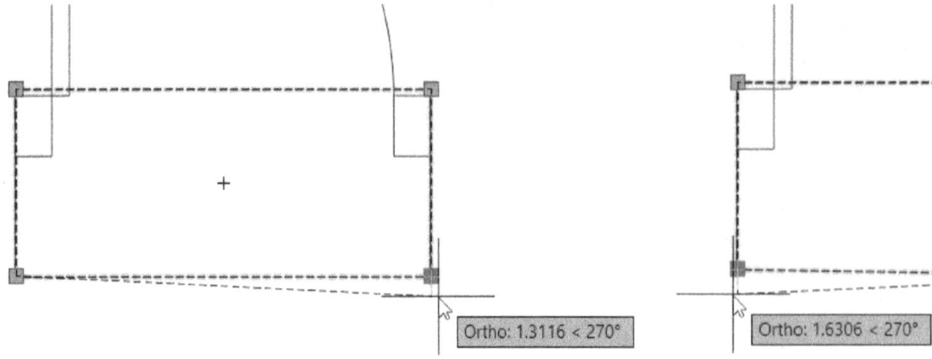

- On the ribbon, click **Insert** tab > **Block Definition** panel > **Create Block > Write Block**. On the **Write Block** dialog, click the **Select objects** icon. Specify the first and second corners of the selection window covering all the entities of the door. Press **Enter** to accept the selection. Click the **Pick point** icon and select the top left corner point of the small rectangle located on the left side. The base point of the block is defined.

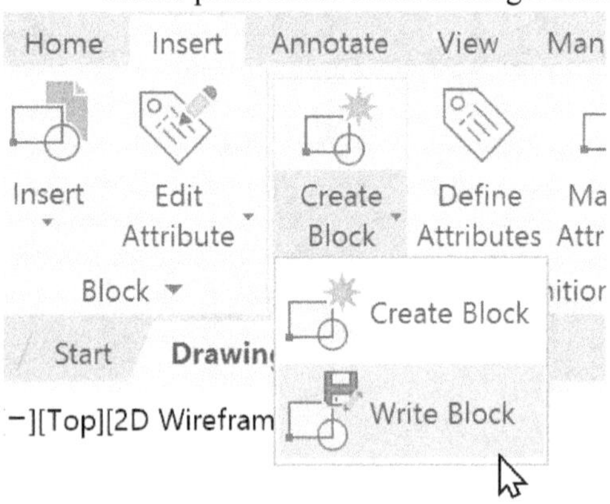

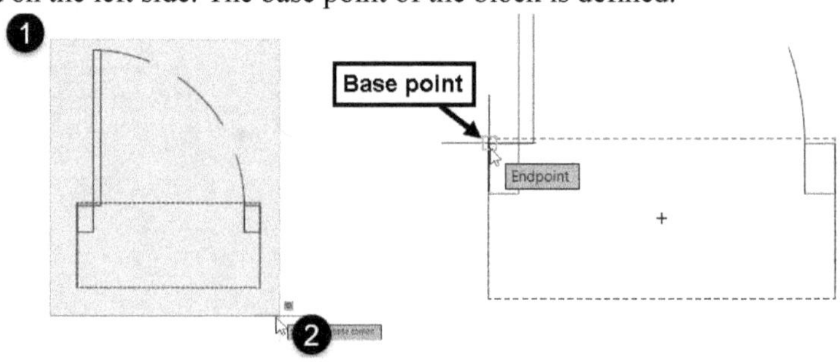

- Click the icon next to the **File name and path** box. Go to the folder location where you saved the **Tutorial 1** drawing file. Type **Single_Door** in the **File name** box and click **Save**. Select **Convert to block** from the **Objects** section and click **OK**. The selected objects are converted into a block.

Now, you need to convert the block into a dynamic block. By doing so, you can change the size, shape, and orientation of the block, dynamically.

- On the ribbon, click **Insert** tab > **Block Definition** panel > **Block Editor** . On the **Edit Block Definition** dialog, select **Single_Door** from the **Block to create or edit** list and click **OK**. The **Block Editor** window appears.
- On the **Block Authoring Palettes**, click the **Parameters** tab and select **Linear** . Specify the start and endpoints of the linear parameter, as shown (select the endpoints of the left vertical line). Move the pointer toward the left and position the parameter.

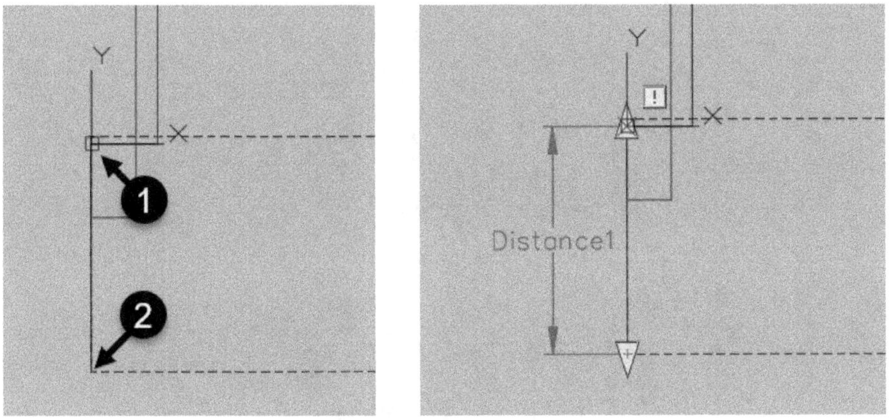

- Select the linear parameter, right click, and then select **Grip Display > 1**; only one grip is displayed on the parameter.

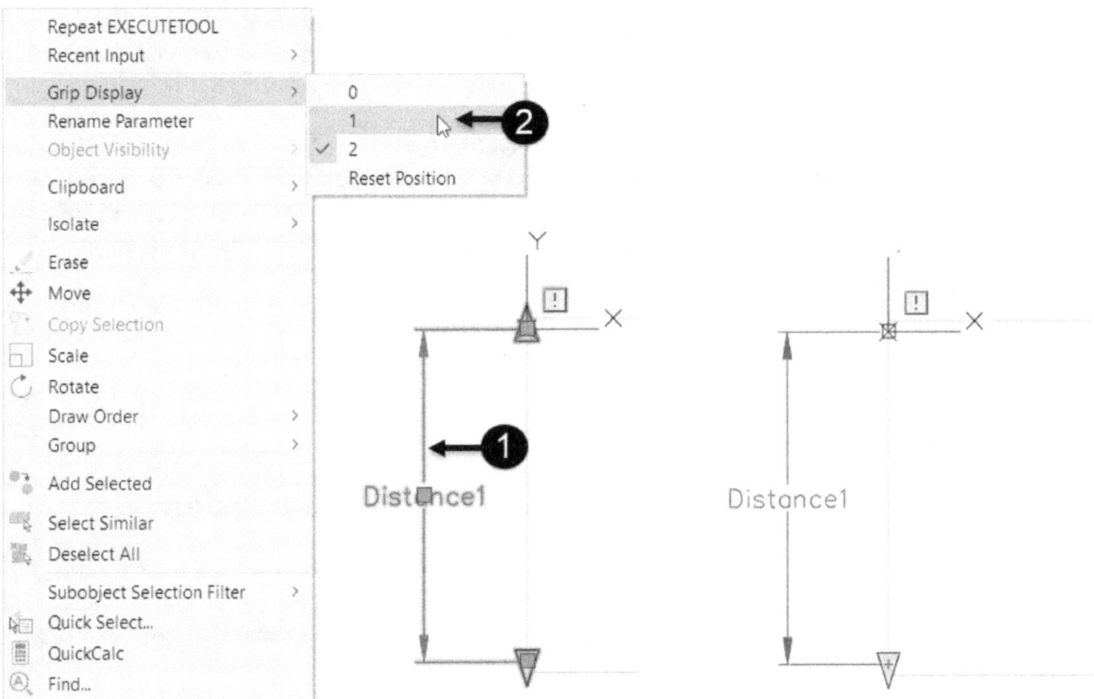

- Select the **Distance 1** parameter and press **CTRL+1** to open the **Properties** palette. On the **Properties** palette, under the **Property Labels** section, set the **Distance name** to **Wall Thickness**.
- Close the **Properties** palette.

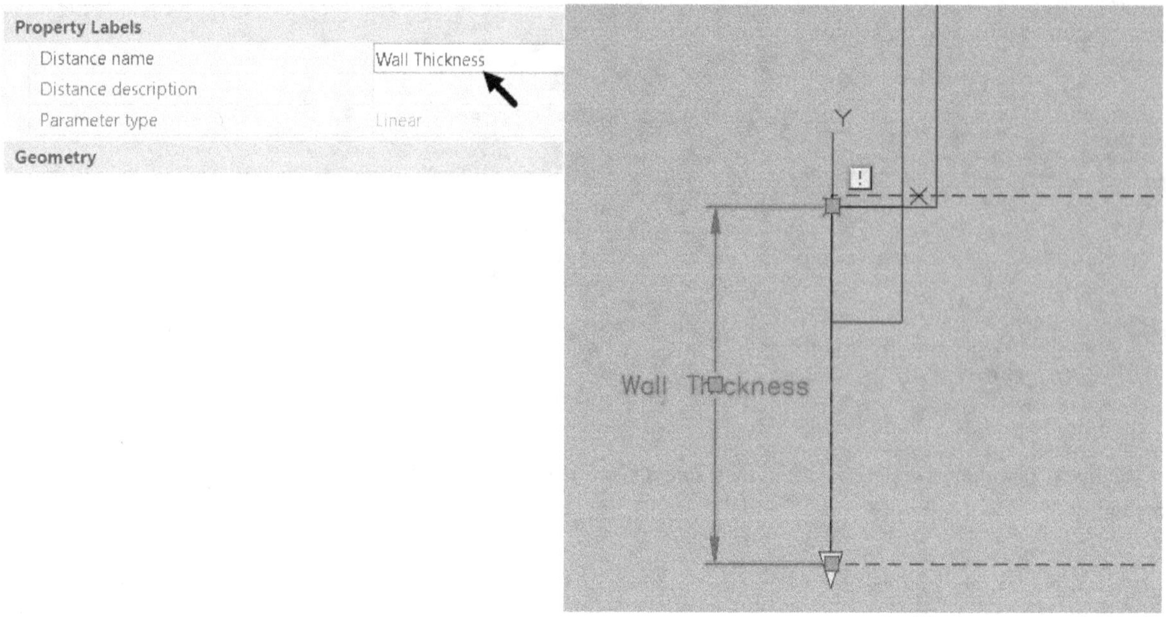

- On the **Block Authoring Palettes**, click the **Actions** tab and select **Stretch** . Select the **Wall Thickness** parameter. Select the endpoint of the **Wall Thickness** parameter. Specify the first corner of the stretch frame, as shown. Drag the pointer and click to specify the opposite corner of the stretch frame, as shown. Select the two vertical lines and the wipeout, and then press **Enter** to specify the objects to be stretched. The **Stretch** action appears at the bottom of the **Wall Thickness** parameter.

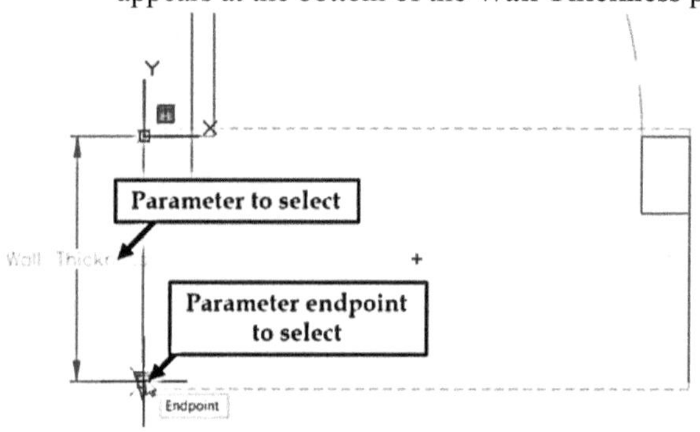

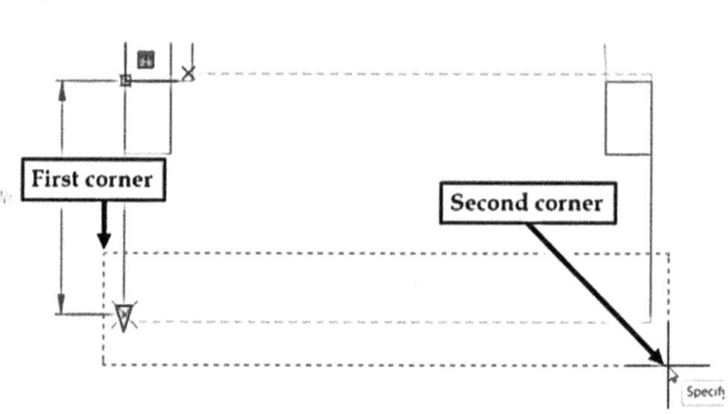

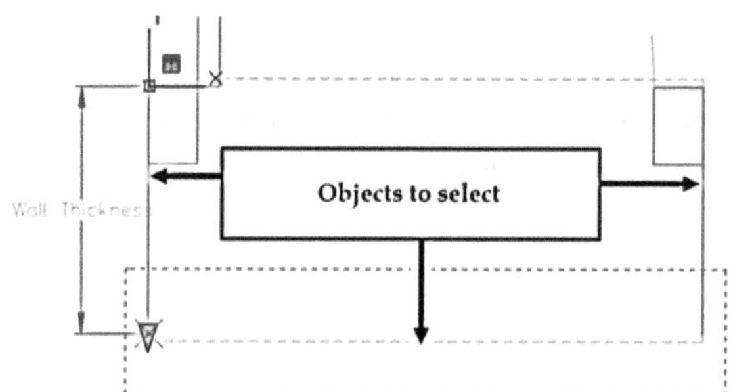

- On the **Block Editor** tab of the ribbon, click **Open/Save** panel > **Test Block** . Select the vertical line of the door and drag the arrow grip. Notice that the wall thickness changes dynamically. On the ribbon, click the **Close Test Block** icon.

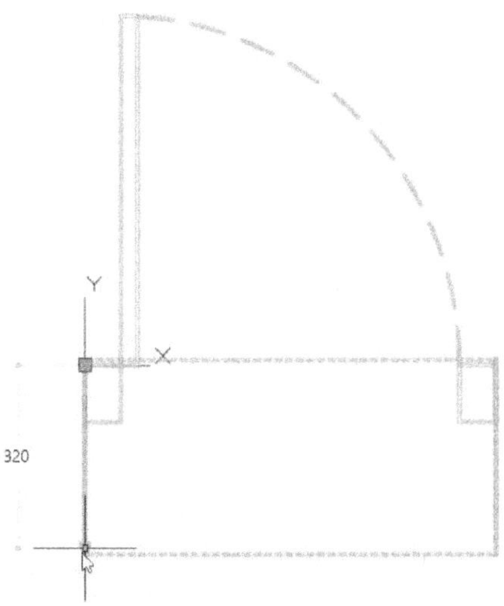

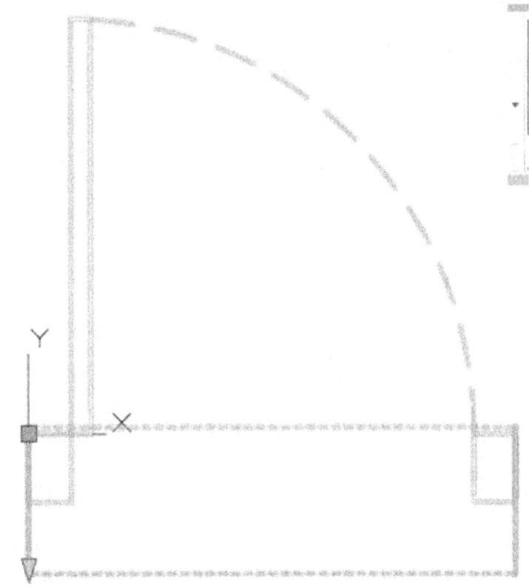

- Create a **Linear** parameter between the inside edges of the door frames, and then change its name to **Door Width**.

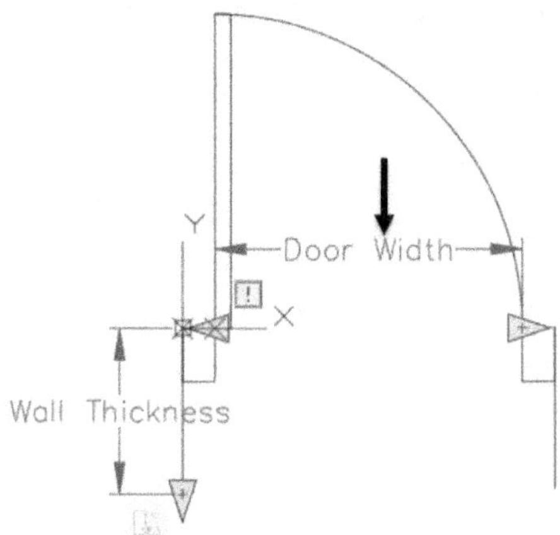

- On the **Block Authoring Palettes**, click **Actions** tab > **Stretch** . Select the **Door Width** parameter and then select its endpoint. Create the stretch frame on the right side of the block, as shown. Select the right vertical line, door frame, and wipeout frame as the objects to stretch. Press **Enter**.

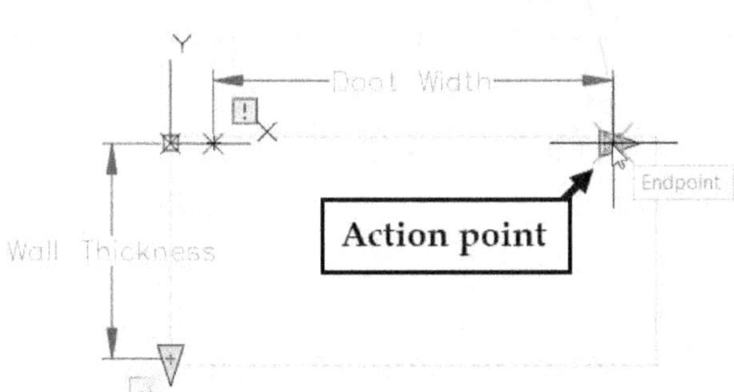

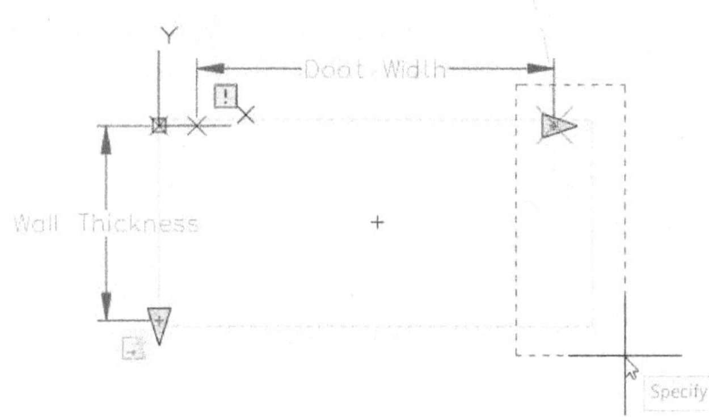

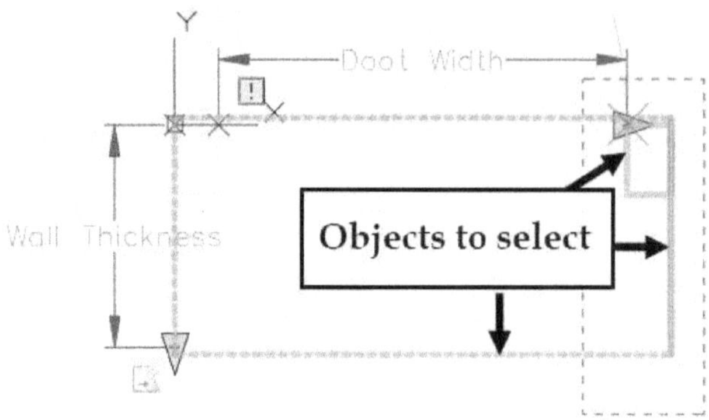

- On the **Block Authoring Palettes**, click **Actions** tab > **Scale** . Select the **Door Width** parameter and the arc. Press **Enter** to create the **Scale** action.

- On the **Block Authoring Palettes**, click **Actions** tab > **Stretch** . Select the **Door Width** parameter and then select its endpoint. Create the stretch frame on the top portion of the door panel, as shown. Select the door panel and press **Enter**.

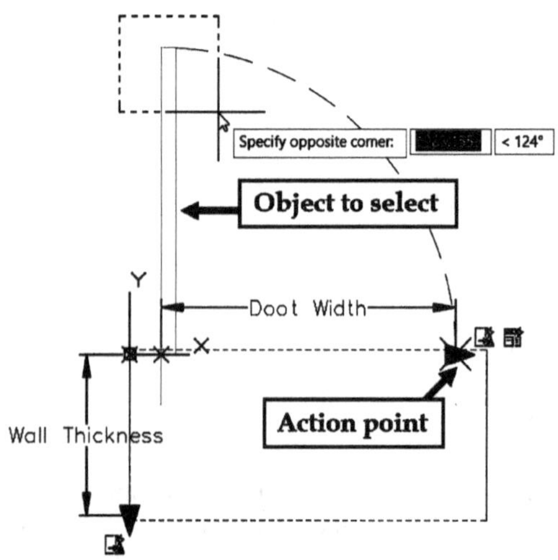

- On the **Block Editor** tab of the ribbon, click **Open/Save** panel > **Test Block** . Select the block and drag the arrow, pointing toward the right. Notice that the door width and door swing are modified. However, the door panel is skewed. Click **Close Test Block** on the ribbon.

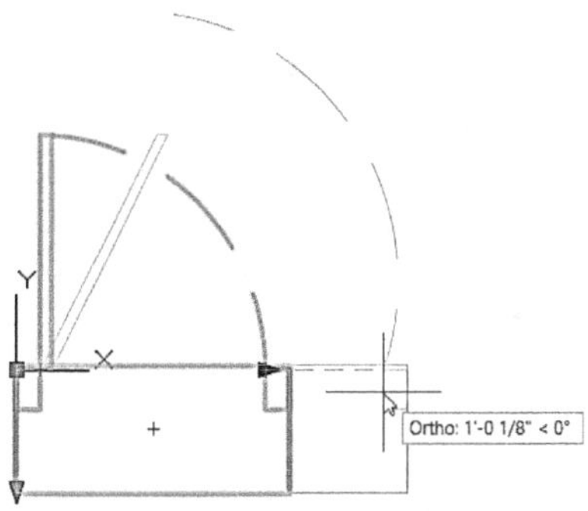

- Select the extreme right **Stretch** icon, and then press **Ctrl+1** on your keyboard.
- On the **Properties** palette, under the **Overrides** section, change the **Angle offset** value to **90**. Press **Enter**. Open the **Test Block Window** and drag the arrow grip, pointing toward the right. Notice that the block changes as desired. However, the size of the door can be changed to any non-standard value. Click **Close Test Block** on the ribbon.

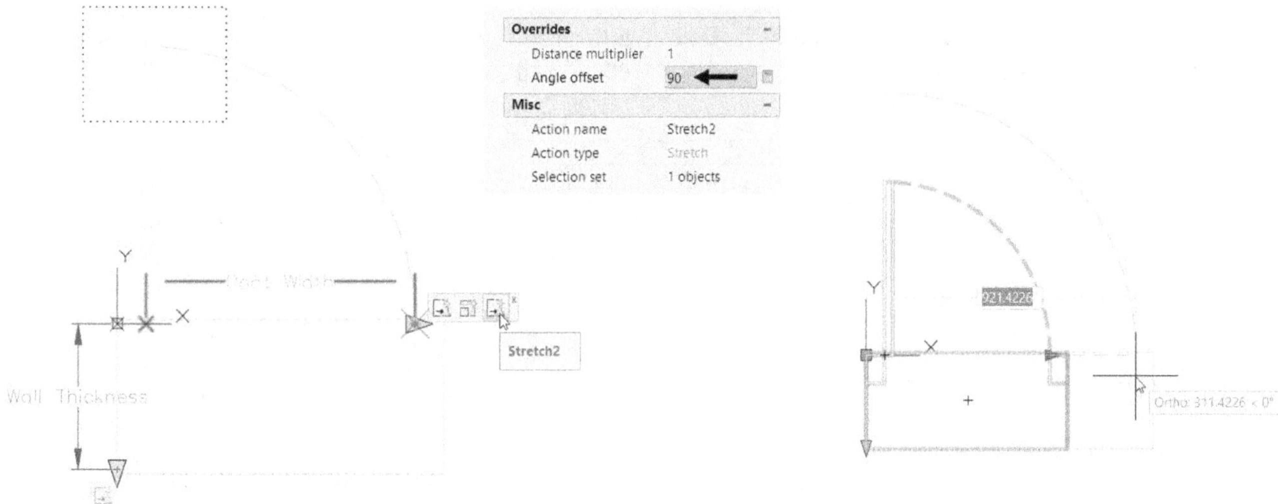

If you want the door to have some standard sizes, you need to change the **Dist type** of the Door Width parameter to **List**.

- Select the **Door Width** parameter. Next, right-click and select **Properties**.
- On the **Properties** palette, under the **Value Set** section, change the **Dist type** to **List**. Click in the **Dist value list** box and select the icon located next to it. On the **Add Distance Value** dialog, type **32.5** in the **Distance to add** box and press **Enter**. Likewise, add other values to the list, as shown. Click **OK** to close the dialog.

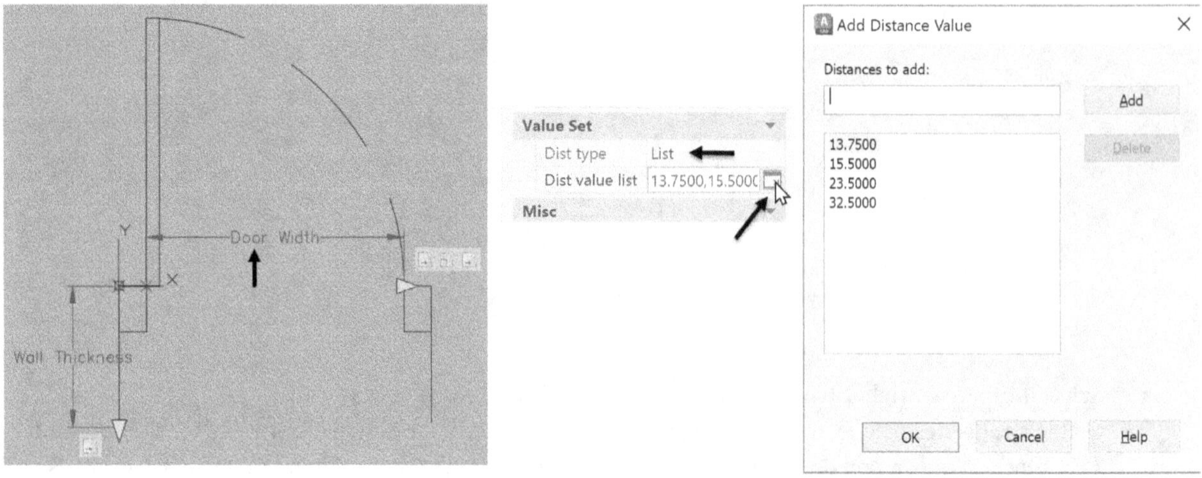

- Open the **Test Block Window** and modify the **Door Width** parameter. Notice the intervals displayed while dragging the stretch arrow. You can change the door width using the intervals. Click **Close Test Block** on the ribbon.

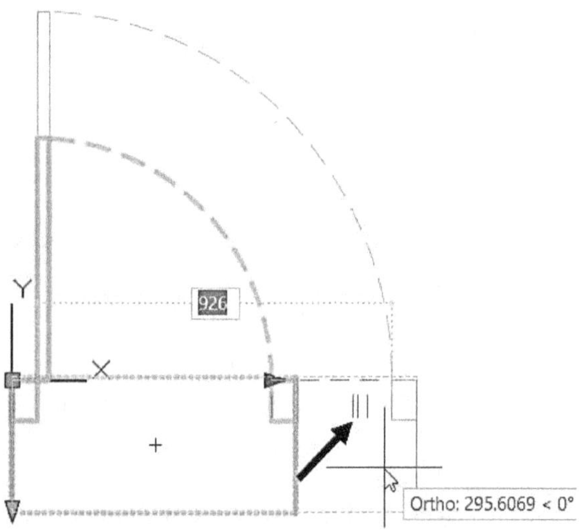

- Click the **Save Block**  button on the **Open/Save** panel of the **Block Editor** ribbon. Next, click **Close Block Editor** on the ribbon.
- Click **Zoom Extents** on the **Navigation Bar** located at the right-hand side in the graphics window.
- On the ribbon, click **Home** tab > **Layers** panel > **Layer** drop-down > **A-DOOR**.
- On the ribbon, click **Insert** tab > **Block** panel > **Insert** drop-down > **Single_Door**. Select **Rotate** from the command line, type **90**, and press **Enter**. Select the intersection point between the grid and the bathroom wall, as shown.

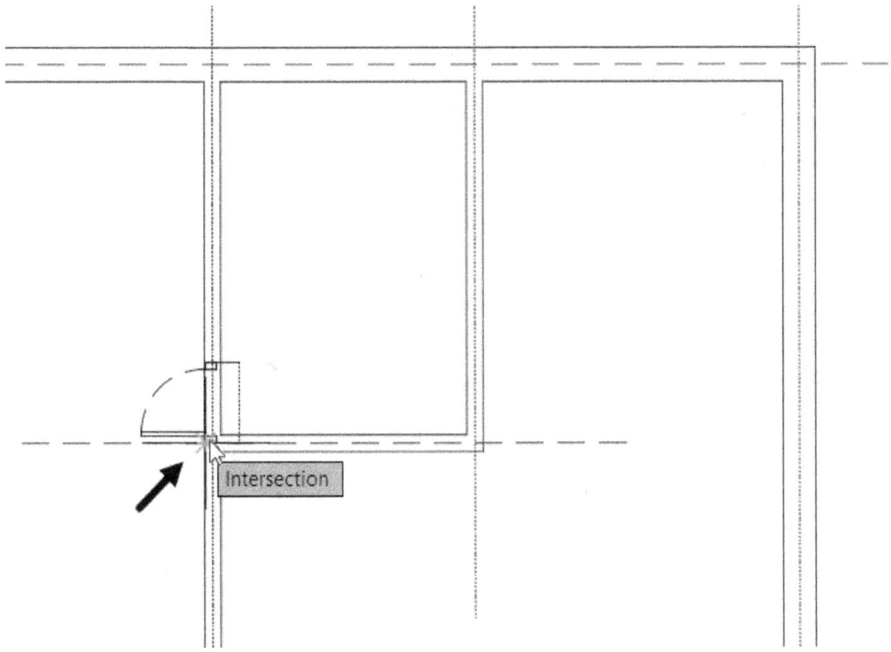

- Select the block, if not already selected. Select the base point of the block and move the pointer up. Type **14.75** and press Enter.

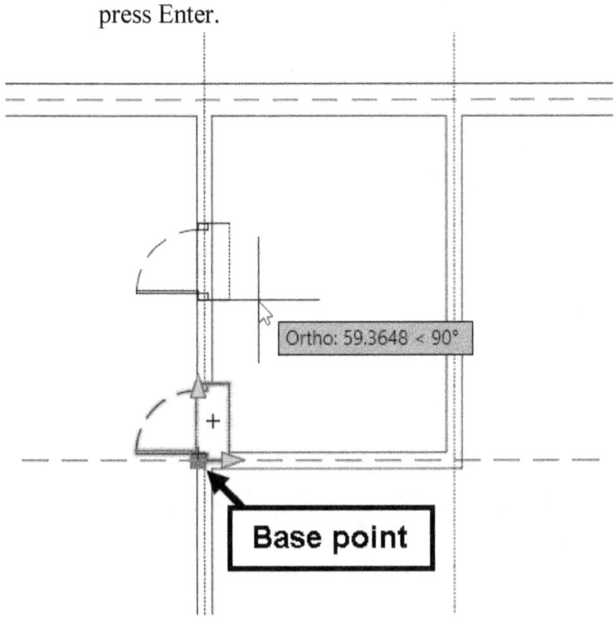

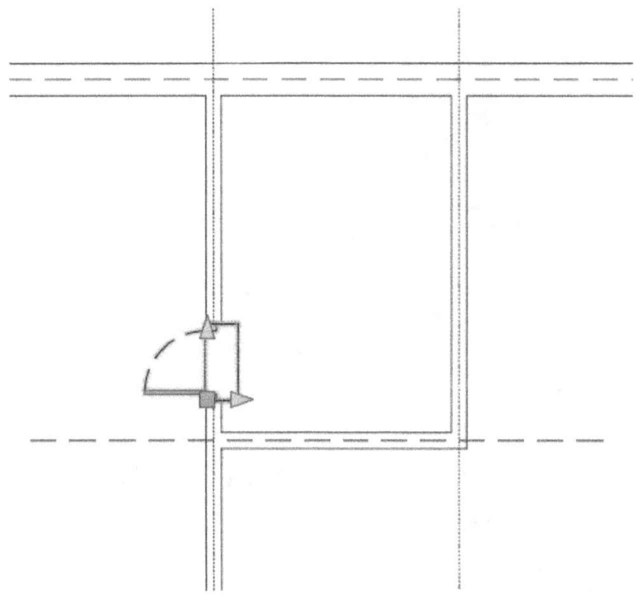

- Click the stretch arrow pointing toward the right. Drag the pointer toward the left and select a point on the wall edge, as shown.

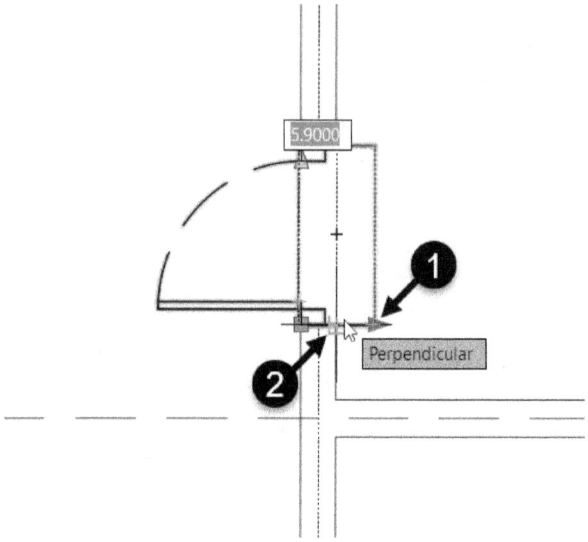

- Click the stretch arrow pointing upwards. Drag the pointer upward and click at the interval, as shown.

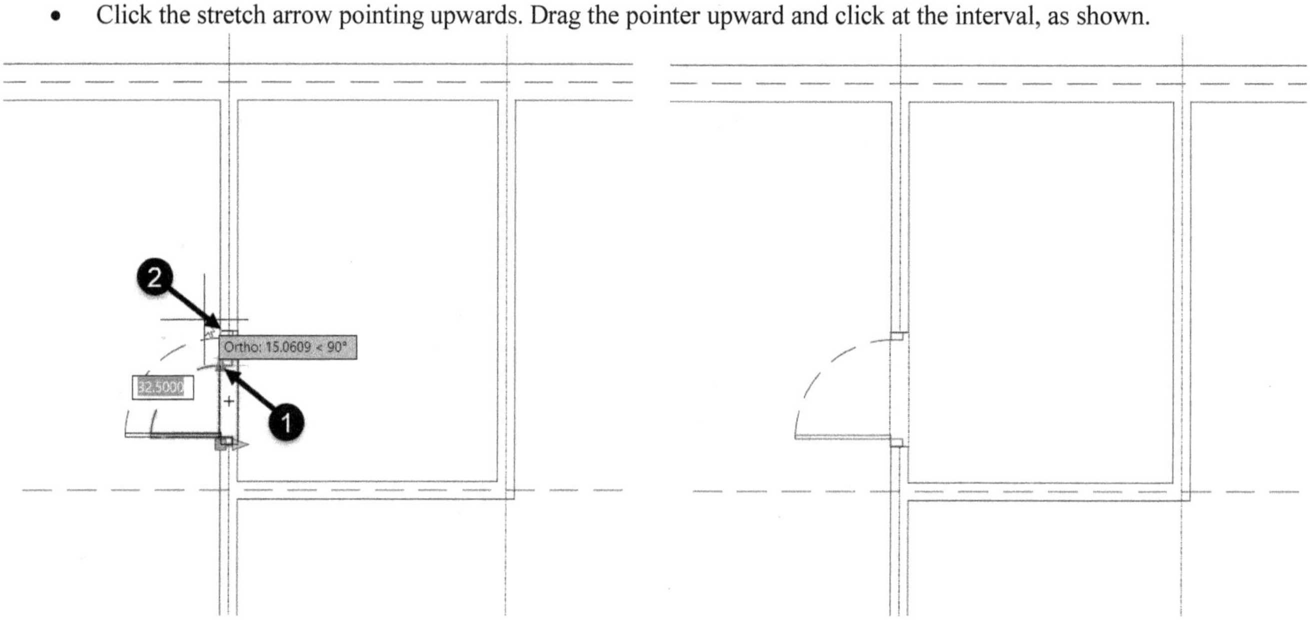

- On the **Home** tab of the ribbon, expand the **Draw** panel and click the **Wipeout** icon. Select **Frames** from the command line. Select the **OFF** option to turn off the wipeout frame.

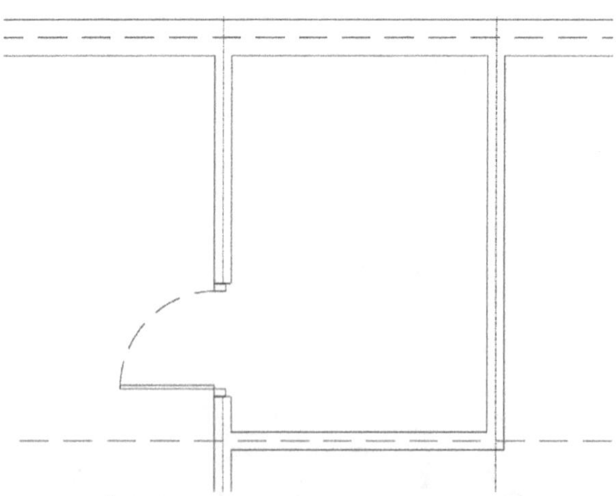

- Insert the other instances of the **Single_Door** blocks, as shown. Note that you need to flip the **Single_Door** block at the utility room.

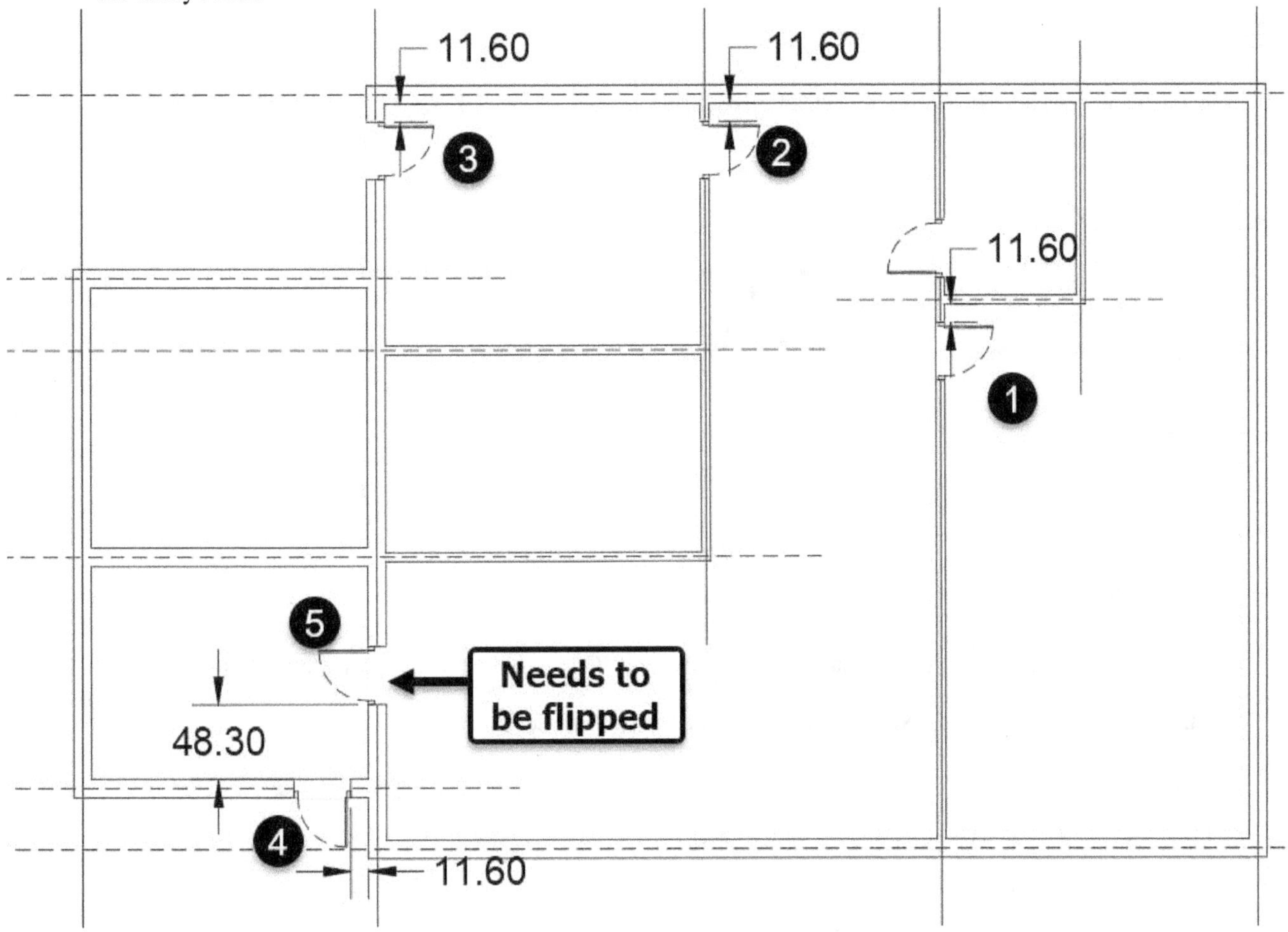

- On the ribbon, click **Home** tab > **Modify** panel > **Mirror**. Select the door to be flipped, and press **Enter**. Select the midpoint of the door. Move the pointer horizontally toward the left and click to define the mirror line. Select **Yes** from the command line to erase the source objects.

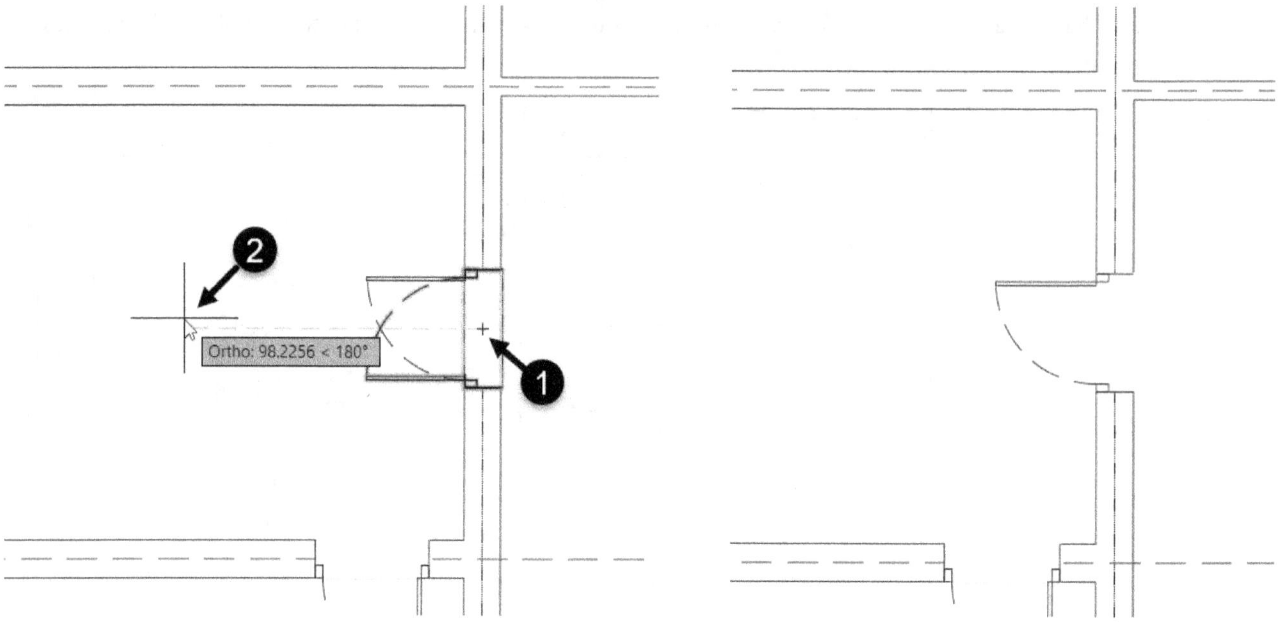

Now, you need to create double doors.

- Select the **Single_Door** block available in the empty area. On the ribbon, click **Home** tab > **Modify** panel > **Explode** . The block is exploded, and individual objects are selectable.

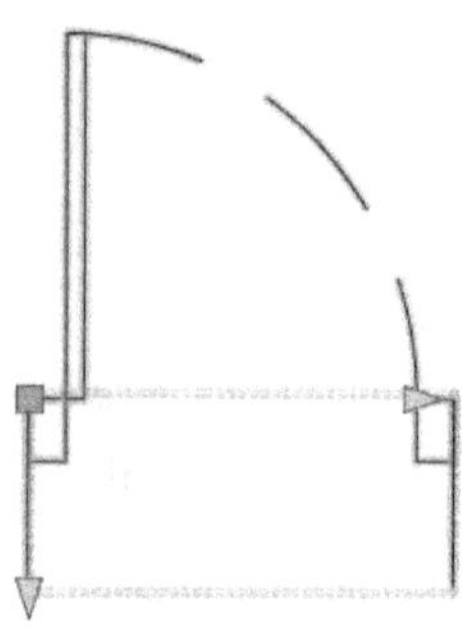

- Select the right vertical line and rectangle, and then press **Delete**.

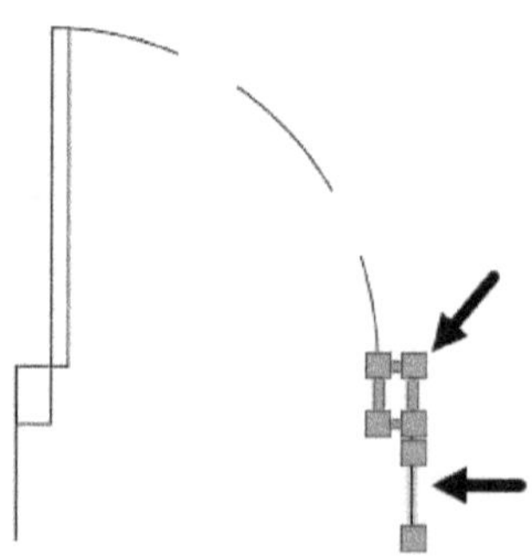

- Select the other objects of the door except the wipeout. On the ribbon, click **Home** tab > **Modify** panel > **Mirror** . Select the start point of the arc, move the pointer upward, and click to define the mirror line. Select **No** from the command line to retain the source objects.

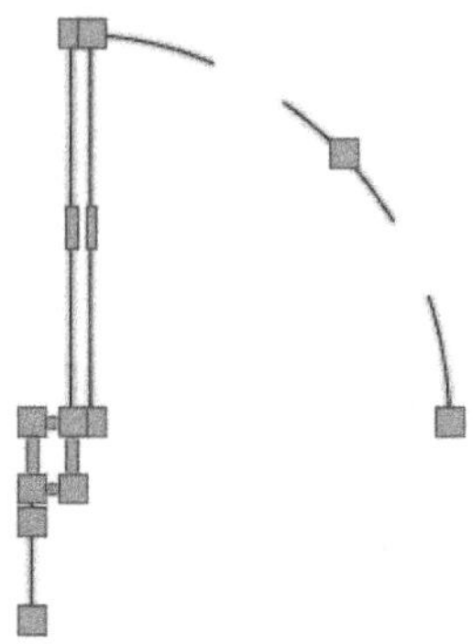

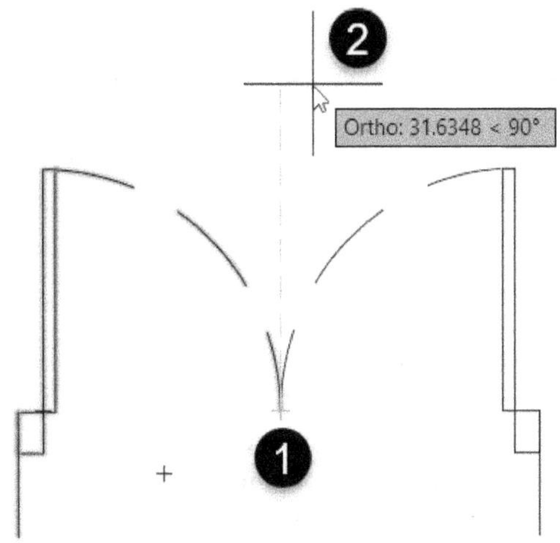

- Place the pointer in the lower portion of the door. The wipeout frame is highlighted. Select the wipeout frame and press **Delete**.

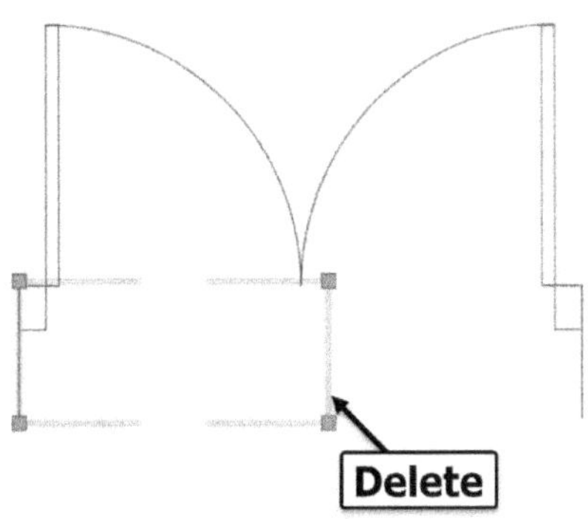

- On the ribbon, click **Home** tab > **Layers** panel > **Layer** drop-down > **WIPEOUT**. Type **REC** in the command line and press **Enter**. Specify the first and second corners of the rectangle, as shown.

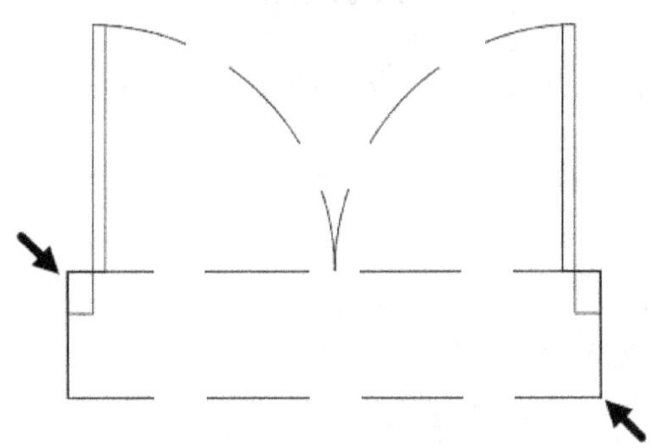

- Select the rectangle to display the grips on it. Select the midpoint grip of the lower horizontal line, and then move the pointer downward. Type **0.4** and press **Enter**. Likewise, stretch the rectangle in the upward direction.

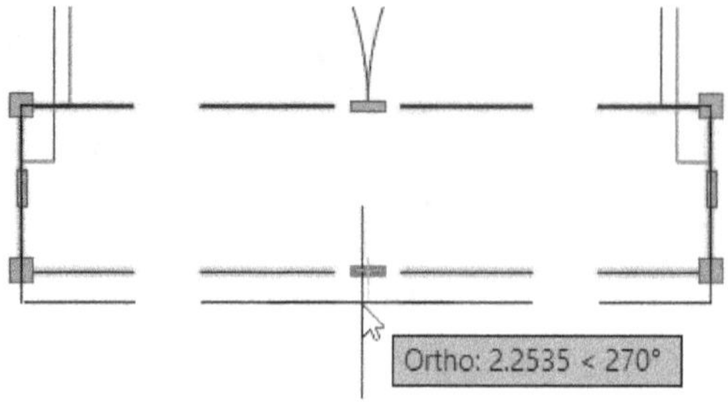

- Type **WIPEOUT** in the command line and press **Enter**. Select **Polyline** from the command line. Select the rectangle, and select **Yes** to erase the source object.
- Place the pointer on the lower portion of the door to highlight the wipeout frame. Select the wipeout frame, right click, and select **Draw order > Send to Back**.
- Select all the objects of the double door.
- On the ribbon, click **Insert > Block Definition > Create Block > Write Block** . On the **Write Block** dialog, click the **Pick Point** icon, and then select the top left corner point, as shown.

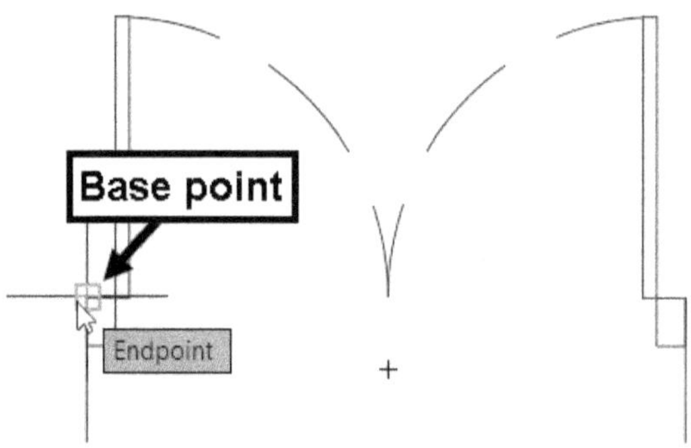

- Click the icon next to the **File name and path** box. Go to the folder location where you saved the **Tutorial 1** drawing file. Type **Double_Door** in the **File name** box and click **Save**. Select **Convert to block** from the **Objects** section and click **OK**. The selected objects are converted into a block.
- Type **BE** and press **Enter**. Select **Double_Door** from the **Block to create or edit** list and click **OK**. The **Block Editor** window appears.
- Create two **Linear** parameters, as shown. Apply the **Stretch** action to the **Wall Thickness** parameter.

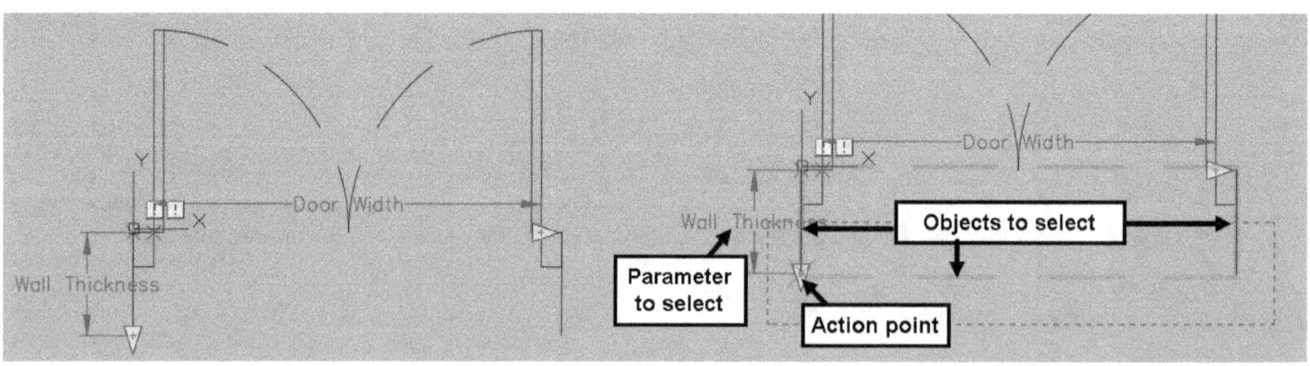

- Apply the **Stretch** action to the **Door Width** parameter, as shown.

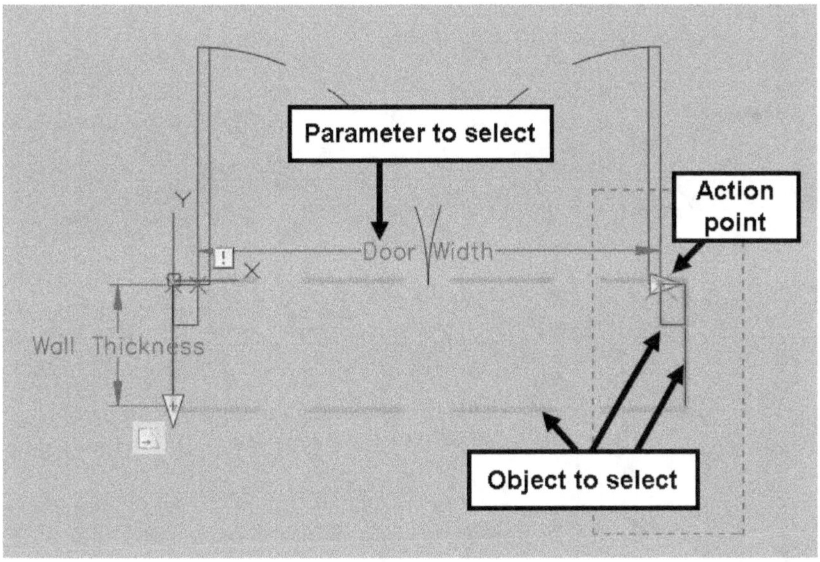

- Apply the **Scale** action to the **Door Width** parameter and select the objects, as shown.

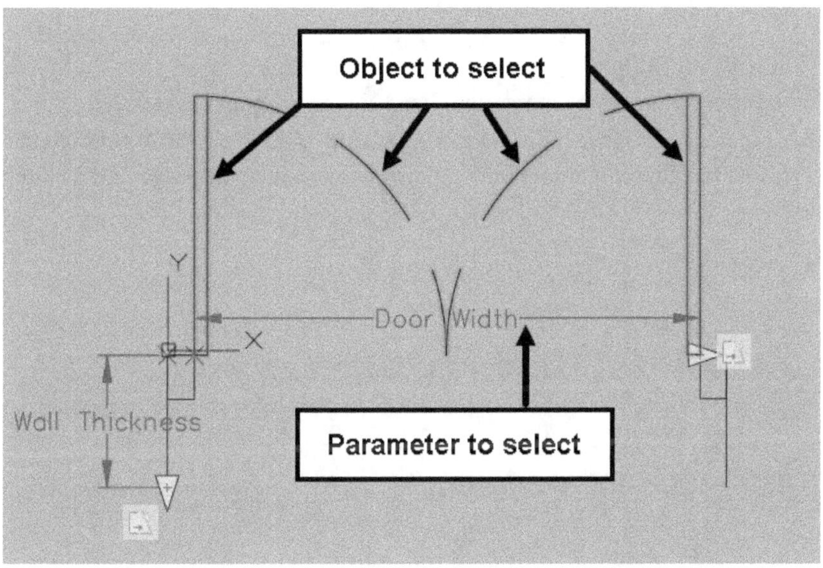

- Select the **Door Width** parameter. Next, right-click and select **Properties**.
- On the **Properties** palette, under the **Value set** section, change the **Dist type** to **List**. Click in the **Dist value list** box and select the icon located next to it. On the **Add Distance Value** dialog, type **65** in the **Distance to add** box and press **Enter**. Likewise, add **48**, **66**, **68,** and **73** to the list, as shown. Click **OK** to close the dialog.

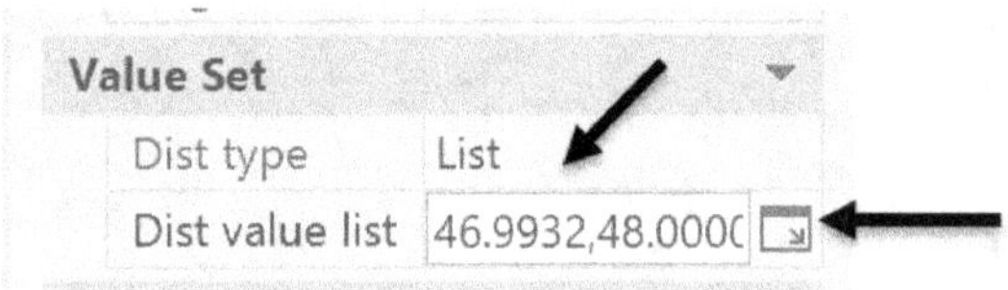

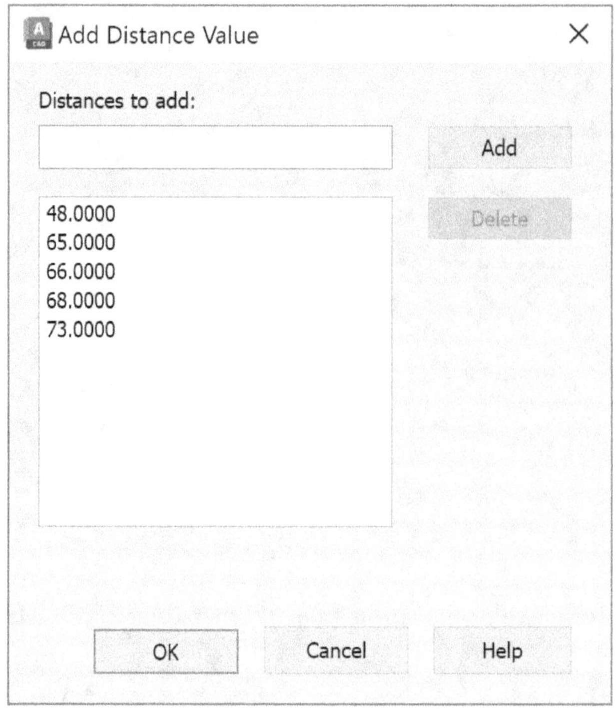

- Test the block, save it, and close the **Block Editor**.
- Click **Zoom Extents** on the **Navigation Pane** located at the right-hand side in the graphics window.
- On the ribbon, click **Insert** tab > **Block** panel > **Insert** drop-down > **Double_Door**. Select **Rotate** from the command line. Type **270** and press **Enter**. Select the intersection point between the outer edge of the extreme right wall and the grid line, as shown.

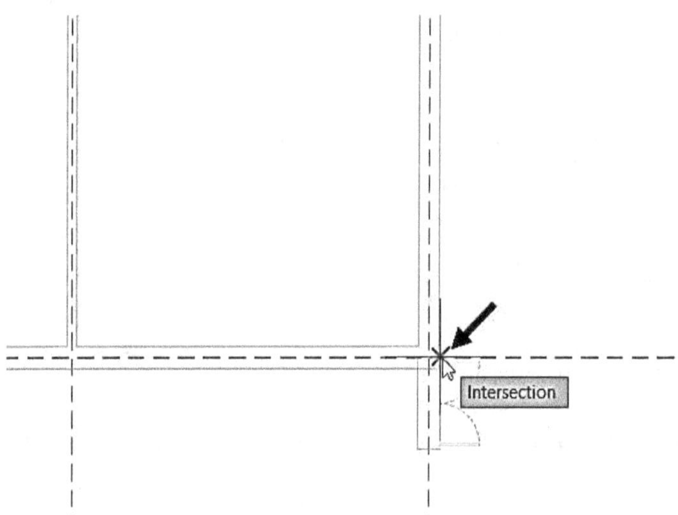

- Select the **Double_Door** block, if not already selected. Click on the base point of the block, and then move it upward. Type **166** and press **Enter**.

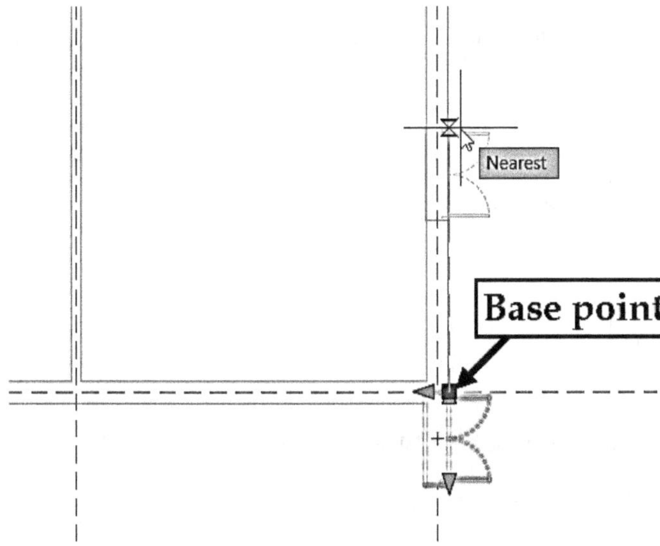

- Click and drag the arrow, pointing downward. Click on the bottom-most interval.

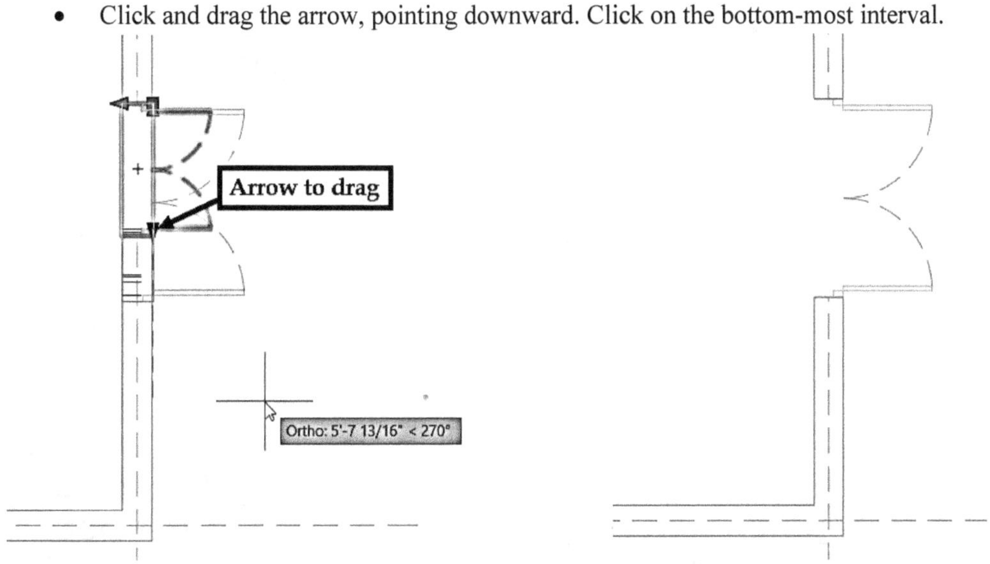

- Likewise, insert another instance of the block, as shown.

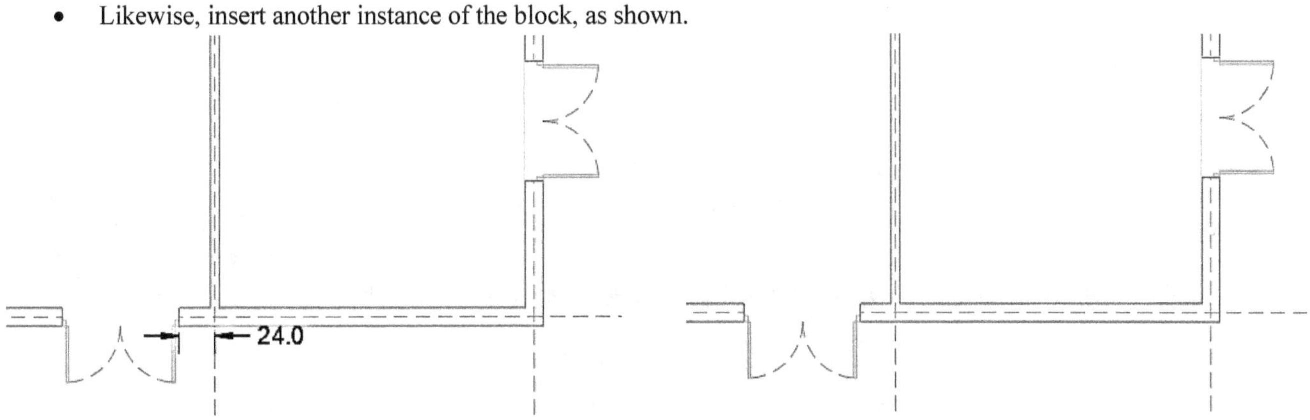

- Create two vertical lines on the **A-WALL** layer and a wipeout on the **WIPEOUT** Layer, as shown.
- Select the wipeout, right click, and then select **Draw Order > Send to Back**.

- Create the 'Opening' block from the objects on the **Write Block** command. Use the top endpoint of the left vertical line as the base point.

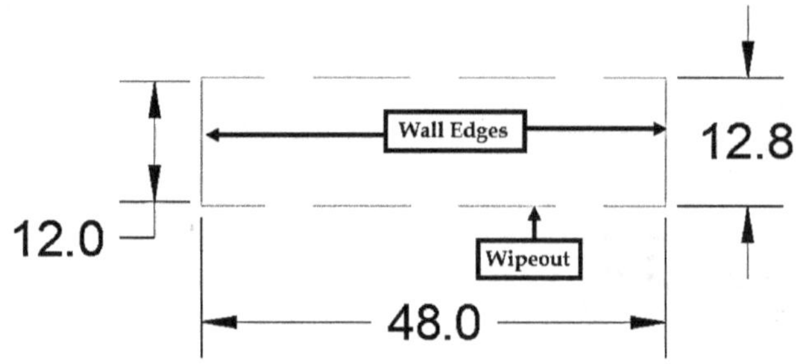

- Type **BE** and press **Enter**. Select the **Opening** block from the **Edit Block Definition** dialog, and then click **OK**.
- Create two Linear parameters, as shown.

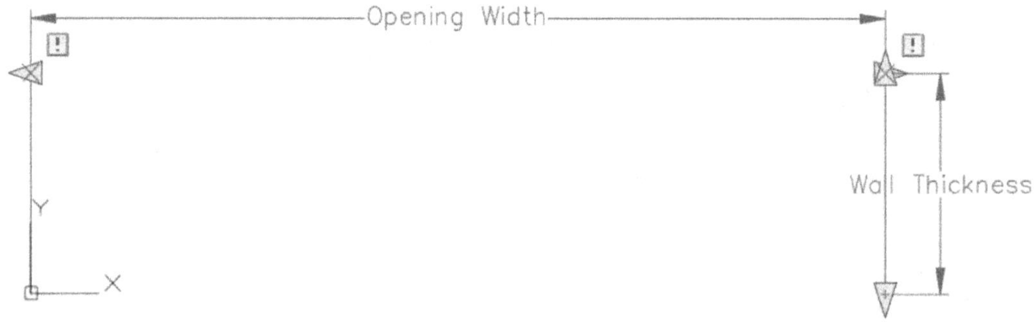

- Apply the **Stretch** action to the **Wall Thickness** parameter.

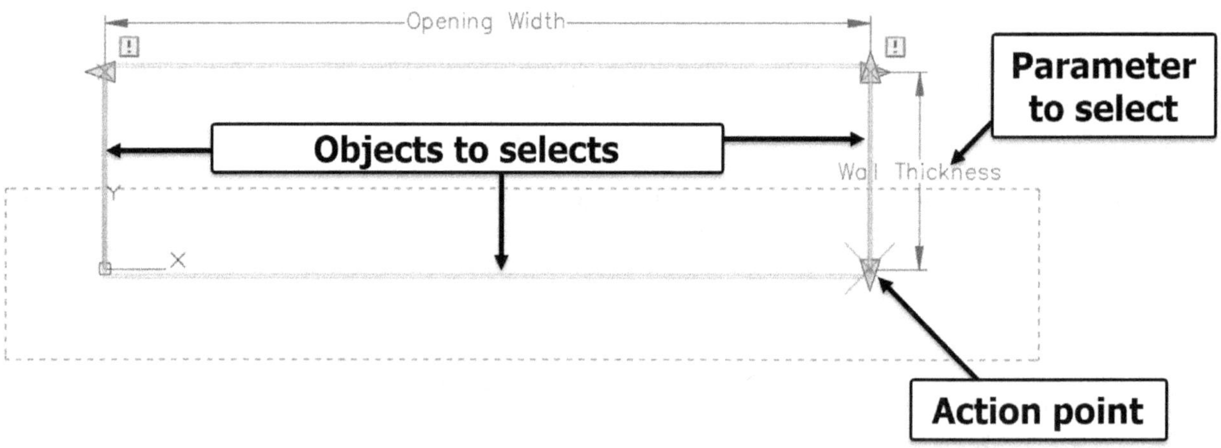

- Apply the **Stretch** action to the **Opening Width** parameter, save the block, and close the Block Editor.

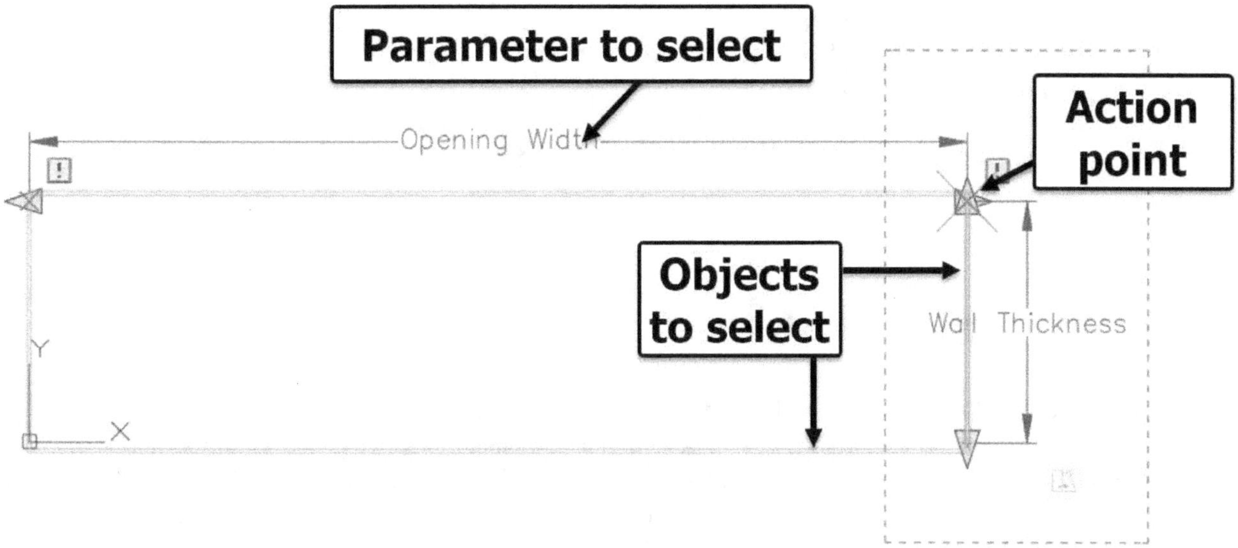

- On the ribbon, click **Home** tab > **Layers** panel > **Layer** drop-down > **A-WALL**. Insert the **Opening** block into the drawing at the locations shown in the figure.

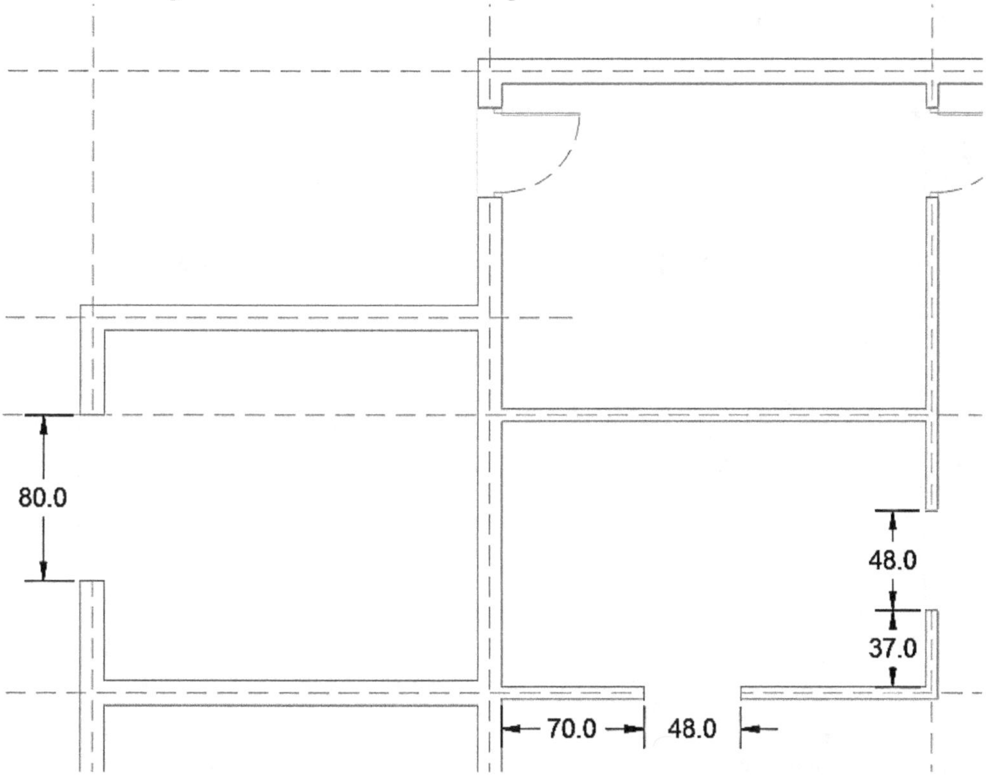

- On the ribbon, click **Home** tab > **Layers** panel > **Layer** drop-down > **A-WINDOWS**. Create the 'Window' block, as shown. Use the top left corner of the left rectangle as the base point.

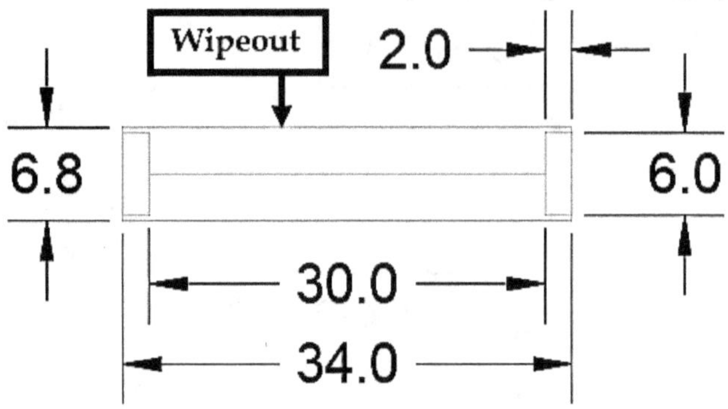

- Open the 'Window' block in the Block Editor. On the **Block Editor** tab of the ribbon, click the **Coincident** tool on the **Geometric** panel. Click the left endpoint of the horizontal line. Click on the middle portion of the vertical line connected to the horizontal line. The **Coincident** constraint is created between the left endpoint of the horizontal line and the midpoint of the vertical line. Likewise, create the **Coincident** constraint between the right endpoint of the horizontal line and the midpoint of the vertical line connected to it.

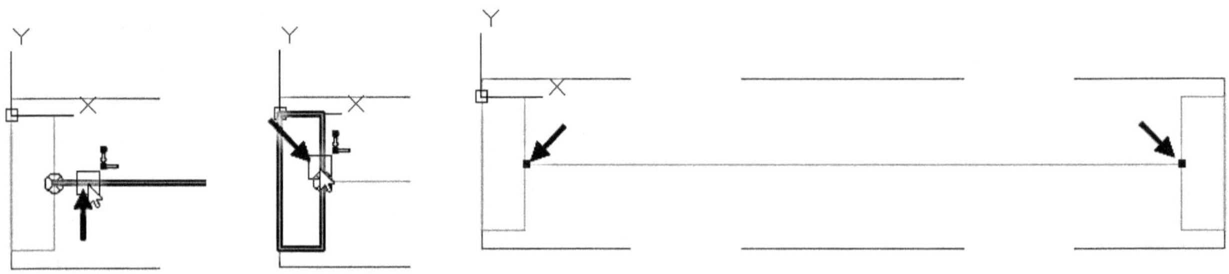

- On the **Block Editor** tab of the ribbon, click the **Horizontal** tool on the **Geometric** panel. Select the horizontal line located at the center.
- Create two linear parameters, as shown.

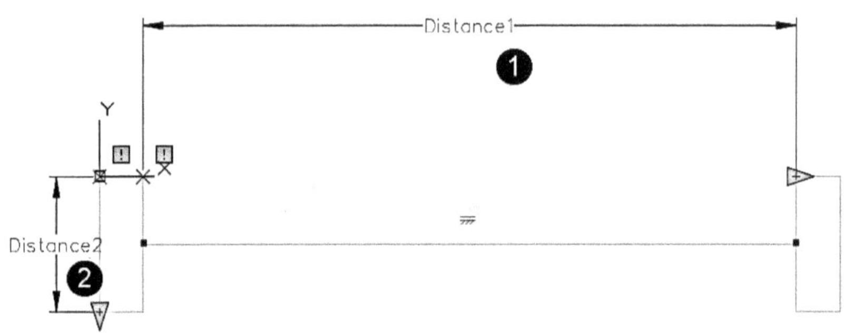

- Apply the **Stretch** action to the first linear parameter.

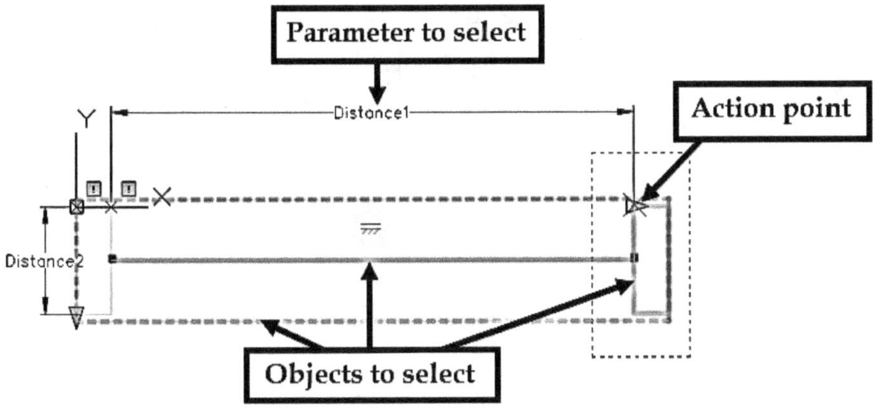

- Apply the **Stretch** action to the second linear parameter.

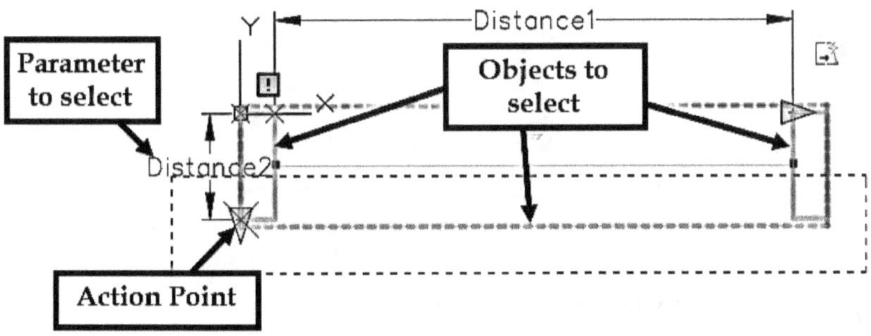

- Select the wipeout, right click, and then select **Draw Order > Send to Back**.
- Test the block, save it, and close the **Block Editor**.
- Insert the window blocks at the locations shown in the figure. Also, change the window lengths.

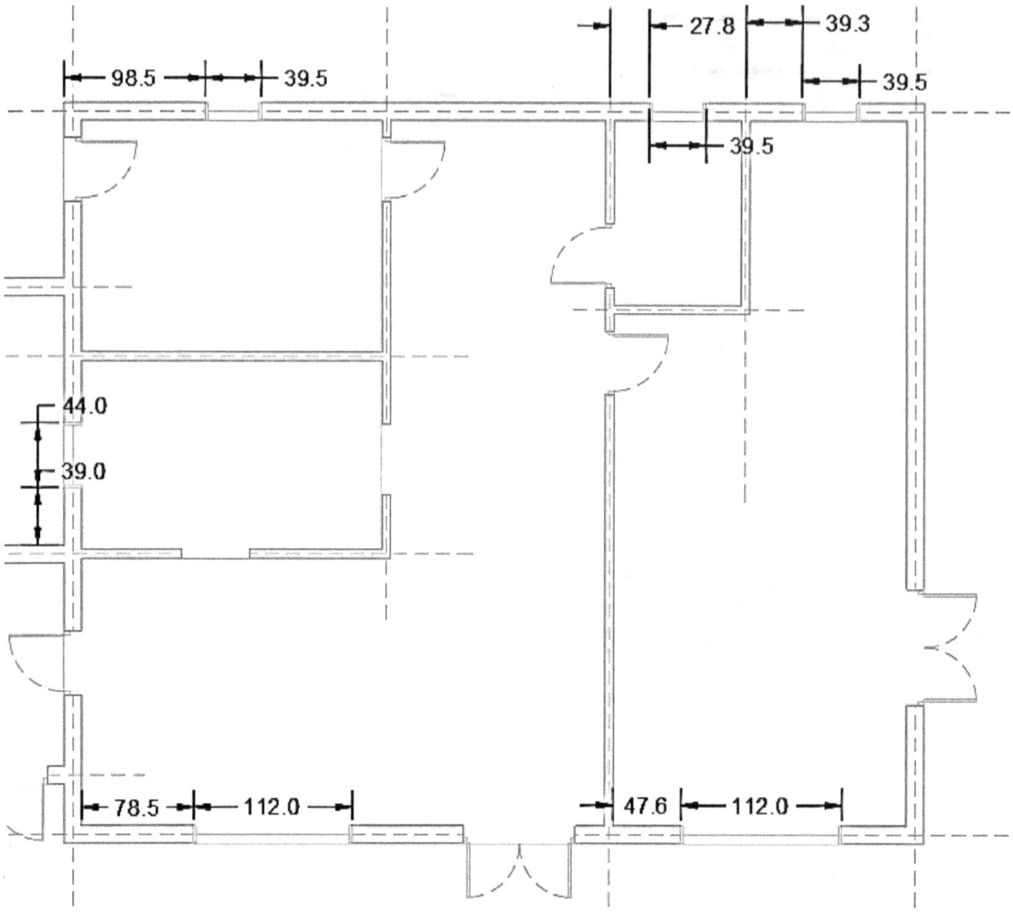

Tutorial 6: Creating Stairs

- On the ribbon, click **Home** tab > **Layers** panel > **Layer** drop-down > **A-STAIRS**.
- Type **O** in the command line and press **Enter**. Type **68** and press **Enter** to define the offset distance. Zoom into the top left corner of the drawing. Select the edge of the horizontal wall, as shown. Move the pointer up and click to create the offset line.

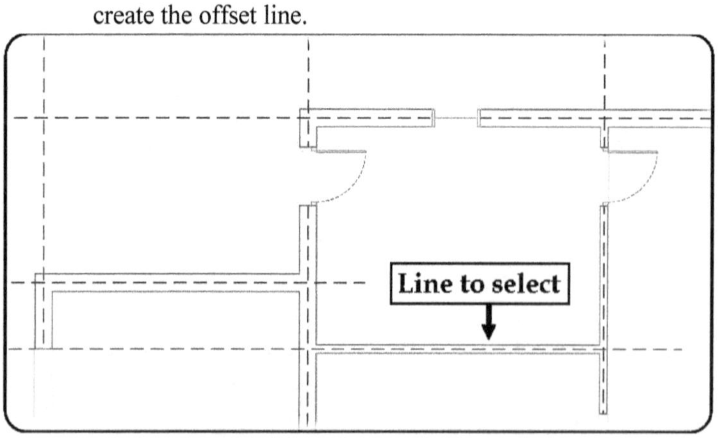

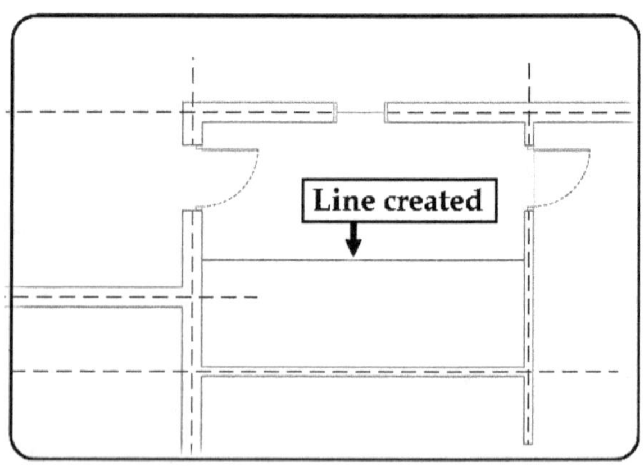

- Likewise, create other offset lines, as shown. The offset distances are also given. Use the **Trim** tool to remove the unwanted portions of the lines, as shown.

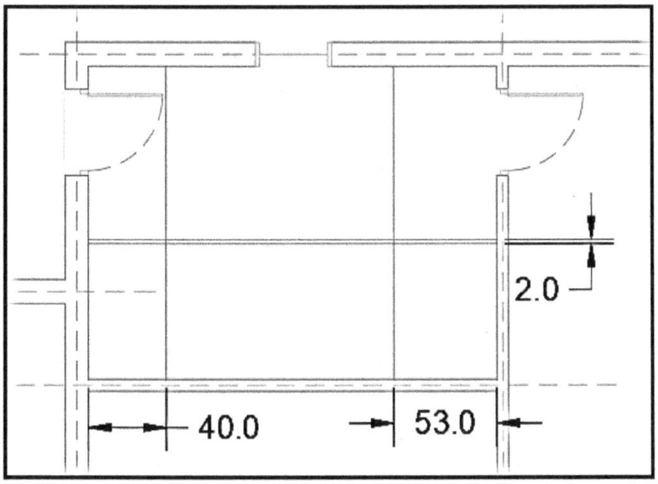

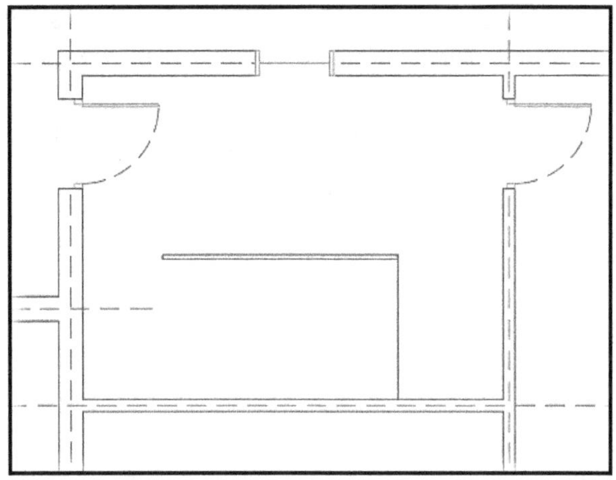

- On the **Home** tab of the ribbon, expand the **Modify** panel and click the **Break at Point** tool. Select the line shown in the figure. Specify the breakpoint, as shown. The selected line is broken at the selected point.

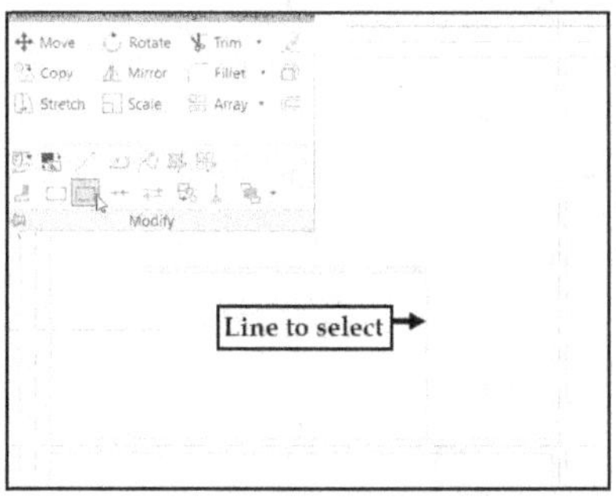

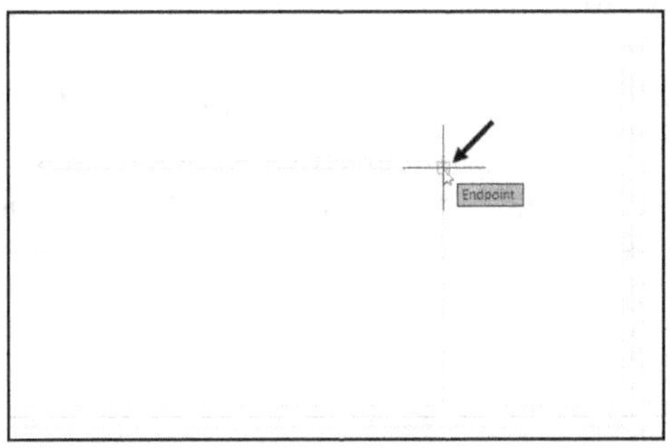

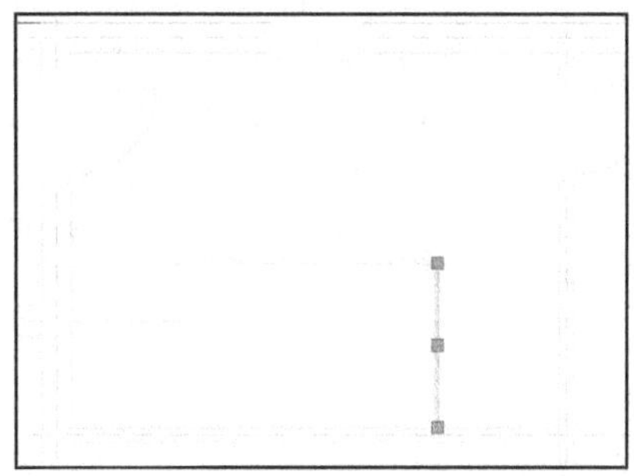

- On the ribbon, click **Home** tab > **Modify** panel > **Array** drop-down > **Rectangular Array**. Select the lower portion of the line that was broken in the previous step, and press **Enter**. On the **Array Creation** tab of the ribbon, change the **Columns** and **Rows** value to 10 and 1, respectively. Change the **Between** value on the **Columns** panel to -12. Click **Close Array** on the **Array Creation** ribbon tab.

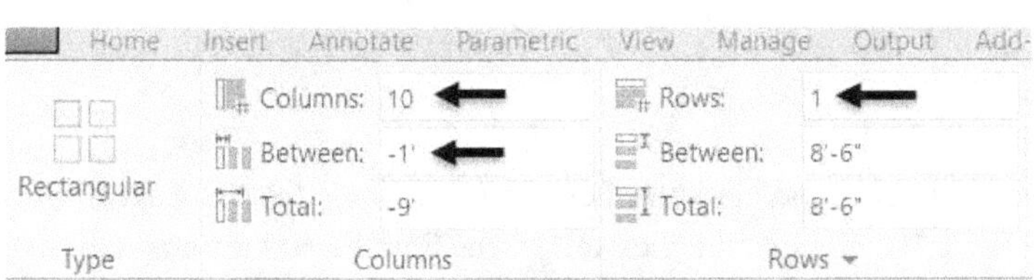

- On the ribbon, click **Home** tab > **Layers** panel > **Layer** drop-down > **CALLOUTS**.
- Click the **Object Snap** drop-down on the Status bar and select the **Midpoint** and **Quadrant** options from the menu.
- Type **C** in the command line and press ENTER. Next, snap to the midpoint of the left-most vertical line of the stairs.

- Move the pointer outward, type **6** and press ENTER to create a circle.
- On the ribbon, click **Home** tab > **Draw** panel > **Line**. Next, select the right quadrant point of the circle.
- Move the pointer horizontally toward right beyond the right-most vertical line of the stairs, and click.
- Move the pointer vertically upward up to a small distance and click.

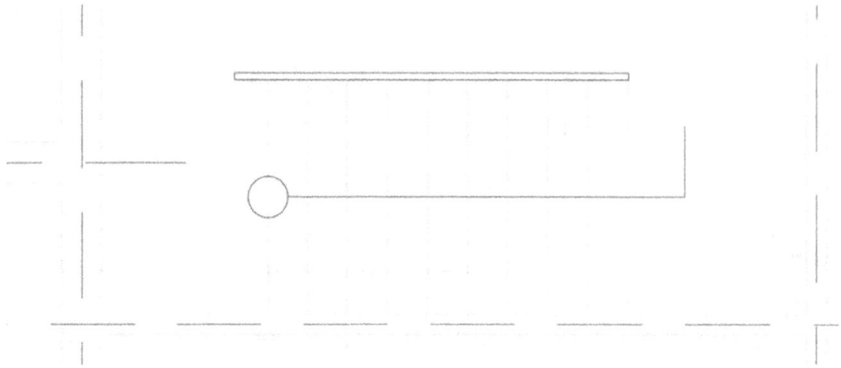

- On the status bar, click the down arrow next to the **Polar Tracking** icon and select **30**. Next, activate the **Polar Tracking** icon on the status bar.
- Type **L** in the command line and press **Enter**. Select the endpoint of the line drawn in the last step. Move the pointer toward the bottom left and click to create an inclined line. Press **Enter** twice. Specify the start point of the new line, as shown. Place the pointer on the endpoint of the inclined line. Move the pointer horizontally toward the right, and then click at the intersection of the trace lines. Press Esc.

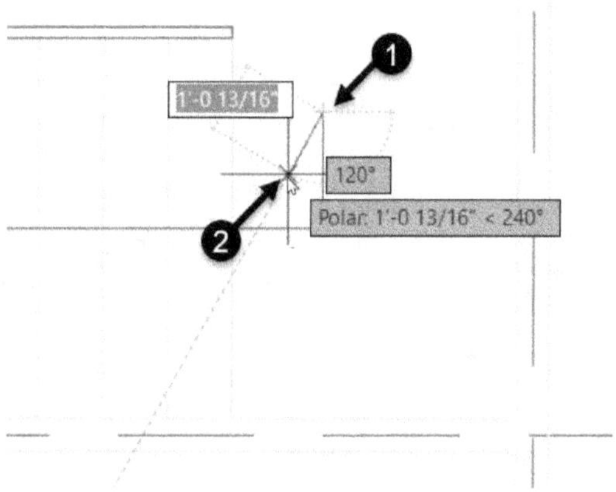

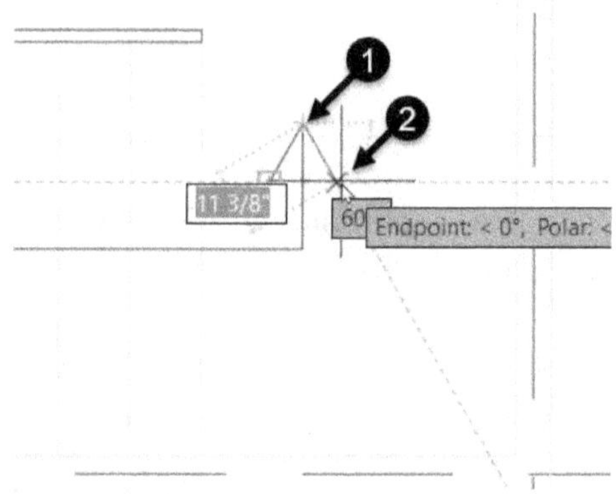

- On the **Home** tab of the ribbon, expand the **Annotation** panel and click the **Text Style** icon. On the **Text Style** dialog, click the **New** button. Type **Callout** in the **Style Name** box and click **OK**. Type **8** in the **Height** box and set the **Width Factor** to **0.75**. Click **Apply** on the dialog and then click the **Set Current** button. Next, close the dialog.

- On the ribbon, click **Home** tab > **Annotation** panel > **Text** drop-down > **Single Line**. Specify the start and endpoints of the text, as shown. Type **STAIR UP** and click anywhere in the graphics window. Press **Esc** to deactivate the command.

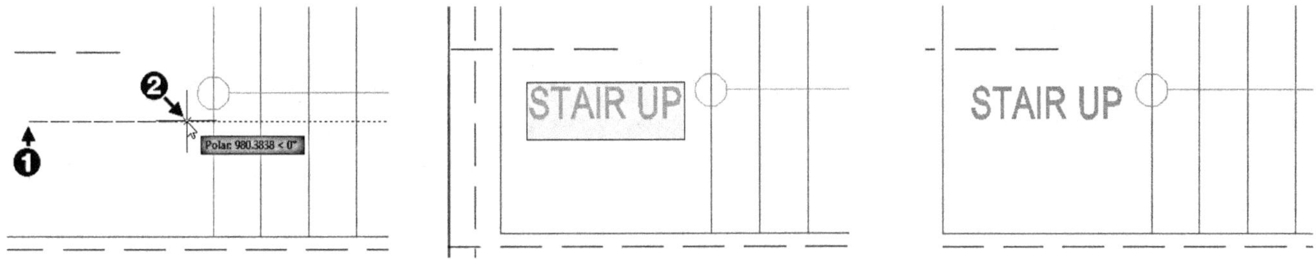

Tutorial 7: Creating the First Floor Plan

Now, you create the upper floor plan by using the walls of the ground floor plan.

- On the Status bar, activate the **ORTHOMODE (F8)** icon.
- Select all the objects of the ground floor plane, including the grid lines. Right click and select **Copy Selection**.

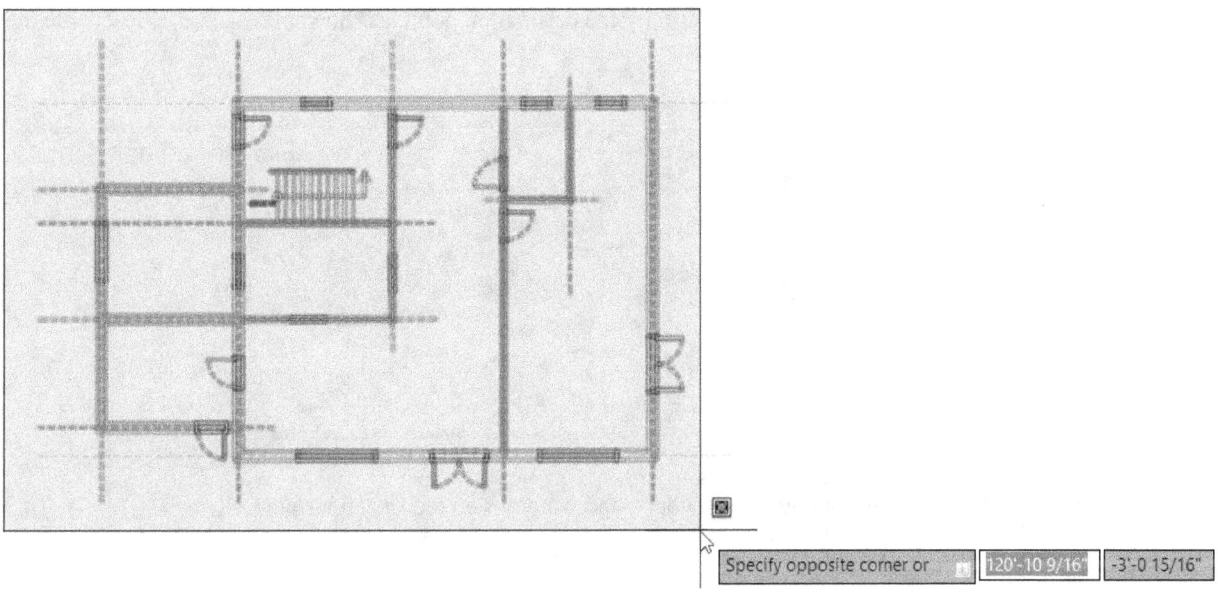

- Select the bottom-left corner point of the ground floor, as shown in the figure.

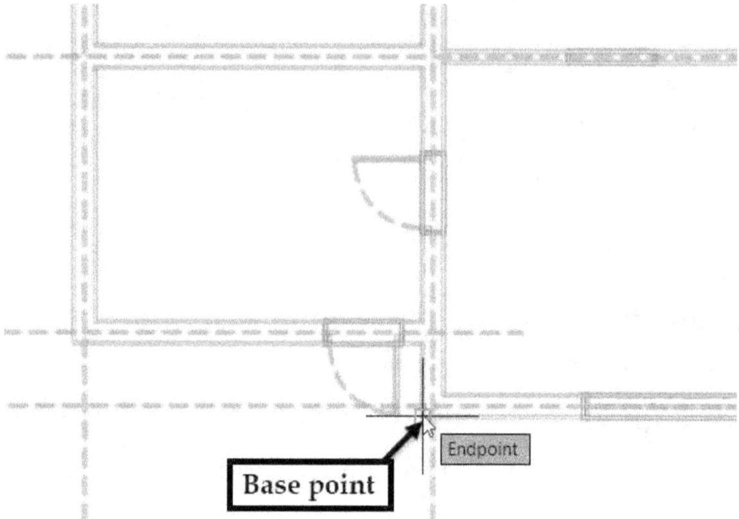

- Move the pointer toward the right and click to specify the destination point, as shown. Press **Esc** to deactivate the **Copy** command.

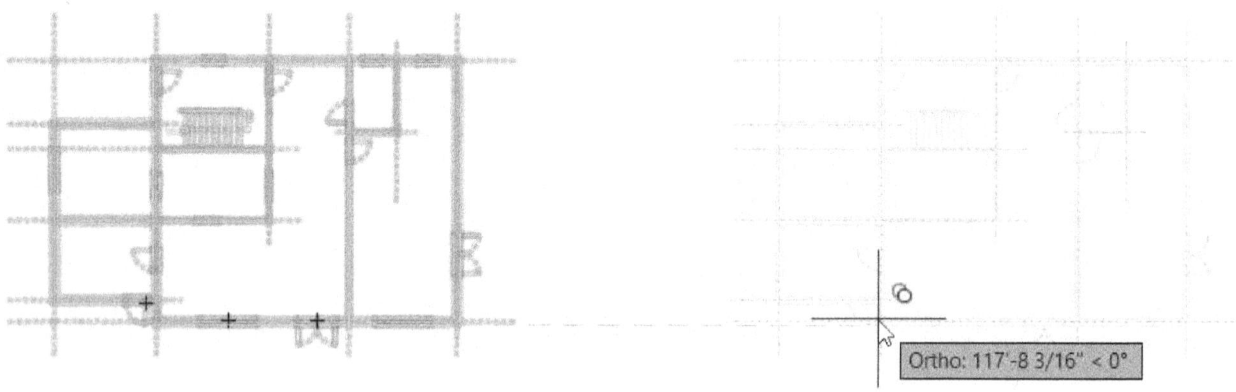

- Delete the unwanted inner walls, garage walls, doors, and windows on the first-floor plan.

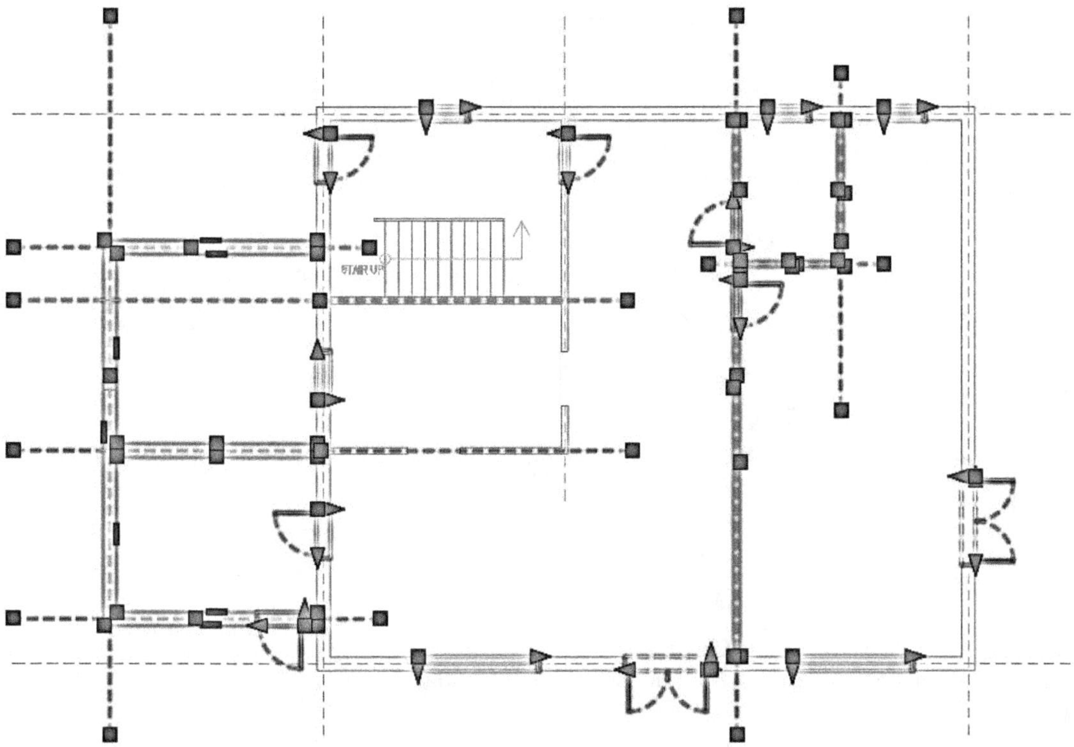

The plan after deleting the unwanted entities is shown next.

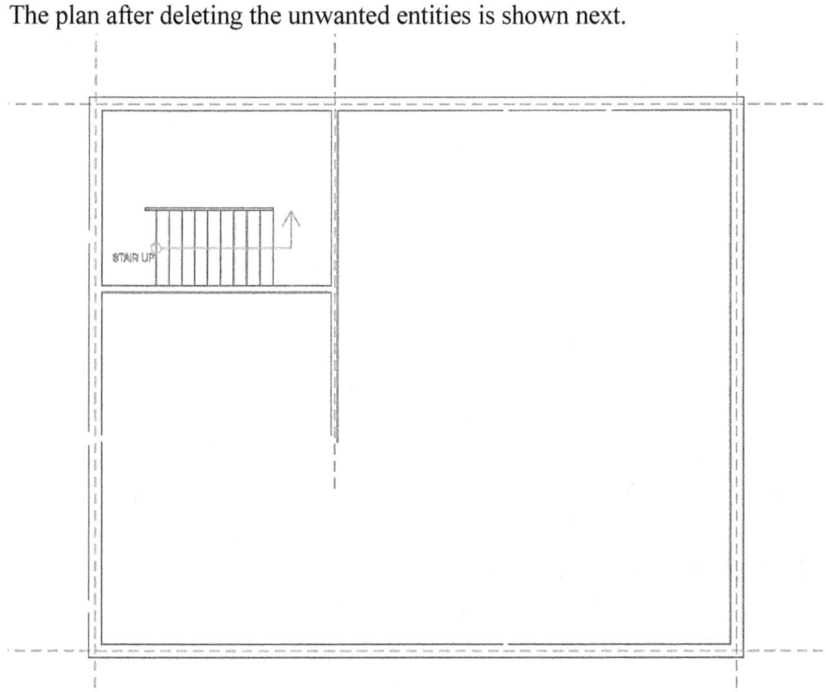

- Create grid lines by using the **Offset** tool.

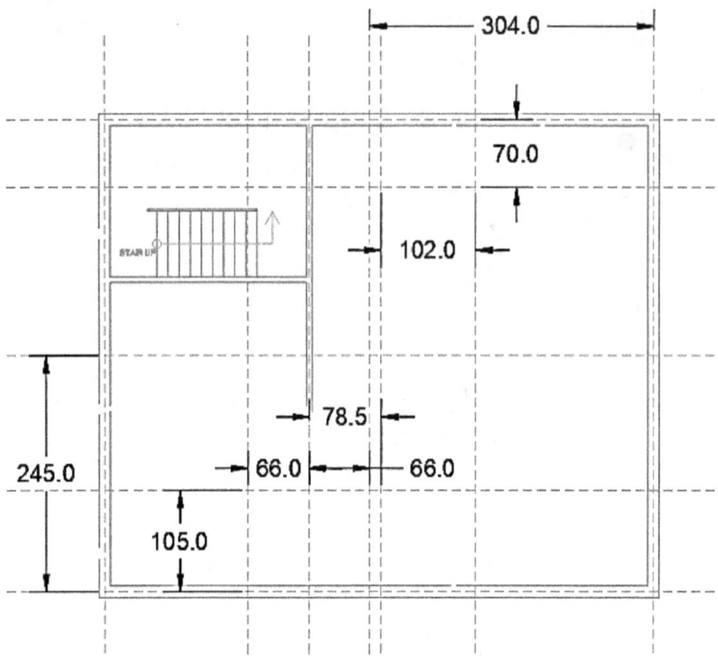

- Create the inner walls using the grid lines. Also, trim the wall intersections.

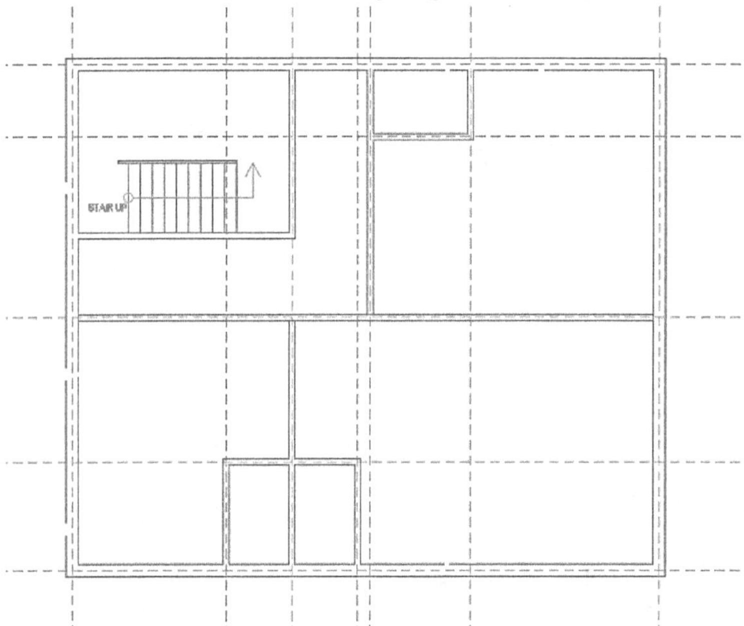

- Zoom to the bottom portion of the drawing and notice a gap on the wall.

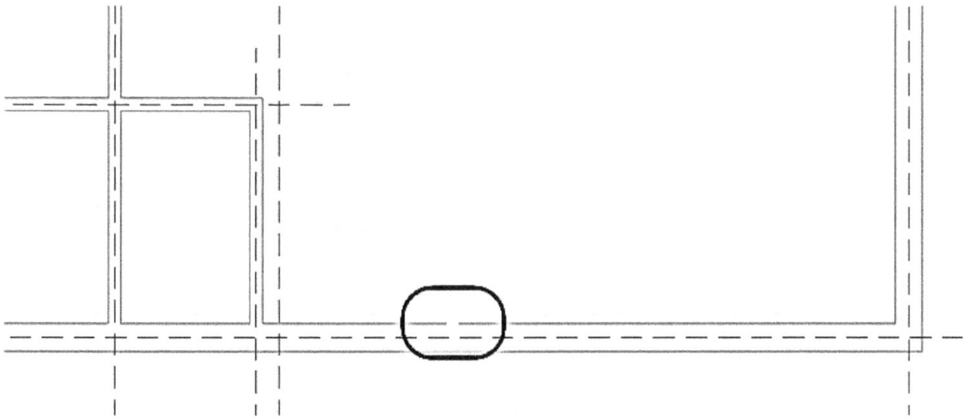

- On the **Home** tab of the ribbon, expand the **Modify** panel and click the **Join** icon.
- Select the two lines adjacent to the gap. Next, press **Enter**; the lines are joined together.

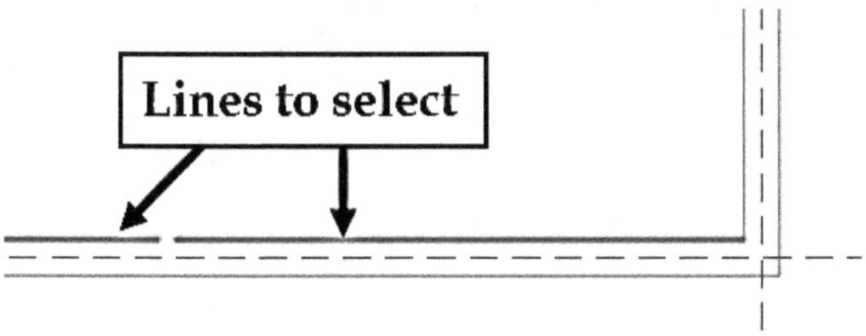

- Activate the **Join** command and select the collinear vertical lines on the left side, as shown. Next, press **Enter** to join the lines.

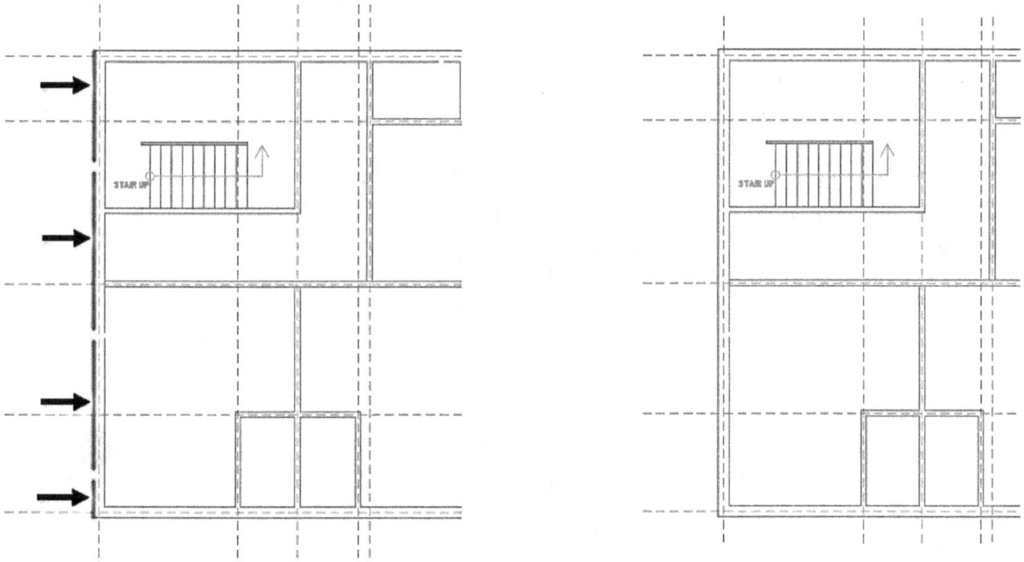

- Likewise, zoom in to the different portions of the walls and remove any existing gaps.
- Add doors and windows to the first-floor plan.

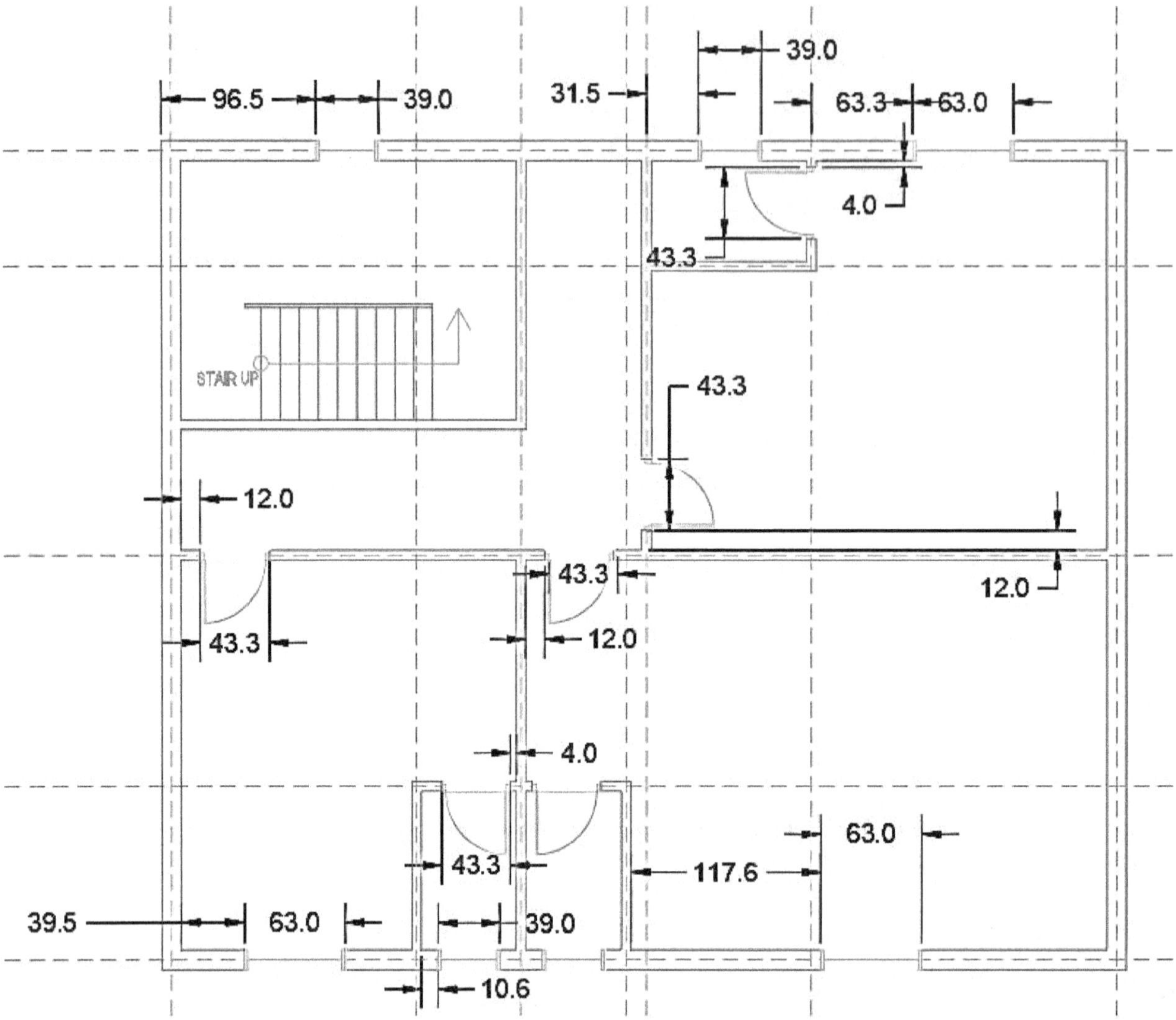

- On the ribbon, click **Home** tab > **Layers** panel > **Layer** drop-down > **A-STAIRS**. Zoom to the stairs portion on the first-floor plan and select the stairs. Type **MI** and press **Enter**. Specify the start and endpoints of the mirror line, as shown. Select **No** from the command line to retain the source objects.

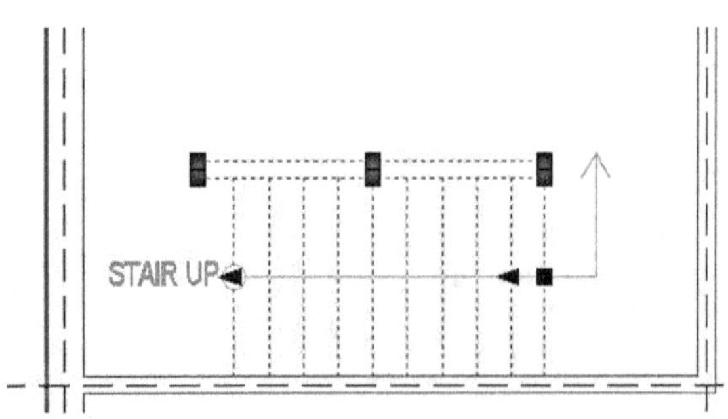

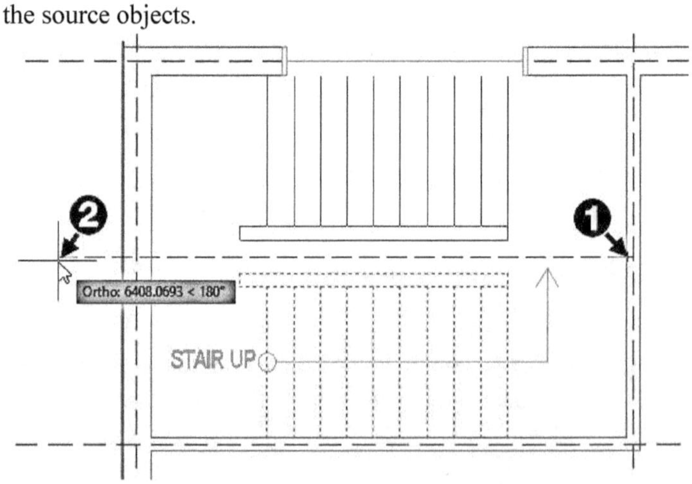

- Delete the right end caps of the railings and create a line connecting both the railings. Create an offset line on the left side of the newly created line. The offset distance is **2**.

- Trim the unwanted portions.

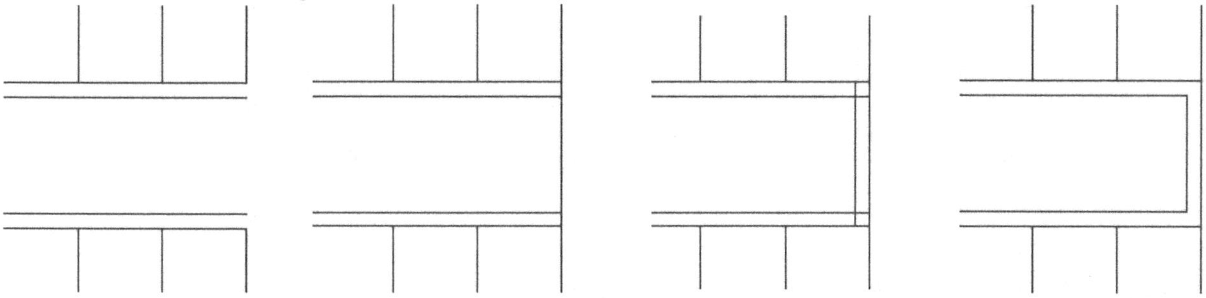

- Activate the **Mirror** command, and then select the callout and text. Press **Enter** and specify the mirror line, as shown. Next, select **Yes** from the command line to delete the source object from the drawing.
- Double click on the text and change it to STAIR DOWN.

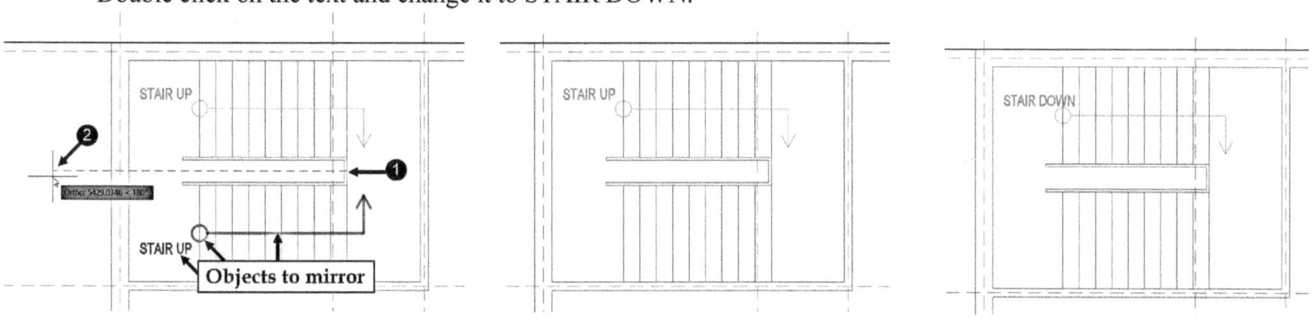

- Delete the wall, as shown. Next, cap the end portion of the wall. Also, join the broken lines of the outer wall.

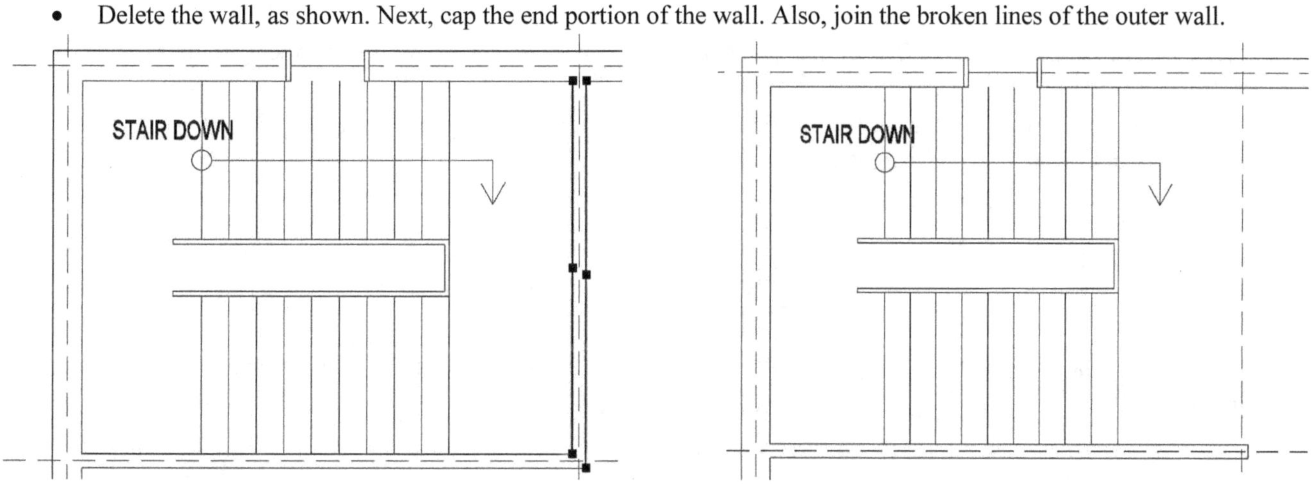

Creating the Sliding Doors

- On the ribbon, click **Home** tab > **Layers** panel > **Layer** drop-down > **A-WALL**. Create two vertical lines of **12** inches long and **60** inches apart.

- On the ribbon, click **Home** tab > **Layers** panel > **Layer** drop-down > **A-DOOR**. Activate the **Rectangle** command and select the lower endpoint of the left vertical line, as shown. Select the **Dimensions** option from the command line. Specify **31** and **2** as the length and width of the rectangle, respectively. Move the pointer upward and click to create the rectangle.

- Type **M** in the command line and press **Enter**. Select the rectangle, and then press **Enter**. Select its lower-left corner point to define the base point. Move the pointer upward and type-in **1** in the command line, and then press **Enter**.

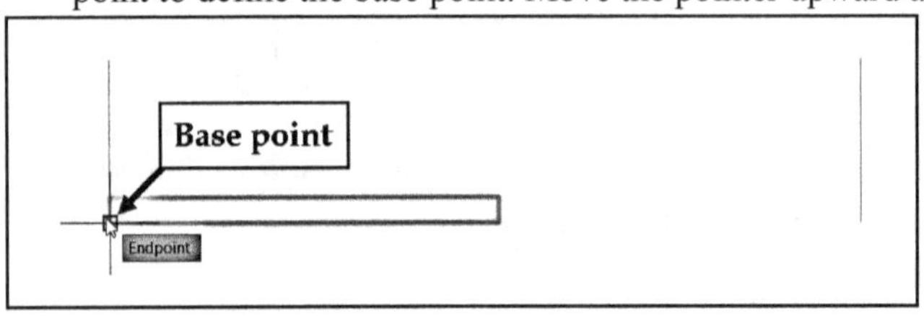

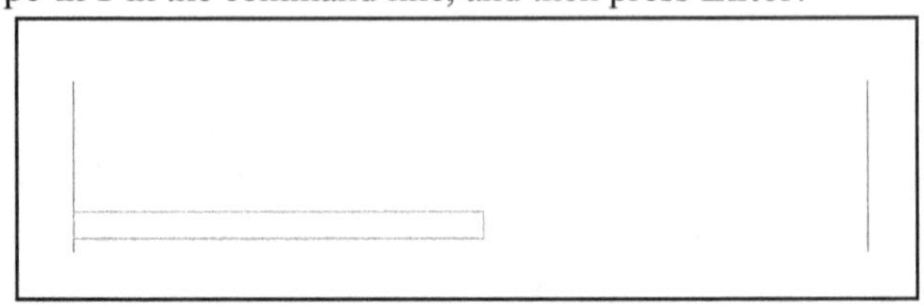

- On the ribbon, click **Home > Modify > Explode**, and select the rectangle. Press **Enter** to explode the rectangle.
- Activate the **Offset** command and specify **2** as the offset distance. Offset the left and right vertical lines of the rectangle.

- Click the down arrow next to the **Object Snap** icon on the status bar, and make sure that the **Midpoint** option is checked.
- Activate the **Line** command and select the midpoints of the offset lines. A line connecting the offset lines is created. Press **Esc** to deactivate the **Line** command.

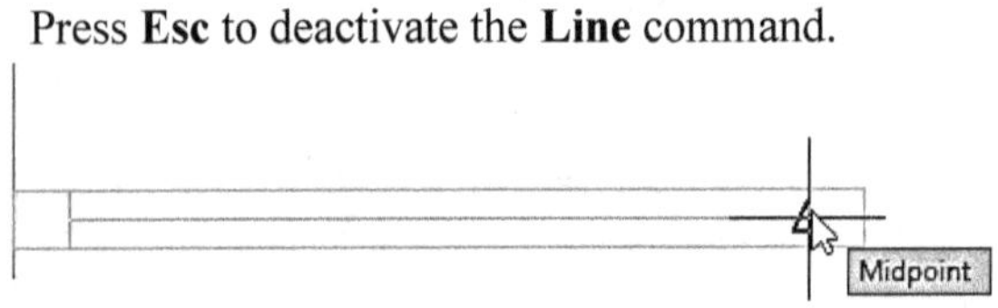

- Type-in **CO** in the command line and press **Enter**. Drag a selection window covering all the elements of the sliding door. Press **Enter**.

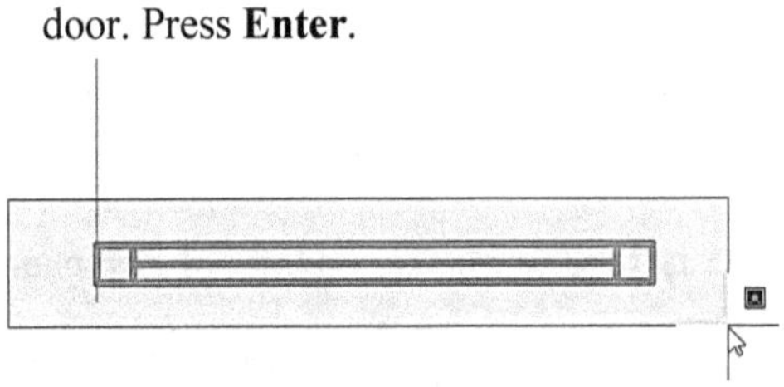

- Select the lower-left corner of the sliding door as the base point. Move the pointer and select the endpoint of the offset line, as shown. Press **Esc** to deactivate the **Copy** command.

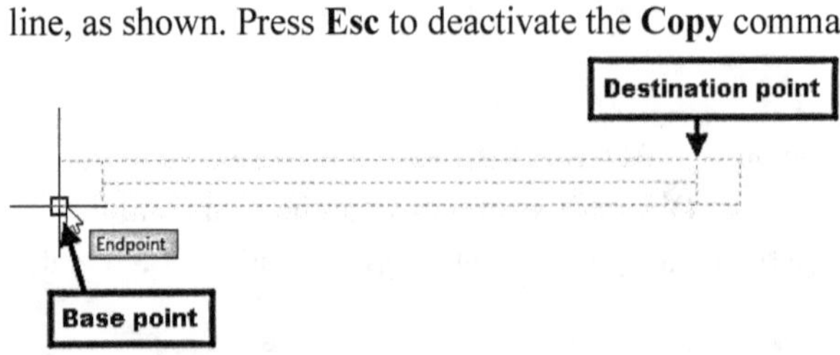

- On the ribbon, click **Home** tab > **Layers** panel > **Layer** drop-down > **WIPEOUT**. Create a rectangle covering all the entities of the sliding door. Extend the width of the rectangle by **1** both sides (select the rectangle and drag the grips that appear of the corners). Activate the **Wipeout** tool and select **Polyline** from the command line. Select the rectangle to convert it into a wipeout. Select **Yes** from the command line to erase the rectangle. Select the wipeout from the graphics window, right click, and select **Draw Order > Send To Back**.

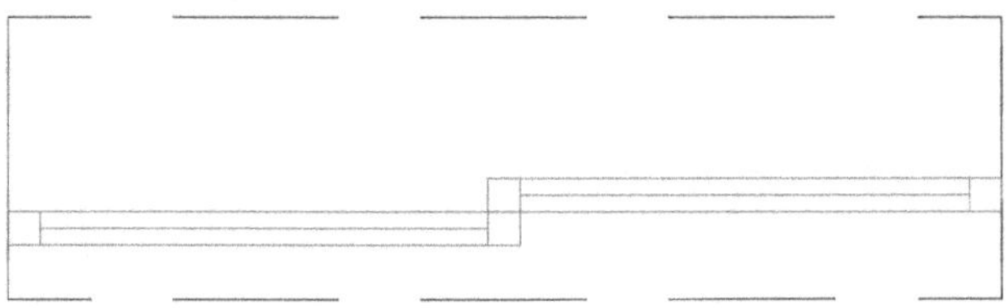

- On the ribbon, click **Insert** tab > **Block Definition** panel > **Blocks** drop-down > **Create Block** . On the **Block Definition** dialog, type **Sliding_Door** in the **Name** box. Click the **Select Objects** icon, create a selection window covering all the entities of the sliding door, and then press **Enter**. Click the **Pick point** icon and select the lower endpoint of the left vertical line. Select the **Delete** option from the **Objects** section. Uncheck the **Open in block editor** option and click **OK**.

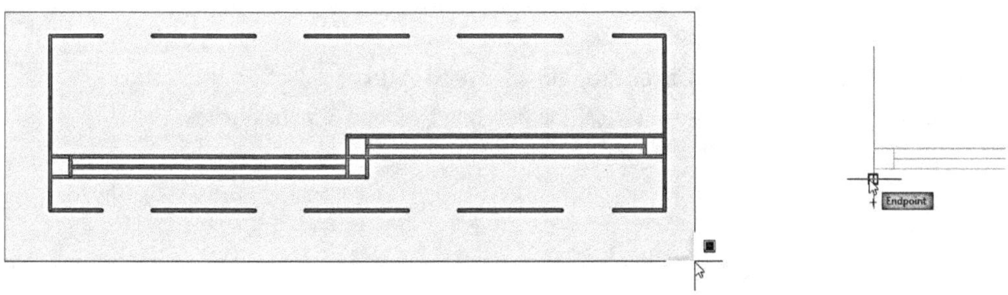

- On the ribbon, click **Insert** tab > **Block** panel > **Insert** gallery > **Sliding _Door**. Select **Rotate** from the command line. Type **270** and press **Enter**. Press the **Shift** key and right click. Select **From** from the shortcut menu. Zoom to the lower right corner of the first-floor plan and select the inner corner point. Move the pointer along the vertical line, type **152**, and press **Enter**. The block is inserted at the specified distance from the inner corner point.

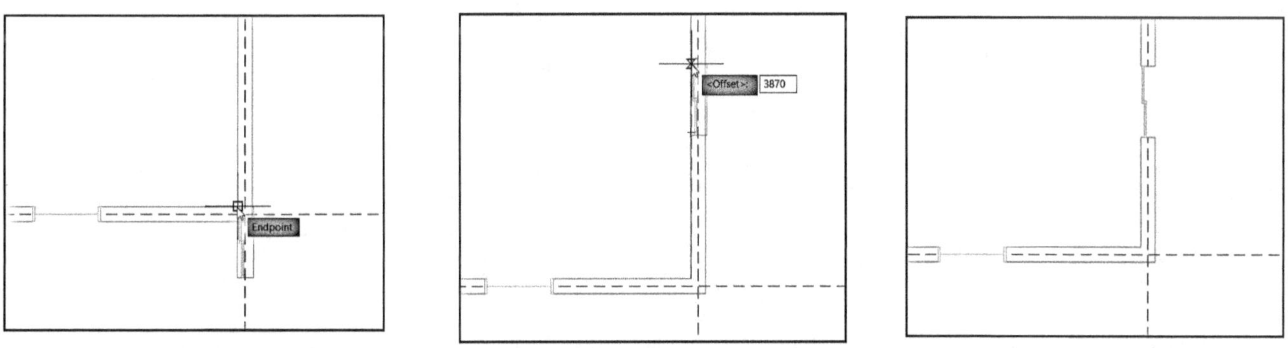

- Likewise, add another slider door to the other bedroom, as shown. The offset distance from the inner corner is given in the figure below.

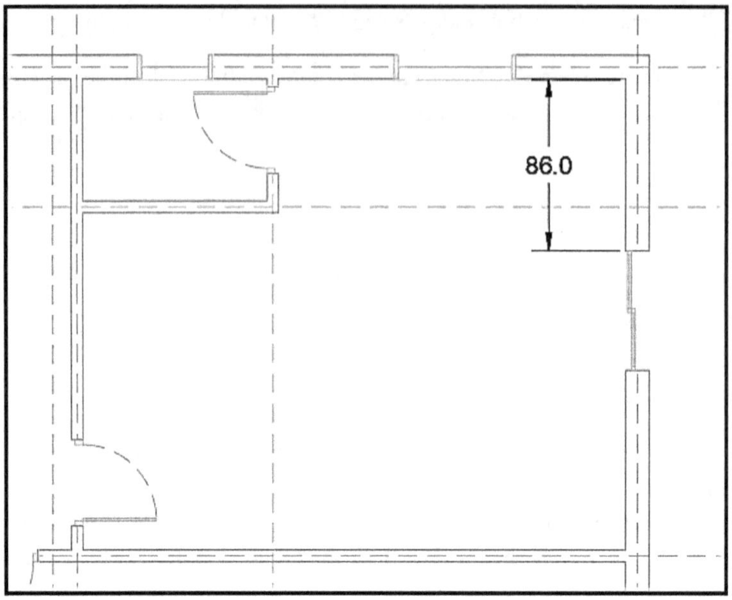

Creating the Balcony

- On the ribbon, click **Home** tab > **Layers** panel > **Layer** drop-down > **A-SLABS**.
- Use the **Polyline** tool to create the balcony, as shown. Offset the polyline by **2** and **3** inches inside.

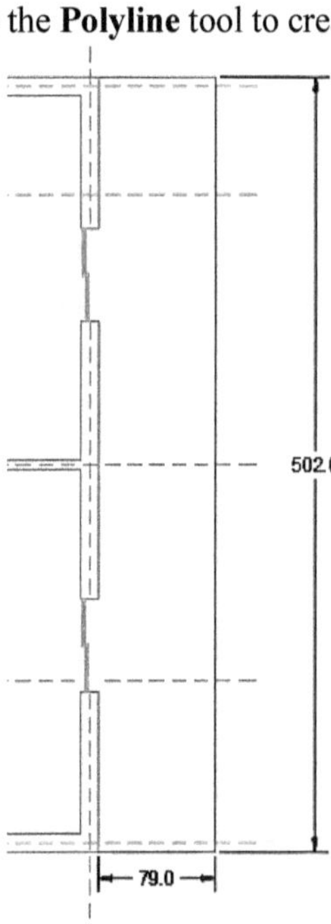

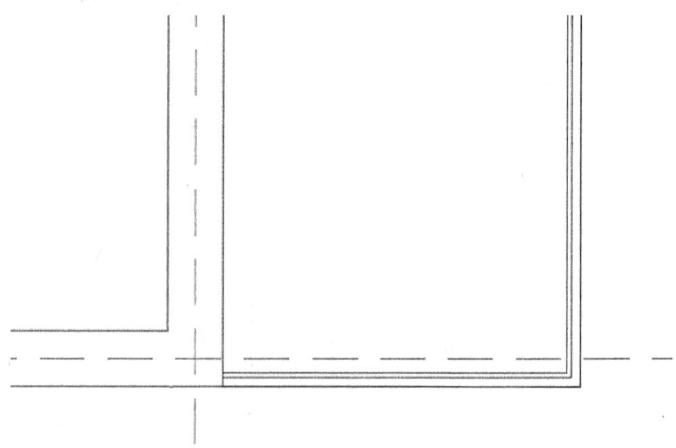

- Select the two offset polylines. On the ribbon, click **Home** tab > **Properties** panel > **Object Color** drop-down > **Index Colors** > **9**.

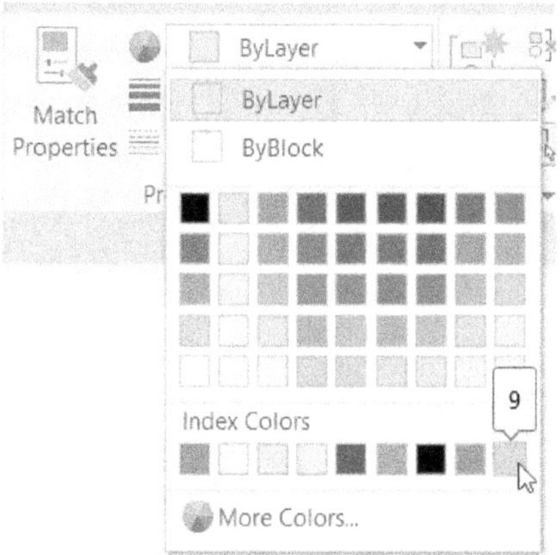

Tutorial 8: Creating Kitchen and Bathroom Fixtures

- On the ribbon, click **Home** tab > **Layers** panel > **Layer** drop-down > **A-KITCHEN**.
- Type **O** and press **Enter**. Select **Layer** from the command line, and then select **Current**. Type **26** and press **Enter**. Zoom to the kitchen area of the ground floor plan. Offset the wall edges, as shown.
- Trim the unwanted portions of the offset lines.

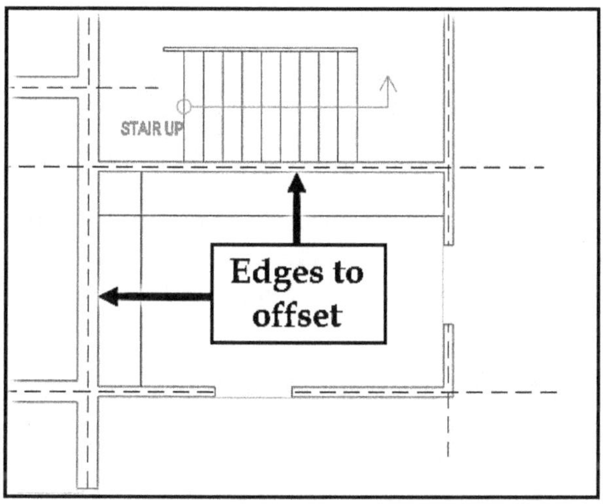

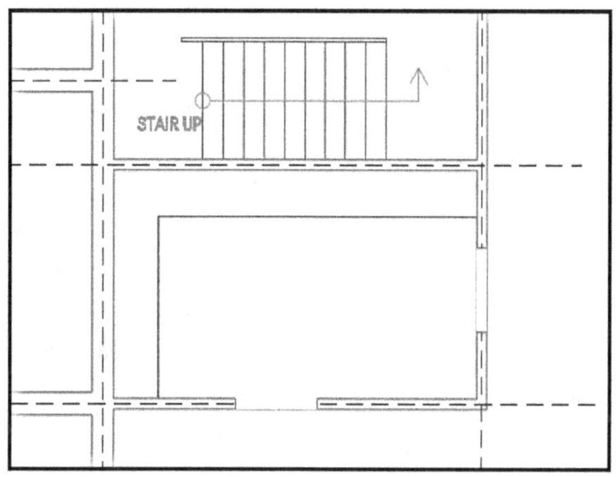

Now, you need to create the sink.

- Create the offset lines, as shown. The offset distances are given in the figure.
- Trim the unwanted entities.

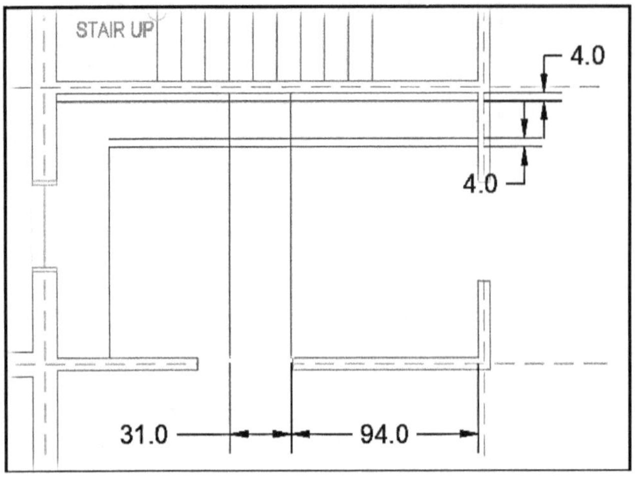

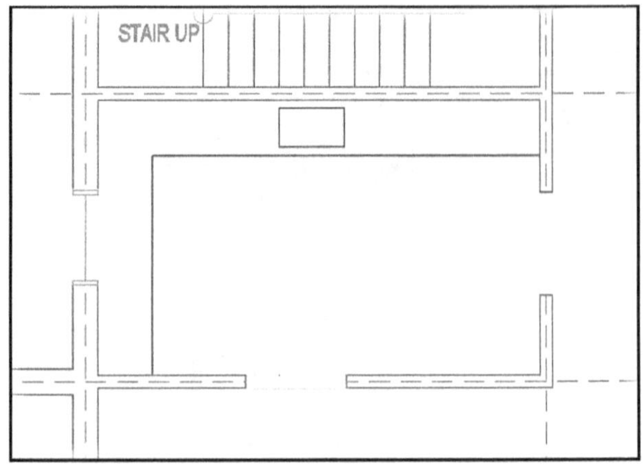

- On the ribbon, click **Home** tab > **Modify** panel > **Fillet** . Select **Radius** from the command line. Type **2** and press **Enter**. Select **Multiple** from the command line. Select the left vertical line and the horizontal line. A fillet is created at the corner. Likewise, create fillets at the other corners.

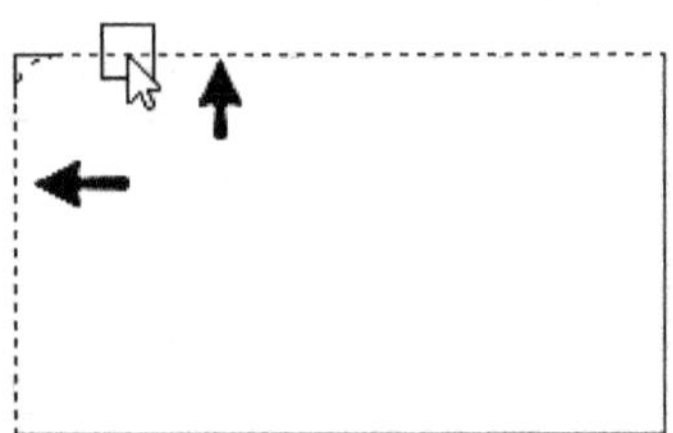
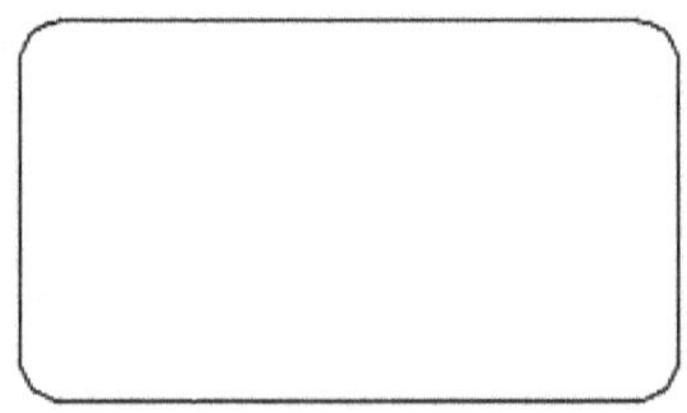

- On the **Home** tab of the ribbon, expand the **Modify** panel and click the **Edit Polyline** tool. Select **Multiple** from the command line. Create a selection window covering all the entities of the sink, and press **Enter**. Select **Yes** to convert the lines and arcs into a polyline. Select **Join** from the command line. Press **Enter** to accept **0** as the distance between the entities. Press **Esc** to deactivate the **Edit Polyline** tool.

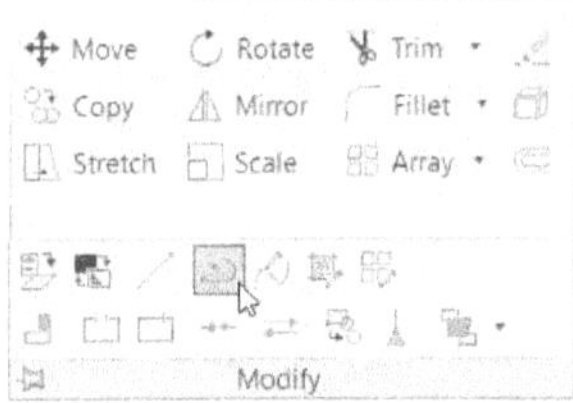

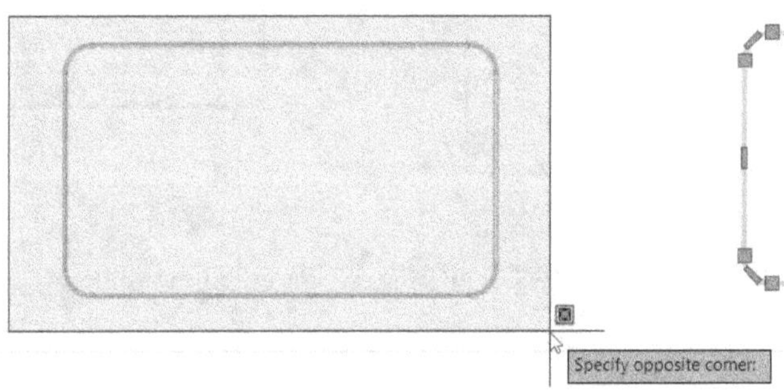

- Type **O** and press **Enter**. Type **1** and press **Enter** to define the offset distance. Select the polyline and click in the area enclosed by it. Press **Esc**.

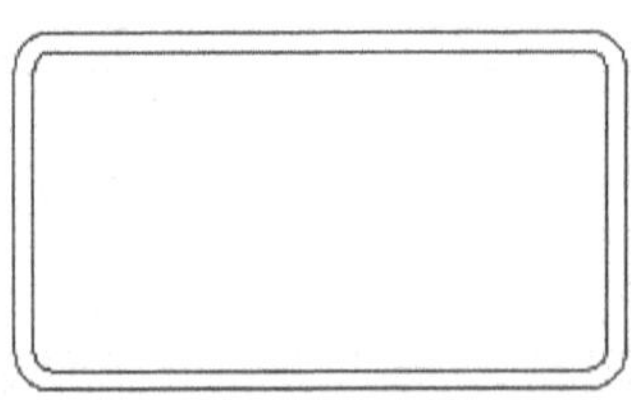

- On the ribbon, click **Home** tab > **Draw** panel > **Circle** drop-down > **Center, Diameter** . Select the midpoint of the upper horizontal line. Move the pointer outward, type **3**, and press **Enter**. Draw a vertical line of **5** inches from the center point of the circle.

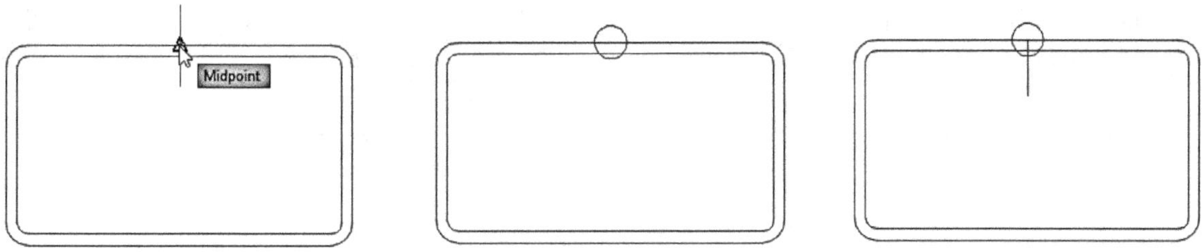

- On the ribbon, click **Home** tab > **Draw** panel > **Circle** drop-down > **Center, Radius** . Select the endpoint of the vertical line. Move the pointer outward, type **1**, and press **Enter**.

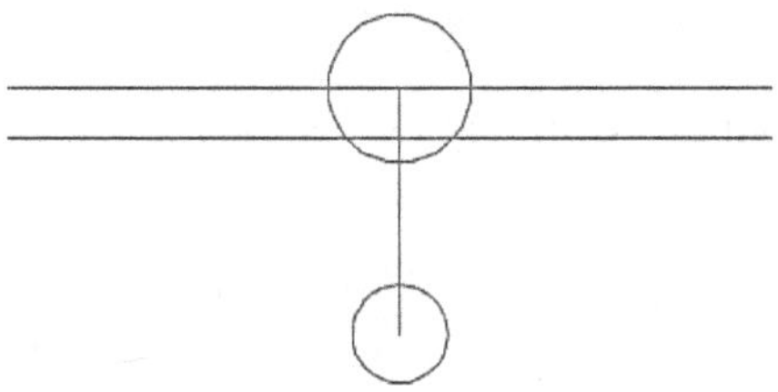

- Type **L** and press **Enter**. Select the left quadrant point of the small circle.
- Make sure that the **Orthomode** icon is not active.
- Move the pointer upward and select the left quadrant point of the large circle. Likewise, create another line by selecting the right quadrant points of the two circles.

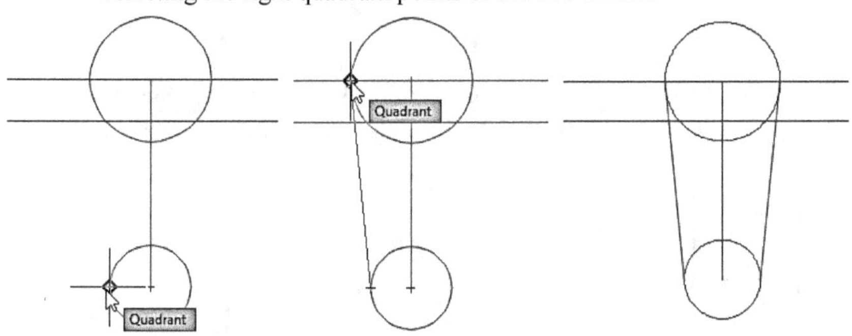

- Delete the vertical line and trim the inner portion of the small circle. Deactivate the **Trim** command.
- Type **M** and press **Enter**. Create a selection window across circles and inclined lines, and press **Enter**. Select the center point of the large circle to define the base point. Move the pointer vertically upward, type **2**, and press **Enter**. Trim the horizontal lines between the inclined lines. Deactivate the **Trim** command.

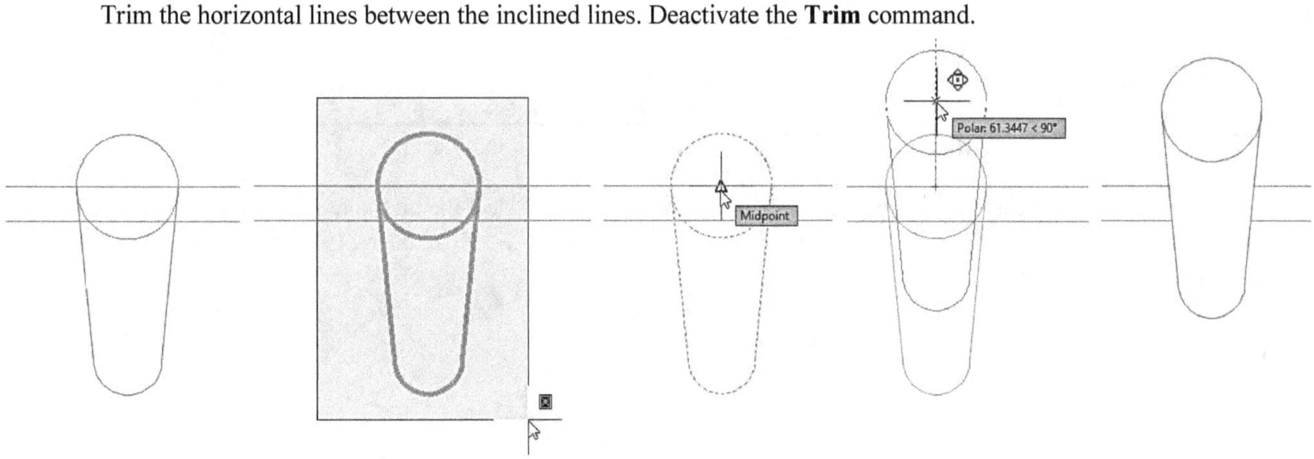

- Type **C** and press **Enter**. Place the pointer on the midpoint of the bottom horizontal line. Move the pointer upward. Place the pointer on the midpoint of the right vertical line. Move the pointer toward left. Click when the trace lines from the two midpoints intersect. Type **1.2** as radius and press **Enter** to create the circle.

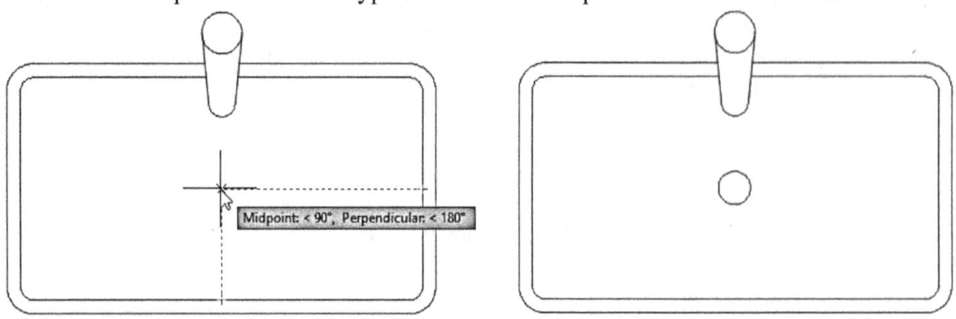

- Press **Enter** to activate the previous command. Select the center point of the previously created circle. Type **0.8** and press Enter.

- Type **REC** in the command line and press **Enter**. Select the lower-left corner of the kitchen. Select **Dimensions** from the command line. Specify **30** as length and width. Move the pointer up and click to create the rectangle.

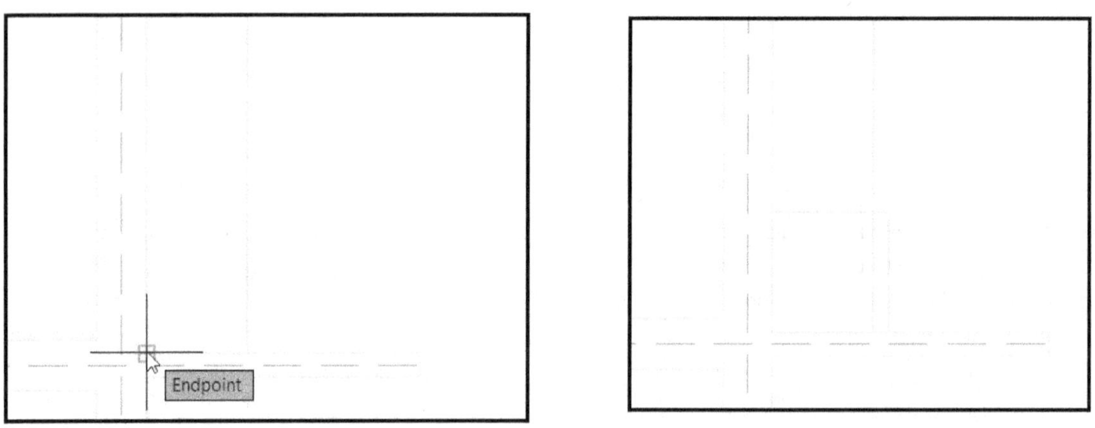

- Select the rectangle and click **Home** tab > **Modify** panel > **Move**. Select the midpoint of the left vertical line of the rectangle. Move the pointer up and select the midpoint of the window. Move the rectangle **0.4** inches toward the right.

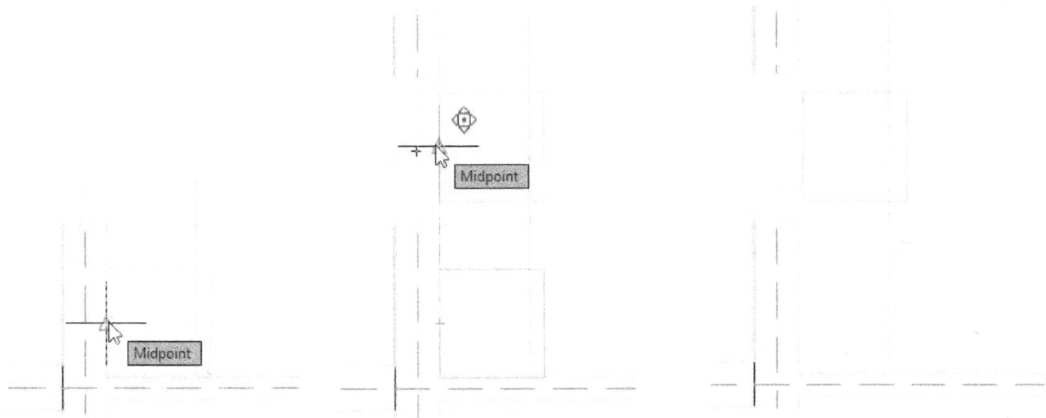

- Create two circles of **10** inch and **8**-inch diameter, respectively. Mirror the two circles about the midpoint of the rectangle.

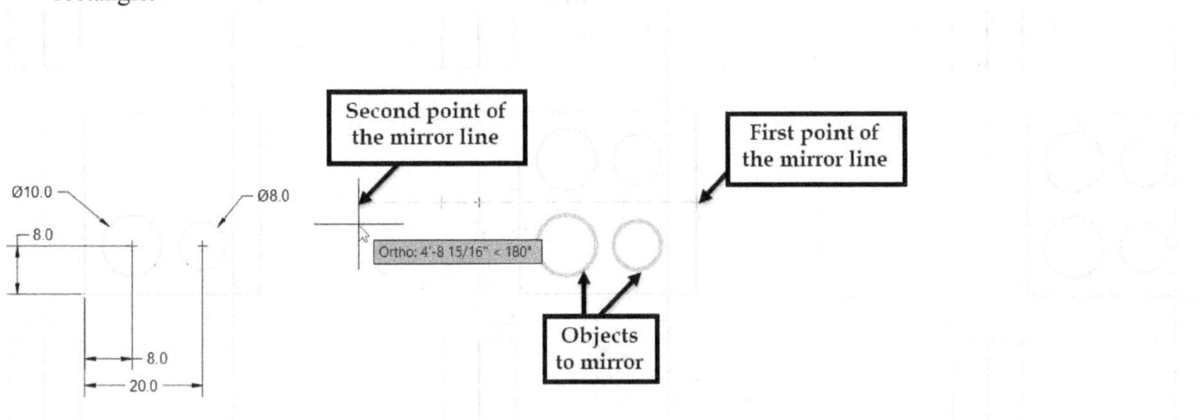

- Create two rectangles, as shown. Use the **Move** tool to create gaps between the rectangles and the wall. The gap should be **4** inches.

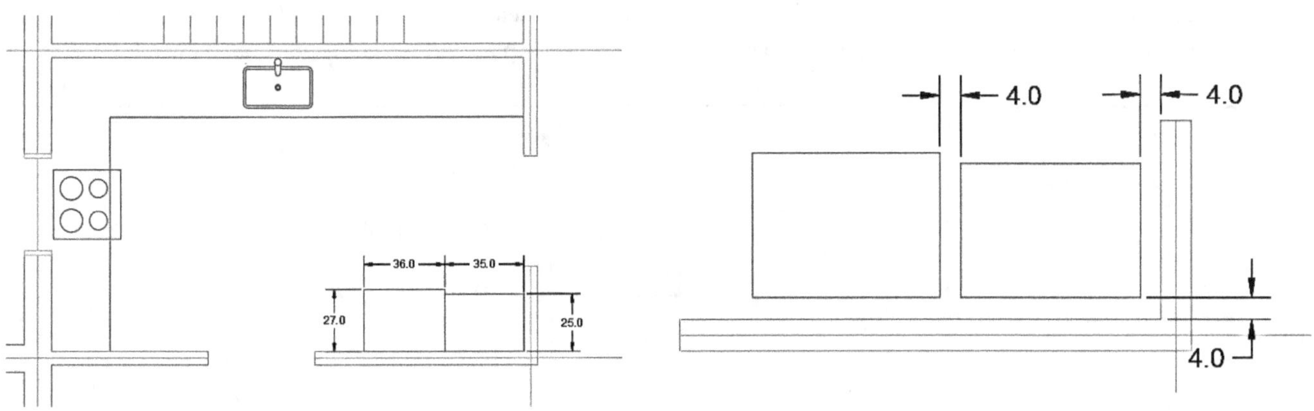

Creating Bathroom Fixtures

- On the ribbon, click **Home** tab > **Layers** panel > **Layer** drop-down > **A-BATHROOM FIXTURES**.
- On the ribbon, click **View** tab > **Palettes** panel > **DesignCenter**. Click on the gear icon on the title bar of the **DesignCenter** palette and select **Allow Docking**. Again, click on the gear icon and select **Anchor Left <**.

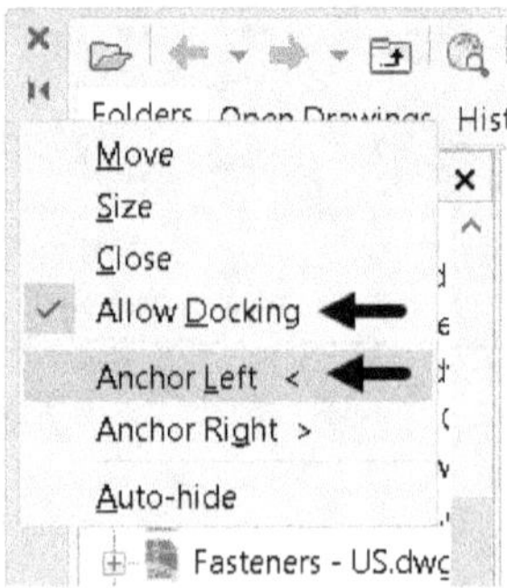

- Click the **DesignCenter** bar on the left side of the graphics window to expand the **DesignCenter** palette. On the **DesignCenter** palette, click the **Home** icon. The **Sample** folder is selected in the **Folder List**. Under the **Sample** node, go to **en-us > DesignCenter** and click the **House Designer.dwg** file. Double click on the **Blocks** icon. Click and drag the **Toilet-top** block from the **DesignCenter** palette into the graphics window. Likewise, click and drag the **Sink – Oval top** block into the graphics window.

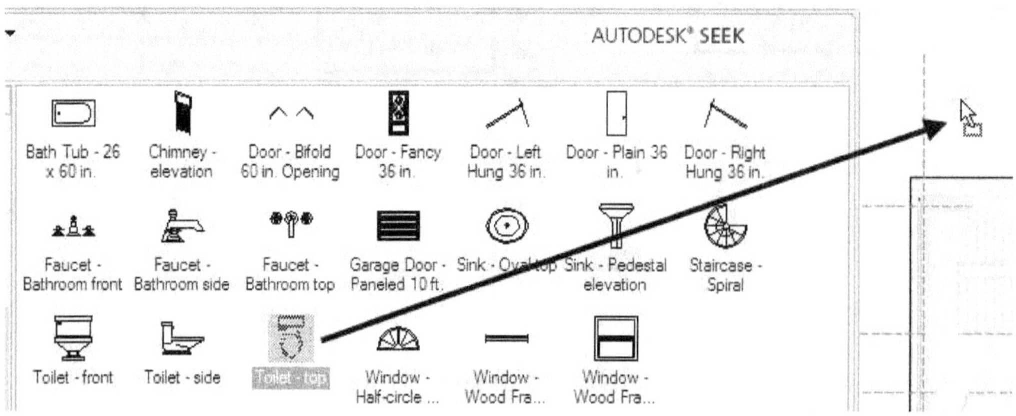

- In the graphics window, click on the **Toilet-top** block. Right click and select **Copy Selection**. Select the midpoint of the horizontal edge of the block. Zoom to the toilet area of the ground floor plan and select the point, as shown. Press **Esc**.

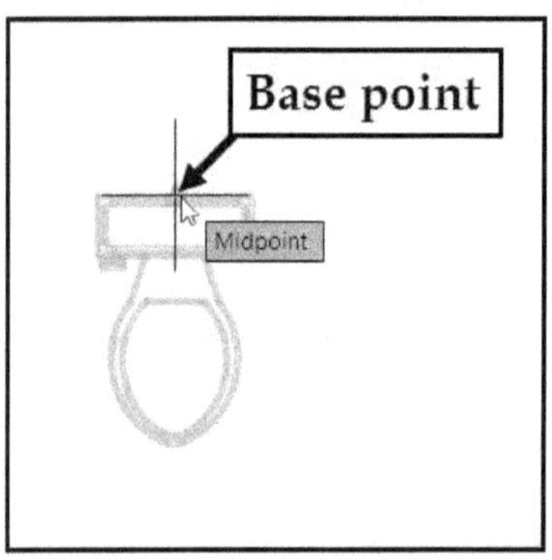

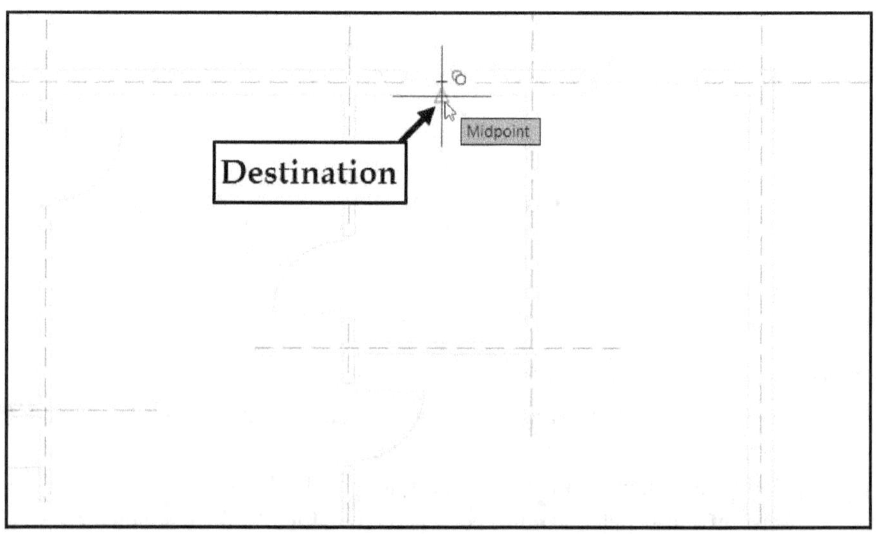

- Select the **Sink Oval** top block and click **Home** tab > **Modify** panel > **Rotate** . Select the center point of the block to define the base point. Type **90** and press **Enter**. Copy the **Sink Oval** top block and place it in the toilet, as shown.

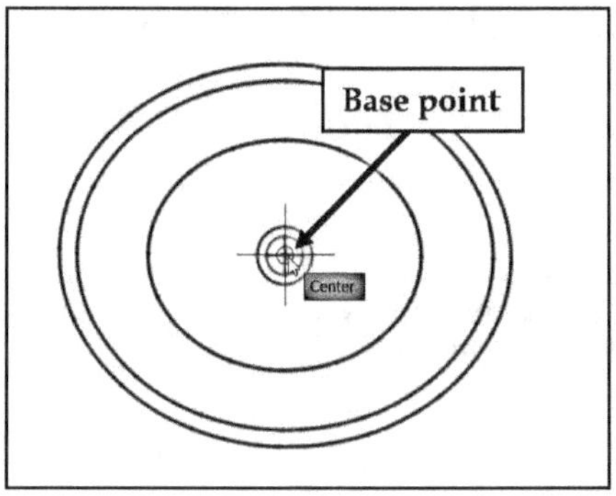

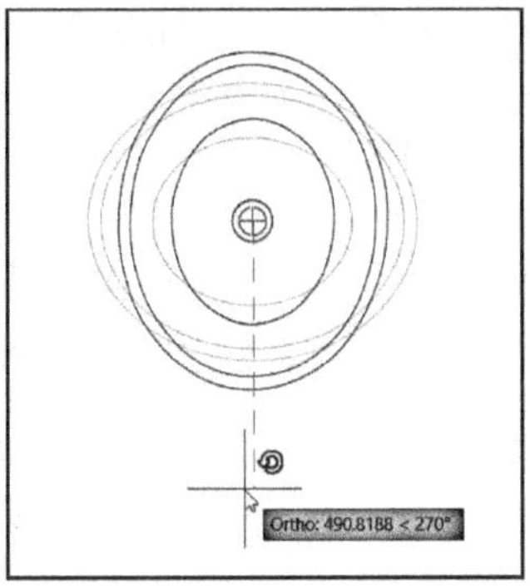

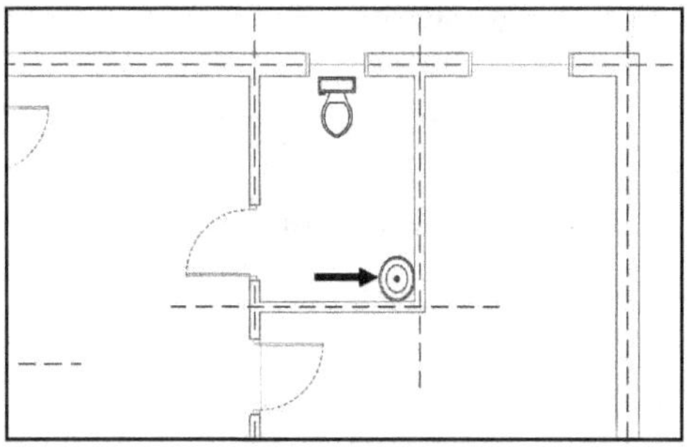

- Likewise, add bathroom fixtures to the first-floor plan.

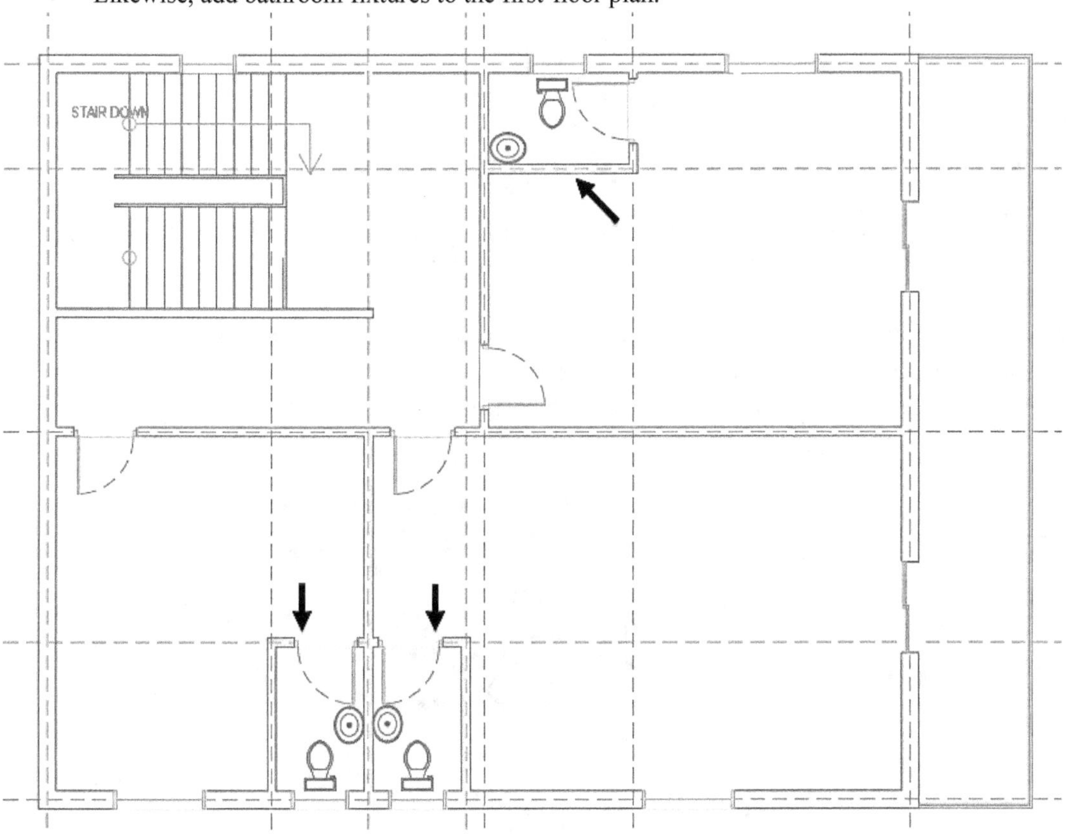

- Go to the following link on the internet and download the bathtub block.

http://www.cadforum.cz/catalog_en/block.asp?blk=3743

You can download different types of free CAD blocks from many websites on the internet. Some of the websites are given below:

https://bimobject.com
http://www.cadforum.cz
http://www.draftsperson.net
http://www.cad-architect.net
http://www.cadcorner.ca

- In the Tutorial 1 drawing file, create a circle on the **A-BATHROOM FIXTURES** layer. Select the circle and press **Ctrl+C**.
- Open the downloaded drawing file of the **Bathtub**. Click **NO** on the **AutoCAD** message box. Press **Ctrl+V** and click to paste the circle in the graphics window. On the ribbon, click **Home** tab > **Properties** panel > **Match Properties** . Select the circle as the source object. Create a selection window across all the entities of the bathtub. Press **Enter** to match the properties of the circle with the bathtub.

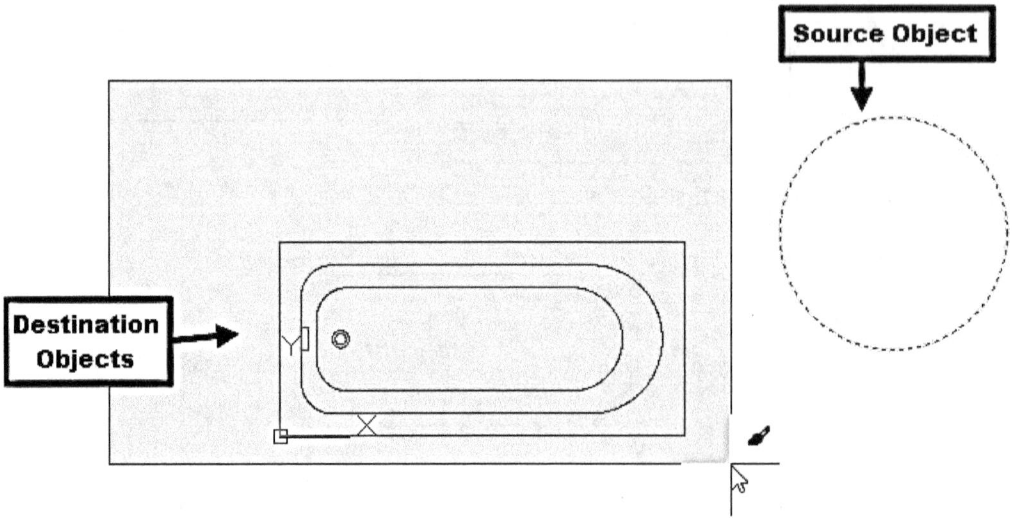

- Type **COPYBASE** and press **Enter**. Select the lower-left corner point of the bathtub. Create a selection window across all the entities of the bathtub. Press **Enter**. Switch to the Tutorial 1 drawing by clicking the Tutorial 1 tab above the graphics window. Press **Ctrl+V** and click in the empty space.

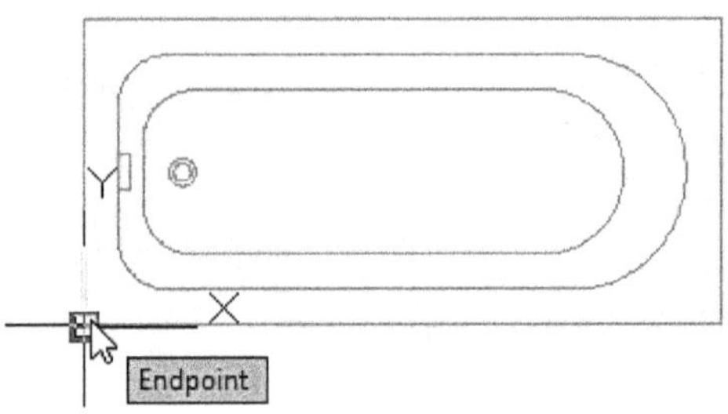

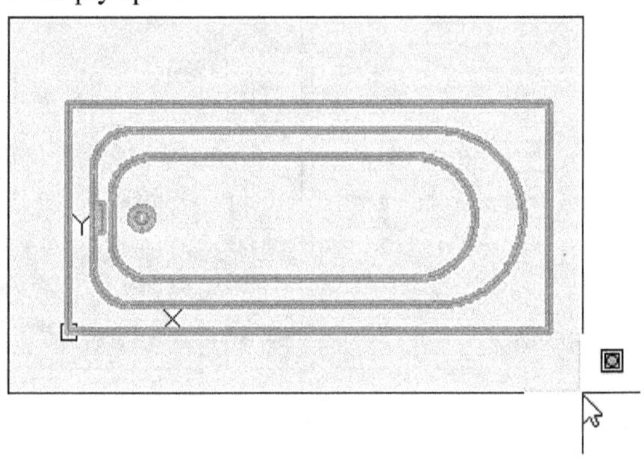

- On the ribbon, click the **Home** tab > **Modify** panel > **Scale**.
- Draw a selection window across all the objects of the bathtub. Next, select the lower-left corner point of the bathtub as the base point.

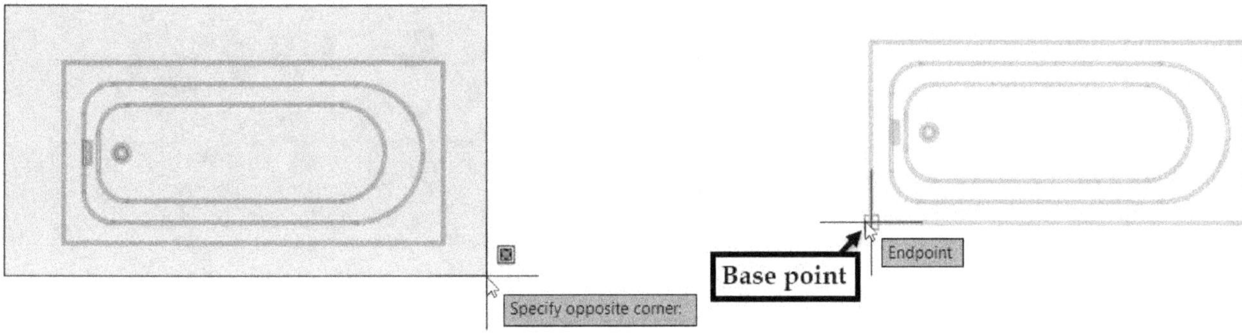

- Select the **Reference** option from the command line. Next, select the endpoints of the bottom horizontal line of the bathtub; the reference length is defined.
- Type **48** and press **Enter** to define the new length; the bathtub is scaled up to the new length.

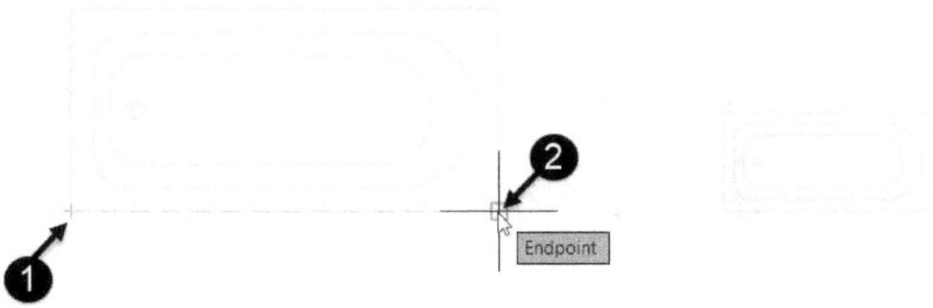

- Select all the entities of the bathtub and rotate them by **90** degrees. Move the bathtub and place it in the bottom left bathroom in the first-floor plan.

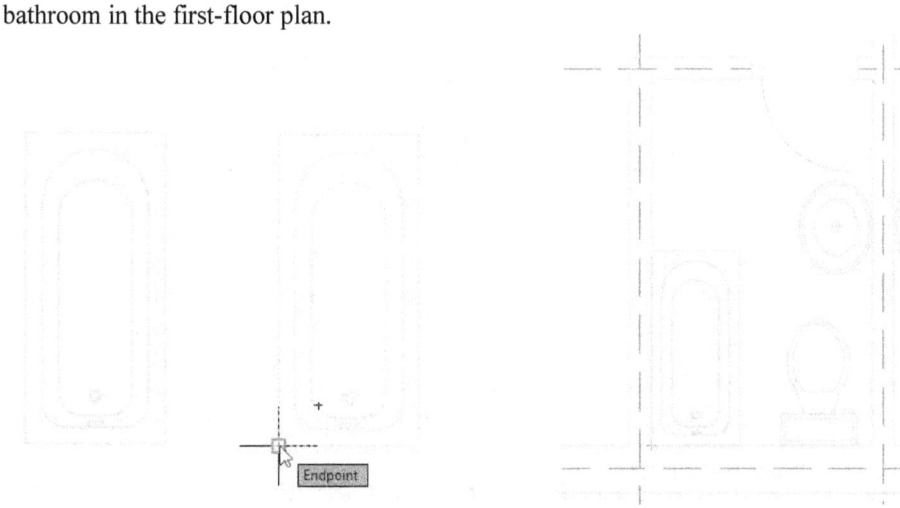

- Zoom to the right side bathroom in the first-floor plan. Select the **Sink Oval** top block, click on the grip, move the block, place it at the corner, as shown. Likewise, move the **Toilet-top** block, as shown.

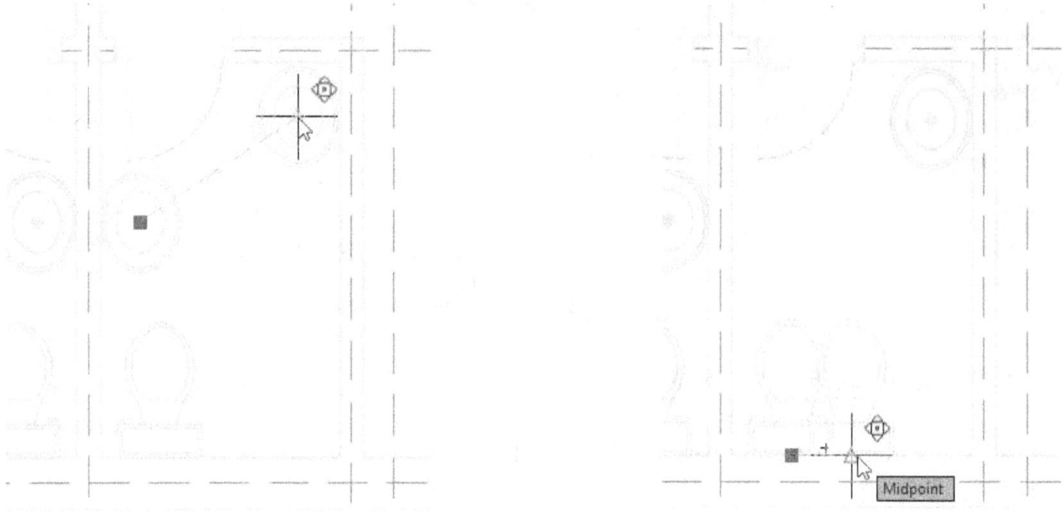

- Draw the shower sink in the right side bathroom.

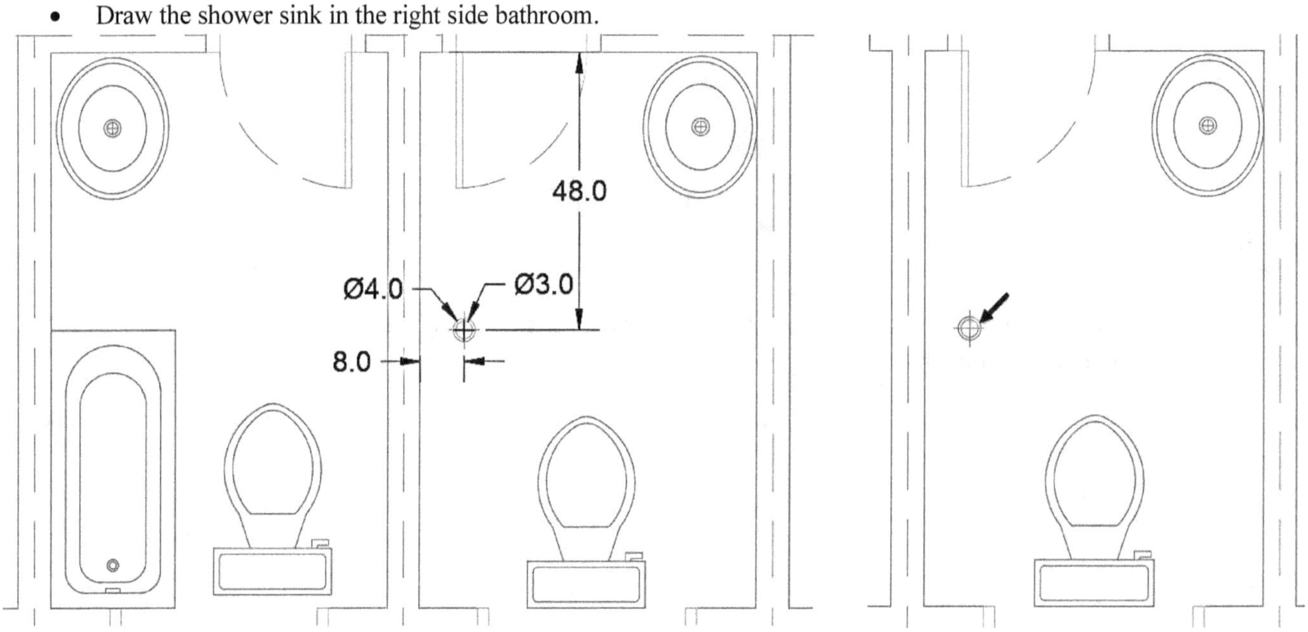

Adding the Furniture Blocks

- On the ribbon, click **Home** tab > **Layers** panel > **Layer** drop-down > **A-FURNITURE**.
- Download the **Blocks.dwg** file from the Companion website. It is a collection of some furniture blocks downloaded from www.cadforum.cz.
- In the Tutorial 1 drawing file, create a circle on the **A-FURNITURE** layer. Select the circle and press **Ctrl+C**.
- Open the **Blocks.dwg** file. Create a selection window across the furniture blocks, and click **Home** tab > **Modify** panel > **Explode**.

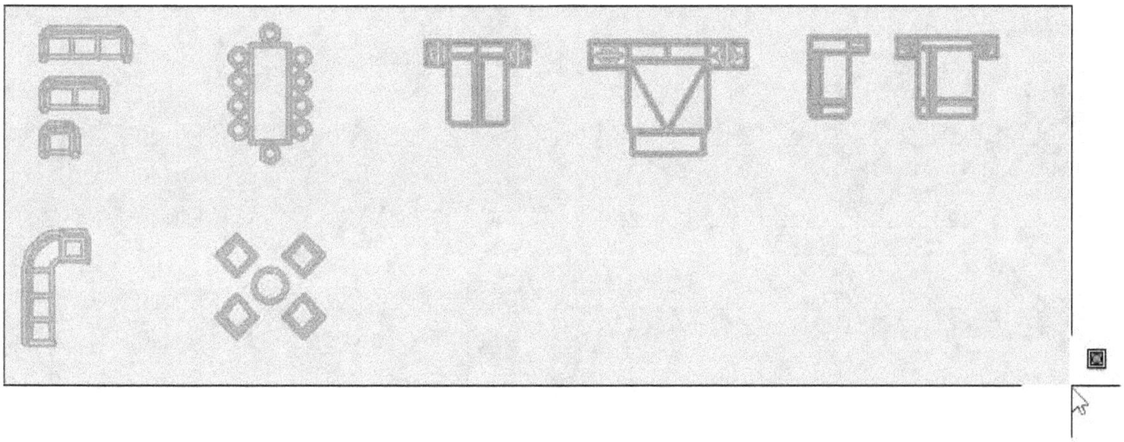

- Press **Ctrl+V** and click to paste the circle in the graphics window. On the ribbon, click **Home** tab > **Properties** panel > **Match Properties**. Select the circle as the source object. Create a selection window across the objects, as shown. Press **Enter** to match the properties of the circle with the selected objects.

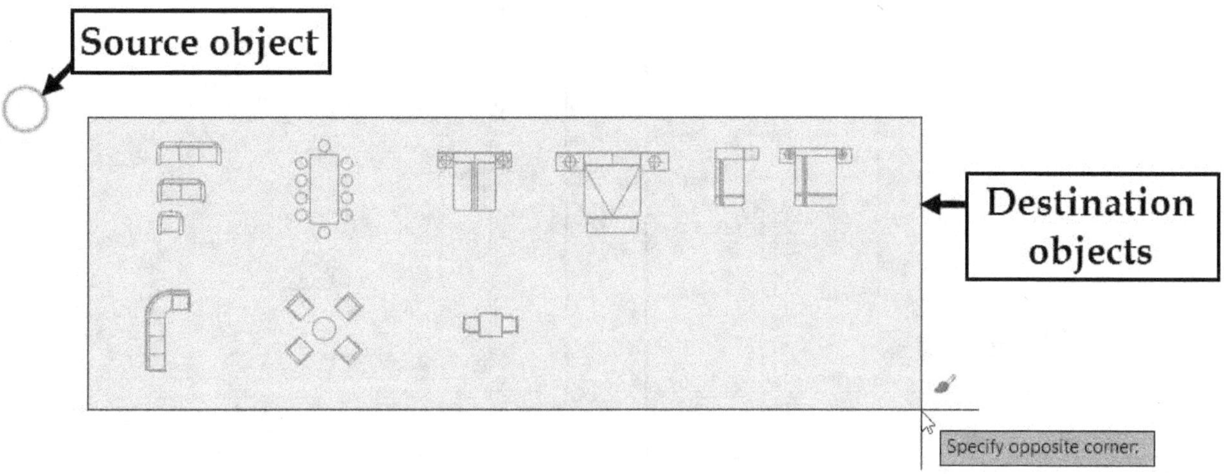

- Add furniture and other objects to the drawing.

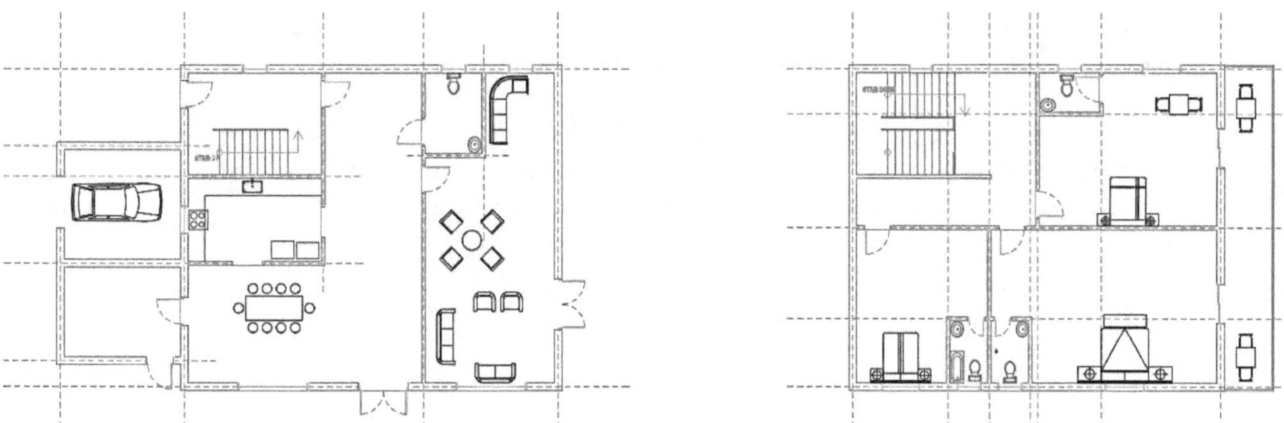

- On the ribbon, click **Home** tab > **Draw** panel > **Ellipse** drop-down > **Center** . Zoom to the sofa set area. Specify the center point, as shown. Next, move the pointer downward and click to specify the major axis. Move the pointer toward the right and click to specify the minor axis radius.

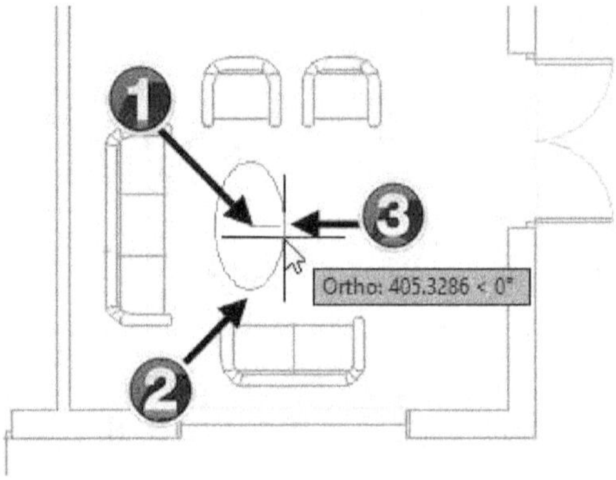

- Draw a rectangle over the sofa set, as shown. Use the **Trim** tool to remove the unwanted portions of the rectangle, as shown.

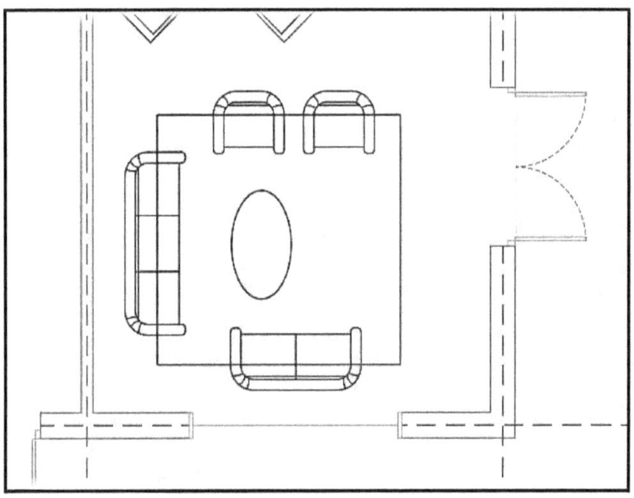

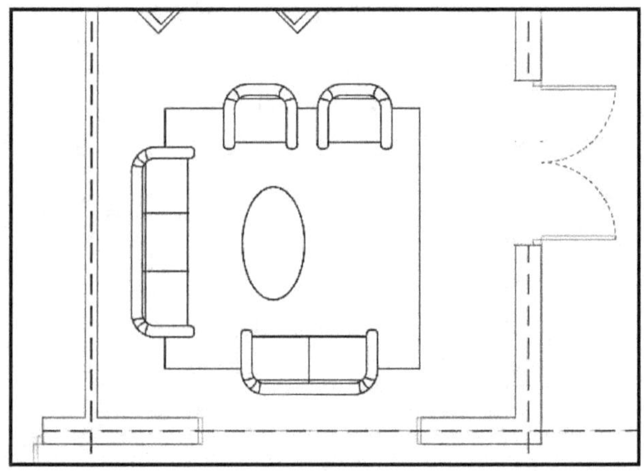

Tutorial 9: Adding Hatch Patterns and Text

- Turn off the **A-GRID** layer.
- On the ribbon, click **Home** tab > **Layers** panel > **Layer** drop-down > **A-WALL**.
- On the ribbon, click **Home** tab > **Draw** panel > **Hatch** drop-down > **Hatch** .
- On the **Hatch Creation** tab, select **SOLID** from the **Pattern** gallery. Click in the area enclosed by the wall edges, as shown. Likewise, click in the other areas of the walls. Note that you need to click in the area only when a preview appears.

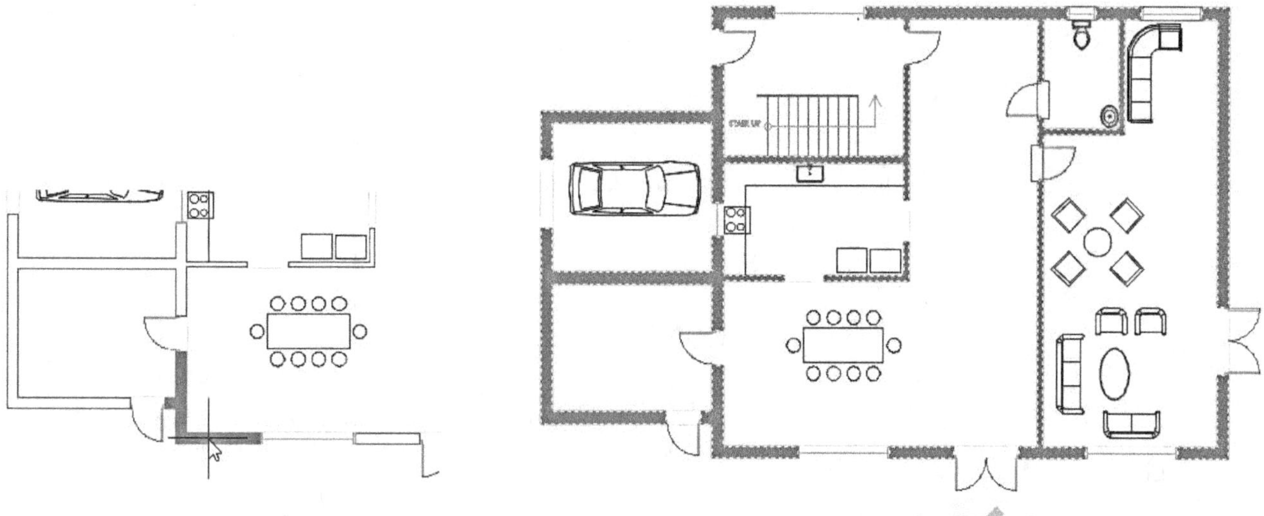

- Add the hatch pattern to the walls on the first-floor plan. Click **Close Hatch Creation** button on the ribbon.

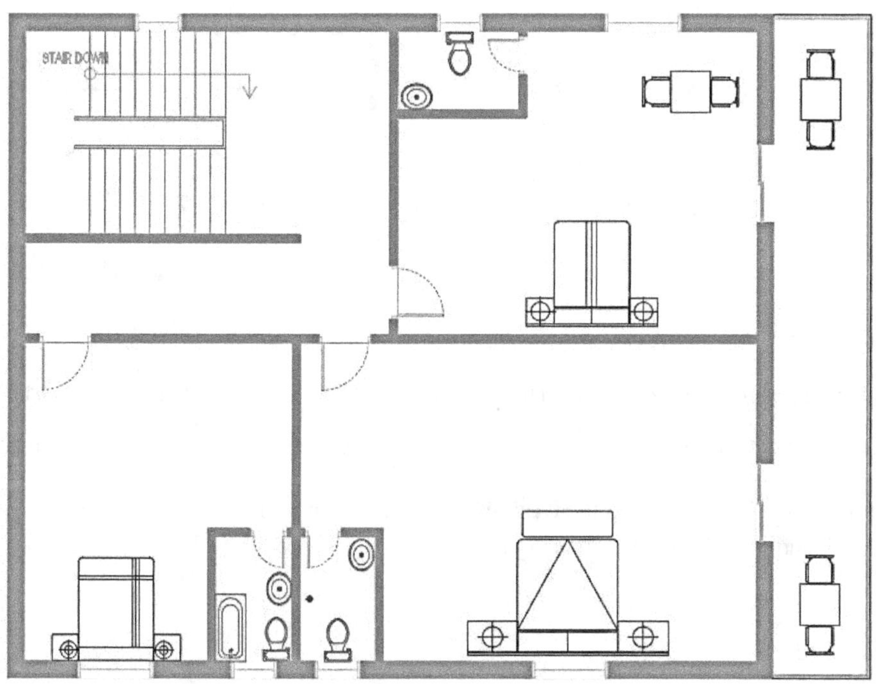

Adding Text Labels

- On the ribbon, click **Home** tab > **Layers** panel > **Layer** drop-down > **A-TEXT**.
- On the **Home** tab of the ribbon, in the **Annotation** panel, click **Text** drop-down > **Multiline Text**.
- Click in the lounge area of the ground floor plan to specify the first corner of the multiline text box. Move the pointer downward-right, and then specify the second corner. Type **Lounge** in the text box. Click and drag the ruler to reduce the width of the text box.
- Click **Close Text Editor** on the ribbon.

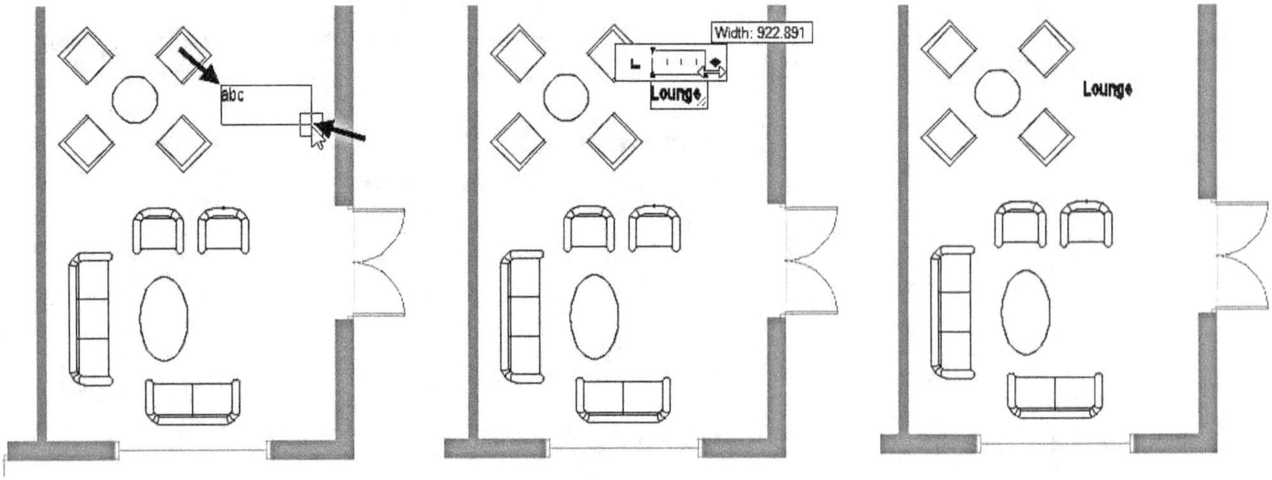

- Likewise, add text labels to the ground and first-floor plans.

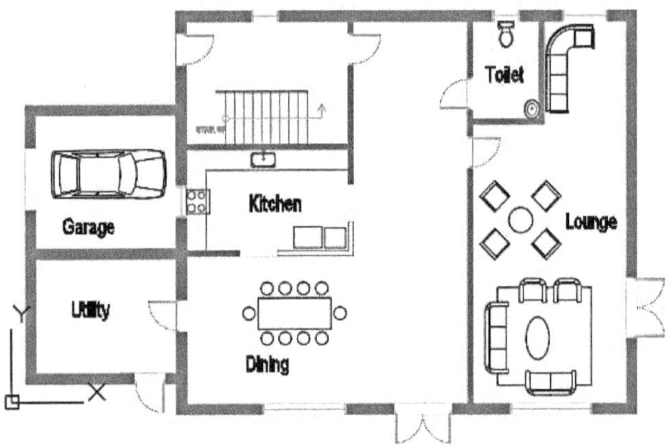

Ground floor plan

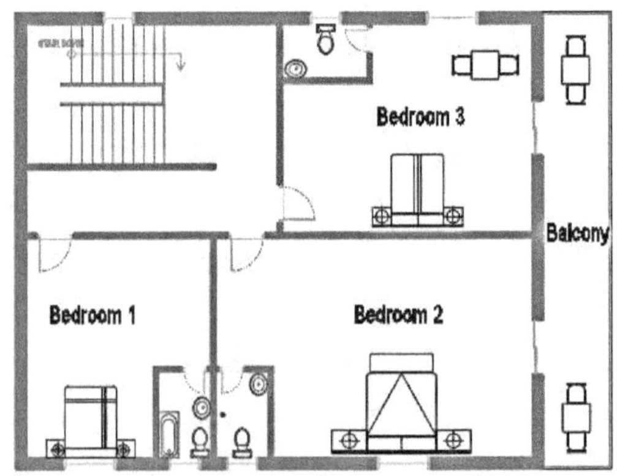

First floor plan

- On the **DesignCenter** palette, click the **Home** icon. The **Sample** folder is selected in the **Folder List**. Under the **Sample** node, go to **en-us > DesignCenter** and click the **Landscaping.dwg** file. Double click on the **Blocks** icon. Click and drag the **North Arrow** block from the **DesignCenter** palette into the graphics window.
- Drag the **North Arrow** block and place it at the bottom right corner of the ground floor plan.

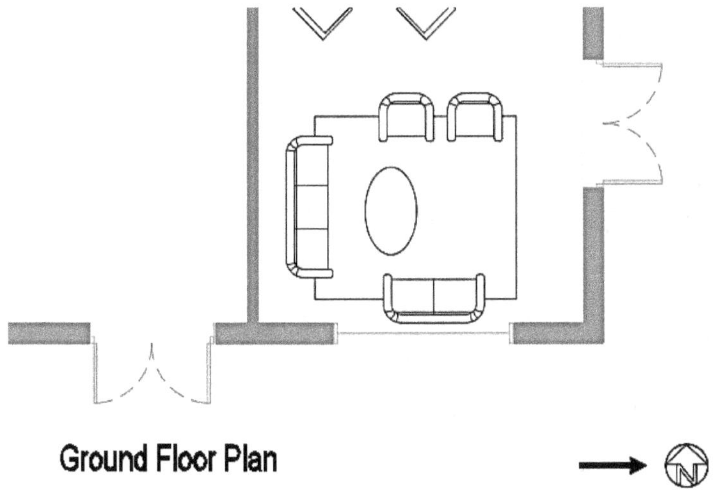

Tutorial 10: Creating Elevations

- Create the layers, as shown next.

Layer Name	Color	Linetype
A-ELEV-WALL	cyan	Continuous
A-ELEV-TEXT	Index Color 7	Continuous
A-ELEV-ROOF	green	Continuous
A-ELEV-FOUNDATION	magenta	Continuous
A-ELEV-FLOORING	blue	Continuous
Reference Lines	Index Color 9	Continuous

- Create a selection window across the ground floor plan. Create a copy of the ground floor plan in the space, as shown. Press **Esc** to deactivate the **Copy** command.

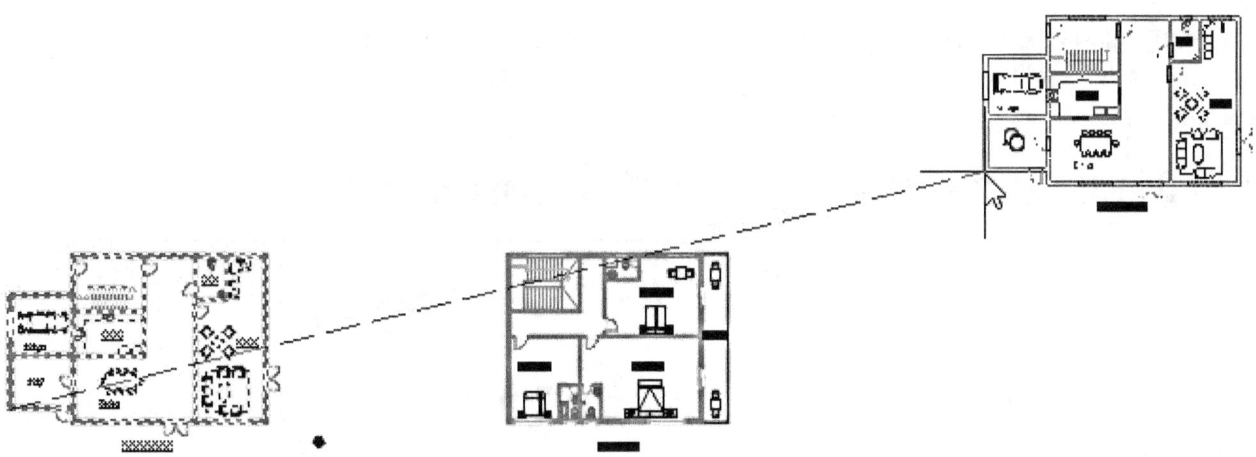

- On the ribbon, click **Home** tab > **Layers** panel > **Layer** drop-down > **A-ELEV-FOUNDATION**. Zoom to the copy of the ground floor plan. Draw a horizontal datum line above the floor plan.

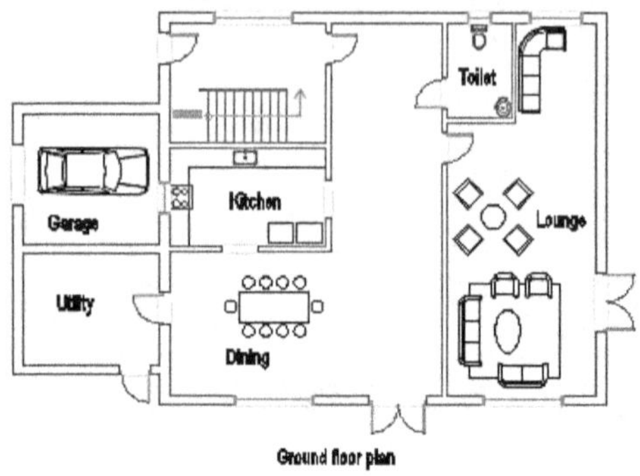

- On the ribbon, click **Home** tab > **Layers** panel > **Layer** drop-down > **A-ELEV-TEXT**.
- Type **PL** and press **Enter**. Select a point on the datum line. Select **Width** from the command line. Type **0** and press **Enter** to define the starting width. Type **10** and press **Enter** to define the end width. Move the pointer vertically upward, type **9**, and press **Enter**. Select **Width** from the command line. Type **0** and press **Enter** twice. Move the pointer horizontally and click. Press **Esc** to deactivate the **Polyline** command.

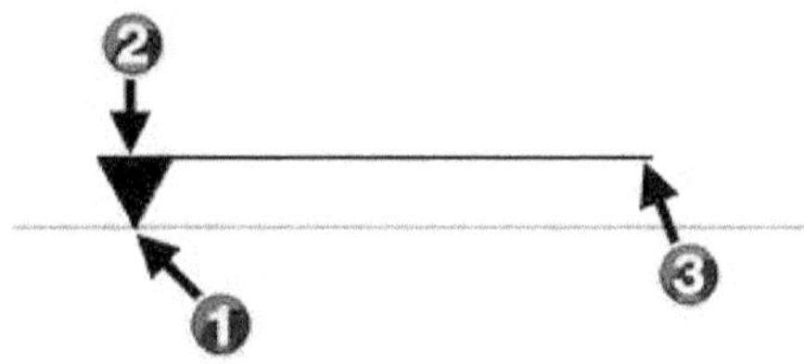

- Create and place the text above the polyline, as shown.

- Offset the horizontal datum up to **98** inches in the upward direction. Copy the floor level annotation and place it above the new line. Double click on the copied text and change it to **8'2"** Ground Floor.

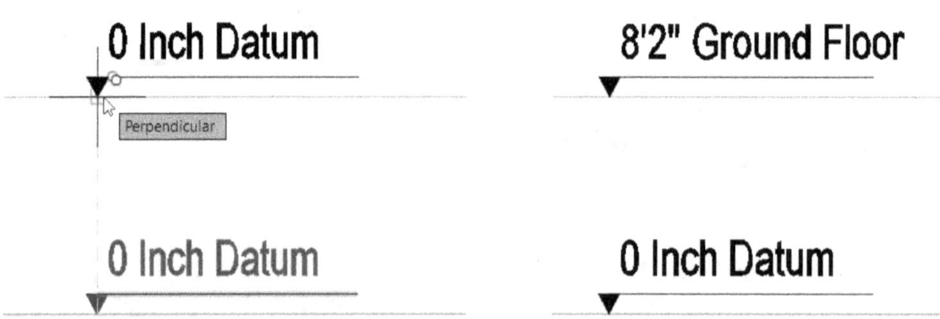

- Offset the ground floor line up to **8"** downward. Press **Esc** to deactivate the **Offset** command; the floor thickness is defined. Select the two lines defining the floor thickness and click **Home** tab > **Layers** panel > **Layers** drop-down **>**

A-ELEV-FLOORING.

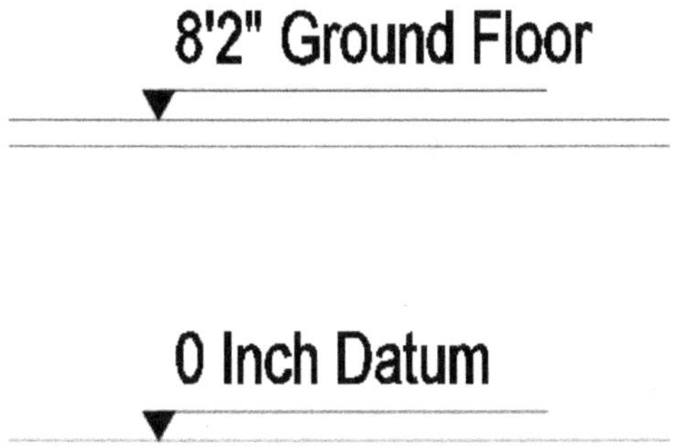

- Create other offset lines, as shown. Select the top three horizontal lines and move them to the **A-ELEV-ROOF** layer.

- On the ribbon, click **Home** tab > **Layers** panel > **Layer** drop-down > **A-ELEV-WALL**. Activate the **Line** tool and select the top left corner of the ground floor plan. Move the pointer upward and click to create a vertical line. Press **Esc**. Likewise, create other vertical lines, as shown.

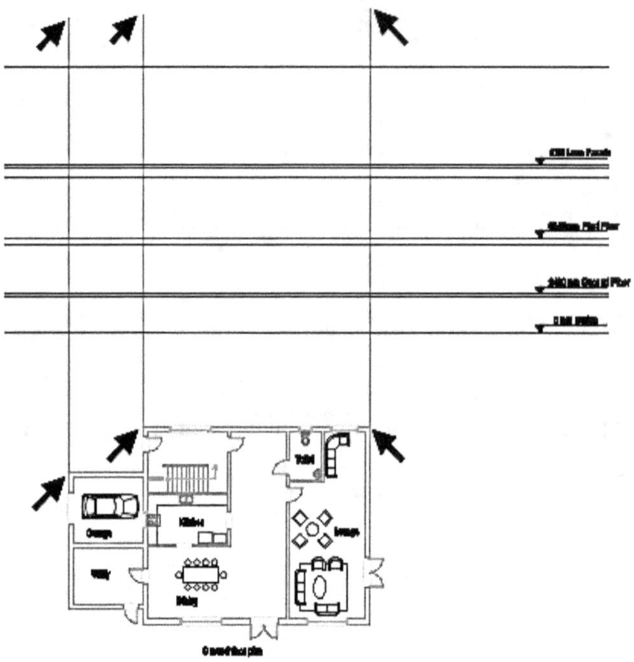

Next, you need to create an overhang for the roof.

- Offset the left vertical lines to the left side. Likewise, offset the right vertical line to the right side. The offset distance is **16** inches.

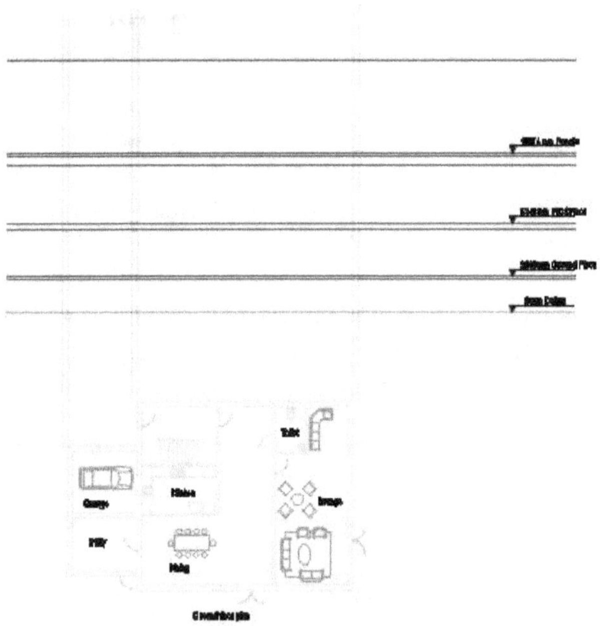

- Type **TR** and press **Enter**. Select the **Crossing** option from the command line. Create a rectangular selection window across the left portions of the horizontal lines, as shown. Likewise, trim the right-side portions of the horizontal lines.

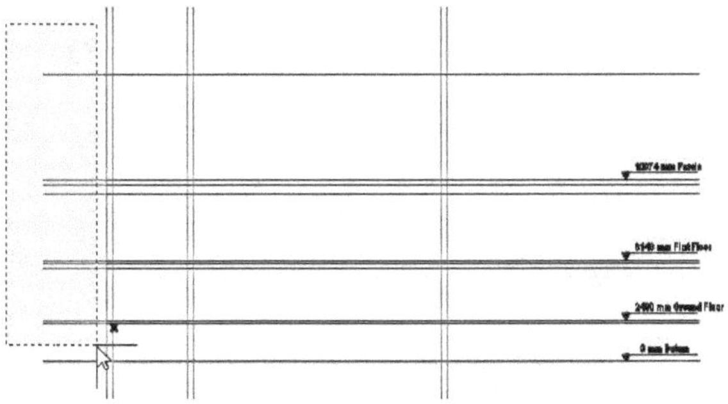

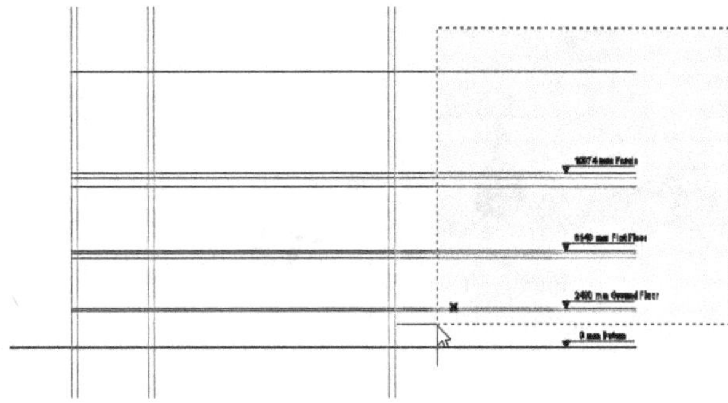

- Trim the upper and lower portions of the vertical lines, as shown.

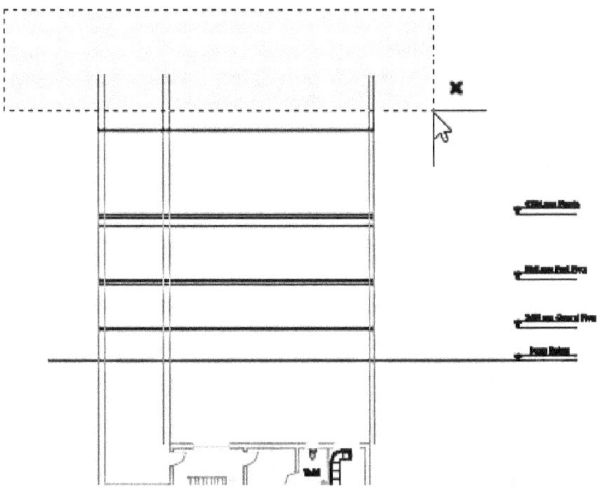

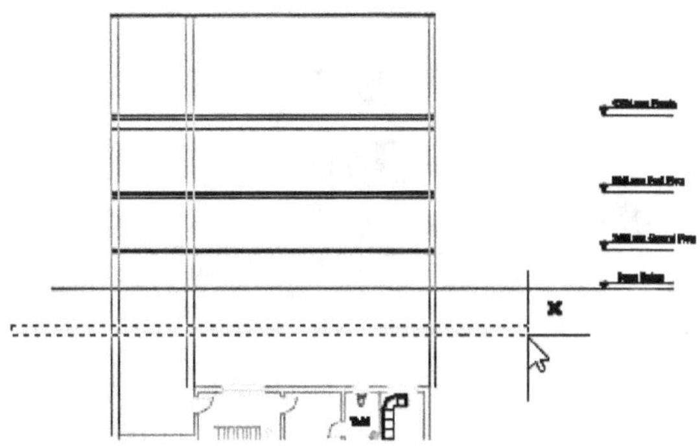

- Trim the other portions of the horizontal lines, as shown. The sequence to trim the horizontal lines is given in the figure below.

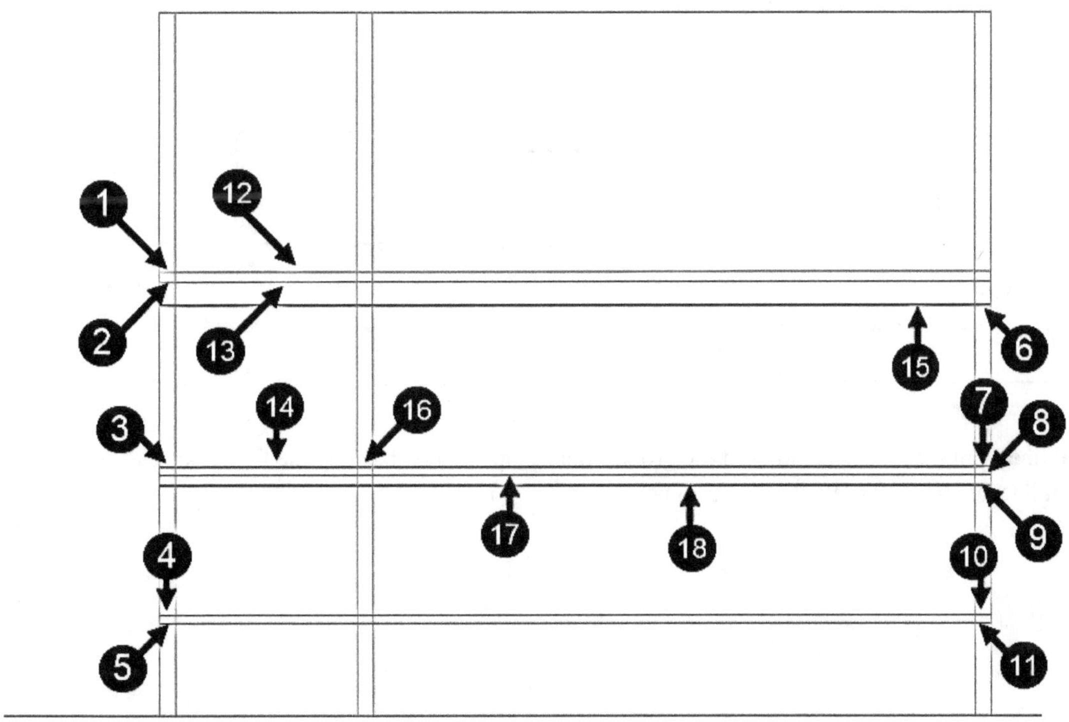

- Trim the other lines in the sequence, as shown.

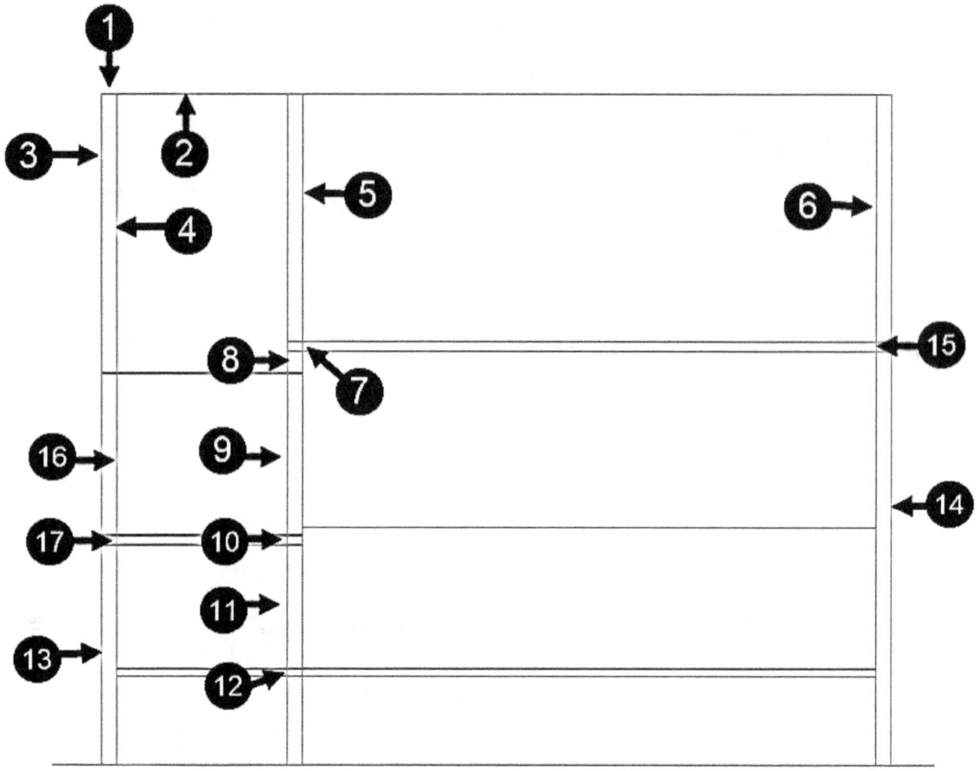

- Select the vertical line, as shown. Press **Delete** on your keyboard.

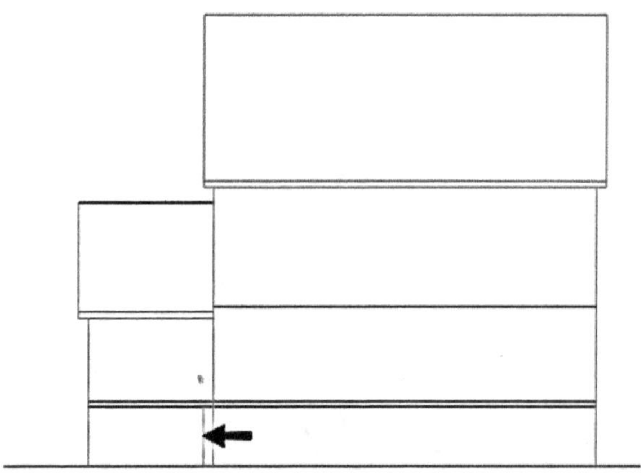

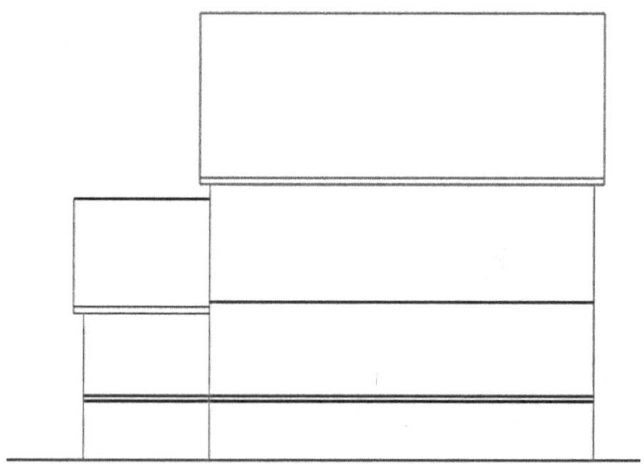

- Draw a vertical line from the top right corner of the ground floor plan, as shown. Copy the first-floor plan and place it on the vertical line, as shown. Delete the vertical line.

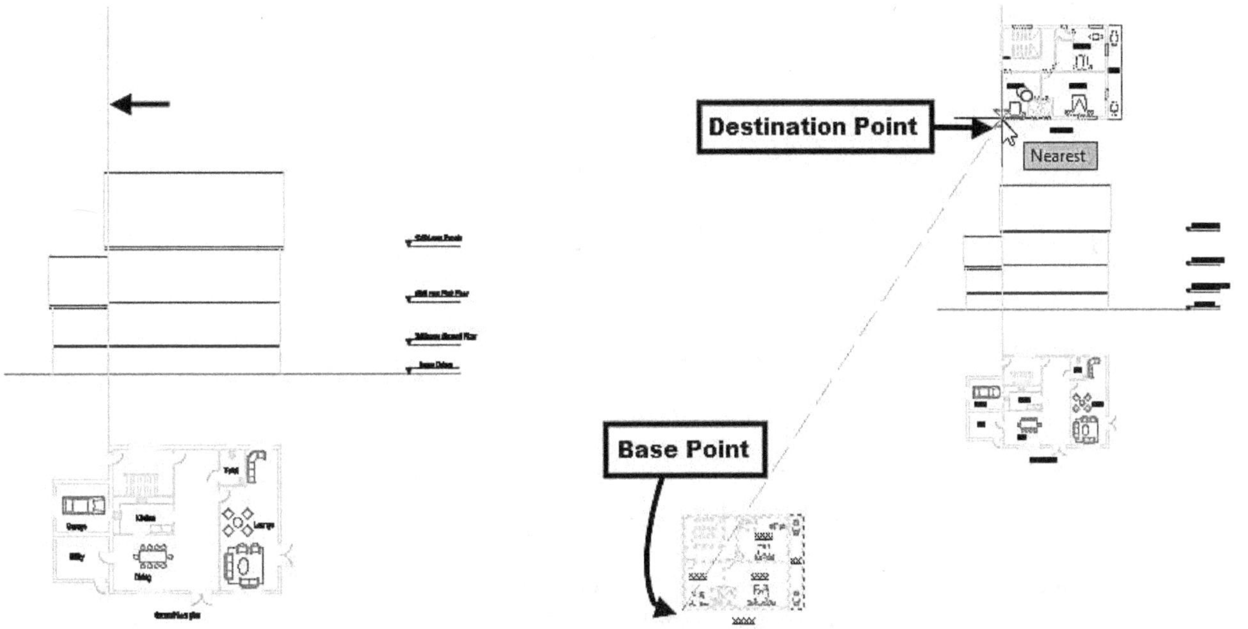

- On the ribbon, click **Home** tab > **Layers** panel > **Layer** drop-down > **Reference Lines**.
- On the **Home** tab of the ribbon, expand the **Draw** panel and click the **Ray** tool. Zoom to the copy of the first-floor plan. Make sure that the **ORTHOMODE** is turned **ON**. Select the corner point of the balcony, move the pointer downward, and click. Press **Esc** to deactivate the tool.

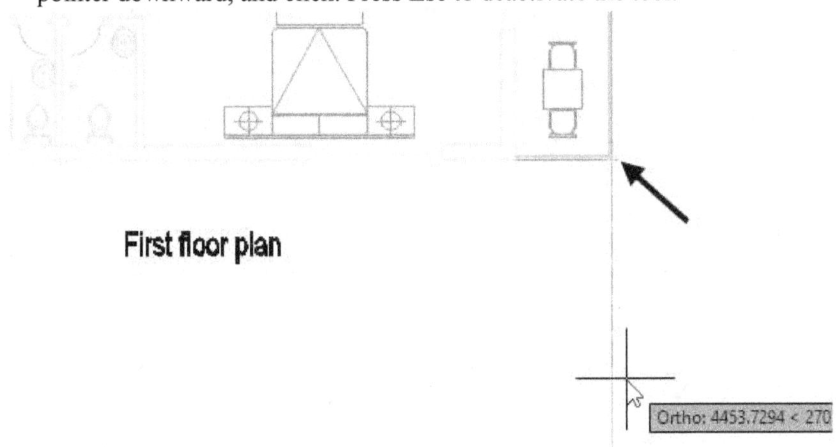

- Likewise, create reference lines from the windows.

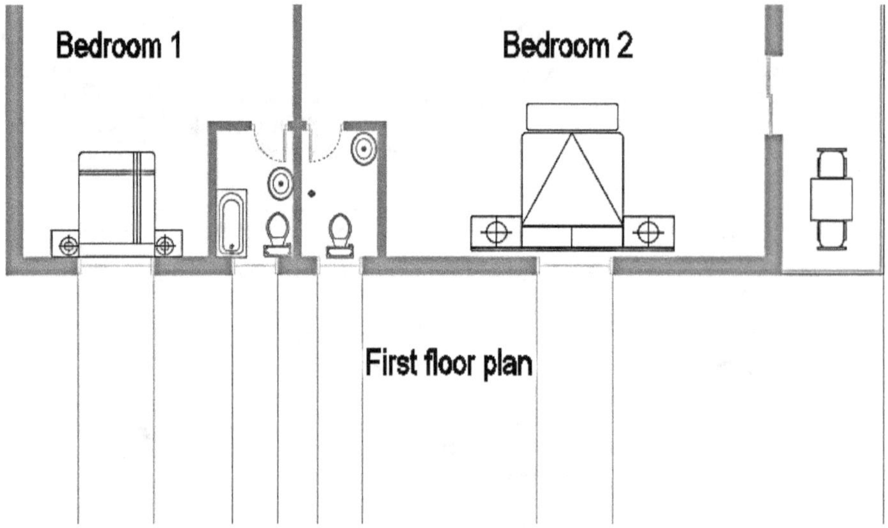

- On the ribbon, click **Home** tab > **Layers** panel > **Layer** drop-down > **A-ELEV-FLOORING**. Create the elements of the balcony using the **Rectangle** tool, as shown.

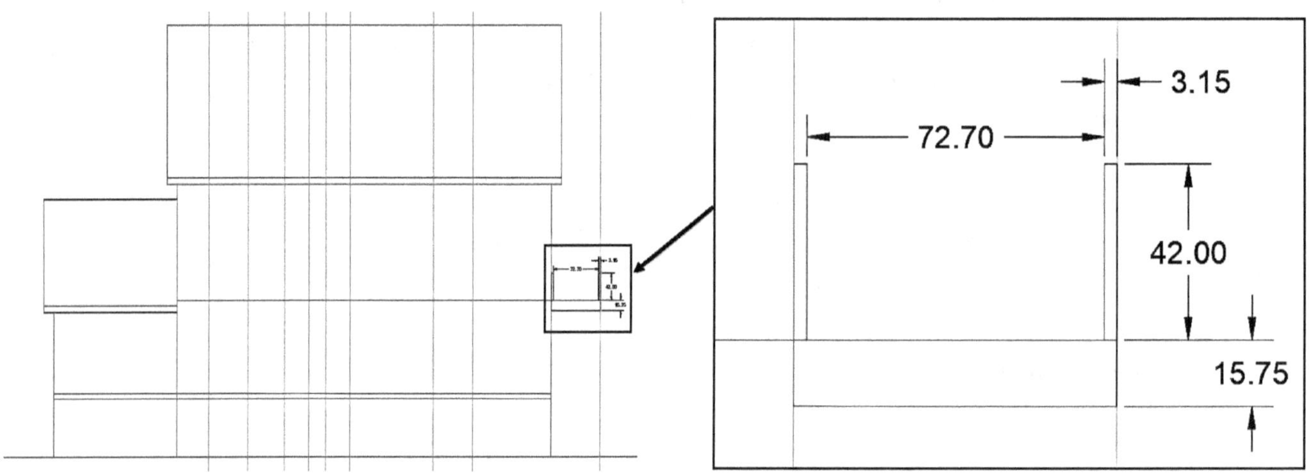

- Use the **Move** tool to move the two rectangles inward by **2.72** inches.

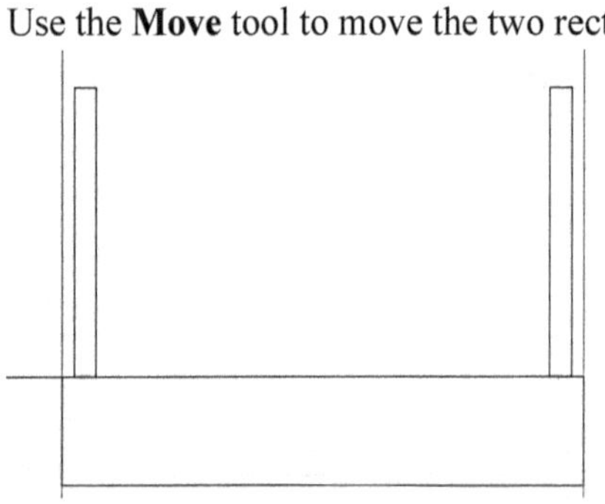

- Type **REC** and press **Enter**. Click in the empty space, and select **Dimensions** from the command line. Type **1** and press **Enter**. Type **2.5** and press **Enter**. Move the pointer upward and click to create the rectangle. Select the rectangle, type **M**, and press **Enter**. Select the midpoint of the lower horizontal line of the rectangle. Move the pointer and select the midpoint of the balcony post, as shown. Likewise, use the **Copy** tool to copy and place the small rectangle on the other post.

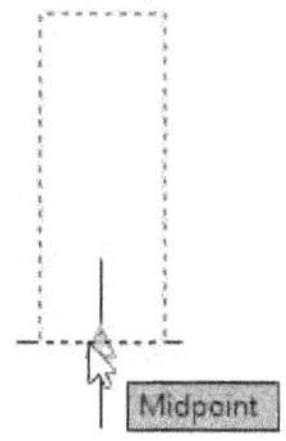

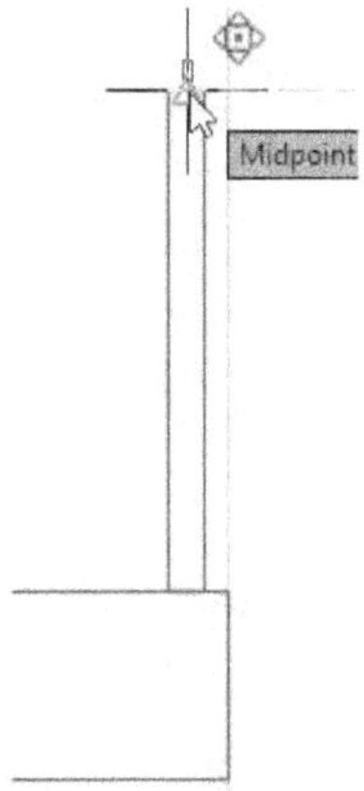

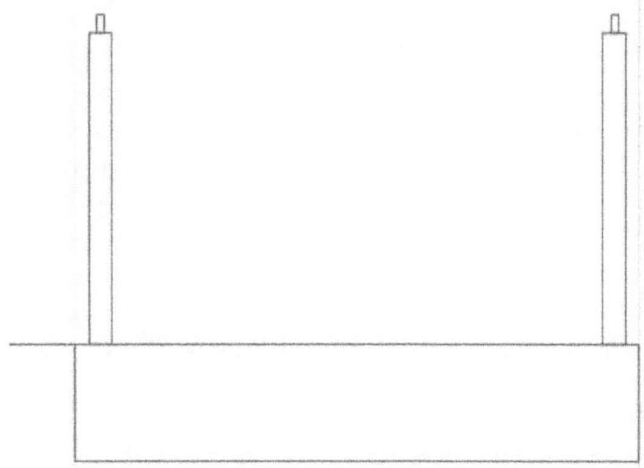

- Create a horizontal line, as shown. Offset the horizontal line by **2** inches.

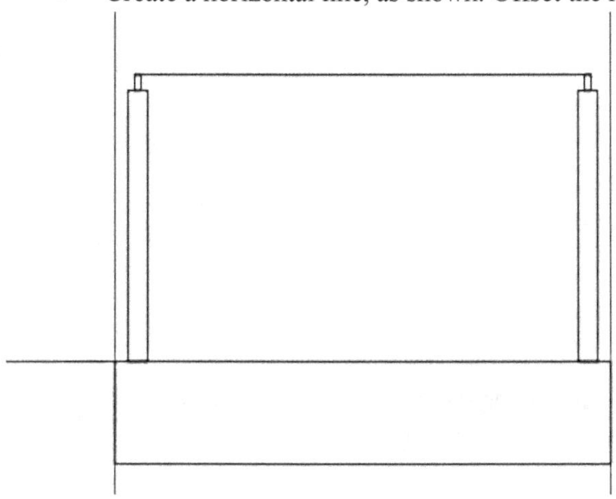

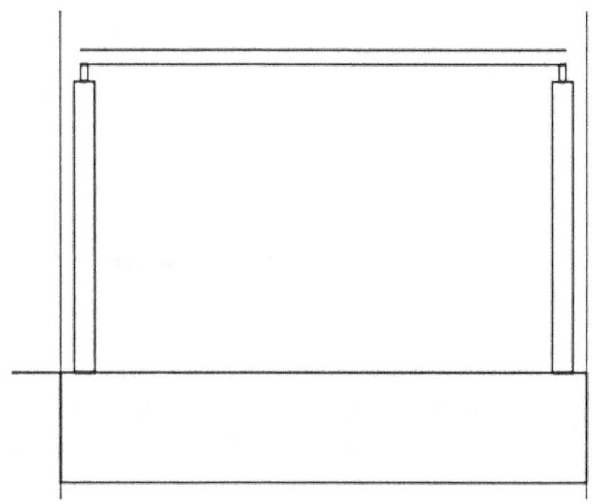

- On the ribbon, click **Home** tab > **Modify** panel > **Trim** drop-down > **Extend** . Press **Enter** to select all entities as boundary edges. Click on the left end of the horizontal line, as shown; it is extended up to the next entity. Likewise, extend the horizontal lines on both sides, as shown.

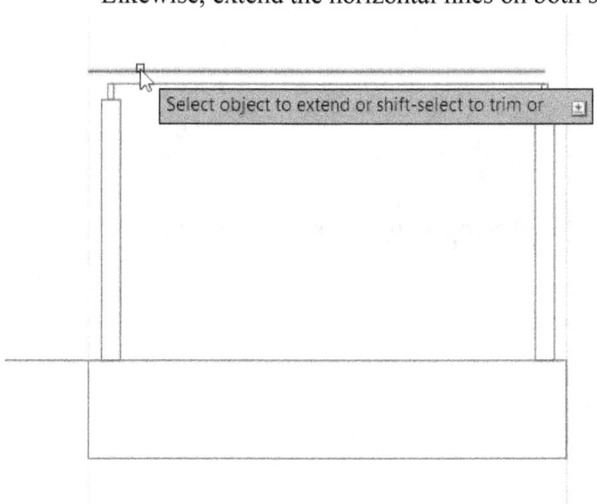

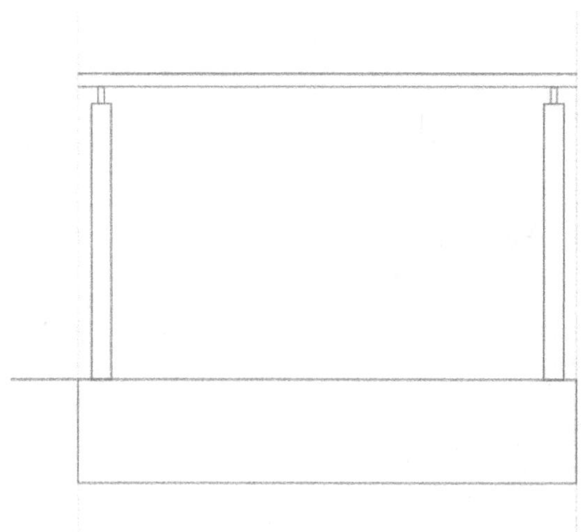

- On the ribbon, click **Home** tab > **Draw** panel > **Arc** drop-down > **Start, End, Direction** . Specify the start and endpoints of the arc, as shown. Move the pointer horizontally toward the right and click.

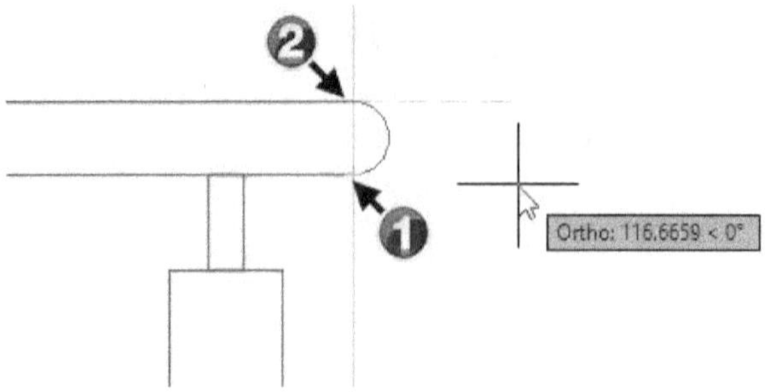

- Create a rectangle by specifying the corner points, as shown. Select the rectangle to display grips on it. Click on the midpoint grip of the lower horizontal line of the rectangle, move the pointer upward, type **3**, and press **Enter**. Likewise, move the vertical lines of the rectangle inward by **0.4** inches.

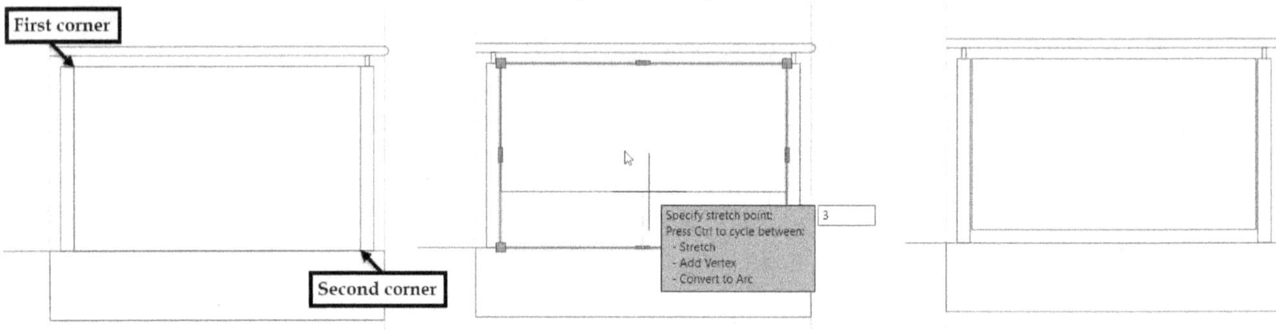

Now, you need to create the sleeve for the glass.

- Type **REC** and press **Enter**. Select the top right corner of the left post, as shown. Select **Dimensions** from the command line. Type **1.5** and press Enter. Type **3** and press **Enter**. Move the pointer downward and click.

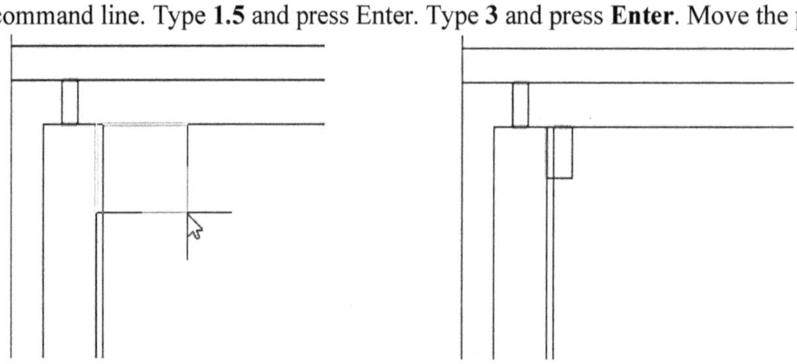

- Select the new rectangle, type **M**, and press **Enter**. Select the top left corner of the rectangle to define the base point. Move the pointer downward, type **4**, and press Enter.

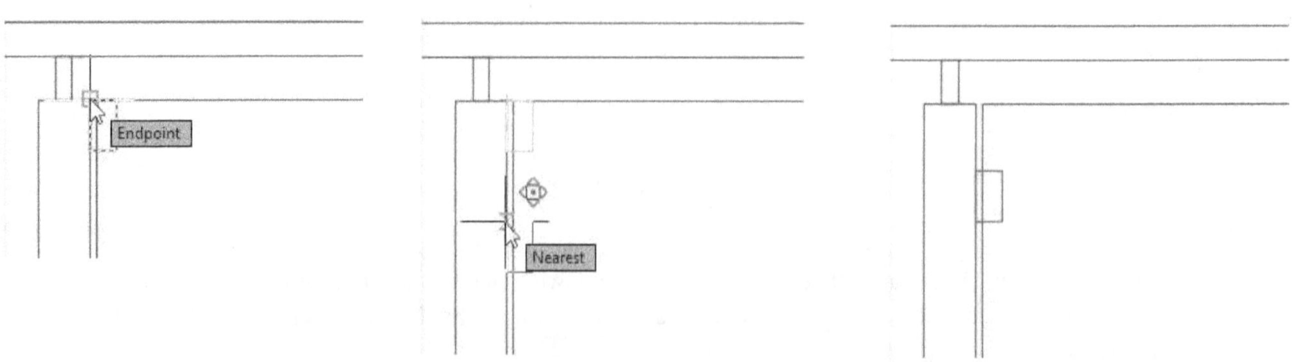

- Activate the **Start, End, Direction**  tool. Select the top right and bottom right corners of the new rectangle. Move the pointer horizontally toward the right and click. Type **TR** and press **Enter** twice. Trim the unwanted portions, as shown. Press **Esc**.

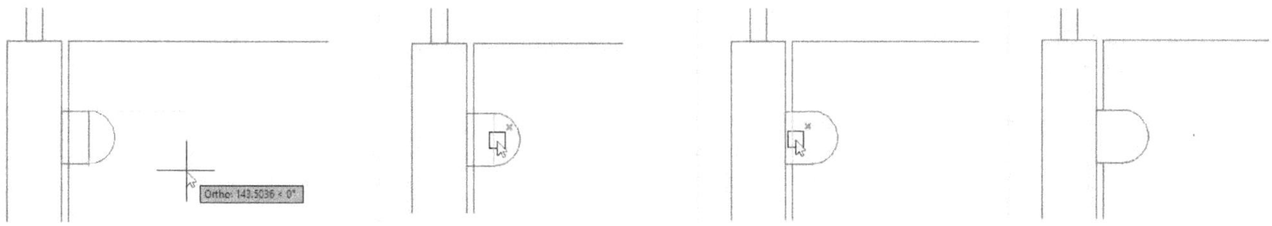

- Select the entities of the sleeve, type **MI**, and press **Enter**. Select the midpoint of the rectangle, move the pointer downward, and click. Select **No** from the command line.

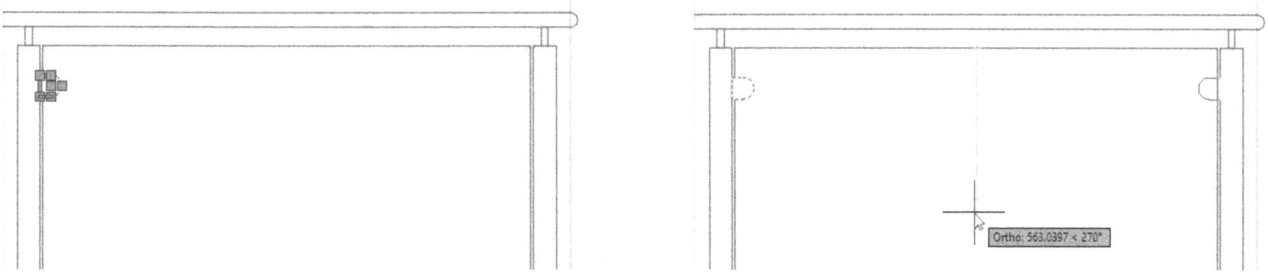

- Select the two sleeves and click **Home** tab > **Modify** panel > **Array** drop-down > **Rectangular Array**. On the **Array Creation** tab of the ribbon, set the **Columns** and **Rows** values to **1** and **2**, respectively. Type **-28** in the **Between** box on the **Rows** panel. Click **Close Array** on the ribbon.

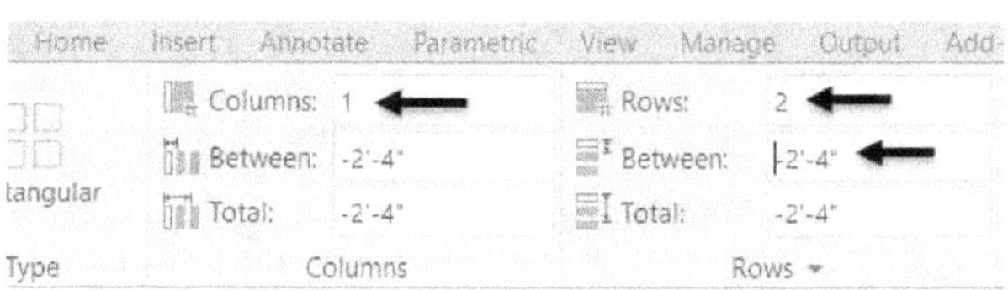

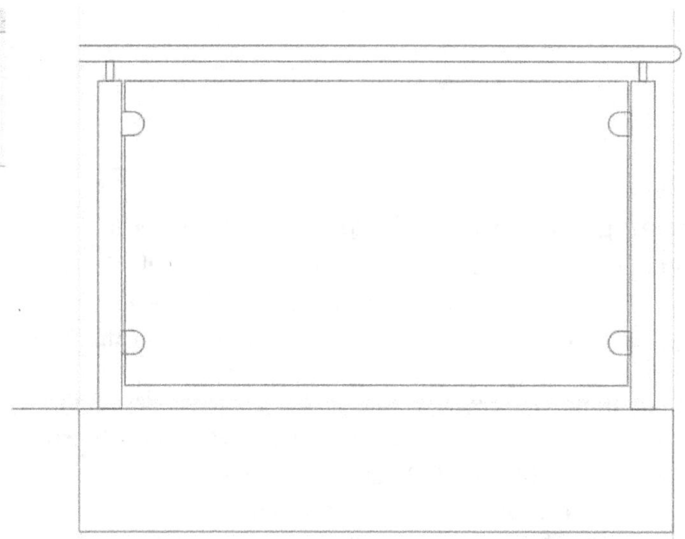

- Trim the unwanted portions of the sleeves, as shown.

- On the Status bar, click the **Polar Tracking** icon. Click the down arrow next to the **Polar Tracking** icon and select **30**. Activate the **Line** command and create an inclined line, as shown. Offset the inclined line on both sides. The offset distance is **4** inches.

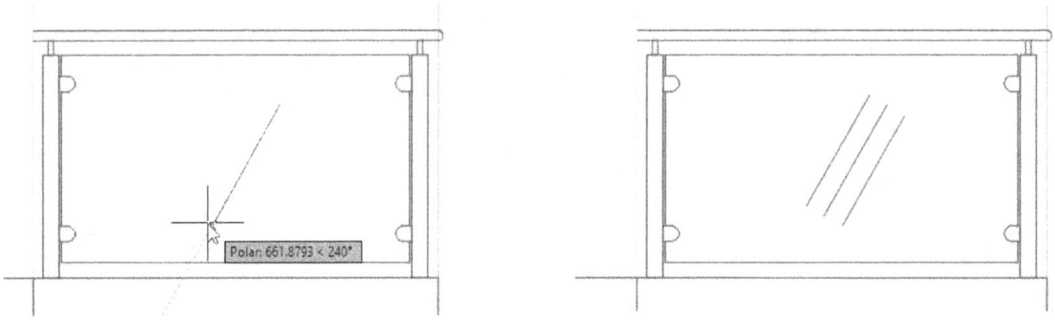

- Select one of the offset lines, type **SC**, and press **Enter**. Next, select the midpoint of the offset line, type **0.5**, and press **Enter**. The line is scaled to half of its size. Likewise, scale the other offset line.

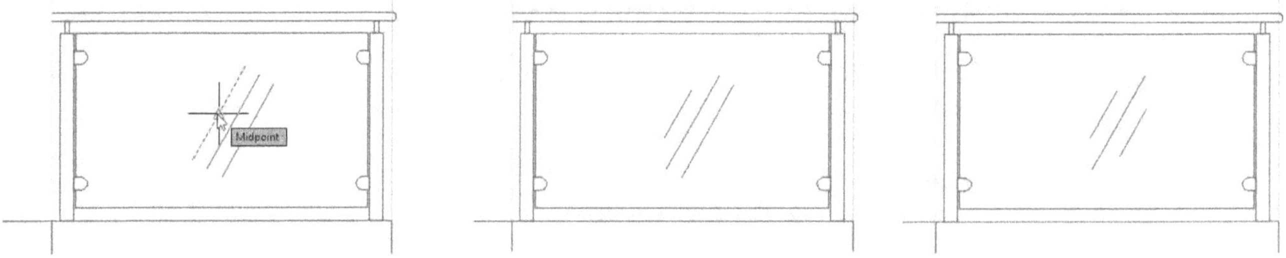

Creating Windows and Doors in the Elevation View

- On the ribbon, click **Home** tab > **Layers** panel > **Layer** drop-down > **A-WINDOW.**
- On the **DesignCenter** palette, click the **Home** button, and go to **Sample > en-us > Dynamic Blocks**. Expand the **Architectural – Imperial.dwg** file and click on the **Blocks** icon. Drag the **Aluminum Window (Elevation) - Imperial** block and place it in the graphics window.
- On the ribbon, click **Insert > Block Definition > Block Editor**.
- On the **Edit Block Definition** dialog, select the **Aluminum Window (Elevation) – Imperial** block from the **Block to create or edit** list. Next, click **OK**.
- Select the **Window Width** parameter from the graphics window. Next, right click and select **Properties** from the shortcut menu.
- On the **Properties** palette, go to the **Value Set** section and click in the **Dist value list** box. Next, click the icon displayed next to the **Dist value list** box.

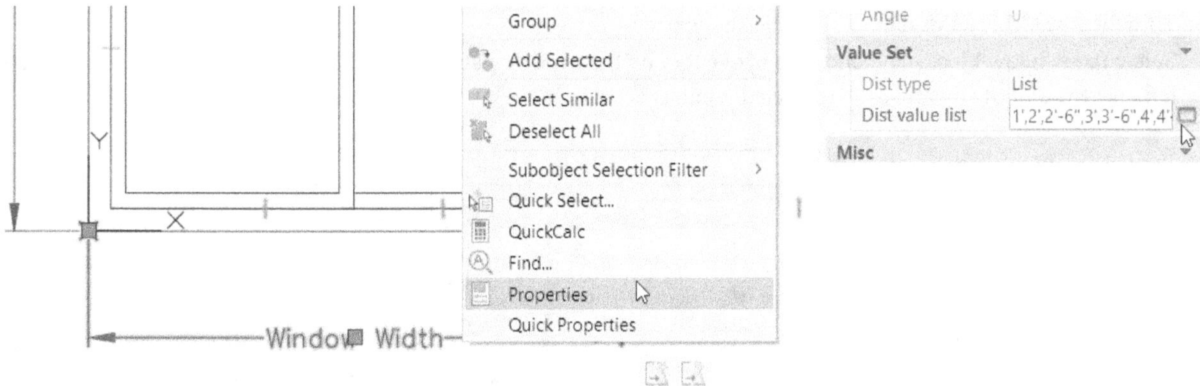

- On the **Add Distance Value** dialog, type **63** in the **Distances to add** box. Next, click the **Add** button.
- Likewise, type **39.5** in the **Distances to add** box, and then click the **Add** button.
- Click the **OK** button on the **Add Distance Value** dialog. Next, click the **Save Block** button on the **Open/Save** panel of the **Block Editor** ribbon.
- Click the **Save the Changes** option on the **Block – Save Parameter Changes?** message box.
- Click the **Close Block Editor** button on the ribbon.
- Select the window block to display the dynamic block grips. Change the window width and height by using the arrow grips.

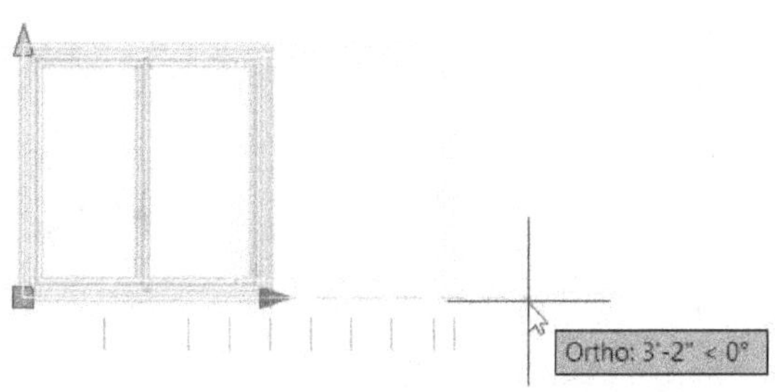

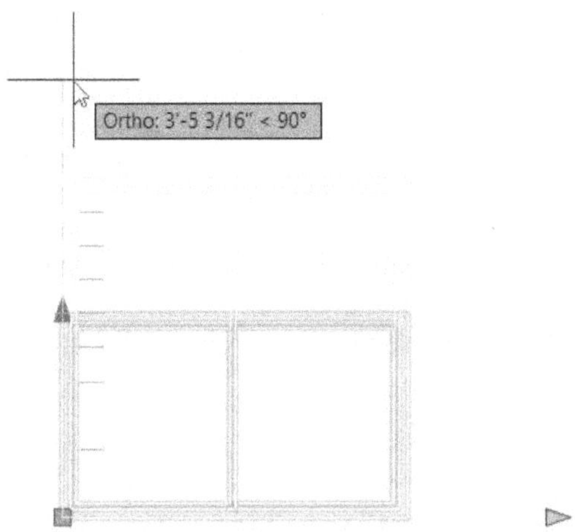

- Copy and place the window block on the elevation view at the locations, as shown.

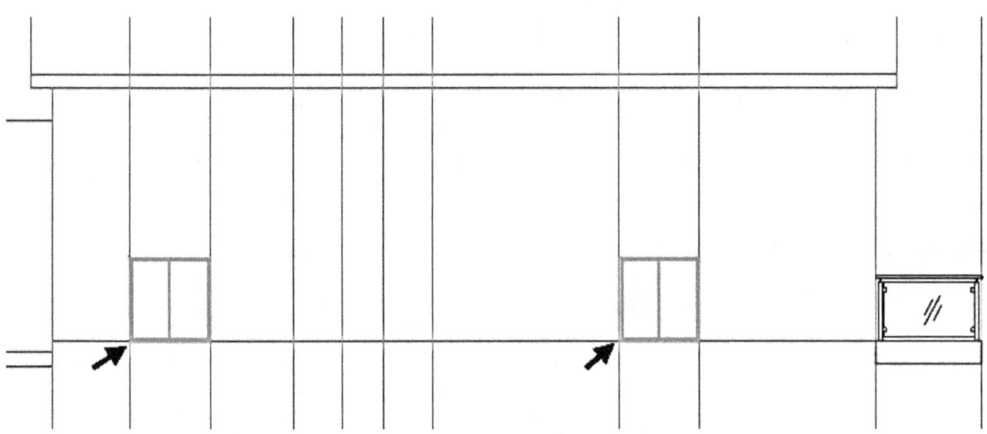

- Turn ON the ORTHOMODE (F8) on the status bar.
- Select the window blocks and click the **Move** tool on the **Modify** panel of the **Home** ribbon tab. Select the lower-left corner point of any one of the selected window blocks. Move the pointer upwards, type **48**, and press **Enter**.

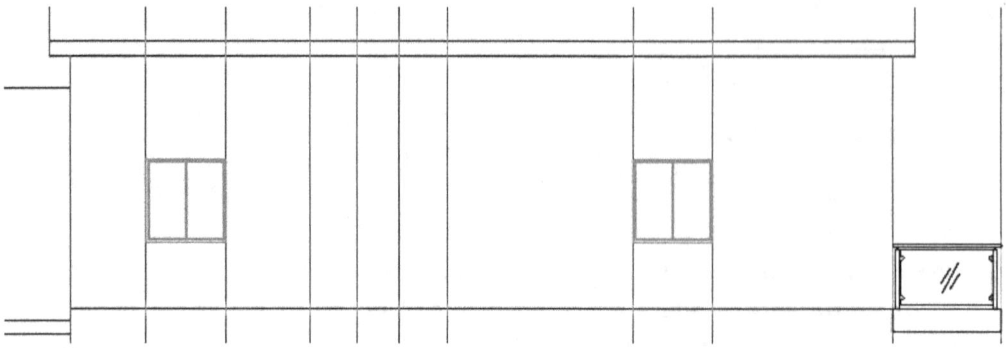

- Create two **39x39** rectangles on the elevation, as shown.

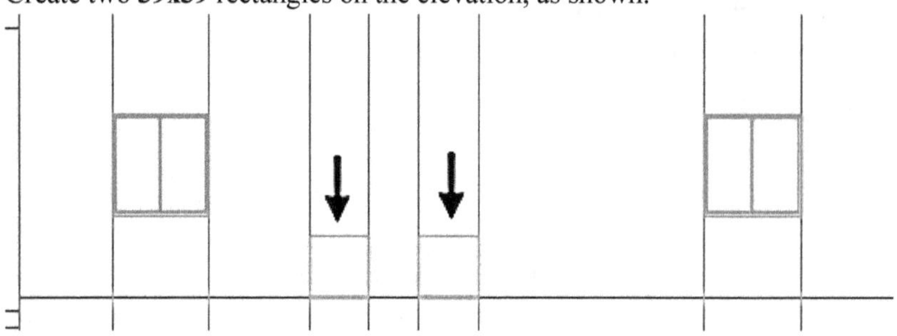

- Move the rectangles upward in the vertical direction up to the distance of **70** inches. Offset the rectangles by **2** inches inside.
- Select the reference lines and press **Delete**.

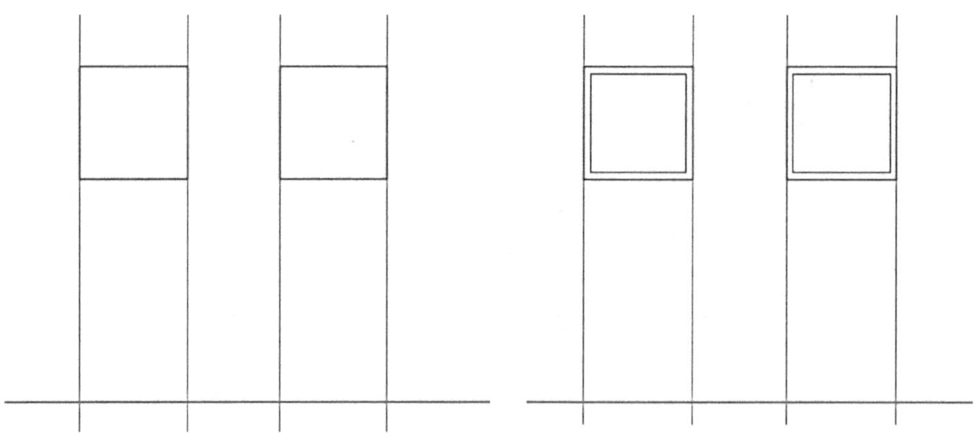

- Select the horizontal line below the ground floor and lengthen it by using the grips.

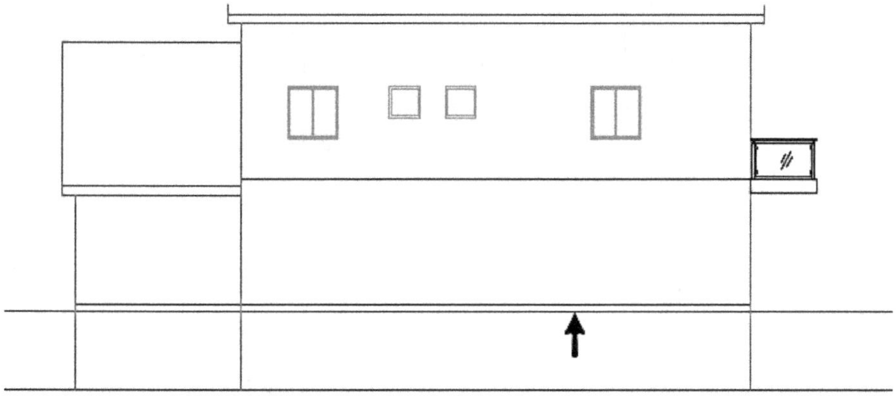

- On the ribbon, click **Home** tab > **Layers** panel > **Layer** drop-down > **Reference Lines**. Create reference lines originating from the door and windows on the ground floor, as shown.

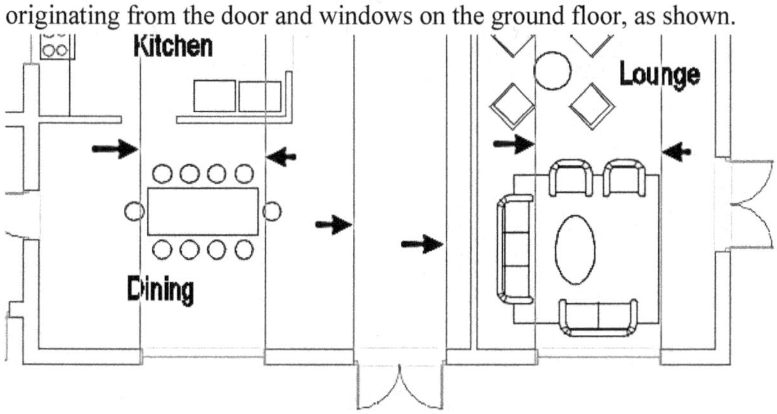

- On the ribbon, click **Home** tab > **Layers** panel > **Layer** drop-down > **A-WINDOWS**. Create a **112x59** rectangle on the elevation view, as shown. Move the rectangle vertically up to **40** inches.

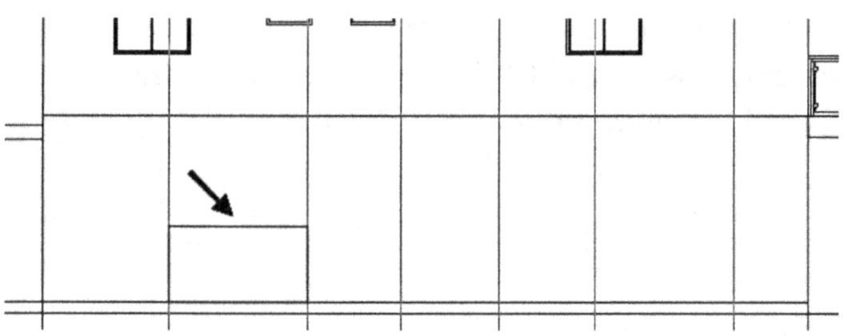
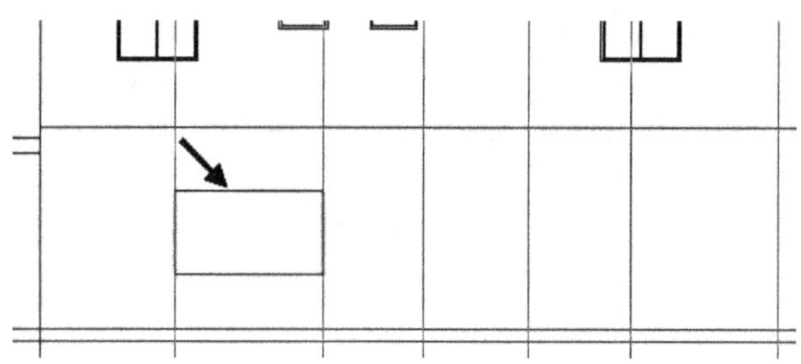

- Offset the rectangle inward by **2** inches. Explode the inner rectangle.

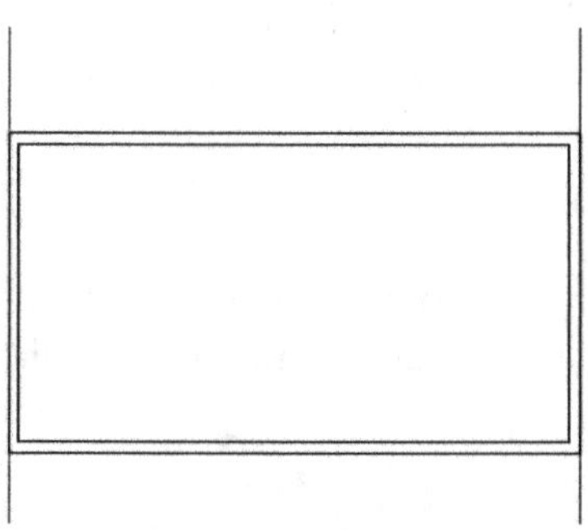
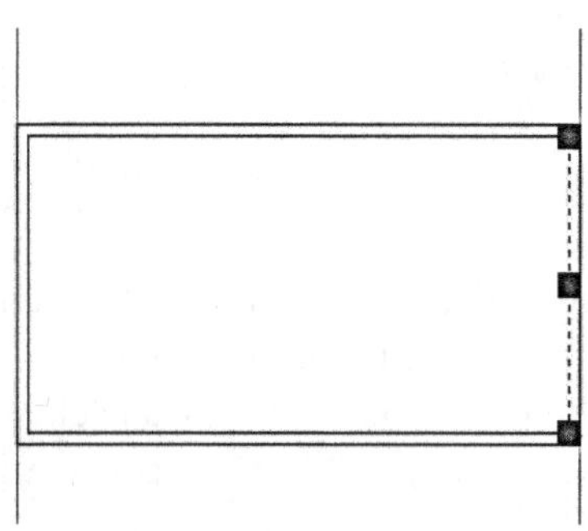

- Offset the inner vertical lines up to **35** inches inside. Again, offset the offset lines up to **2** inches inside.

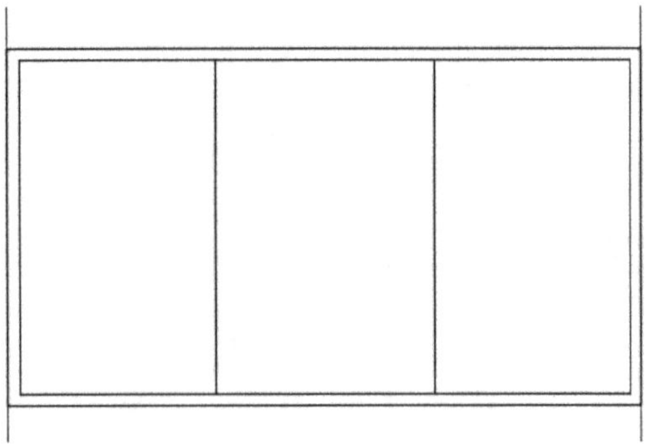

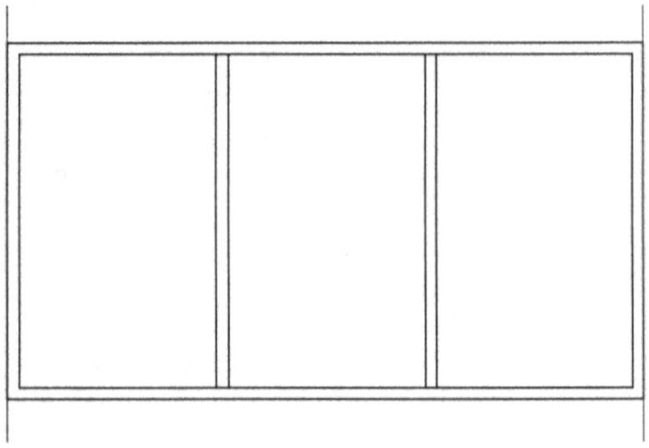

- Create a selection window across all the entities of the window, and click the **Copy** tool on the **Modify** panel of the **Home** ribbon tab. Select the lower-left corner of the window to define the base point. Move the pointer toward the right and select a point on the reference line, as shown.

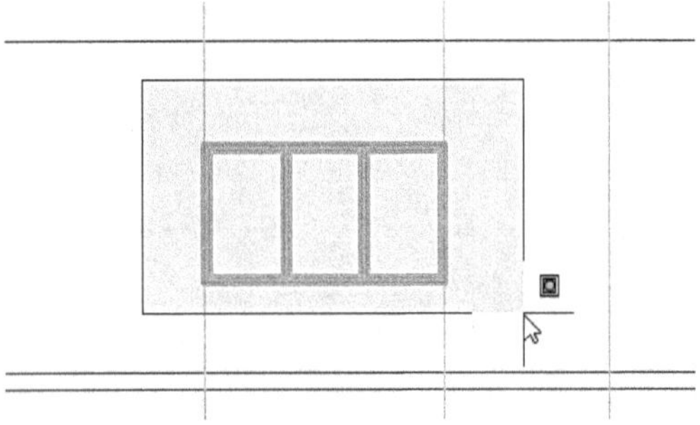

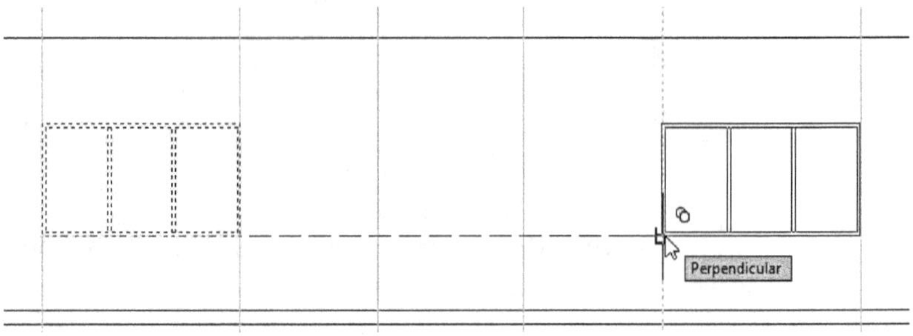

- On the ribbon, click **Home** tab > **Layers** panel > **Layer** drop-down > **A-DOOR**. Type **REC** and press **Enter**. Select the intersection point between the reference line and ground floor line, as shown.

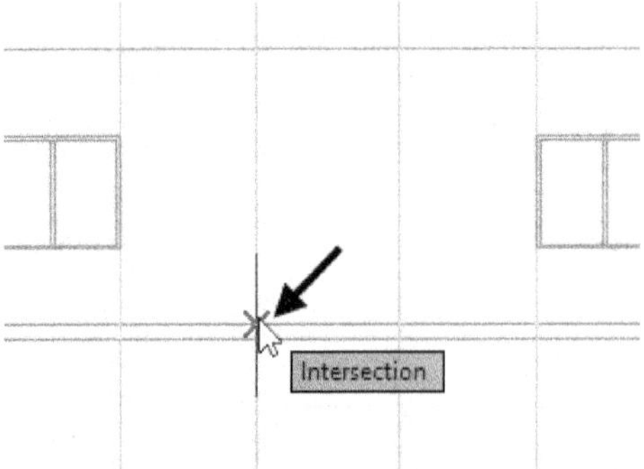

- Select **Dimensions** from the command line. Select the two intersection points on the elevation view, as shown. The distance between the selected points defines the length of the rectangle. Type **98** and press **Enter** to define the width of the rectangle. Move the pointer upward and click to create the rectangle.

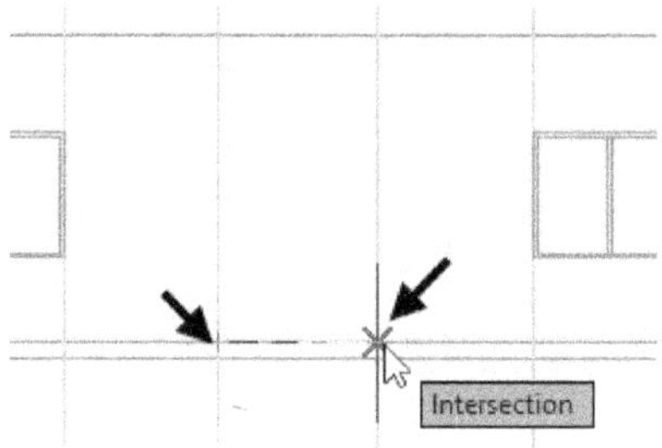

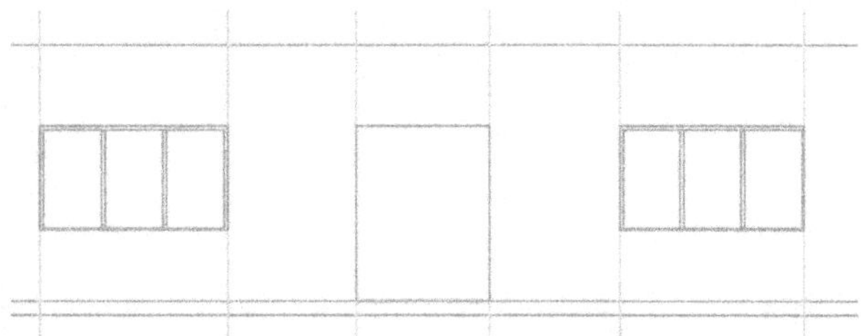

- Offset the rectangle up to **2.5** inches inside. Select the two rectangles and click the **Explode** tool on the **Modify** panel of the **Home** ribbon tab. Select the lower horizontal line of the inner rectangle and press **Delete**. Type **EX** and press **Enter** twice. Click on the lower end portions of the inner vertical lines. The selected lines are extended up to the intersecting horizontal line. Press **Esc**.

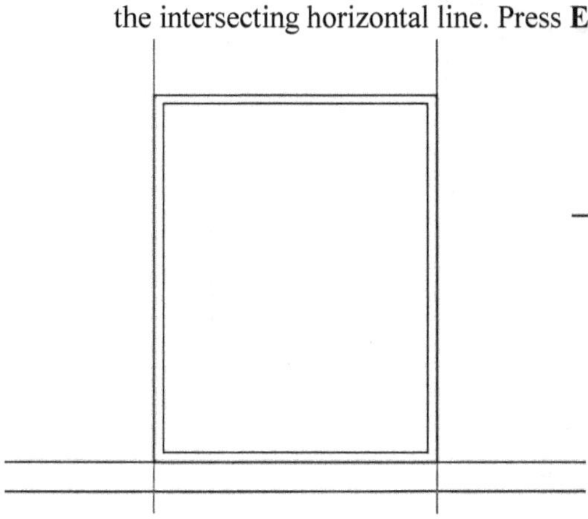

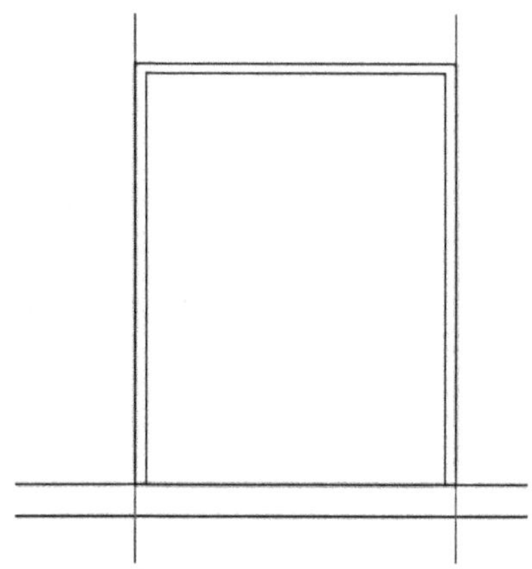

- Type **L** and press **Enter**. Create a vertical line by selecting the midpoints of the horizontal lines of the door, as shown. Press **Enter** twice. Select the upper-end point of the new vertical line. Select the midpoint of the left vertical line of the door. Likewise, create other lines by selecting the points, as shown. The inclined lines indicate the hinge direction of the door.

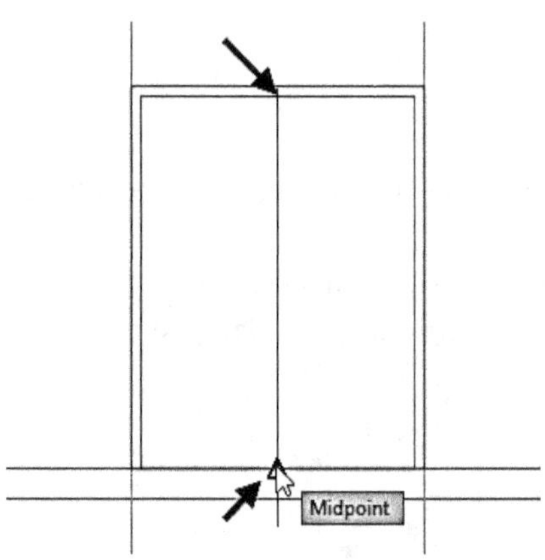

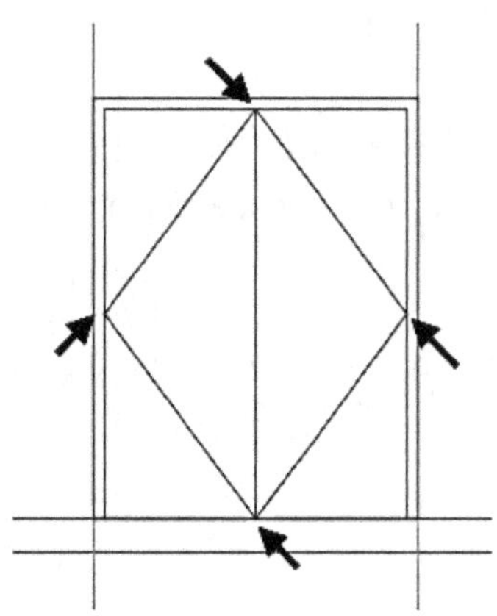

- Select the inclined lines, type **PR**, and press **Enter**. On the **Properties** palette, change the **Linetype** and **Linetype Scale** to **DASHED** and **10,** respectively.

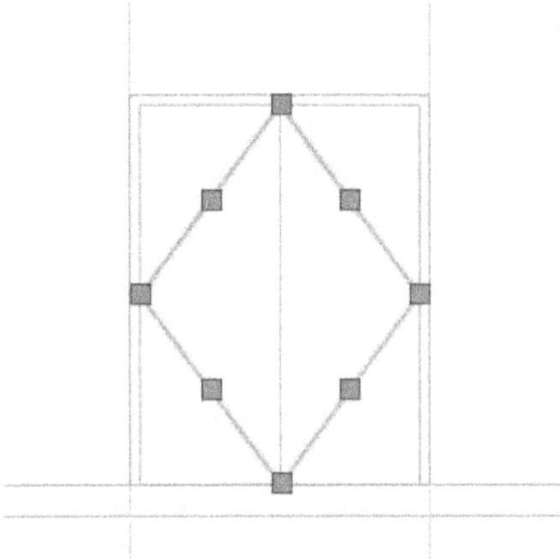

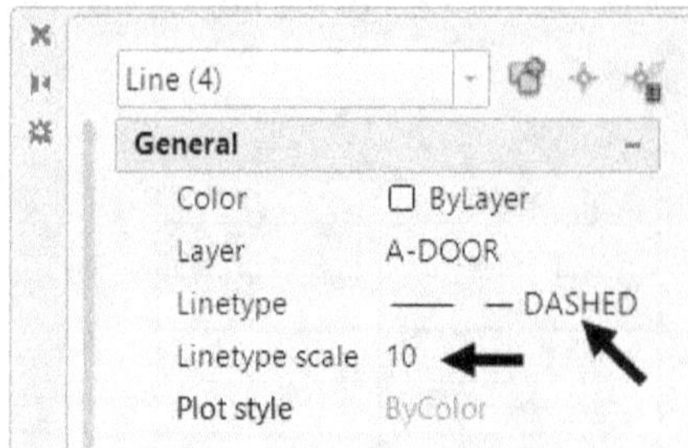

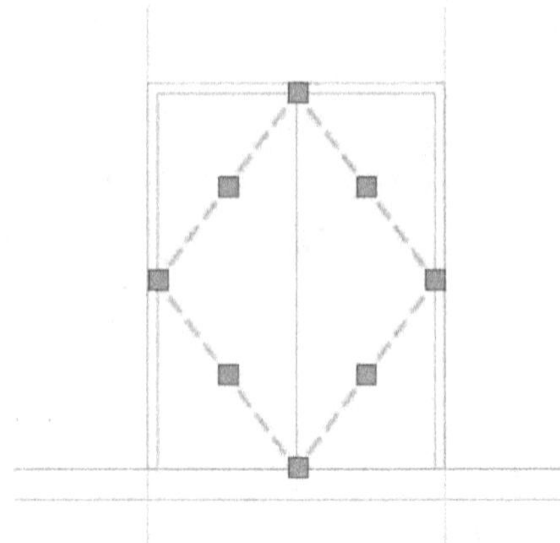

- Likewise, create the utility room door, as shown.

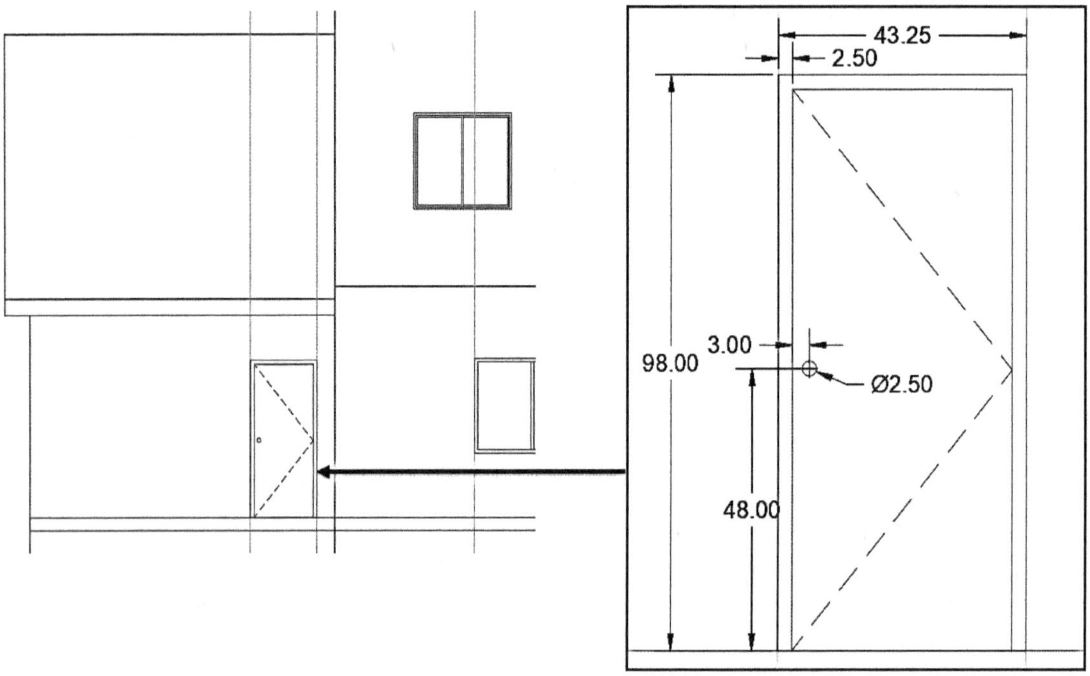

- Select the reference lines and press **Delete**.

Creating the Opposite Elevation

You can create the elevation opposite to the front elevation by just mirroring it and modifying the internal objects.

- Create a selection window across all the objects of the elevation view. On the ribbon, click **Home** tab > **Modify** panel > **Move**. Select any point on the elevation view, move the pointer downward, and place the elevation view below the ground floor plan.

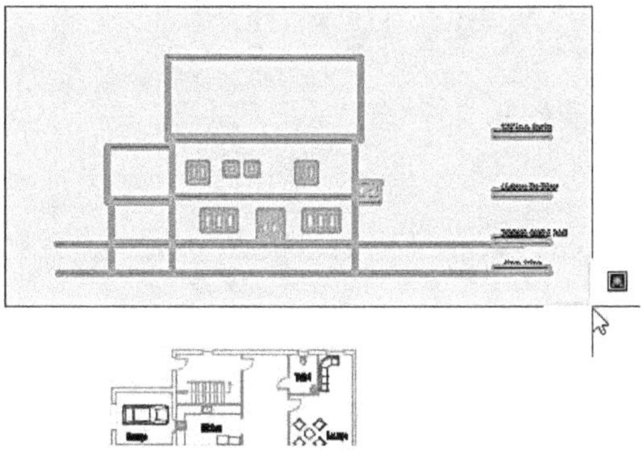

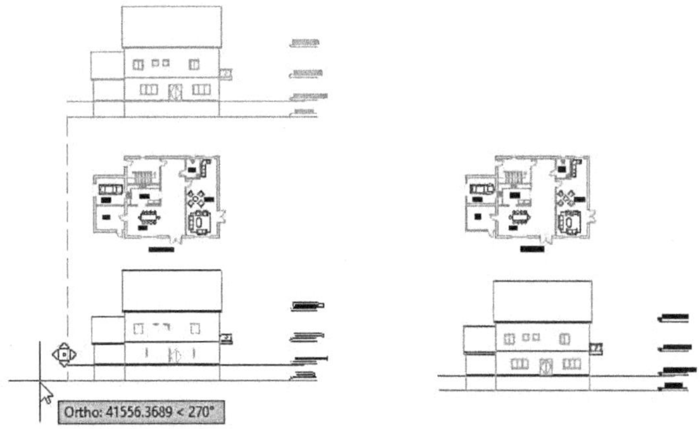

- Create a selection window across the elevation view, type **MI**, and press **Enter**. Select the midpoint of a vertical line on the ground floor elevation, as shown. Move the pointer horizontally toward the right and click to mirror the elevation view. Select **No** from the command line.

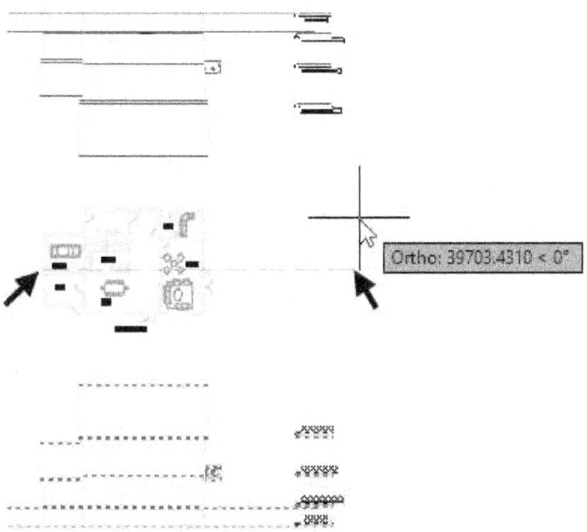

Now, you need to change the orientation of the UCS (User Coordinate System) to match the mirrored elevation view.

- Type **UCS** and press **Enter**. Select **Z** from the command line. Type **180** and press **Enter**. The UCS is rotated about the Z-axis by **180** degrees.

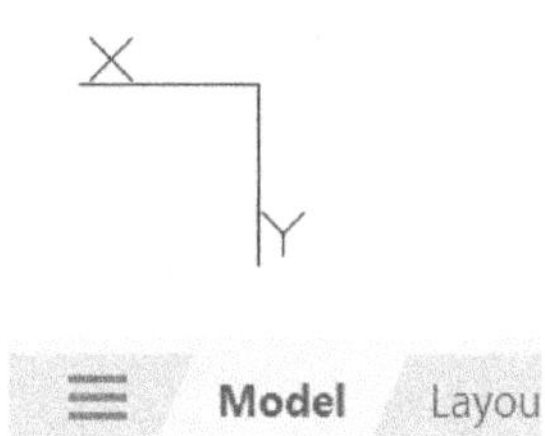

- Type **PLAN** and press Enter. Select **Current ucs** from the command line to orient the drawing with UCS.
- Type **Z** and press Enter. Select **Center** from the command line. Type **0** and press **Enter** to specify the zoom center. Type **2000** and press **Enter** to specify the magnification height. Press and hold the middle mouse button and drag the pointer to bring the elevation view to the center. Scroll the mouse wheel to magnify the elevation view.

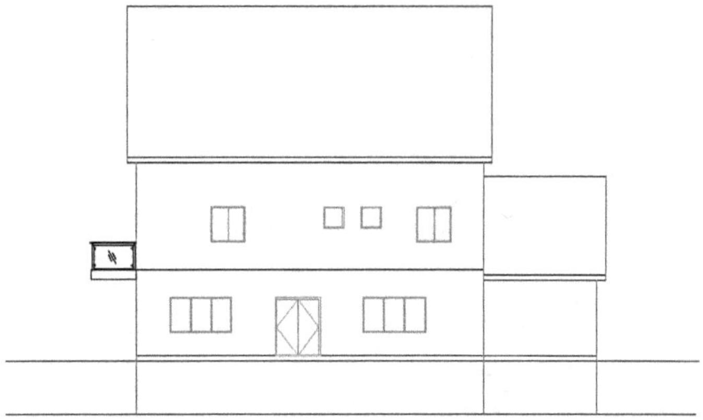

- Select the doors and windows on the elevation view and press **Delete**.

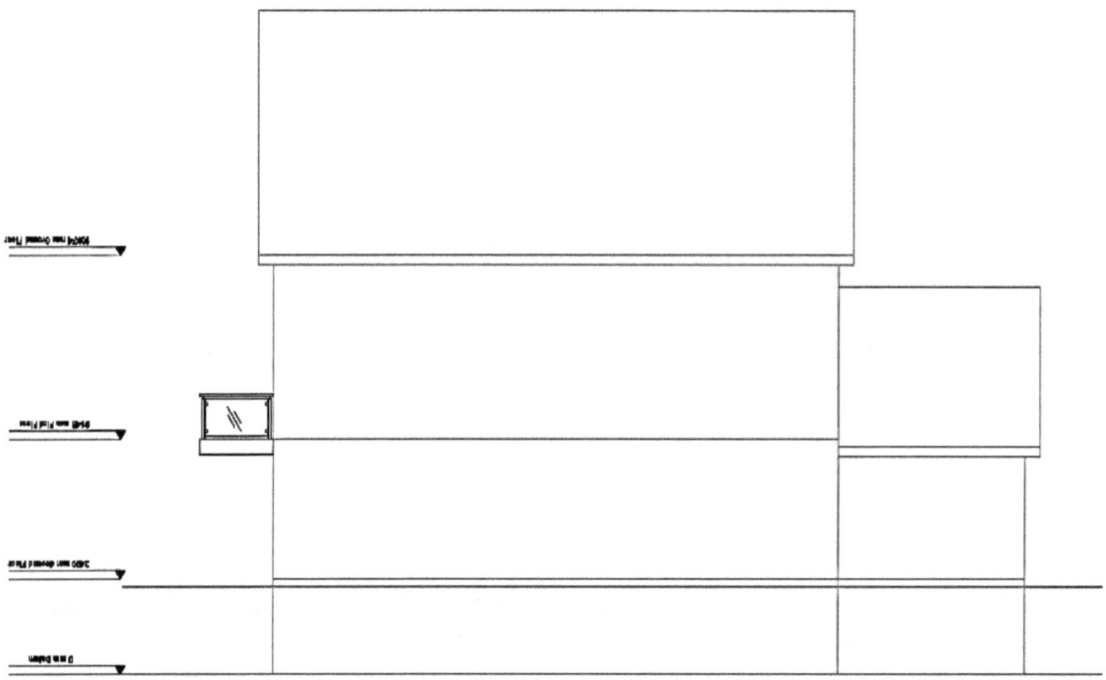

- On the ribbon, click **Home** tab > **Layers** panel > **Layer** drop-down > **Reference Lines**. Create reference lines from the rare windows of the ground floor plan.

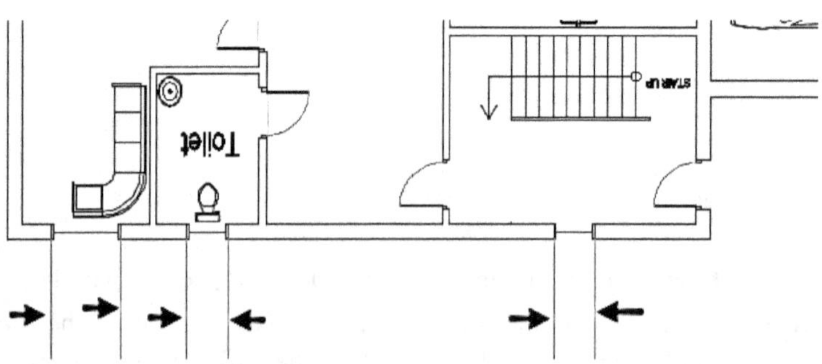

- On the ribbon, click **Home** tab > **Layers** panel > **Layer** drop-down > **A-WINDOWS**.
- On the ribbon, click **Insert** tab > **Block** panel > **Insert** gallery > **Aluminum Window (Elevation) – Imperial**.

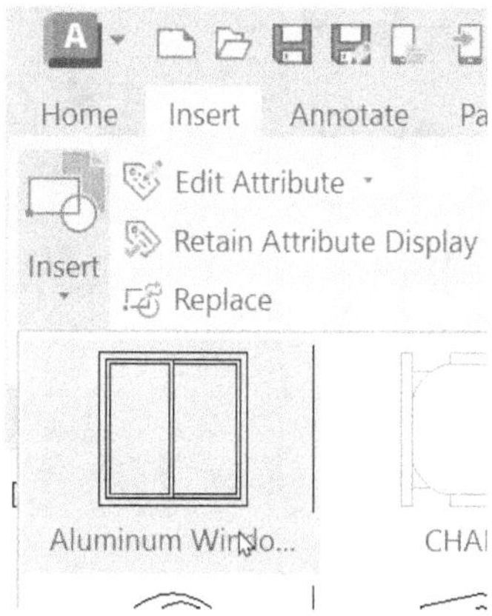

- Select the intersection point between the ground floor line and the reference line from the left-side window, as shown. Select the window block and then select its base point. Move the pointer along the reference line, type **48**, and press **Enter**.

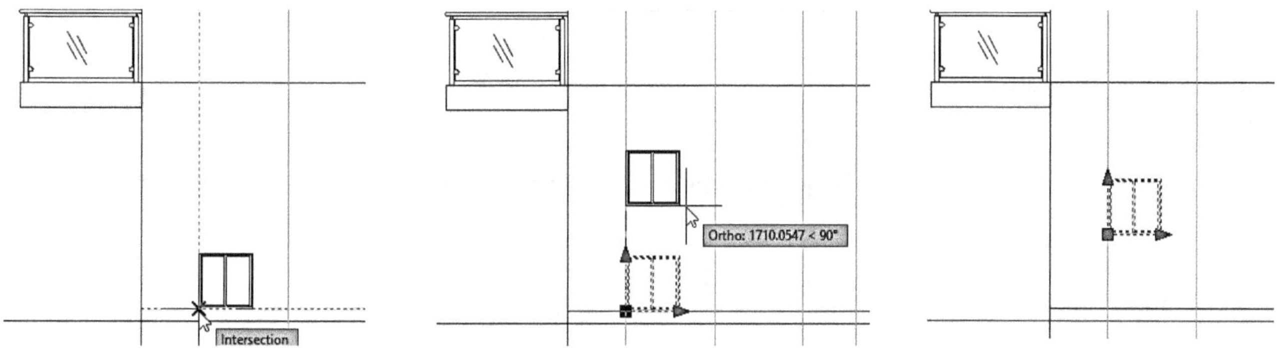

- Use the arrow grips of the window block to set its width and height.

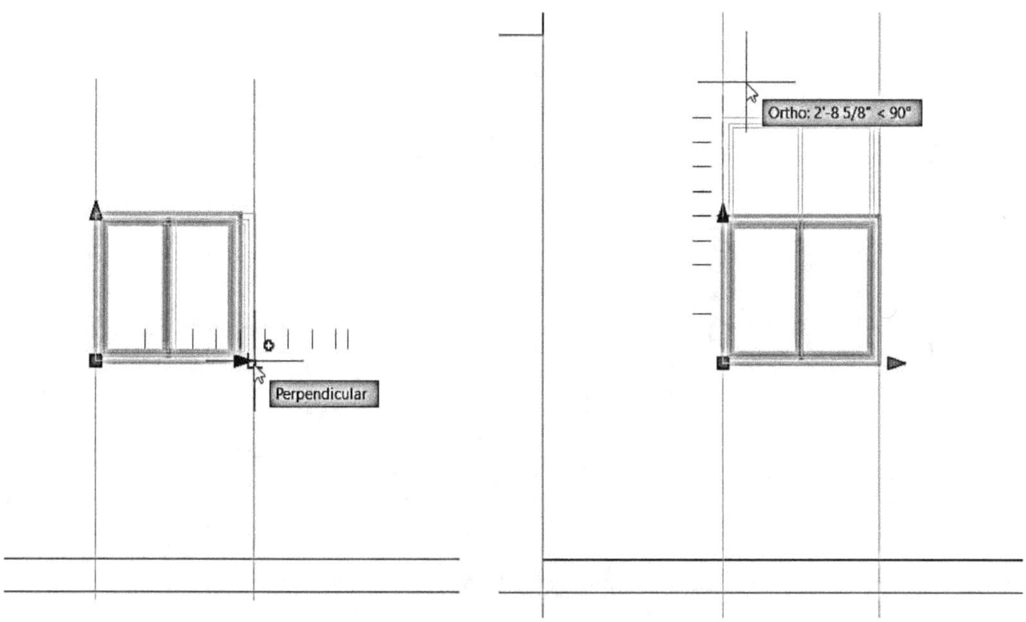

- Create the bathroom window using the **Rectangle** tool, as shown.

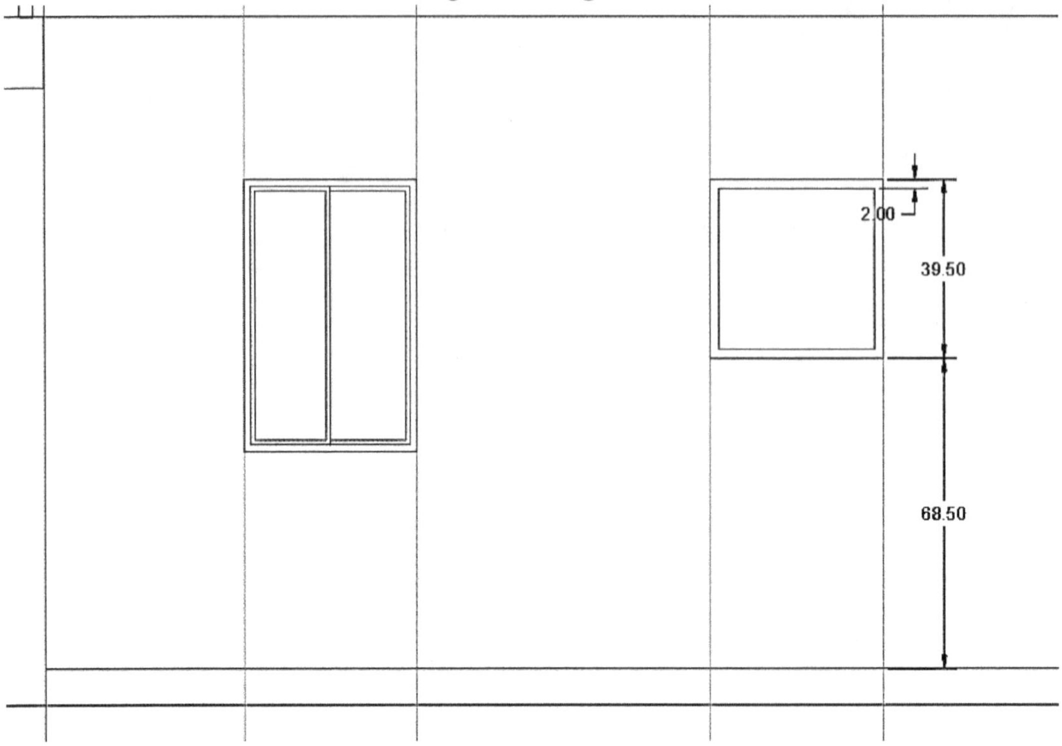

- Create the stair window using the **Rectangle**, **Explode**, and **Offset** tools, as shown. Select the reference lines and press **Delete**.

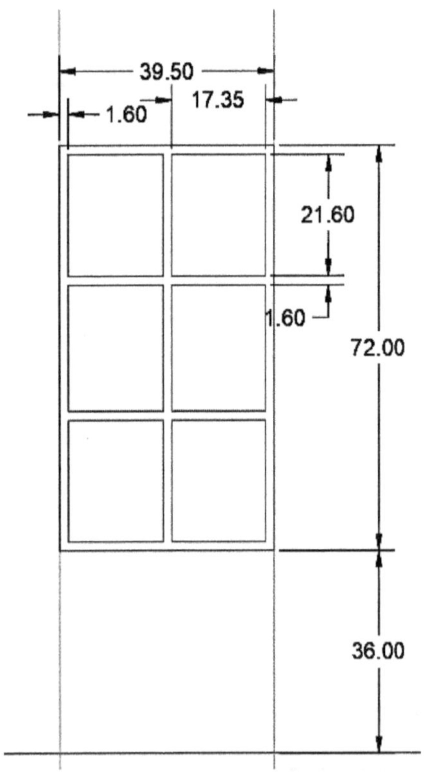

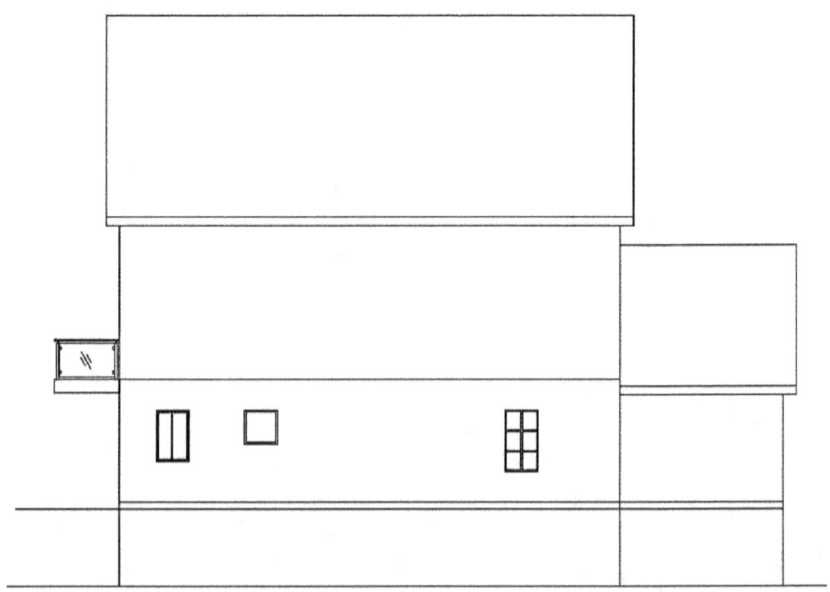

- Switch to the **Reference Lines** layer and create the rays from the windows of the rear side of the first-floor plan.

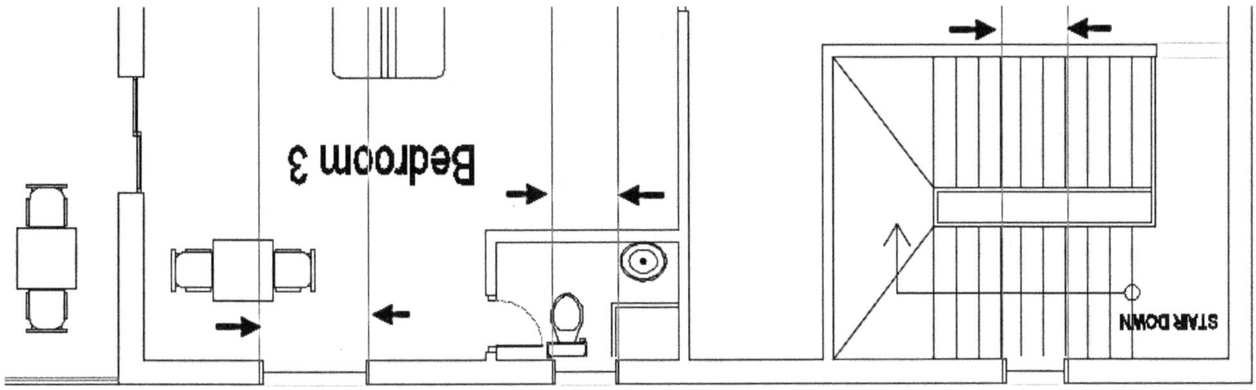

- Copy the existing windows one-by-one and place them at the locations, as shown.

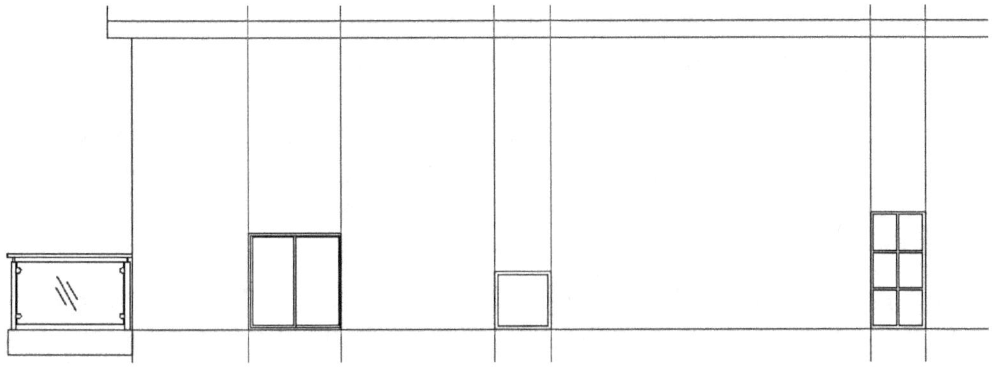

- Move the windows up to the distances, as shown. Delete the reference lines.

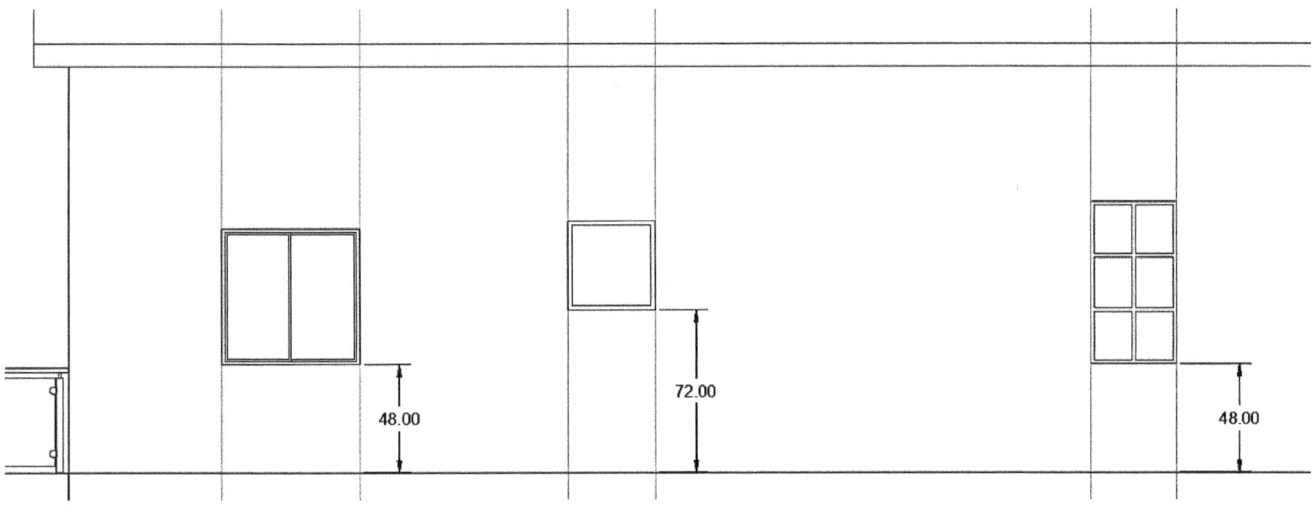

- On the **View** tab of the ribbon, click the right mouse button on any one of the panels and select **Show Panels > Coordinates**. The **Coordinates** panel appears on the **View** tab of the ribbon.
- On the **Coordinates** panel, click the **UCS, Named UCS** tool.

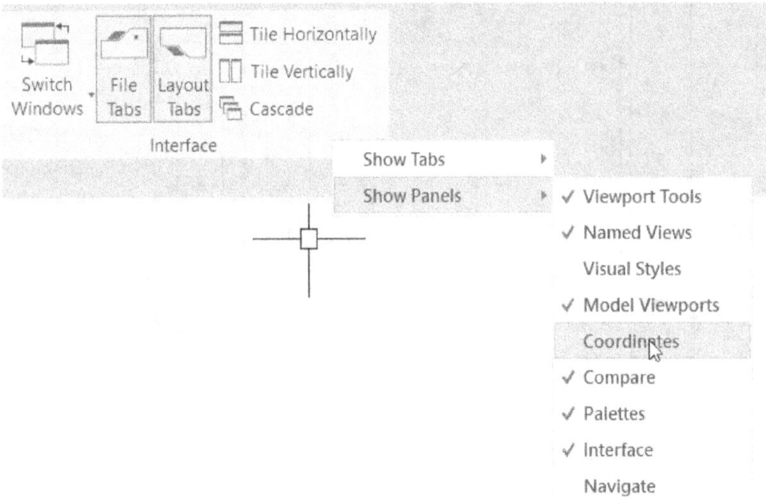

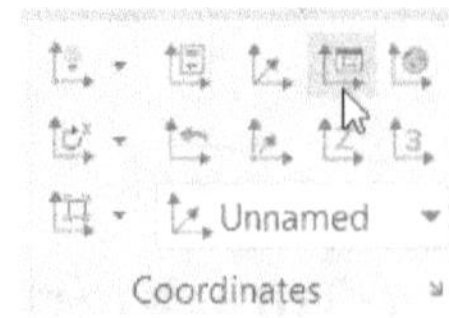

- On the **UCS** dialog, click the **Named UCSs** tab. Right click on the **Unnamed** ucs and select **Rename**. Type **North Elev** and click **OK**.
- On the **Named Views** panel of the **View** ribbon, click the **View Manager** tool to open the **View Manager** dialog. Click the **New** button on the **View Manager** dialog to open the **New View/Shot Properties** dialog — type **North Elev** in the **View name** box.
- Select the **Define window** option and create a window enclosing the elevation view. Press **Enter** to accept.
- Click the **More options** icon located at the bottom left corner of the dialog. Click the **View Properties** tab and make sure that **North Elev** is selected in the **UCS** drop-down and click **OK**. The **Views** list in the **View Manager** dialog displays the **North Elev** view.

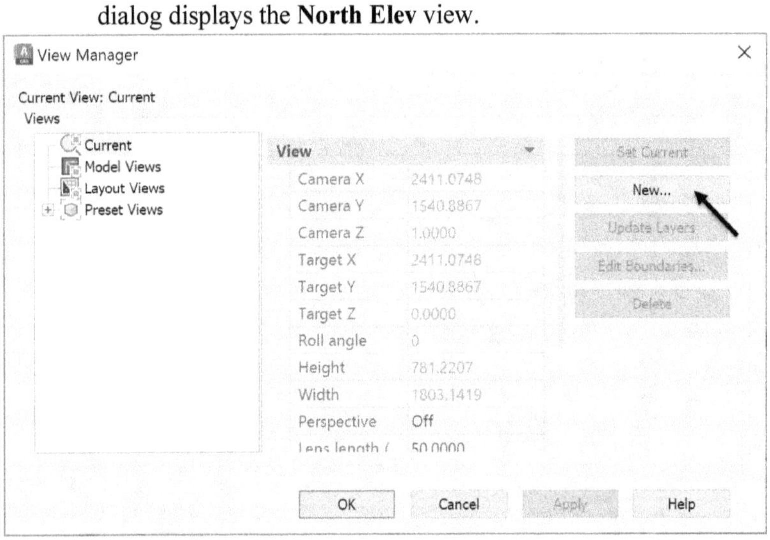

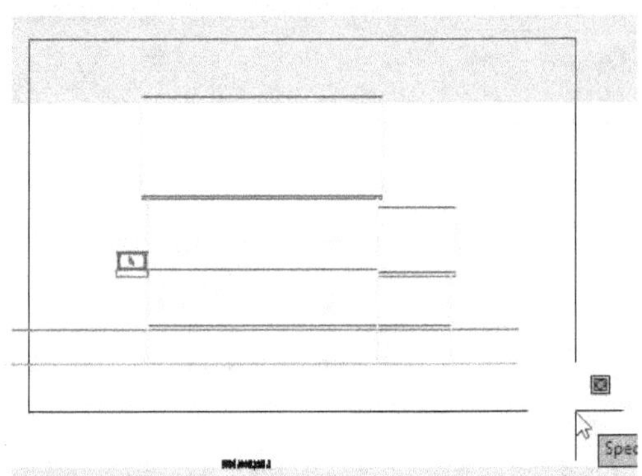

- Click **OK** on the **View Manager** dialog.

Now, you need to switch back to the default view orientation.

- On the **View** tab of the ribbon, in the **Named Views** panel, select **Top** from the **Restore View** drop-down. The default orientation of the drawing is displayed.

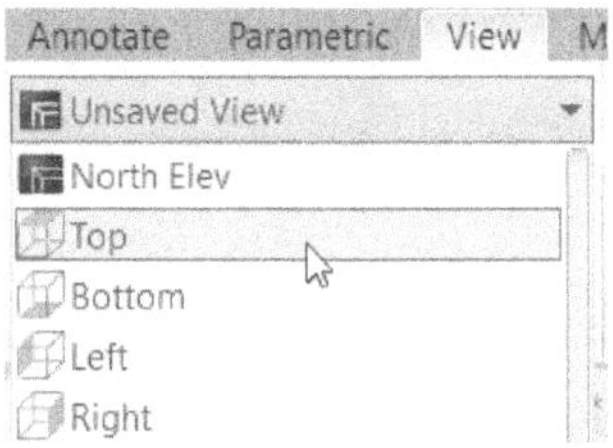

- Type **Z** and press **Enter**. Select **Center** from the command line. Type **0** and press **Enter** to specify the zoom center. Type **2000** and press **Enter** to specify the magnification height. Press and hold the middle mouse button and drag the pointer to bring the elevation view to the center.
- Select all the annotations showing the floor levels and mirror them about the midpoint of the elevation.

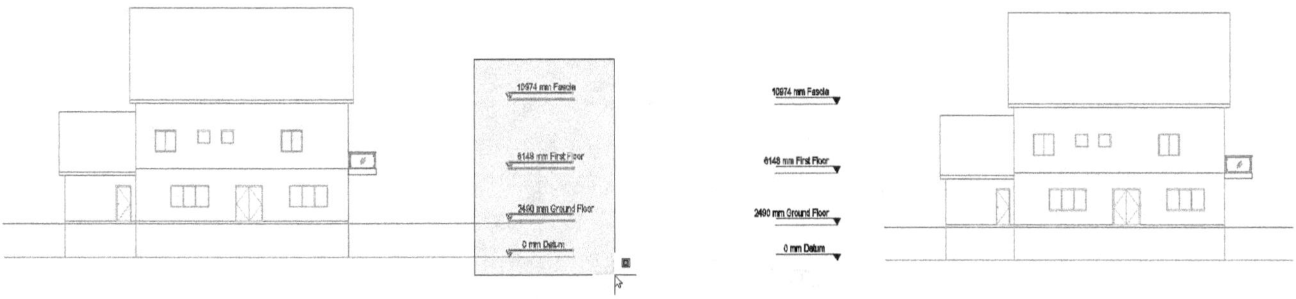

Creating the Front and Rear Elevations

- On the ribbon, click **Home > Layers > Layer** drop-down **> Reference Lines** to make it current.
- Create a **45**-degree line from the lower right corner point of the ground floor plan. You can use the polar tracking to create the inclined line.

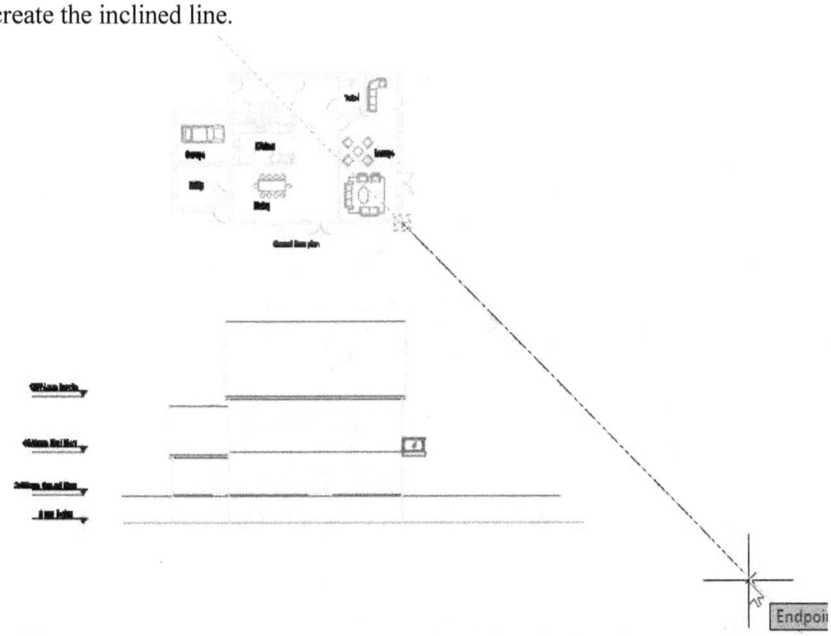

- On the **Home** tab of the ribbon, expand the **Draw** panel and click the **Construction Line** tool. Select **Hor** from the command line. Select the top corner point of the South Elevation, as shown. A horizontal construction line is created, passing through the selected point.

- Likewise, create other construction lines, as shown. Press **Esc**.

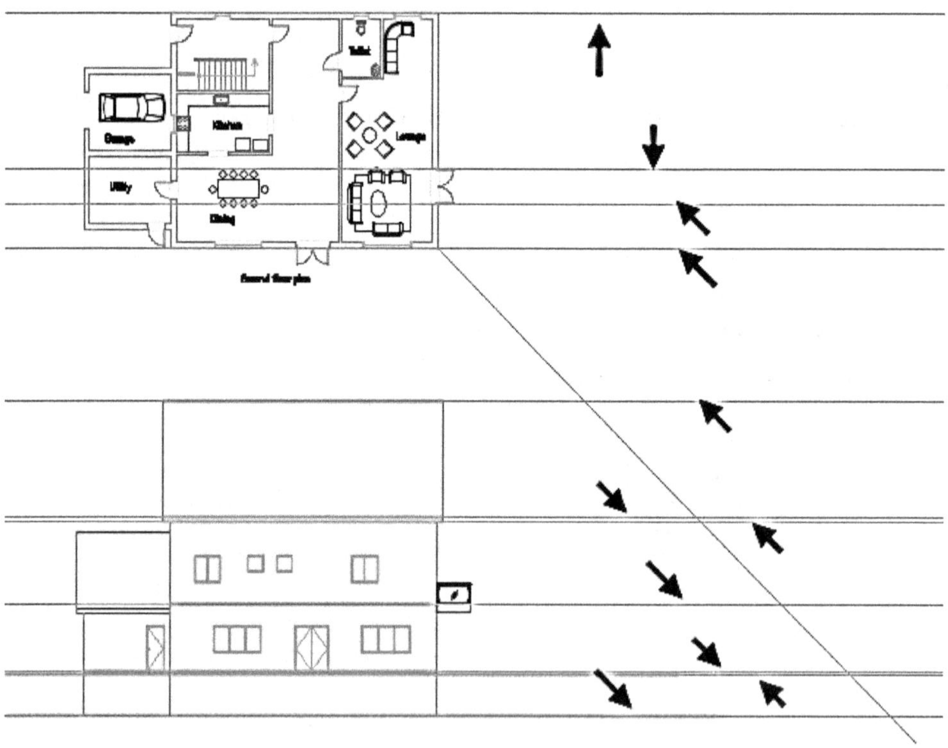

- Type **XL** and press **Enter**. Select **Ver** from the command line. Select the intersection point between the horizontal construction line and the inclined line, as shown. Likewise, select the intersection points between the inclined and other horizontal construction lines. Press **Esc** to deactivate the command.

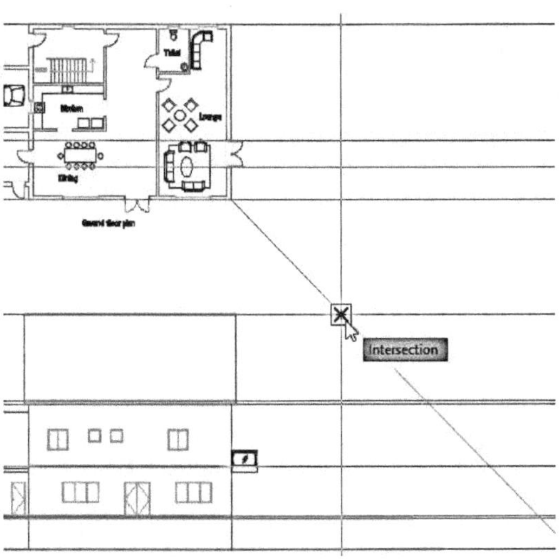

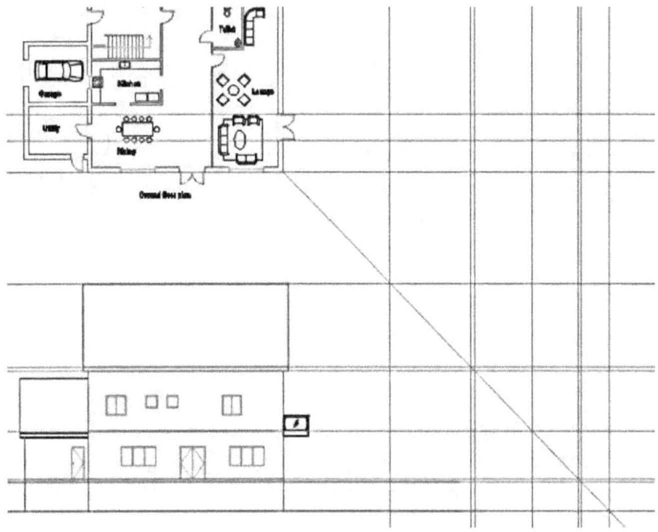

- Type **UCS** and press **Enter**. Select **Z** from the command line. Type **90** and press **Enter**. Type **PLAN** and press **Enter** twice. The **UCS** is rotated by **90** degrees about the Z-axis. Zoom to the area below the ground floor plan, as shown.
- Create a construction line passing through the center of the ground floor plan, as shown.

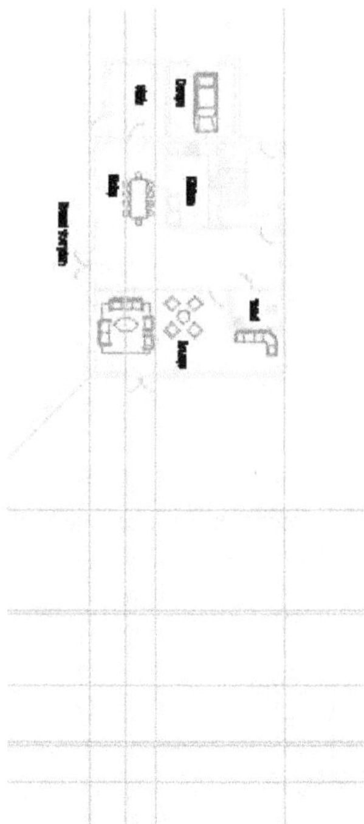

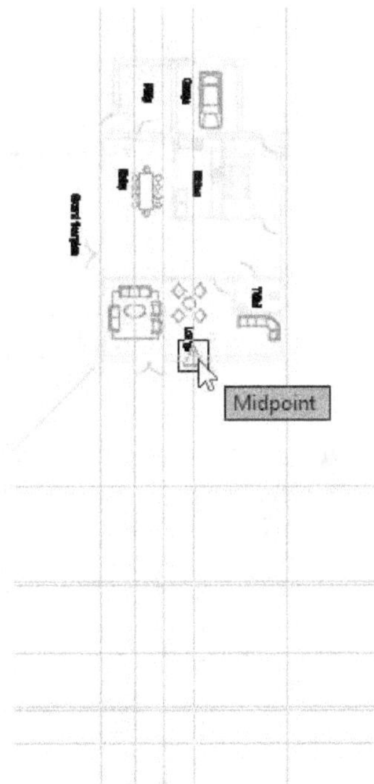

- Create two construction lines at **16** inches distance from the exterior walls, as shown. These lines help you to draw the roof overhang.

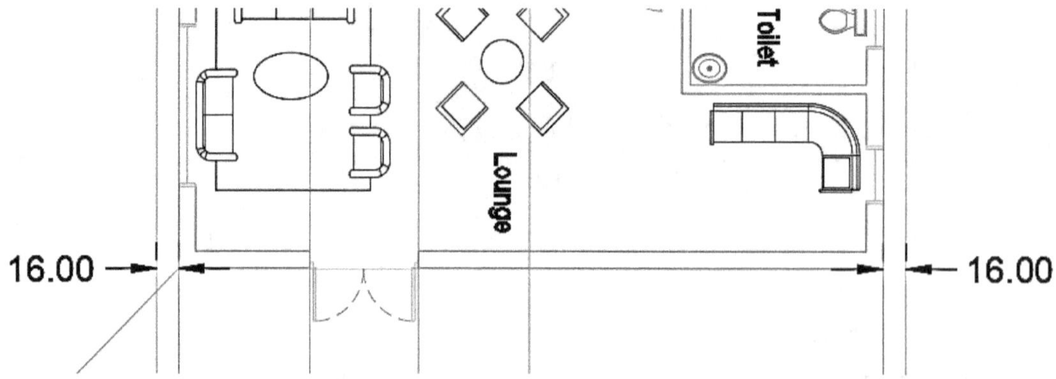

- Create the foundation, floors, and walls on **A-ELEV-FOUNDATION**, **A-ELEV-FLOORING**, and **A-ELEV-WALL** layers, respectively.

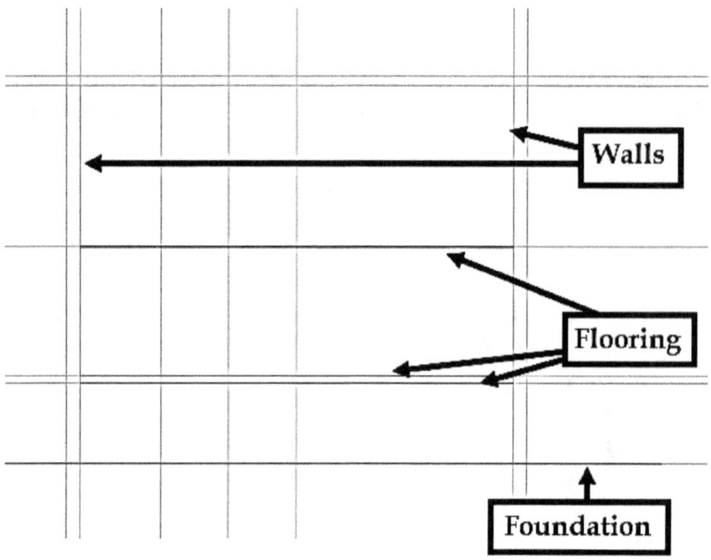

- On the ribbon, click **Home** tab > **Layers** panel > **Layer** drop-down > **A-ELEV-ROOF**. Type **REC** and press **Enter**. Select the intersection point between the construction lines, as shown. Select **Dimensions** from the command line. Type **44** and press **Enter** to define the length. Type **10** and press **Enter** to define the width. Move the pointer toward the right and click.

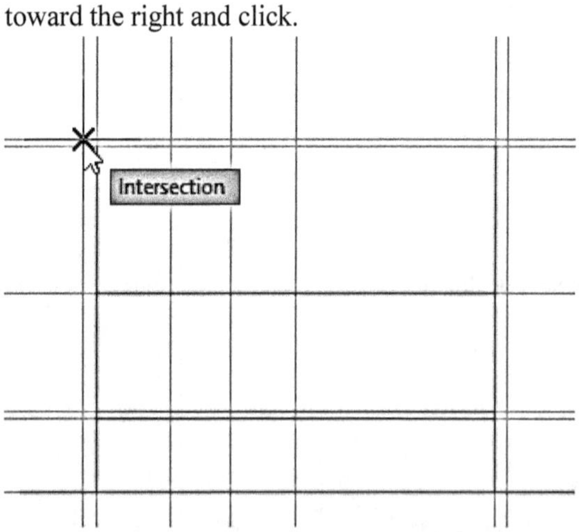

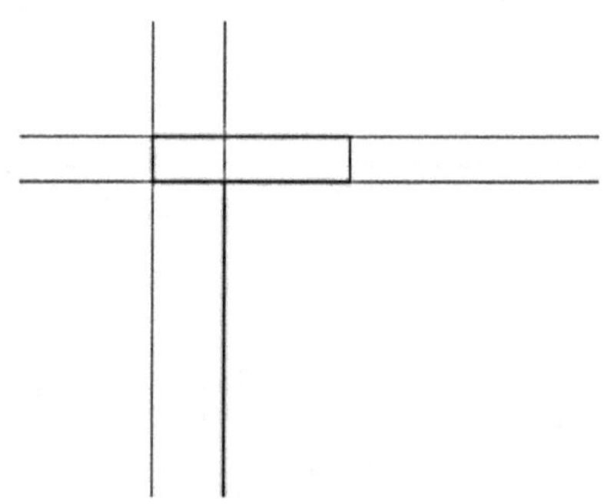

- On the ribbon, click **Home** tab > **Modify** panel > **Fillet** drop-down > **Chamfer** . Select **Angle** from the command line. Select the two intersection points to define the chamfer length on the first line, as shown. Type **15** and press **Enter** to define the chamfer angle. Select the lower horizontal and left vertical line of the rectangle.

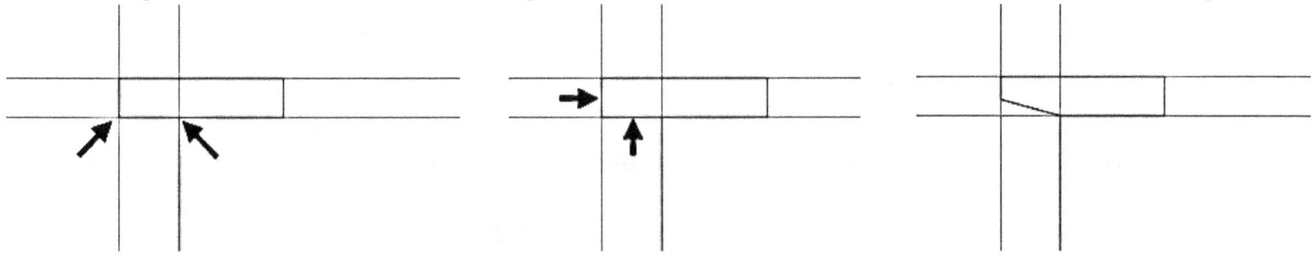

- Type **L** and press **Enter**. Select the intersection points between the construction lines, as shown. Press Esc.

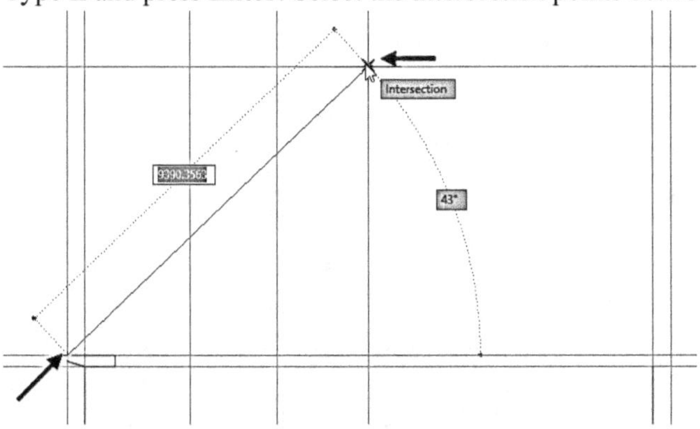

- Type **O** and press Enter. Type **4** and press Enter. Select the newly created inclined line. Move the pointer downwards and click. Trim the intersecting portion between the offset line and the rectangle, as shown. Press **Esc** to deactivate the **Trim** command.

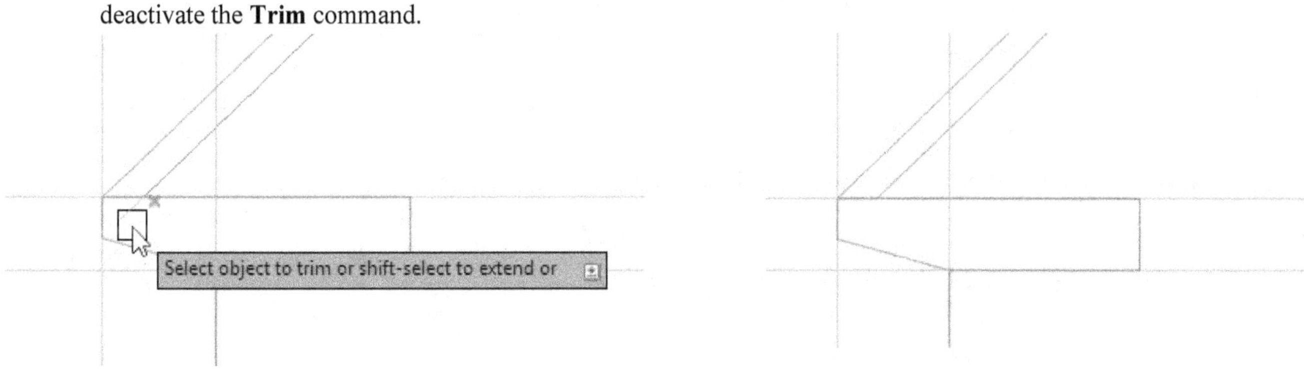

- Select the two inclined lines and the rectangle. Type **MI** and press Enter. Select the top endpoint of the inclined line, move the pointer vertically downward, and click. Select **No** from the command line to retain the source objects.

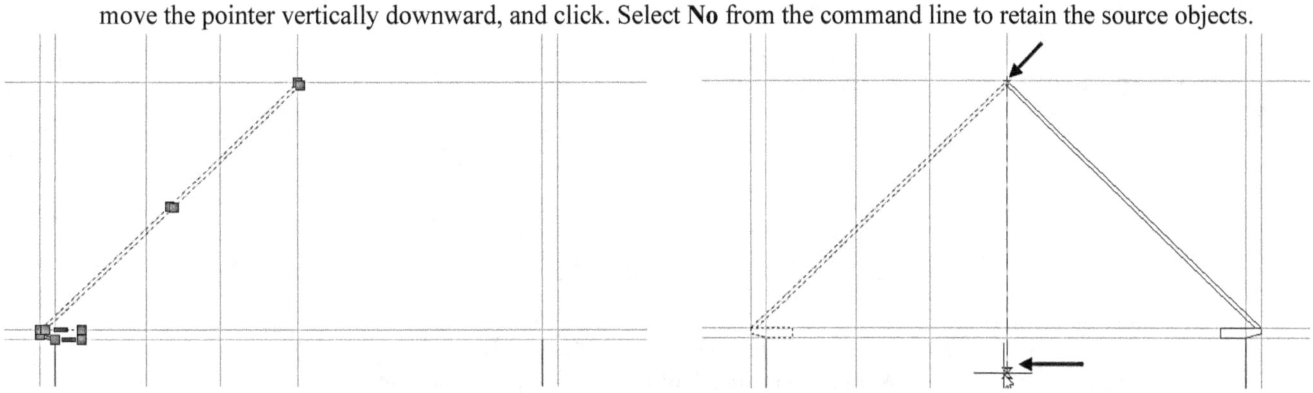

- Zoom to the top portion of the roof and trim the unwanted portions, as shown.

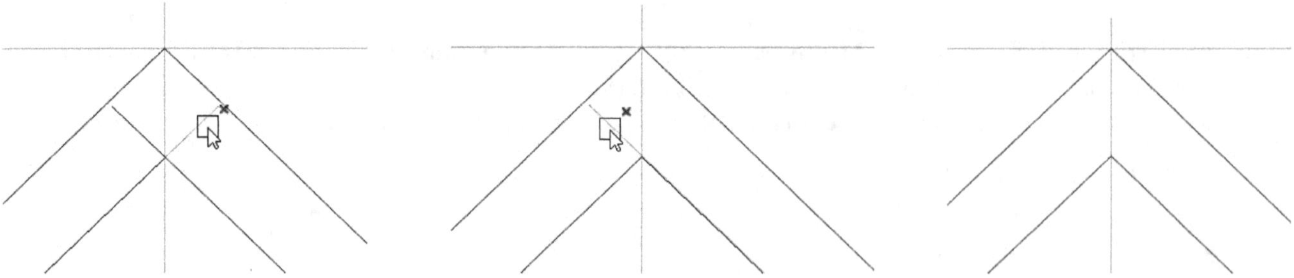

- On the ribbon, click **Home** tab > **Draw** panel > **Rectangle**. Select the intersection point on the front elevation view, as shown.
- Select the **Dimensions** option from the command line. Next, type **502** and press Enter.
- Type **15.75** and press Enter. Next, move the pointer downward and click to create the rectangle.

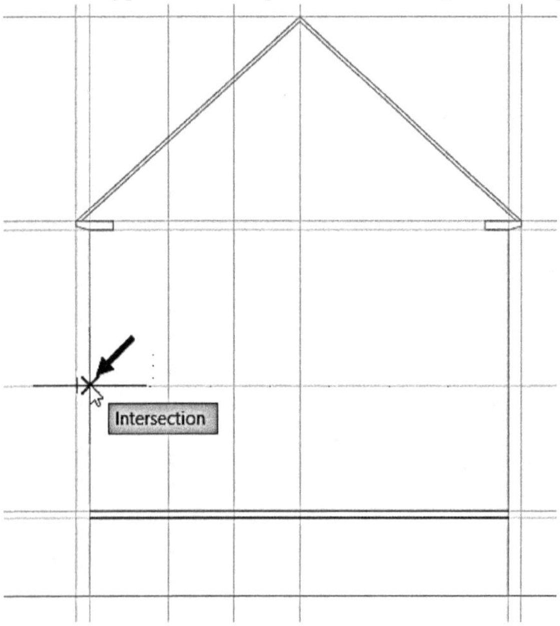

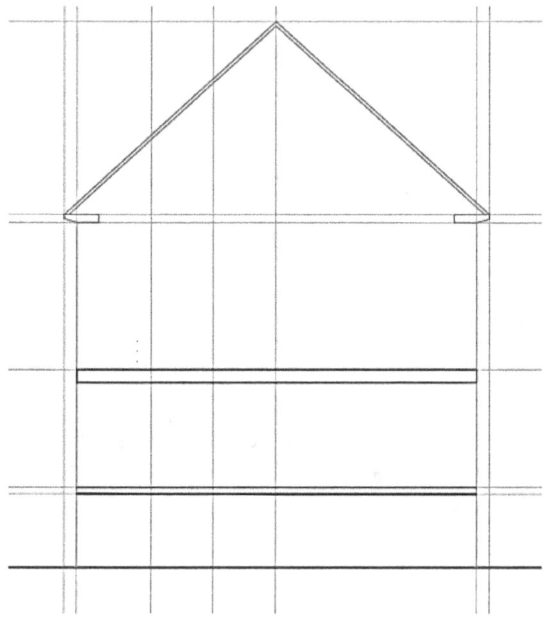

- Create the railing post on the left side on the front elevation view, as shown.

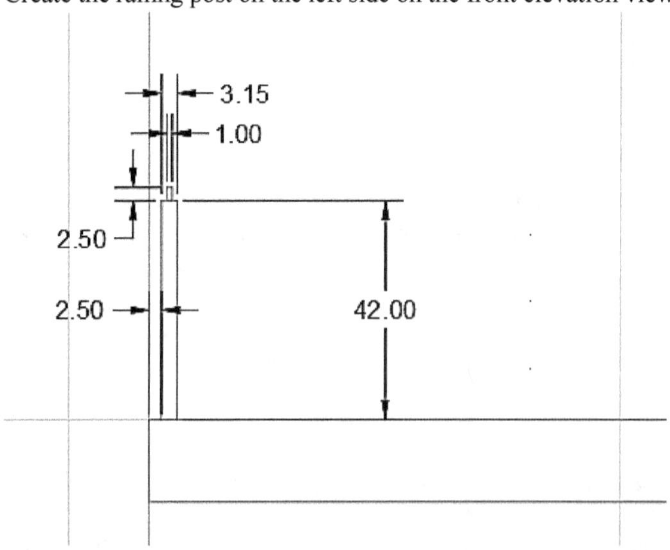

- Select the railing post of the balcony, as shown. On the ribbon, click **Home** tab > **Modify** panel > **Array** drop-down > **Rectangular Array**. On the **Array Creation** tab of the ribbon, type **8** and **1** in the **Columns** and **Rows** boxes, respectively. Type **493.85** in the **Total** box on the **Columns** panel. Click **Close Array**.

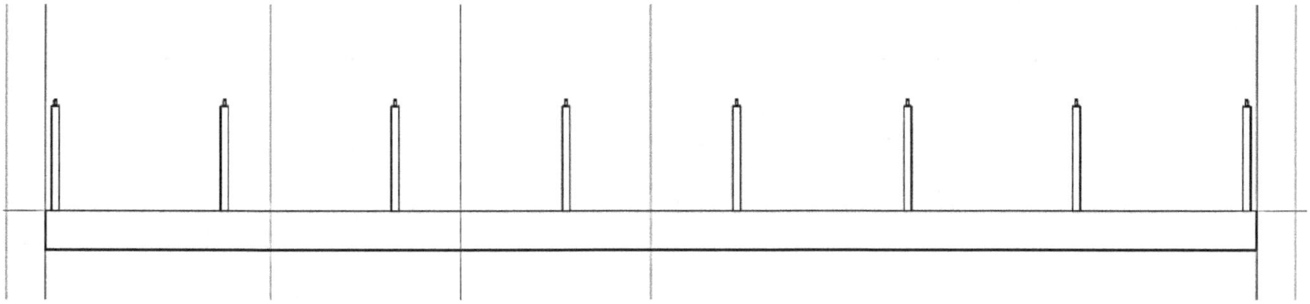

- Create the elements of the balcony railing, as shown.

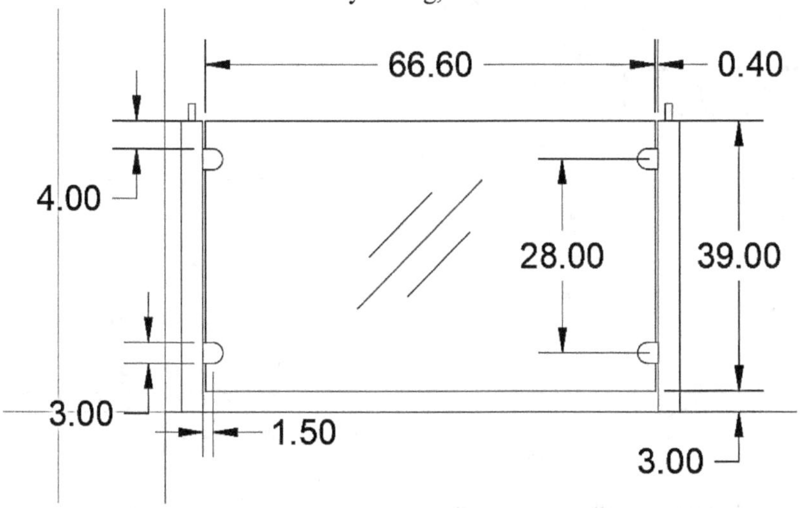

- Select the elements, as shown. Type **CO** and press Enter. Select the corner point of the rectangle, as shown.

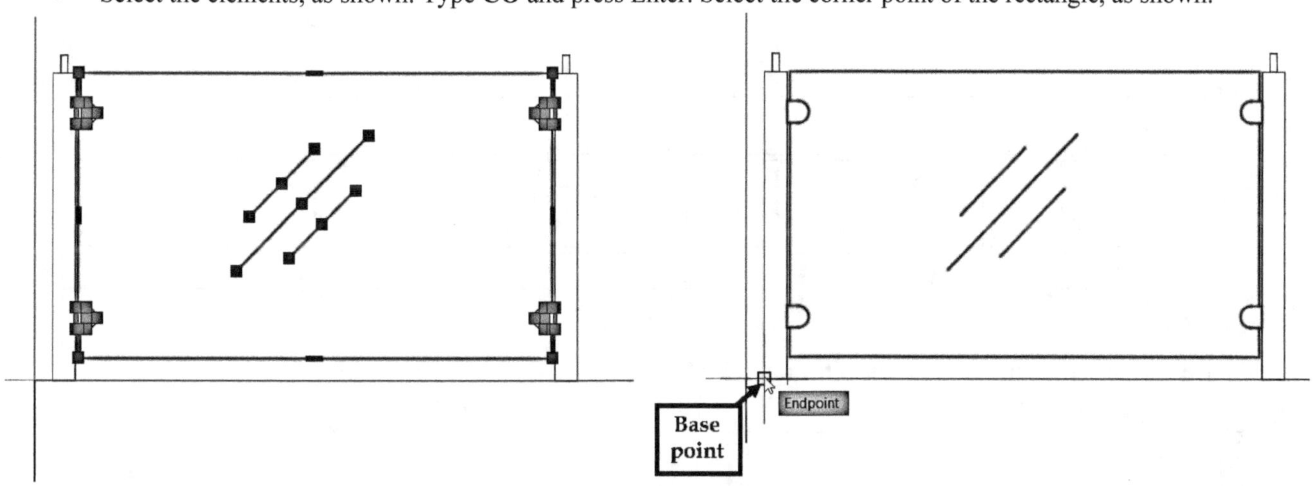

- Move the pointer horizontally and select the corner point of the rectangle, as shown. Likewise, place the glass and sleeve copies, as shown.

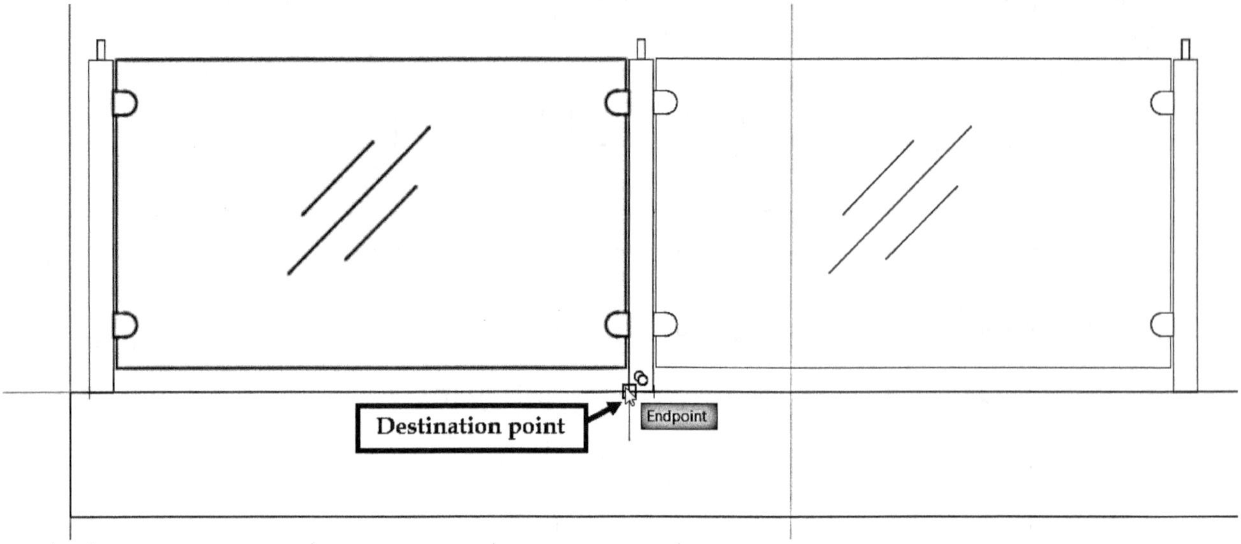

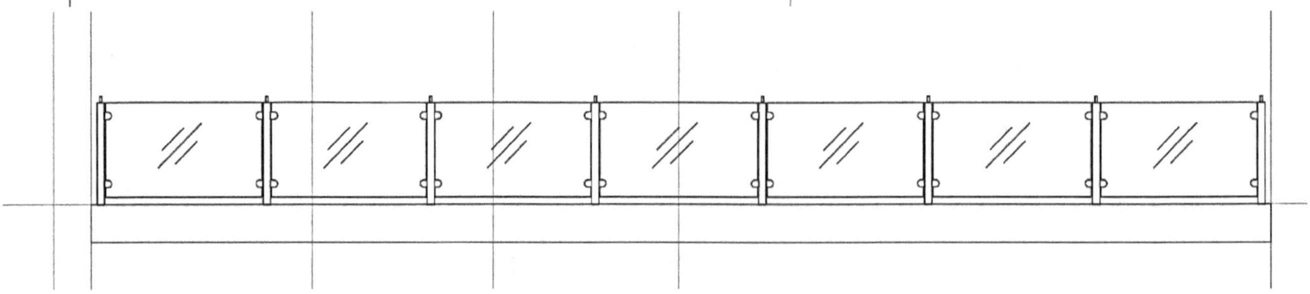

- Create two parallel lines using the dimensions shown in the figure.

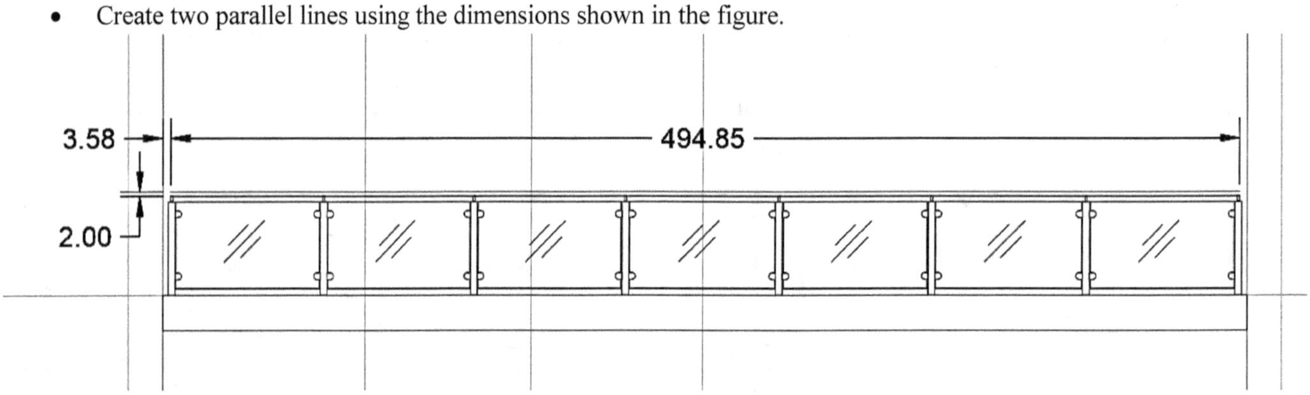

- Next, create arcs on both the ends of the railing.

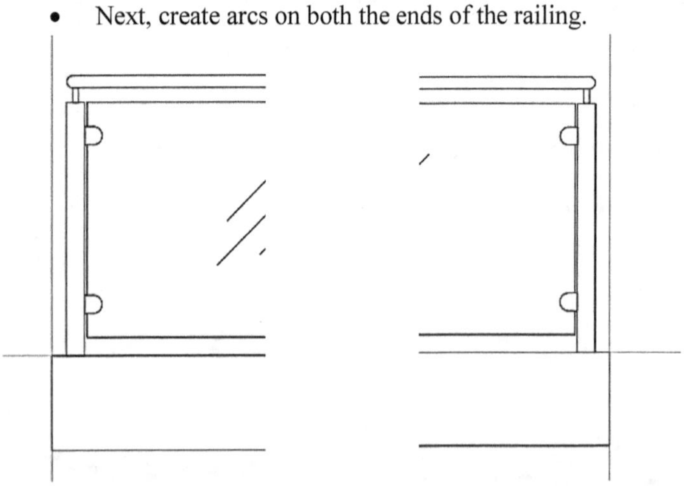

- Copy the double door from the South elevation, rotate it, and then place it between the construction lines, as shown. Likewise, copy the bathroom window, rotate it, and place it at the location, as shown. Delete the construction lines, as shown.

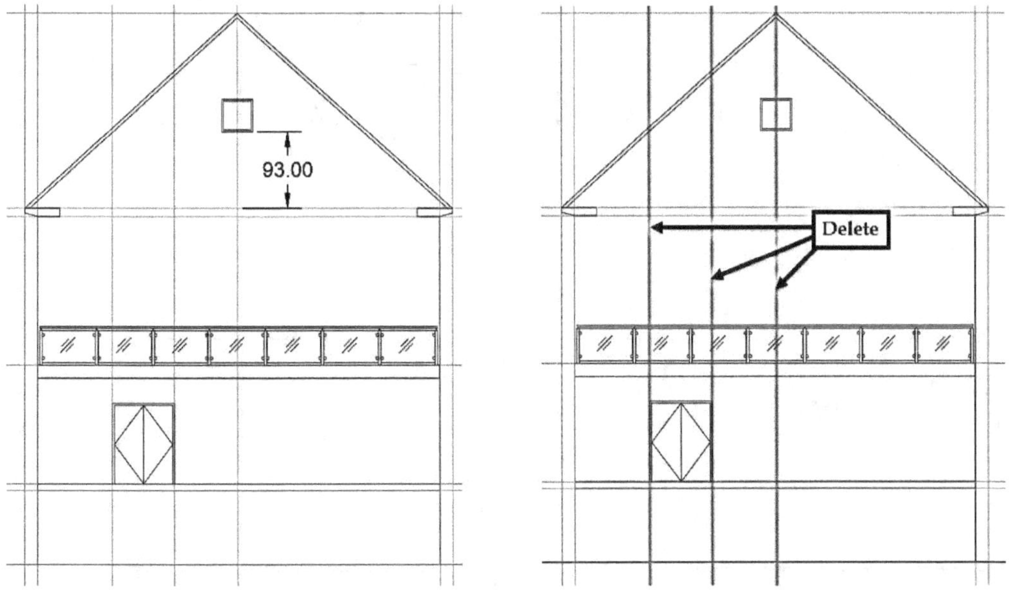

- Create construction lines passing through the sliding doors on the first-floor plan, as shown.

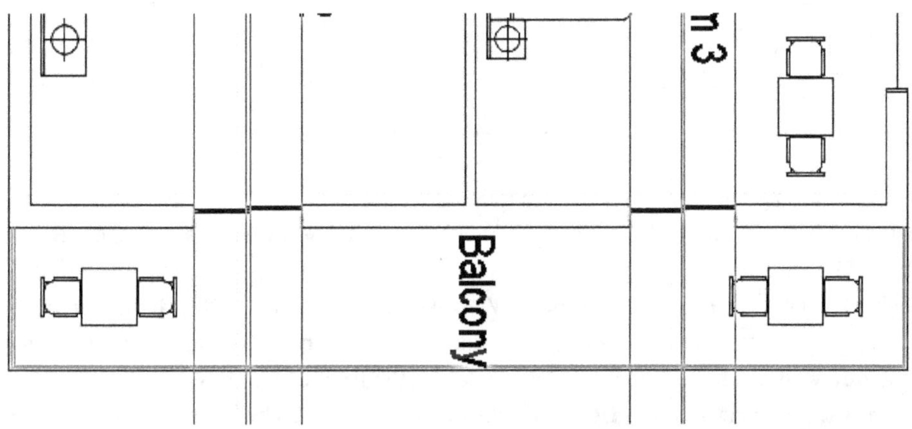

- Select the construction lines and click the **Move** tool on the **Modify** panel of the **Home** ribbon tab. Select the base point on the first-floor plan, as shown. Move the pointer and select the destination point on the ground floor plan, as shown.

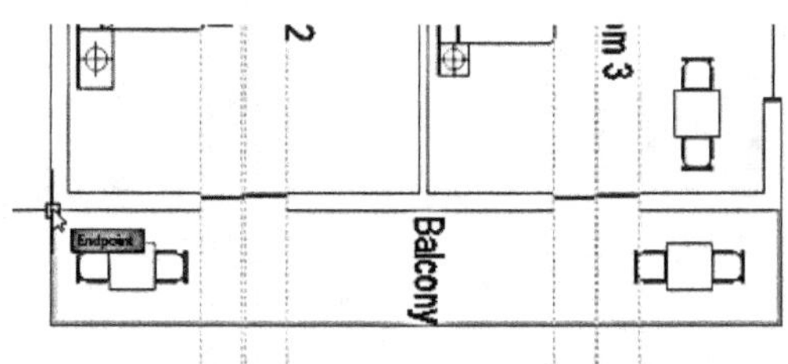

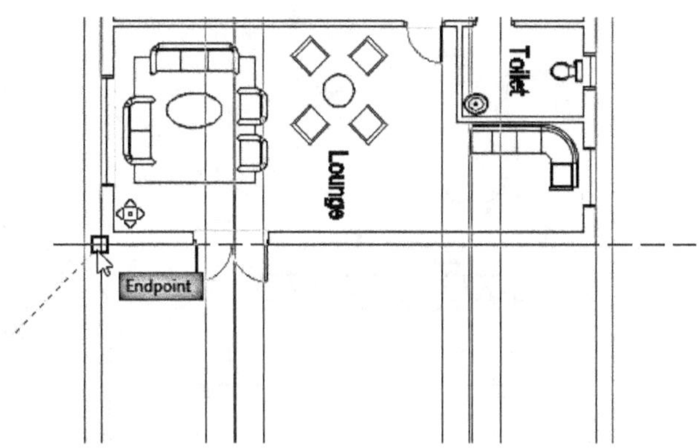

- Create the sliding doors on the Front elevation, as shown.

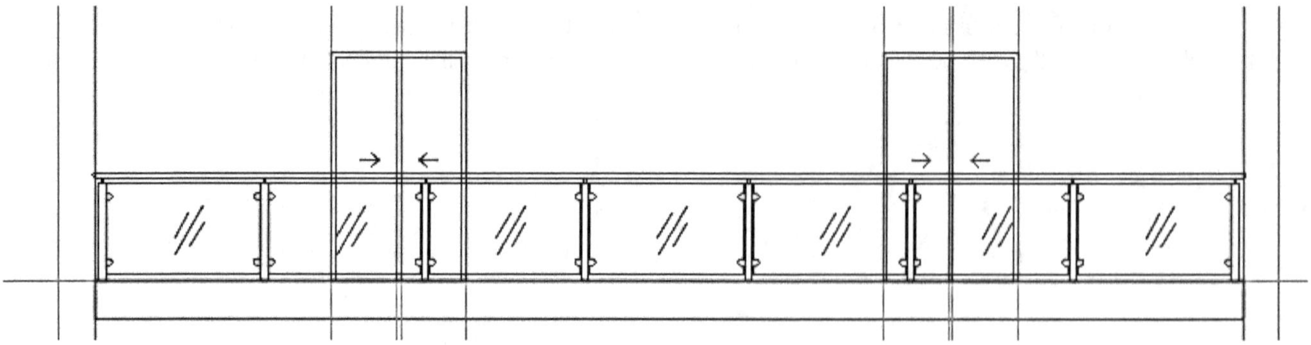

The dimensions of the sliding doors are given next.

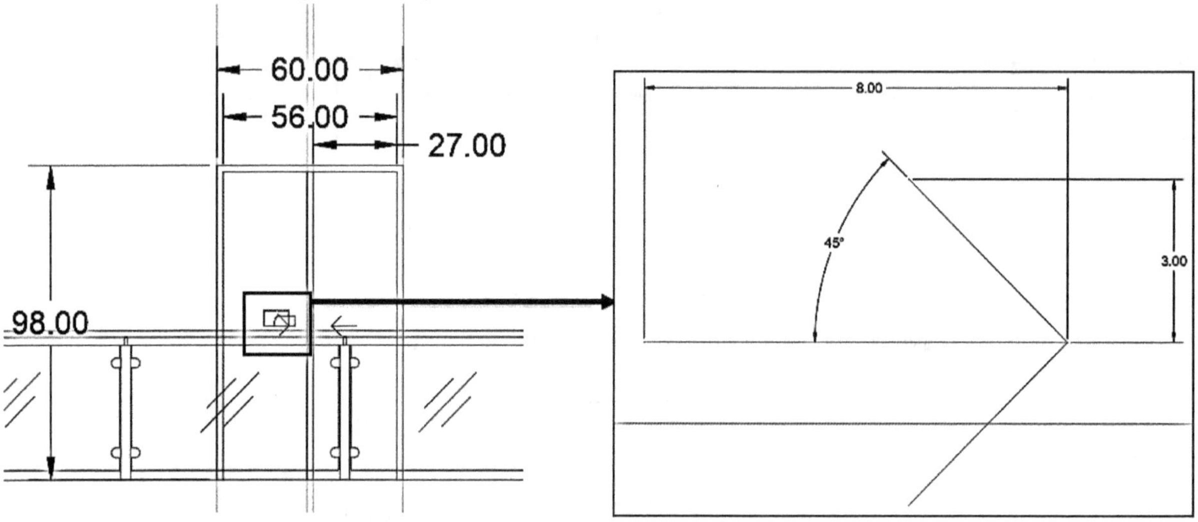

- Delete the construction lines passing through the sliding doors.
- Type **UCSMAN** and press Enter. On the **UCS** dialog, right click on the **Unnamed** ucs and select **Rename**. Type **Front-Elev** and click **OK**.
- On the ribbon, click **View** tab > **Named Views** panel > **View Manager**. Click the **New** button on the **View Manager** dialog to open the **New View/Shot Properties** dialog — type **Front Elev** in the **View name** box.
- Select the **Define window** option and create a window enclosing the front elevation view. Press Enter to accept. Make sure that **Front Elev** is selected in the **UCS** drop-down and click **OK**. The **Views** list in the **View Manager** dialog displays the **Front Elev** view.
- Click **OK** on the **View Manager** dialog.

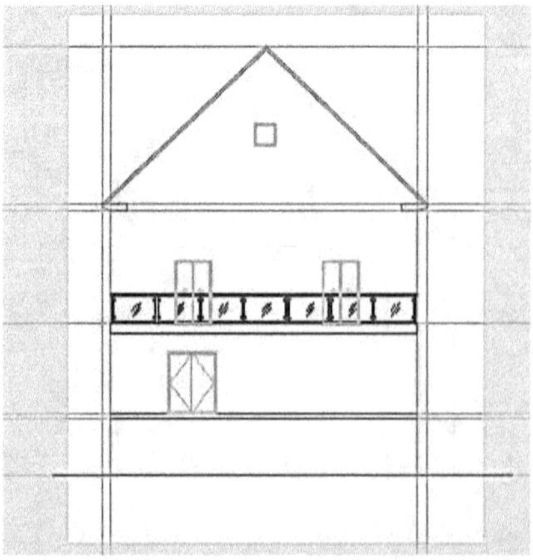

- In the top left corner of the graphics window, select **Top** from the **View Controls** menu. Zoom to the elevation views.

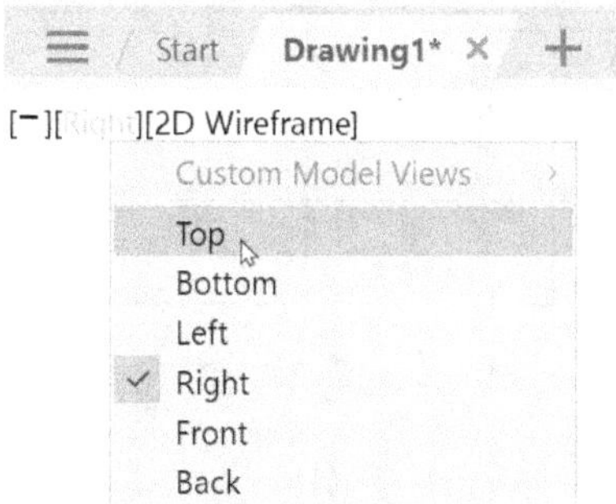

- Mirror the Front elevation about the approximate center of the ground floor plan.

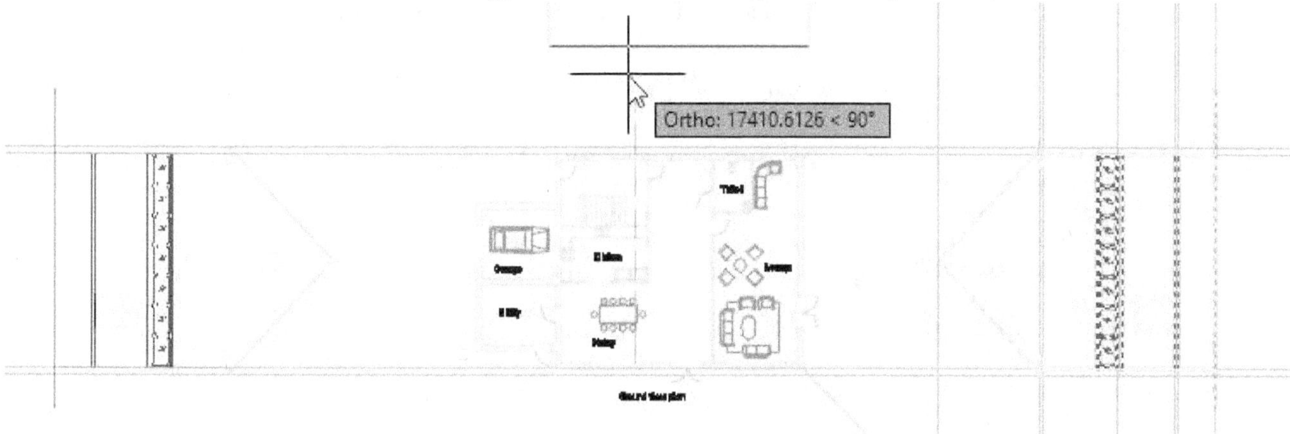

- Type **UCS** and press Enter. Select **Z** from the command line. Type **270** and press Enter. Type **PLAN** and press Enter twice. The UCS is rotated by 270 degrees about the Z-axis. Zoom to the elevation views.
- Delete the doors and balcony on the mirrored elevation view.

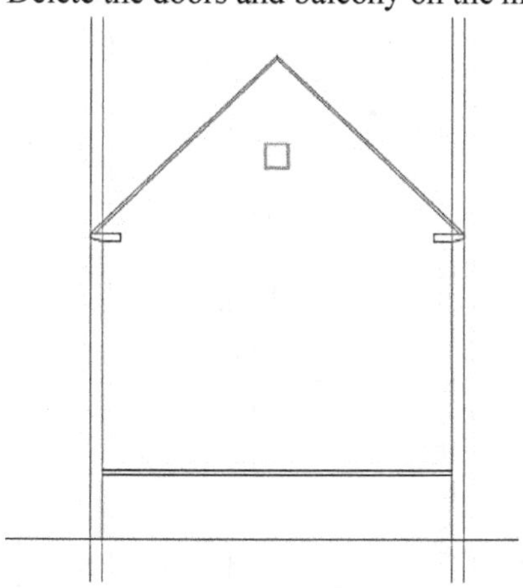

- Activate the **Reference Lines** layer. Create the construction lines projecting from the garage, and rear entrance. Also, create a construction line from the center of the garage.

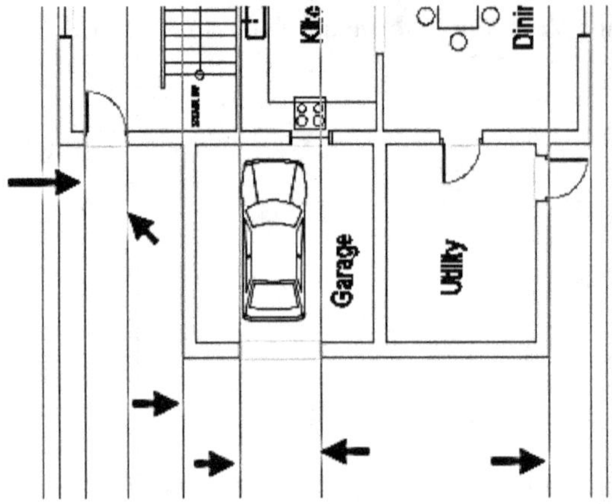

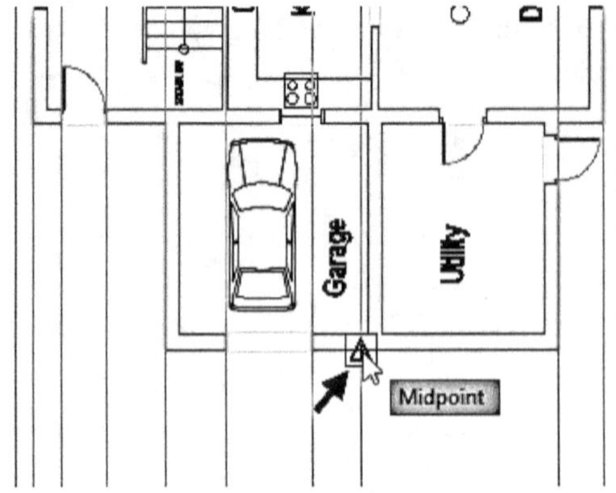

- Create two construction lines at **16** inches distance from the exterior walls, as shown. These lines help you to draw the roof overhang for the garage.

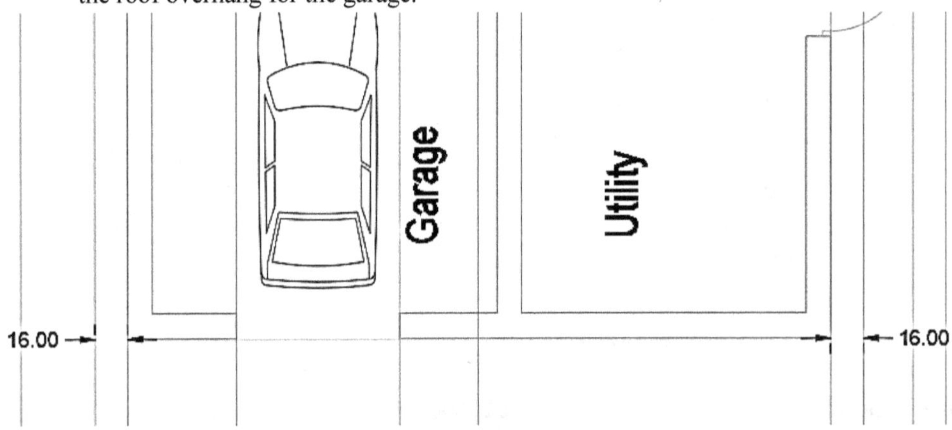

- Type **XL** and press Enter. Select **Offset** from the command line. Type **126** and press Enter. Select the ground level line, move the pointer up, and click to create a construction line. Use the **Offset** tool to create other construction lines, as shown.

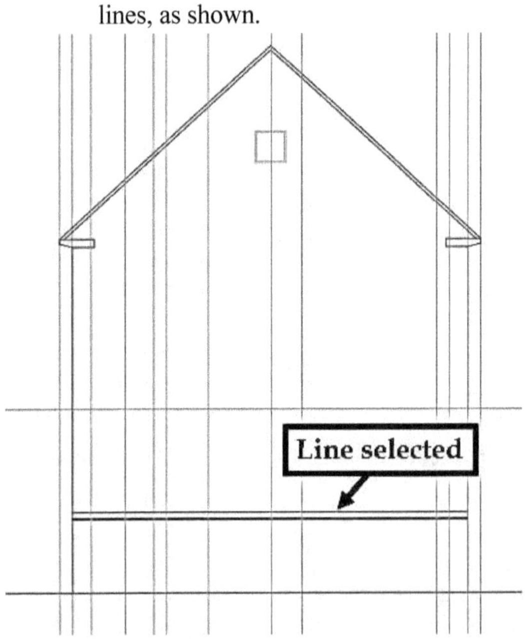

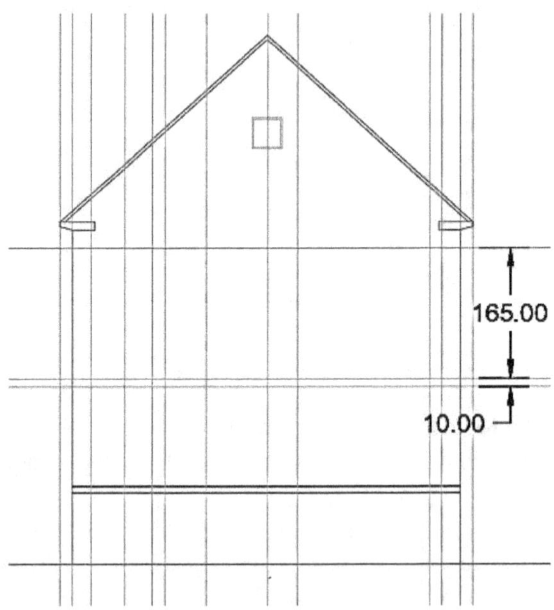

- Create the walls, door, roof, window, and opening on the Rear elevation, as shown.

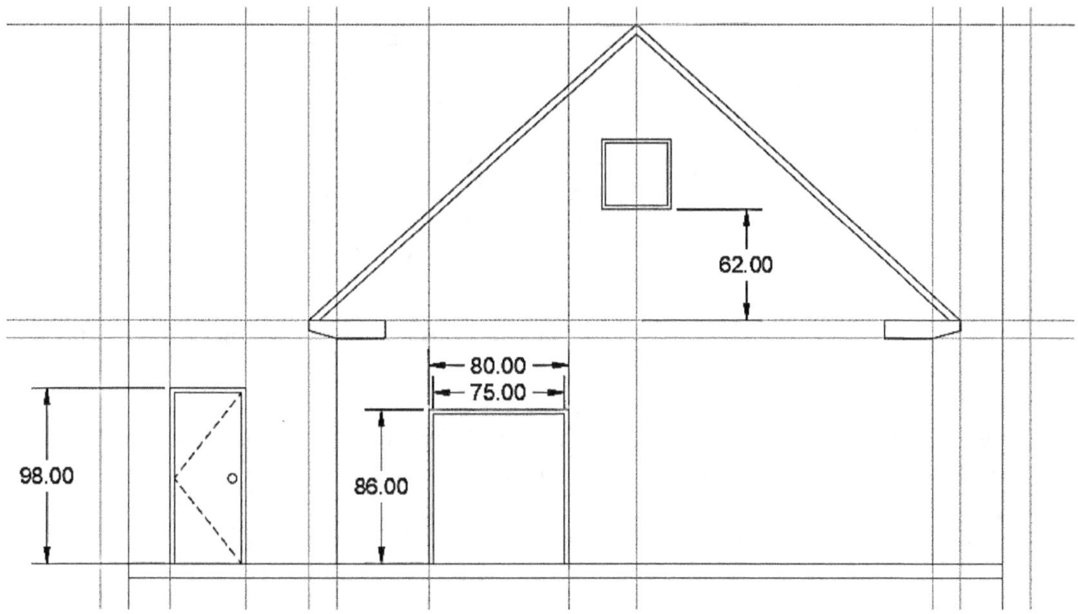

- Save the view as Rear-Elev and switch to the default orientation of the UCS.

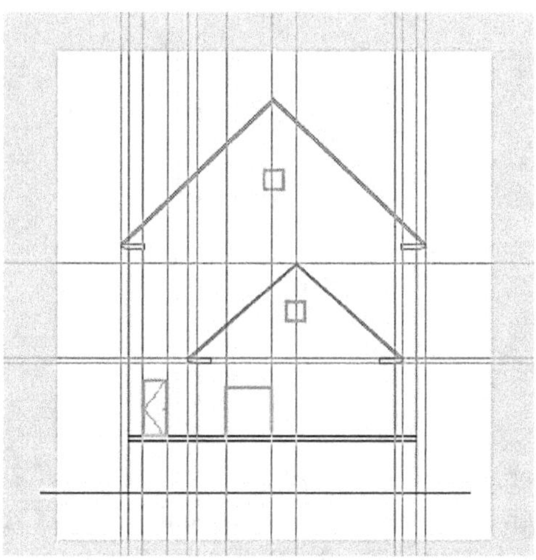

- Switch to a different layer.
- Freeze the **Reference lines** layer by clicking the sun icon next to **Reference Lines** on the **Layer** drop-down.

Hatching the Elevation Views

- In the graphics window, click the **Top** option in the In-Canvas Controls located at the top left corner.

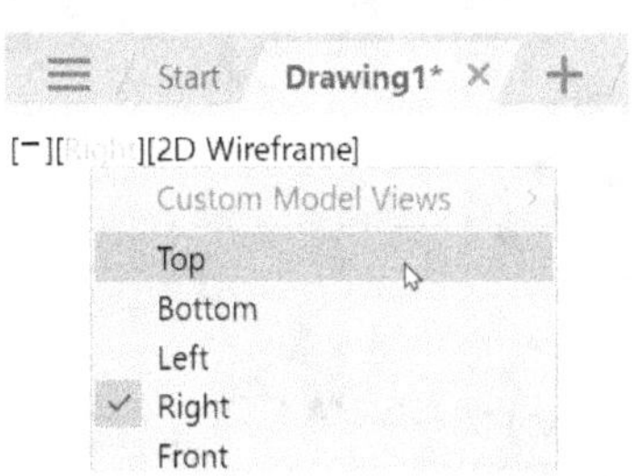

- Create the following layers:

Layer Name	Color	Linetype
A-ELEV-WALL-PATT	cyan	Continuous
A-ELEV-ROOF-PATT	green	Continuous
A-ELEV-FOUNDATION-PATT	Index Color 6	Continuous

- Activate the A-ELEV-ROOF-PATT layer. On the ribbon, click **Home** tab > **Draw** panel >**Pattern** drop-down > **Hatch** .
- On the **Hatch Creation** tab of the ribbon, on the **Pattern** panel, expand the gallery and select the **AR-RSHKE** pattern. Zoom to the South elevation and click in the roof area.

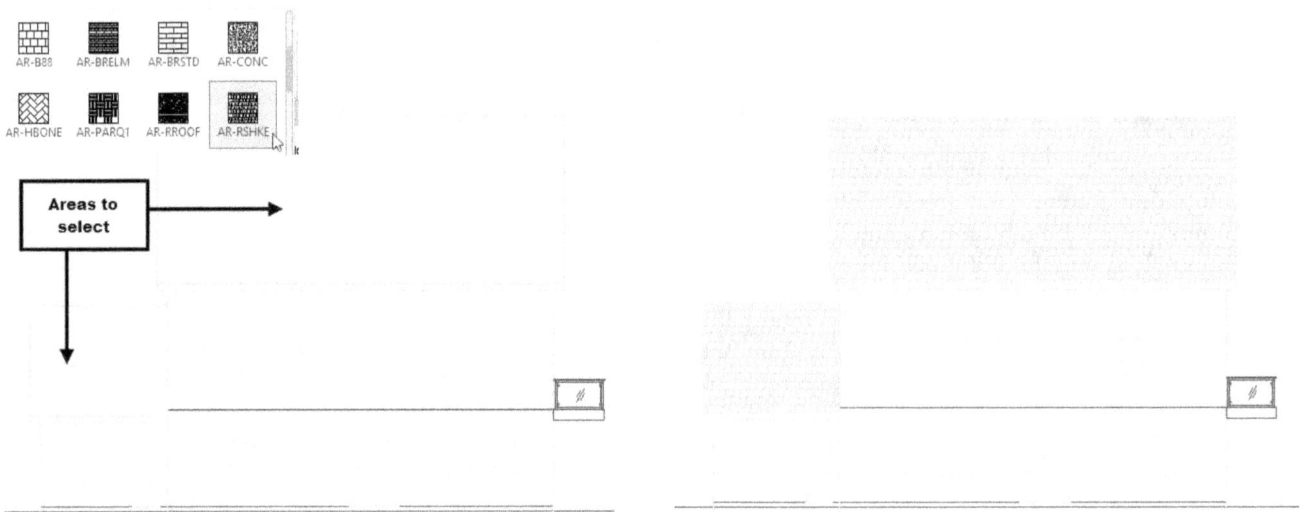

- Click the **Close Hatch Creation** icon on the **Hatch Creation** tab.
- Select the roof hatch pattern and notice that a single hatch pattern is created in two areas. On the **Hatch Creation** tab of the ribbon, expand the **Options** panel and click the **Separate Hatches** tool. The hatches are separated. Press Esc to deselect the hatch pattern.

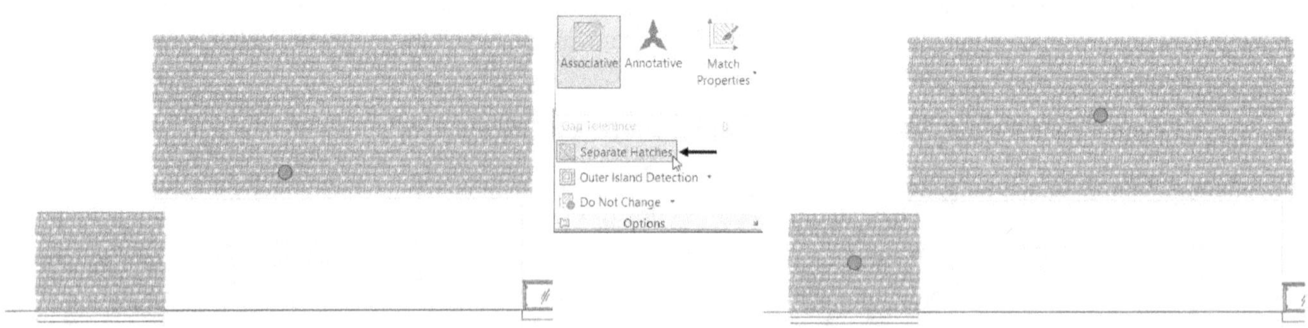

- On the ribbon, click **Home** tab > **Layers** panel > **Layer** drop-down > **A-ELEV-WALL-PATT**.
- Type **Hatch** and press Enter. On the **Hatch Creation** tab of the ribbon, on the **Pattern** panel, expand the gallery and select the **AR-B816C** pattern. On the **Hatch Creation** tab of the ribbon, expand the **Options** panel and click the

Create Separate Hatches tool. Click on the areas, as shown. Click **Close Hatch Creation**.

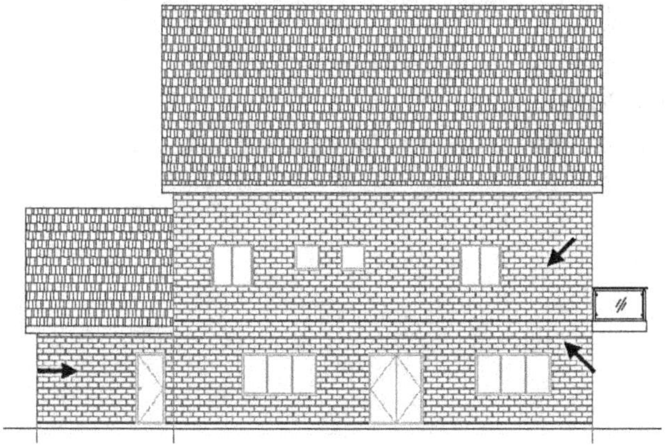

- Activate the A-ELEV-FOUNDATION-PATT layer and fill the AR-CONC hatch, as shown.

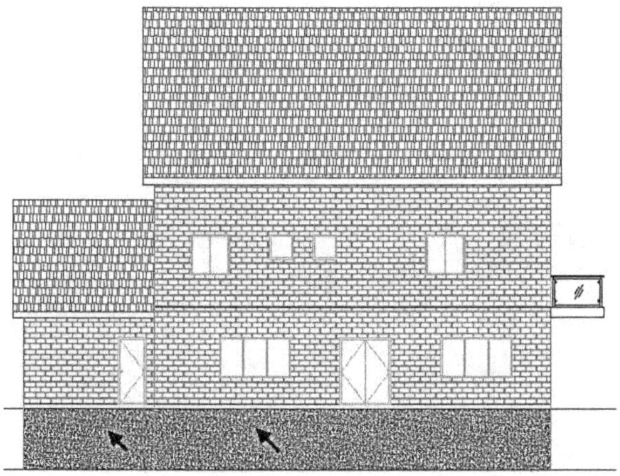

Tutorial 11: Adding Dimensions

- On the ribbon, click **Home > Layers > Layer** drop-down > **DIMENSIONS** to make it current.
- Type **D** in the command line and press Enter. On the **Dimension Style Manager** dialog, select the **Standard** dimension style and click the **New** button. Type-in **Architectural** in the **New Style Name** box and click **Continue**.
- Click the **Primary Units** tab and select **Unit format > Architectural.**
- Set **Precision** to **0'-0 1/16".**
- Click the **Symbol and Arrows** tab.
- Under the **Arrowheads** section, select **First > Architectural tick**. The second arrowhead is automatically changed to **Architectural tick**.
- Select **Leader > Closed Filled** and enter 12 in the **Arrow Size** box.
- Click the **Lines** tab and set **Extend beyond dim lines** and **Offset from origin** to 3 and 1.5, respectively.
- Click the **Text** tab and click the button ... next to the **Text Style** drop-down.
- On the **Text Style** dialog, type 12 in the **Height** box and click **Apply**. Next, click **Close.**Type **1** in the **Fraction height scale** box.
- In the **Text placement** section, set the following settings.
  Vertical-Centered
  Horizontal-Centered
  View Direction-Left-to-Right

- In the **Text alignment** section, select the **Aligned with dimension line** option.
- Click the **Fit** tab, and select **Either text or arrows (best fit)** option from the **Fit options** section.
- In the **Text placement** section, select the **Over dimension line, without Leader** option.
- Click **OK** and click **Set Current** on the **Dimension Style Manager**. Click **Close**.
- On the **Home** tab of the ribbon, click **Layers** panel > **Layers** drop-down, and then click the bulb icon of the **A-GRID** layer. The grid lines are turned on.
- On the ribbon, click **Annotate > Dimensions > Dimension**.
- Select the points on the vertical grid lines, as shown below.
- Move the pointer and click to locate the dimension.

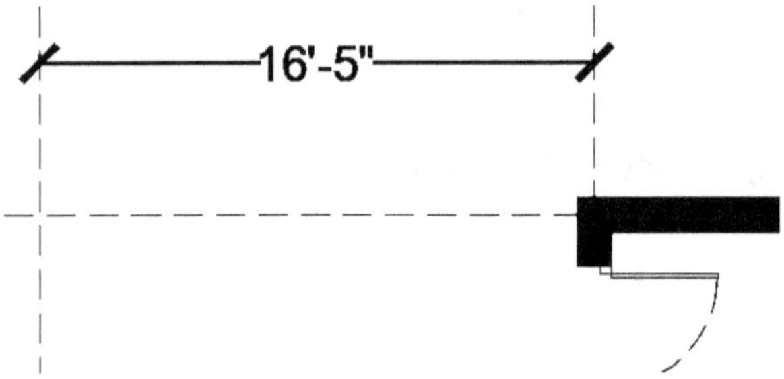

- On the ribbon, click **Annotate > Dimensions > Continue** . You notice that a dimension is attached to the pointer.
- Move the pointer and click on the next grid line.
- Likewise, create the other continuous dimensions, as shown. Next, press Esc to deactivate the **Continue** command.

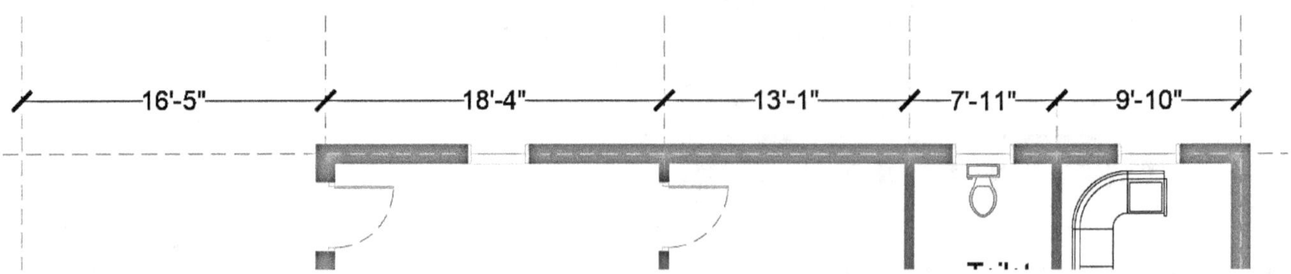

- Activate the **Dimension** command to create the overall horizontal dimension.

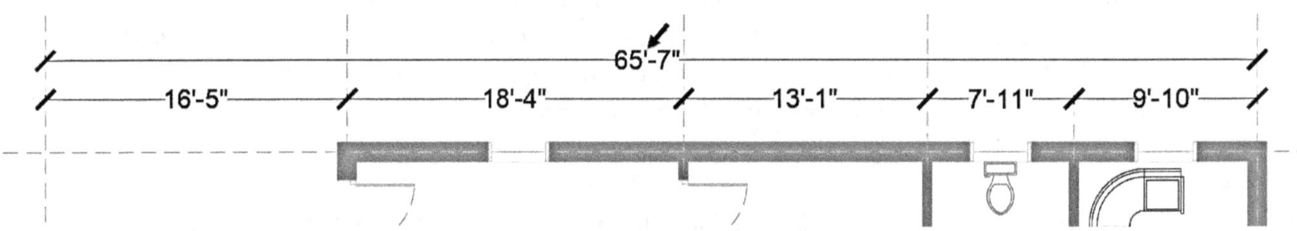

- Likewise, add vertical dimensions to the grid lines.

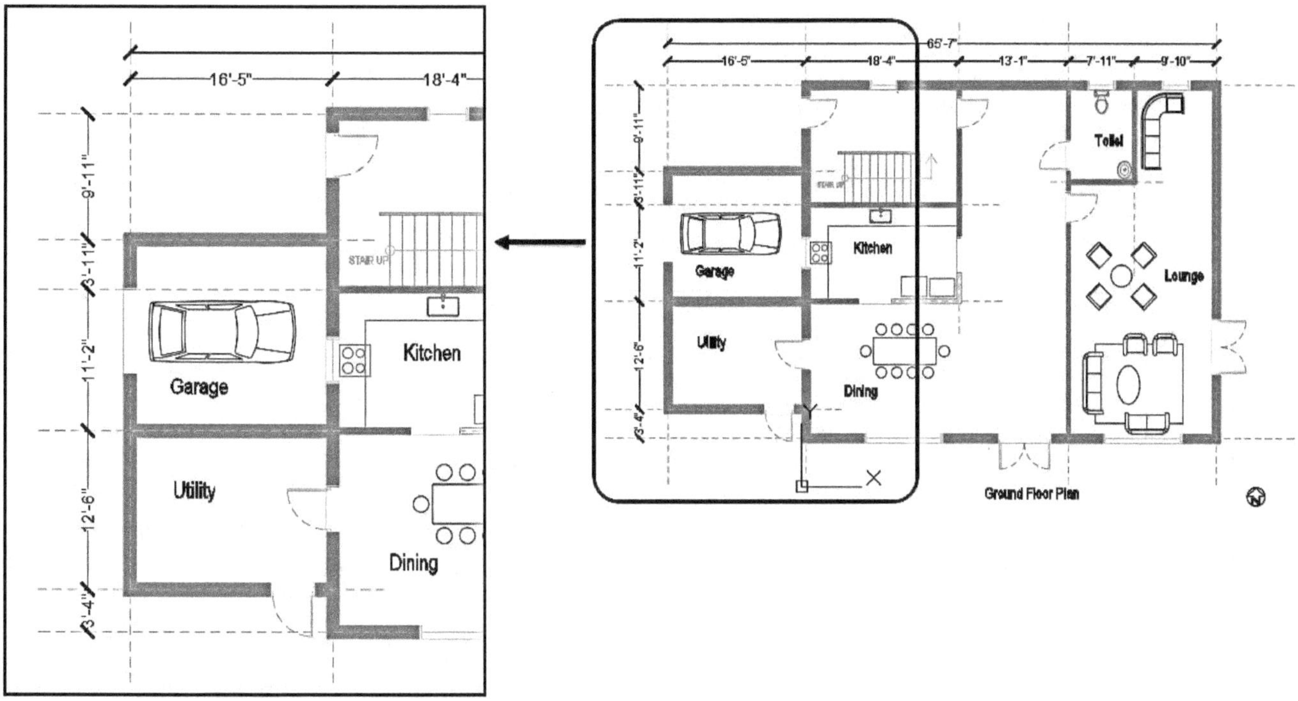

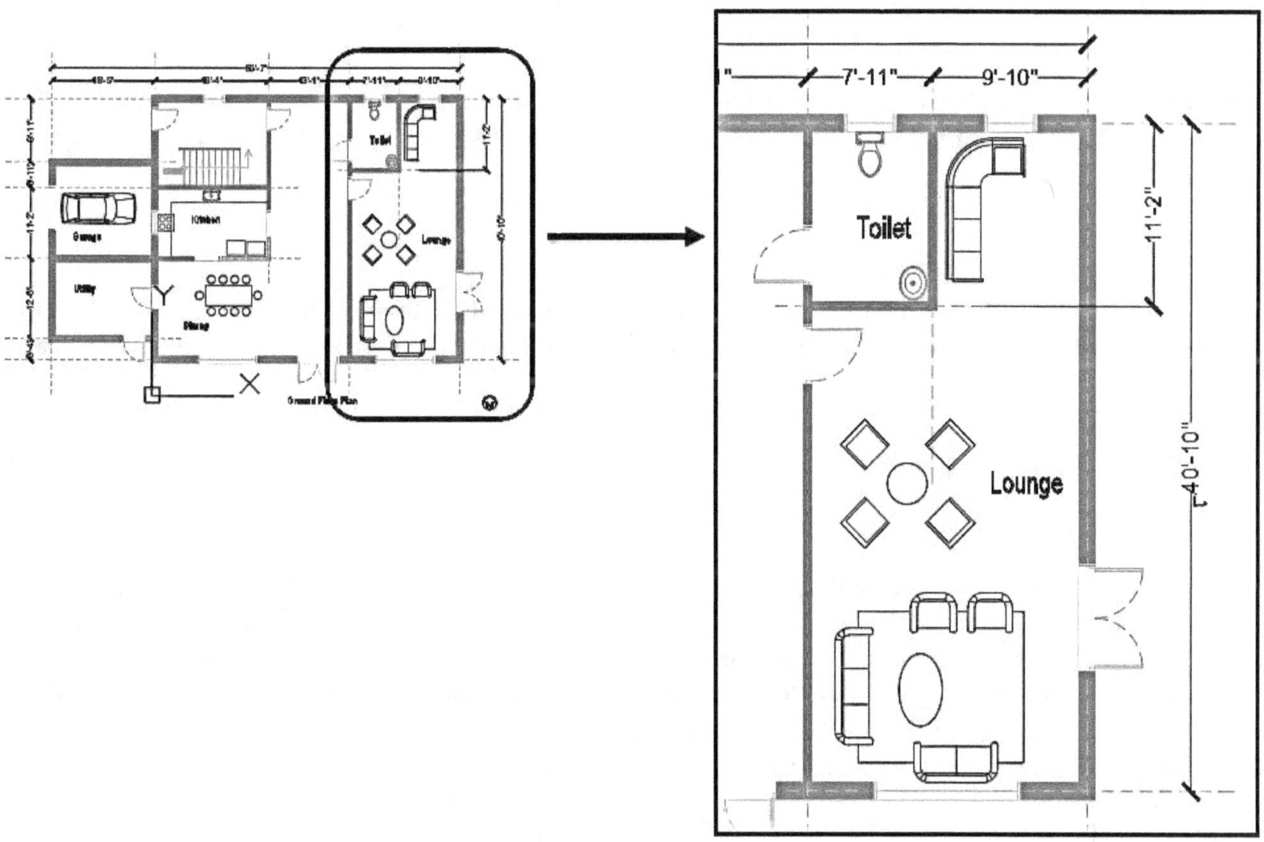

- Complete adding dimensions to the drawing, as shown below.

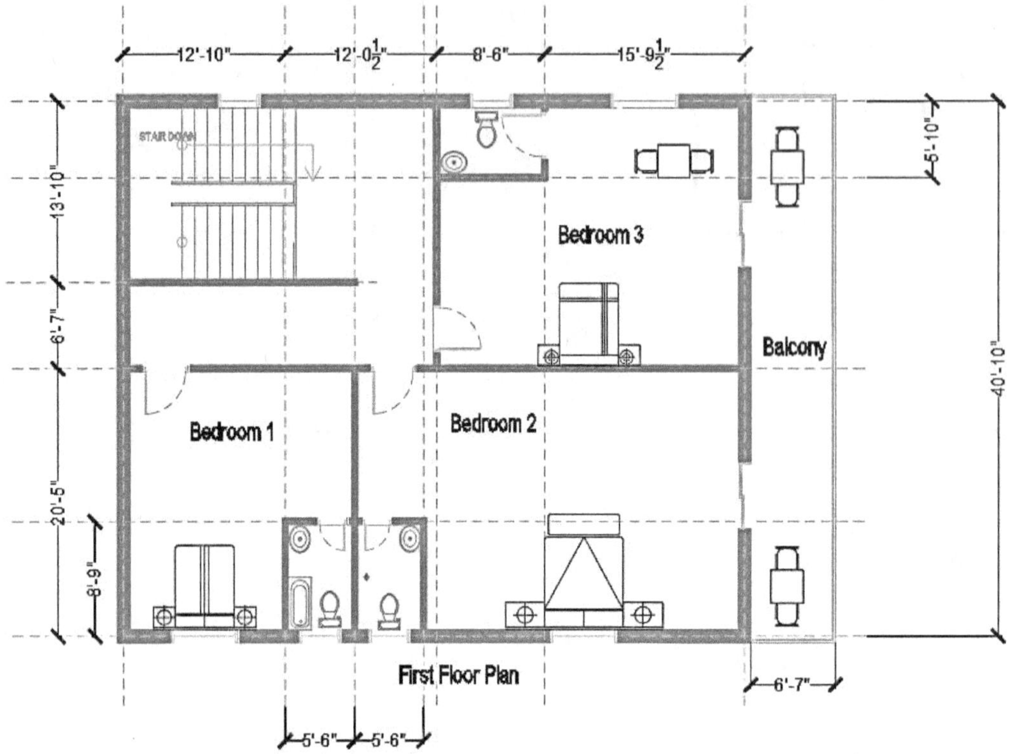

Tutorial 12: Creating Grid Bubbles

- Create the **A-GRIDBUBBLE** layer, set the layer color to Index color 9, and activate it. Create a circle of 12-inch diameter.
- On the ribbon, click **Insert > Block Definition > Define Attributes**  .
- On the **Attribute Definition** dialog, type-in GRIDBUBBLE in the **Tag** box and select **Justification > Middle center**. Select **Text Style > Standard** and click **OK**. Select the center point of the circle. The attribute text is placed at the center of the circle.

- On the ribbon, click **Insert > Block Definition > Create Block**. Type-in Grid bubble in the **Name** box and click the **Select objects** button. Draw a crossing window to select the circle and attribute. Press Enter to accept the selection.
- Click the **Pick point** option under the **Basepoint** section. Select the lower quadrant point of the circle to define the base point of the block. Uncheck the **Open in block editor** option. Select **Delete** from the **Objects** section and click **OK**.
- On the ribbon, click **Insert > Block > Insert > Grid bubble**.
- Select the top endpoint of the first vertical grid line; the **Edit Attributes** dialog pops up. Type-in **A** in the GRIDBUBBLE box and click **OK**.

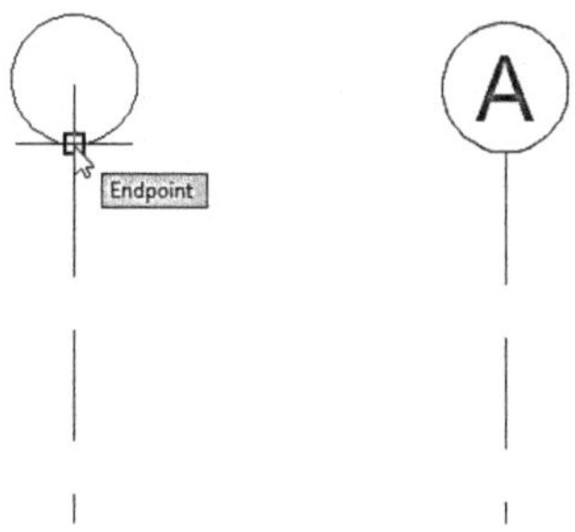

- Likewise, add other grid bubbles to the vertical grid lines.

- Create another block with the name Vertical Grid bubble. Make sure that you select the right quadrant point of the circle as the base point.

- Insert the vertical grid bubbles, as shown below. Enter numbers in the grid bubbles.

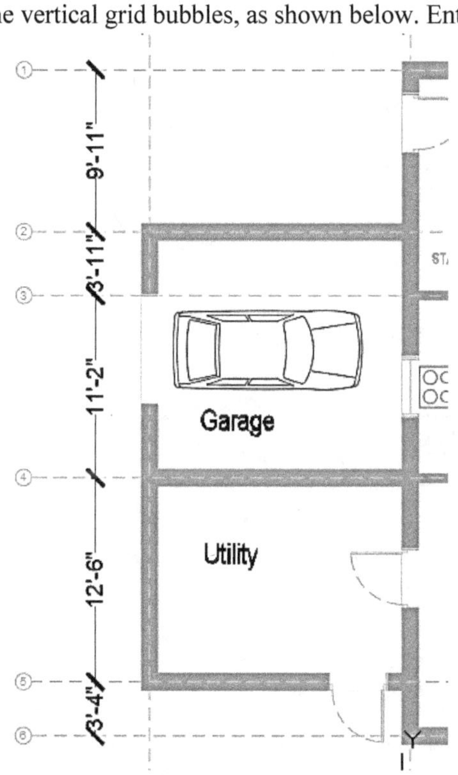

- Likewise, add grid bubbles to the first-floor plan.

Tutorial 13: Layouts and Title Block

- Click the **Layout 1** tab at the bottom of the graphics window.

Notice the layout tab menu adjacent to the Model tab. It offers a range of functions, allowing you to effortlessly switch between layouts, create layouts from templates, publish layouts, and much more.

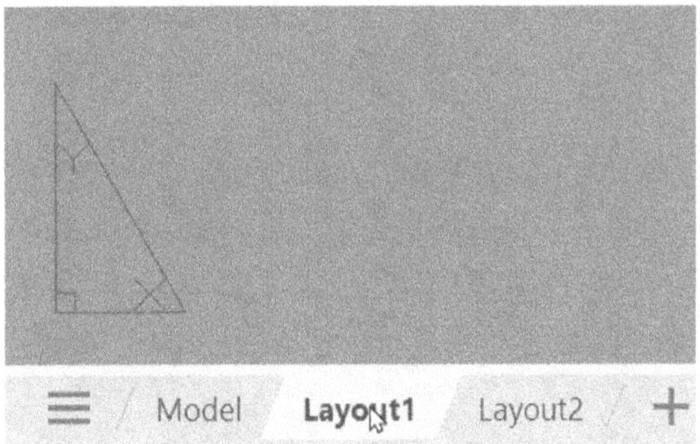

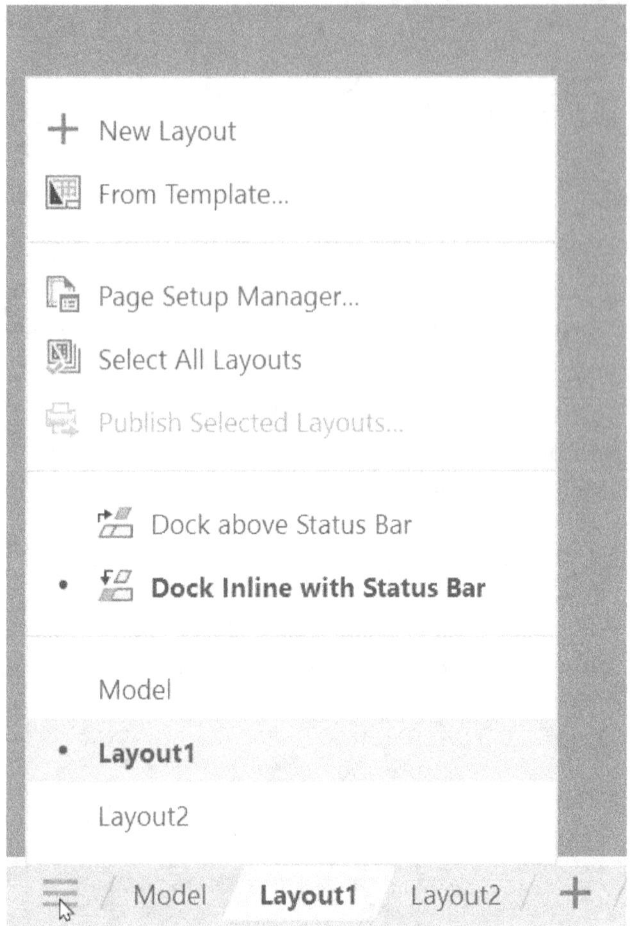

Notice that a white paper is displayed with a viewport created automatically. The components of a layout are shown in the figure below.

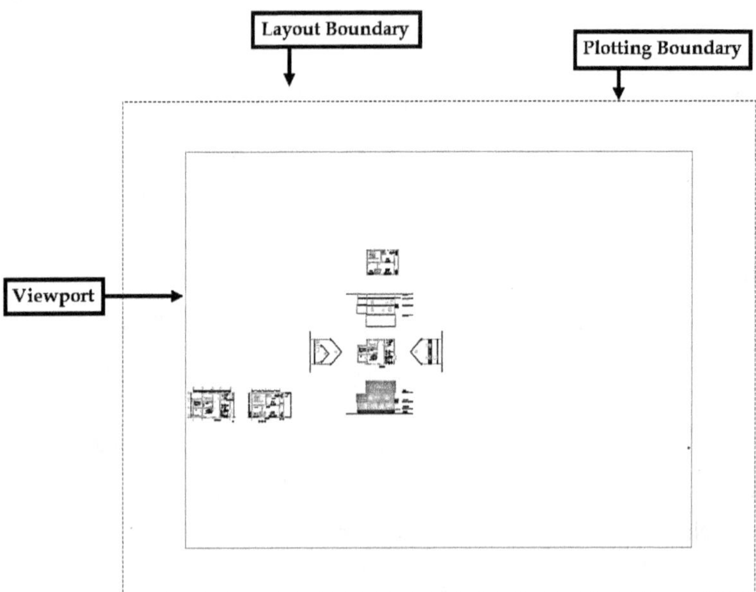

- Click **Output > Plot > Page Setup Manager** on the ribbon; the **Page Setup Manager** dialog appears. On the **Page Setup Manager** dialog, click the **Modify** button; the **Page Setup –Layout1** dialog appears.

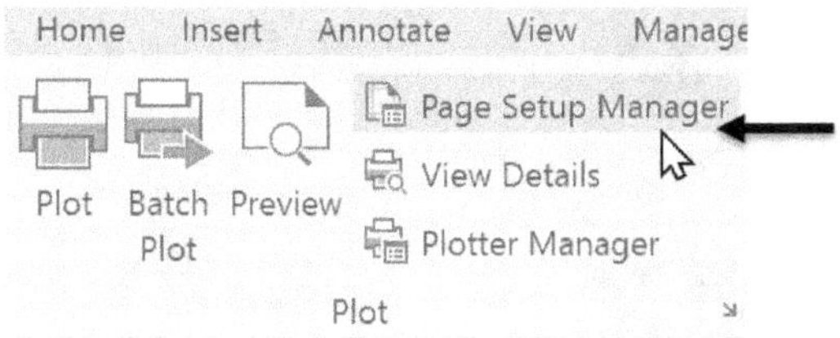

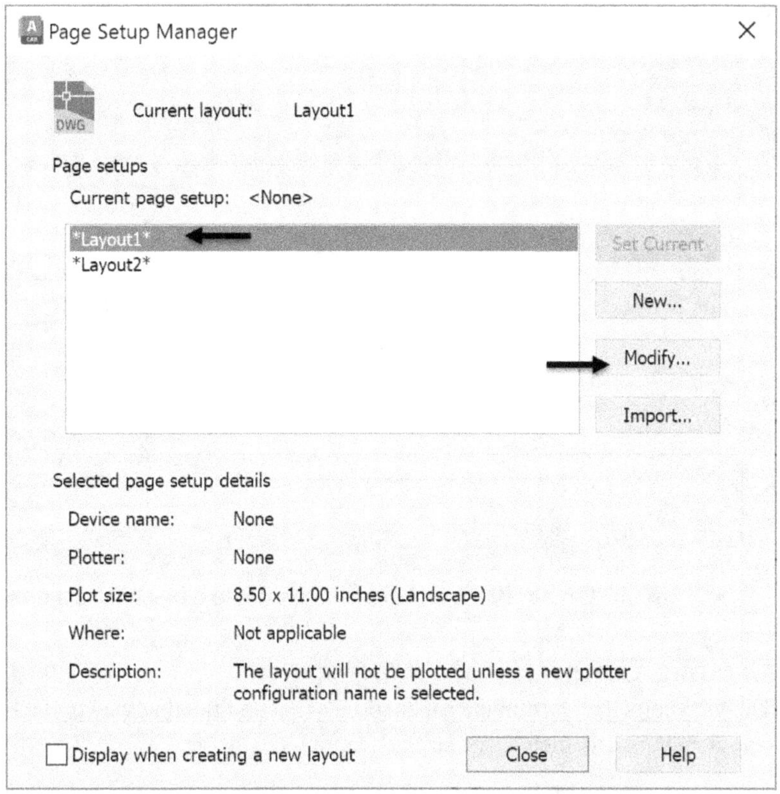

- On the **Page Setup** dialog, select **DWG to PDF.pc3** from the **Name** drop-down under the **Printer/Plotter** group. Set the **Plot Style table** to **acad.ctb**. Set the **Paper size** to **ARCH D (36.00 x 24.00 inches)**. Set the **Plot scale** to **1:1**. Click **OK**, and then click **Close** on the **Page Setup Manager** dialog.
- Double-click on the **Layout1** tab and enter **ARCH D**; the **Layout1** is renamed.

Creating the Title Block on the Layout

You can draw objects on layouts to create title blocks, borders, and viewports. However, it is not recommended to draw the actual drawing on layouts. You can also create dimensions on layouts.

- Click the **ARCH D** layout tab.
- Create the **Title Block** layer and make it current. Select the viewport on the layout and press Delete.
- Create the border and title block, as shown. Insert text inside the title block, as shown.

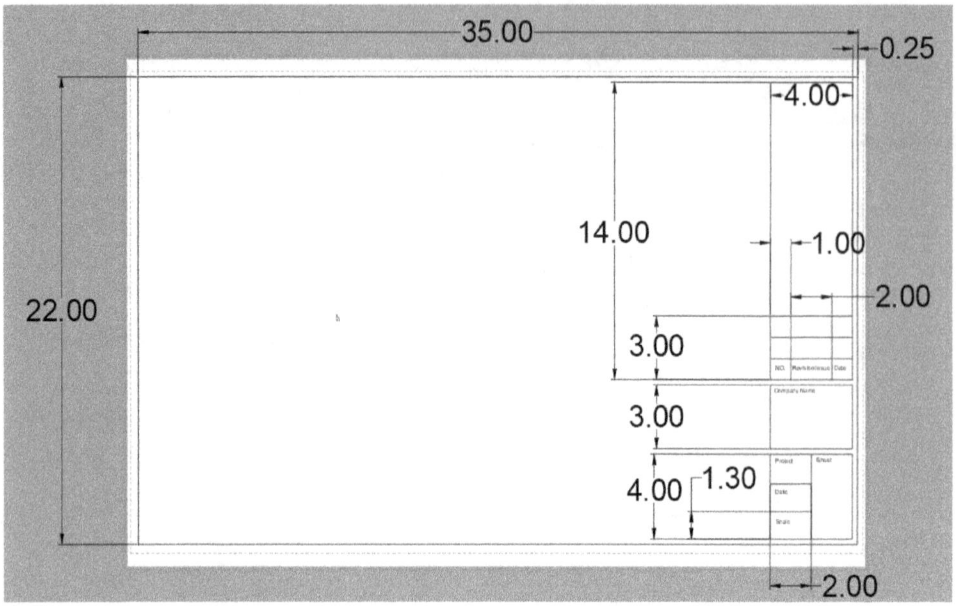

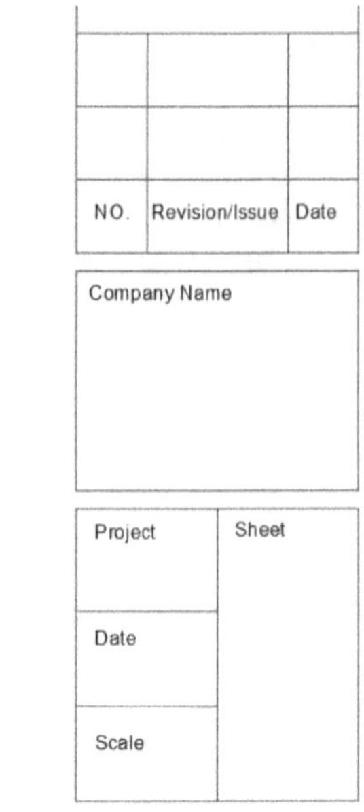

- Use the **Create Block** tool and convert it into a block. Use the **Insert** tool and insert the block on the layout.

Creating Viewports in the Paper space

The viewports that exist in the paper space are called floating viewports. Because you can position them anywhere in the layout, and modify their shape size concerning the layout.

- Open the **ARCH D** layout, if not already open.
- Click **Layout > Layout Viewports > Rectangular** on the ribbon.

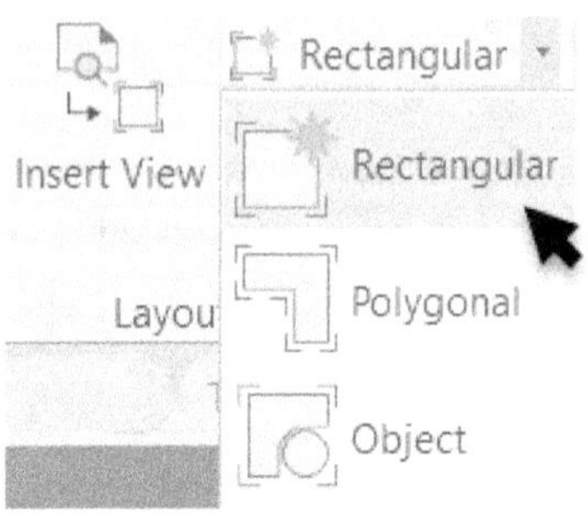

- Create the rectangular viewport by picking the first and second corner points, as shown in the figure.

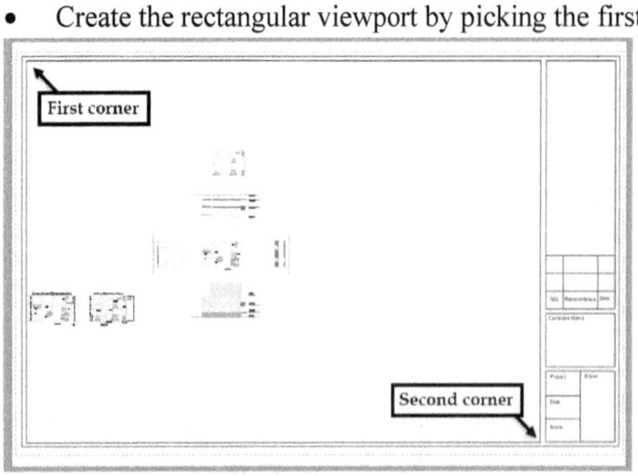

- Click the **Model** tab at the bottom left corner of the window.
- On the ribbon, click **View > Named Views > View Manager**. Create two named views of the ground and first-floor plans. Also, create another named view of the South Elevation.

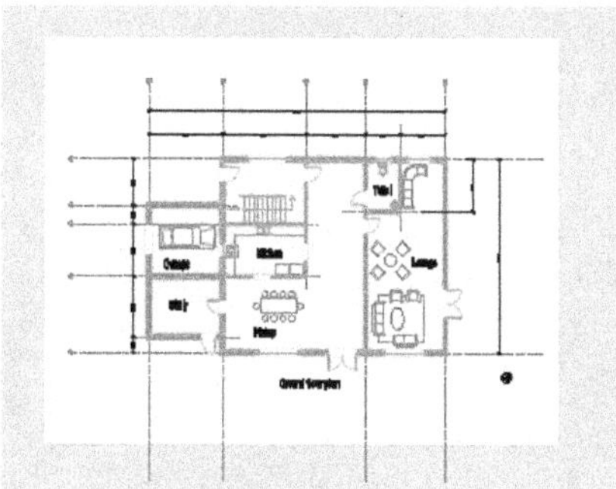

Ground Floor

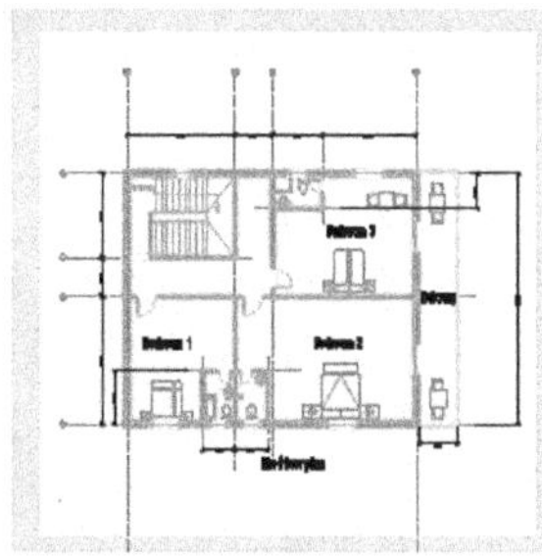

First Floor

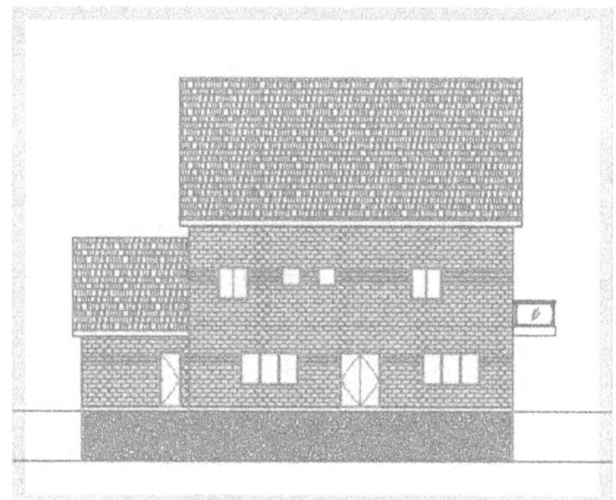

South Elevation

- Click the **ARCH D** tab.
- Click the **PAPER** button on the status bar; the model space inside the viewport is activated. Also, the viewport frame becomes thicker when you are in model space.
- On the ribbon, click **View** tab > **Named Views** panel > **Restore Views** drop-down > **Ground Floor**.

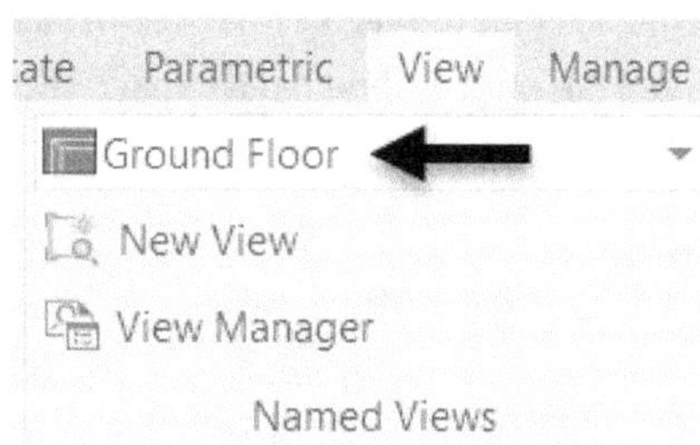

- Click the **Viewport Scale** button and select **1:50** from the menu; the drawing is zoomed out.
- After fitting the drawing inside the viewport, you can lock the viewport position by clicking the **Lock/Unlock Viewport** button on the status bar.

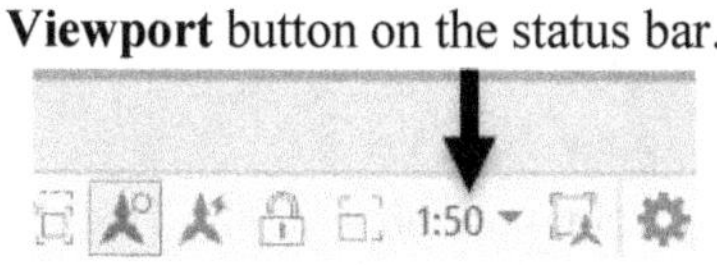

After locking the viewport, you cannot change the scale or position of the drawing.

- Click the **MODEL** button on the status bar to switch back to paper space.

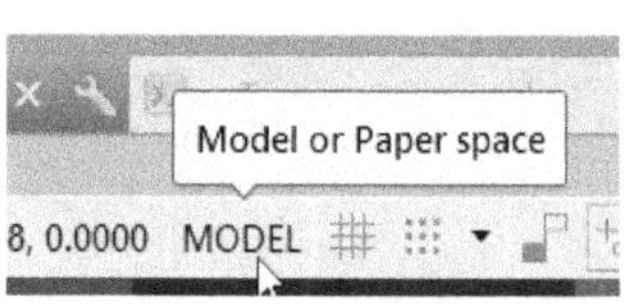

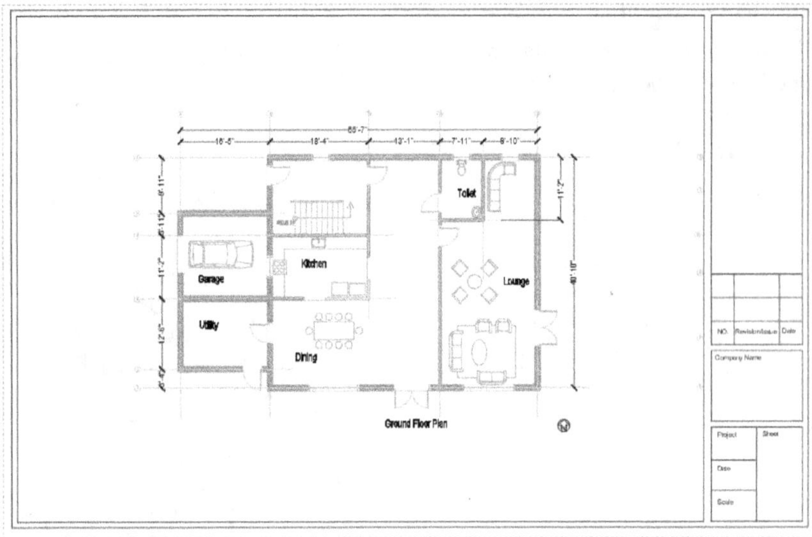

To hide viewport frames while plotting a drawing, follow the steps given below.

- Type **LA** in the command line and press Enter; the **Layer Properties Manager** appears.
- In the **Layer Properties Manager**, create a new layer called **Hide Viewports** and make it current.
- Deactivate the plotter symbol under the **Plot** column of the **Hide Viewports** layer; the object on this layer will not be plotted. Close the **Layer Properties Manager**.
- Click the **Home** tab on the ribbon and expand the **Layers** panel. Click the **Change to Current Layer** button on the **Layers** panel.

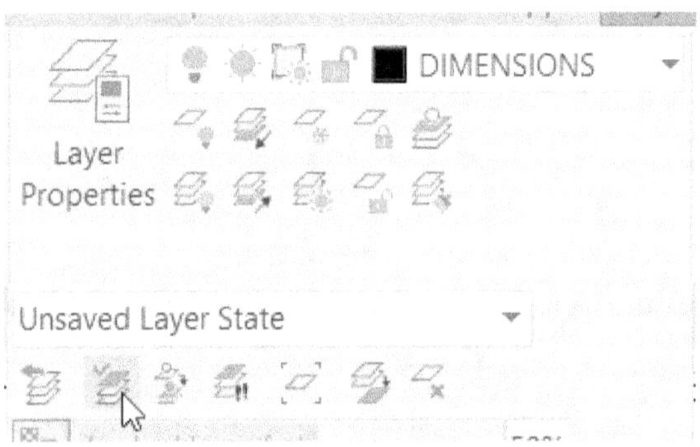

- Select the viewport in the **ARCH D** layout and press ENTER; the viewport frames are unplottable. To check this, click the **Preview** button on the **Plot** panel of the **Output** ribbon tab; the plot preview appears as shown below.

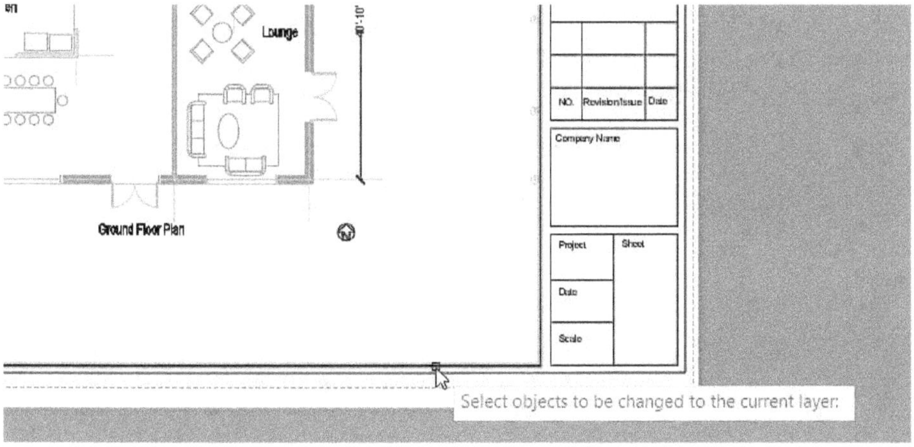

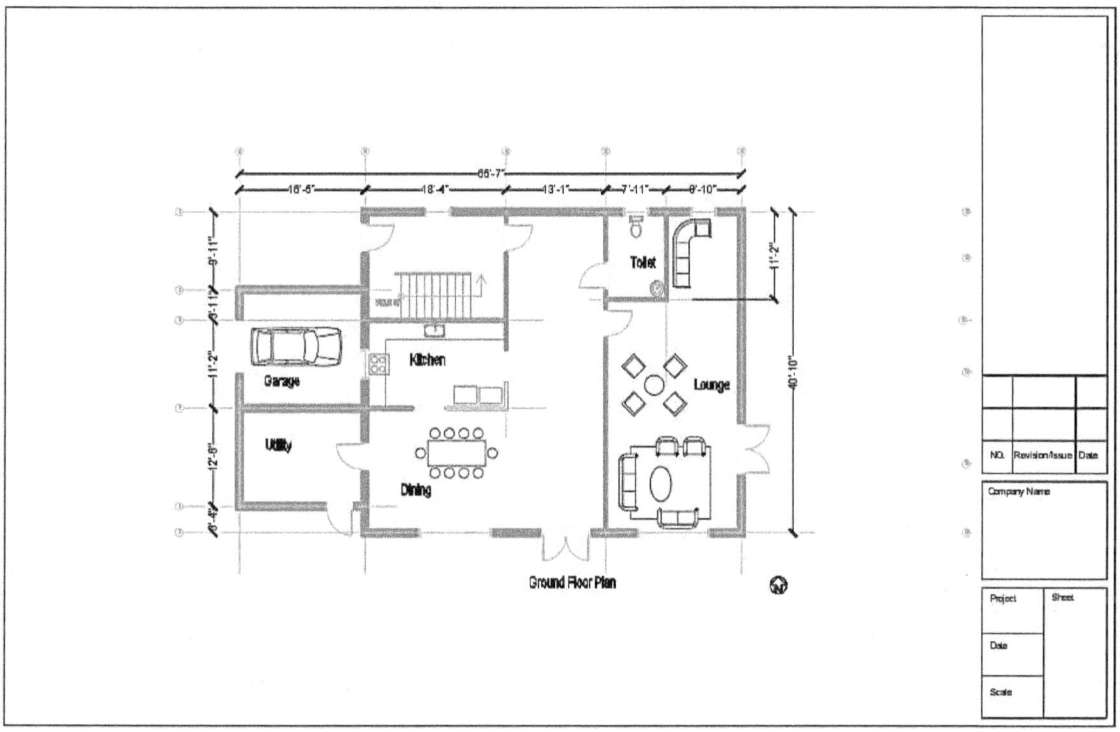

- Click the **Close preview window** icon.

Creating layouts for the other views

- Right click on the Layout2 and select **Delete**. Click **OK**.

- Click the right mouse button on the **ARCH D** layout and select **Move or Copy**. Select (move to end) from the **Move or Copy** dialog. Check the **Create a copy** option and click **OK**.
- Likewise, create four more copies of the **ARCH D** layout.

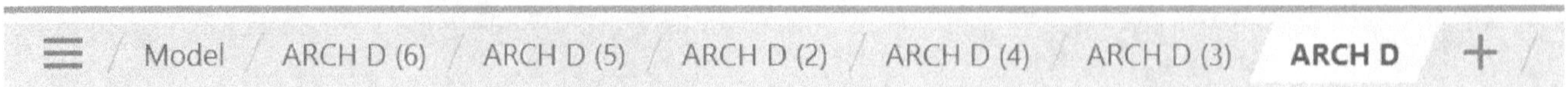

- Rename the layouts, as shown.

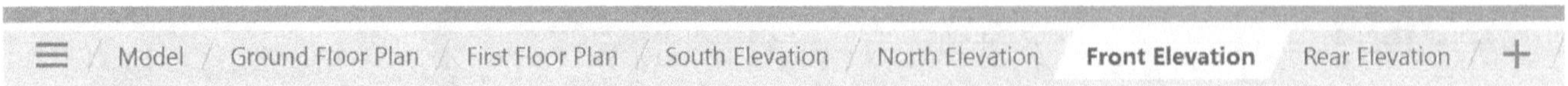

- Select the **First Floor Plan** layout tab. Double click in the viewport, and then click the **Lock** icon on the status bar; the viewport is unlocked. On the ribbon, click **View** tab > **Named Views** panel > **Restore Views** drop-down > **First Floor**. Click the **Viewport Scale** button and select **1:50** from the menu. Click the **Lock/Unlock Viewport** button on the status bar.

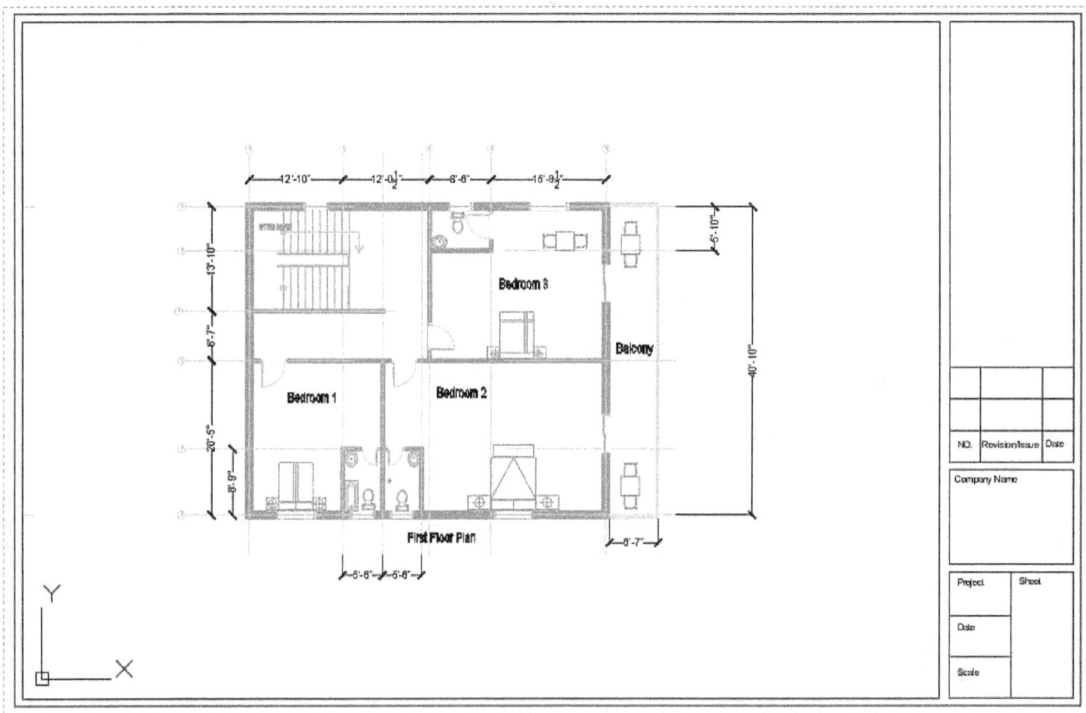

- Likewise, compose the **South Elevation**, **North Elevation**, **Front Elevation**, and **Rear Elevation** layouts.

Changing the Layer Properties in Viewports

The layer properties in viewports are not related to the layer properties in model space. You can change the layer properties in viewports without any effect in the model space.

- Select the **Front Elevation** layout tab. In the **Layer Properties Manager**, click the icon in the **VP Freeze** column of the **Reference Lines** layer; the reference lines disappear in the viewport, as shown below.

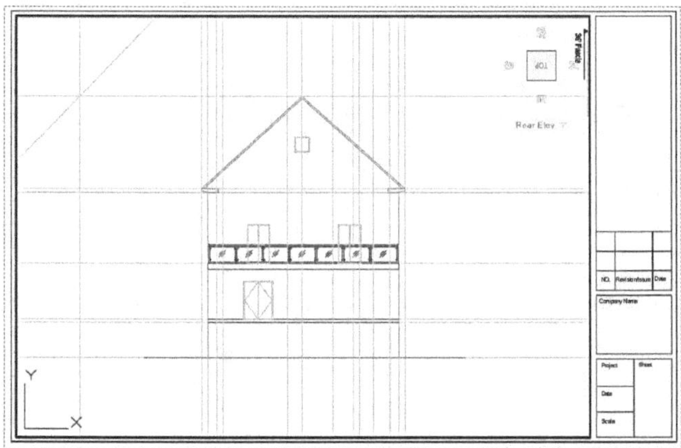 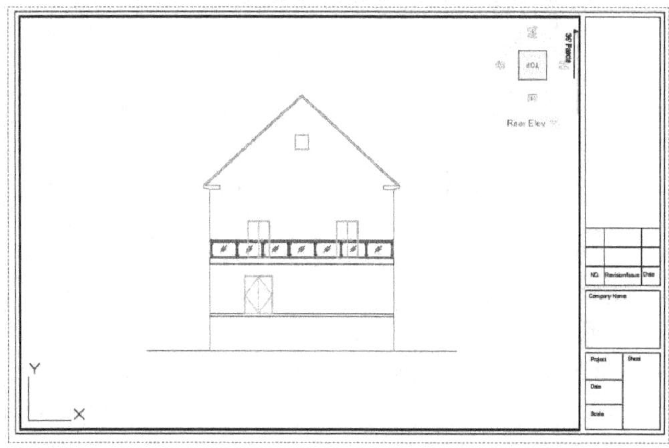

- Double-click outside the viewport to switch to the paper space.
- Click the **Model** tab below the graphics window.
- Save the drawing file.

Tutorial 14: Printing

- On the Application Menu, click **Print > Manage Plot Styles** . Next, double click on the **acad.ctb** icon (**AutoCAD Color-dependent Plot Style Table File** type).

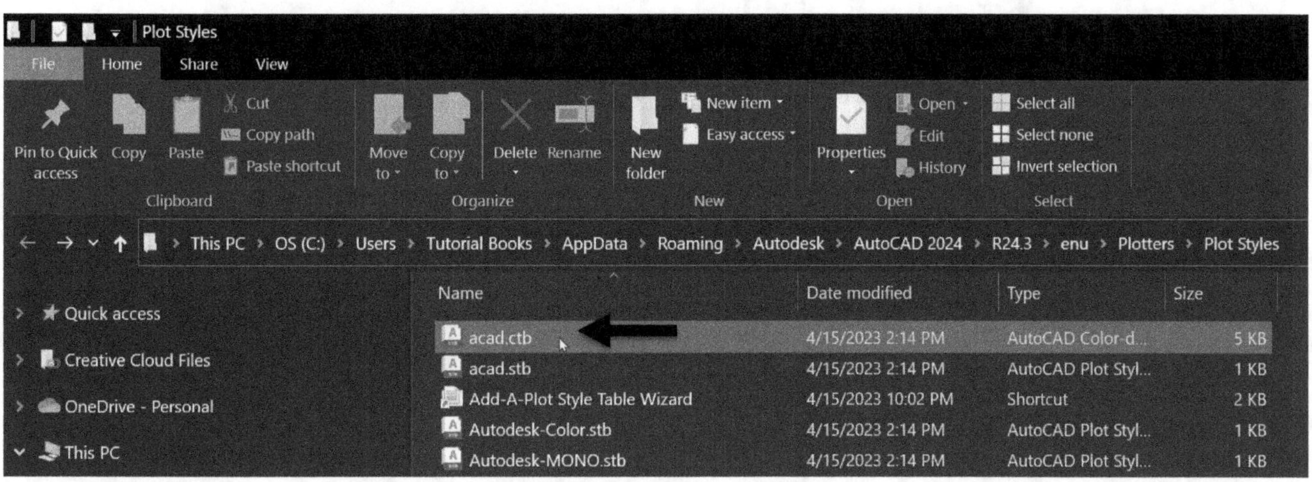

- Click the **Form View** tab on the **Plot Style Table Editor** dialog. Select **Color 1** from the **Plot Styles** list. In the **Properties** section, set the Lineweight to 0.1. Likewise, change the lineweights of the other colors, as shown.

Color	Lineweight
Color 1	0.1 mm
Color 2	0.2 mm
Color 3	0.4 mm
Color 4	0.5 mm
Color 5	0.7 mm
Color 6	1.0 mm
Color 8	0.09 mm
Color 9	0.05m

- Press and hold the Shift key and select Color 1 and Color 9. Set **Color** to **Black** in the **Properties** section. Click **Save & Close**.
- Click the **Ground Floor Plan** layout tab at the bottom of the window.
- On the ribbon, click **Output** tab > **Plot** panel > **Preview** ; the print preview of the drawing appears. Notice that the linetype scale of the dashed lines is changed. You need to change the PSLTSCALE variable value to 0 to retain the original linetype scale of the lines.
- Click **Close Preview Window** on the top right corner.
- Type PSLTSCALE and press Enter. Type 0 and press Enter.
- On the ribbon, click **Output** tab > **Plot** panel > **Plot** . On the Batch Plot dialog, click the **Continue to plot a single sheet** option.
- On the **Plot** dialog, select **Layout** from the **Plot area** section. Set the **Scale** and **Drawing orientation** to **1:1** and **Landscape**, respectively. Click **OK** to print the drawing. Likewise, print other layouts.

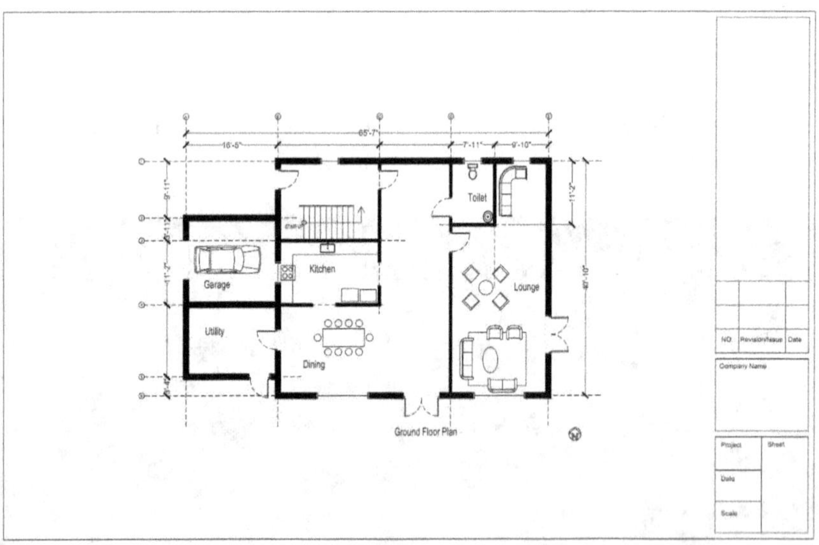

- Save and close the drawing.

Tutorial 15: Share Views

In this tutorial, you publish the drawings to a web browser. In doing so, you can view the drawings without any application installed on your device.

- Open the Tutorial 1 file.
- On the ribbon, click **View** tab > **Named Views** panel > **Restore View** drop-down > **Ground Floor**; the ground floor plan is displayed on the screen.
- Click **Application Menu > Publish > Share View.**

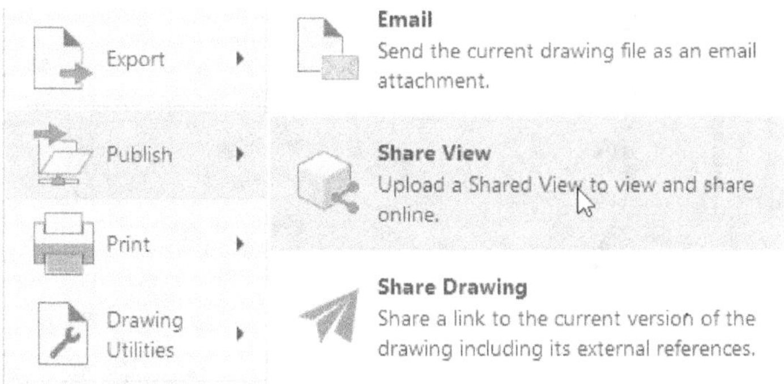

The **Autodesk Sign In** dialog appears if you have not signed in to your Autodesk Account.

- Enter your Autodesk ID and password, and then click **Sign in**; the **Share View** dialog appears.
- Enter Tutorial1 in the **Name** box.
- Select the **Share current view only** option from the **View to share** section.
- Click **Share** and **Proceed** to share the views online.
- To view the shared drawing, click the **View in Browser line** displayed at the bottom right corner of the application window; the drawing view opens in the internet browser.

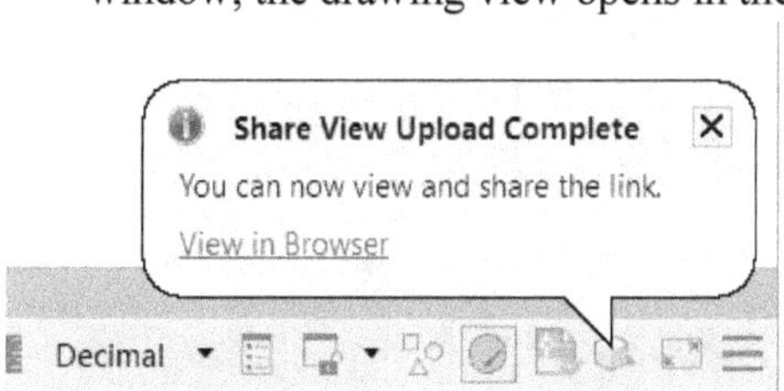

- To add comments to the shared views, click **Collaborate > Share > Shared Views** on the ribbon.
- On the **Shared Views** palette, click the **Refresh** icon to display the shared views.
- Select the shared view from the palette and click **Add Comment.**

Tutorial 16: Compare Drawings

In this tutorial, you use the **DWG Compare** command to compare two revisions of a drawing or two different drawings.

- Download the DWG_compare drawing file from the companion website.
- Open the DWG_compare drawing.

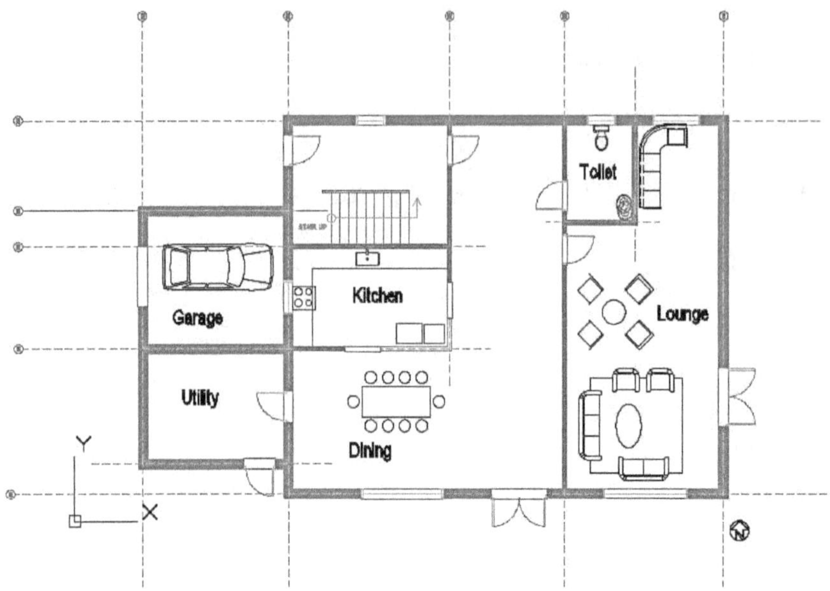

- Create two objects on the drawing at the locations, as shown.

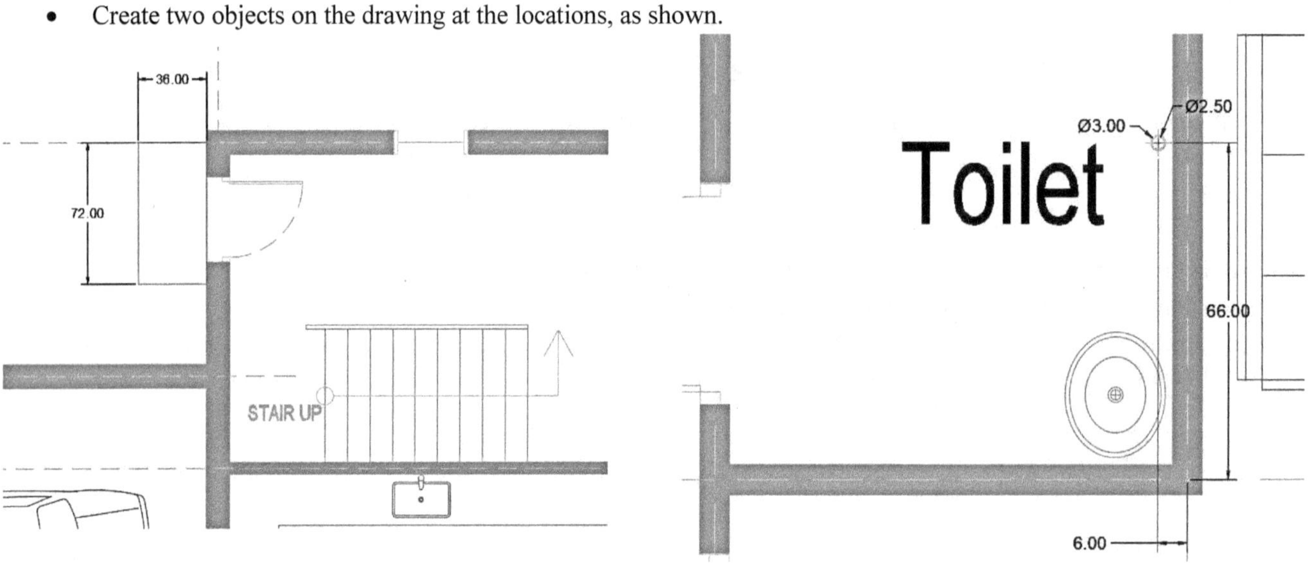

- On the **Quick Access Toolbar**, click **Save As**. Next, specify the location of the drawing file, type DWG_compare2 in the **File name** box, and then click **Save**.
- Next, close the **DWG_compare2.dwg** file.
- Open the **DWG_compare.dwg** file.
- On the ribbon, click the **Collaborate > Compare > DWG Compare**. The **Select drawing to compare** dialog pops up on the screen.
- Browse to the location of the **DWG_compare2** file and double click on it.
- Click **Close** on the message box; a revision cloud highlights the differences between the two drawings.

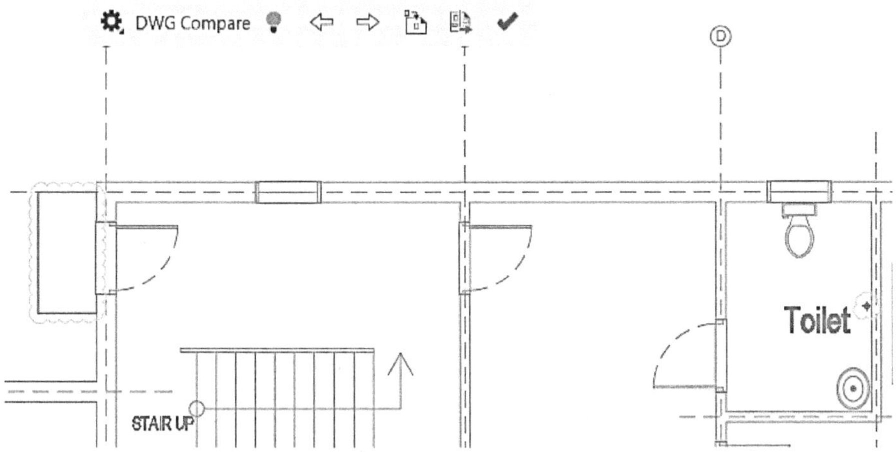

You can click the **On or off** icon to turn **ON** or **OFF** the comparisons.

Use the **Next** and **Previous** icons to zoom to different results.

On the **DWG Compare** toolbar, click the **Settings** drop-down to specify the color settings, revision cloud settings, and objects to be filtered.

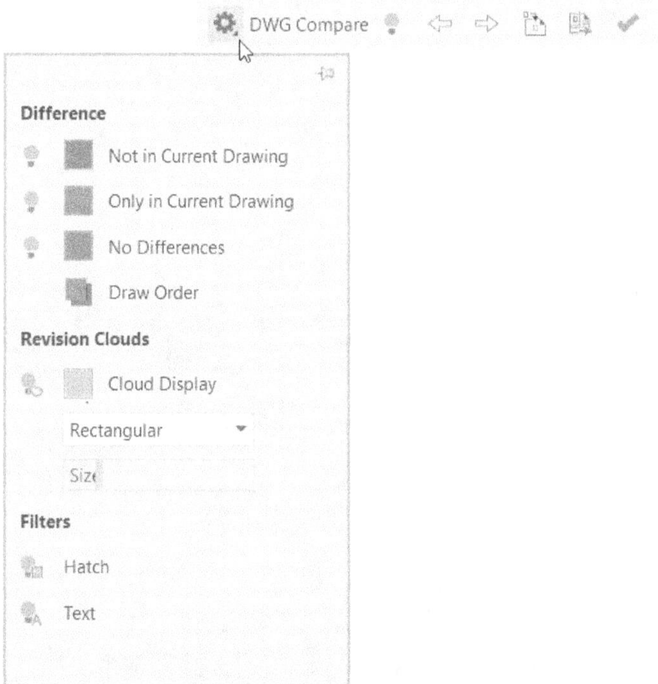

- Select the **Polygonal** option from the drop-down in the **Revision Clouds** section.
- Click and drag the **Margin** dragger to change the margin between the revision cloud and highlighted objects.

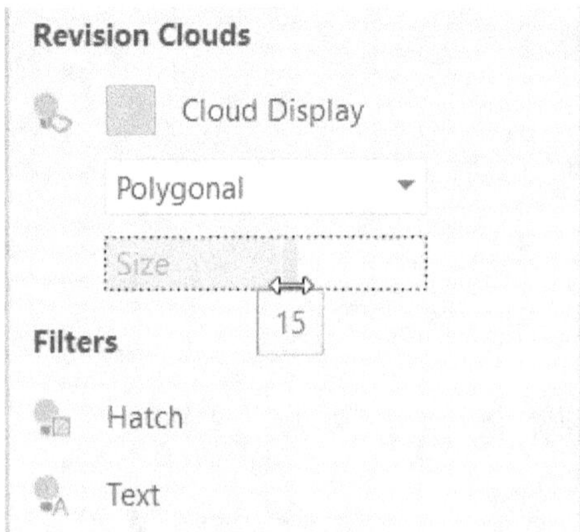

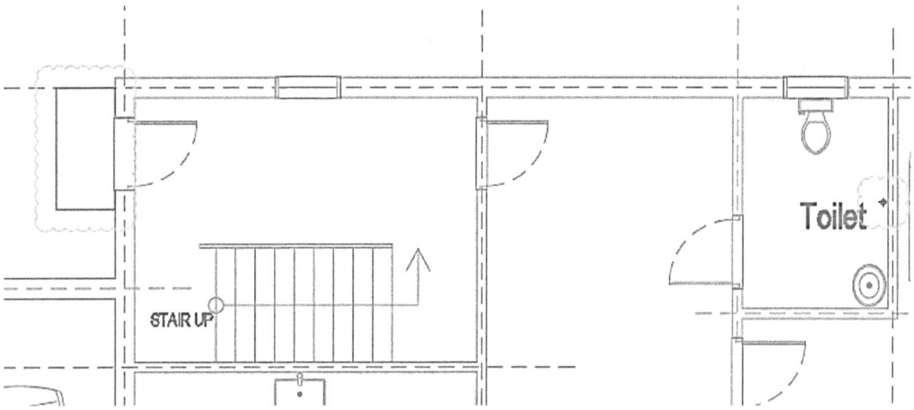

- Click the **Import Objects** icon on the **DWG Compare** toolbar.

- Select the objects highlighted in red color.

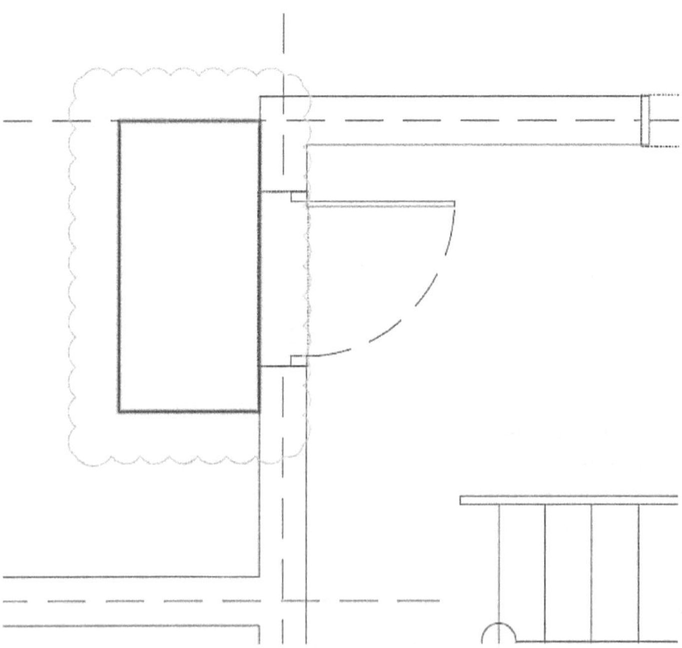

- Press **Enter**; the selected objects are imported into the current drawing.
- Click the **Exit Compare** icon on the **DWG Compare** toolbar.
- Close the **DWG_compare** file without saving.

Part 2: Creating 3D Architectural Model

In this chapter, you learn to do the following:

- **Work with Visual Styles**
- **Create Doors and Window openings**
- **Create the Ceiling**
- **Create Doors and Windows**
- **Create Stairs**
- **Create Balcony**
- **Create Railing**
- **Create Roof**
- **Create Terrain surface**

Tutorial 1: Importing 2D Drawings

- Download the **2D-Drawings.dwg** file from the companion website.
- Start a new drawing file using the **acad** template.
- On the ribbon, click **Insert** tab > **Block** panel > **Insert drop-down** > **Blocks from Libraries**.

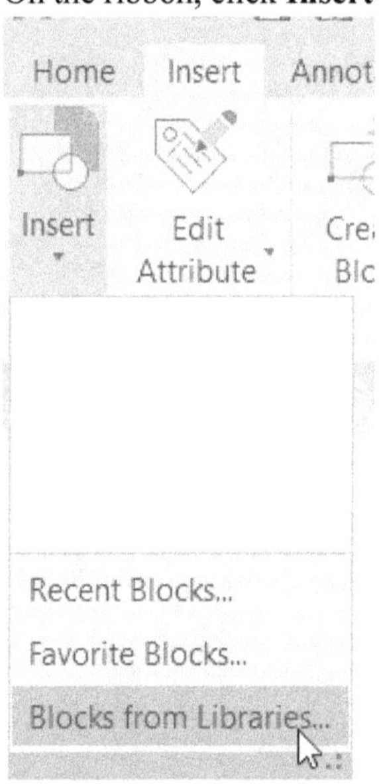

- On the **BLOCKS** palette, click the **Libraries** button. Go to the location of the **2D-Drawings.dwg**, select it, and then click **Open**.
- On the **BLOCKS** palette, right-click on 2D-Drawings file, and then select **Insert and Explode**.
- Type **0,0** and press **Enter**. Next, type **0** and press ENTER.
- Close the **BLOCKS** palette.
- Type **Z** and press **Enter**. Type **A** and press **Enter**. The entire drawing is visible in the graphics window.

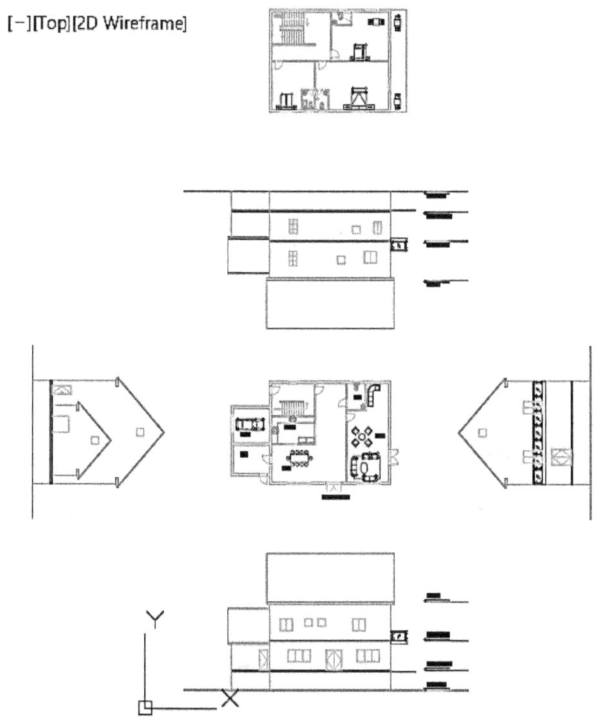

After inserting the 2D drawings into the graphics window, you need to remove the entities of the drawing that are not used to create the 3D model. For example, the texts and annotations are not used to create the 3D model. You can delete the unwanted entities by deleting the entire layer associated with it. However, AutoCAD will not allow you to delete a layer, which has objects on it. There is a unique tool to delete all the objects on a layer and then purge the layer.

- On the **Home** tab of the ribbon, expand the **Layer** panel, and select the **Delete** tool. Select the text and the stair callout, and then press **Enter**. Select **Yes** from the command line.

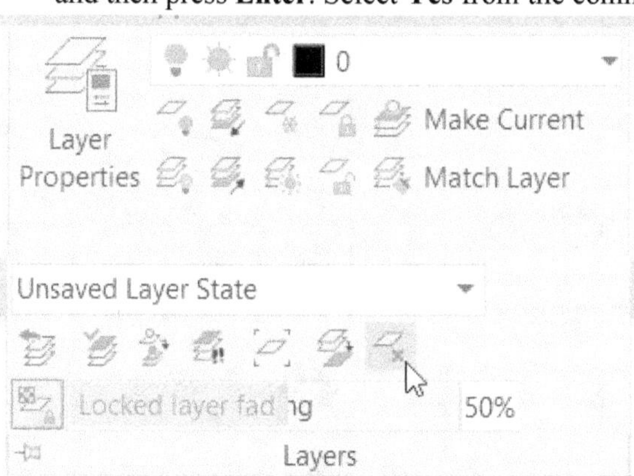

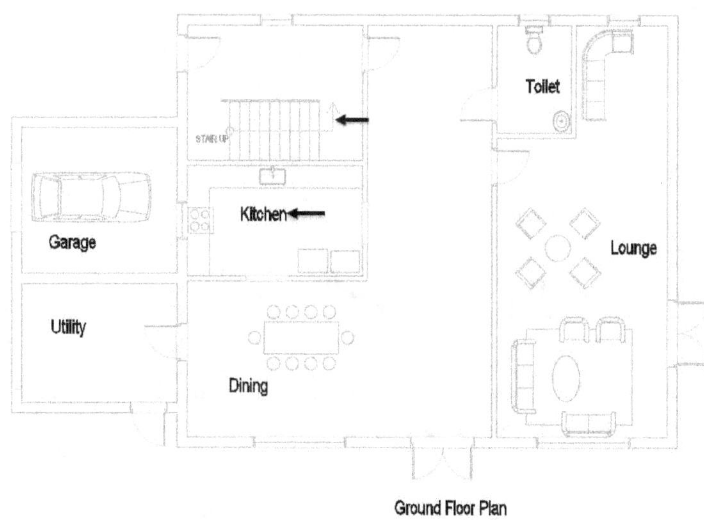

- Type **WIPEOUT** and press Enter. Select **Frames** from the command line. Select **OFF** to turn off the wipeout frames of the drawing.
- On the ribbon, click **Home** tab > **Layers** panel > **Off** . Select the car block, kitchen fixtures, and bathroom fixtures. Press **Esc**.

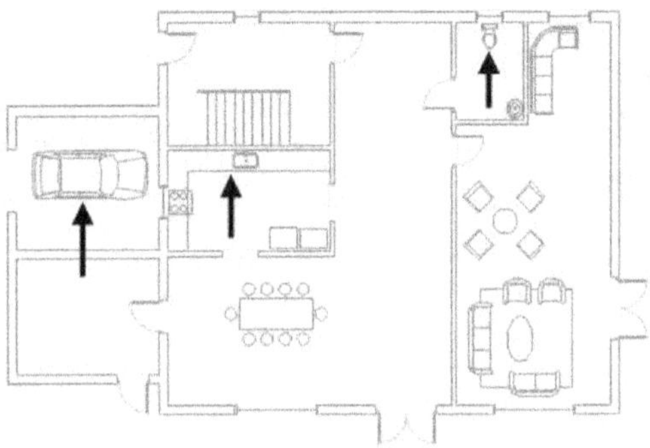

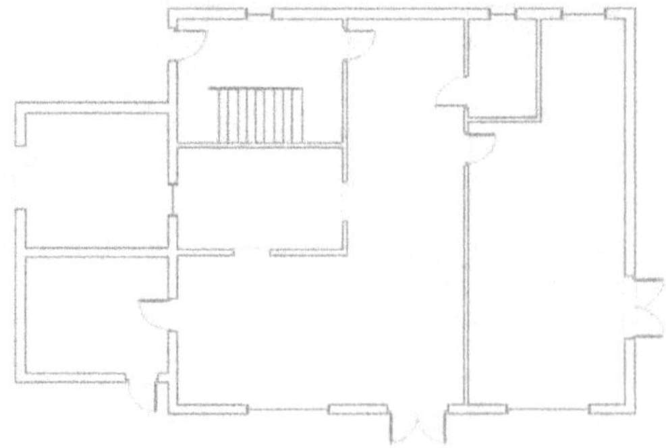

Tutorial 2: Creating 3D Walls

- Create a new layer with the name **3D-Walls** and set its color to Index color **8**. Activate the new layer.
- On the status bar, activate the **Object Snap** icon and click the down-arrow next to it. Make sure that the **Endpoint** option is checked.
- On the ribbon, click **Home** tab > **Draw** panel > **Polyline**. Create a closed polyline by selecting the corner points of the ground floor plan, as shown.

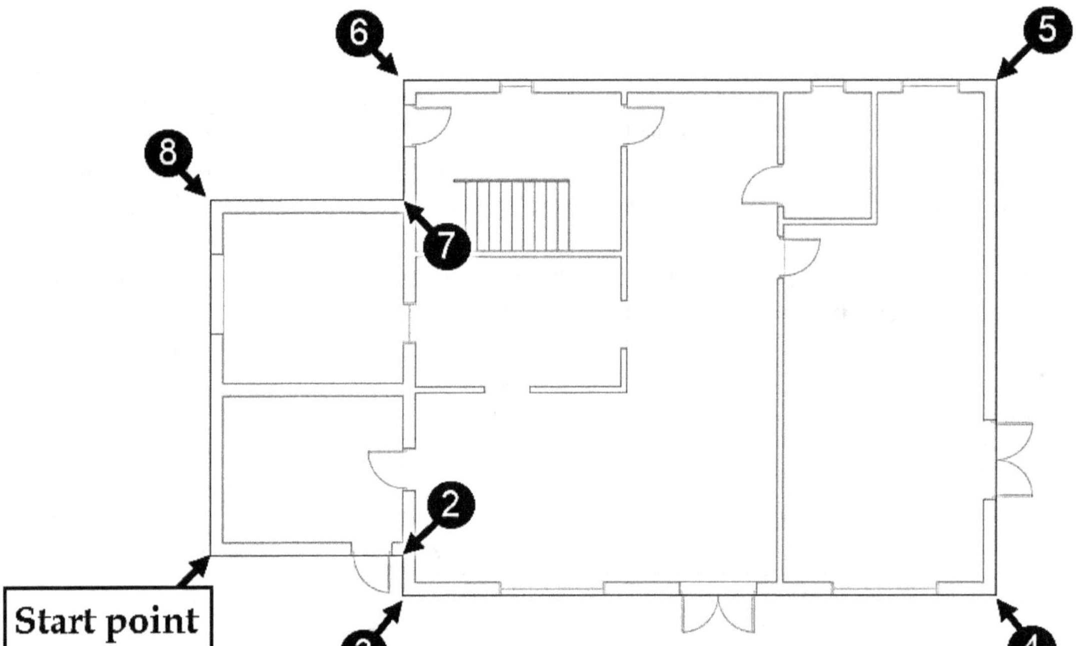

- Activate the **Rectangle** tool and create rectangles by selecting the corners, as shown. Activate the **Polyline** tool and create the other loops, as shown.

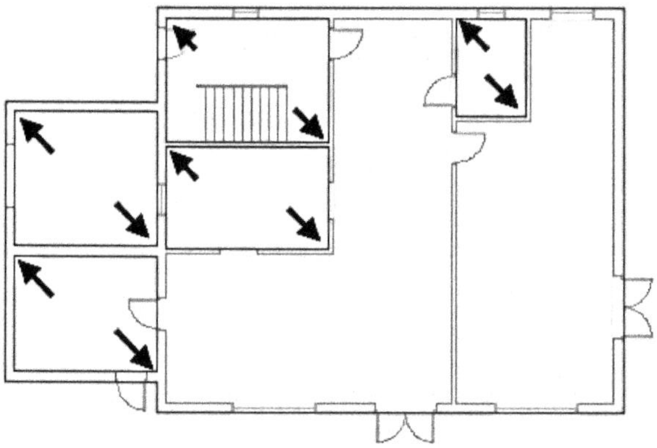

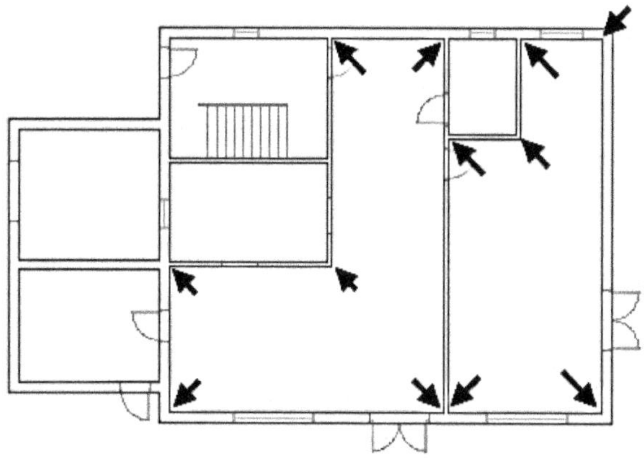

- Change the Workspace to **3D Modeling** by using the **Workspace** drop-down on the **Quick Access Toolbar** or the **Workspace Switching** menu on the status bar.

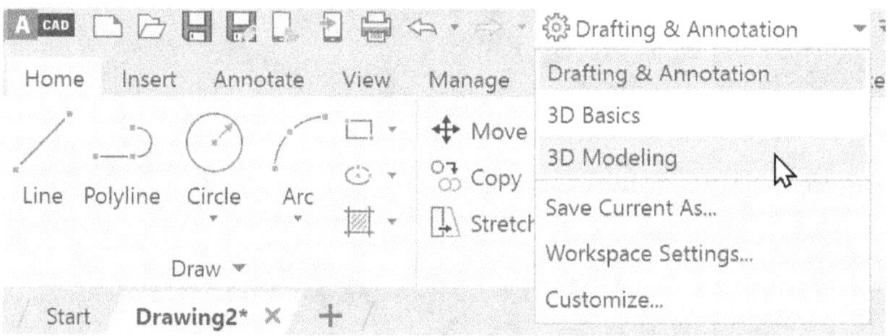

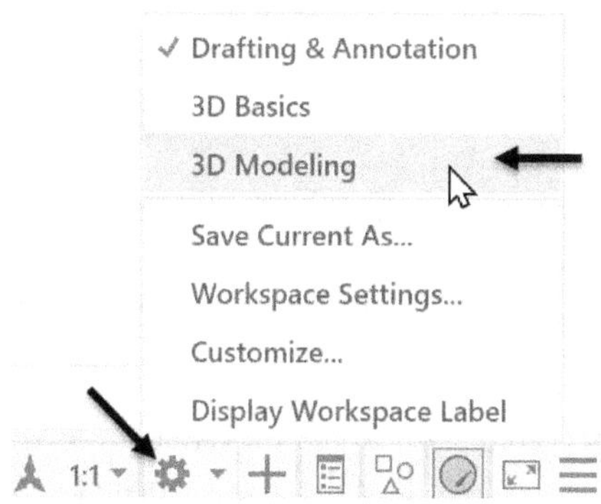

- On the ribbon, click **Home** tab > **Groups** panel > **Group**  . Create a selection window covering all the entities of the South elevation. Press **Enter** to group the selected entities. Likewise, create groups of the other elevations.

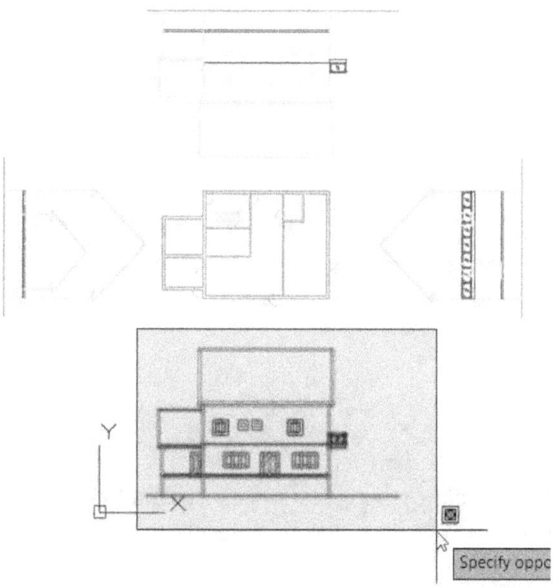

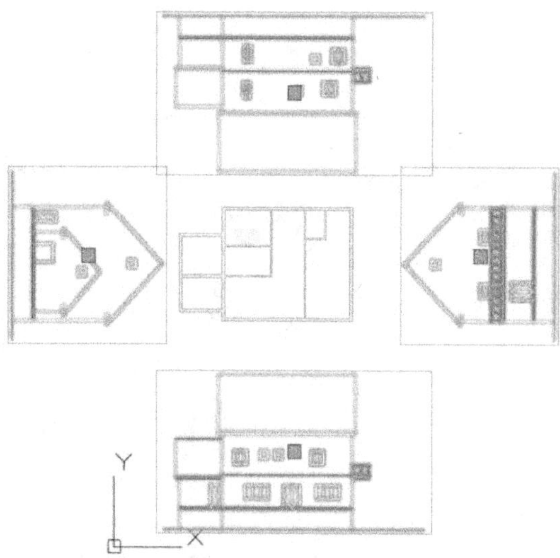

Now, you need to change the orientation of the drawing using the **ViewCube** located at the top right corner of the graphics window.

- On the **ViewCube**, click the lower right corner. The orientation of the drawing changes along with the ViewCube.

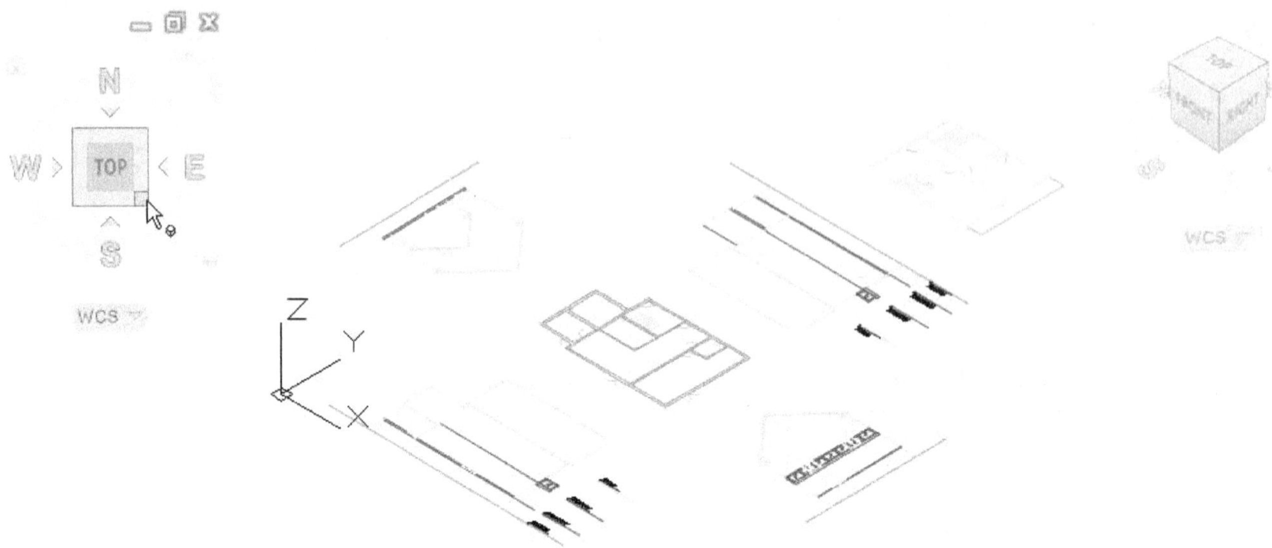

Now, you need to rotate the elevation views by **90 degrees** using the **Rotate Gizmo**.

- Make sure that the **ORTHOMODE** is turned **ON**.

- Select the South Elevation group from the drawing. On the ribbon, click **Home** tab >**Modify** panel > **3D Rotate** . The Rotate Gizmo appears on the selected group.
- Select the endpoint of the ground level line, as shown; the base point of the rotation is defined.

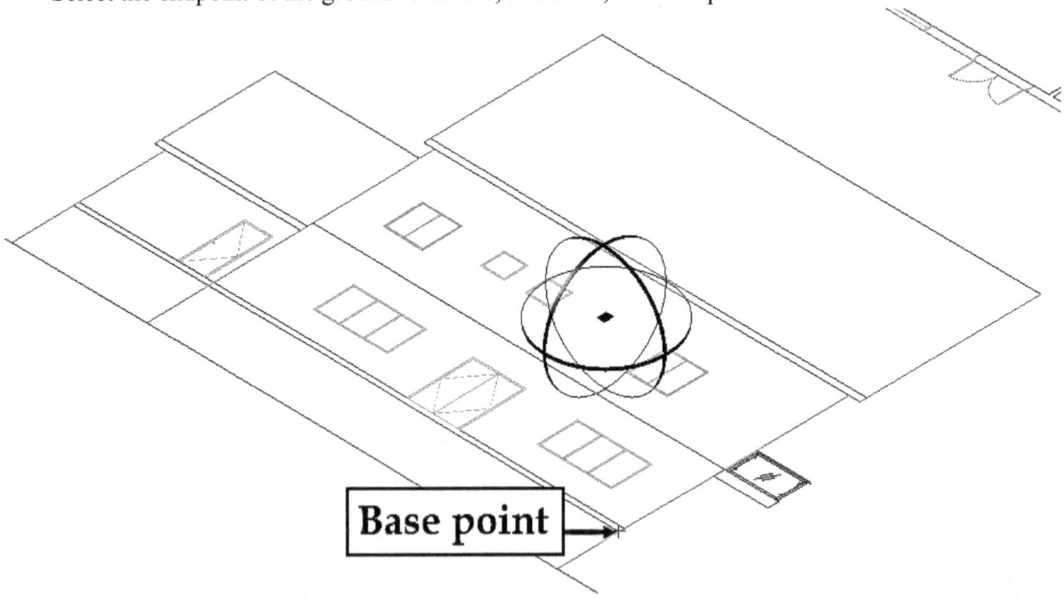

- Click on the red ring of the Rotate Gizmo to define the rotation axis. Move the pointer toward the right and click to define the start point rotation angle. Move the pointer upward and click to rotate the elevation view by 90 degrees.

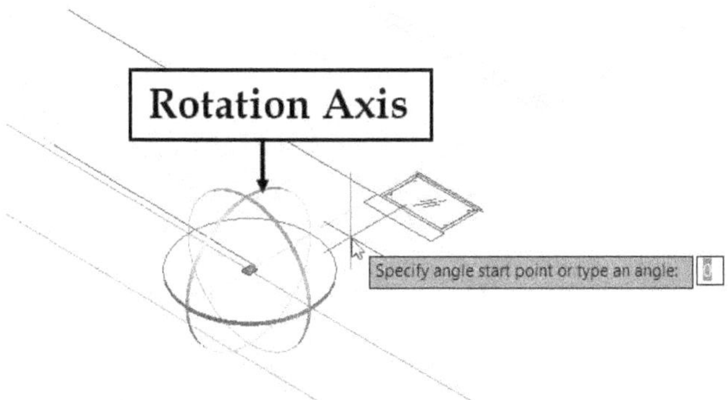

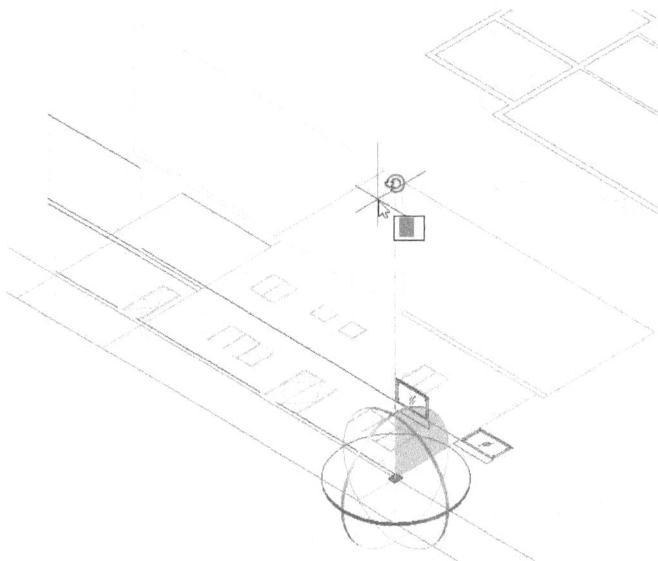

- Click the **Front** face of the ViewCube. The elevation view becomes parallel to the screen. Notice that the ground level coincides with the **X-axis** of the UCS. Click the top right corner of the ViewCube to switch back to the previous orientation.

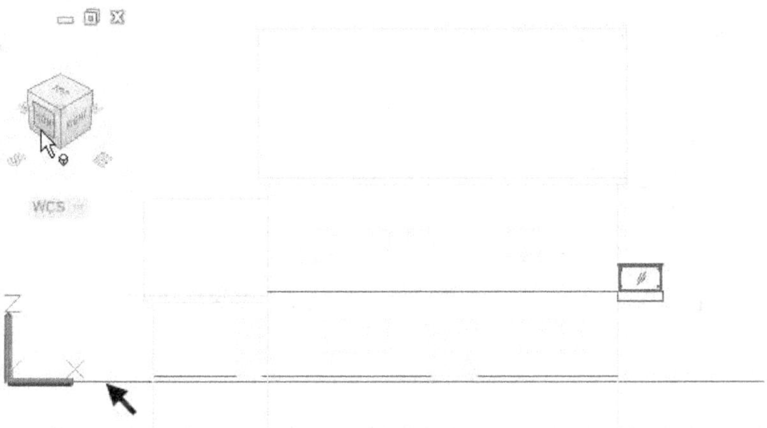

- Rotate the other elevations about the ground level lines.
  Front Elevation

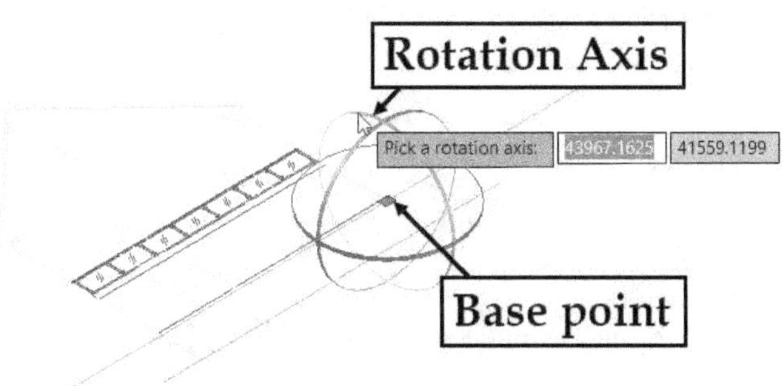

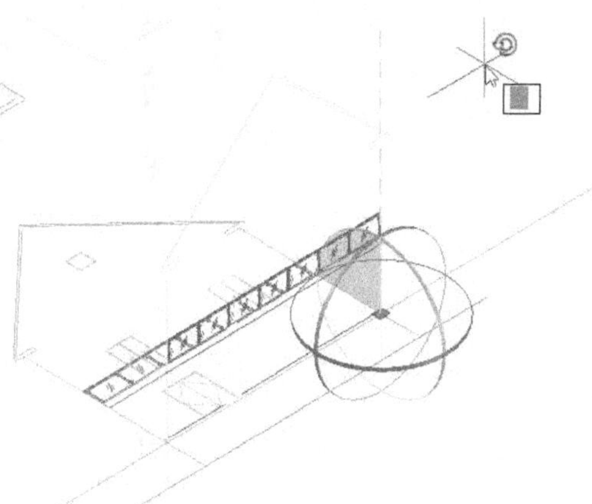

Rear Elevation

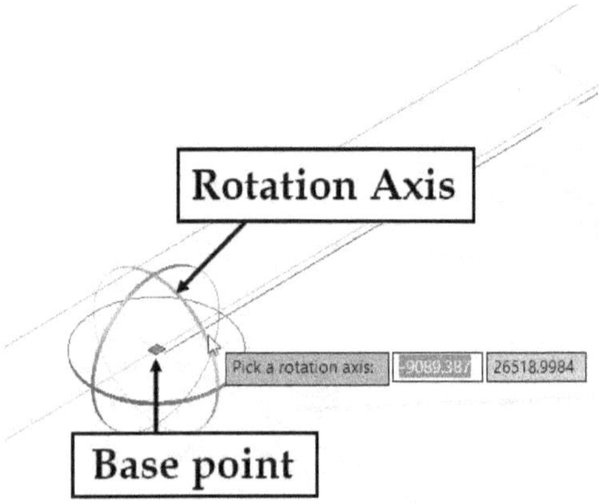

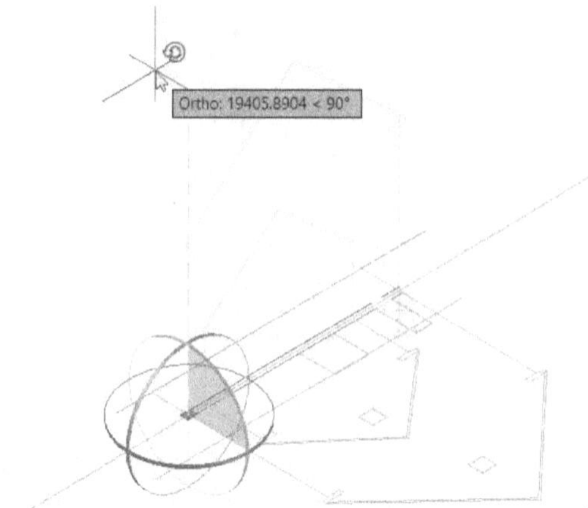

North Elevation

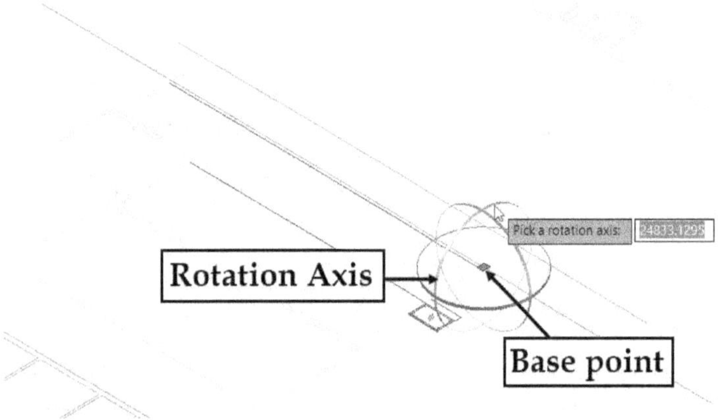

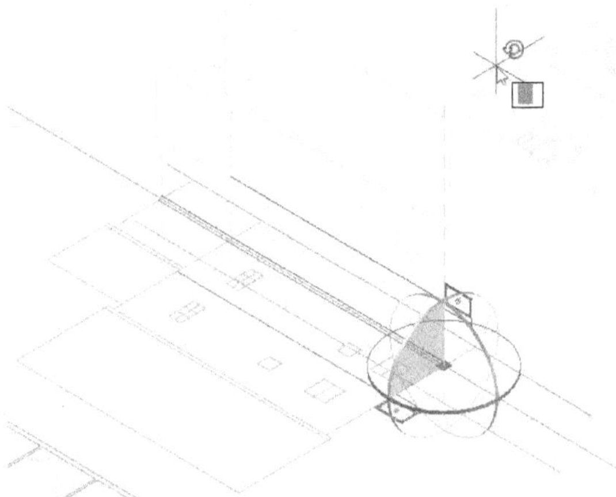

- Open the **Layers Properties Manager** and turn off the A-WALL, A-WINDOWS, A-DOORS, A-SLAB, WIPEOUT, and DOOR_SWING layers.

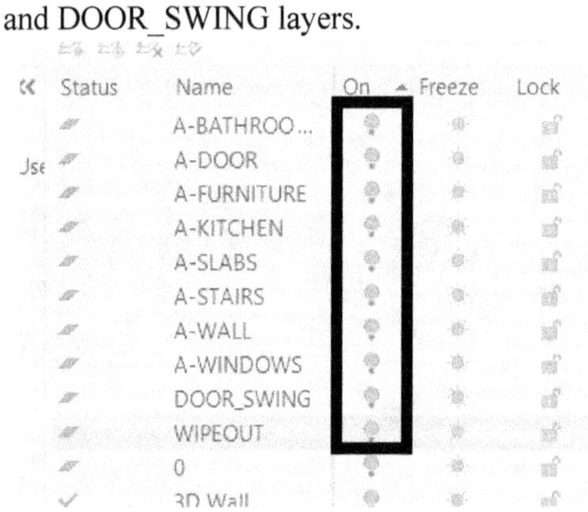

- In the top left corner of the graphics window, click **Wireframe** and select **Shades of Gray** from the Menu.
- On the ribbon, click **Home** tab > **Modeling** panel > **Presspull** .

- Zoom to the ground floor plan and click in the area enclosed by the polyline. Zoom-out of the floor plane and select a point on the first floor level on the South elevation. The 3D walls are created up to the first-floor level.

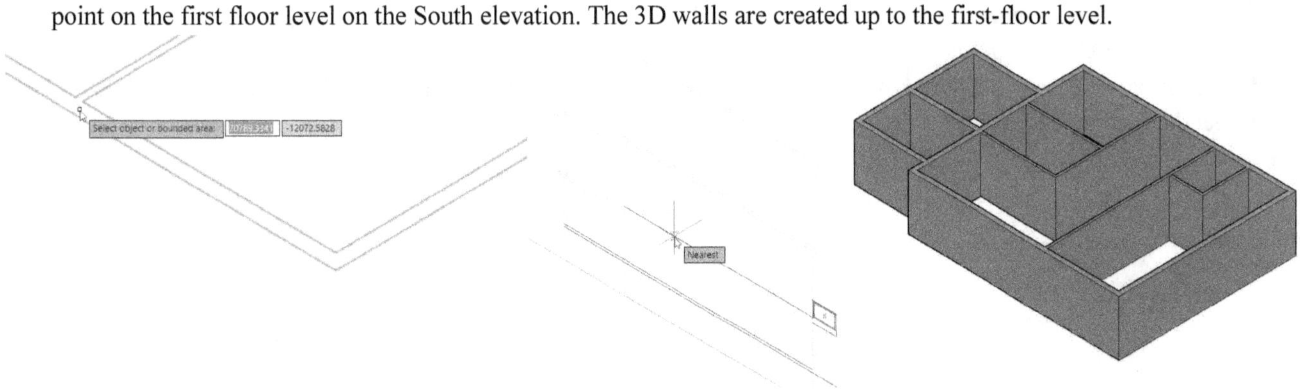

- On the ribbon, click **Home** tab > **Layers** panel > **Layer Properties Manager**. On the Layer Properties Manager, turn **ON** the light bulb icons of A-WINDOWS, A-WALL, A-DOORS, and DOOR_SWING layers.
- On the ribbon, click **Home** tab > **View** panel > **View Styles** drop-down > **Wireframe**.

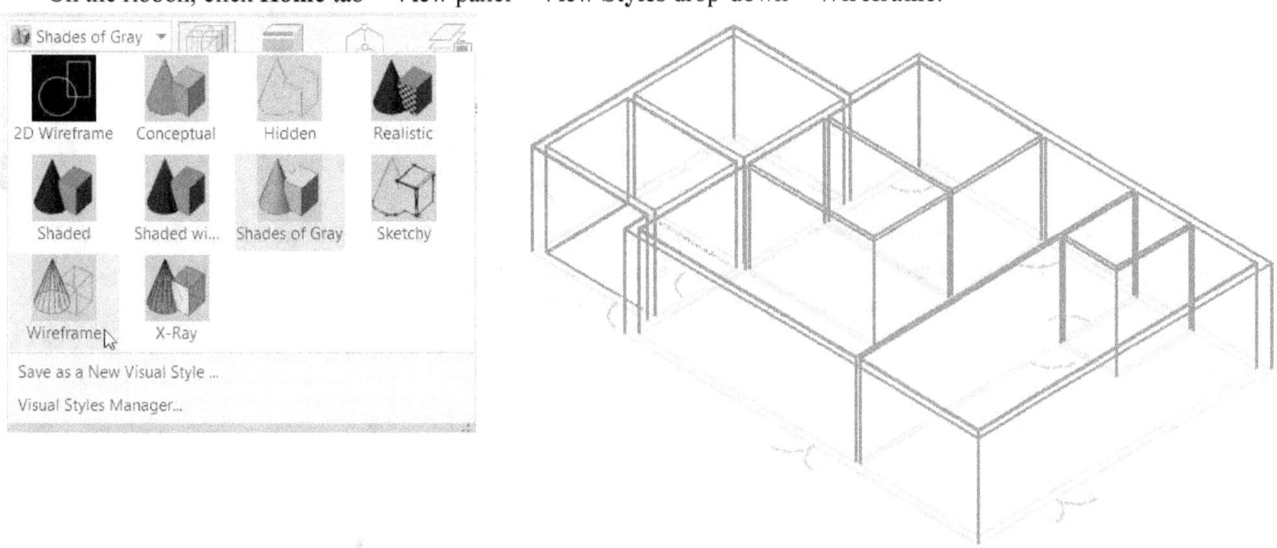

- Deactivate the **Dynamic UCS** icon on the status bar. Click the down-arrow next to the **Object Snap** icon and make sure that the **Apparent Intersection** option is checked.

- On the ribbon, click **Home** tab > **Modeling** panel > **Primitive** drop-down > **Box**. Specify the first and second corners of the box, as shown. Zoom to the South elevation (using the mouse wheel) and select the corner point of the double-door, as shown. The box is created.

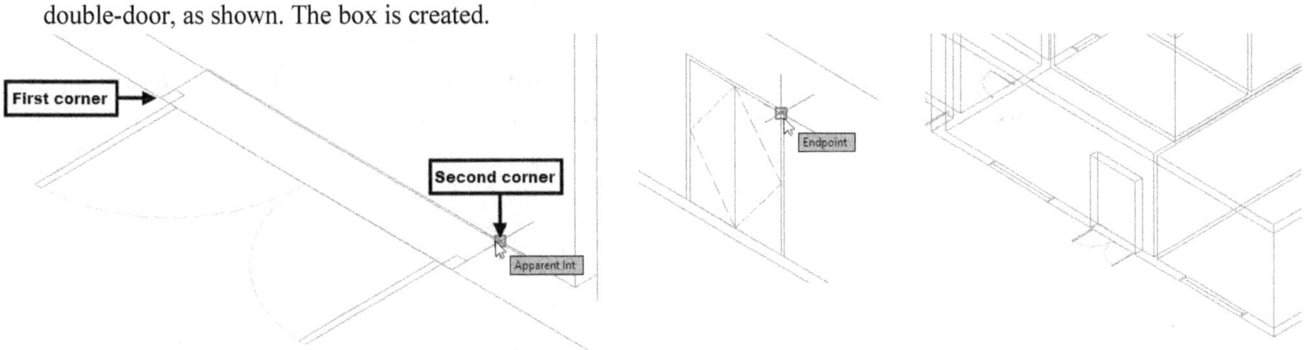

Now, you use the **3D Align** tool to copy the box and place it on the other double-door location.

- On the ribbon, click **Home** tab > **Modify** panel > **3D Align**. Select the box from the graphics window and press Enter — select **Copy** from the command line.
- Select the base, second, and third points on the box, as shown. Zoom to the other double-door location on the floor plan. Select the first, second, and third destination points, as shown.

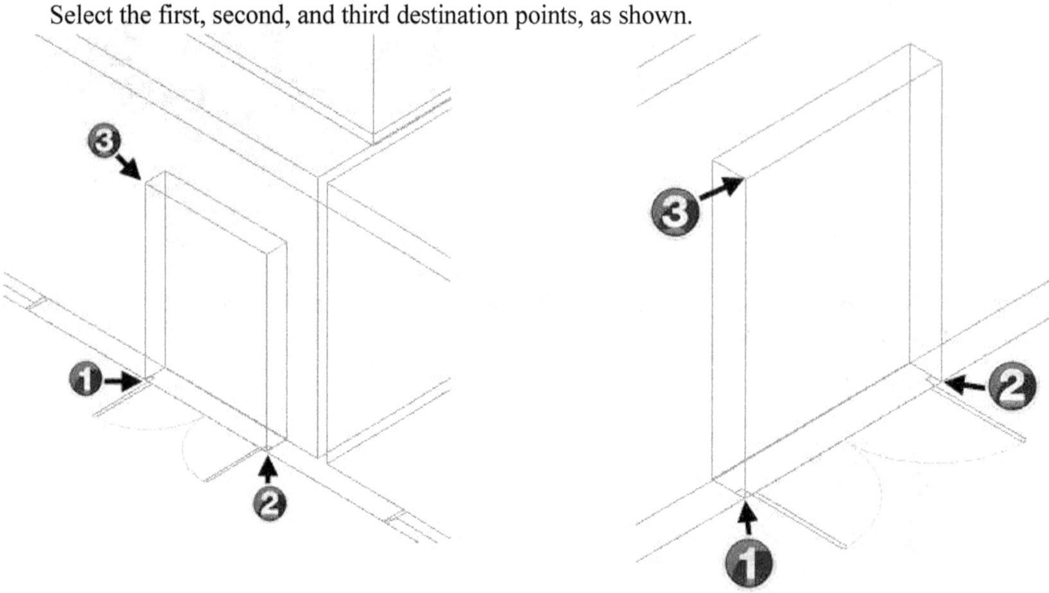

- On the Navigation Bar, click **Zoom** drop-down > **Zoom Window**. Specify the first and second corners of the Zoom window, as shown. Type **BOX** and press Enter. Select the first and second corners of the box. Zoom to the South elevation and select the top right corner of the single door, as shown.

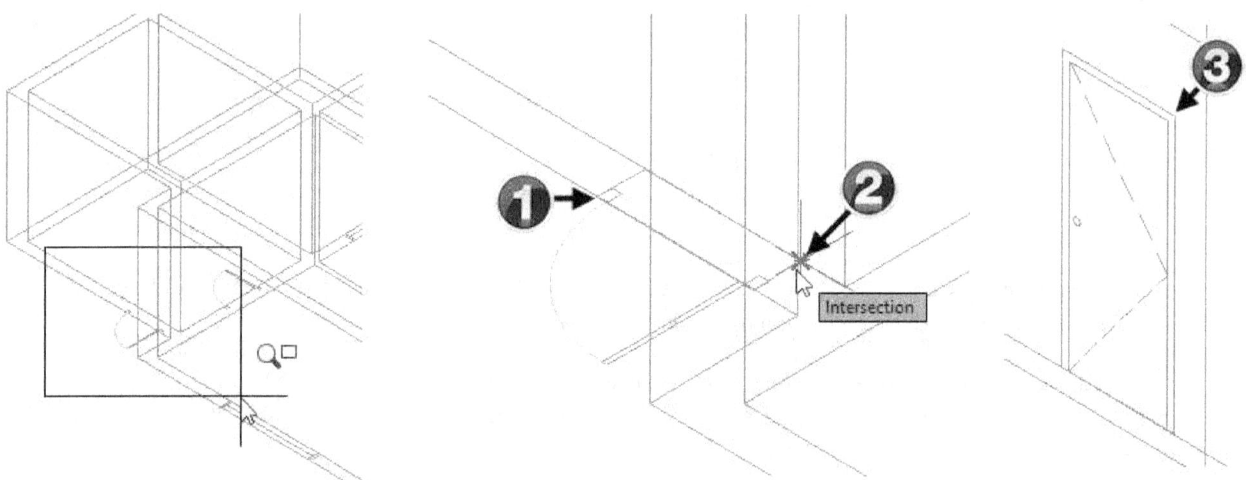

- Zoom to the utility room by using the **Zoom Window** tool. Activate the **Box** tool and specify the first and second corners of the box. Move the pointer upward and select the top right corner of the box created in the last step.

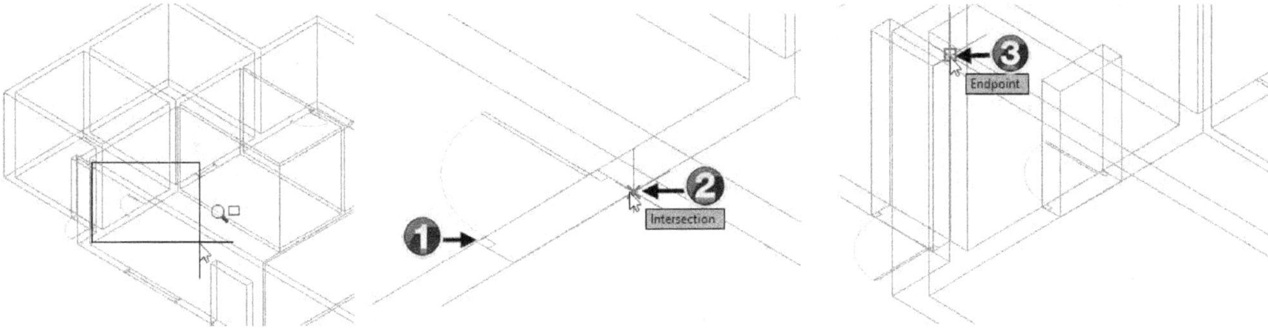

- Likewise, create other boxes at the other single door locations, as shown.

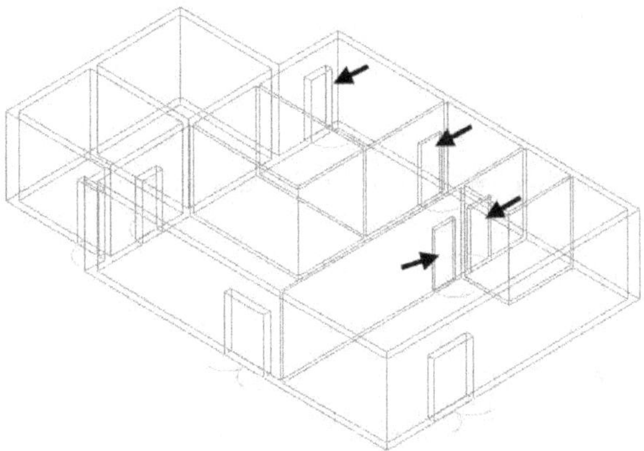

- Create two boxes at the kitchen openings.

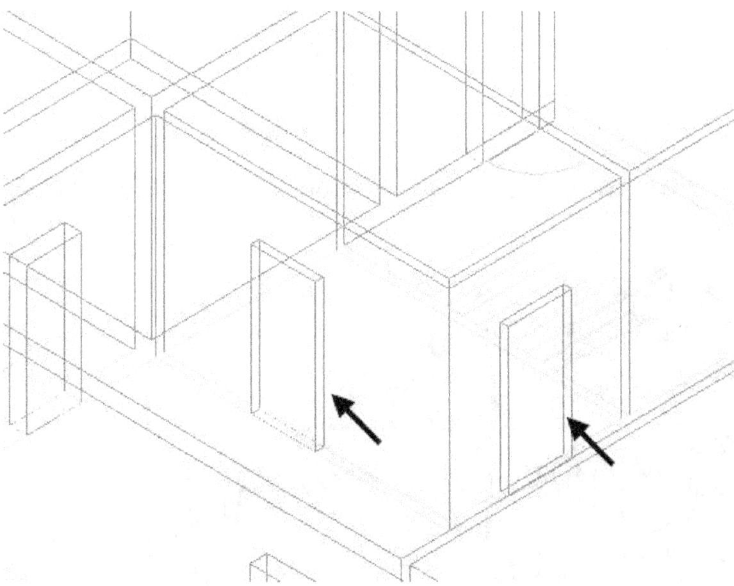

- Zoom to the garage area and create a box on the garage opening. Use the garage opening on the Rear elevation to define the box height.

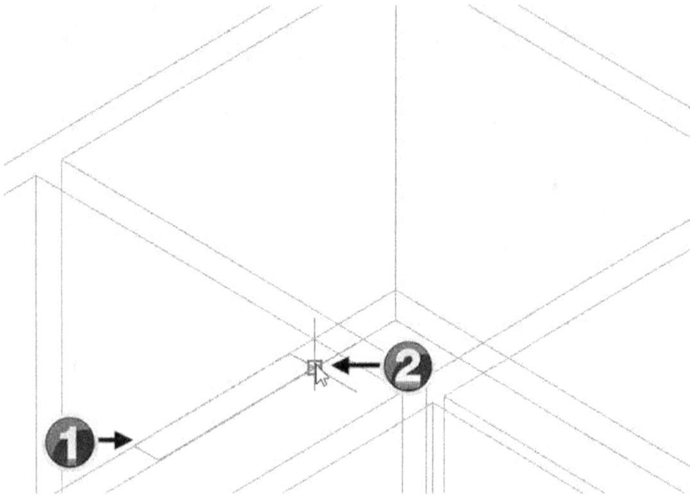

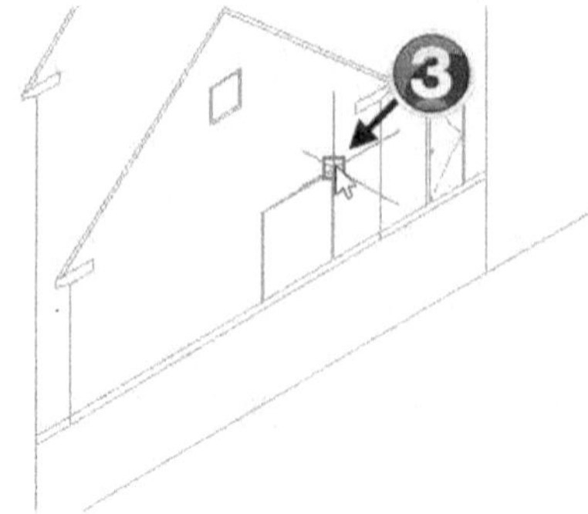

- On the ribbon, click **Home** tab > **Solid Editing** panel > **Solid, Subtract** . Select the 3D walls and press Enter. Select all the boxes created at the doors and opening locations. Press Enter to subtract the boxes from the walls.

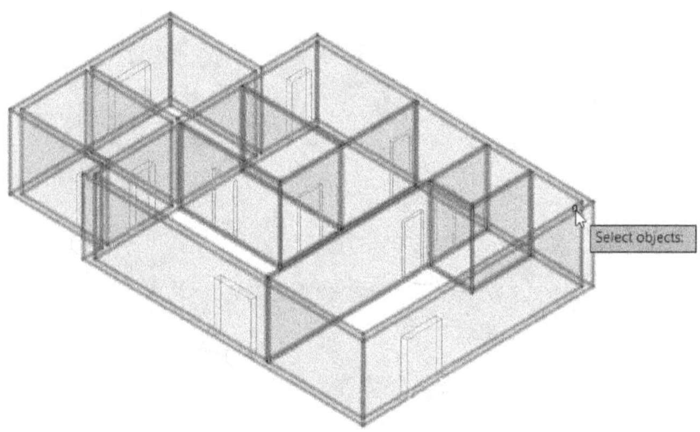

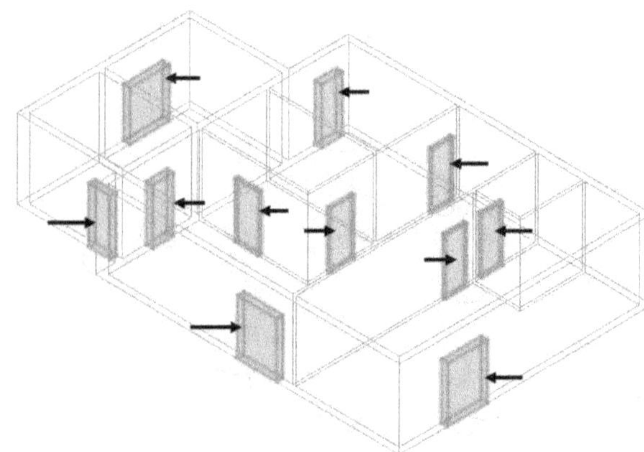

- In the top left corner of the graphics window, click **Wireframe** from the In-canvas tools, and select **Shades of Gray** from the menu.

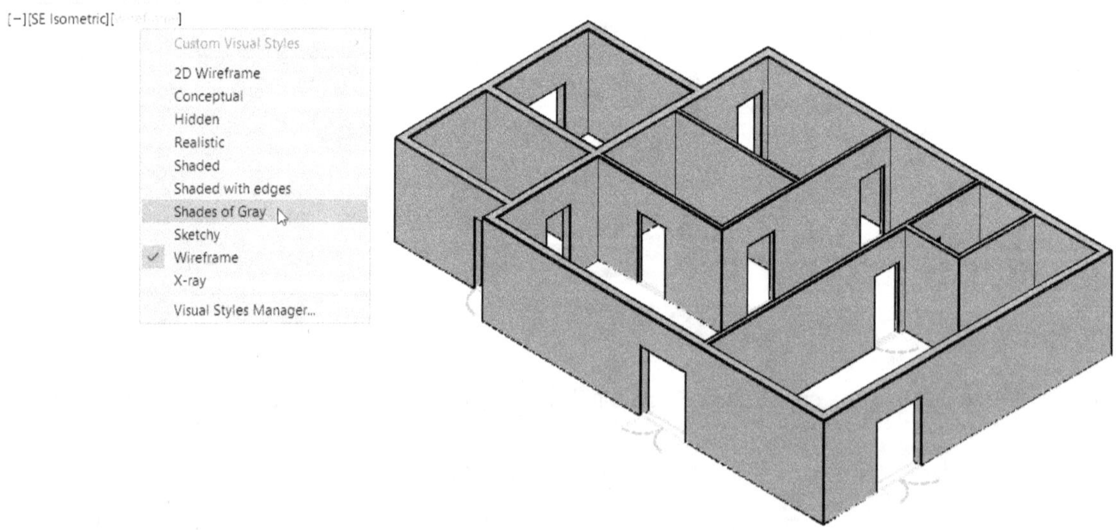

- On the ribbon, click **Home** tab > **Modeling** panel >**Presspull** . Zoom to the right side window on the South elevation. Select the outer rectangle of the window. Move the pointer toward the walls and select the corner point, as shown.

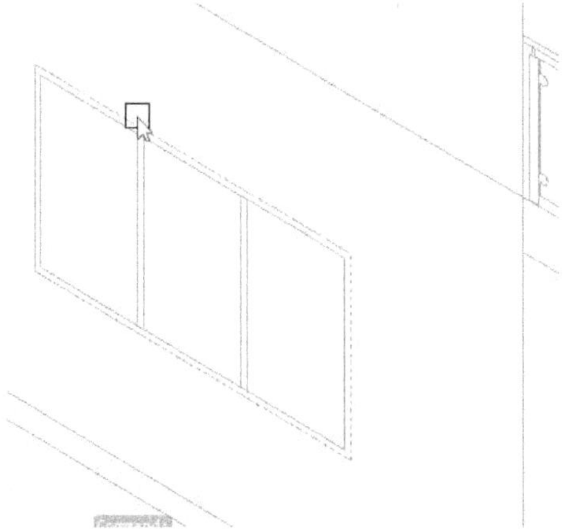

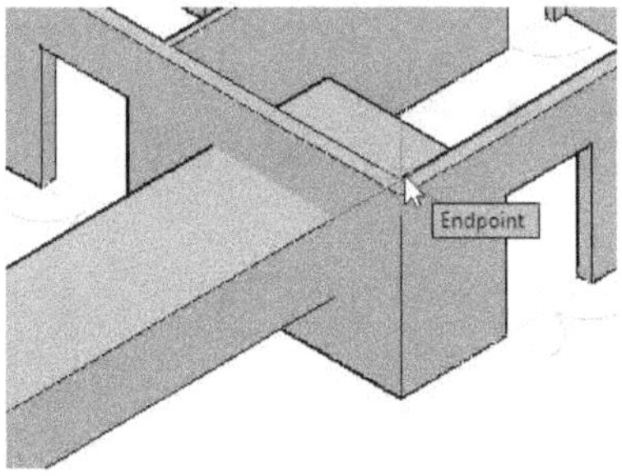

- Zoom to the left side window of the South elevation and select the outer rectangle. Move the pointer towards the walls and select the corner point, as shown.

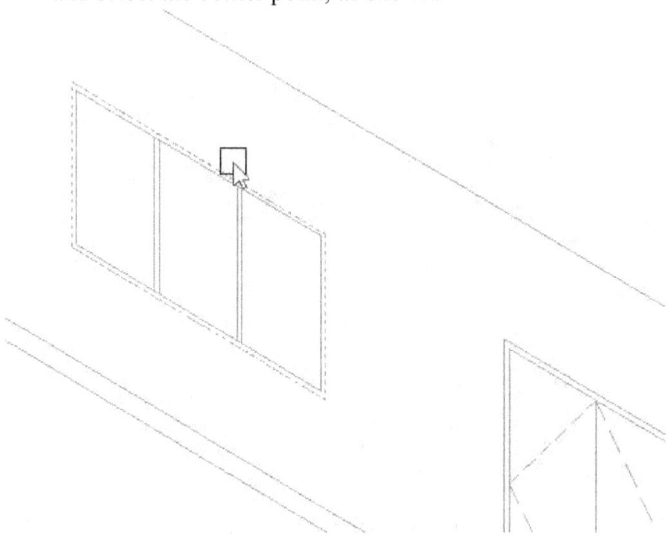

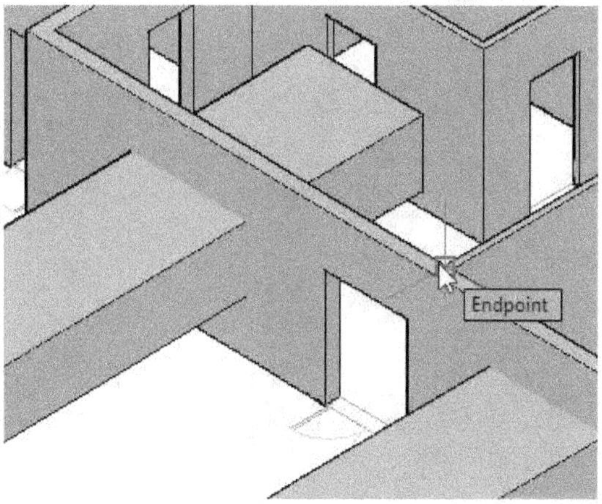

- Zoom to the middle window of the North elevation and select the outer rectangle, as shown. Move the pointer toward the walls and select the corner point, as shown.

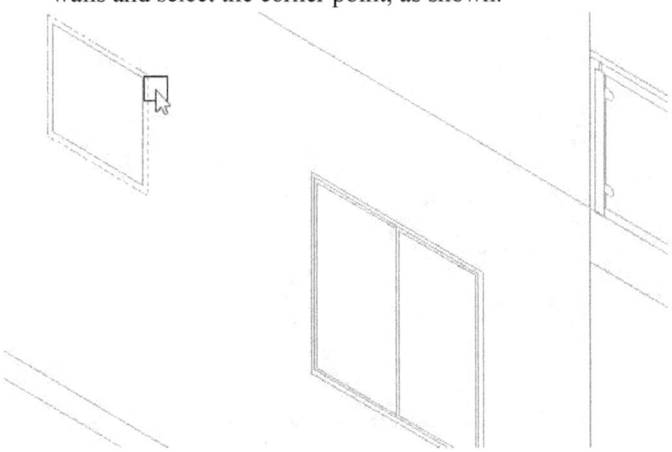

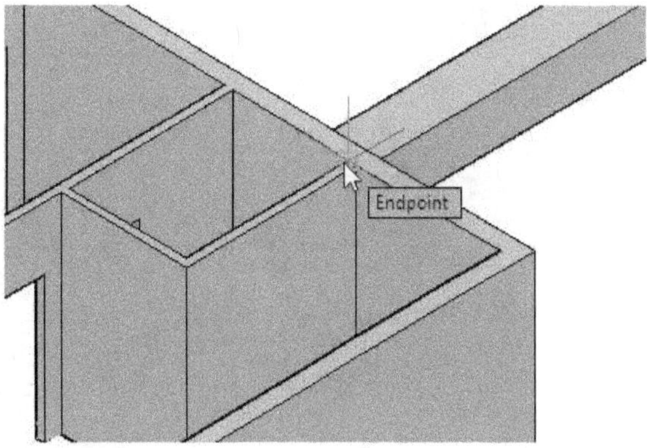

- On the ribbon, click **Home** tab > **Coordinates** panel > **UCS** . Zoom to the extreme right window of North elevation, and select the top left corner of the window. Make sure that the ORTHOMODE(F8) is active. Move the pointer downward and select the lower-left corner of the window. Move the pointer toward the right and select the top right corner of the window. The UCS is positioned, as shown.

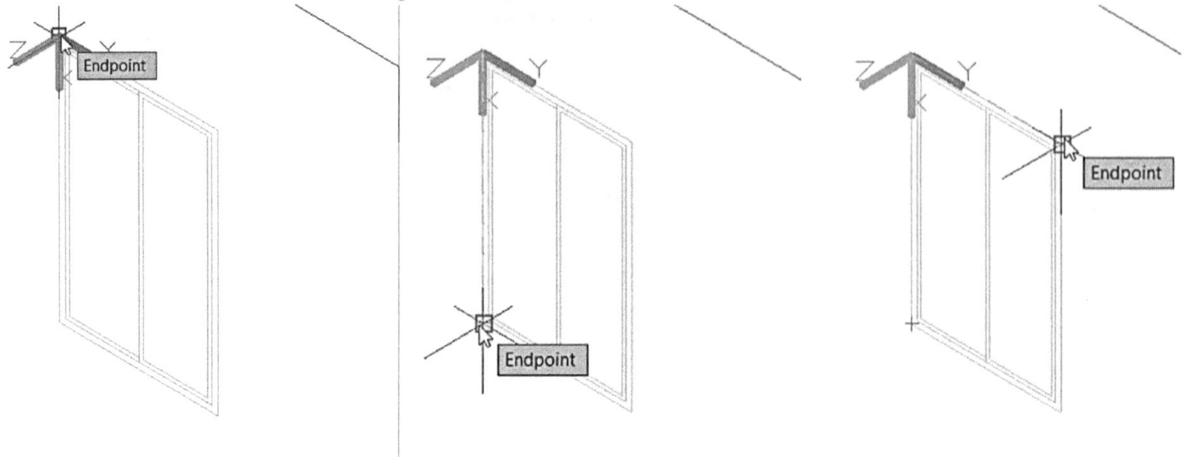

- Create a box by specifying the first, second, and third corners, as shown.

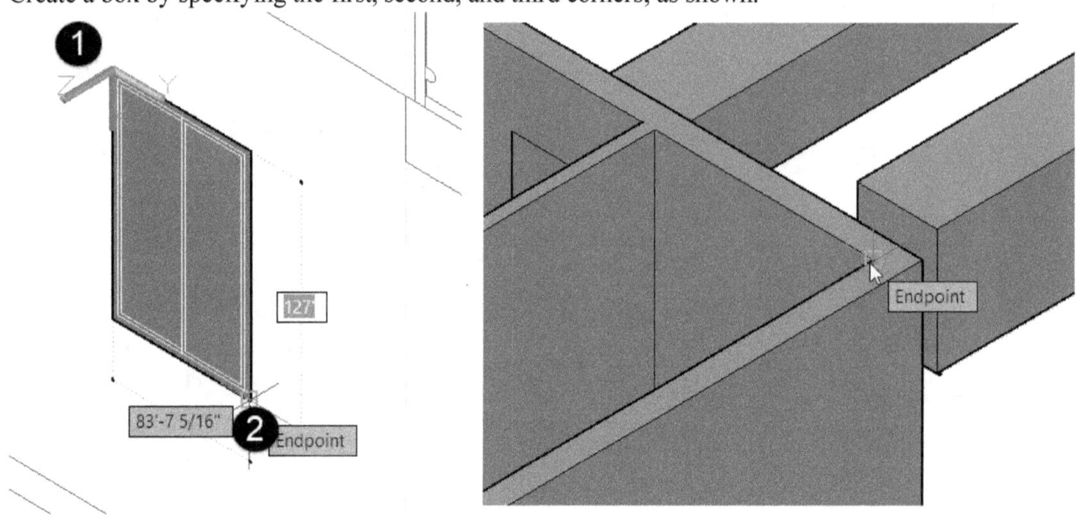

- Zoom to the left side window of the North elevation. Next, create a box by specifying the first, second, and third corners, as shown.

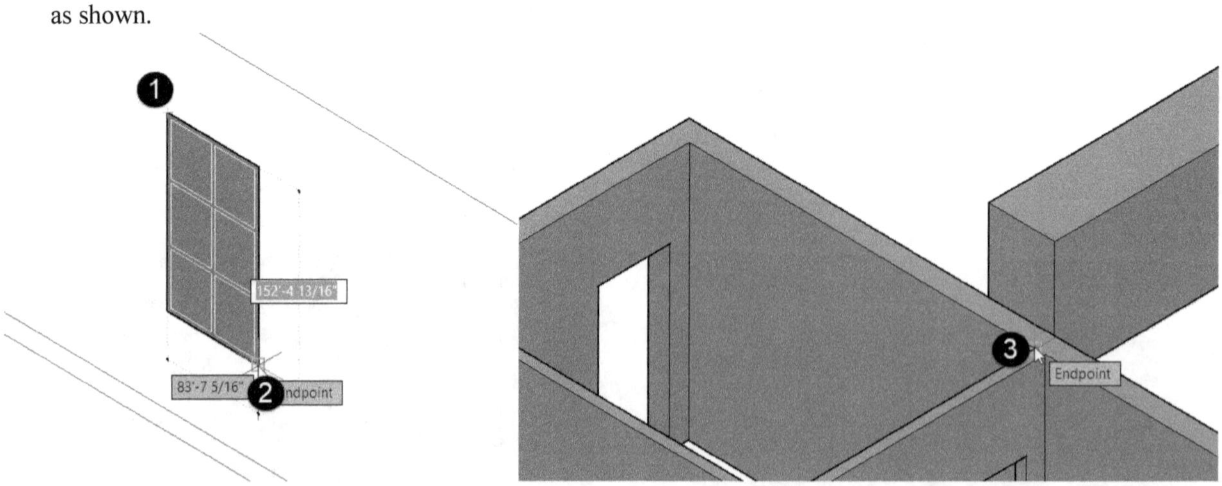

- On the ribbon, click **Home** tab > **Coordinates** panel > **UCS, World** . The UCS is brought to its default position and orientation.

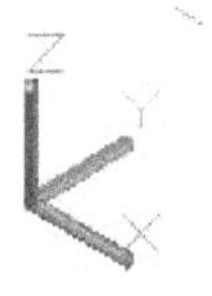

- On the ribbon, click **Home** tab > **Solid Editing** panel > **Solid, Subtract** . Select the 3D walls and press Enter. Select all the boxes created using the **Presspull** and **Box** tools. Press Enter to create the window openings.

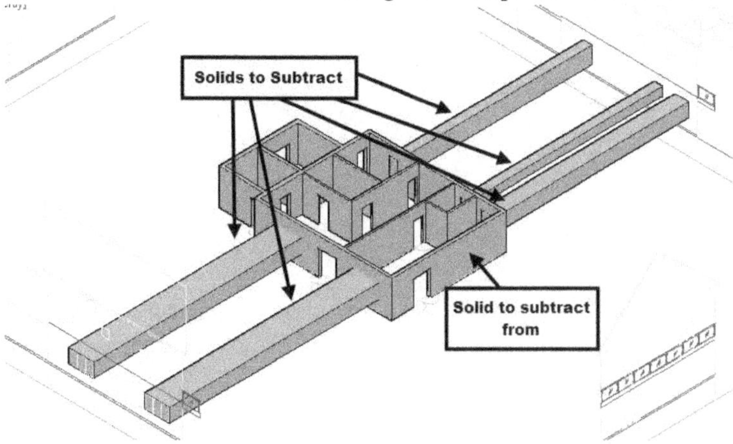

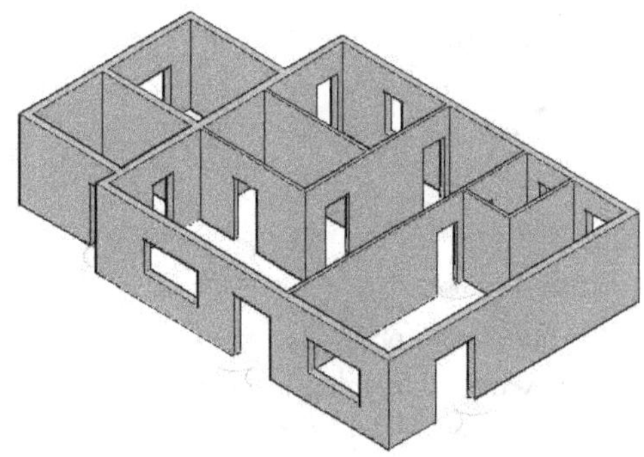

- On the ribbon, click **Visualize** tab > **Visual Styles** panel > **Visual Styles** drop-down > **Wireframe**.
- Zoom to the kitchen area. Activate the **Box** tool and specify the first and second corners, as shown. Select **2Point** from the command line. Select the two points to define the height of the box, as shown.

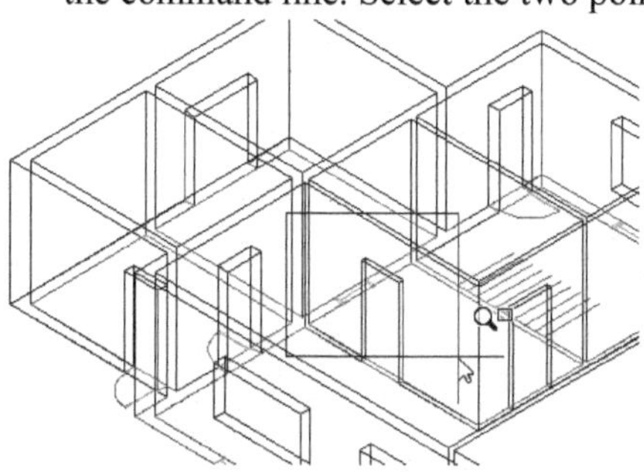

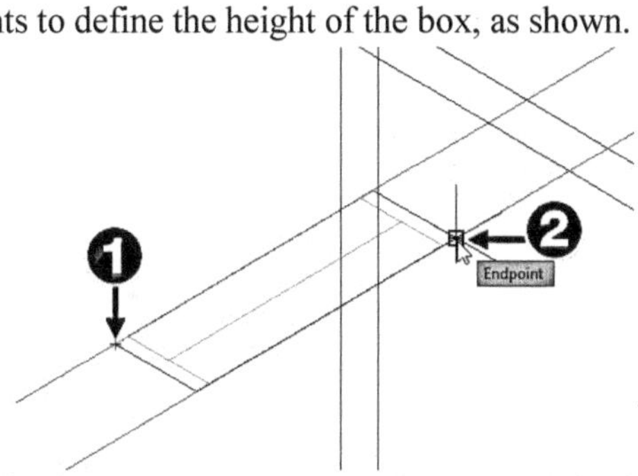

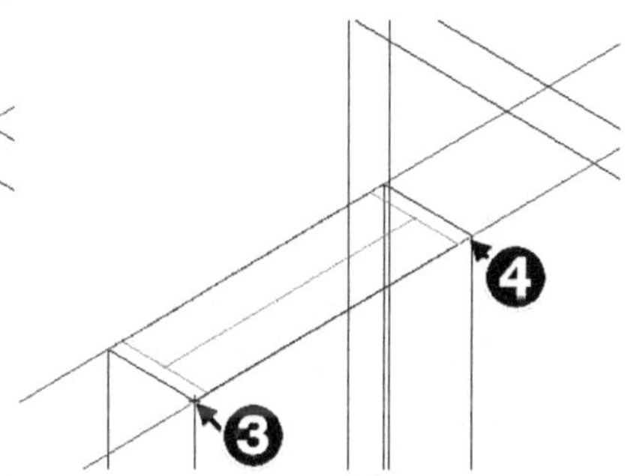

- On the ribbon, click **Home** tab > **Selection** panel > **Gizmo** drop-down > **Move Gizmo** . Select the box created in the last step. Select the origin of the **Move Gizmo**, move the pointer, and select the lower-left corner of the box. Select the **Z-axis** (blue vertical arrow) of the **Move Gizmo**, move the pointer upward, type **71**, and press **Enter**.

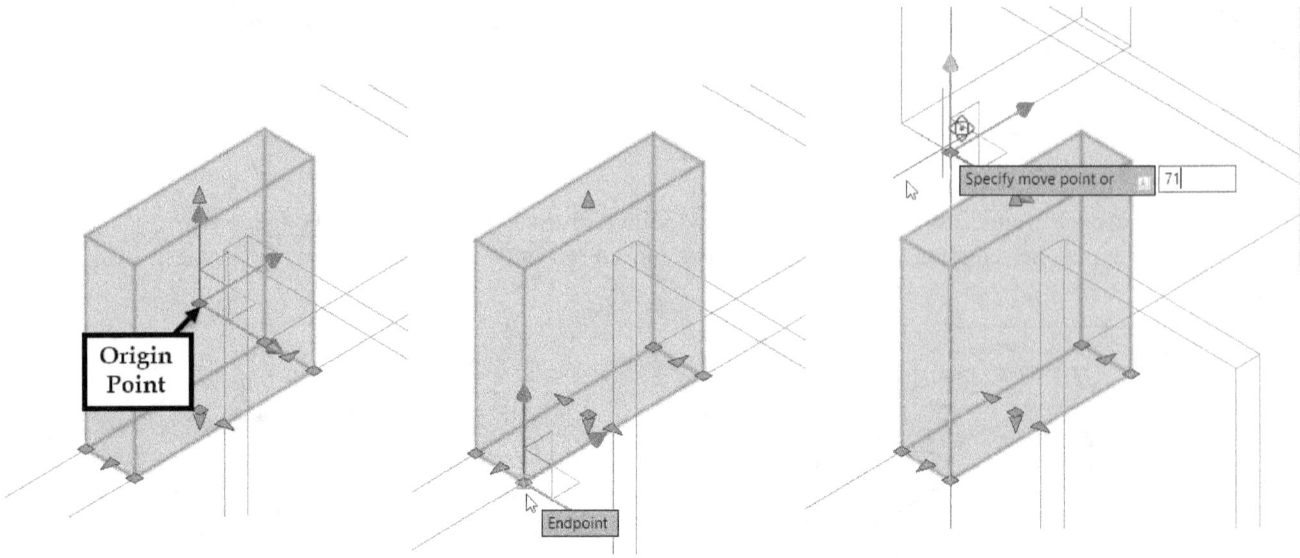

- Type **SU** and press **Enter**. Select the 3D walls and press **Enter**. Select the box created in the last step and press **Enter**. The window opening is created.

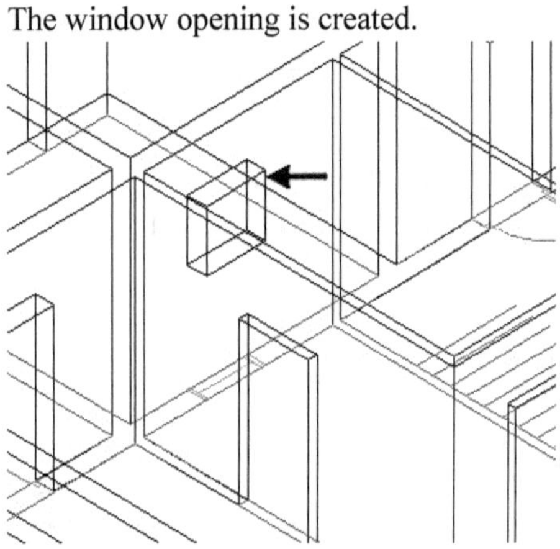

Tutorial 3: Create the Ceiling

- Create a new layer with the name **3D-Floor**. The layer color should be **Yellow**. Make the **3D-Floor** as current.
- On the ribbon, click **Home** tab > **View** panel > **Restore View** drop-down > **Top**. The view orientation is changed to Top.
- Type **Z** and press Enter. Next, select the **All** option from the command line.
- On the ribbon, click **Home** tab > **Draw** panel > **Polyline**. Activate the **Dynamic UCS** icon on the Status bar. Place the pointer on the top face of the 3D walls. Move the pointer and select the lower-left corner point, as shown. Likewise, select the other corner points, as shown. Select **Close** from the command line.

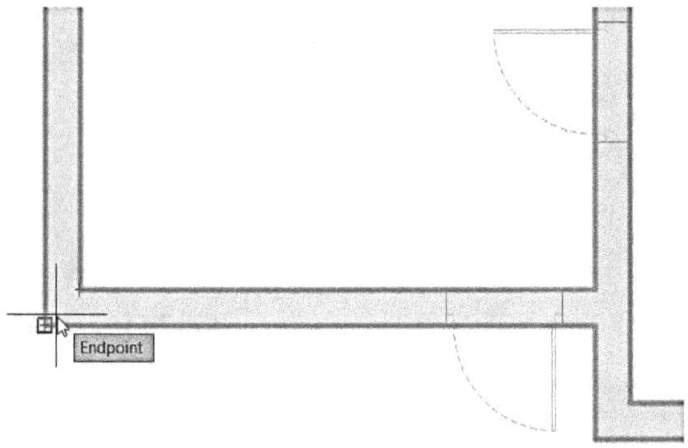

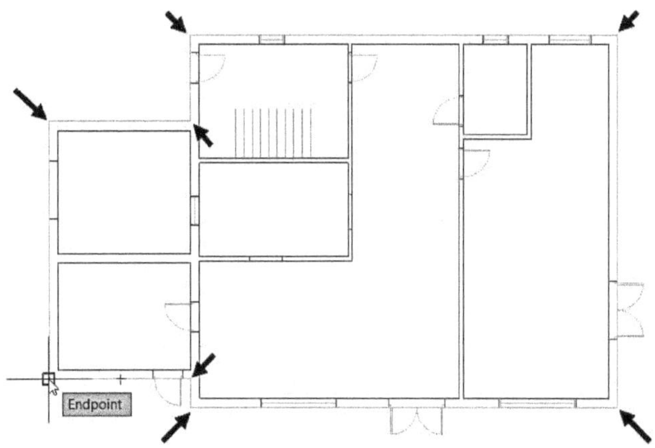

- On the status bar, click the **Customization** button, and then select the **Selection Cycling** option; the **Selection Cycling** icon is displayed on the status bar.
- Activate the **Selection Cycling** icon on the status bar.

- Type **O** and press Enter. Type **12** and press Enter to define the offset distance. Select the polyline and click inside to specify the offset side. Press **Esc** to deactivate the tool.

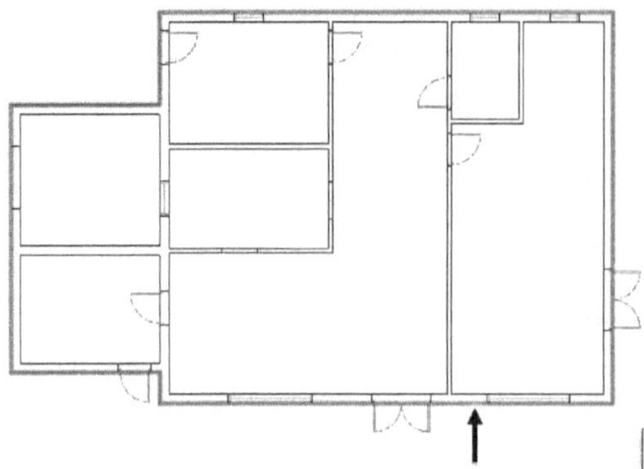

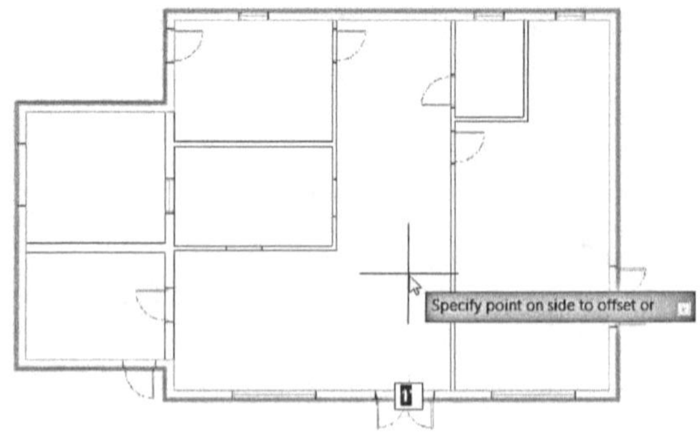

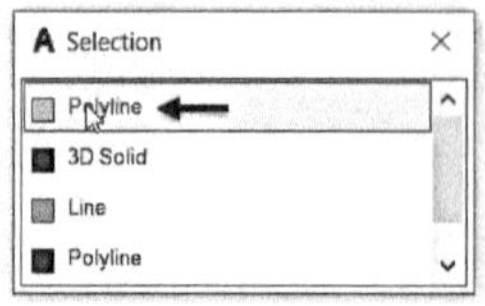

- On the ribbon, click **Home** tab > **Modeling** panel > **Extrude** . Select the offset line and press Enter. Type **-8** and press Enter. On the ribbon, click **Home** tab > **View** panel > **Restore View** drop-down > **SE Isometric**. The view orientation is changed to SE Isometric. Change the **View Style** to **Shades of Gray**.

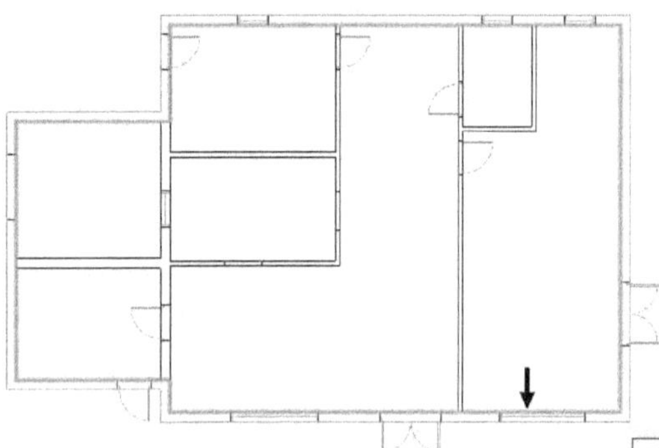

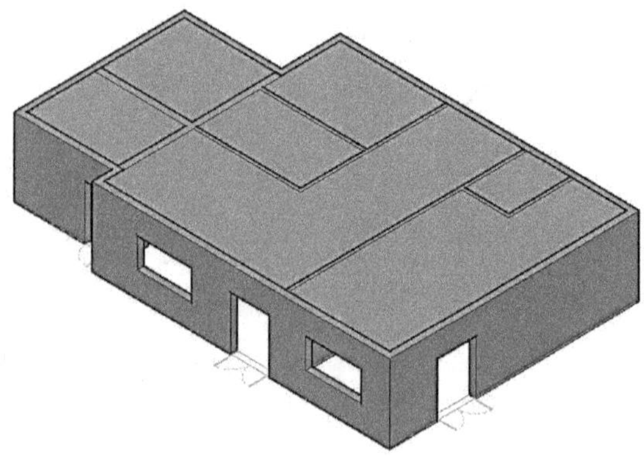

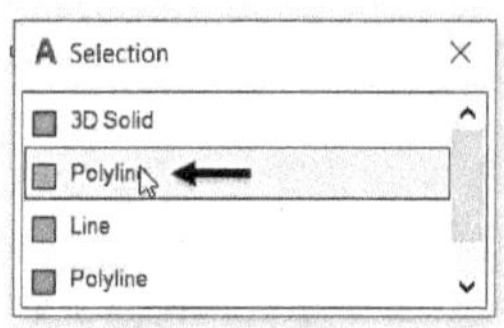

- Select the extruded solid and notice the Move Gizmo attached to it. Click on the Z-axis (blue arrow) of the Move Gizmo, and then select **Copy** from the command line. Move the pointer upward and click to create a copy of the extruded solid. Select **eXit** from the command line. Press Esc to deselect the extruded solid.

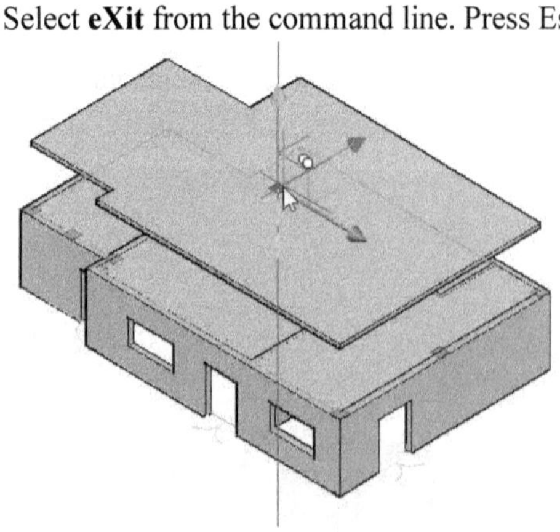

- On the ribbon, click **Home** tab > **Solid Editing** panel > **Solid, Subtract** . Select the 3D walls and press Enter. Select the extruded solid and press Enter.

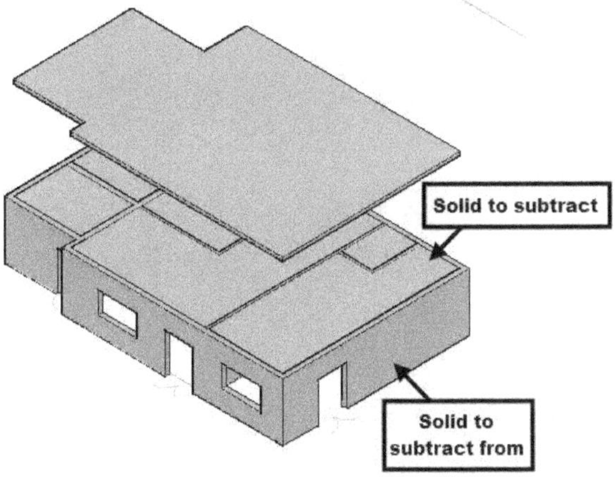

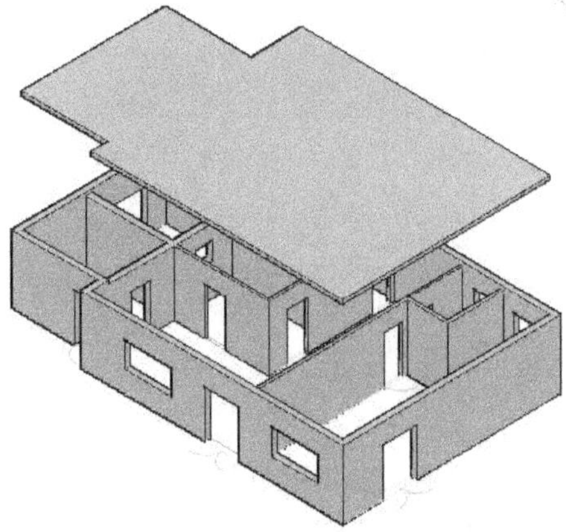

- Select the copied extruded solid and click **Home** tab > **Modify** panel > **Move** . Select the base point and destination point, as shown. The extruded solid is positioned above the walls.

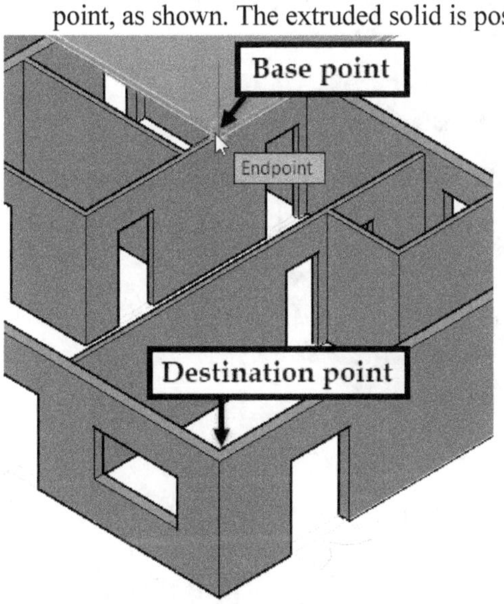

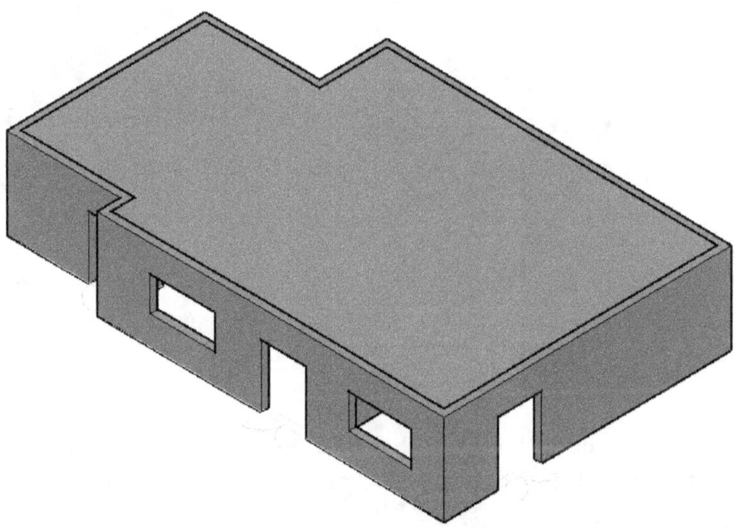

Now, you need to create the slab.

- Type EXT and press Enter. Select the polyline created on the top face of the 3D walls, and then press Enter.
- Move the pointer upward, type 8, and then press Enter.

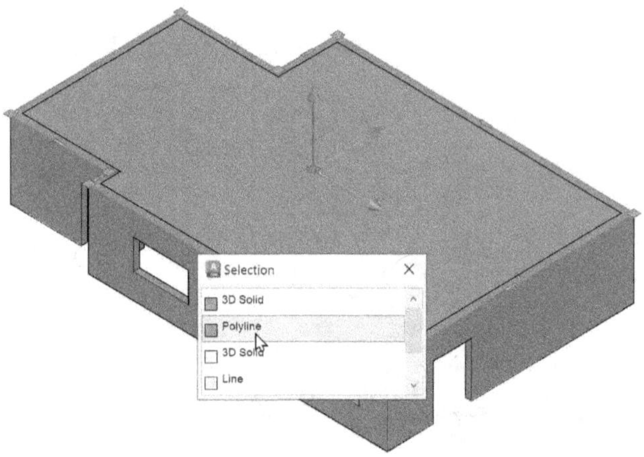

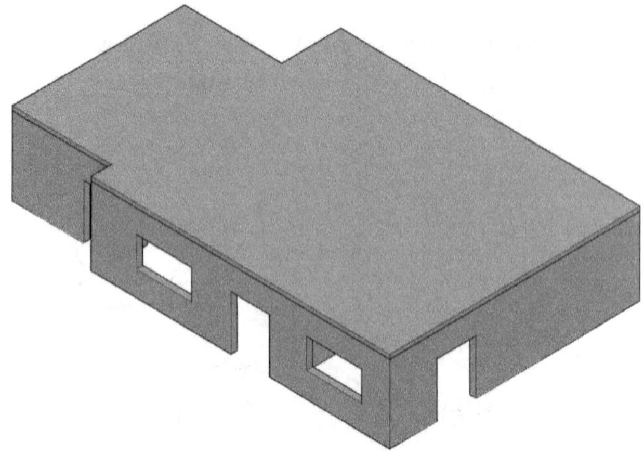

- Select the newly created extruded solid. On the ribbon, click **Home** tab > **Modify** panel > **Copy** . Select the base point and destination point, as shown. Press **Esc** to deactivate the **Copy** command.

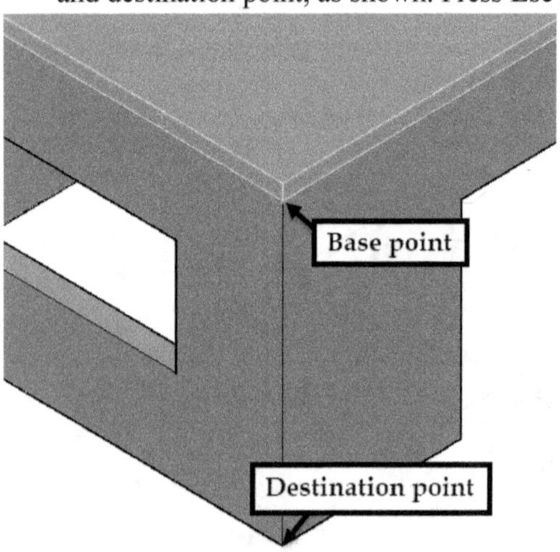

- On the ribbon, click **Home** tab > **Solid Editing** panel > **Solid, Subtract** . Select the 3D walls and press **Enter**. Select the extruded solid at the bottom of the 3D walls, and press Enter.

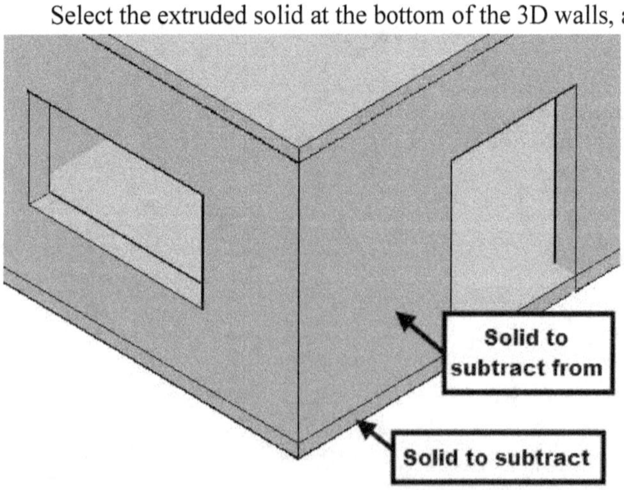

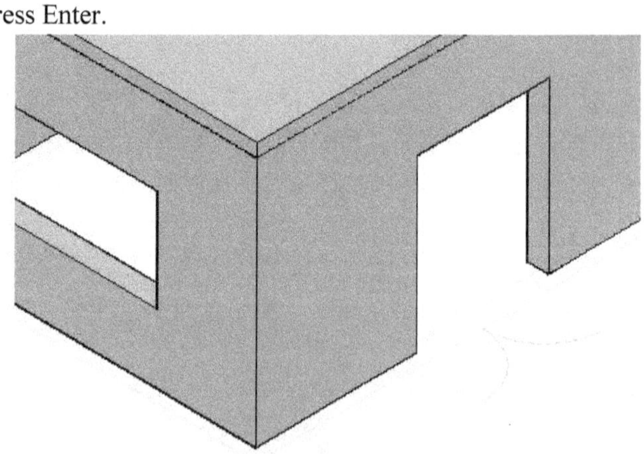

- Select the extruded solid and click **Home** tab > **Modify** panel > **Move** . Select the base point and destination point, as shown. The extruded solid is positioned below the walls.

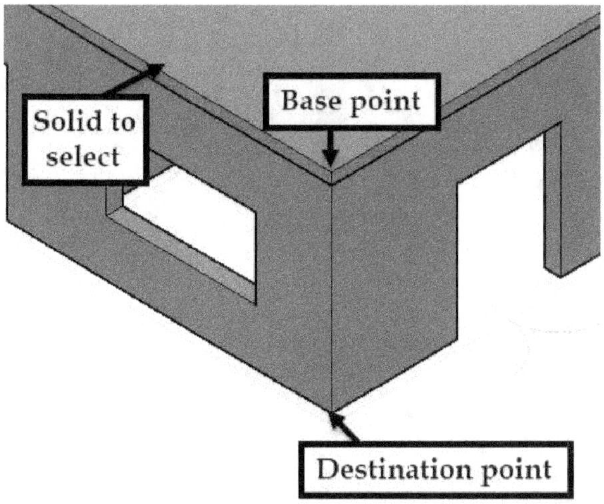

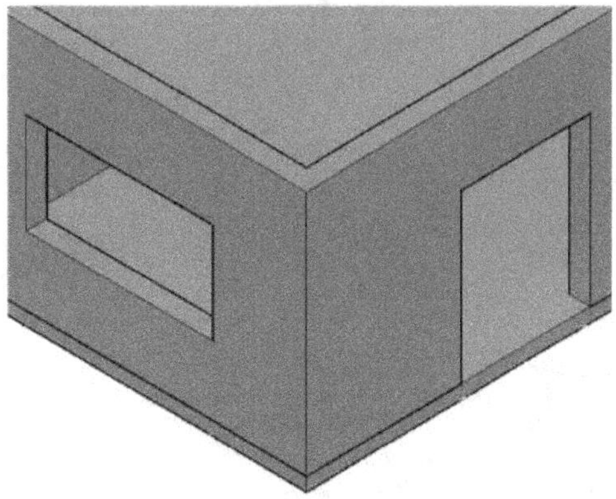

Tutorial 4: Creating Doors on the Ground Floor

- Create two layers "3D-Door" and "3D-Doorframe". Set the colors to Index color **30** and **22**, respectively. Set the 3D-Doorframe layer as current.
- On the ribbon, click **Home** tab > **Layers** panel > **Off** . Select any one of the 3D floors to turn off its layer. Deactivate the **Off** command.
- Type **PL** and press Enter. Make sure that the **Dynamic UCS** icon is turned **ON** on the Status bar. Zoom to the double-door location and place the pointer on the outer face of the wall. Move the pointer on the highlighted face and select the lower left corner of the door opening.

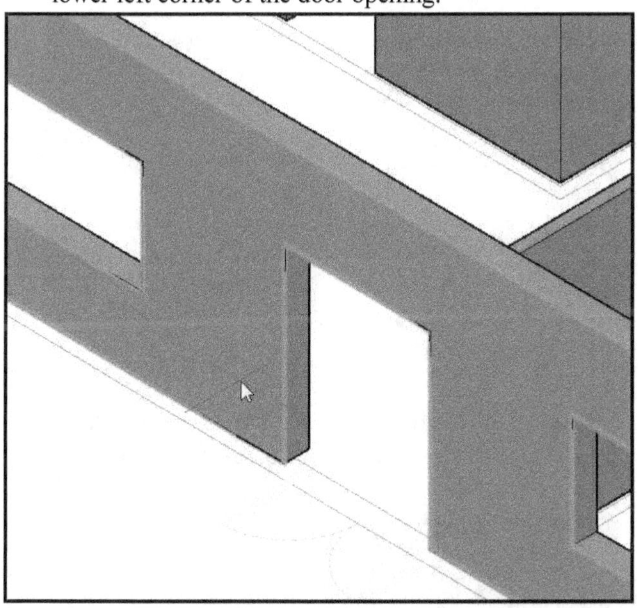

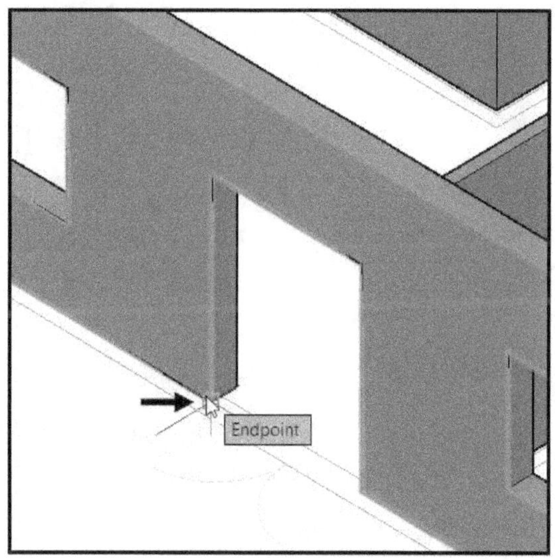

- Select the other corners of the door opening in the clockwise direction. Press **Esc** to deactivate the tool.

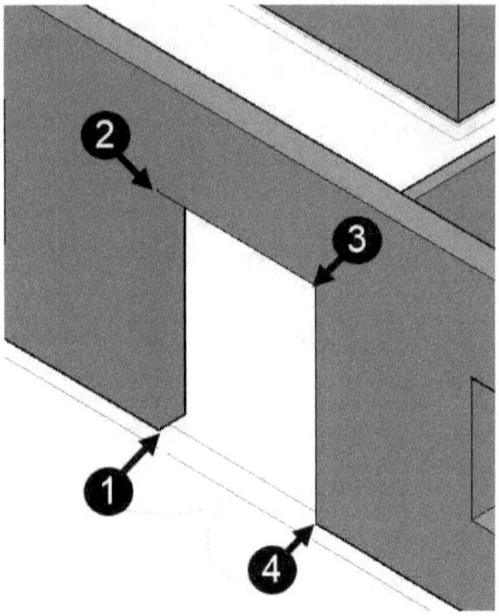

- On the **Home** tab of the ribbon, expand the **Modify** panel and click the **Explode** tool. Select the 2D door block and press **Enter**. The block is exploded into individual entities.

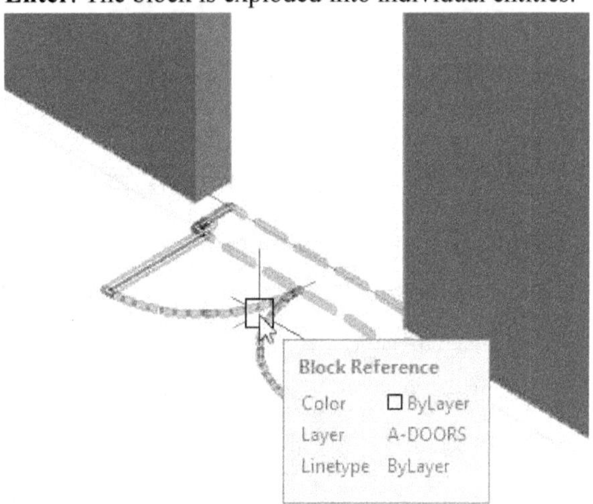

- On the ribbon, click **Home** tab > **Modeling** panel > **Extrude** drop-down > **Sweep** . Select the rectangle of the 2D door and press **Enter**. Select **Base point** from the command line and select the corner point of the rectangle, as shown.

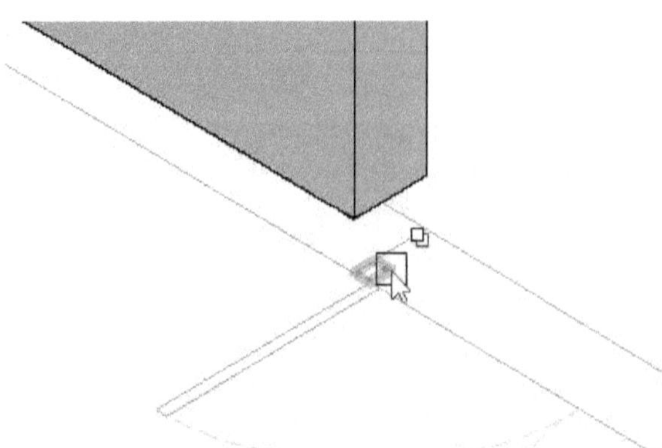

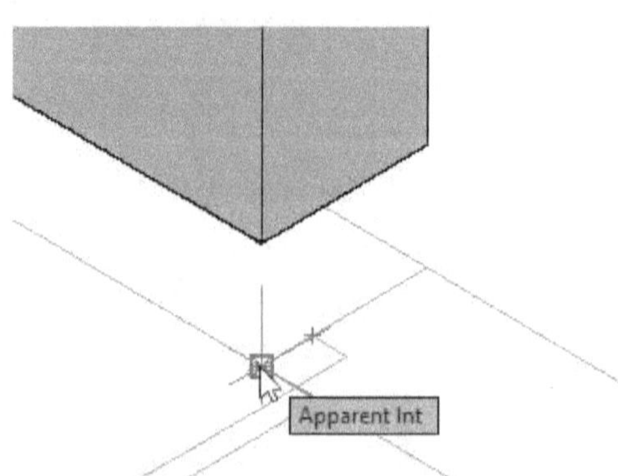

- Select the polyline created on the door opening edge; the door frame is created, as shown.

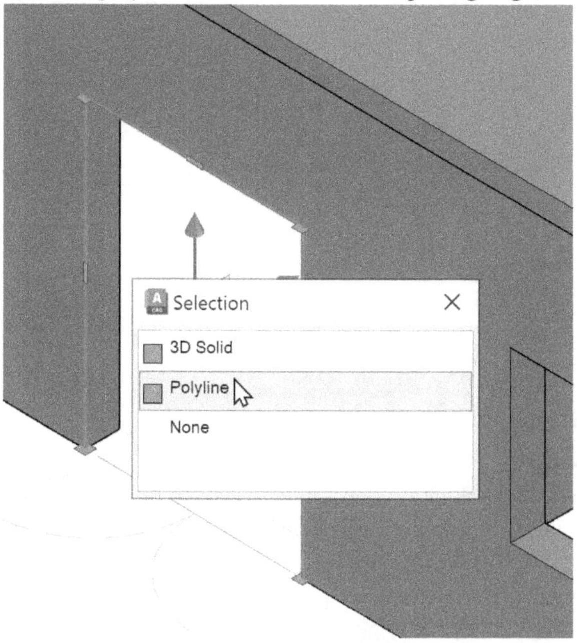

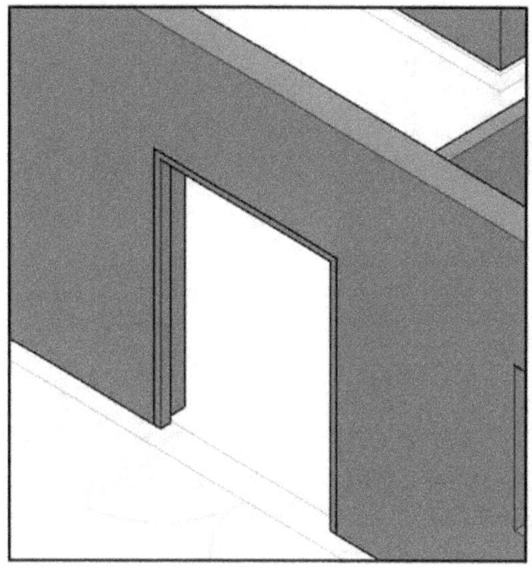

- On **Navigation Bar**, click the **Orbit** tool. Press and hold the left mouse button and drag the mouse toward the right; the model is rotated toward the right. Place the pointer on the single door opening of the utility room, move the mouse wheel in the forward direction.

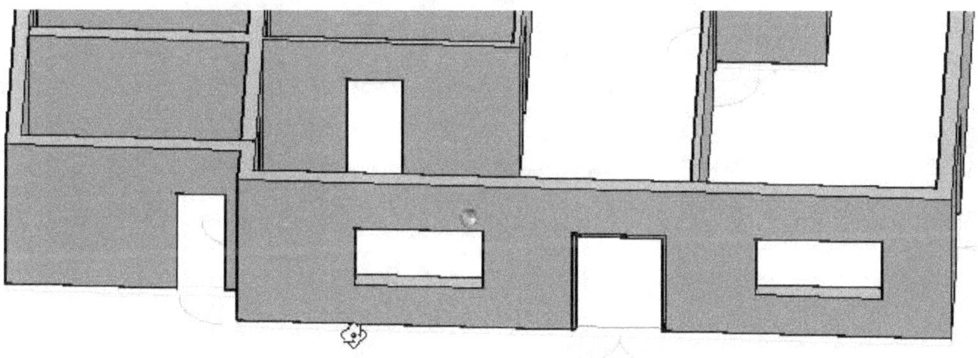

- Create the door frame using the **Sweep** tool.

- On the ribbon, click **Home** tab > **View** panel > **Restore View** drop-down > **SE Isometric** .
- On the ribbon, click **Home** tab > **Layers** panel > **Layer** drop-down > **3D-Door**.
- Type **BOX** and press **Enter**. Place the pointer on the front face of the double-door frame. Move the pointer on the highlighted face and select the lower left corner point, as shown. On the status bar, click the down arrow next to the **Object Snap** icon and make sure that the **Midpoint** option is selected. Move the pointer upward and select the midpoint of the horizontal portion of the door frame. Type **1.78** and press **Enter** to create the door.

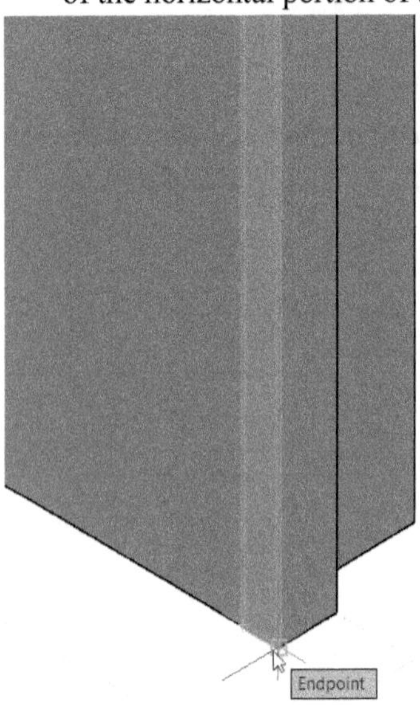

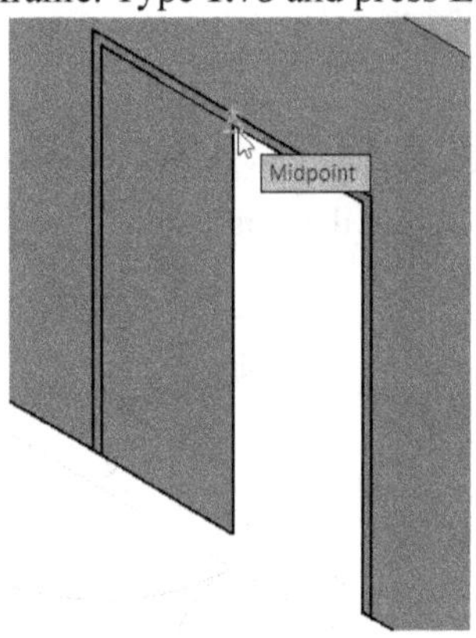

- Select the door and click the **Move** tool on the **Modify** panel of the **Home** ribbon tab. Select the corner point of the door, as shown. Move the pointer inwards, type **4**, and press **Enter**.

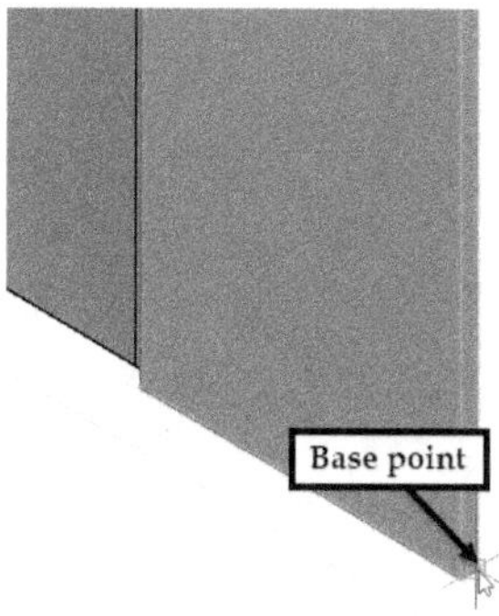

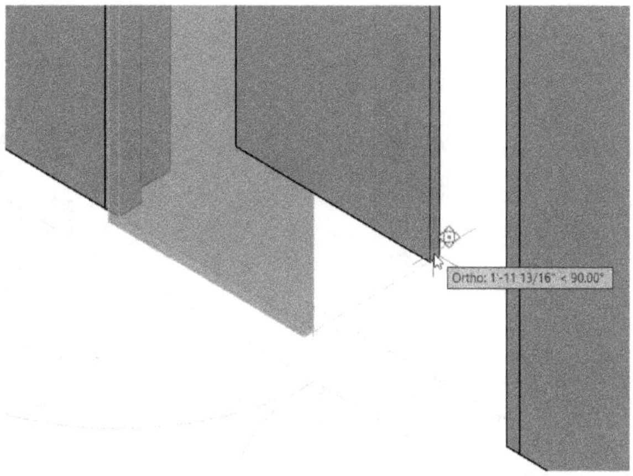

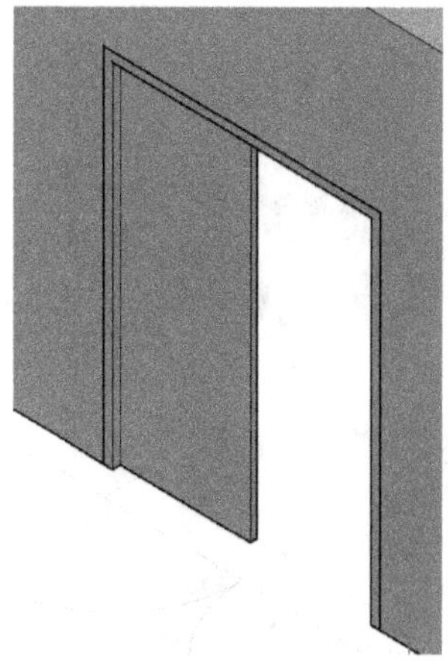

Now, you need to create the door handle.

- On the ribbon, click **Home** tab > **Modeling** panel > **Primitives** drop-down > **Sphere**. Select the lower right corner of the door to specify the center of the sphere. Move the pointer outward, type **1.57**, and press **Enter**.

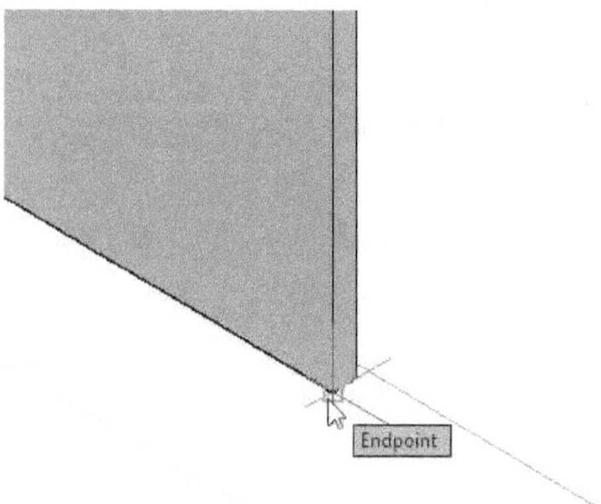

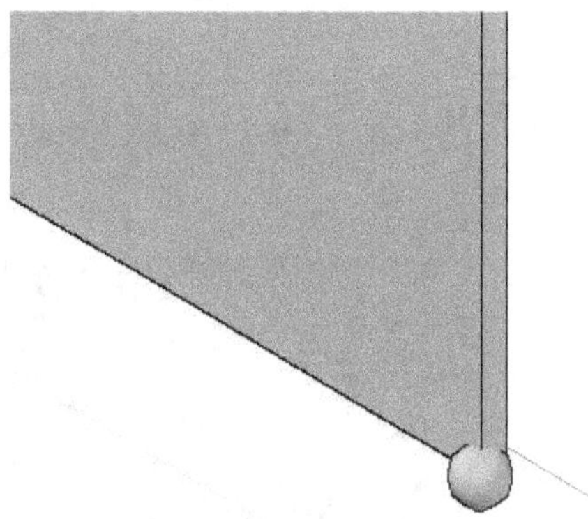

- Select the sphere and click the **Move** tool on the **Modify** panel of the **Home** ribbon tab. Select the corner point of the door, as shown. Move the pointer upwards and select the midpoint of the door edge.

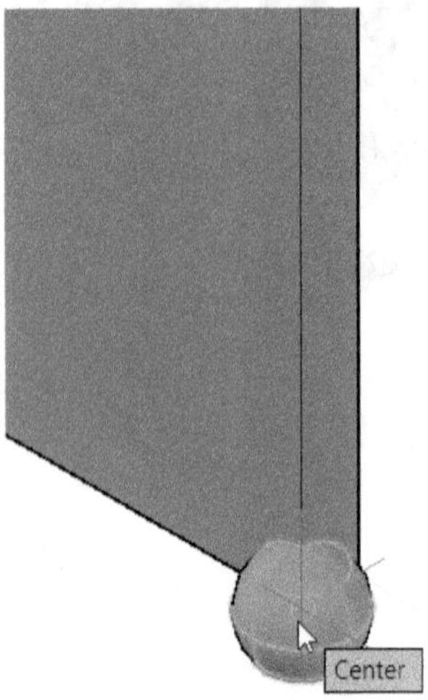

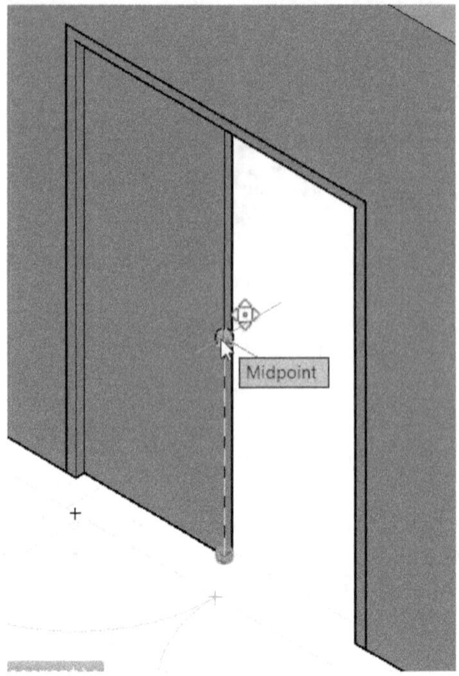

- Select the sphere and click on the **X-axis** (red arrow) of the **Move Gizmo**. Move the pointer toward the left, type **3.5**, and press **Enter**.

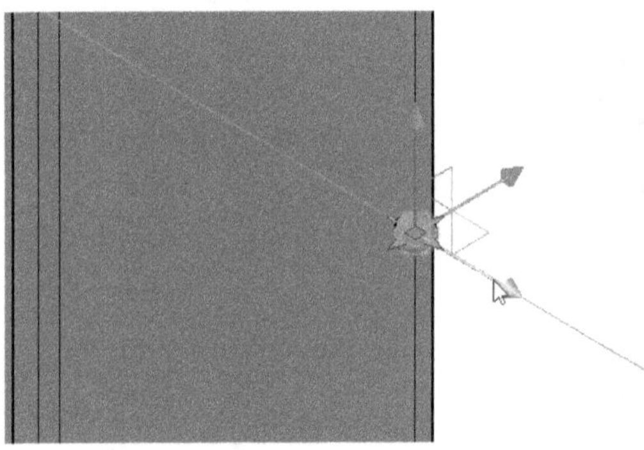
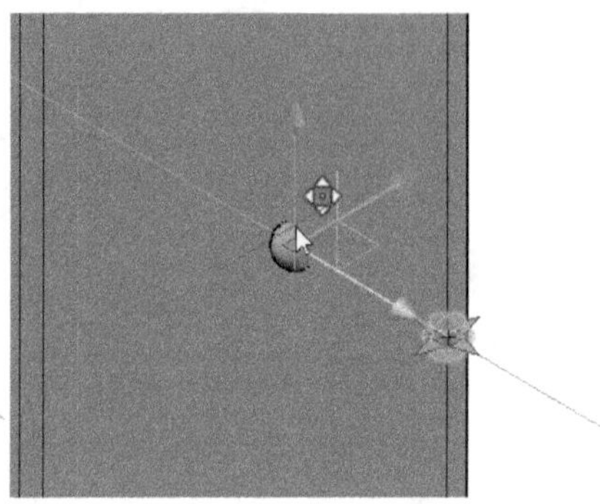

- Select the **Y-axis** (green arrow) of the **Move Gizmo** and move the sphere toward left. Type **1** and press **Enter**. Press **Esc** to deselect the sphere.

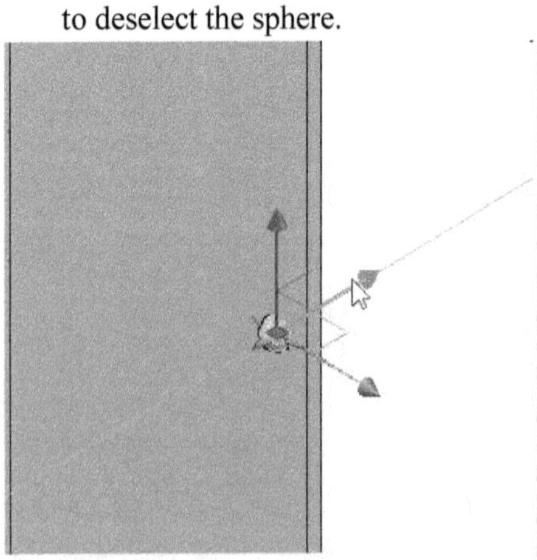
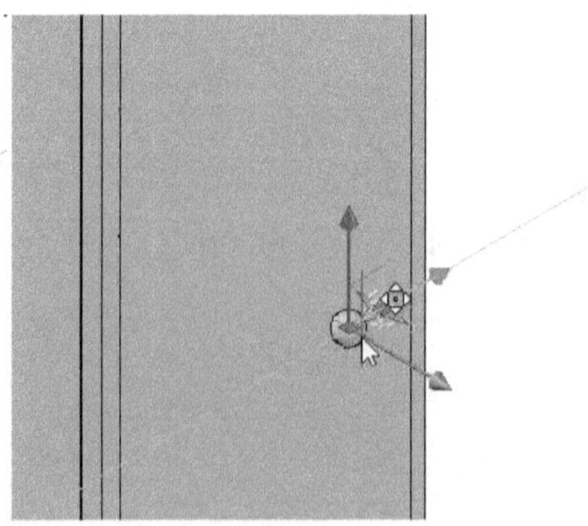

- On the ribbon, click **Solid** tab > **Solid Editing** panel > **Offset Edge** . Select the front face of the door. Select **Distance**

from the command line. Type **7** and press **Enter**. Click on the door to offset the edges. Again, select the front face of the door. Select **Distance** from the command line. Type **8** and press **Enter**. Click on the door to create another offset edge. Press **Esc** to deactivate the tool.

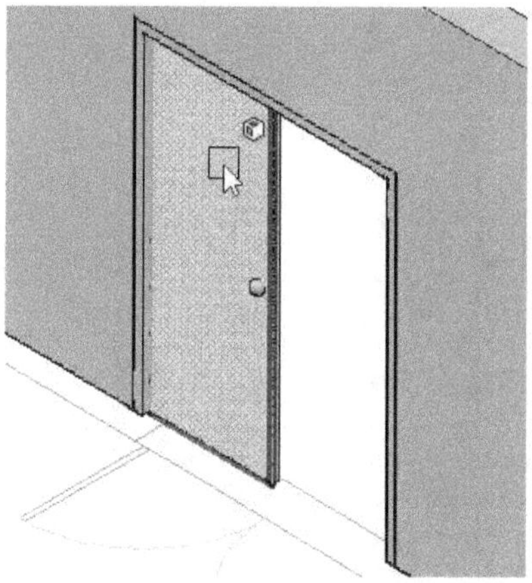
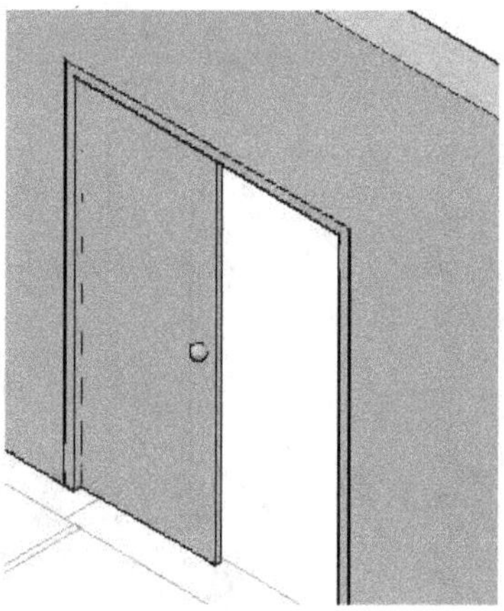
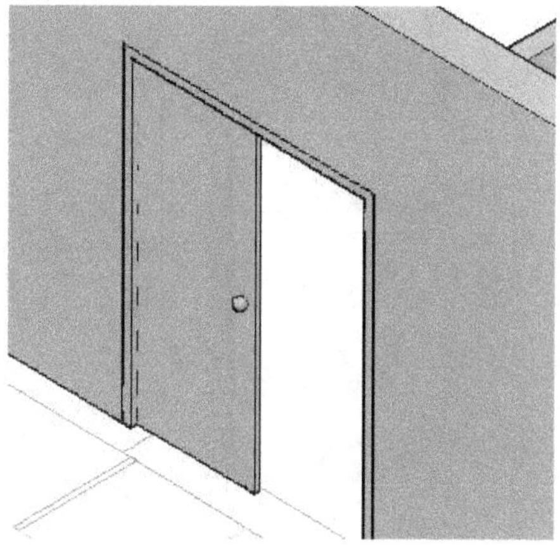

- On the ribbon, click **Solid** tab > **Solid Editing** panel > **Imprint** . Select the door, and then select any one of the offset polylines. Select **Yes** from the command line; the selected polyline is imprinted onto the front face of the door. Select the other offset polyline, and then select **Yes** from the command line. Press **Esc** to deactivate the command.
- On the ribbon, click **Home** tab > **Solid Editing** panel > **Union** . Select the door and sphere, and then press **Enter**; both the solids are combined together.
- Select the door, type **MI**, and press **Enter**. Place the pointer on the front face of the door frame and select the midpoint of its horizontal edge. Move the pointer downward and click to mirror the door. Select **No** from the command line to retain the source object.

- On the Navigation Bar, click the **Orbit** tool and rotate the model such that the single door opening on the utility room appears.

- Select the mirrored door, type **CO**, and press **Enter**. Select the lower left corner of the door as the base point. Move the pointer toward the left and select the lower left corner of the door frame, as shown. Press **Esc** to deactivate the **Copy** command.

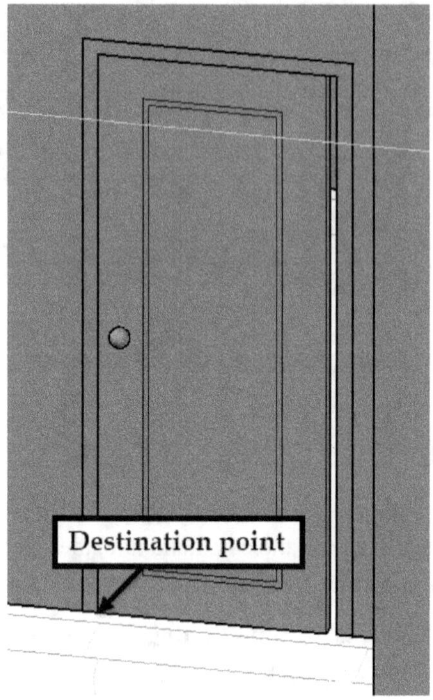

- Zoom-in to the single door and notice a gap between the door and the doorframe.
- On the ribbon, click the **Home** tab > **Solid Editing** panel > **Extrude Faces** drop-down > **Offset Faces**.

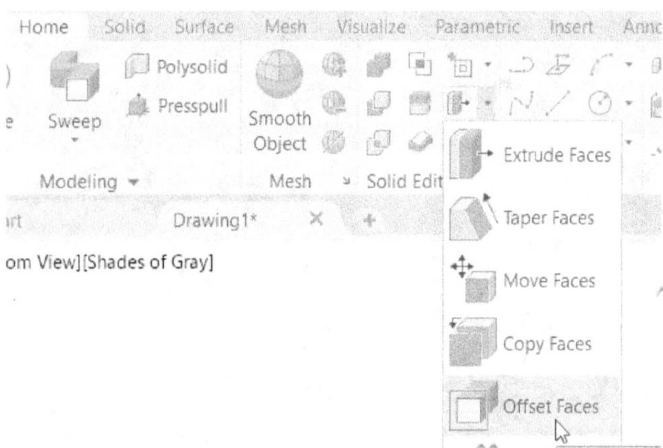

- Select the side face of the door and press **Enter**.
- Select the corner points of the door and the doorframe, as shown; the side face of the door is offset.

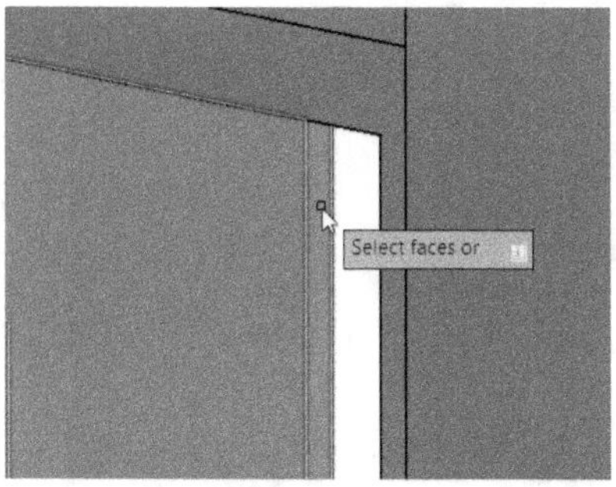

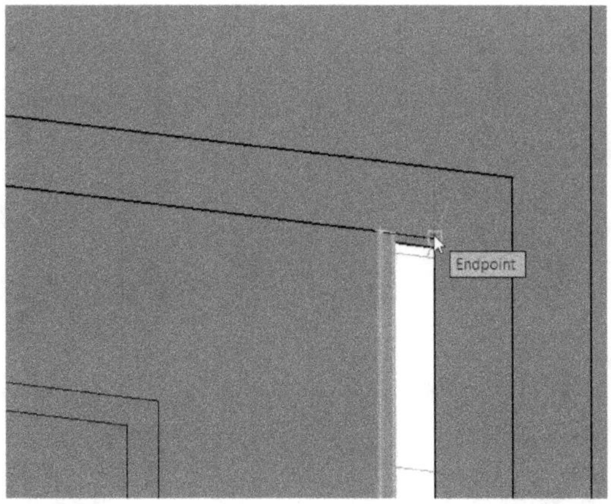

- Press **Esc** to deactivate the active command.
- Press and hold the **Ctrl** key, and then select all the imprinted edges on the door.
- Press the **Delete** key on your keyboard to delete them.

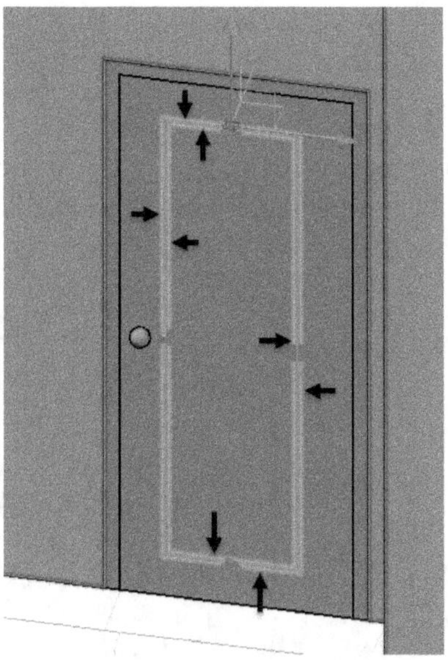

- Zoom-in to the double-door and select the doors and door frame. On the ribbon, click **Home** tab > **Groups** panel > **Group** . The three solids are grouped.

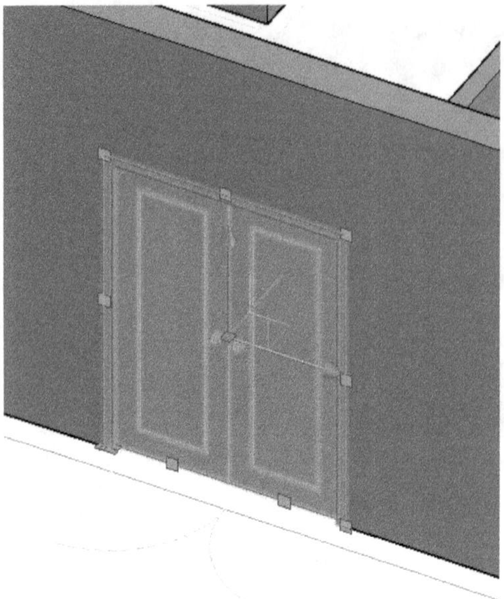

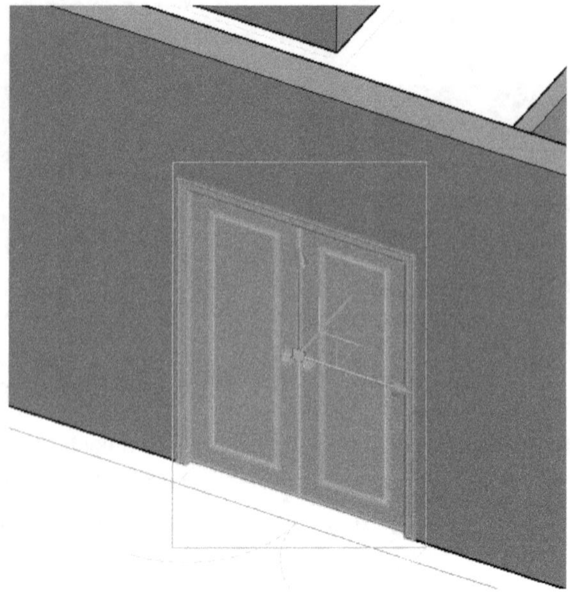

- On the ribbon, click **Home** tab > **Modify** panel > **3D Align**. Select the double-door group and press **Enter**. Select **Copy** from the command line. Select the first, second, and third base points, as shown. On the Navigation Bar, click the **Orbit** tool and rotate the model such that the double-door opening on the front elevation side is visible. Right click and select **Exit** to deactivate the **Orbit** tool. Select the first, second, and third destination points, as shown.

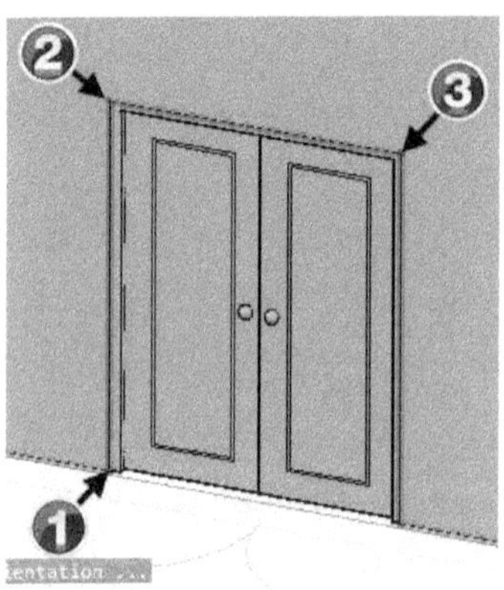

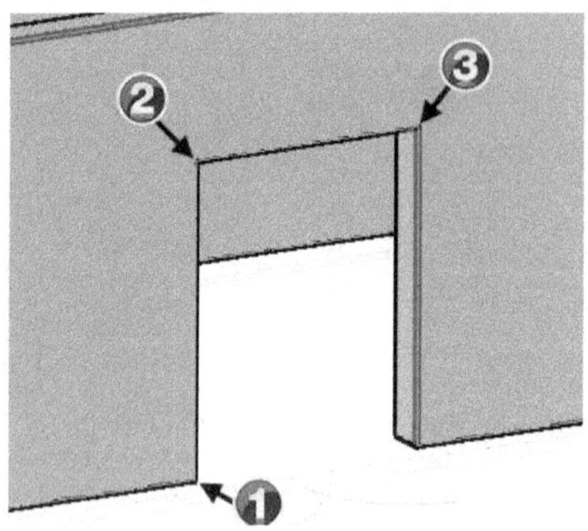

- On the ribbon, click **Home** tab > **View** panel > **Restore View** drop-down > **SW Isometric**.
- On the ribbon, click **Insert** tab > **Block Definition** panel > **Create Block**. Type **3D-Single door** in the **Name** box. Click the **Select Objects** icon on the dialog, and then select the single door and its door frame. Press **Enter** to display the dialog. Click the **Pick point** icon. Zoom to the single door and select the top left corner of the door frame. Select **Retain** from the **Objects** section on the dialog. Uncheck the **Open in block editor** option and click **OK**.

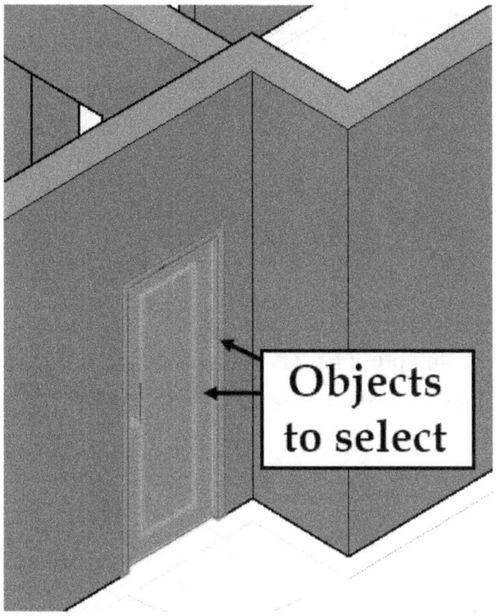

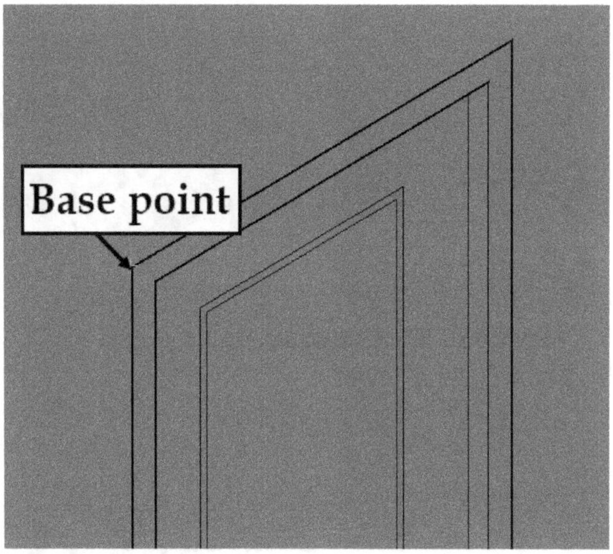

- On the ribbon, click **Insert** tab > **Block** panel > **Insert** gallery > **3D-Single door**. Click in the empty space to position the block.
- On the ribbon, click **Home > Modify > 3D Rotate** 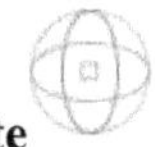 . Select the block and press **Enter**. Select the top right corner of the block to define the base point.
- Select the horizontal ring of the move gizmo to define the rotation axis.
- Move the pointer forward and click to specify the start point of the rotation. Move the pointer toward the right and click to rotate the block by 90 degrees.

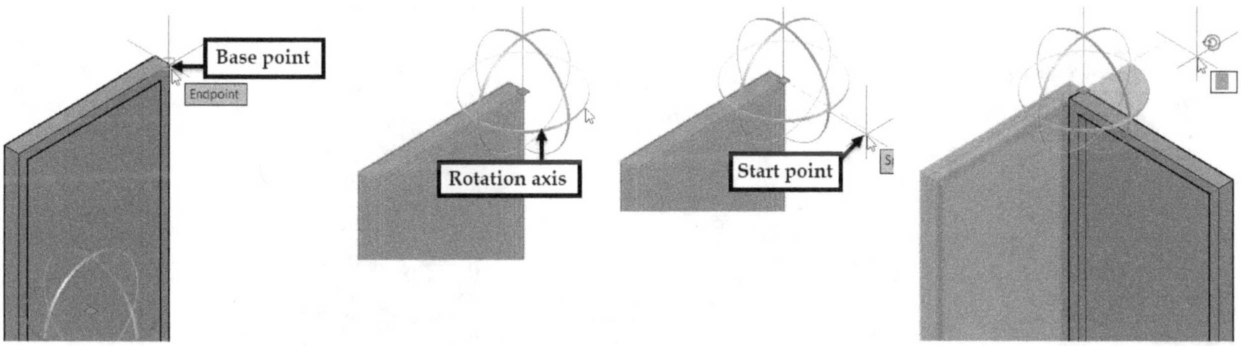

- Select the block, type **M**, and press Enter. Select the top right corner as the base point, as shown. Use the **Orbit** tool to rotate the model such that the door opening of the utility room appears. Right click and select **Exit** to deactivate the orbit mode. Select the top right corner of the door opening, as shown.

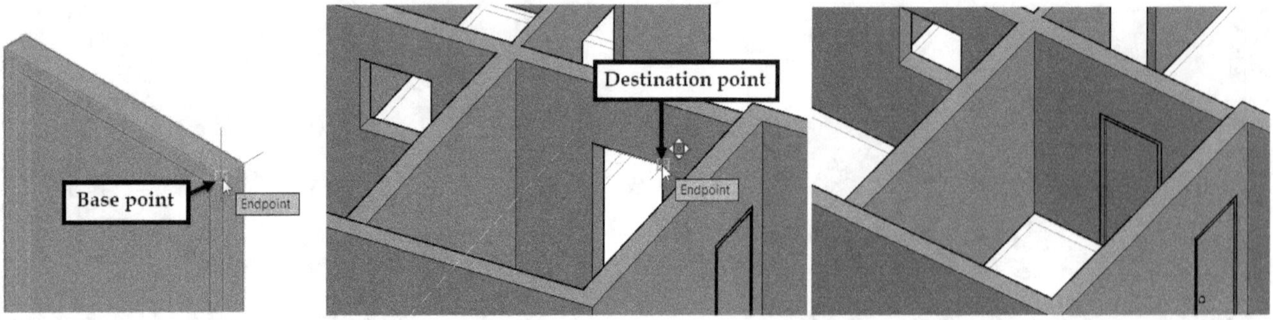

- Insert another instance of the **3D-Single door** block. Select the block, type **MI**, and press **Enter**. Select the top right corner of the door frame, move the pointer upward, and then click to mirror the door block. Select **Yes** to delete the source object.

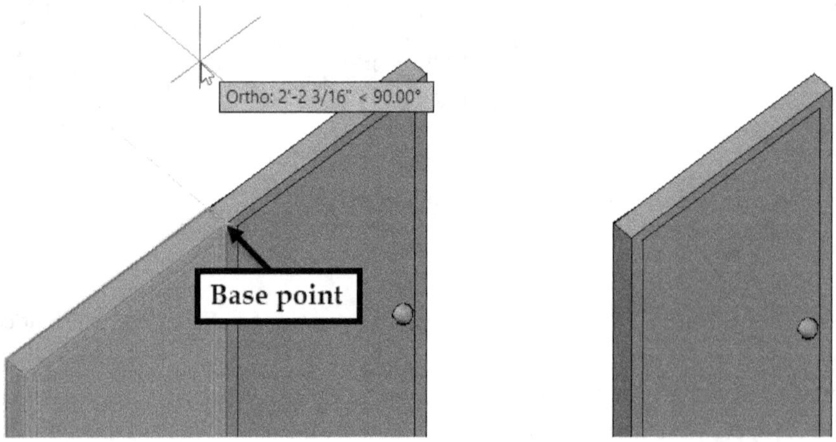

- Rotate the door by **270** degrees. Copy the door block and place it at the door opening on the rear elevation, as shown.

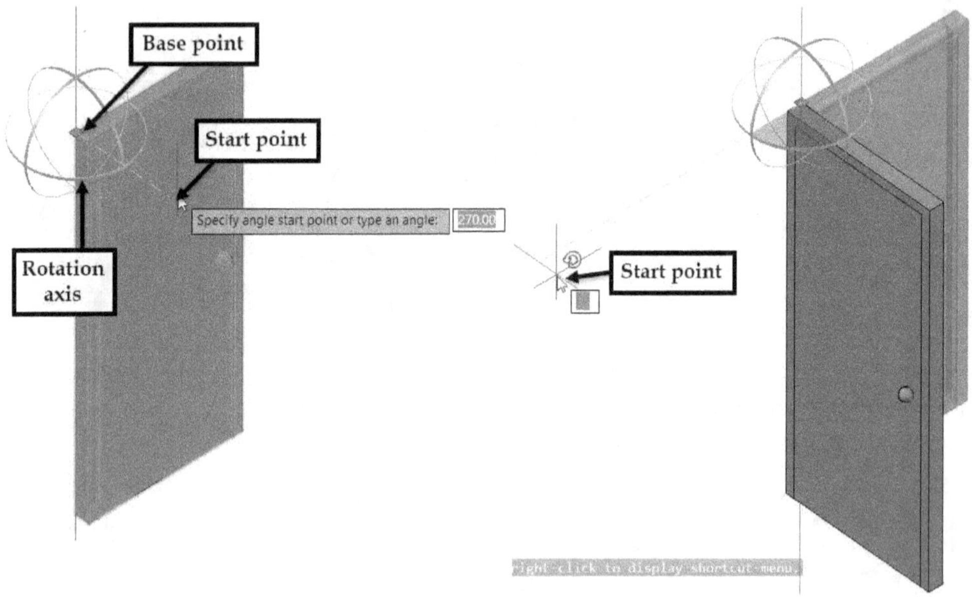

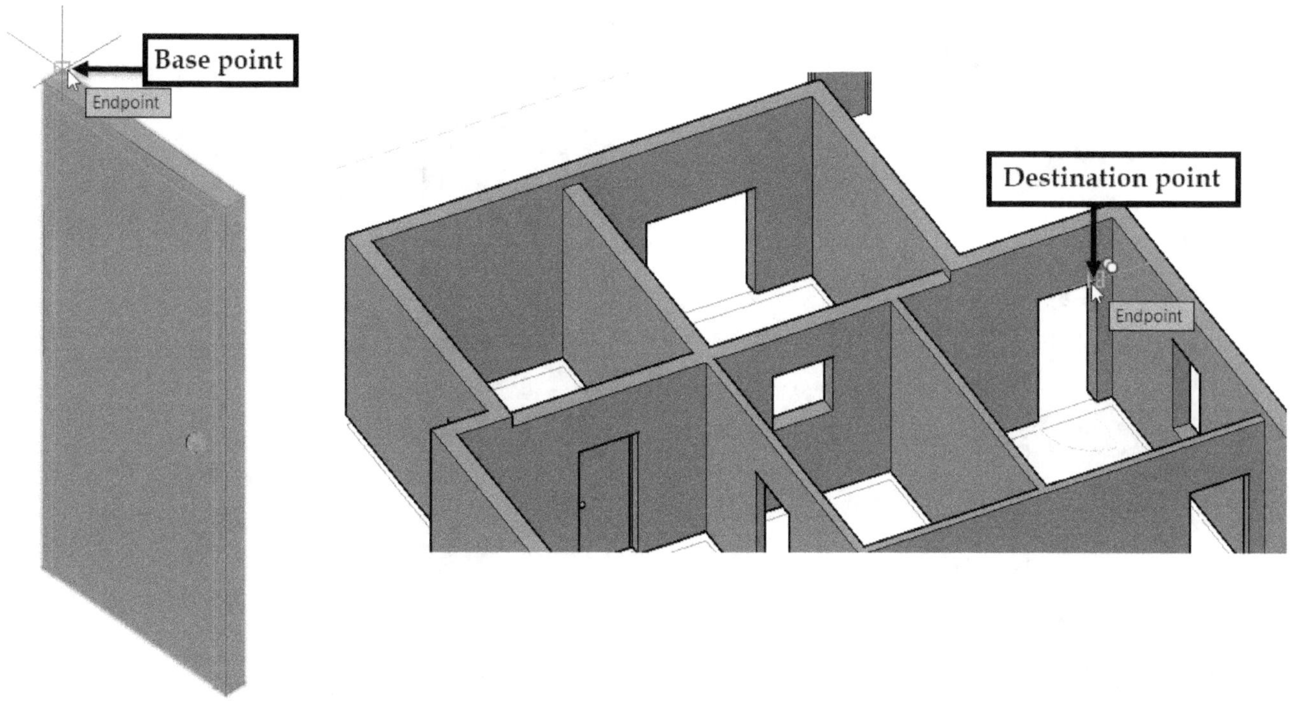

- Place the copy of the door block at other openings, as shown.

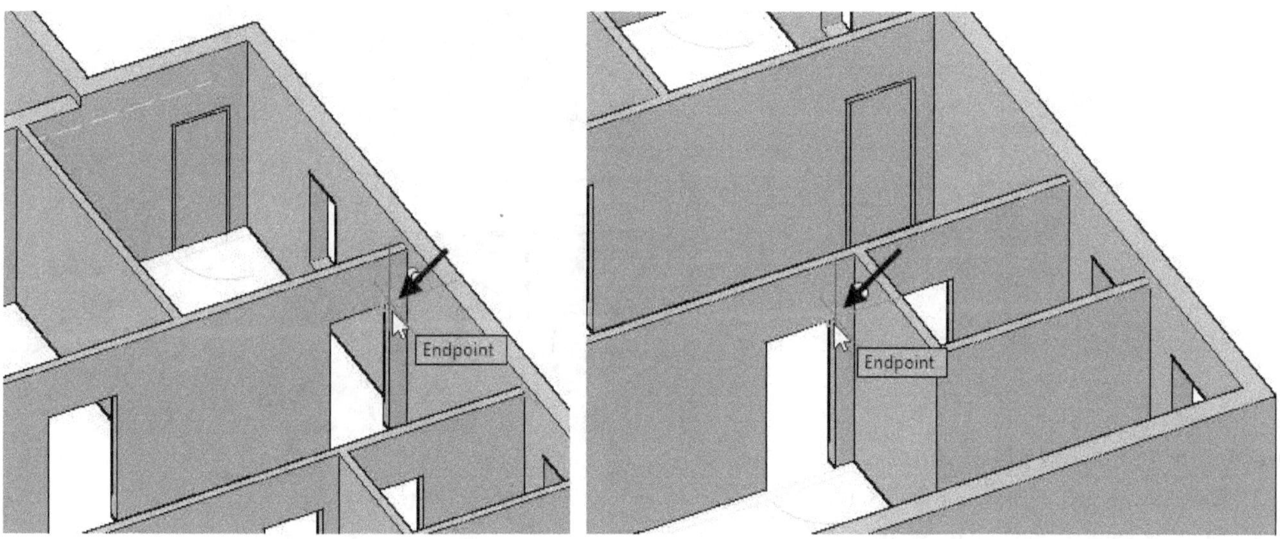

- Change the view orientation to **SW Isometric**.
- On the ribbon, click **Home** tab > **Modify** panel > **3D Mirror**. Select the **3D-Single Door** block and press **Enter**.
- Select **3points** from the command line, and then select the three points from the door block, as shown.
- Select **Yes** from the command line to delete the source object.

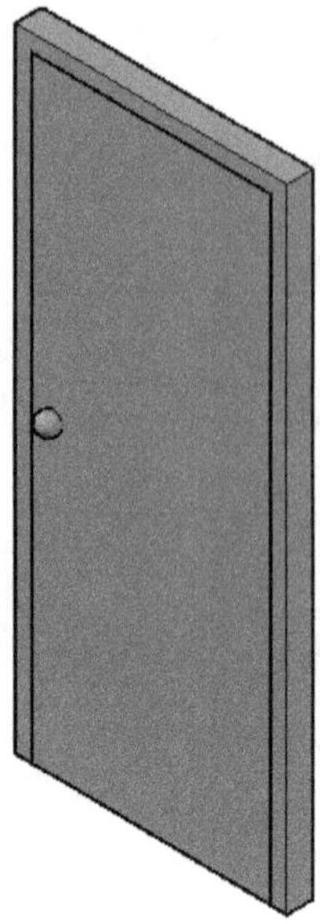

- Move the mirrored door block and place it on the bathroom door opening.

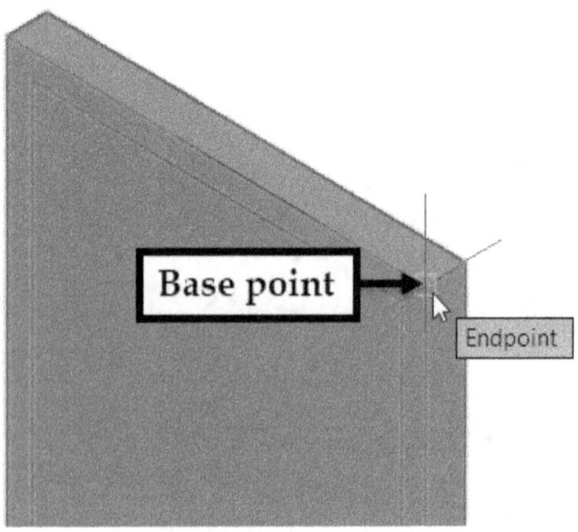

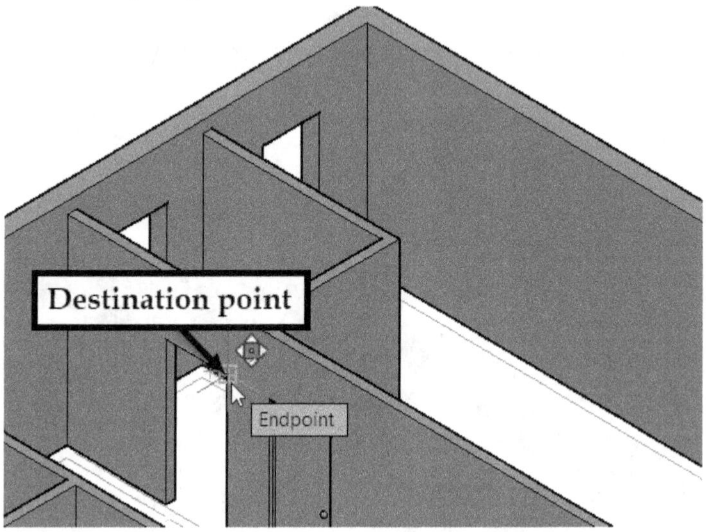

Tutorial 5: Creating 3D Windows

- Create a new layer, "3D-Windows". Set the layer color to yellow, and then activate the layer.
- Change the view orientation to **SE Isometric**.
- Select the South Elevation group, and then click **Home** tab > **Groups** panel > **Ungroup** .
- Zoom to the South elevation and create a selection window over the 2D-window. Type **CO** and press **Enter**. Select the top right corner of the window, move the pointer toward the 3D walls, and then select the top right corner of the window opening. Press **Esc** to deactivate the **Copy** command.

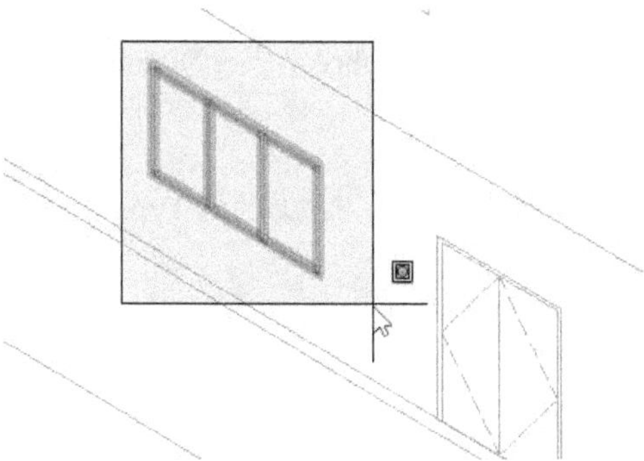

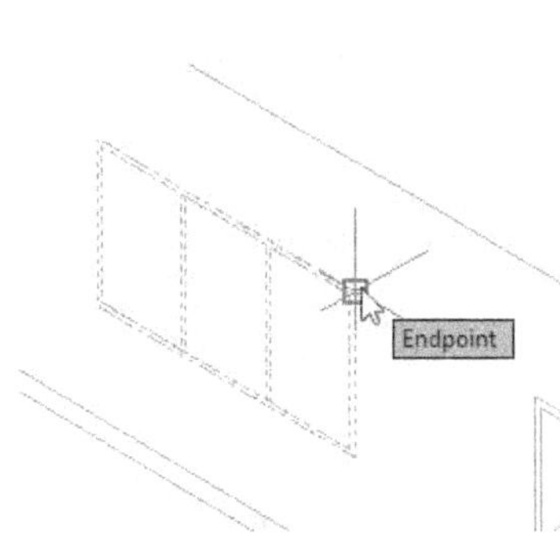

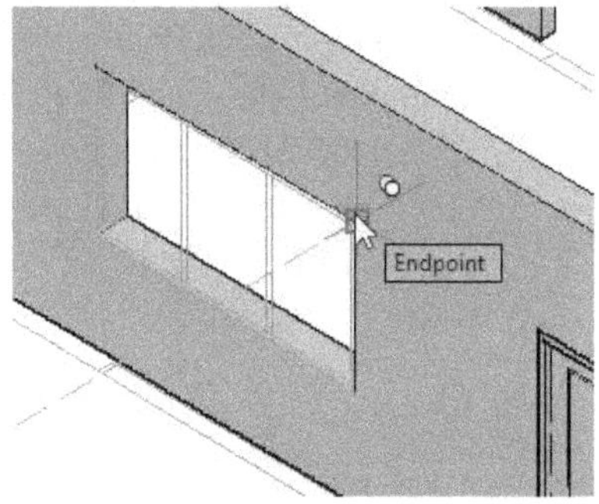

- Type **EXT** and press **Enter**. Select the outer polyline of the window, as shown. Next, press **Enter** to accept the selection. Type **-2** and press **Enter** to extrude the polyline.

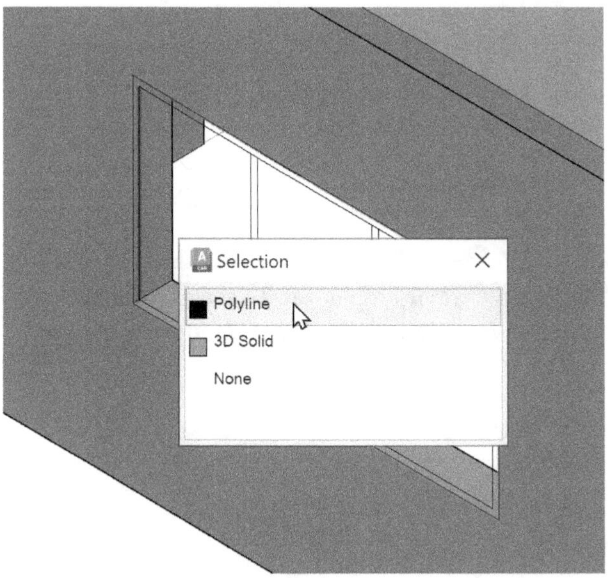

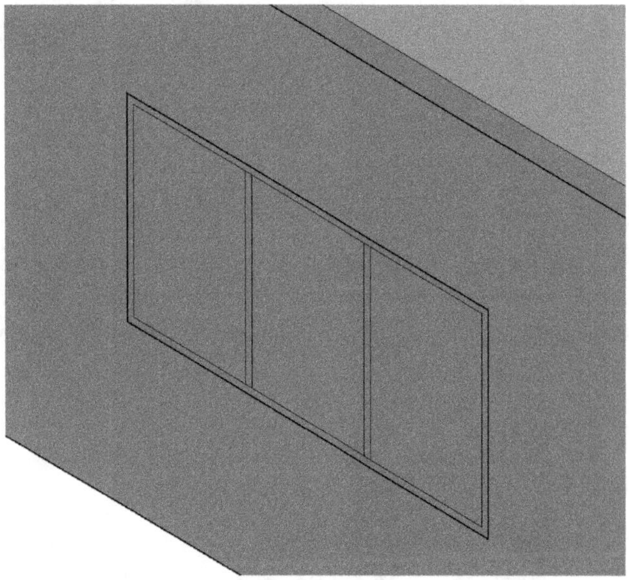

- Turn off the **3D-Walls** layer. On the ribbon, click **Home** tab > **Modeling** panel > **Presspull** . Click in the region enclosed by the rectangle, as shown. Move the pointer, type **-0.4**. Likewise, presspull the other two regions, as shown.

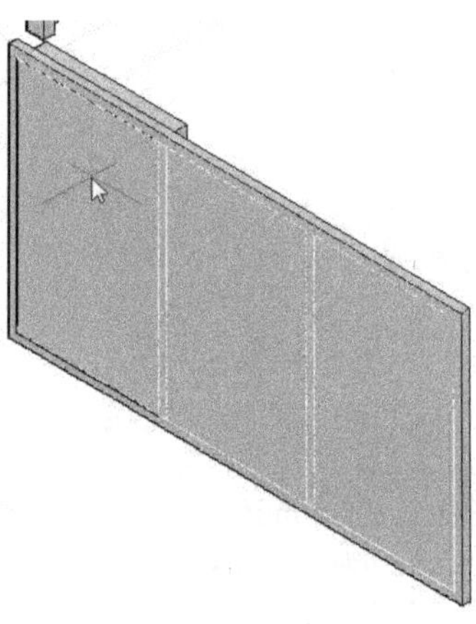

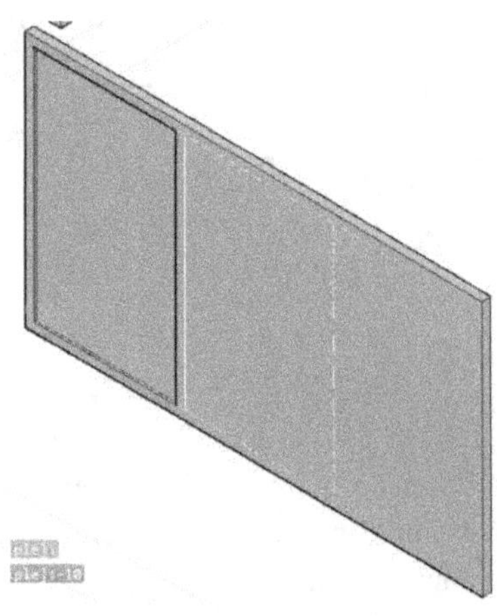

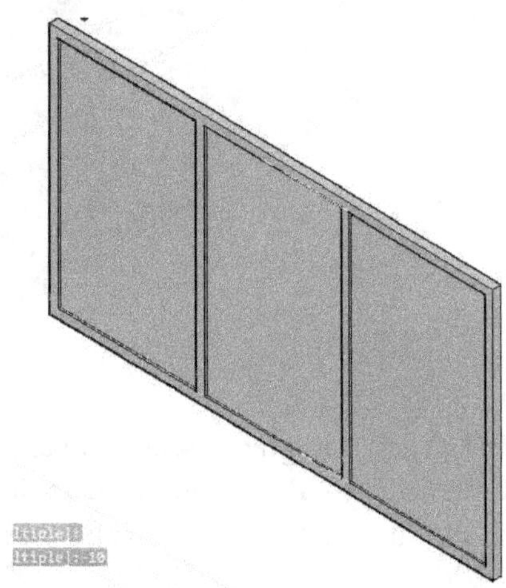

- On the ribbon, click **Solid** tab > **Solid Editing** panel > **Offset Edge**. Select a press-pulled face. Select **Distance** from the command line. Type **1** and press **Enter**. Click on the selected face to offset the face edges.
- Likewise, offset the other edges.
- On the ribbon, click **Solid** tab > **Solid** panel > **Presspull**. Select the press-pulled face and move the pointer. Type **-1.5** and press **Enter**.
- Likewise, press pull the remaining two faces, as shown. Press **Esc** to deactivate the **Presspull** command.

- On the ribbon, click **Home** tab > **Selection** panel > **Filter** drop-down > **Face**. Select the faces, as shown. Right click and select **Properties**. On the **Properties** palette, select **Blue** from the **Color** drop-down. The color of the selected faces is changed to blue. You can notice the difference when you set the **View Style** to **Shaded with edges**. Press **Esc**.

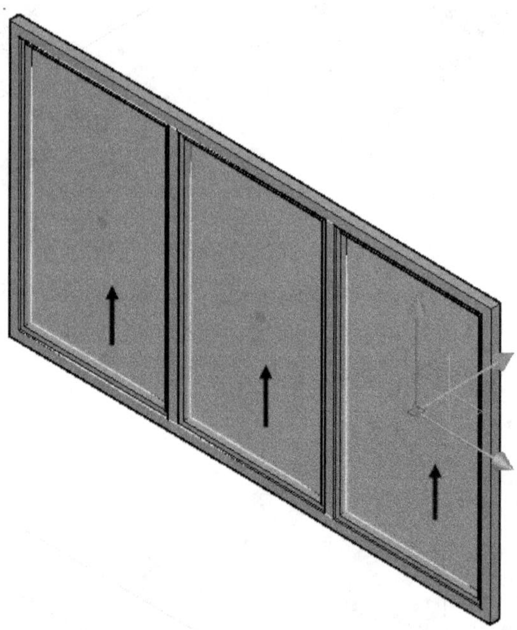

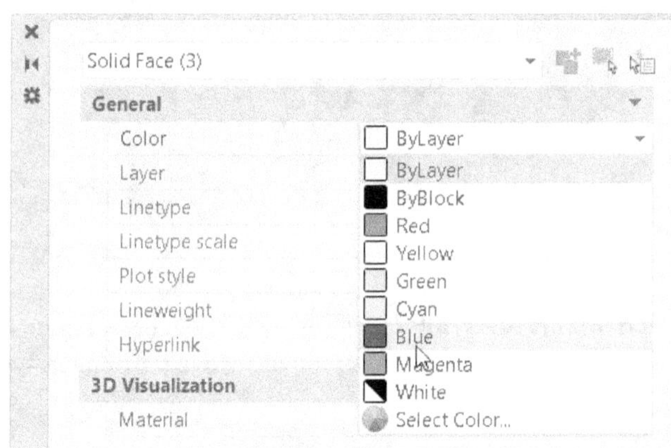

- On the ribbon, click **Home** tab > **Selection** panel > **Filter** drop-down > **No Filter**. Select the window, type **3DMIRROR**, and press **Enter**. Select the **3points** option from the command line. Select the corner points of the window, as shown. Select the **No** option from the command line.

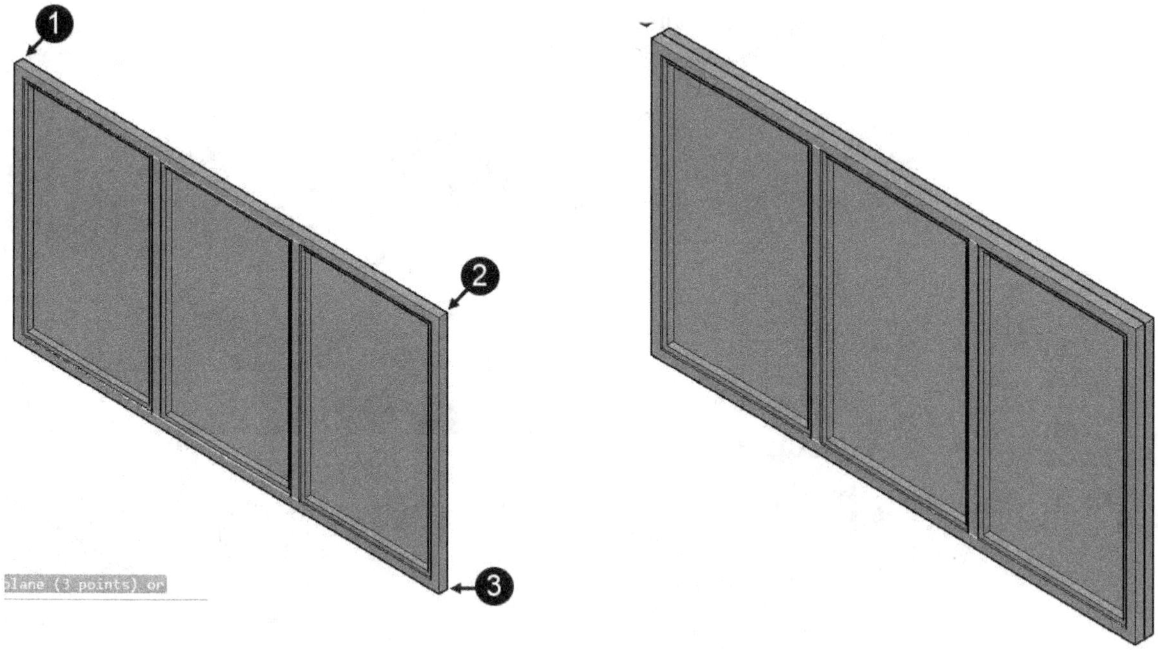

- Type **UNI** and press **Enter**. Select two window pieces and press **Enter**. The selected solids are united together.

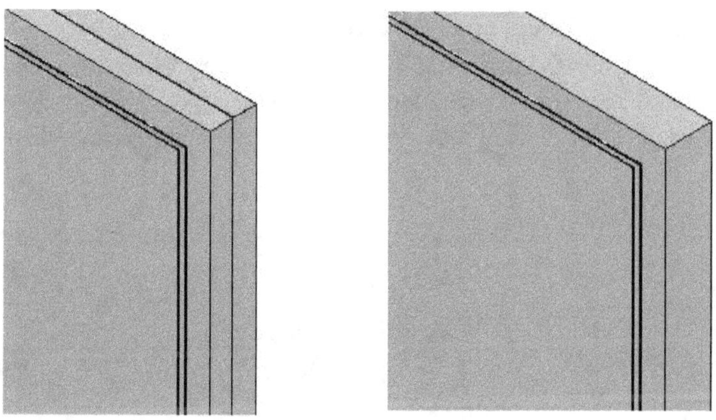

- Turn on the **3D-Walls** layer. Select the window, click on the **Y-axis** (green arrow) of the Move gizmo, and move the pointer inside the 3D wall. Type **6** and press **Enter**. Press **Esc** to deselect the window. Select the lines and polyline placed on the window opening, and press **Delete**.

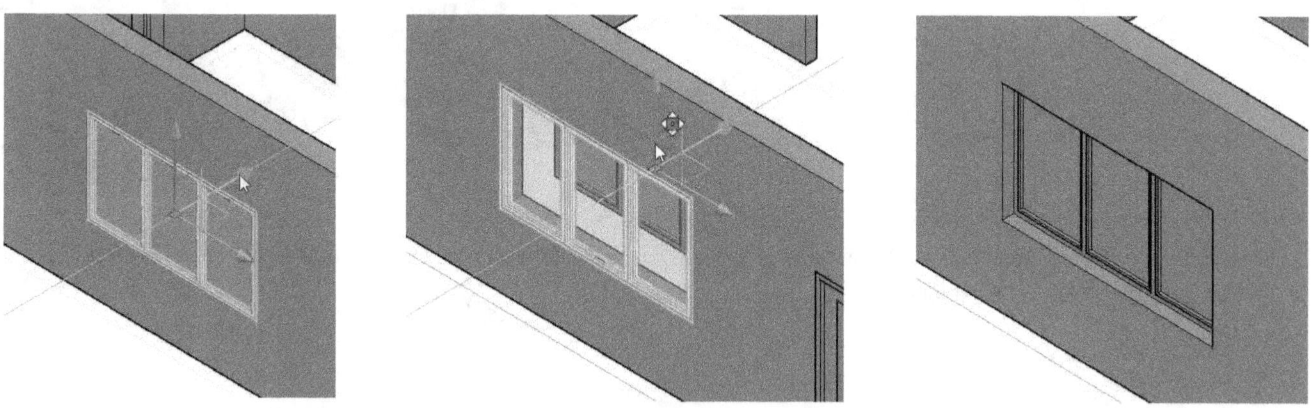

- Select the window, type **CO**, and press **Enter**. Select the lower left corner of the window opening to define the base point. Move the pointer toward the right side window opening, and then select its lower left corner point. Press **Esc**.

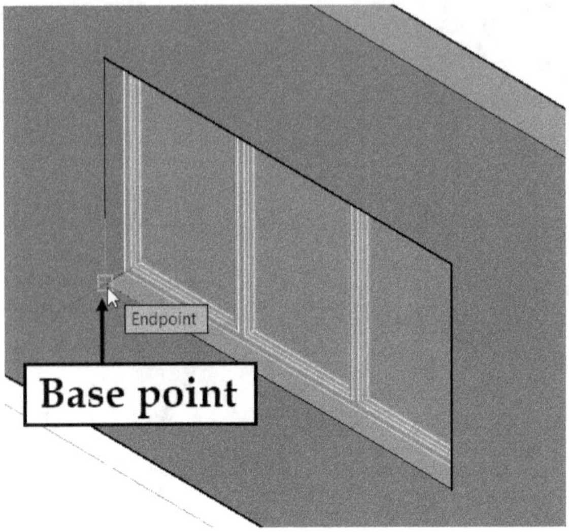

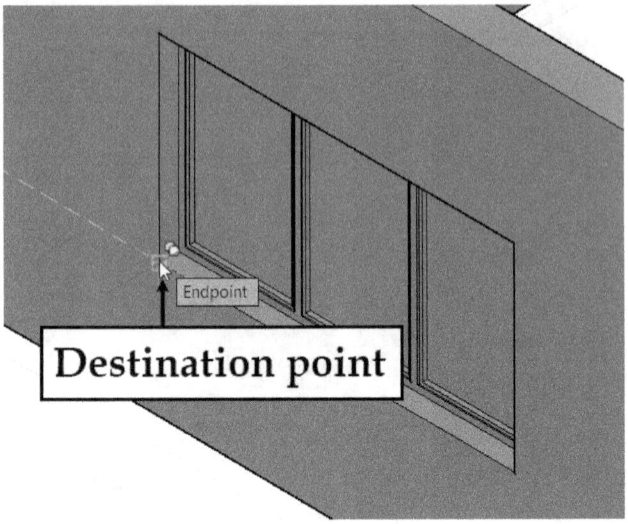

- Select the North elevation group, and then click **Home** tab > **Groups** panel > **Ungroup** 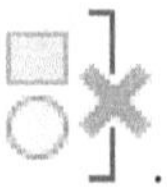 .
- Change the view orientation to **NW Isometric**. Select the 2D windows on the North elevation view by creating selection windows over them. Type **CO** and press **Enter**. Zoom to the extreme left window and select its lower left point. Move the pointer toward the 3D walls and select the lower left corner point of the extreme left window opening. Press **Esc** to deactivate the **Copy** command.

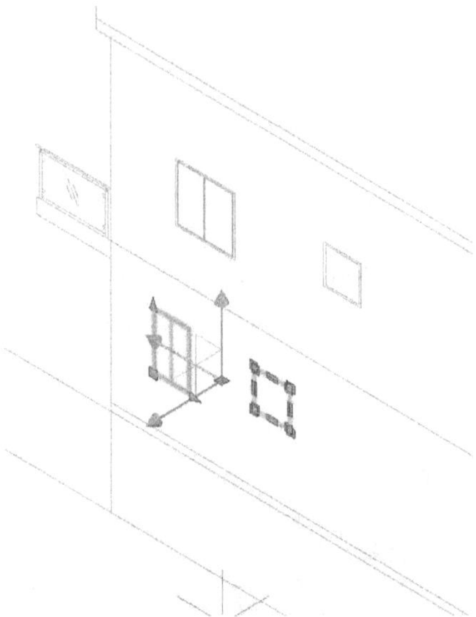

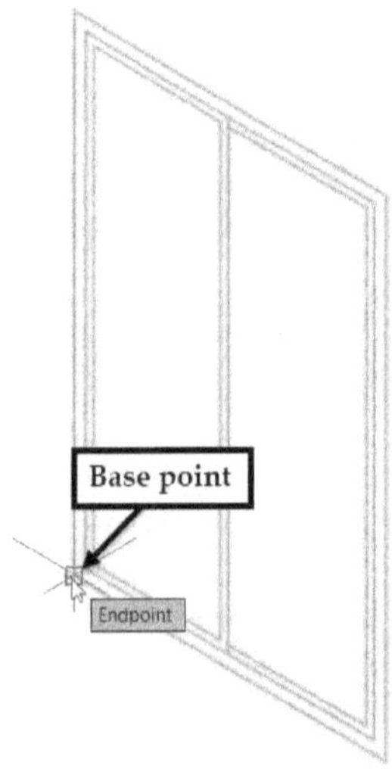

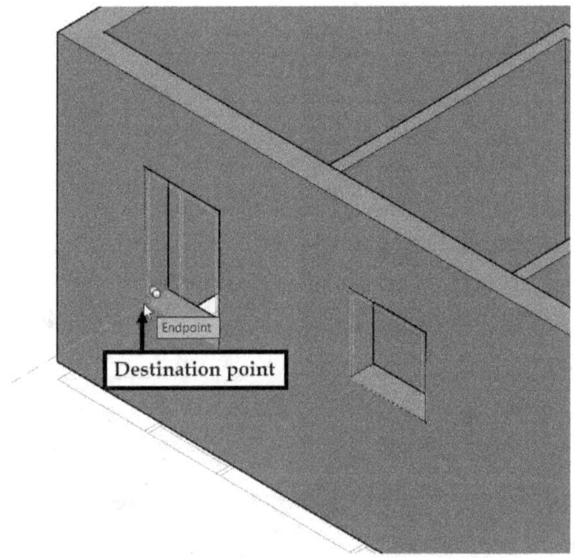

- Select the copy of the extreme left 2D-window. On the **Home** tab of the ribbon, expand the **Modify** panel and click the **Explode** tool; the block is exploded.

- Turn **OFF** the **3D Walls** layer.
- On the ribbon, click **Home** tab > **Modeling** panel > **Polysolid**. Select the **Height** option from the command line. Type **4** and press **Enter**. Select the **Width** option from the command line and enter **1.5**. Press **Enter**. Select **Justify** from the command line, and then select **Right**. Select **Object** from the command line. Select the outer rectangle of the window, as shown.

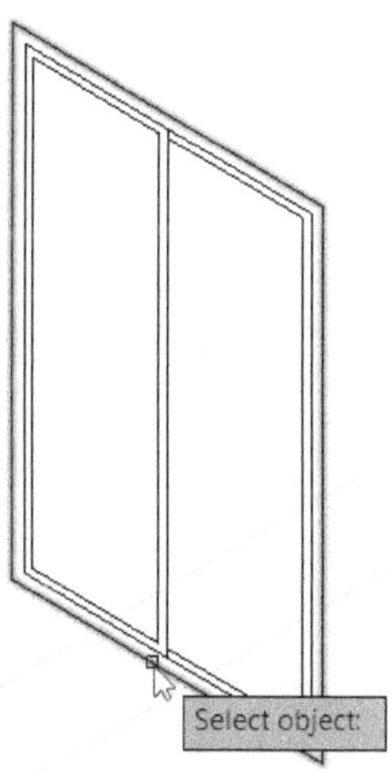

- Type **UCS** in the command line and press **Enter**. Next, select the three corners of the poly solid, as shown. The origin, X-axis, and Y-axis are defined.

- Deactivate the **Dynamic UCS** icon on the Status bar.
- On the ribbon, click **Home** tab > **Modeling** panel > **Box**. Specify the first and second corners of the box, as shown. Type **2** and press **Enter** to create the box.

- On the ribbon, click **Solid** tab > **Solid Editing** panel > **Offset Edge** . Select the front face of the box. Select **Distance**, and then enter **1**. Press **Enter**. Click on the front face of the box to offset the edges of the selected face.
- Activate the **Presspull** tool and click in the area enclosed by the offset edge. Move the pointer inside the box and click to

remove the material.

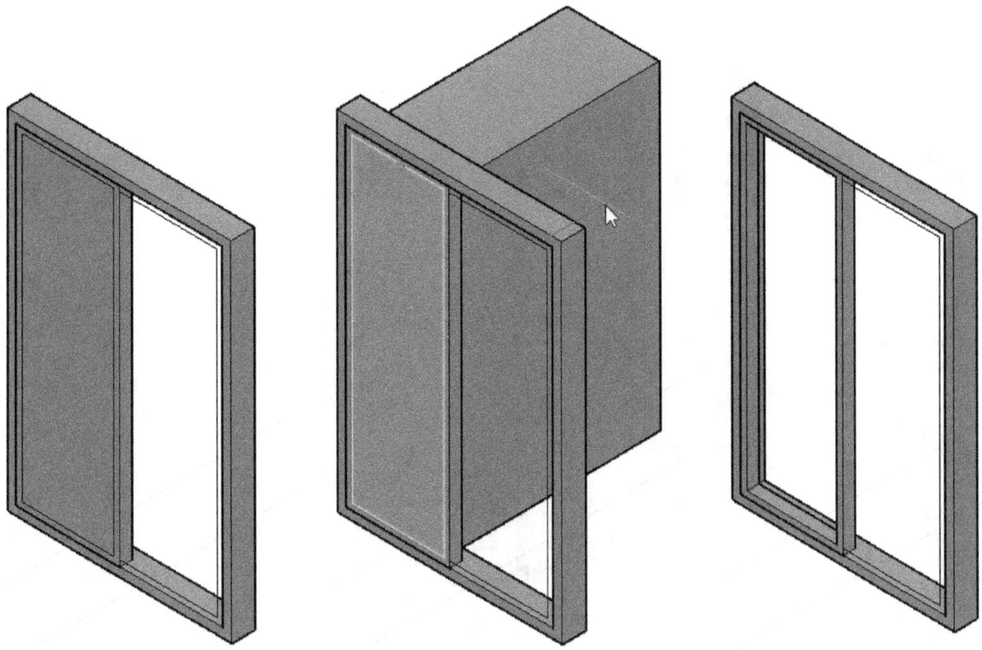

- On the ribbon, click **Home** tab > **Modeling** panel > **Box**. Specify the first and second corners of the box, as shown. Type **0.16** and press **Enter** to create the box. Select the newly created box, click on the **Y-axis** (green arrow) of the Move gizmo, and move the pointer inside the 3D wall. Type **1** and press **Enter**.

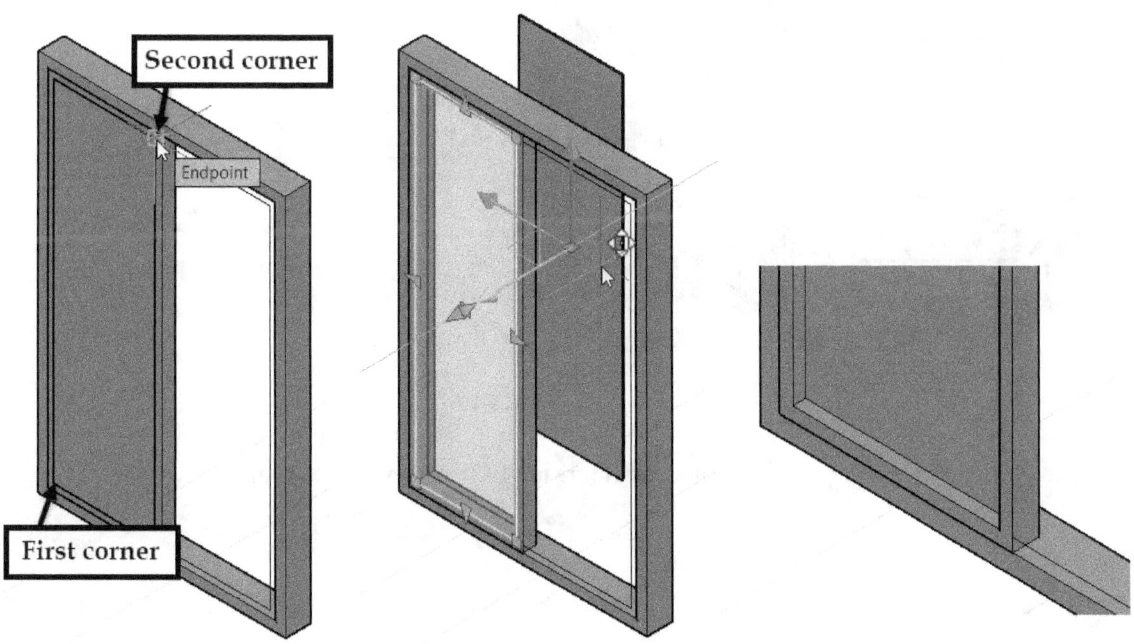

- Select the box, right click, and select **Properties**. On the **Properties** palette, select **Blue** from the **Color** drop-down.
- Type **UNI** and press **Enter**. Select the box created in the last step and the press-pulled solid. Press **Enter** to unite them.

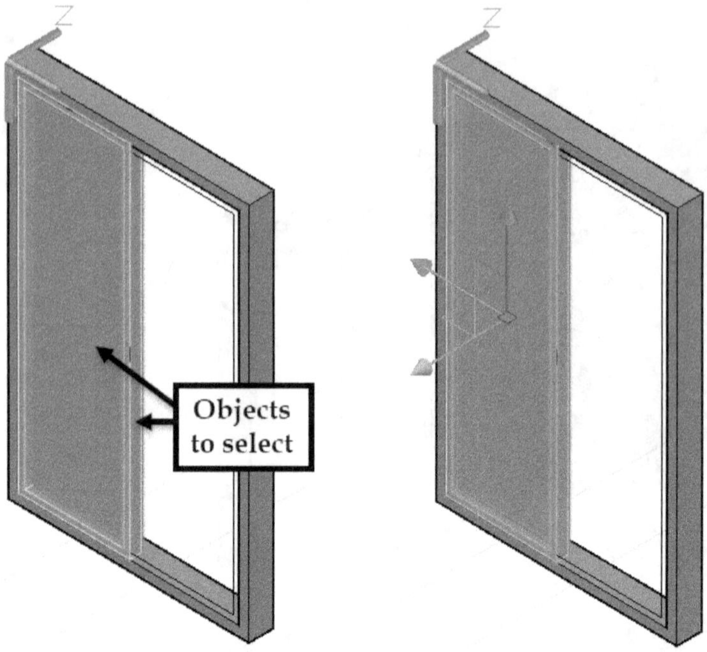

- Select the combined solid, type **CO**, and press **Enter**. Select the lower left corner point of the combined solid. Select the lower right corner point on the backside. Press **Esc**.

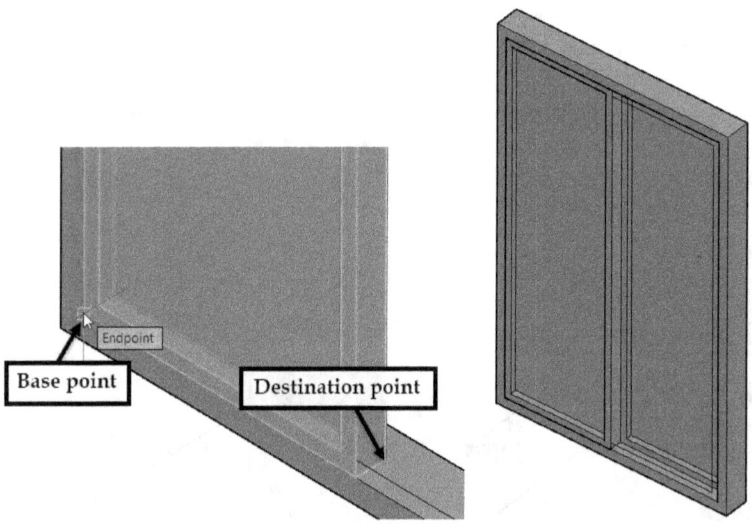

- Create a selection box over the window. On the ribbon, click **Home** tab > **Groups** panel > **Group**.

- Turn **ON** the **3D-Walls** layer.
- Select the window group, type **M**, and press **Enter**. Select the top left corner point of the window group. Move the pointer inside the wall, type **8**, and press **Enter**.

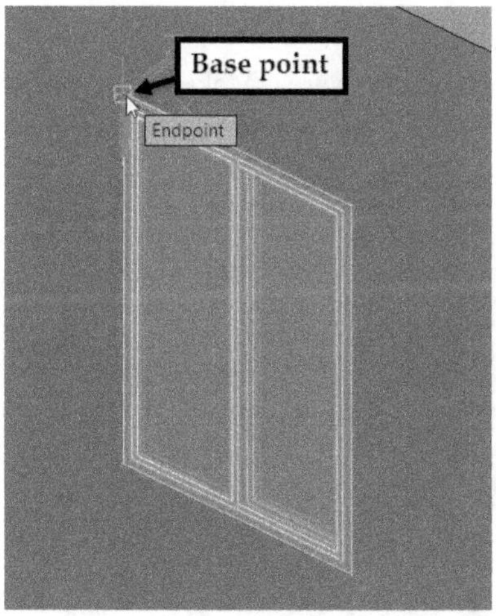

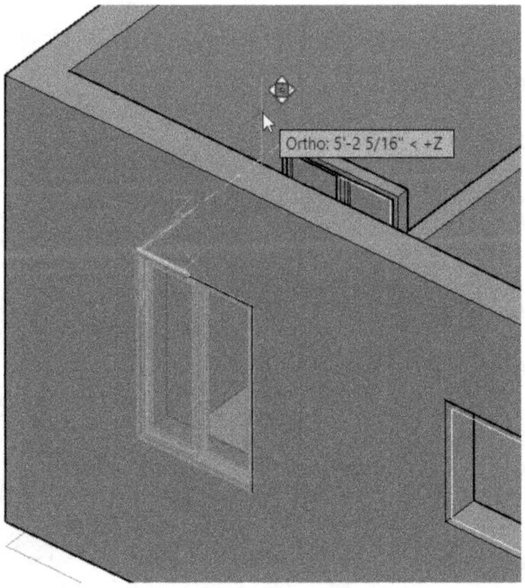

- Likewise, create other windows, as shown.

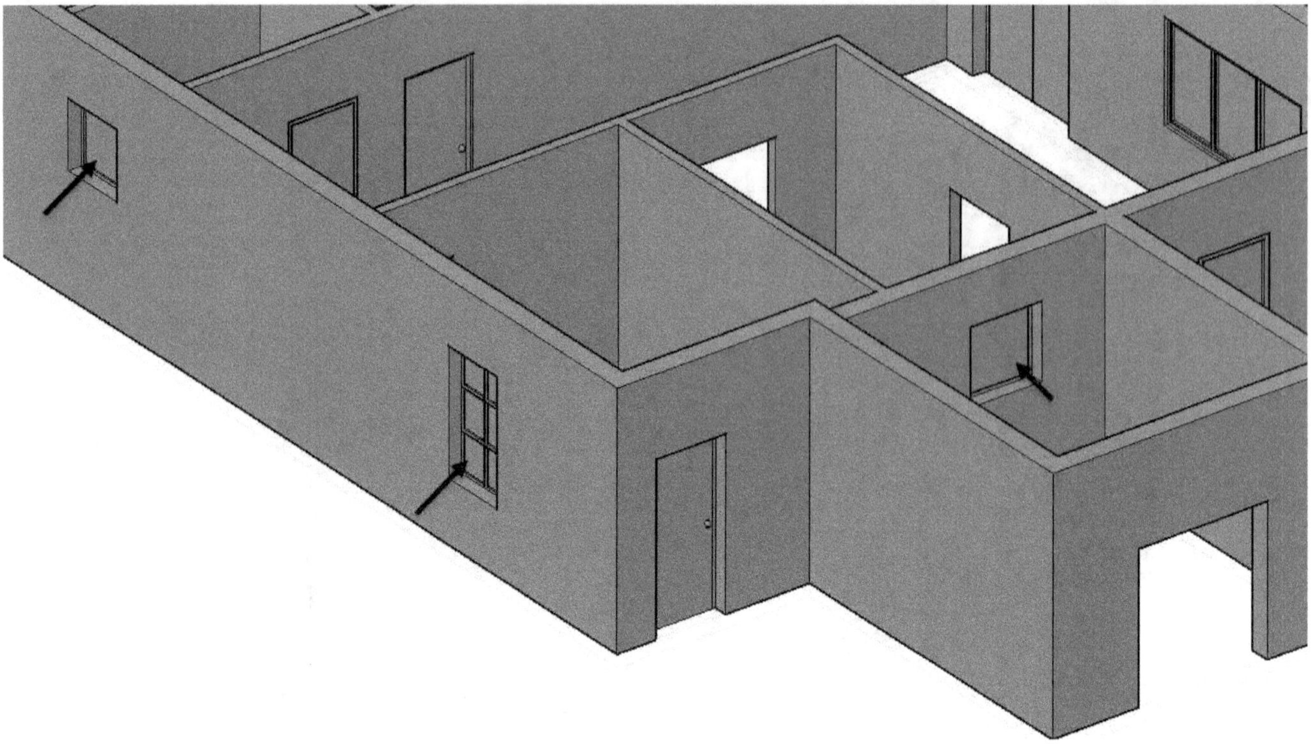

- Click **Home** tab > **Coordinates** panel > **UCS, World** on the ribbon.

Tutorial 6: Creating 3D Stairs

- Create a layer "3D-Stair" and set the color to Index color 150. Set the **3D-Stair** layer as current.
- On the ribbon, click **Home** tab > **Modeling** panel > **Primitive** drop-down > **Box**. Zoom to stairs area. Make sure that the **Dynamic UCS** icon is activated on the status bar. Place the pointer on the top face of the inner walls and select the corner point, as shown. Select the diagonally opposite corner, as shown.

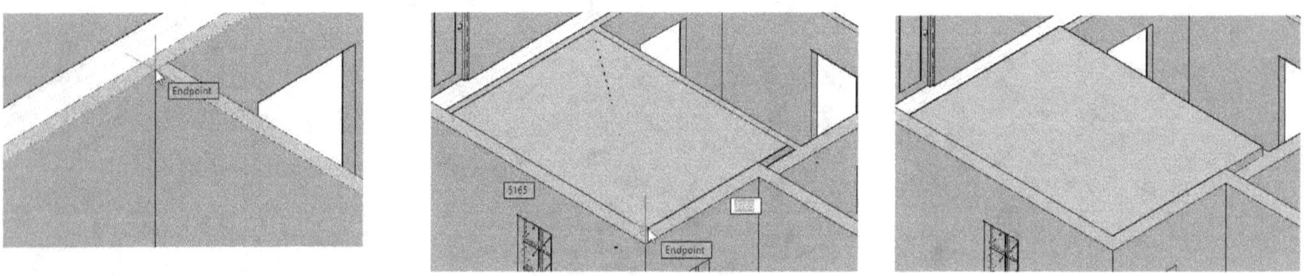

- Turn on the **3D-Floor** layer. Type **SU** and press **Enter**. Select the first floor and press **Enter**. Select the box created in the last step and press **Enter**.

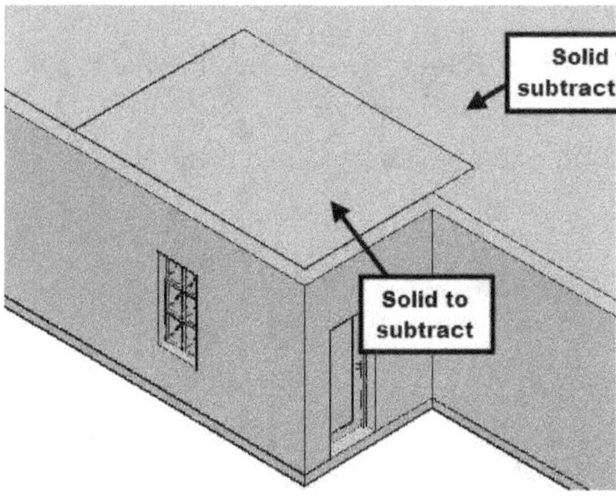

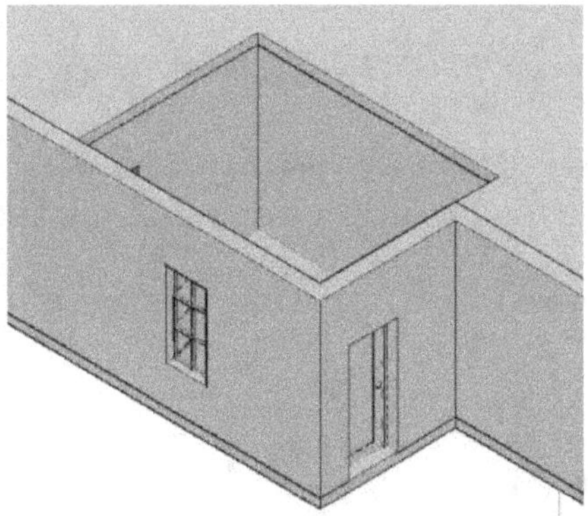

- Type **3DO** and press **Enter**. Rotate the model, as shown. Press **Esc**.

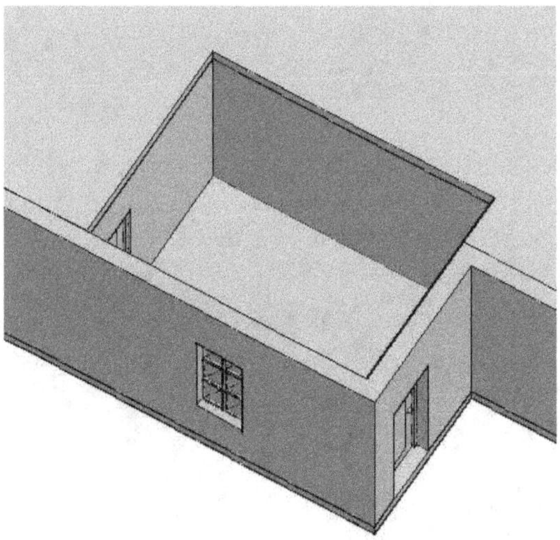

- Make sure that the **Dynamic Input** icon is activated on the status bar.
- On the ribbon, click **Home** tab > **Modeling** panel > **Primitive** drop-down > **Wedge**. Place the pointer on the ground floor, and then select the corner point, as shown. Move the pointer toward the right. Type **171.65** and press **Tab**. Type **68.2** and press **Enter**. Move the pointer upward, type **144**, and press **Enter**.

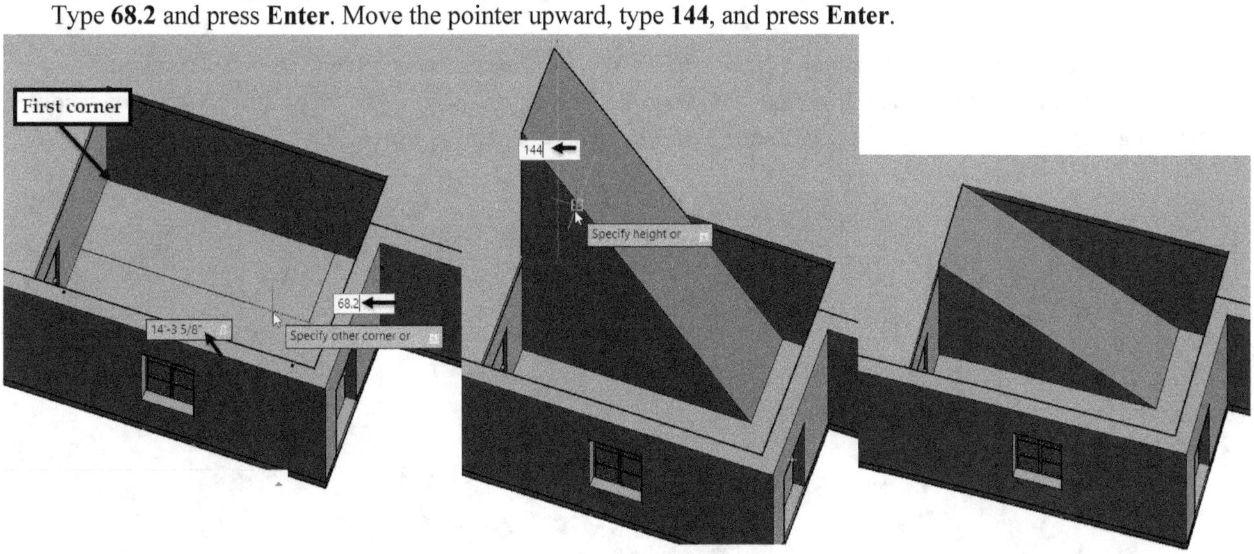

- On the ribbon, click **Home** tab > **Solid Editing** panel > **Edges** drop-down > **Extract Edges**. Select the wedge and press Enter.
- Type **UCS** and press **Enter**. Select **Face** from the command line. Select the side face of the wedge, and then select **accept** from the command line. The UCS is positioned on the selected face.

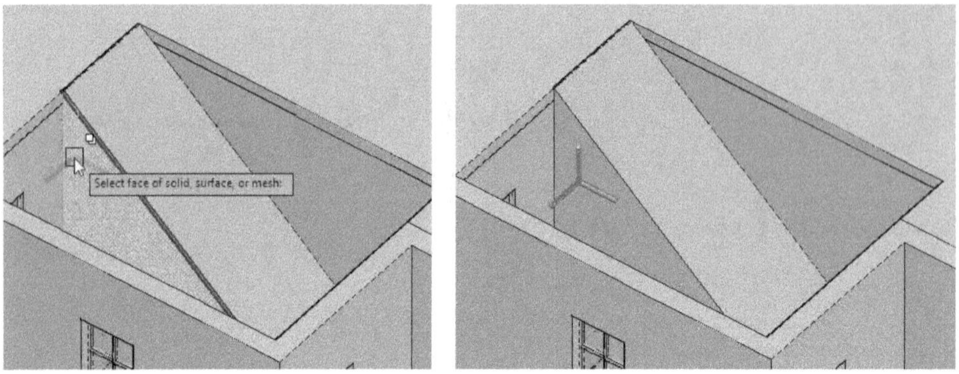

- Type **O** and press **Enter**. Type **18** and press **Enter**. Select the inclined extracted edge. Move the pointer downward and click to offset the line. Press **Esc**.

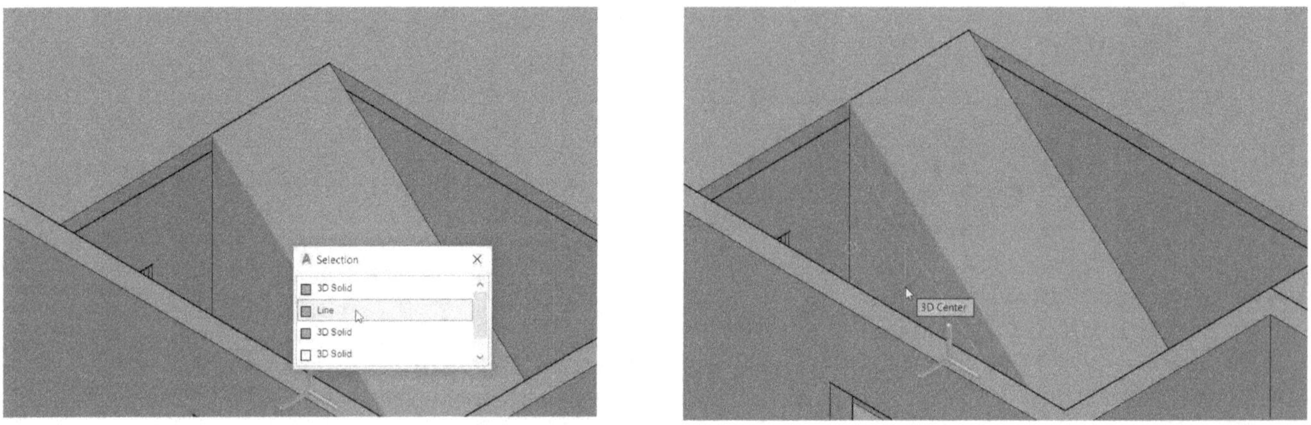

- On the ribbon, click **Home** tab > **Coordinates** panel > **UCS, World**. The UCS is restored to its default position.
- On the ribbon, click **Home** tab > **Modeling** panel > **Presspull**. Click on the side face of the wedge in the region below the offset edge, as shown. Move the pointer into the wedge, type **68.2**, and press **Enter**. Press **Esc**.

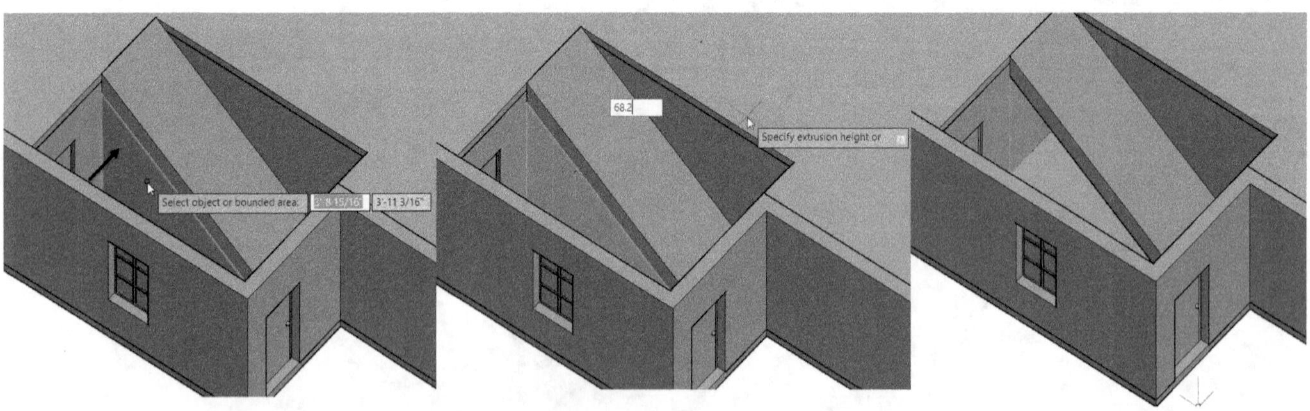

- Activate the **Box** tool and place the pointer on the top face of the first floor. Move the pointer and select the corner point, as shown. Move the pointer forward. Specify the length and width as **68.2** and **8.58**, respectively, and then press **Enter**. Move the pointer downward, type **7.2**, and press **Enter**.

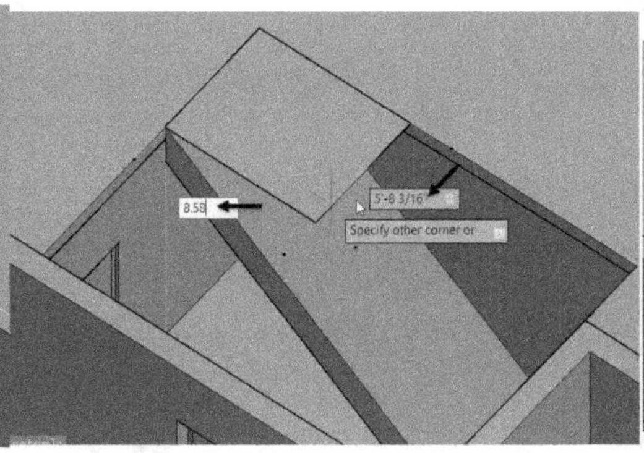

- On the ribbon, click **Home** tab > **Modify** panel > **Array** drop-down > **Path Array**. Select the box and press **Enter**. Select the extracted inclined line. On the **Array Creation** tab, on the **Properties** panel, click **Measure Method** drop-down > **Divide**. On the **Items** panel, change the **Items** value to **21**.
- Deactivate the **Associative** icon on the **Properties** panel. Click **Close Array** on the **Array Creation** ribbon tab.

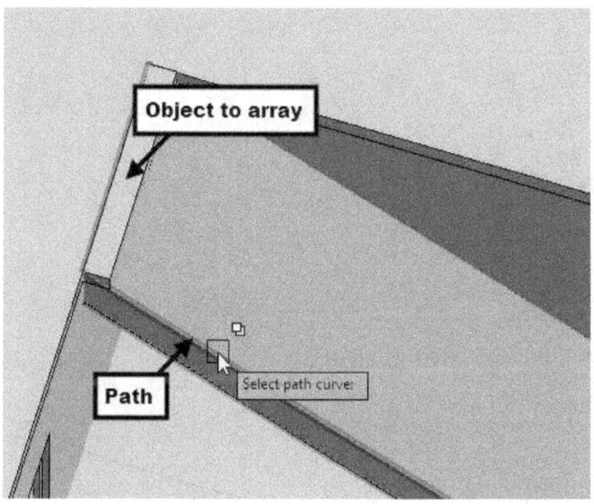

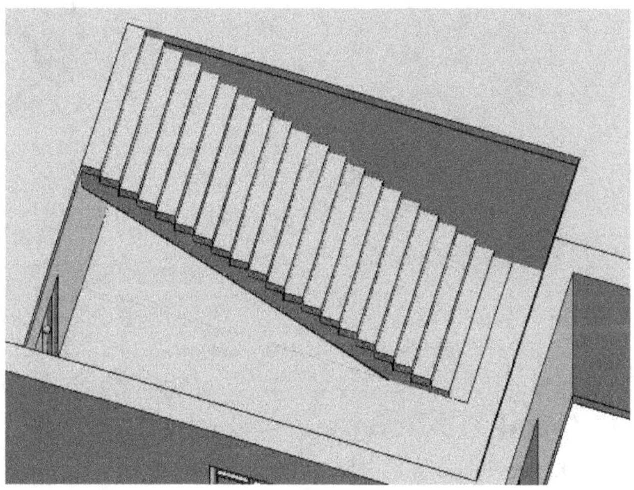

- Select the bottom-most stair and press **Delete**.

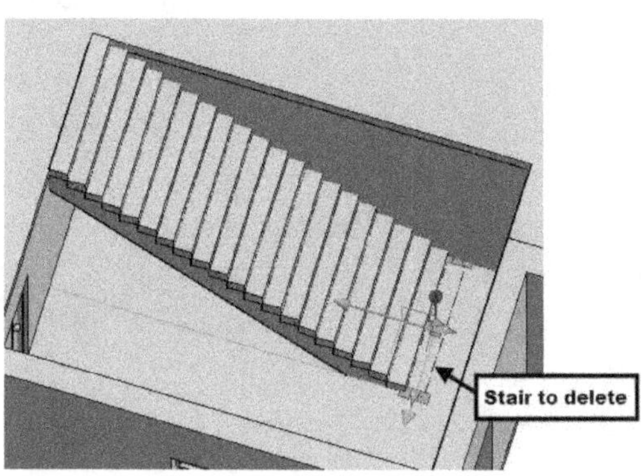

- On the ribbon, click **Home** tab > **Layers** panel > **Isolate**. Select any one of the stairs and press Enter; all the layers except the layer of the selected object are hidden.
- Select any one of the extracted edges. Right click and select **Select Similar**; all the extracted edges are selected. Press **Delete** to delete all the selected edges.

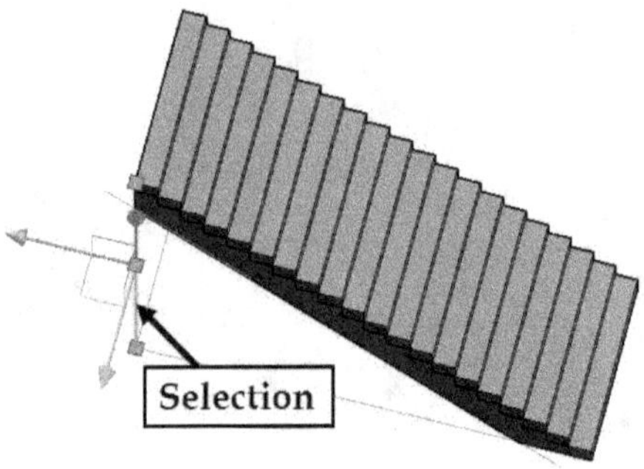

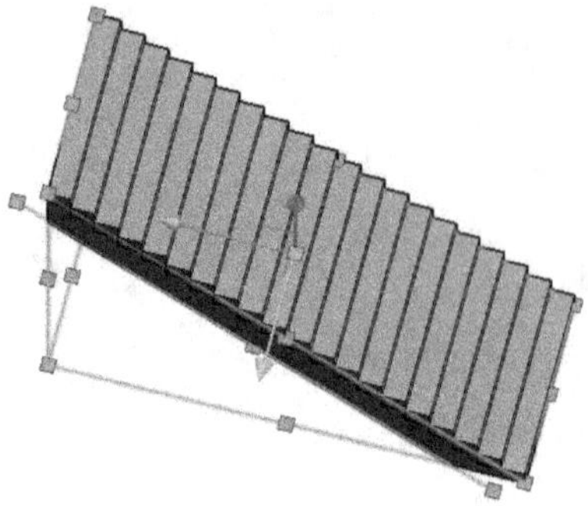

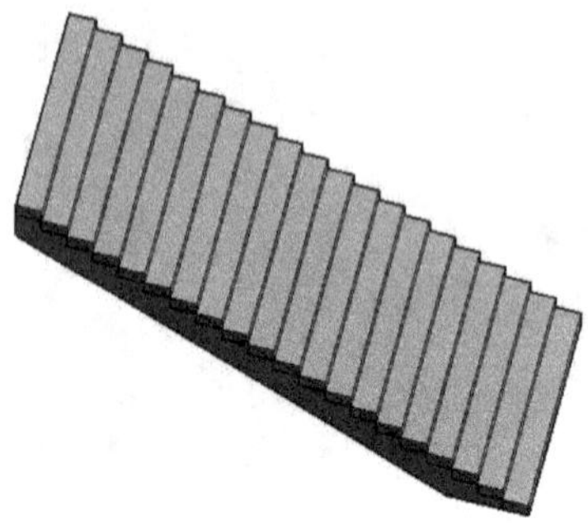

- Type **UNI** and press **Enter**. Create a selection window over all the objects of the staircase and press **Enter**.

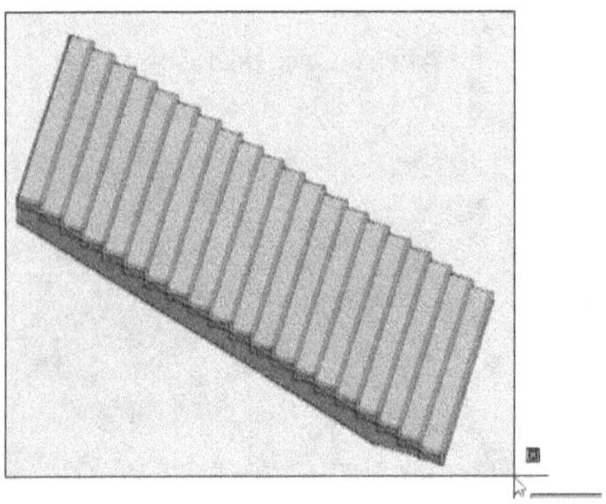

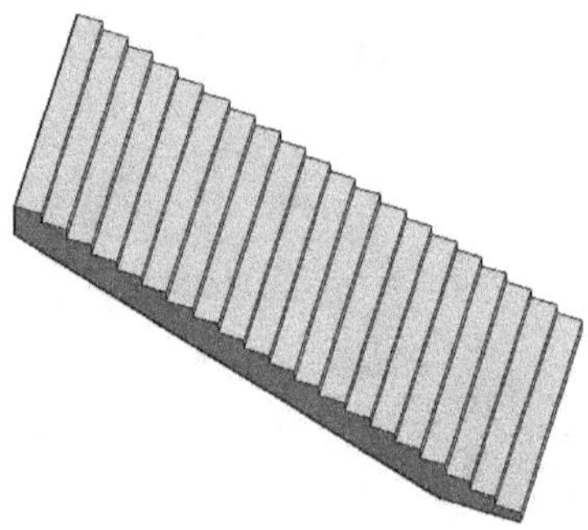

- On the ribbon, click **Home** tab > **Layers** panel > **Unisolate**. All the layers are turned on.

Tutorial 7: Modeling the First Floor

- On the ribbon, click **Home** tab > **View** panel > **Restore View** drop-down > **Top**.
- On the ribbon, click **Home** tab > **Layers** panel > **Off** . Zoom to the first-floor plan and select the objects, as shown.

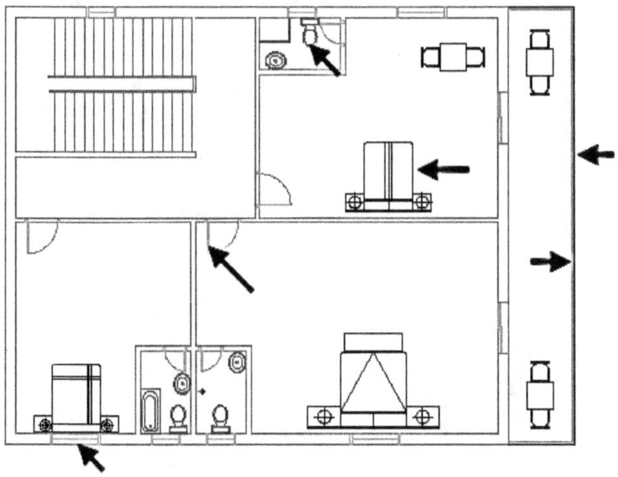

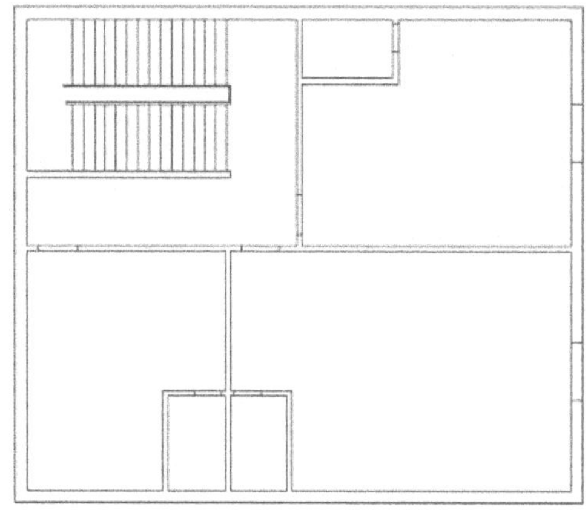

Note: Skip the above step if the fixtures are hidden already.

- Create a selection window over the first-floor plan. On the ribbon, click **Home** tab > **Layers** panel > **Copy Objects New Layer** . Select any one of the 3D walls. Select the lower left corner point of the first floor, move the pointer toward the right and click to place the copy.

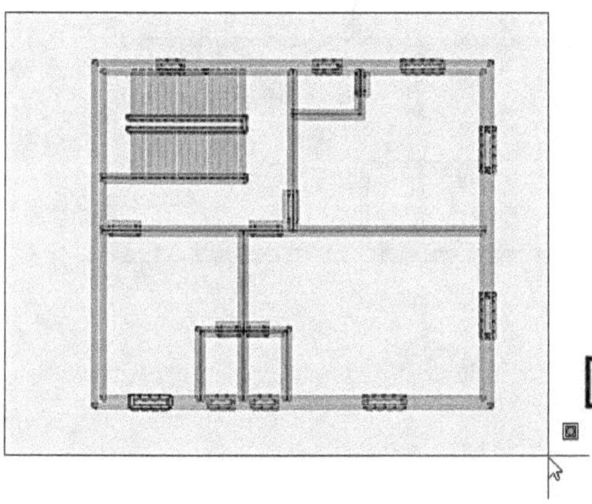

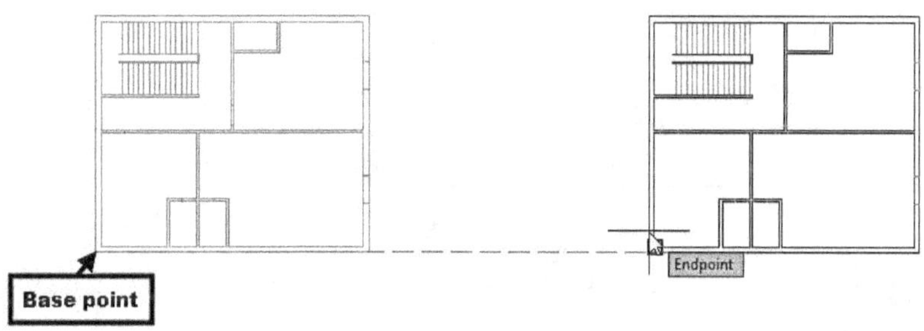

- Select the stairs from the copy of the first-floor plan and press **Delete**.
- On the **Home** tab of the ribbon, expand the **Draw** panel and click the **Region** tool. Create a selection window over the copy of the first-floor plan, and then press **Enter**.

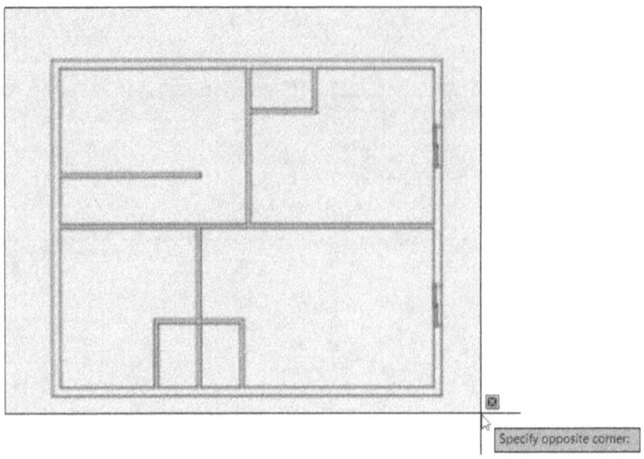

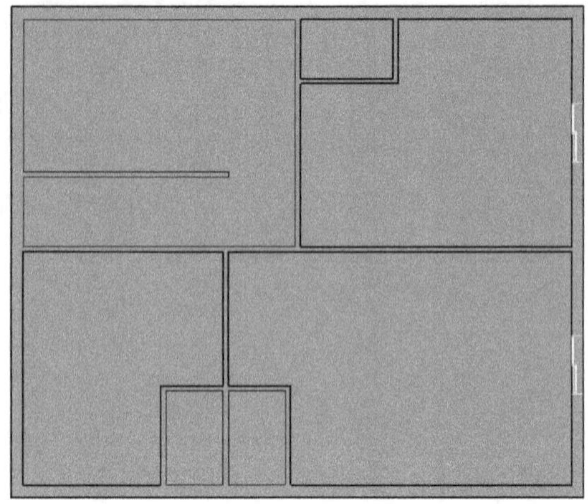

- Activate the **3D Walls** layer from the **Layer Property Manager**.
- Type **SU** and press **Enter**. Select the outermost region and press **Enter**. Select the inner regions and press **Enter**.

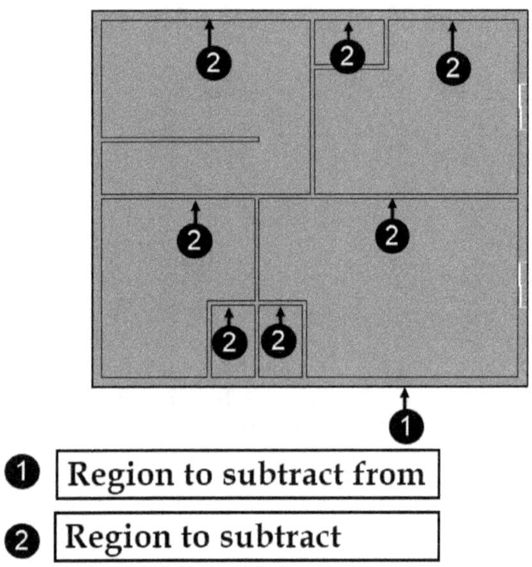

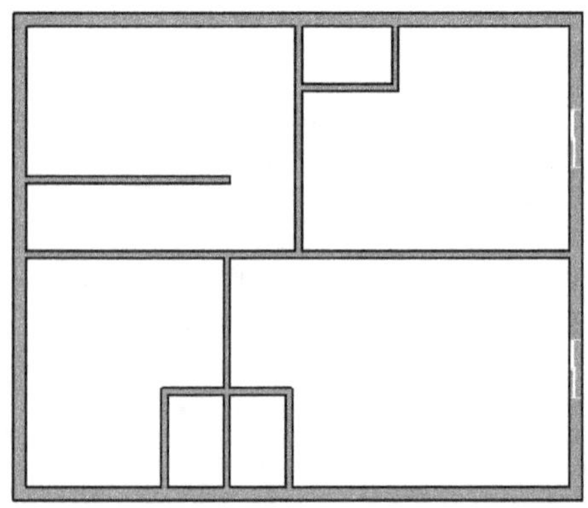

- Change the view orientation to **SE Isometric**.

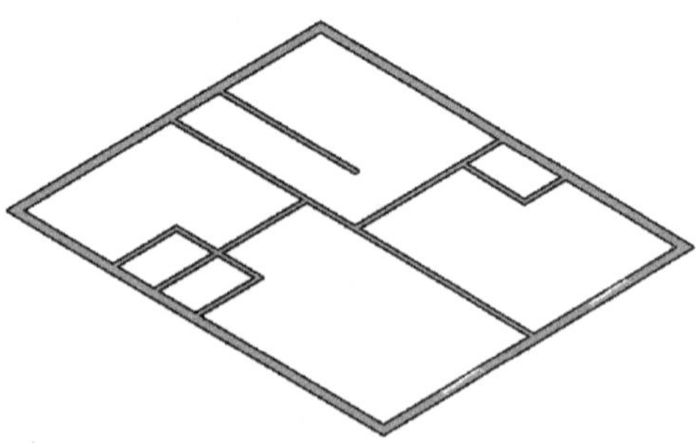

- Type **MEA** in the command line and press **Enter**. Next, select **Distance** from the command line. Zoom to the North Elevation, and then select the two points, as shown. The distance between the two points is displayed as 15' above the command line. Press **Esc** to deactivate the **Measure** command.

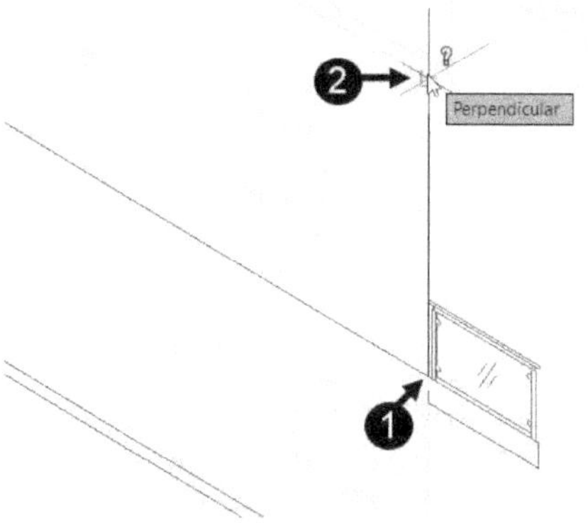

- Type **EXT** and press **Enter**. Select the region and press Enter. Move the pointer upward, type **180**, and then press **Enter**.

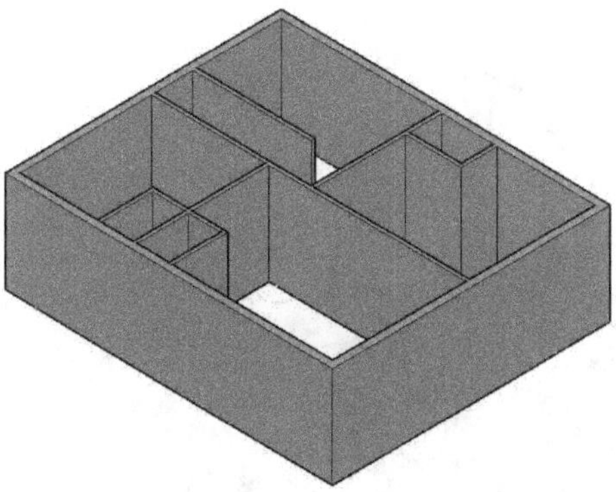

- Select the extruded solid, type **M**, and press **Enter**. Select the lower corner point, as shown. Select the corner point on the ground floor wall, as shown.

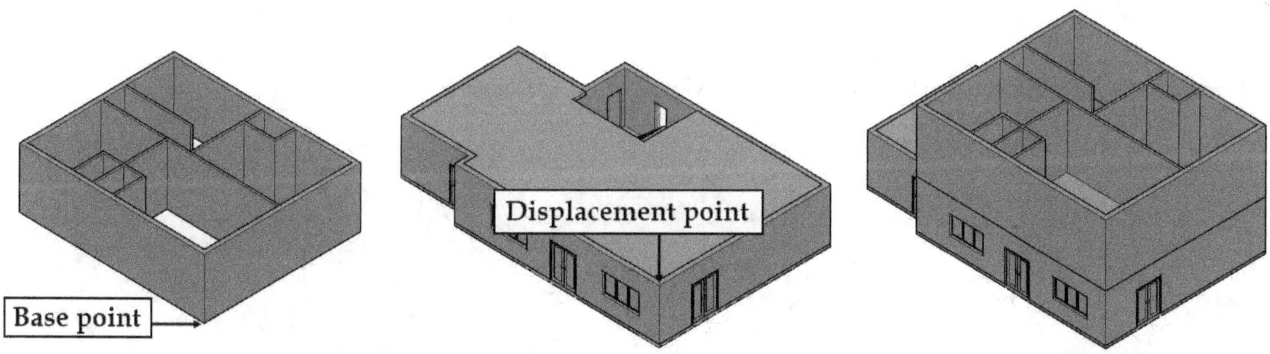

- Activate the **Rectangle** tool and create a rectangle on the top face of the outer wall, as shown.

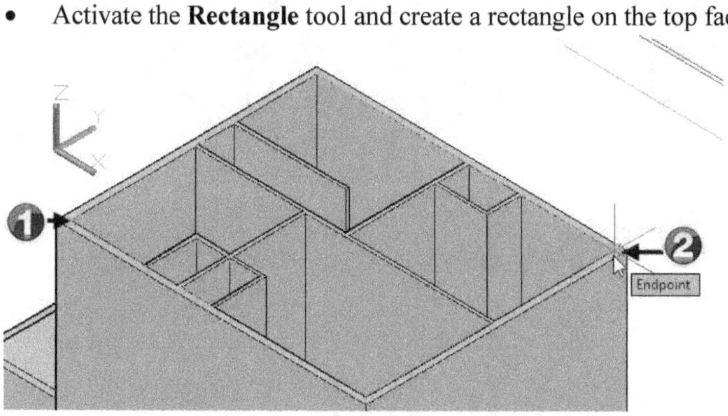

- Activate the **Presspull** tool and click on the top face of the inner wall, as shown. Zoom to the North elevation and select the point, as shown.

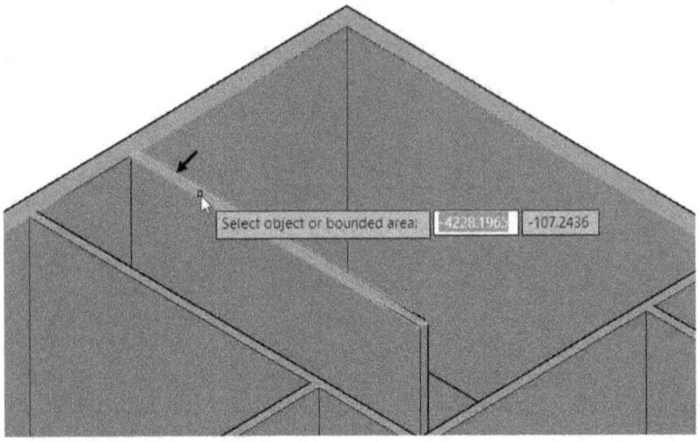

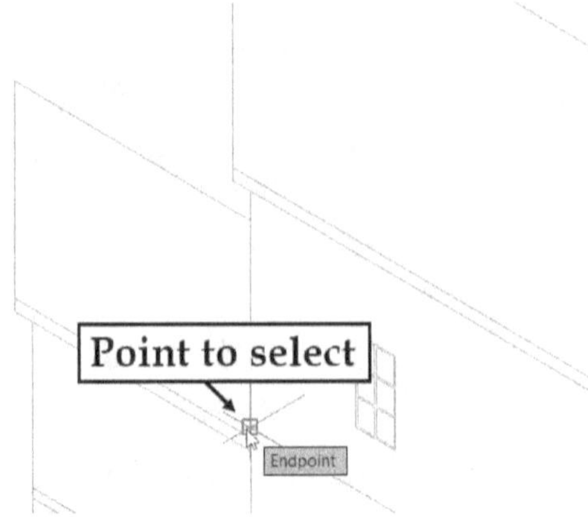

- Use the **Presspull** tool and decrease the height of the inner walls by **8** inches.

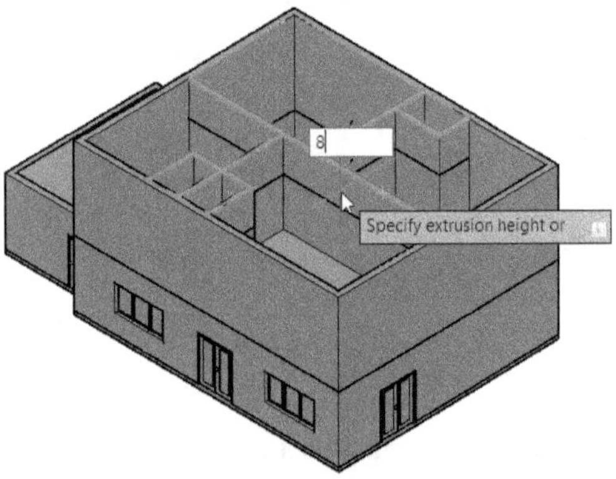

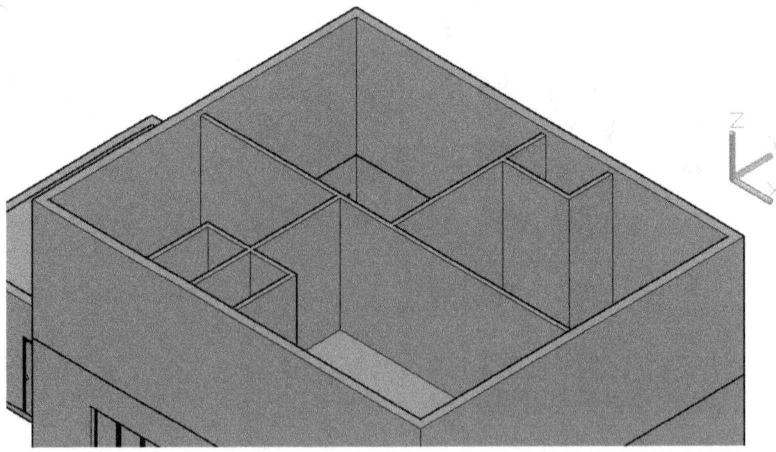

- Copy the 2D doors and windows from the elevation views onto the 3D walls.

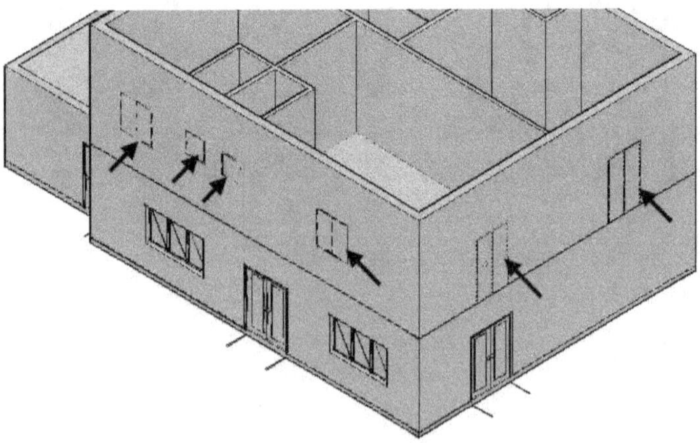

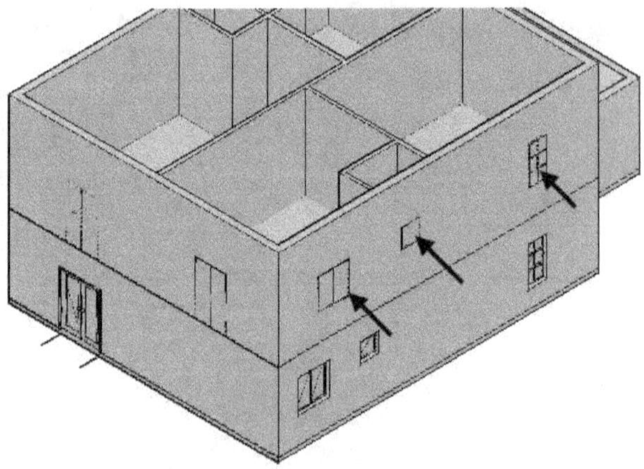

- Create doors and window openings using the **Box** and **Subtract** tools.

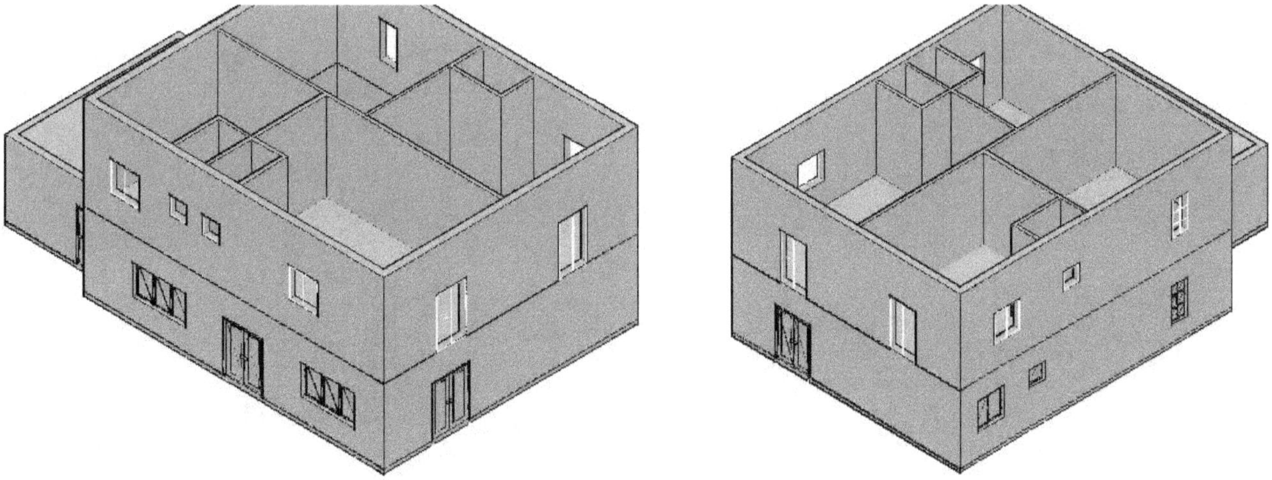

- Create boxes on the first-floor plan, as shown. The height of the boxes is **98** inches.

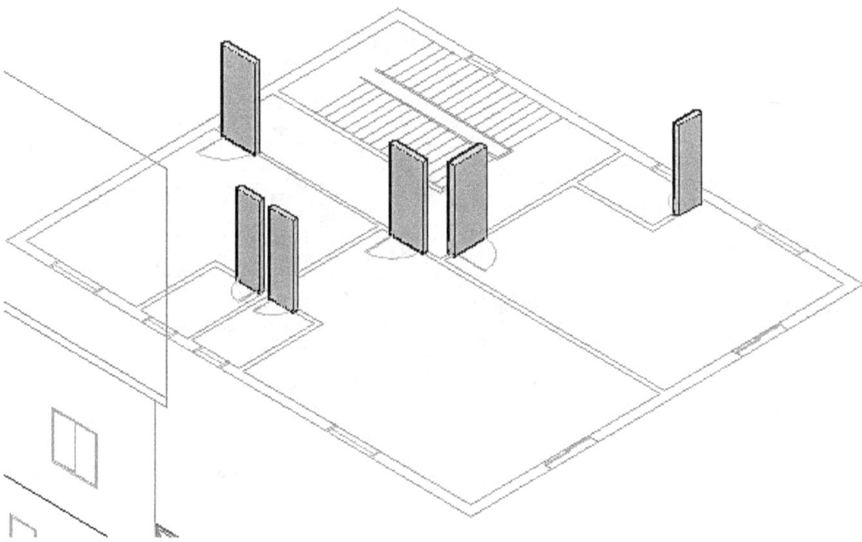

- Select all the boxes on the first-floor plan, type M, and press Enter. Select the corner point on the first-floor plan to define the base point, as shown. Specify the destination point on the 3D wall, as shown.

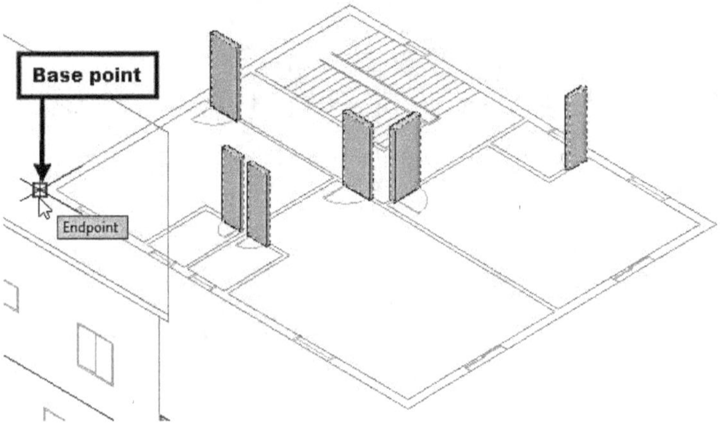

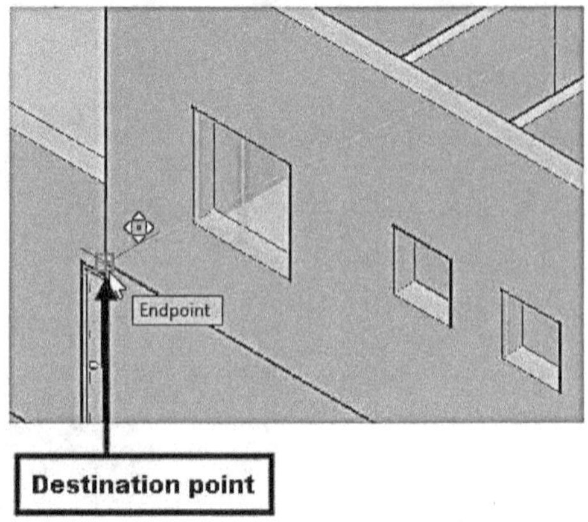

- Subtract the boxes from the 3D walls.

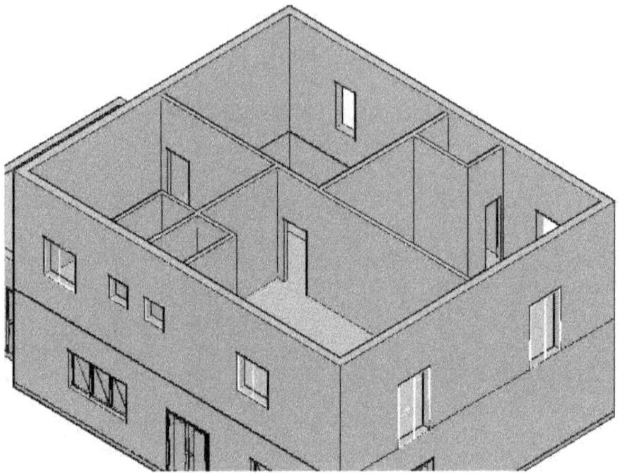

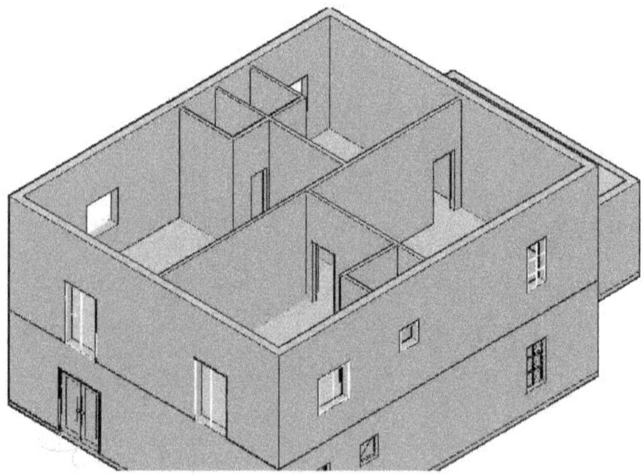

- Copy the doors and windows from the ground floor and place them on door and window openings. Also, create sliding doors, bathroom doors, and windows with different dimensions. The procedure to create doors and windows has been described already.

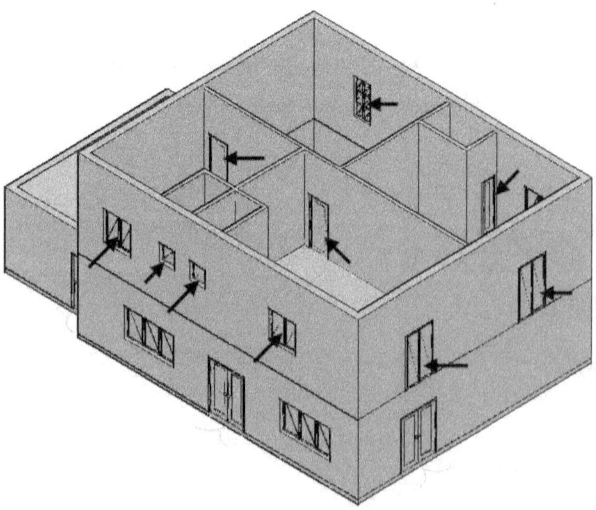

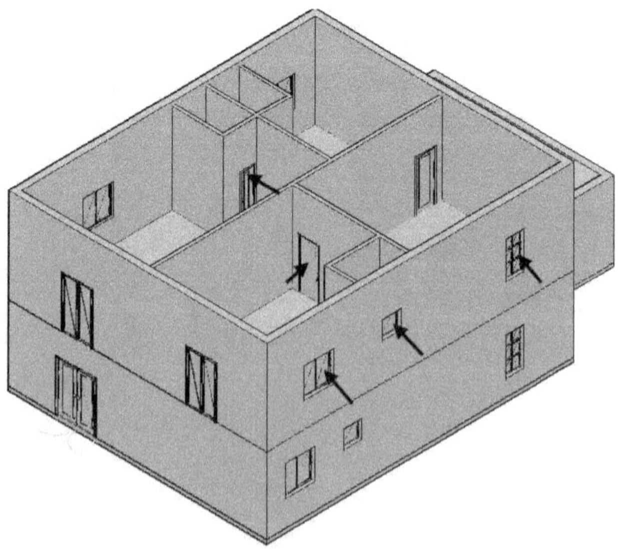

Tutorial 8: Creating the Balcony

- Create a new layer "3D-Balcony", set its color to green, and activate the layer.
- On the ribbon, click **Home > Group > Ungroup** 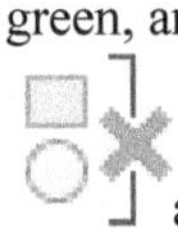 and select the North elevation.

Note: Skip the above step, if the North elevation is ungrouped already.

- Zoom to the North elevation and create a selection window over the balcony. Type **CO** and press **Enter**. Specify the base and destination points, as shown. Press **Esc**.

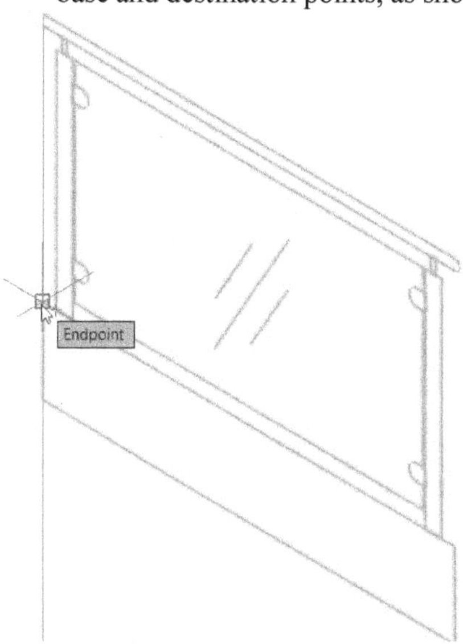

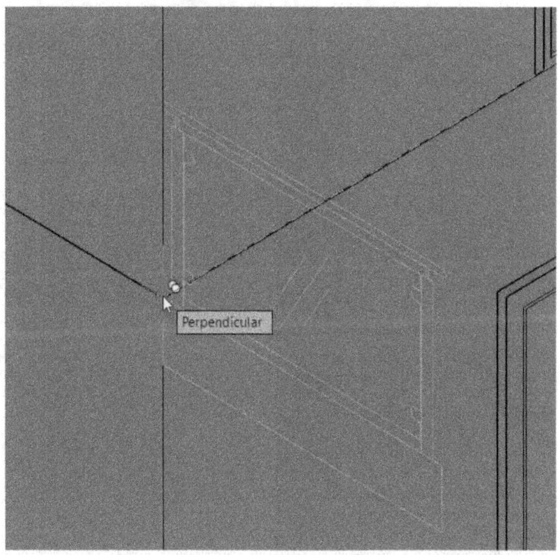

- Type **EXT** and press **Enter**. Select the large rectangle of the balcony, press **Enter**, and move the pointer toward the right. Select the corner point of the ground floor wall, as shown.

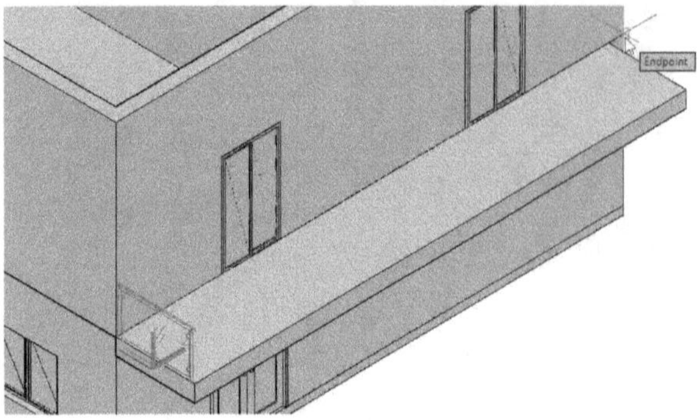

- On the ribbon, click **Home** tab > **Modeling** panel > **Primitives** drop-down > **Cylinder** . Select **2P** from the command line. Place the pointer on the top face of the extruded solid, and select lower corner points of the rectangle, as shown. Move the pointer upward and select the top left corner point of the rectangle, as shown; the cylinder is created.

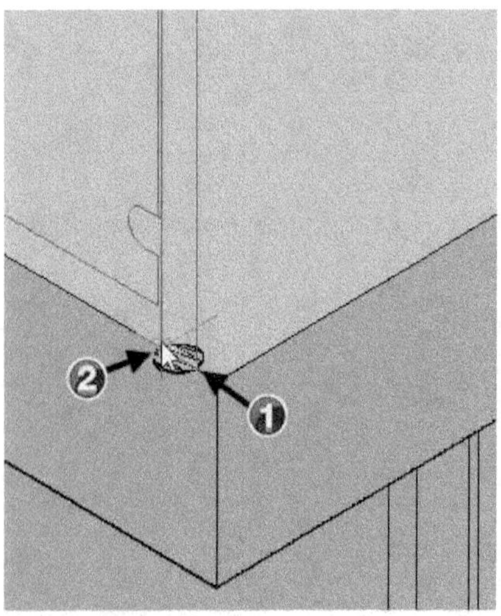

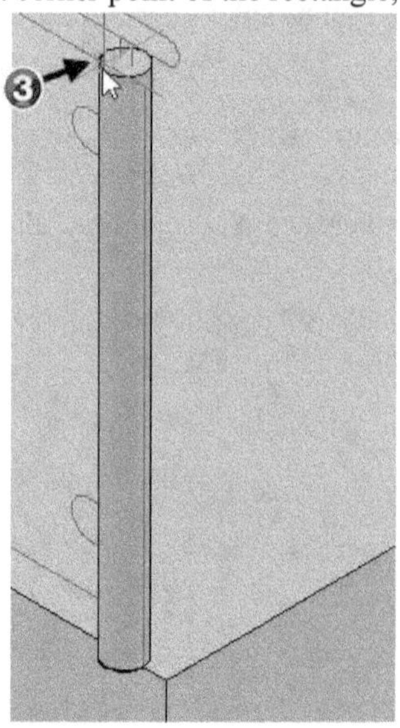

- Activate the **Cylinder** tool and create another cylinder, as shown.

- Select the rectangular array of the sleeve. On the **Home** tab of the ribbon, expand the **Modify** panel and click the **Explode** tool (skip this step if the rectangular array is exploded already).

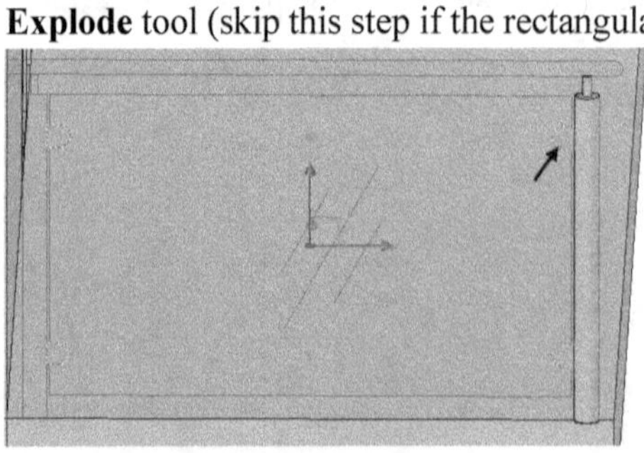

- On the **Home** tab of the ribbon, expand the **Draw** panel and click the **Region** tool. Select the arc and polyline of the sleeve and press **Enter**. Type **EXT** and press **Enter**. Select the region, press Enter, move the pointer toward the right, type **0.8**, and press **Enter**.

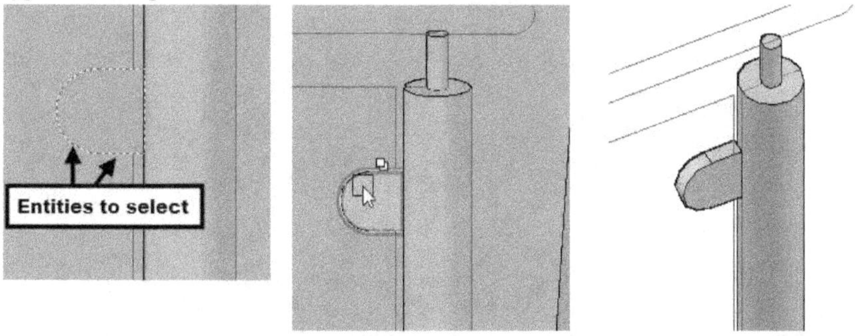

- Select the extruded solid. Select the Y-axis of the Move gizmo, move the pointer backward, type **0.4**, and press **Enter**.

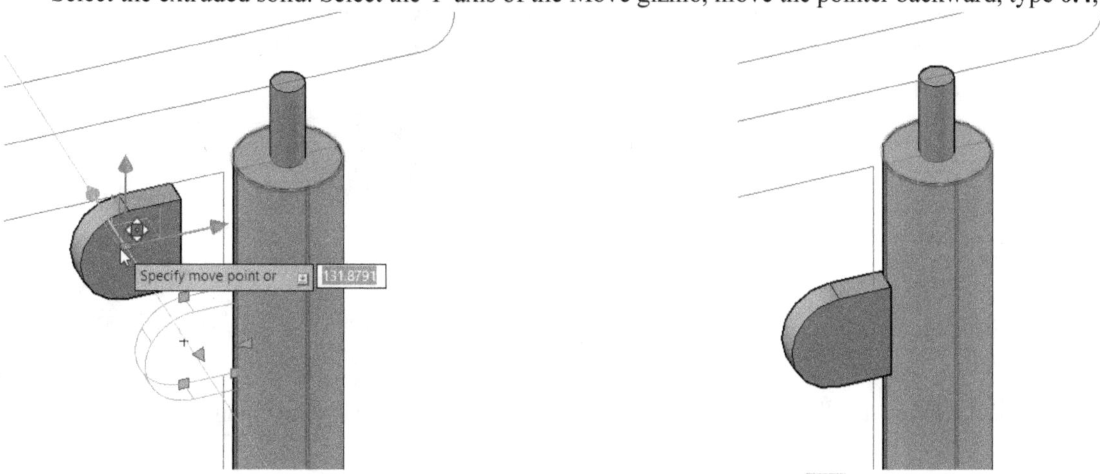

- On the ribbon, click **Solid** tab > **Solid Editing** panel > **Offset Edges**  . Select the top face of the sleeve, and then select **Distance** from the command line. Type **0.1** and press **Enter**. Click on the top face of the sleeve to create an offset edge. Press **Esc**. Select the offset edge to display grips. Click on the midpoint grip of the width, move the pointer toward left and click; the rectangle is stretched.

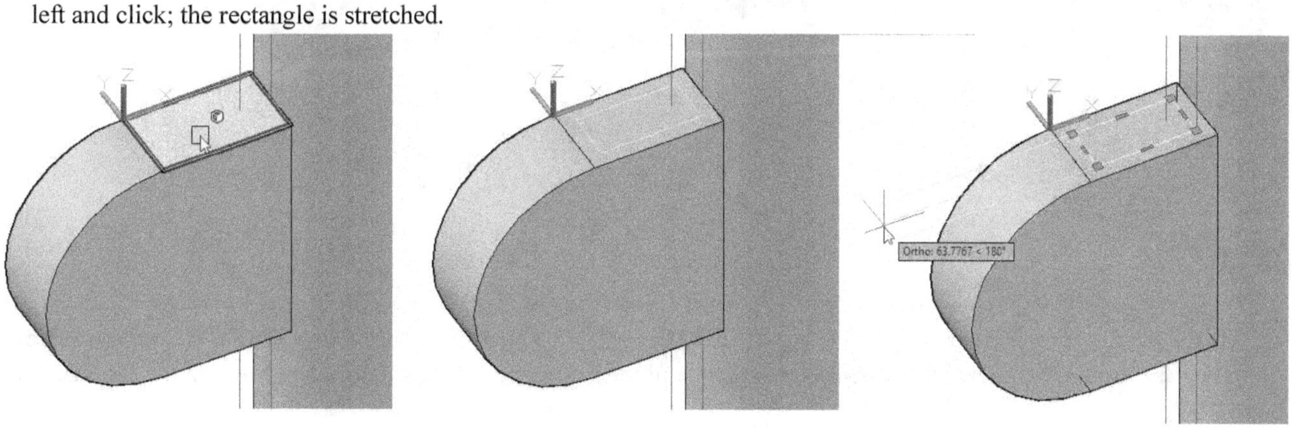

- Extrude the offset rectangle, and then subtract it from the sleeve.

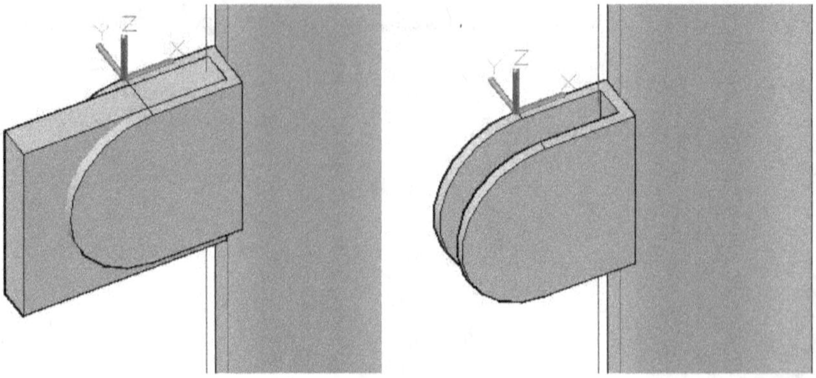

- Select the sleeve, type **CO**, and press **Enter**. Select the midpoint of the top edge of the sleeve to define the base point. Move the pointer downward and select the corner point of the 2D sleeve as the destination point. Press **Esc**.

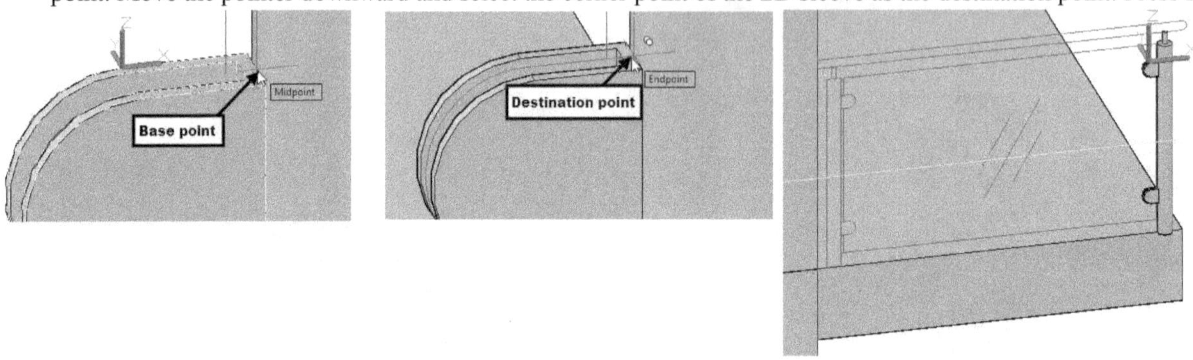

- Select the two cylinders and sleeves, and then click on the Y-axis of the Move gizmo. Move the pointer forward, type **4.075**, and press **Enter**.

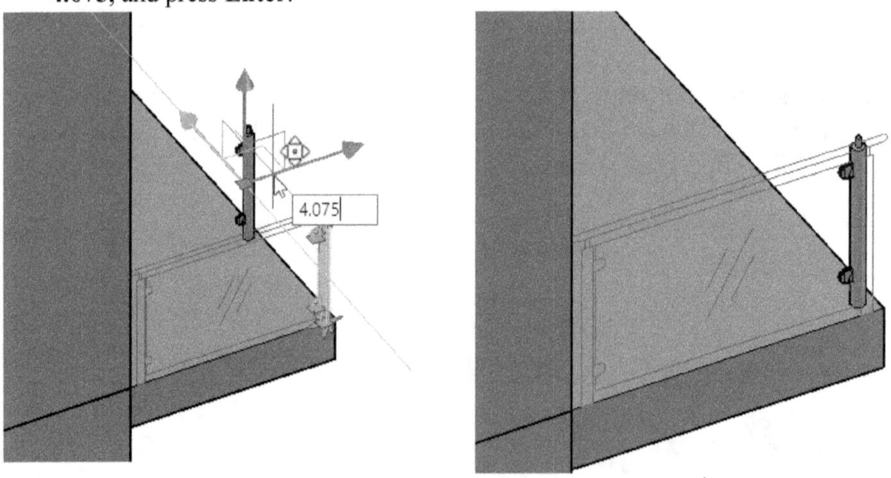

- On the ribbon, click **Home** tab > **Modify** panel > **3D Mirror** . Select the two cylinders and sleeves and press **Enter**. Select **YZ** from the command line. Select the midpoint of the top edge of the balcony. Select **No** from the command line.

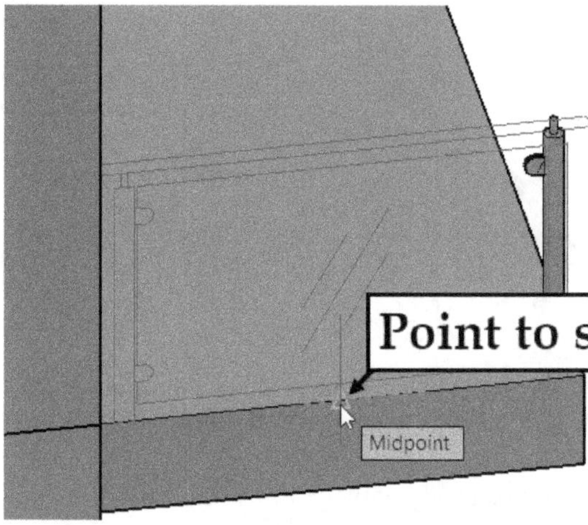

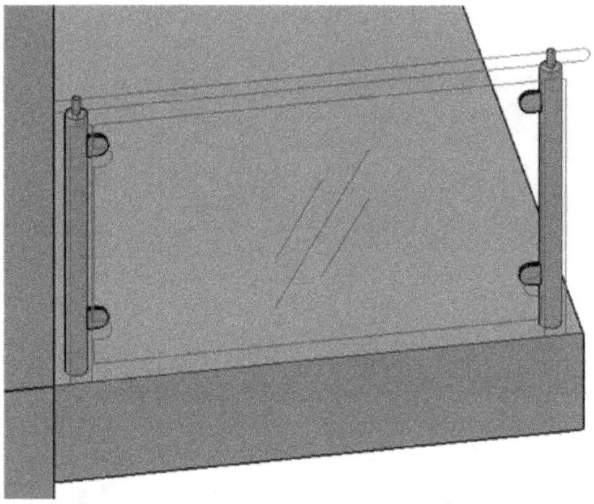

- Select the two sleeves on the right post, type **RO**, and press **Enter**. Select the center point on the top face of the cylinder. Select **Copy** from the command line. Type **270** and press **Enter** to create the rotated copies of the sleeves.

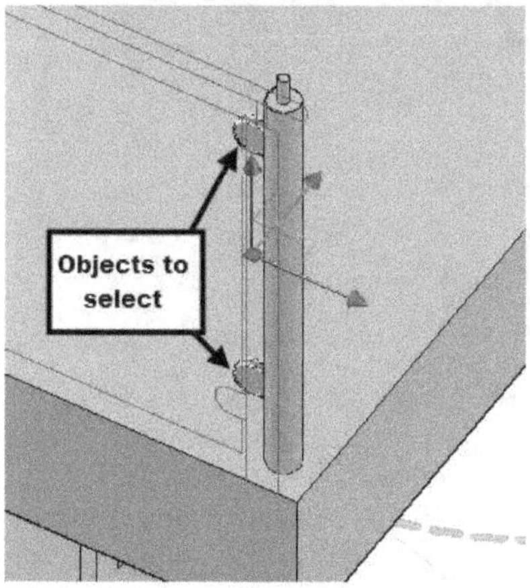

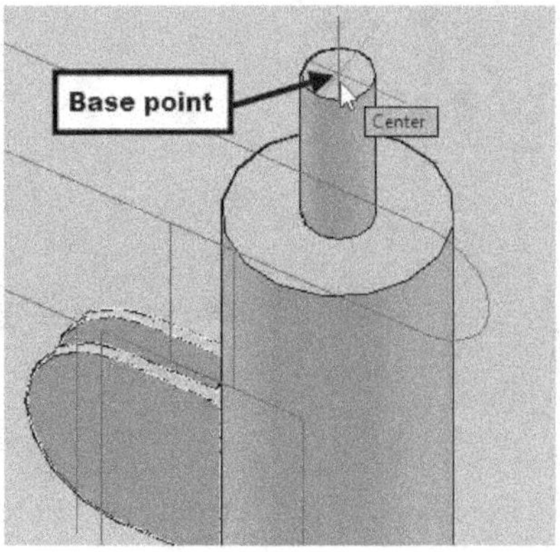

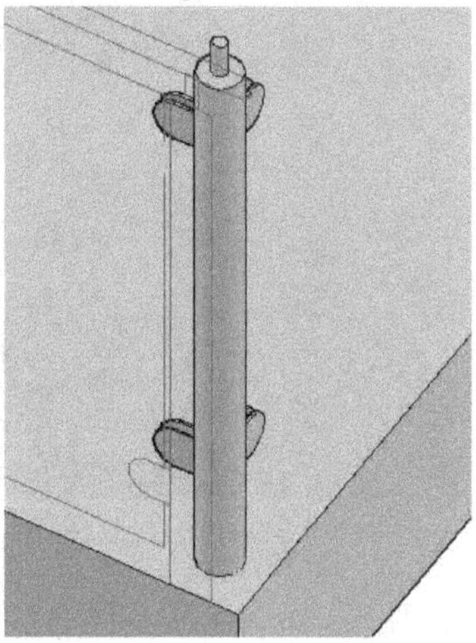

- Select the right side post and rotated copies of sleeves. On the ribbon, click **Home** tab > **Modify** panel > **Array** drop-down > **Rectangular Array** . On the **Array Creation** tab, enter **1** and **8** in the **Columns** and **Rows** boxes, respectively. Enter **493.85** in the **Total** box on the **Rows** panel. Click **Close Array** on the ribbon.

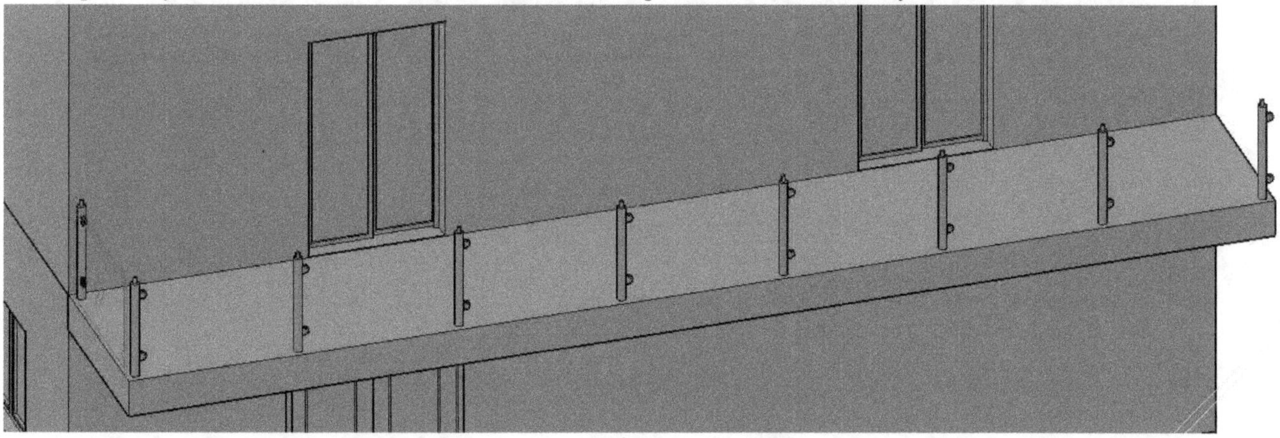

- On the ribbon, click **Home** tab > **Modify** panel > **3D Mirror**. Zoom to the second left post and select the two sleeves and press **Enter**. Select the **ZX** option from the command line. Select the center point on the top face of the cylinder. Select **No** from the command line.

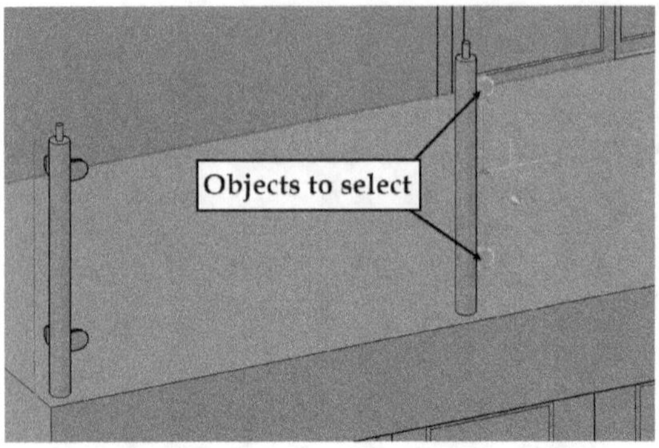

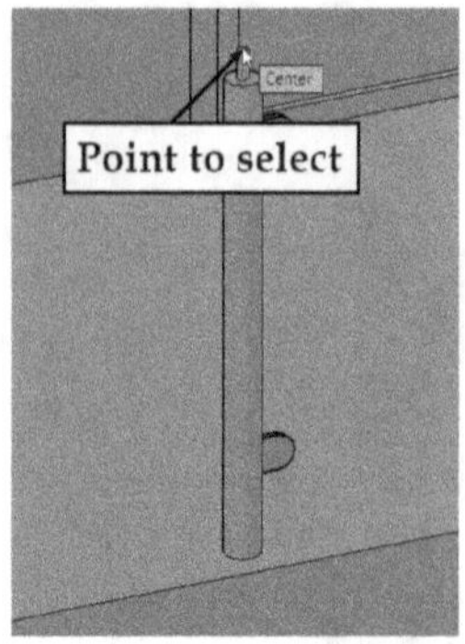

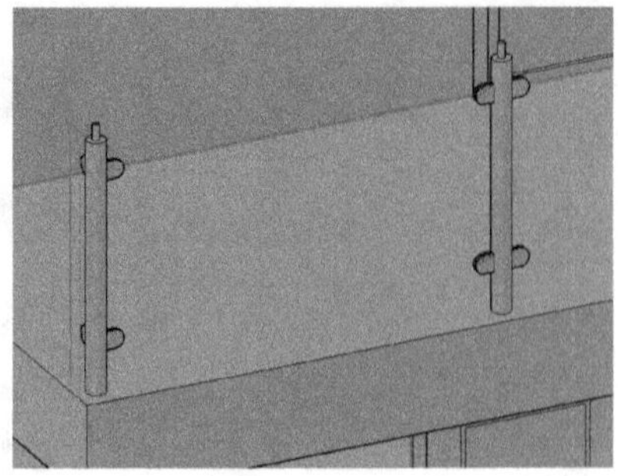

- Select the mirrored sleeves. On the ribbon, click **Home** tab > **Modify** panel > **Array** drop-down > **Rectangular Array** . On the **Array Creation** tab, enter **1** and **7** in the **Columns** and **Rows** boxes, respectively. Enter **423.31** in the **Total** box on the **Rows** panel. Click **Close Array** on the ribbon.

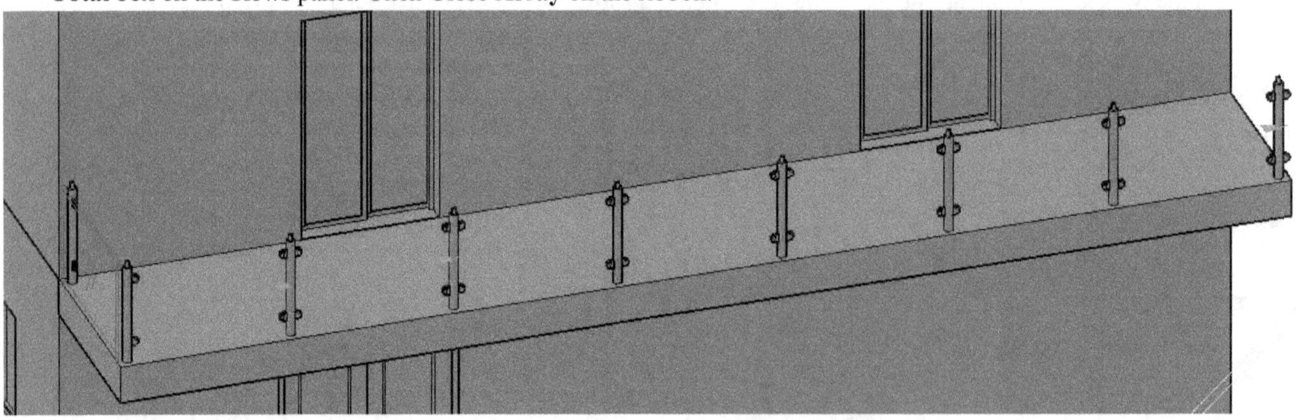

- Select the post and the sleeves next to the wall, as shown. Type **CO** and press Enter. Specify the base point by selecting the center point of the post, as shown. Move the pointer toward the right and select the center point of the extreme right post, as shown. Press **Esc** to deactivate the **Copy** command.

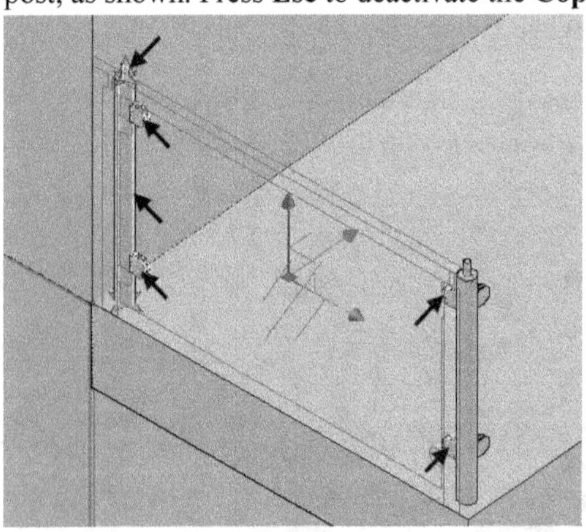

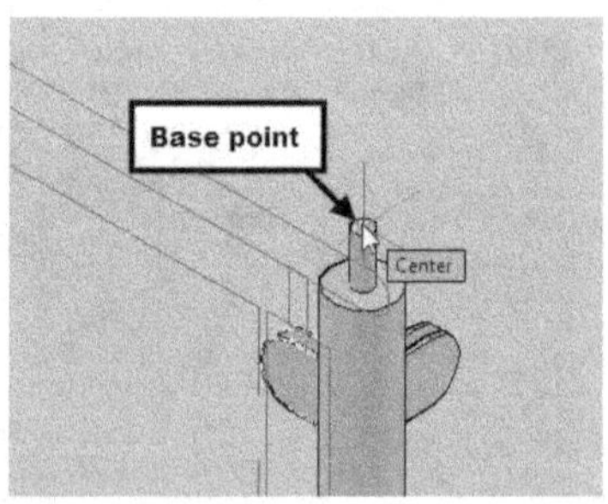

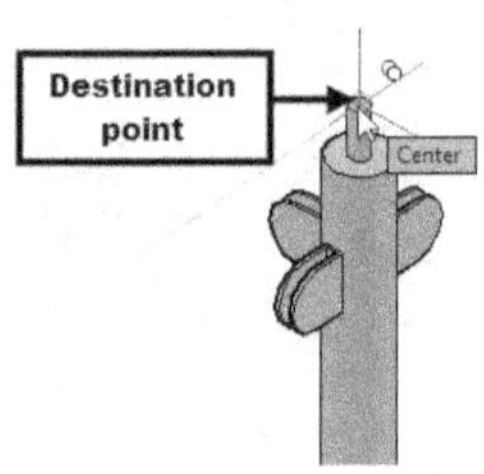

- Select the two unwanted sleeves on the extreme right post and press **Delete**.

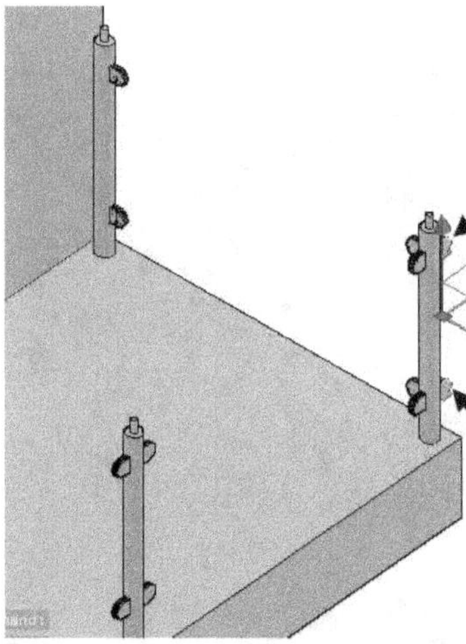

- On the ribbon, click **Home** tab > **Coordinates** panel > **3 Point** . Select the points on the side face of the balcony in the sequence shown below. The first point defines the UCS origin. The second and third points define the X and Y axes.

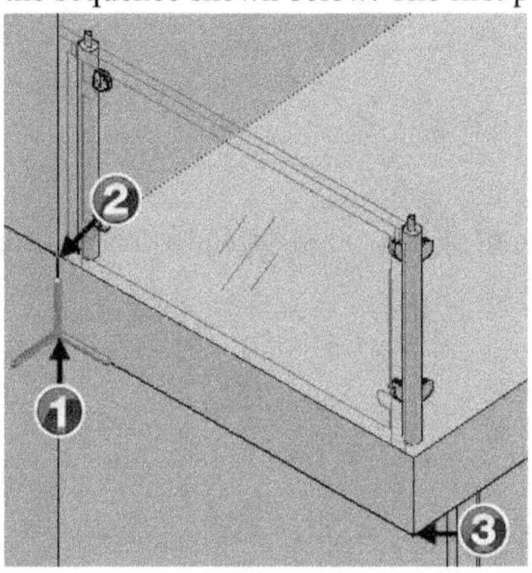

- Turn off the **Dynamic UCS** icon on the status bar. Activate the **Box** tool and specify the first and second corners of the box, as shown. Move the pointer towards the right, and then type **0.6** and press **Enter**.

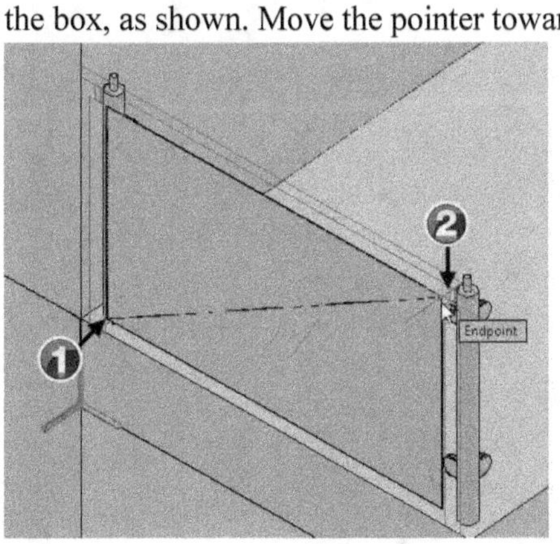

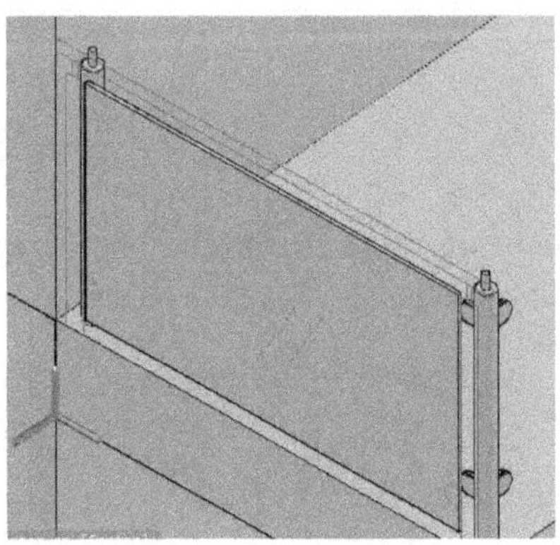

- Select the box to display the Move gizmo. Click on the Y-axis of the Move gizmo, move the pointer forward, type **3.775**, and press Enter.

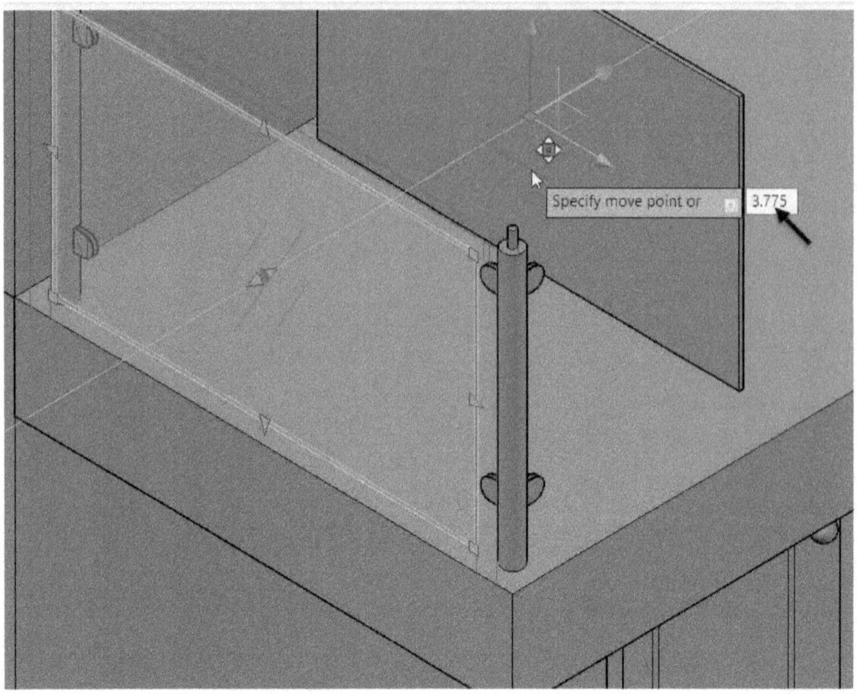

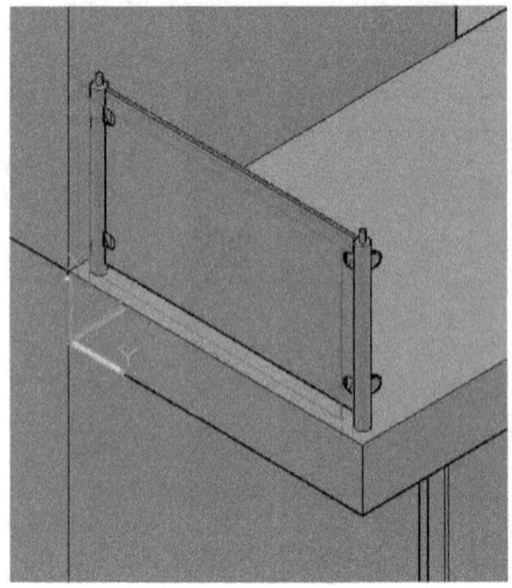

- On the ribbon, click **Home** tab > **Coordinates** panel > **3 Point** . Zoom-in to the Front elevation and select the points of the balcony in the sequence shown below.

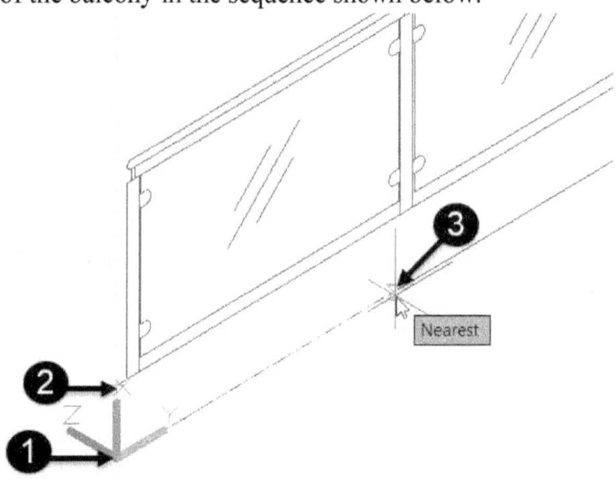

- On the ribbon, click **Home** tab > **Modeling** panel > **Primitive** drop-down > **Box**.
- Select the corner points of the rectangle, as shown. Move the pointer toward the left, type **0.6**, and then press **Enter**.

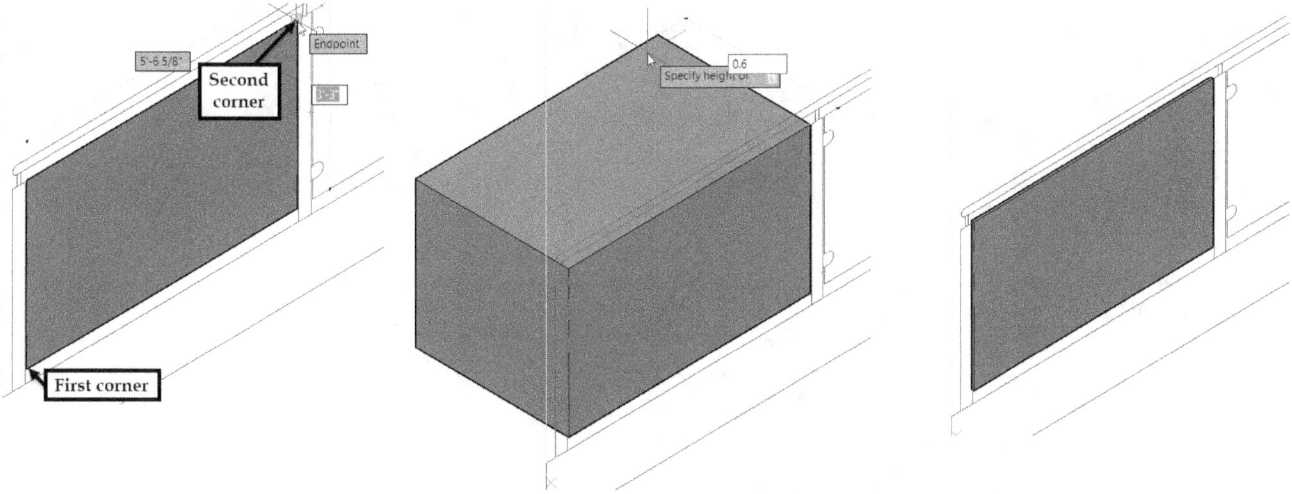

- Select the box created in the earlier step. Type **M** and press **Enter**. Select the midpoint of the rectangle, as shown.
- Move the pointer toward the 3D Model and select the center point of the cylinder, as shown.

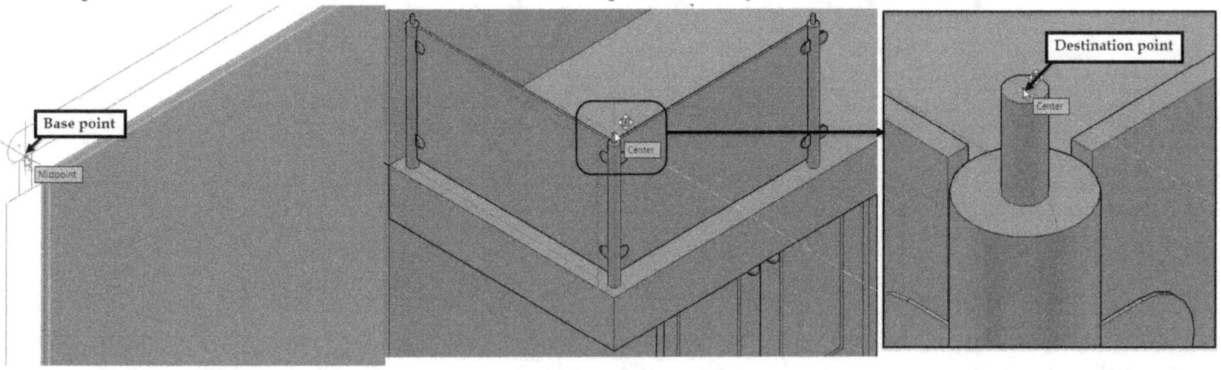

- Select the box and click on the X-axis of the move gizmo. Next, move the pointer toward the right, type **0.3**, and then press **Enter**.

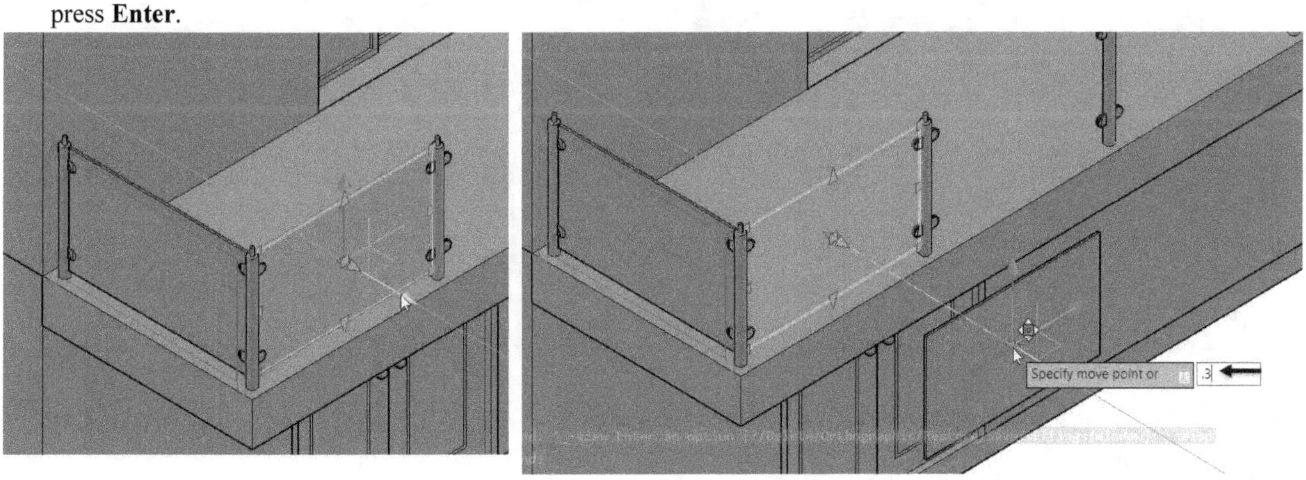

- Select the newly created box. On the ribbon, click **Home** tab > **Modify** panel > **Array** drop-down > **Rectangular Array** . On the **Array Creation** tab, enter **1** and **7** in the **Columns** and **Rows** boxes, respectively. Enter **423.31** in the **Total** box on the **Rows** panel. Click **Close Array** on the ribbon.

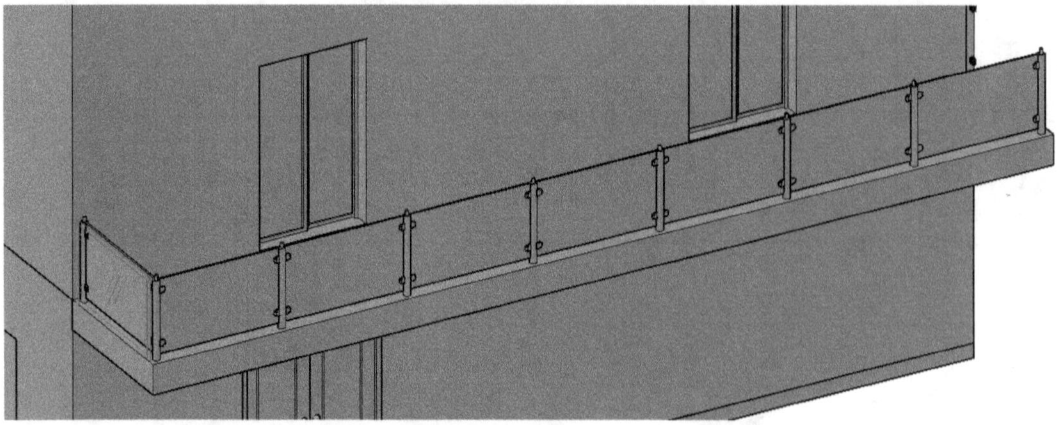

- Copy the box on the left end and place it on the right end.

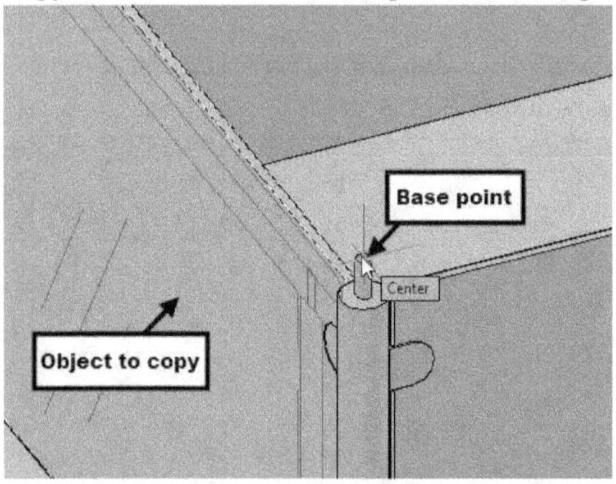

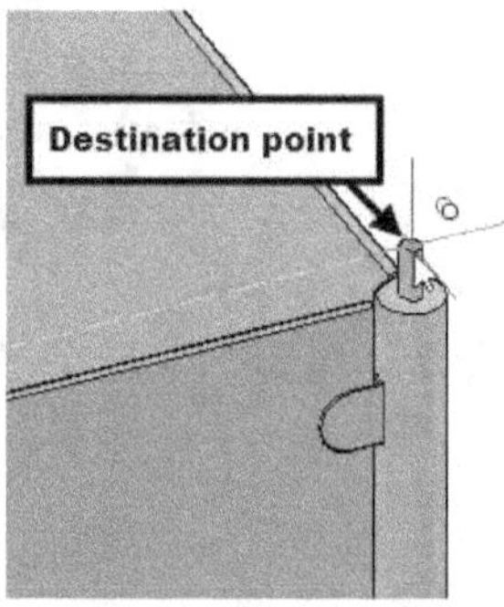

- On the ribbon, click the **Home** tab > **Coordinates** panel > **UCS, World**; the UCS is moved to its default position.
- Type **PL** and press **Enter**. Select the center points of the top faces of the posts, as shown.

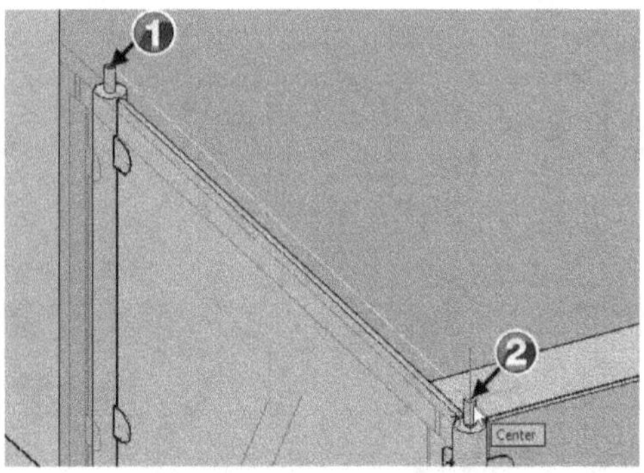

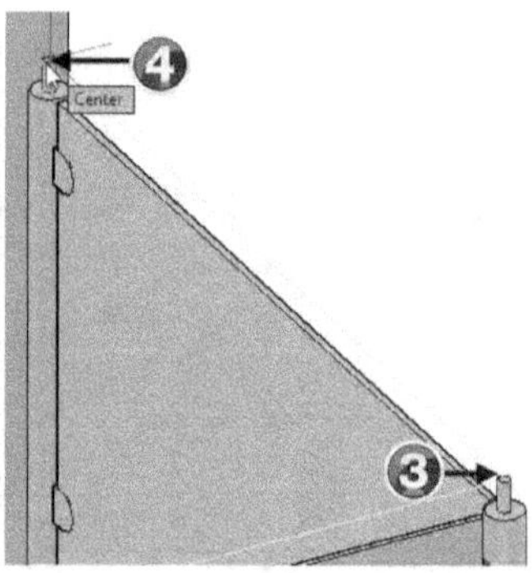

- On the ribbon, click **Home** tab > **Coordinates** panel > **Z-Axis Vector** . Specify the first and second points of the Z axis, as shown.

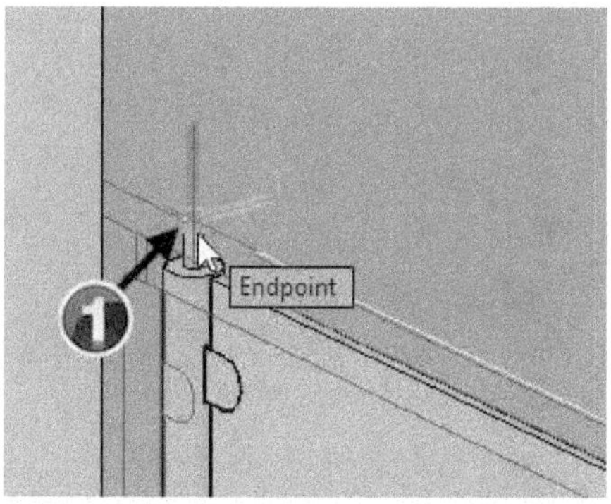

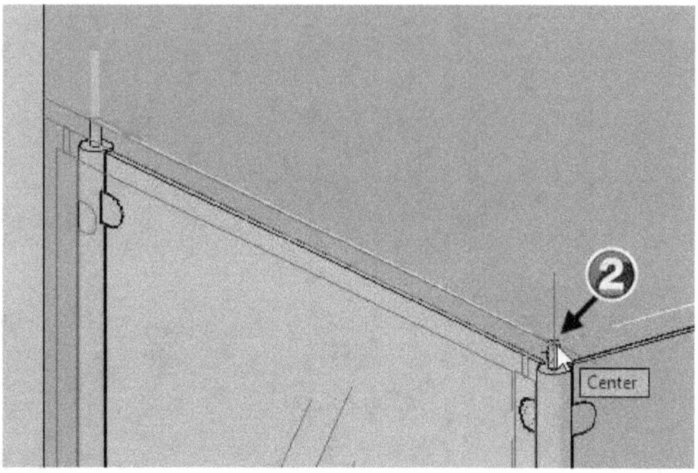

- Deactivate the **Dynamic Input** icon on the Status bar.
- Type **C** and press **Enter**. Select the origin point of the UCS. Type **1** and press **Enter**.

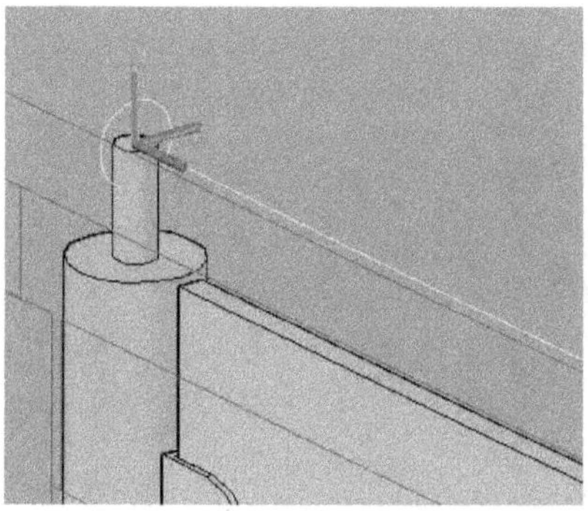

- On the ribbon, click **Home** tab > **Modeling** panel > **Extrude** drop-down > **Sweep** . Select the circle and press **Enter**. Select the polyline and press Enter.

- Select the swept solid to display the Move gizmo. Select the Y-axis of the move gizmo, move the pointer upward, type **0.95**, and then press **Enter**.

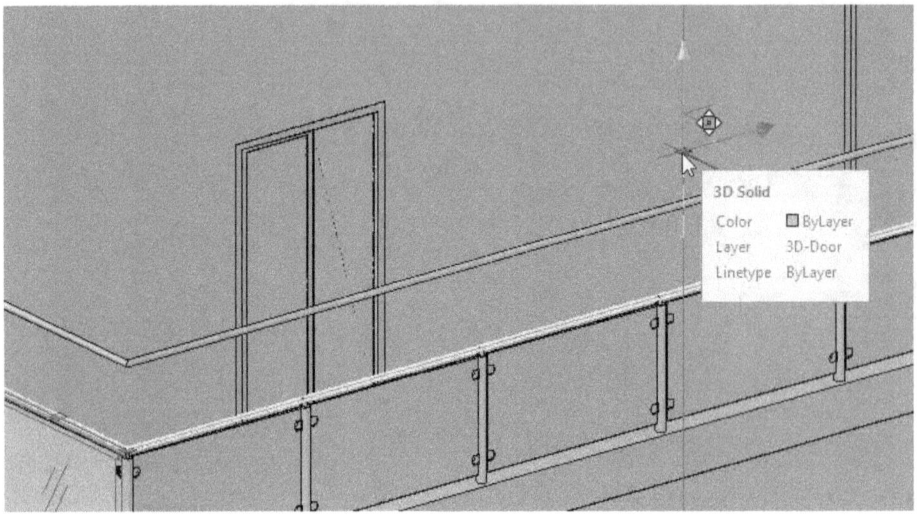

- Extend the swept solid up to the wall by using the **Presspull** tool.

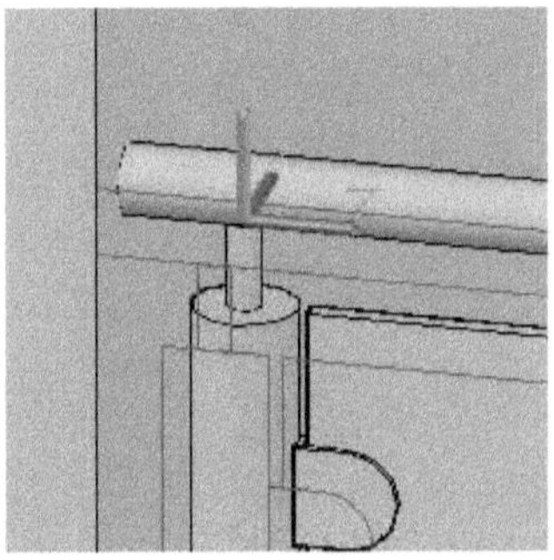

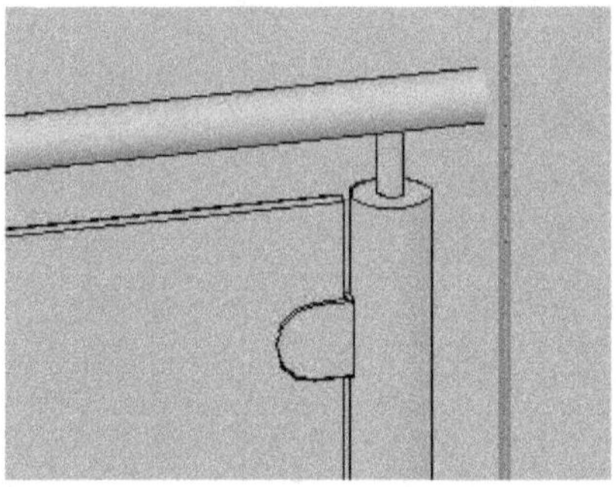

- On the ribbon, click **Home** tab > **Coordinates** panel > **UCS, World**. The UCS is restored to its default position.

Tutorial 9: Creating the Staircase on the first floor

- Activate the **3D-Floor** layer from the Layer Properties Manager.
- Create the 8-inch thickness floor on top of the first floor.

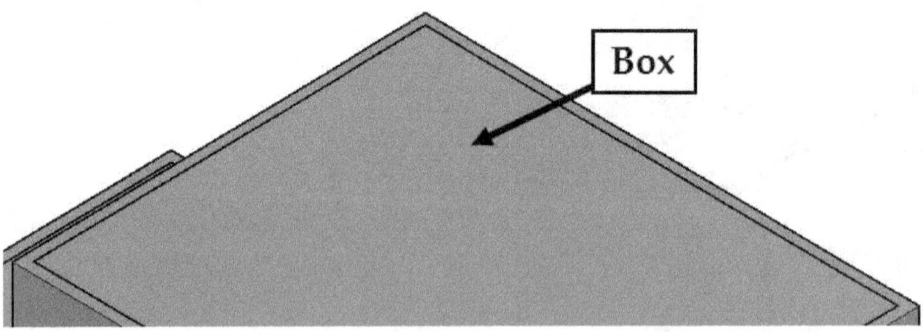

- Create a 211x157x8 box at the corner of the floor, as shown. Subtract the box from the floor.

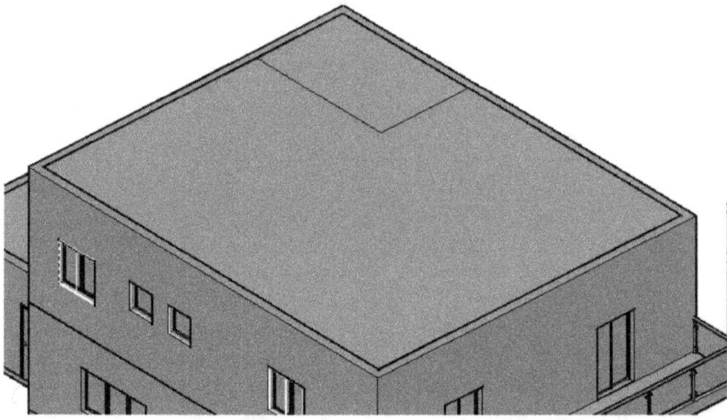

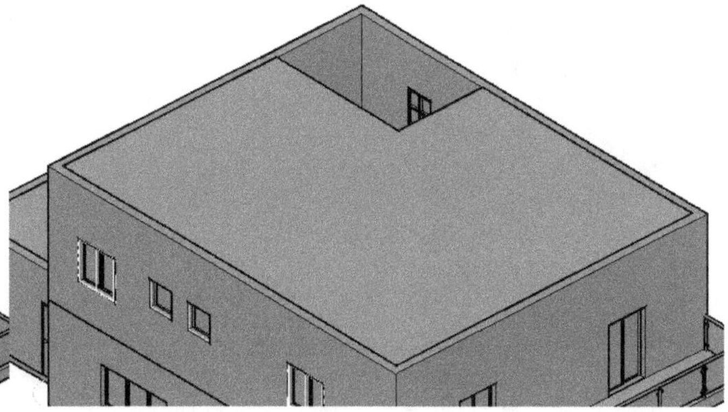

- Deactivate the **Dynamic UCS** icon on the status bar. On the ribbon, click **Home** tab > **Coordinates** panel > **UCS** . Specify the origin, X, and Y axes of the UCS, as shown.

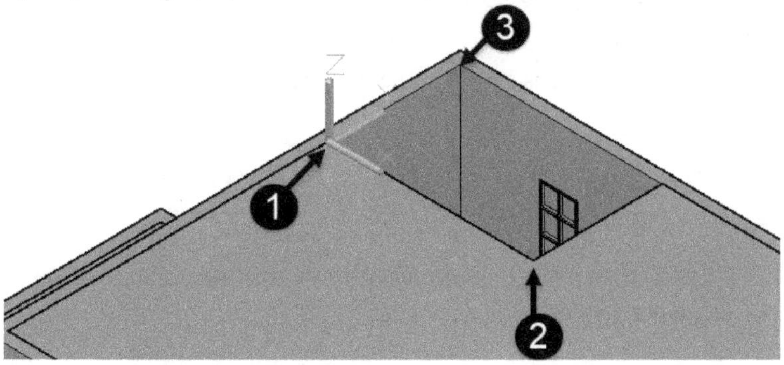

- Set the "3D-Stairs" layer as current.
- Activate the **Dynamic Input** icon on the status bar.

- On the ribbon, click **Home** tab > **Modeling** panel > **Primitives** drop-down > **Wedge** . Specify the first corner of the wedge, as shown.
- Type 145.9 and press the Tab key. Next, type 68.2 and press Enter.
- Move the pointer upward, type 122.5, and press Enter.

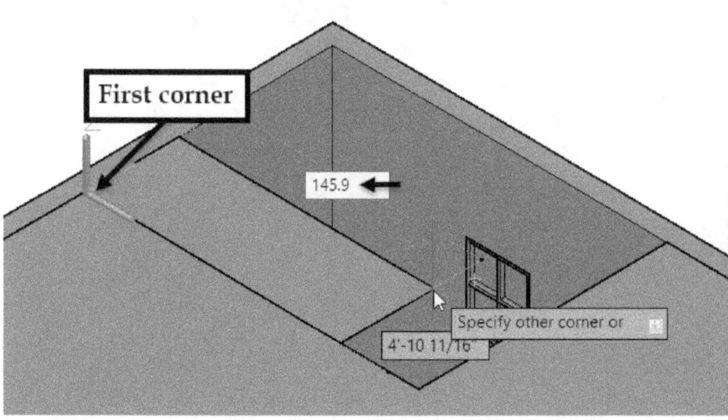

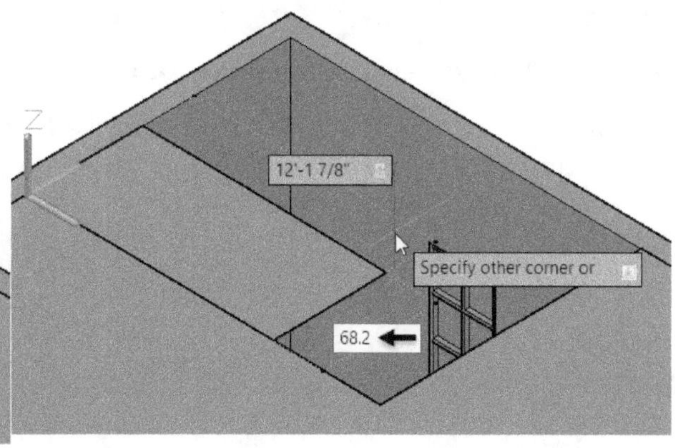

- Select the newly created wedge, type **M** in the command line, and then press ENTER. Next, select the lower right corner of the wedge to define the base point. Select the corner point of the opening, as shown.

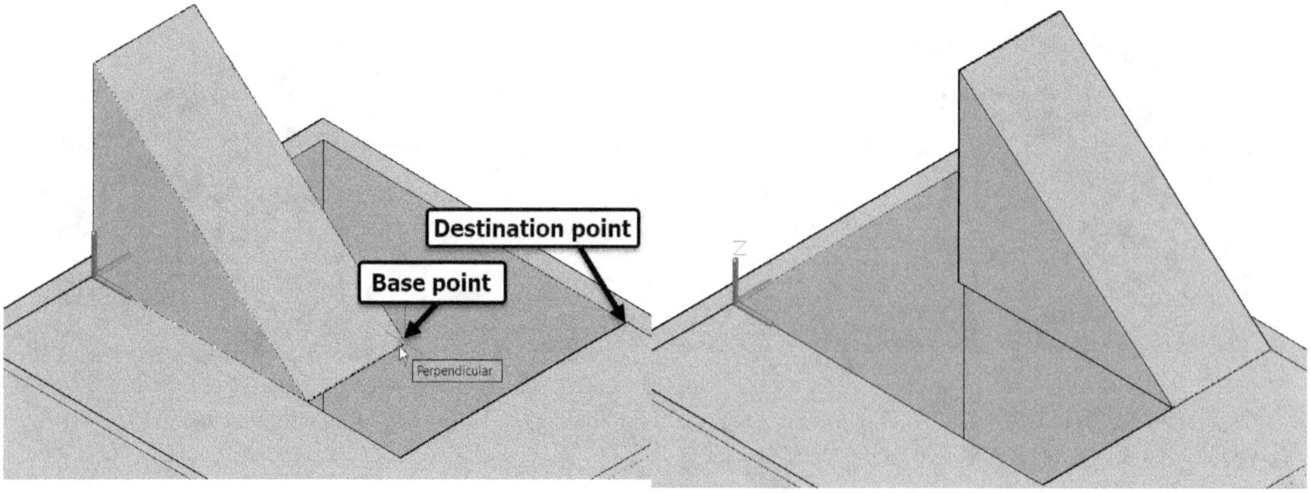

- Type **UCS** and press Enter twice to restore the **UCS** to its default position.
- Type L and press Enter. Select the endpoints of the inclined edge, as shown — next, right click, and select Enter.
- Create an 8.6x68.2x-7.2 box on the top edge of the wedge.
- On the ribbon, click **Home** tab > **Modify** panel > **Array** drop-down > **Path Array** . Select the box and press Enter. Select the line coinciding with the inclined edge. On the **Array Creation** tab, on the **Properties** panel, click **Measure Method** drop-down > **Divide** . On the **Items** panel, change the **Items** value to **18**. Next, deactivate the **Associative** icon on the Properties panel. Click **Close Array** on the **Array Creation** ribbon tab.

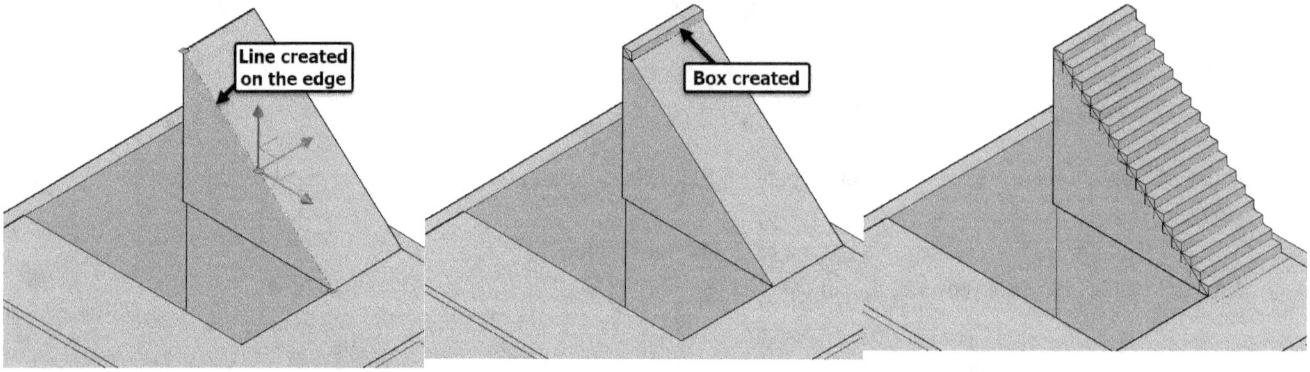

- Select the bottom-most stair and press **Delete**.
- On the ribbon, click **Home** tab > **Layers** panel > **Isolate** . Select any one of the stairs and press Enter; all the layers except the layer of the selected object are hidden.

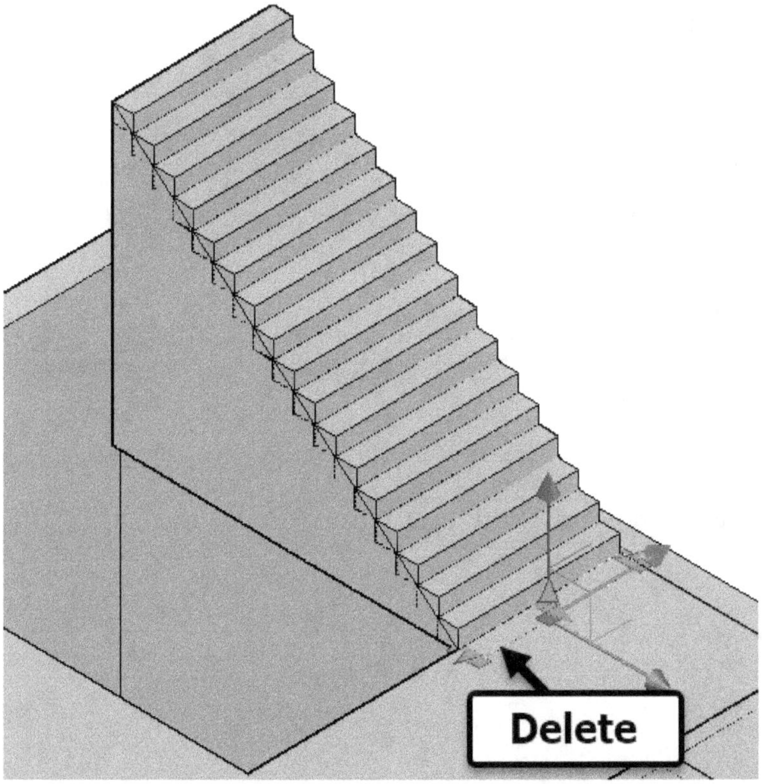

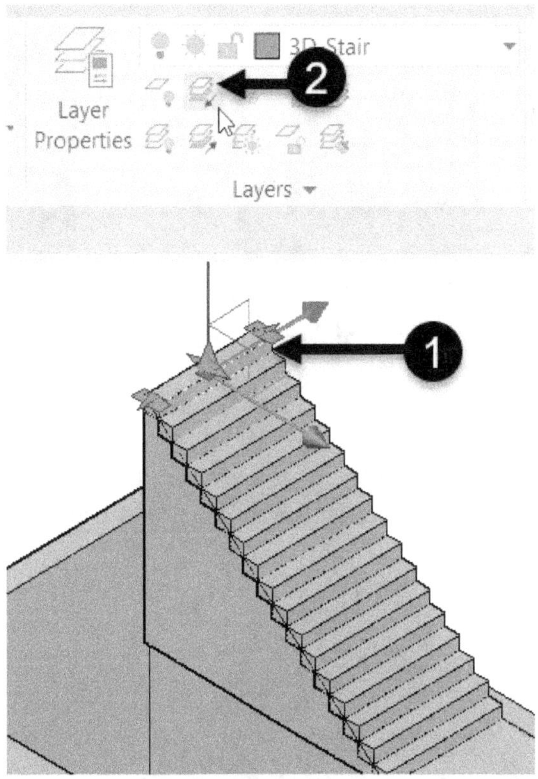

- Type UCS and press Enter. Select **Face** from the command line. Select the side face of the wedge. Click **Next** until the X and Y axes of the UCS are displayed on the side face. Next, select **accept** from the command line. The UCS is positioned on the selected face.

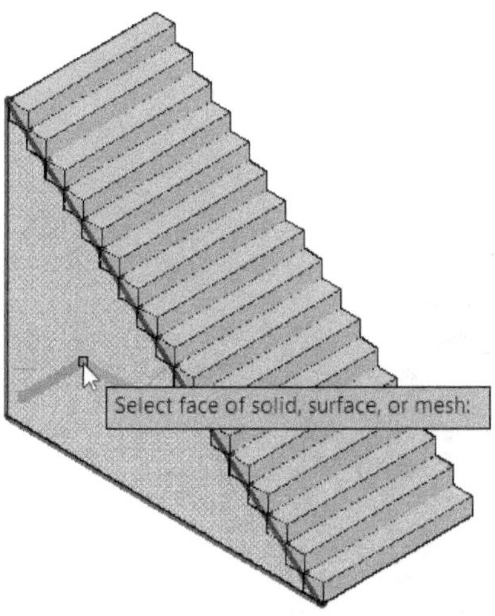

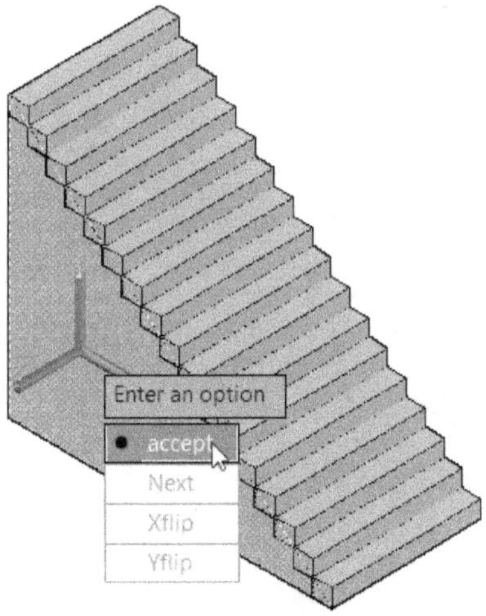

- Offset the line used to create the path array by 18 inches. Next, use the **Presspull** tool to remove material on the wedge. Press Esc to deactivate the **Presspull** command.

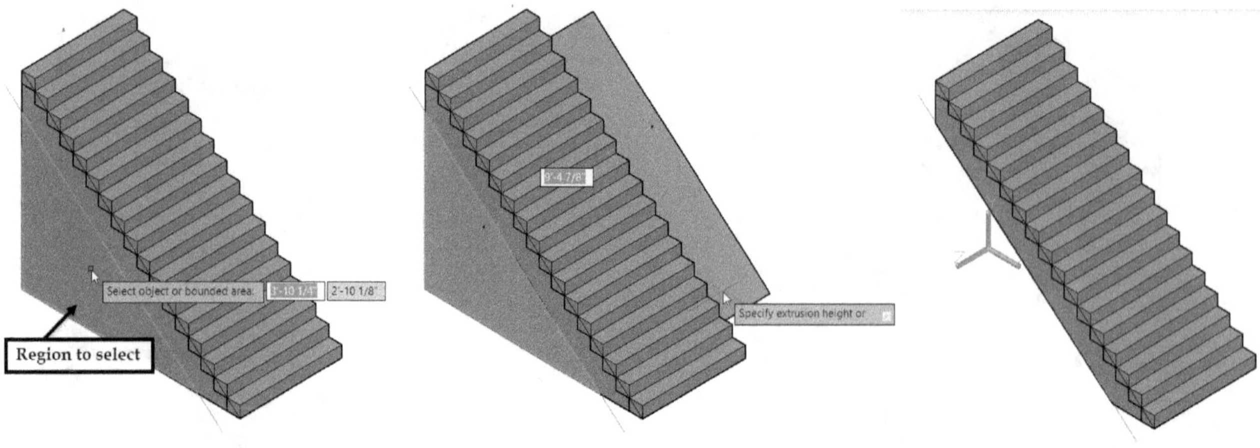

- Type UCS and press Enter twice to restore the UCS to its default position.
- Select the offset line and the line used to create the polar array. Press Delete.

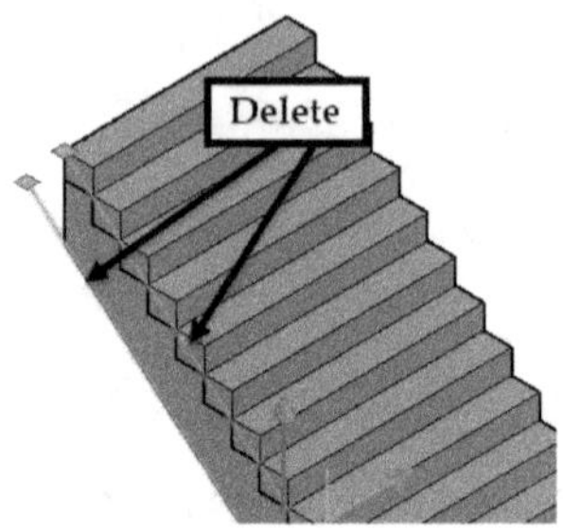

- Type UNI and press Enter. Create a selection window over the stairs and press Enter.

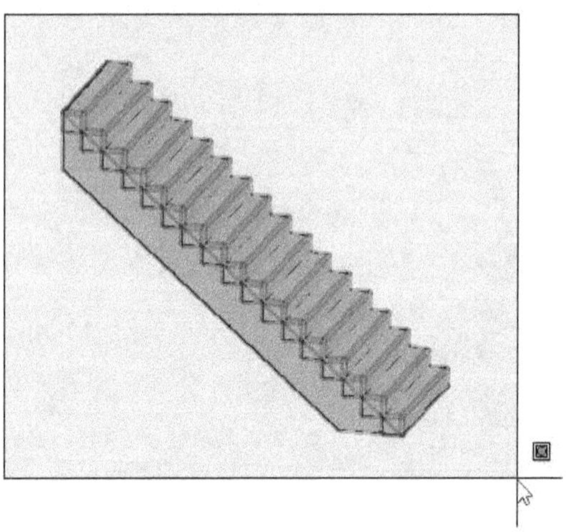

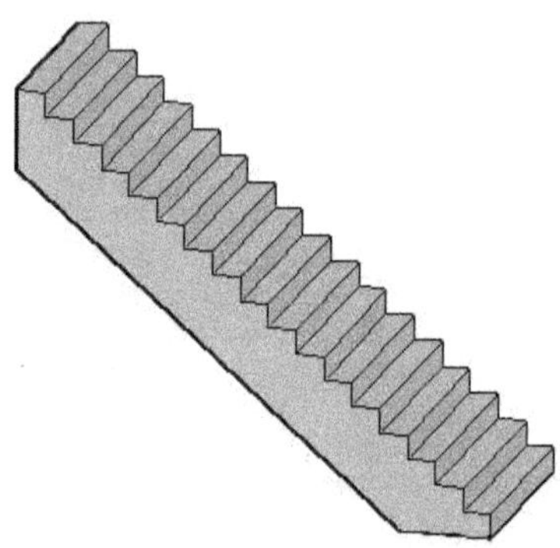

- Select the staircase, type M, and press Enter. Specify the base point, as shown. Move the pointer downward, type 180, and press Enter.

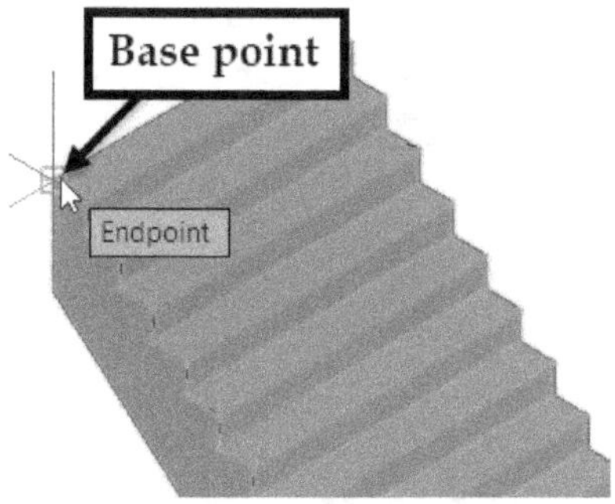

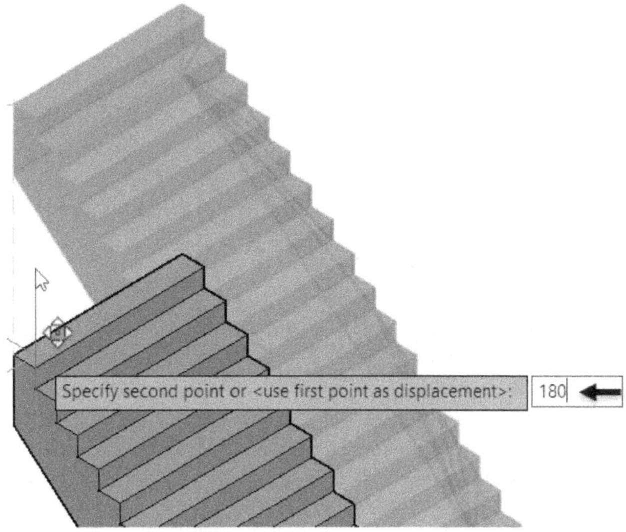

- On the ribbon, click **Home** tab > **Layers** panel > **Turn All Layers On**. All the layers are turned on.
- On the ribbon, click **Home** tab > **Modeling** panel > **Primitives** drop-down > **Box**. Next, select the first and second corners of the box, as shown.
- On the ribbon, click **Home** tab > **Coordinates** panel > **UCS**. Specify the origin, X, and Y axes of the UCS, as shown.

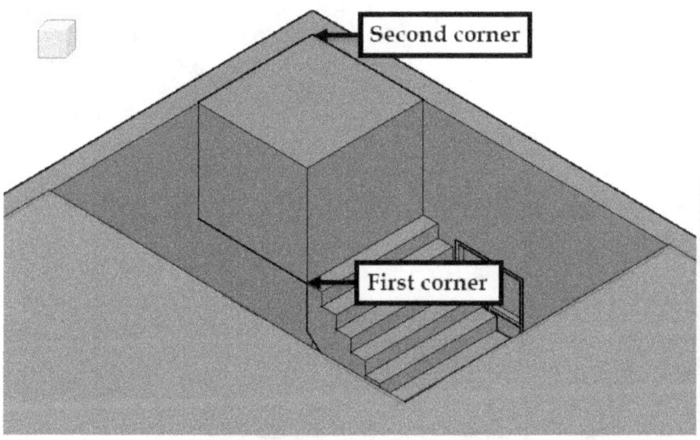

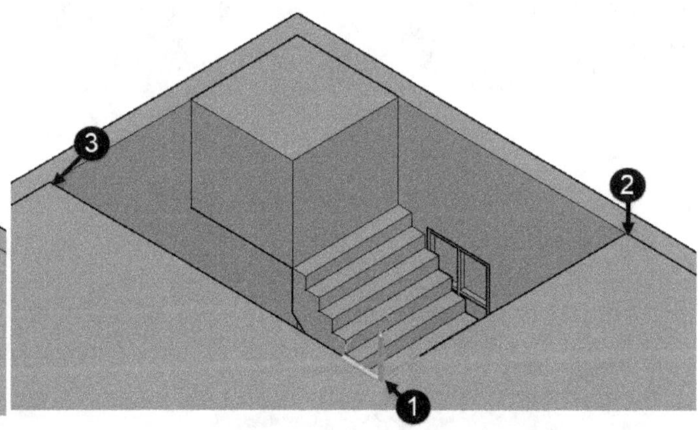

- Activate the **Presspull** command and pull the left side face of the box up to 20 inches.

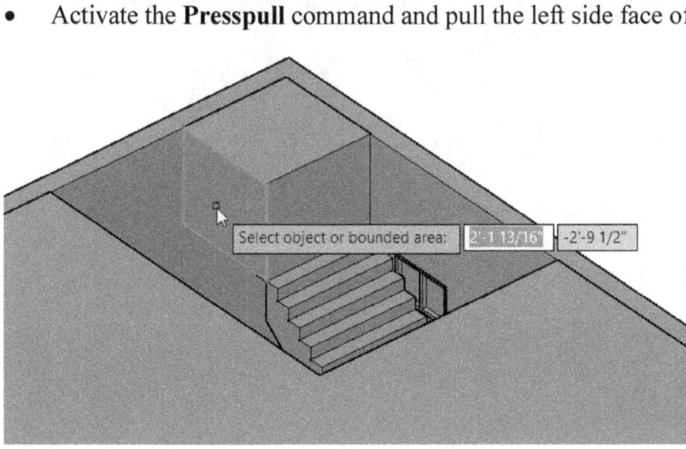

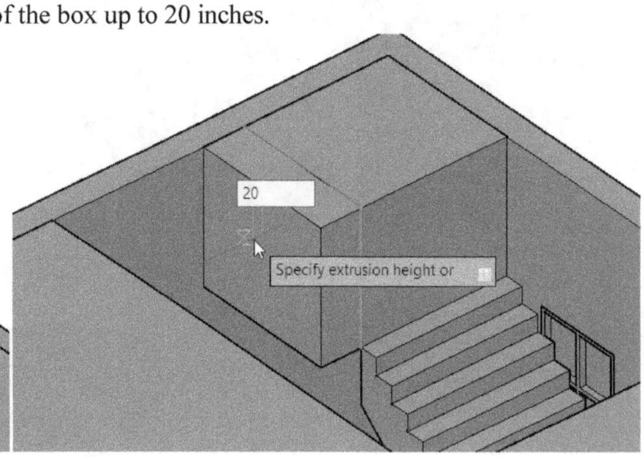

- Activate the **Wedge** command and select the corner points, as shown. Move the pointer upward, type 57.52, and press

Enter.

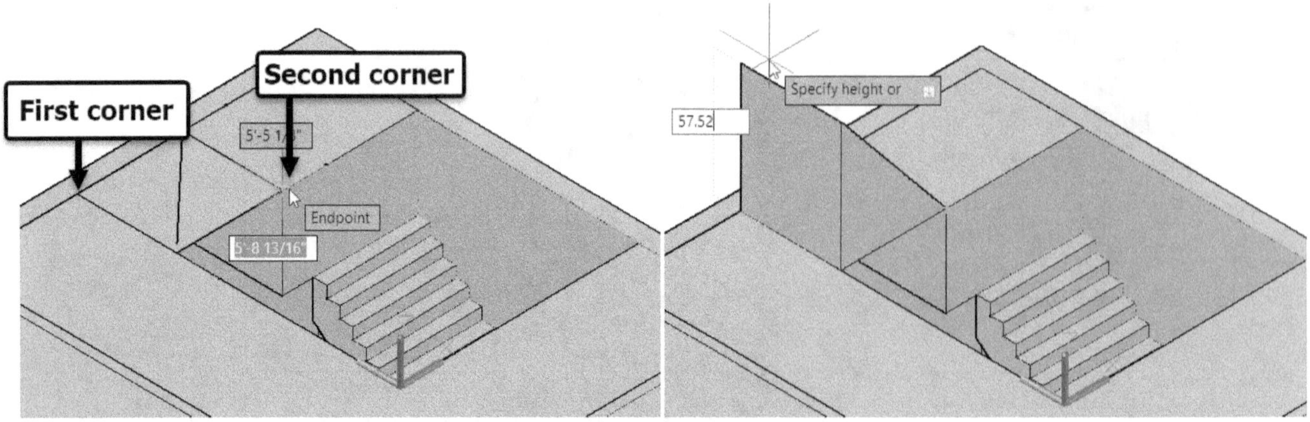

- Create the remaining 9 stairs on the wedge, as shown. Delete the bottom stair.

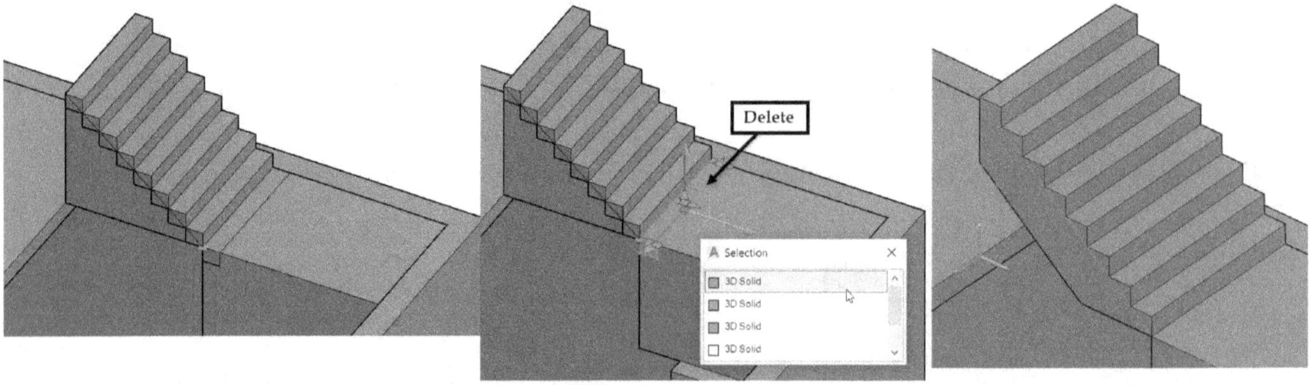

- Activate the **Presspull** command and select the top face of the box. Next, move the pointer downward, type 49.5, and then press Enter.

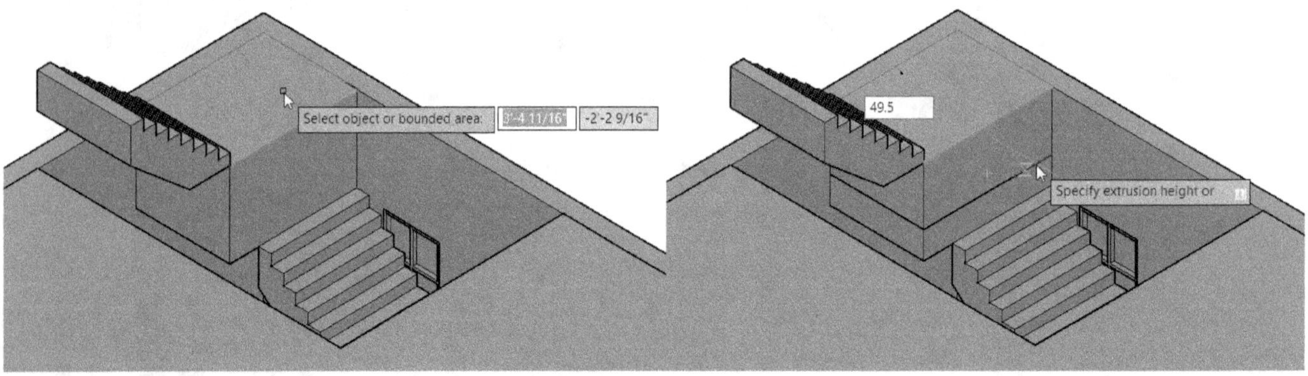

- Select the box and activate the **Move** command. Next, specify the Basepoint and Destination points, as shown.

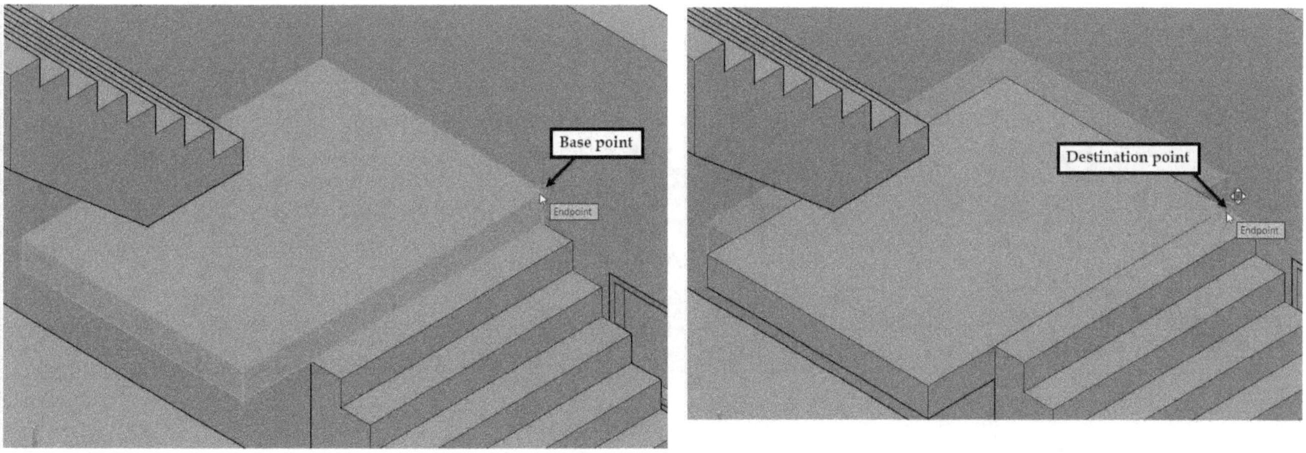

- Select the first stair and activate the **Move** command. Next, specify the Basepoint and Destination point, as shown.
- Type UCS and press Enter twice to restore the UCS to its default position.

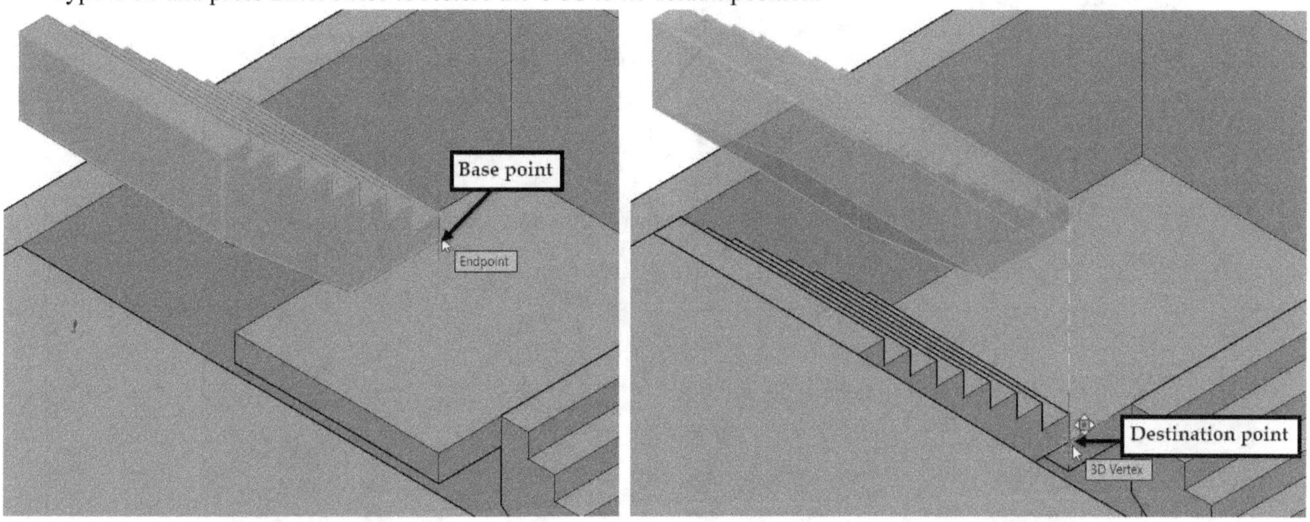

Notice that the staircase is placed in front of the window. You need to change the location of the window.

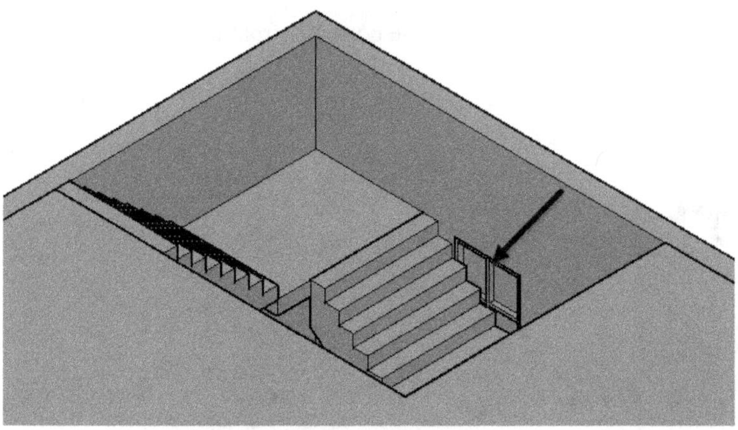

- Select the window, click on the X-axis of the move gizmo, and move the pointer toward the right. Type 146 and press Enter.

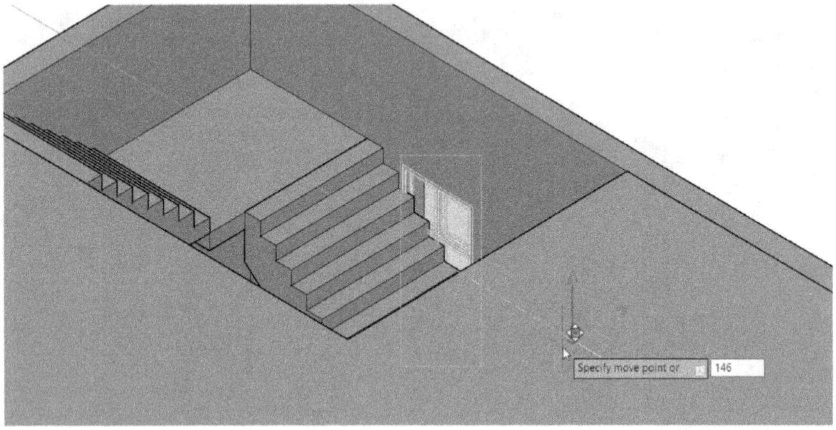

- Change the orientation to NW Isometric. Create a box on the window opening by selecting its corner points. The depth of the box is 12 inches.

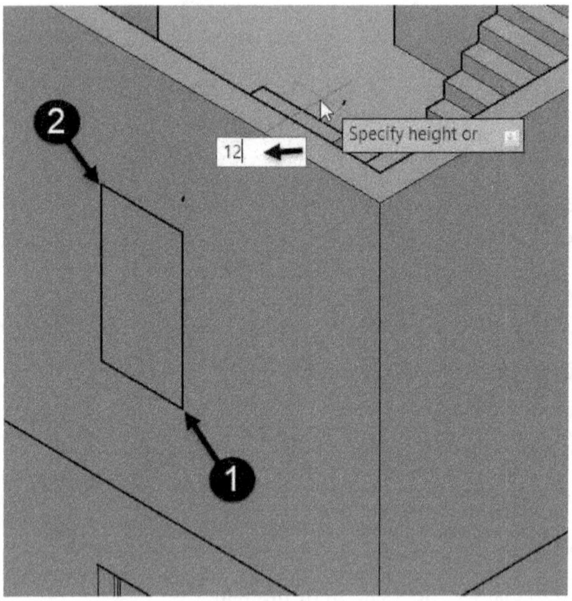

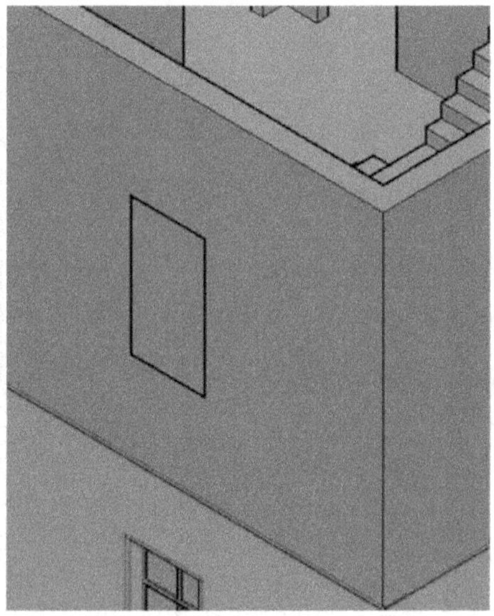

- Create a copy of the box at 146 inches in the positive X –direction. Subtract the box copy from the walls.

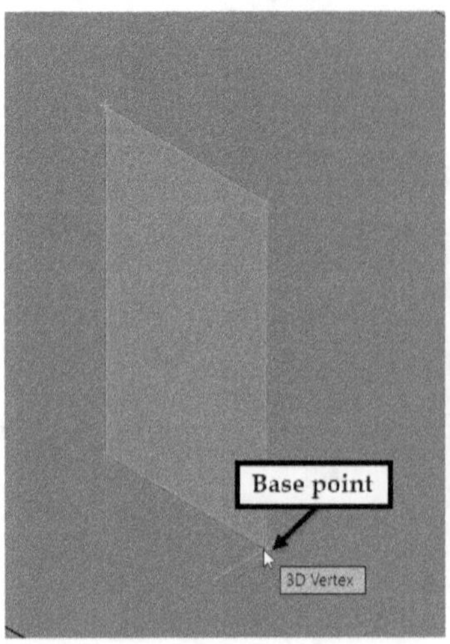

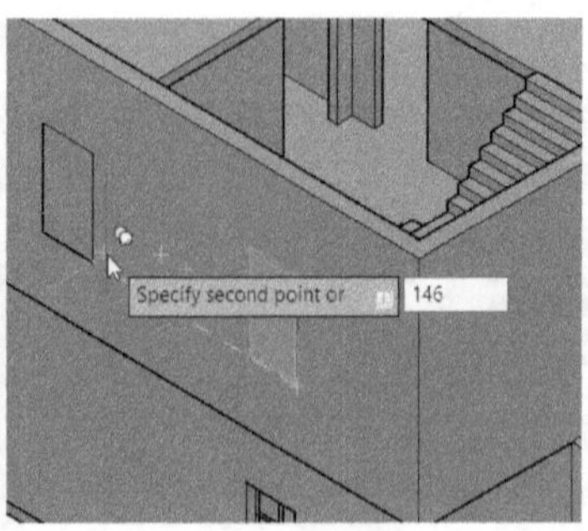

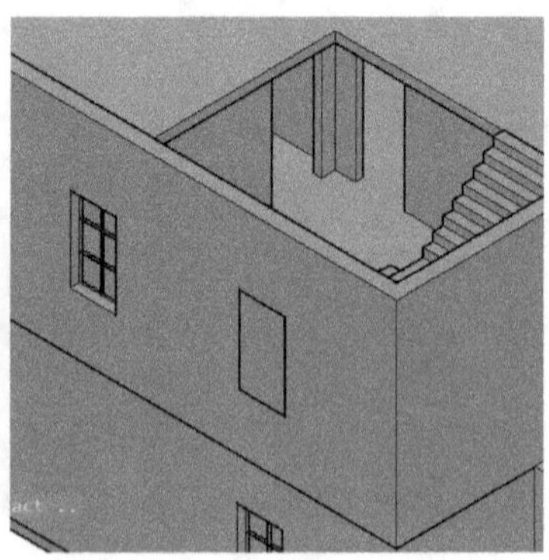

- Unite the box with the walls.

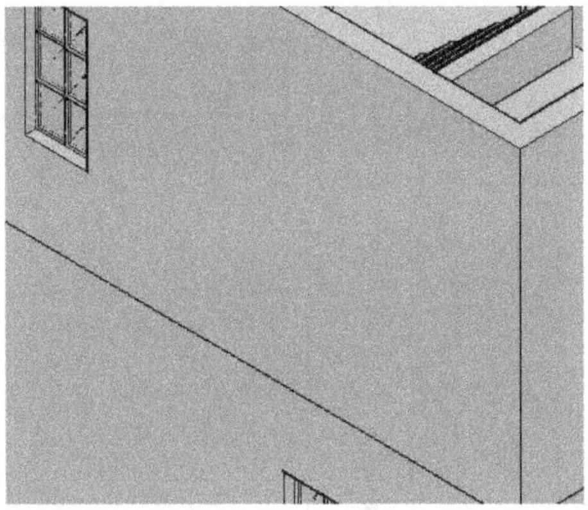

Creating Railing

- On the ribbon, click **Home** tab > **Layers** panel > **Isolate**. Next, select any one of the stairs, and then press Enter; the stairs are isolated.
- On the ribbon, click **Home** tab > **View** panel > **Restore View** drop-down > **SW Isometric**.

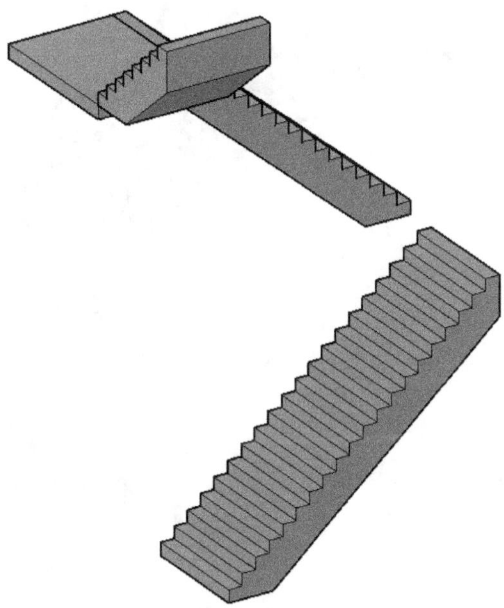

- Create a new layer "3D-Railing" and set its color to Index color 12. Set the **3D-Railing** layer as current.
- Deactivate the **Dynamic Input** icon on the status bar.
- Make sure that the ORTHOMODE (F8) icon is active on the status bar.
- On the ribbon, click **Home** tab > **Draw** panel > **3D Polyline** . Specify the first and second points of the 3D polyline, as shown. Move the pointer horizontally toward the left, type 18, and press Enter.
- Move the pointer and place it on the corner point of the stair, as shown.
- Move the pointer toward the right and notice a trace line. Next, click to select the intersection of the trace line with the dashed line, as shown.

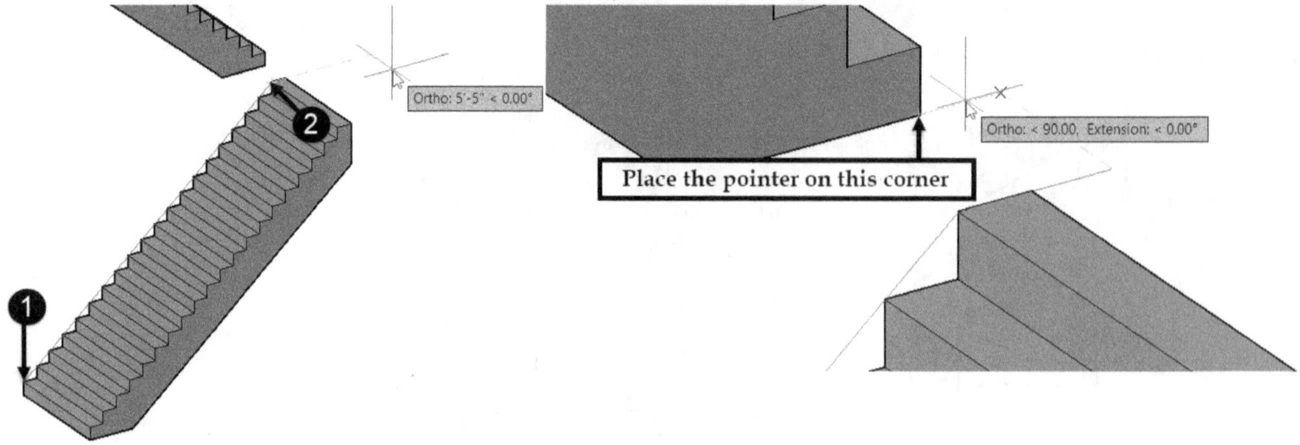

- Rotate the model view and specify the remaining points of the 3D polyline in the sequence shown in the figure. Press Esc.

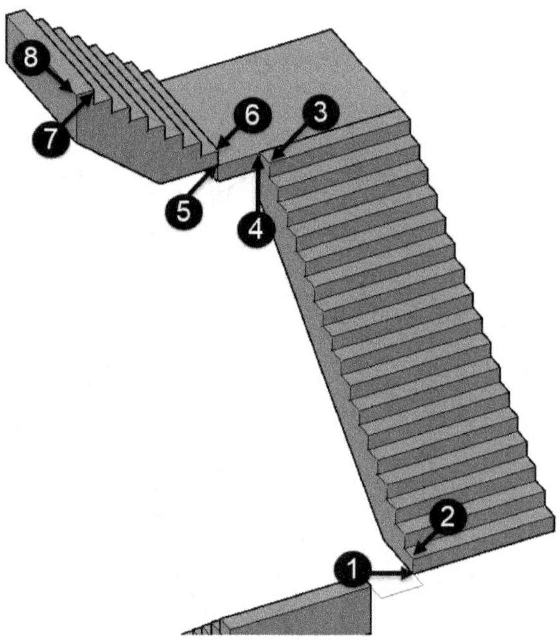

- Click the **Unisolate** icon on the **Layers** panel of the ribbon.
- Select the first floor walls and the top-most floor of the model, and then select **Isolate > Hide Objects**.

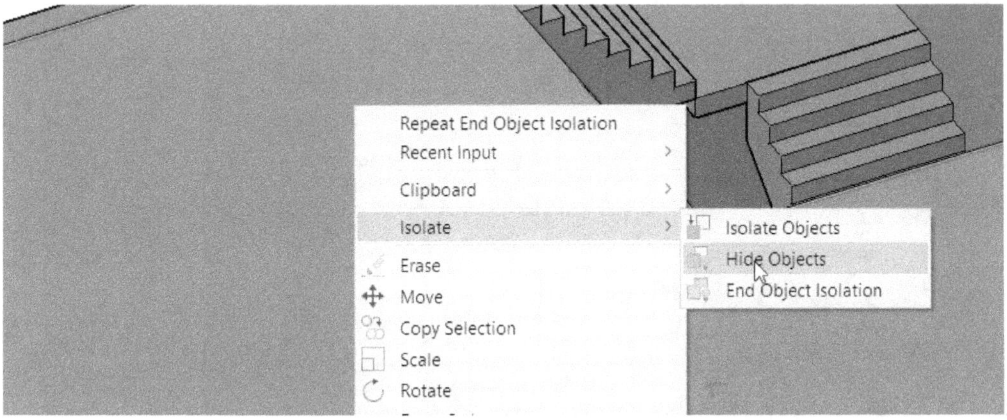

- Create a horizontal line by selecting the endpoints of the edge, as shown. Select the line and move it by 4 inches in the Y-direction, as shown.

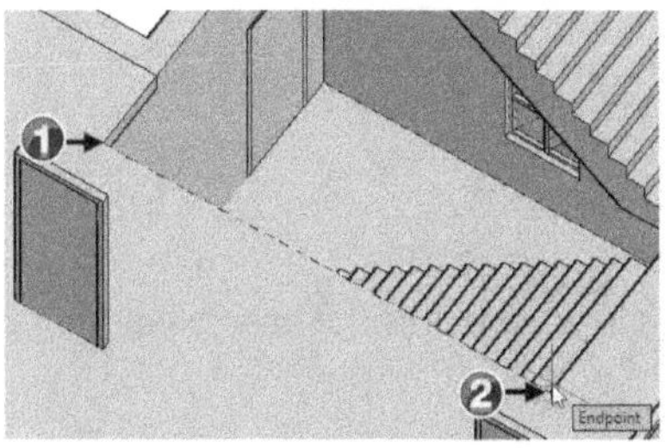

- Select the polyline, click on the Z-axis of the Move gizmo, and move the pointer upward. Type 40 and press Enter. Likewise, move the horizontal line upwards.

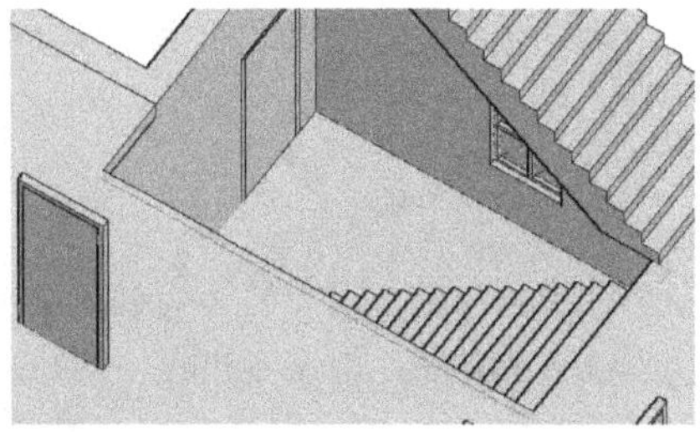

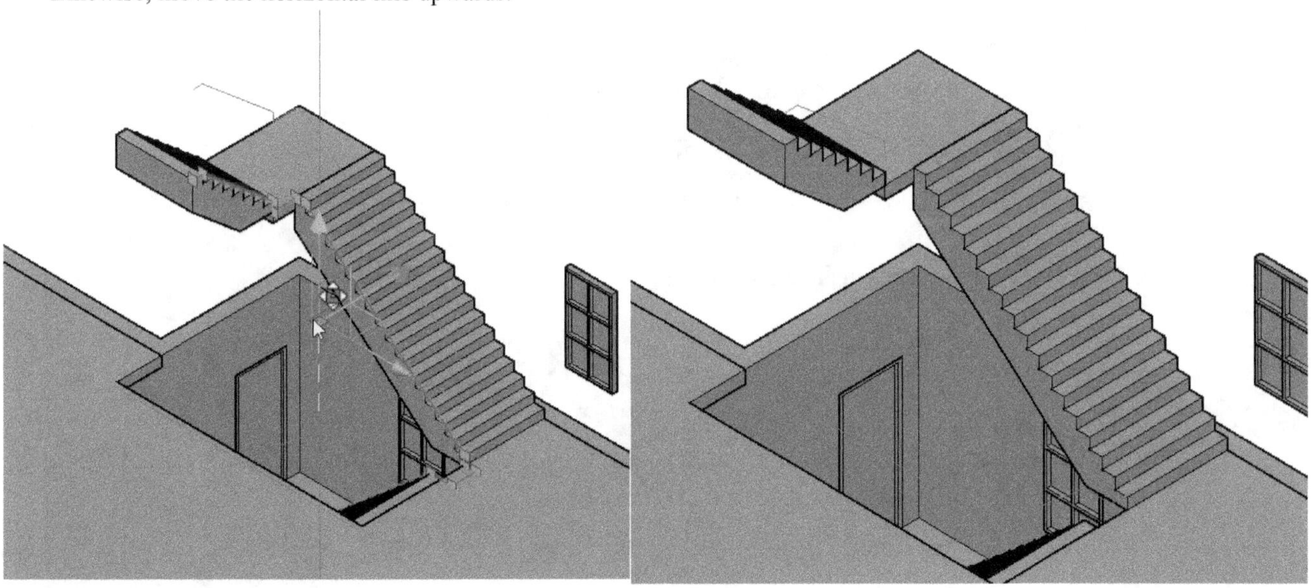

- Type UCS and press Enter. Select Z-axis from the command line and select the endpoint of the 3D polyline. Move the pointer forward and select the corner point of the polyline, as shown.

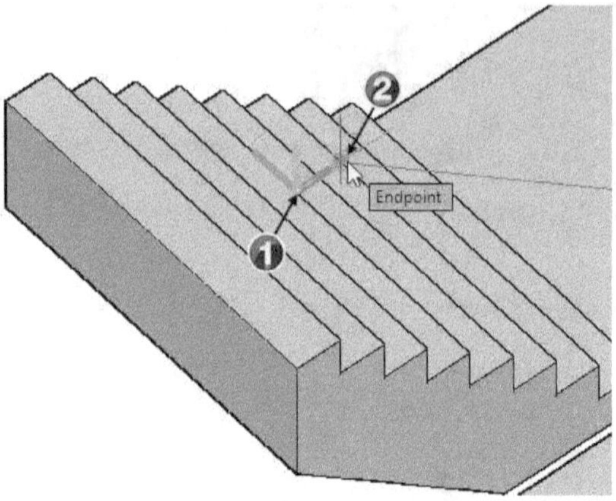

- Create a 4x4 filleted rectangle at the endpoint of the polyline, as shown. The fillet radius is 0.4 inches.

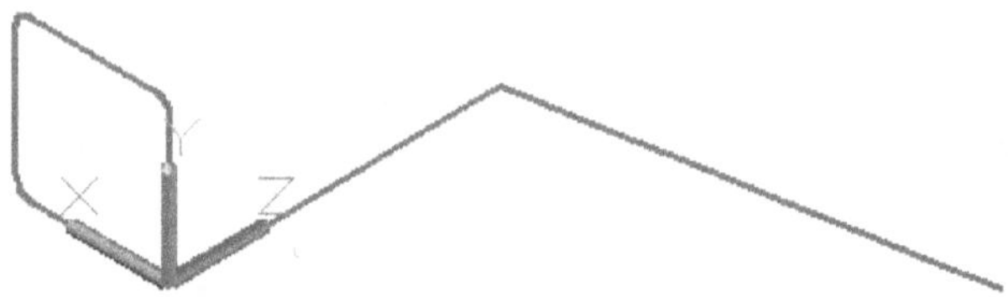

- Use the **Sweep** tool to create a swept solid, as shown. Likewise, create a rectangle at the endpoint of the horizontal line on the ground floor ceiling, and then sweep it.

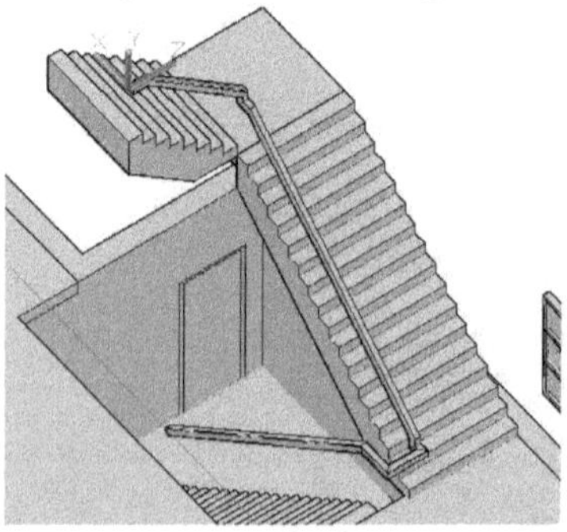
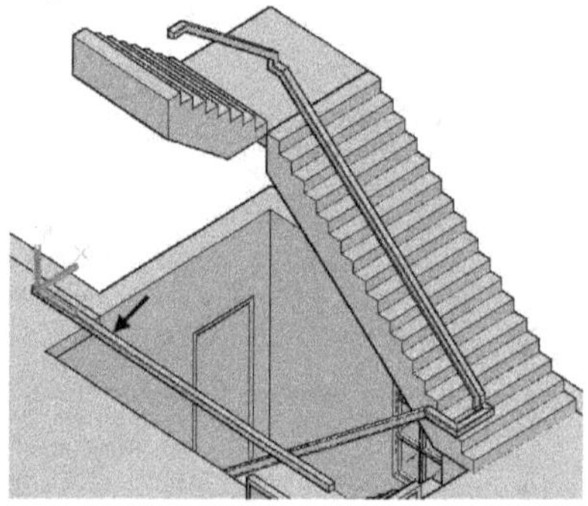

- Pull the side faces of the top two stairs up to 2 inches.

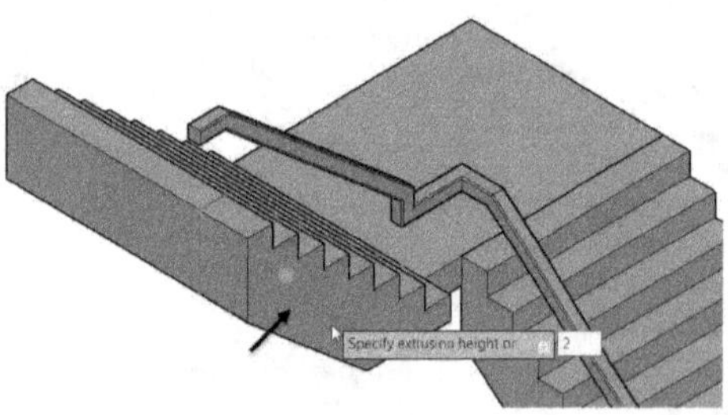
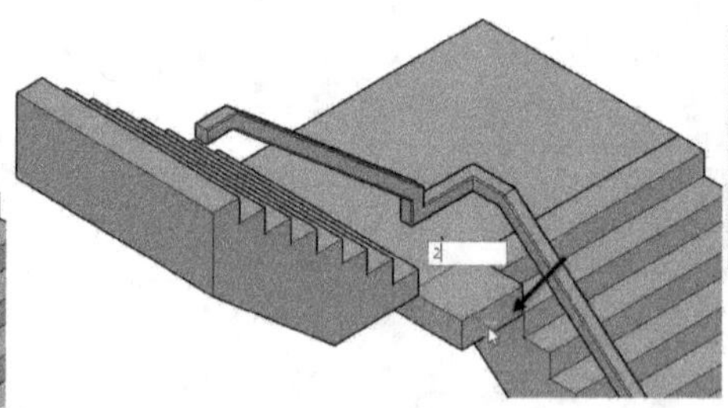
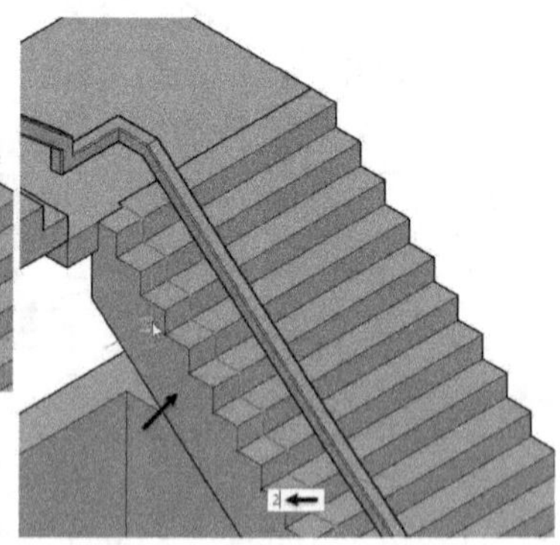

- Select all the staircases and railing. Right click and select **Isolate > Isolate Objects**. Change the view orientation to **SW Isometric**.

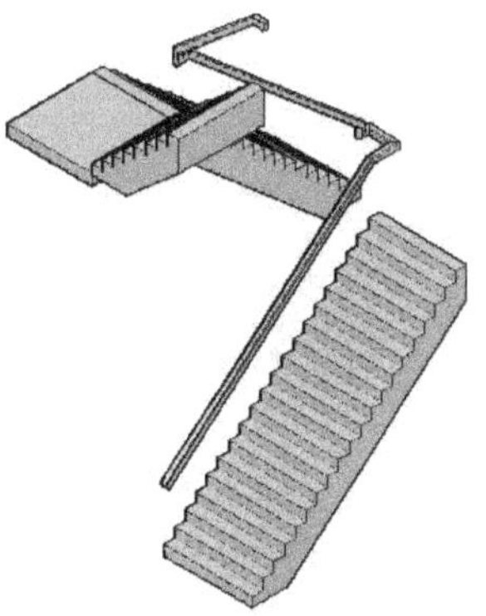

- Type UCS and press Enter twice. Next, click **Home** tab > **View** panel > **Restore View** drop-down > **SW Isometric** on the ribbon.
- Create a 3.15x3.15x45.4 box on the bottom stair, as shown. Move the box 0.4 inches towards the right and 2.7 inches backward.

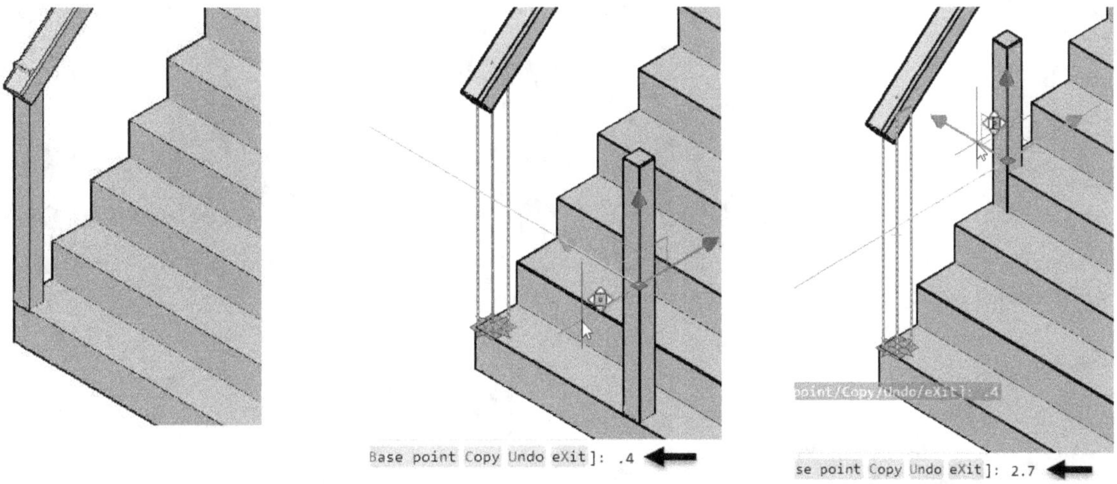

- Select the box, type CO, and press Enter. Specify the base point, as shown. Select the **Array** option from the command line. Type 7 and press Enter. Select the second point of the copy array, as shown; the copy array is created, as shown. Press Esc.

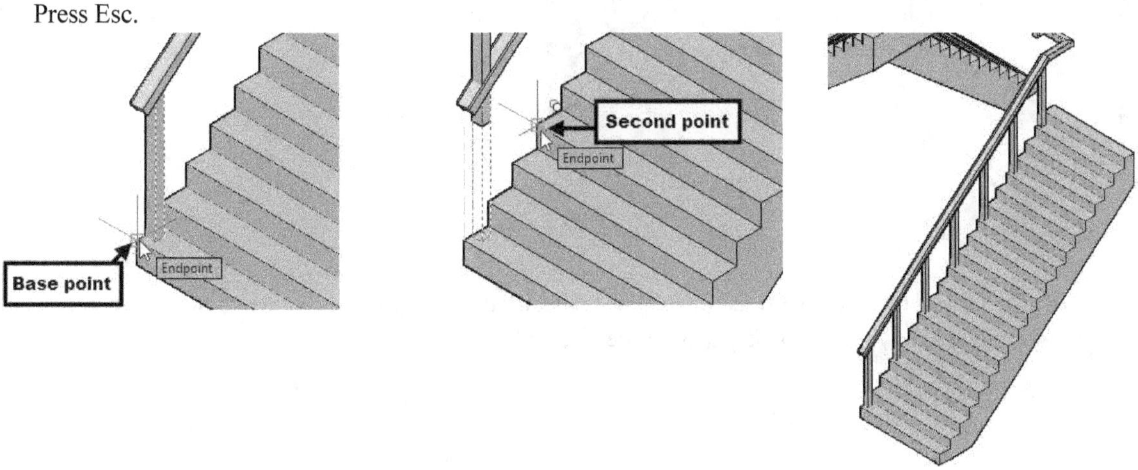

- Select the first box of the copy array, type CO, and press Enter. Specify the base and destination points, as shown.

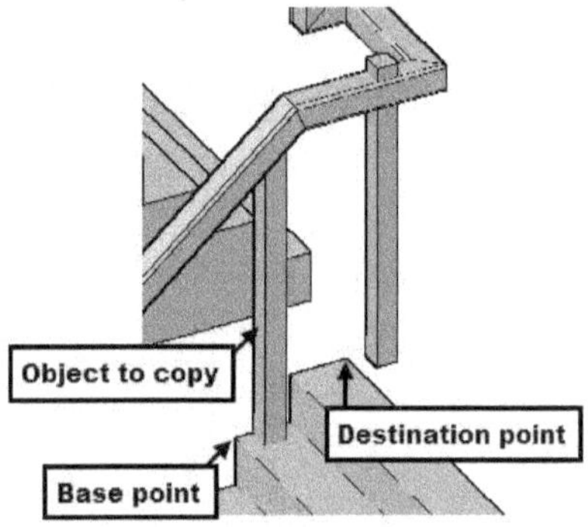

- Activate the **Dynamic Input** icon on the status bar.
- Activate the **Presspull** command and click on the top face of the copied box, as shown in the figure. Next and move the pointer downward. Type 4 and press Enter.

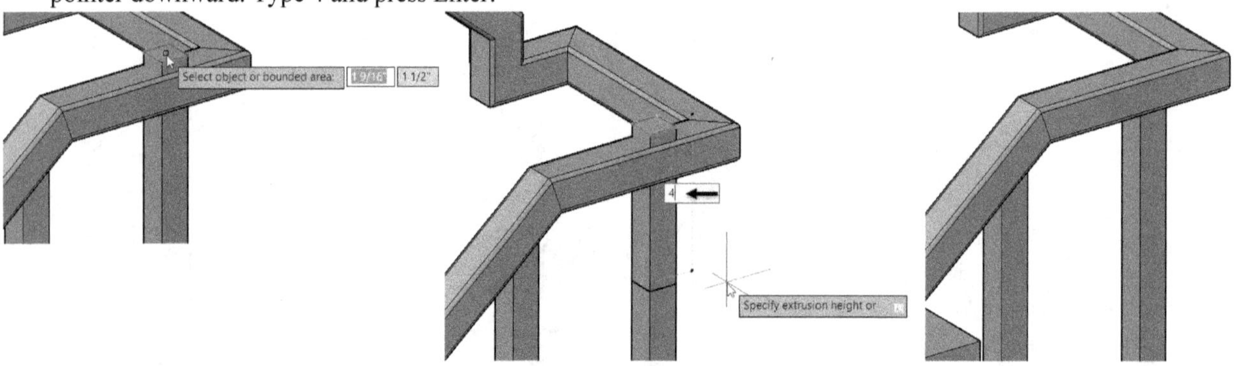

- Move the copied box by 6 inches in the X-direction (red arrow).

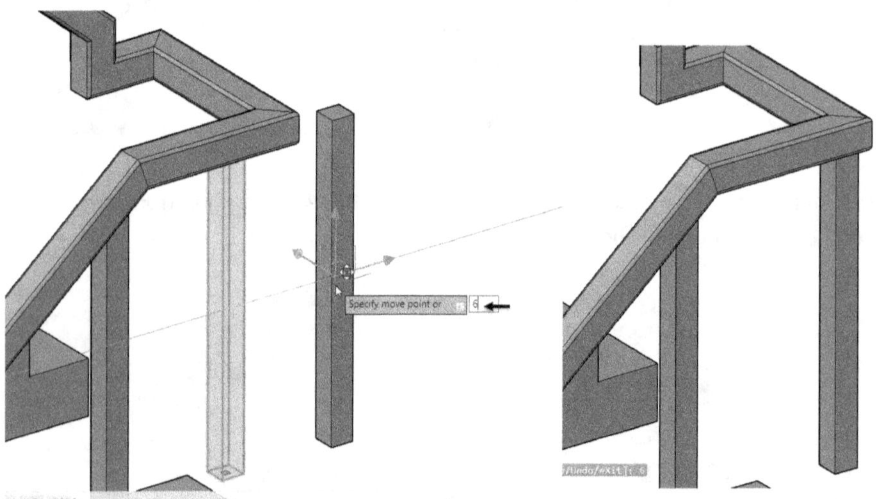

- Select the first box of the copy array, type CO, and press Enter. Specify the base point, as shown. Select the corner point of the stair, as shown; another copy of the box is placed at the selected point. Press Esc.

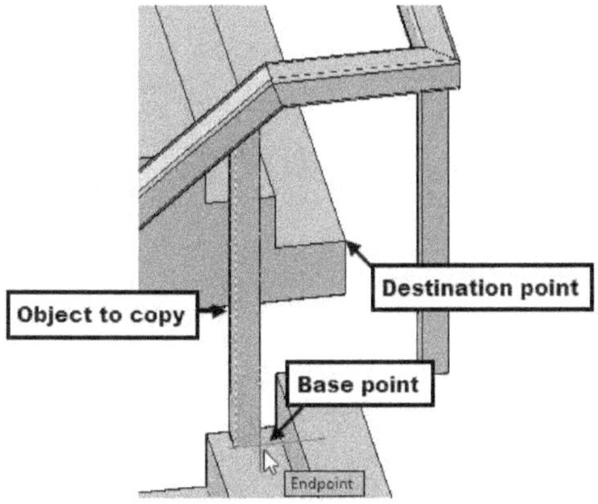

- Orbit the model, as shown. Move the box on the bottom stair up to 2.36 inches towards the right and 2.71 inches backward.

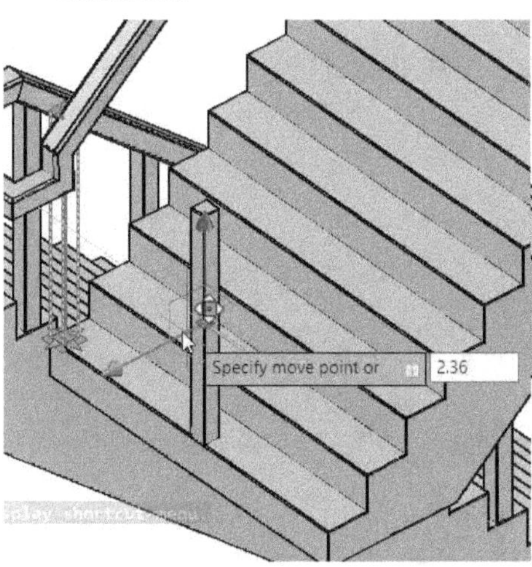

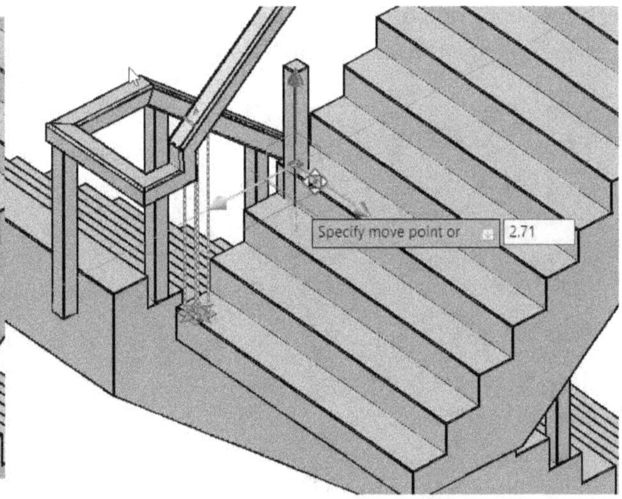

- Create the copy array of the box, as shown. Select the box located on the topmost stair, type CO, and press Enter. Specify the base point, as shown. Select the corner point of the bottom stair, as shown. Press Esc.

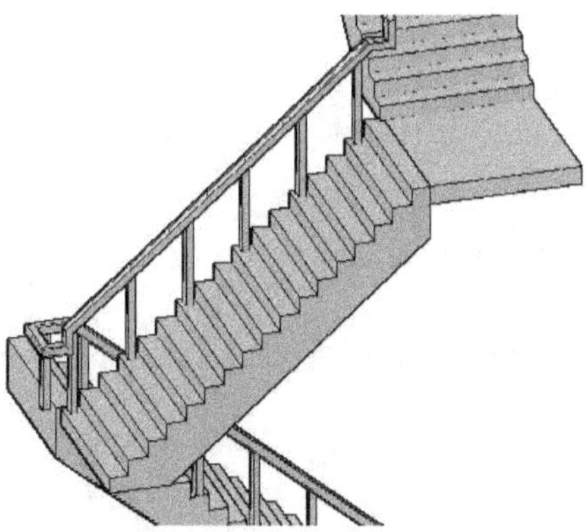

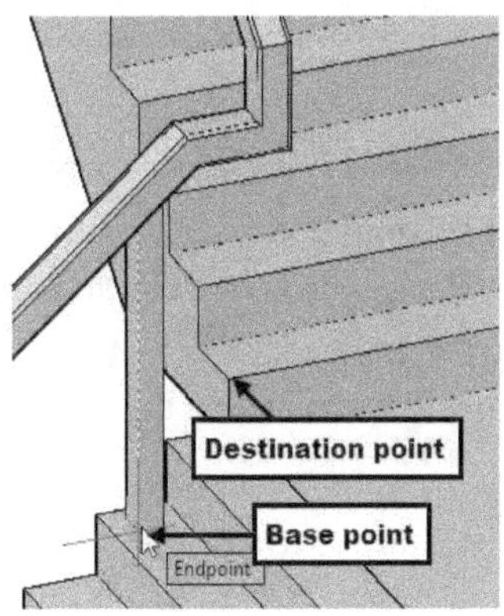

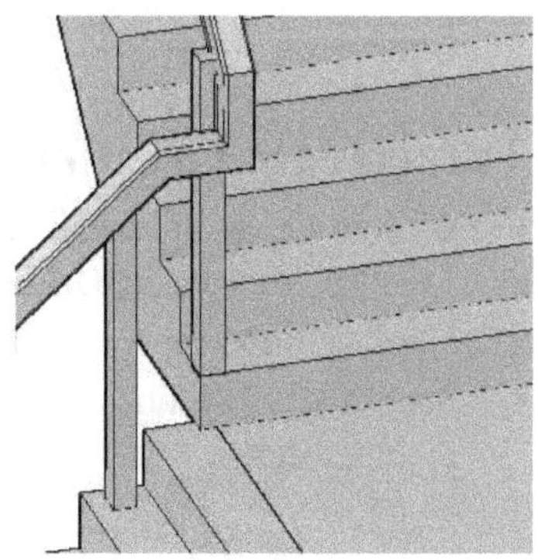

- Move the box on the bottom stair 2.36 inches towards the right and 2.71 inches backward.
- Create the array copy of the box, as shown. Press Esc.

- Right click and select **Isolate > End Object Isolation**.
- Hide the first-floor ceiling, and then create a railing on the ground floor ceiling. The spacing between the posts in 25.6 inches.

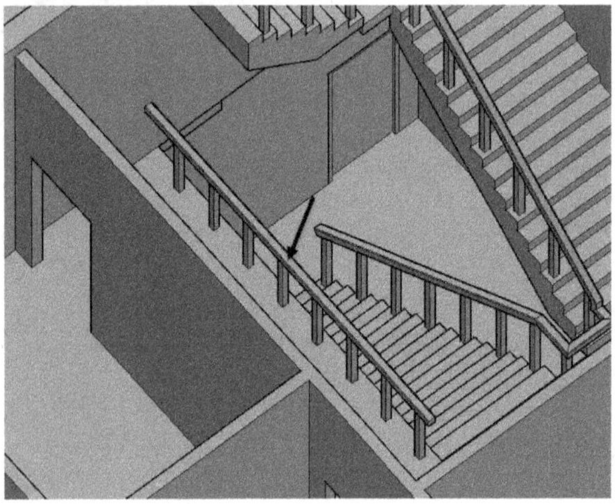

- Right and select **Isolate > End Object Isolation**.

Tutorial 10: Creating the Roof

- Change the view orientation to **SE Isometric**.
- Create a new layer, "3D-Roof". Change the layer color to green, and then set the layer as current.
- Ungroup the Front Elevation, if it is grouped.
- Select the roof entities of the Front elevation view, type CO, and press Enter. Specify the base point and destination point, as shown.

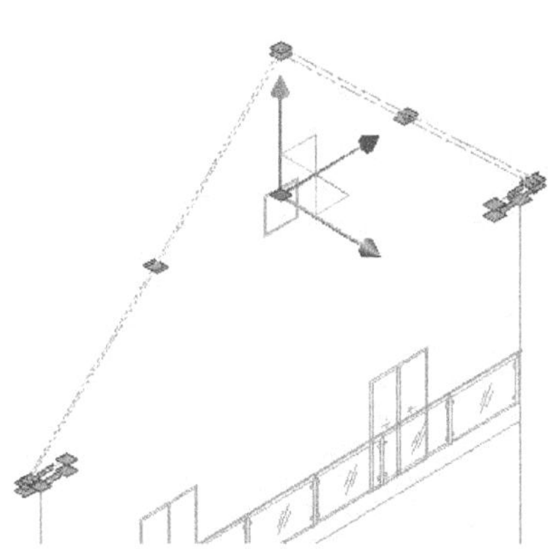

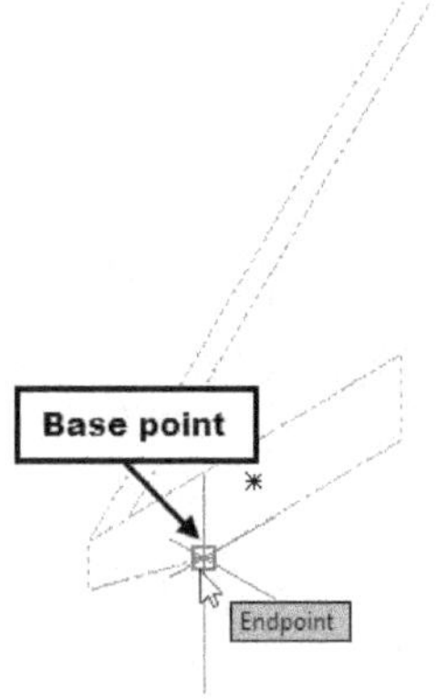

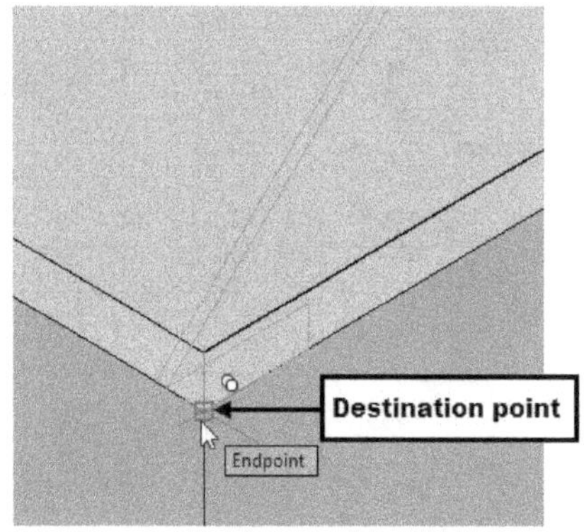

- Activate the **Extrude** tool and select the two entities of the roof, as shown. Press Enter and select the endpoint of the roof on the South East Elevation view.

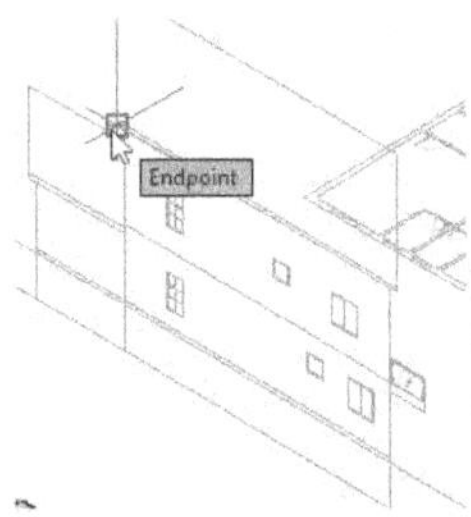

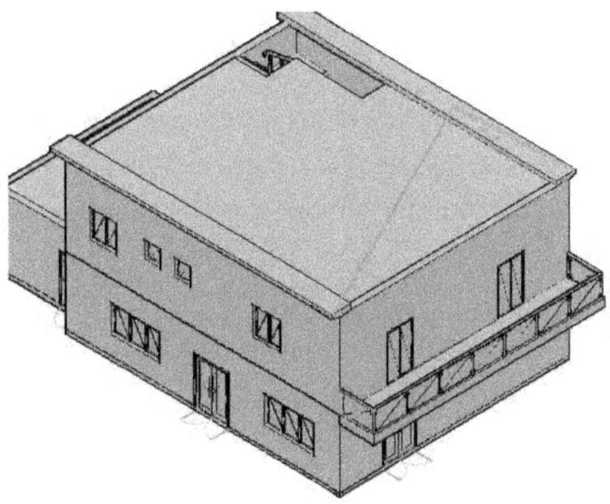

- Type L and press Enter. Close the openings of the roof, as shown.

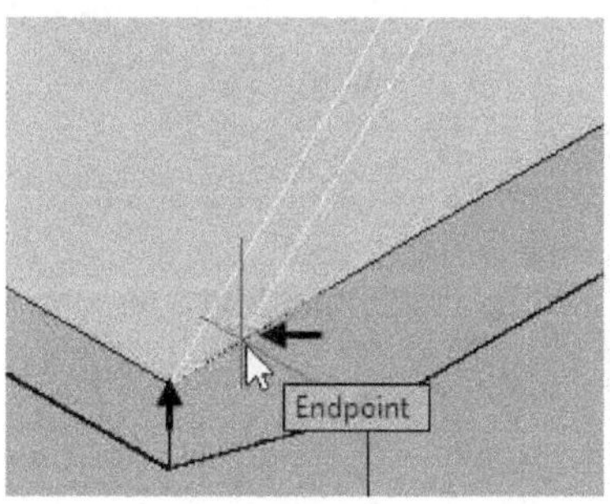

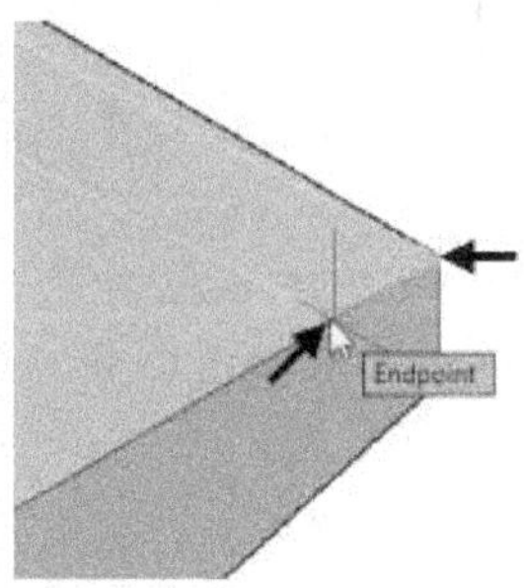

- Activate the **Dynamic UCS**  icon on the status bar. On the ribbon, click **Home** tab > **Draw** panel > **Polyline**. Place the pointer on the wall and select the corner point of the roof support. Select points in the sequence shown below. Select **Close** from the command line.

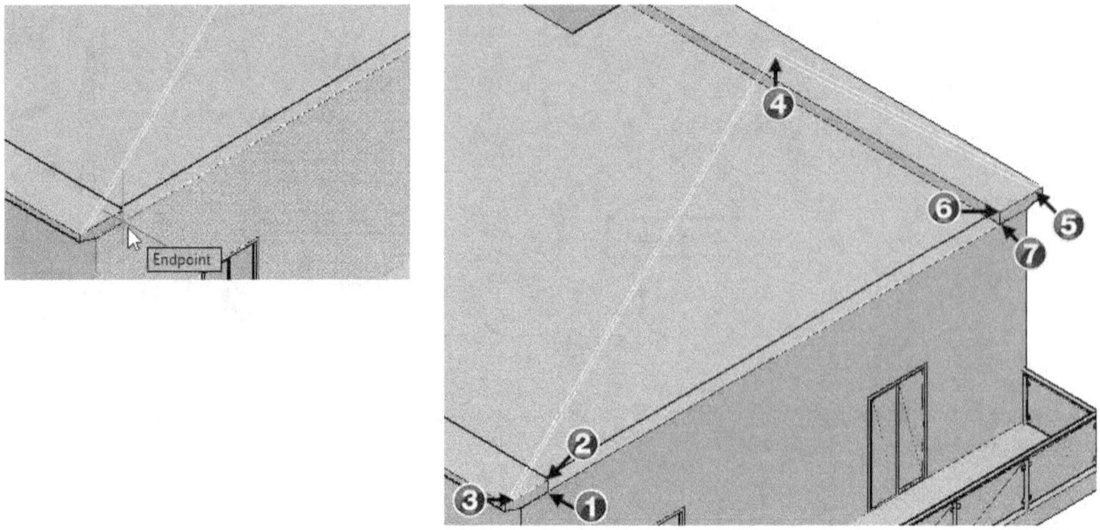

- Extrude the polyline up to 12.6 inches inward. Select the extruded solid, type MI, and press Enter. Select the midpoint of the horizontal edge of the wall, as shown. Move the pointer vertically upward and click to mirror the extruded solid. Select **No** from the command line.

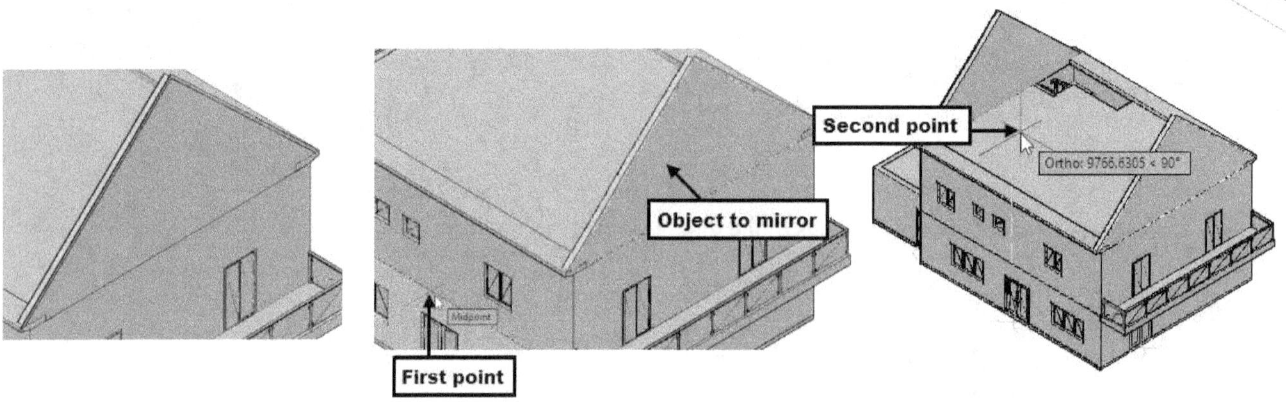

- Type REG and press Enter. Select the 2D lines of the roof, as shown. Press Enter to convert the lines into a region.

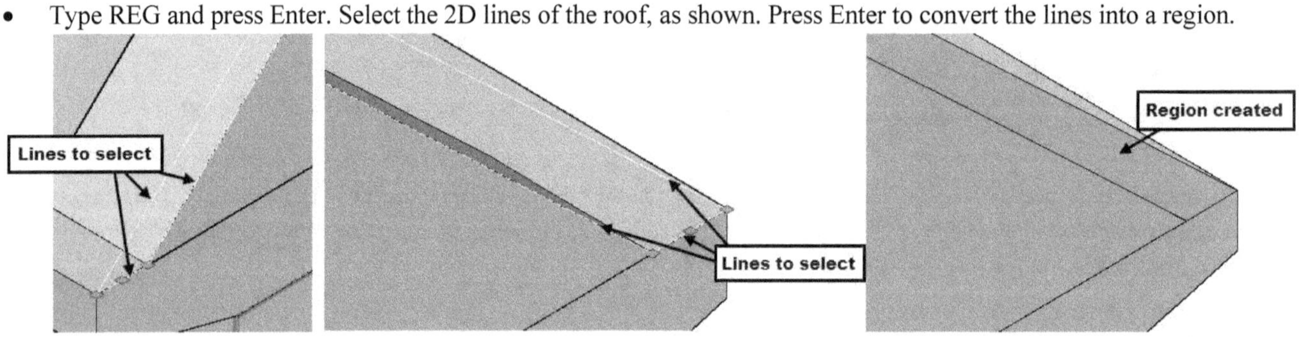

- Extrude the region up to the other end of the roof support.

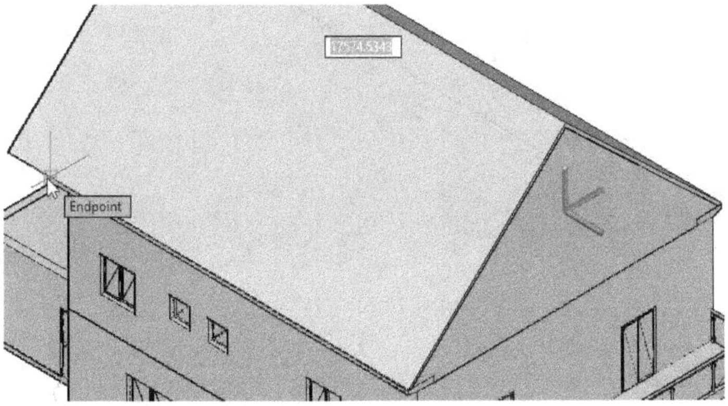

- Press-pull the front faces of the roof and roof supports up to 16 inches.

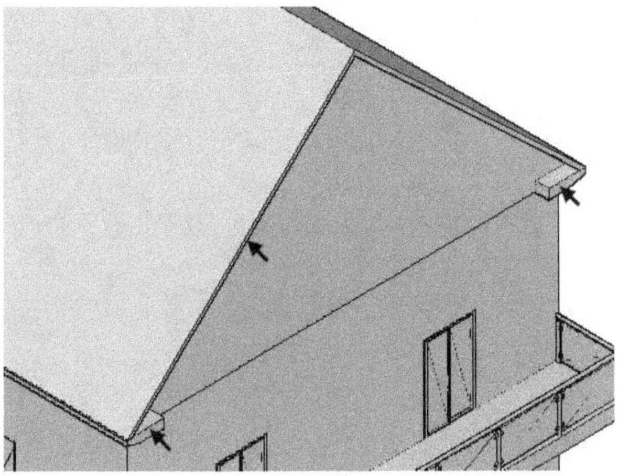

- Change the view orientation to **SW Isometric**. Press-pull the ceiling of the garage, and then create the roof, as shown.

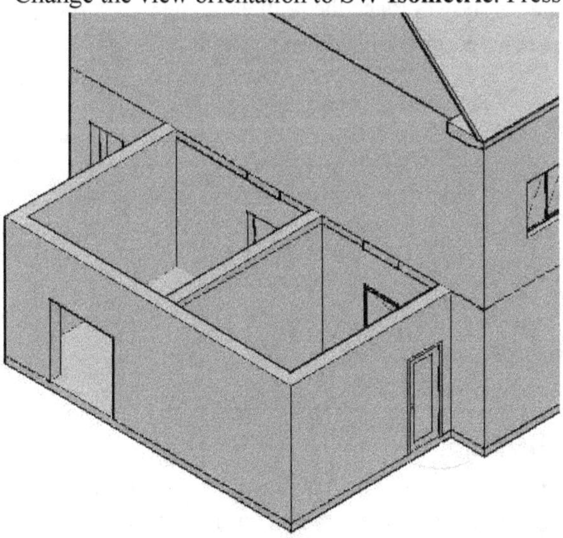

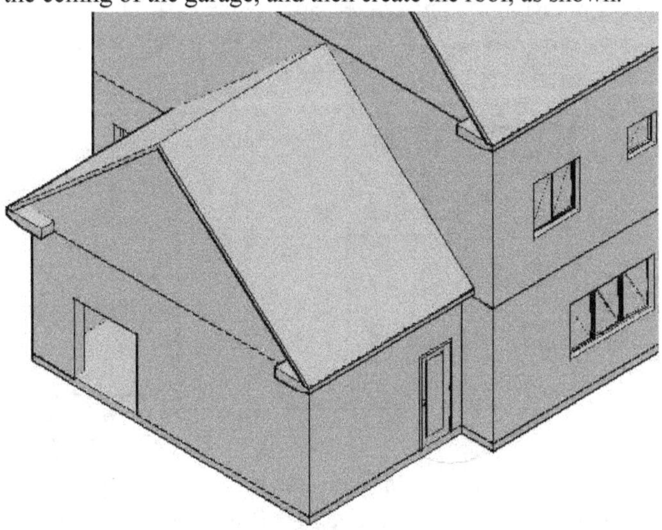

- Create windows on the rear and front walls, as shown.

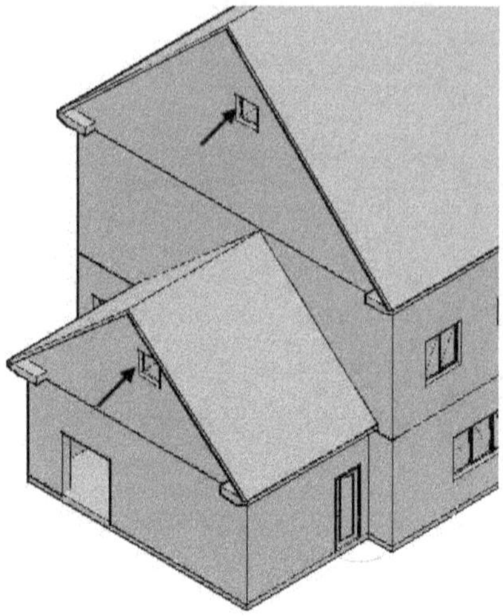

Tutorial 11: Creating the Terrain surface

- On the Quick Access Toolbar, click **Workspace** drop-down > **3D Modeling**.
- Download the Site_plan.dwg file the companion website and open it in AutoCAD.

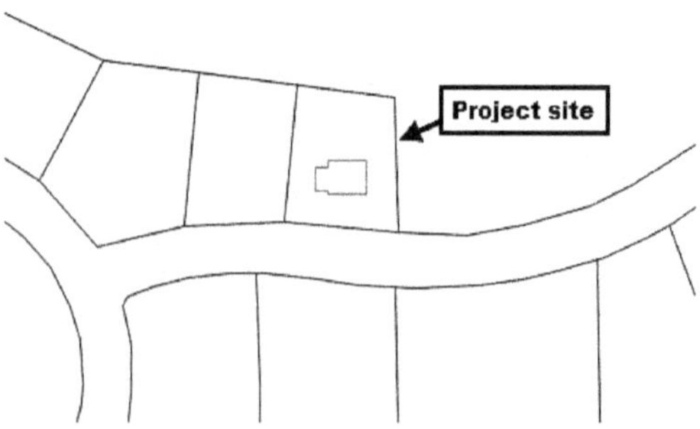

- Type REC and press Enter. Specify the first corner of the rectangle, as shown. Place the pointer on the two corner points, as shown. Select the intersection of the trace lines to specify the second corner. Offset the rectangle by 71 inches outwards.

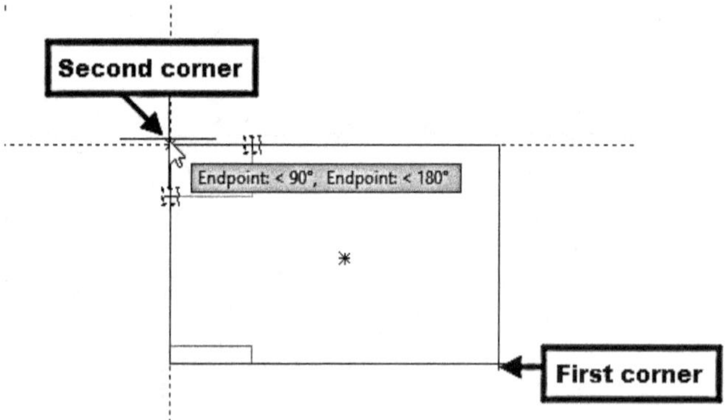

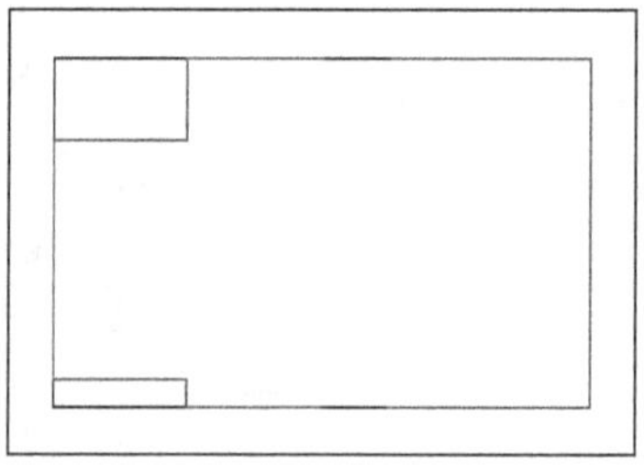

- Offset the left vertical line of the site boundary by 95 inches inside. Again, offset the new line by 240 inches. Create two horizontal lines intersecting the offset lines, as shown. Trim the unwanted portions of the offset lines, as shown.

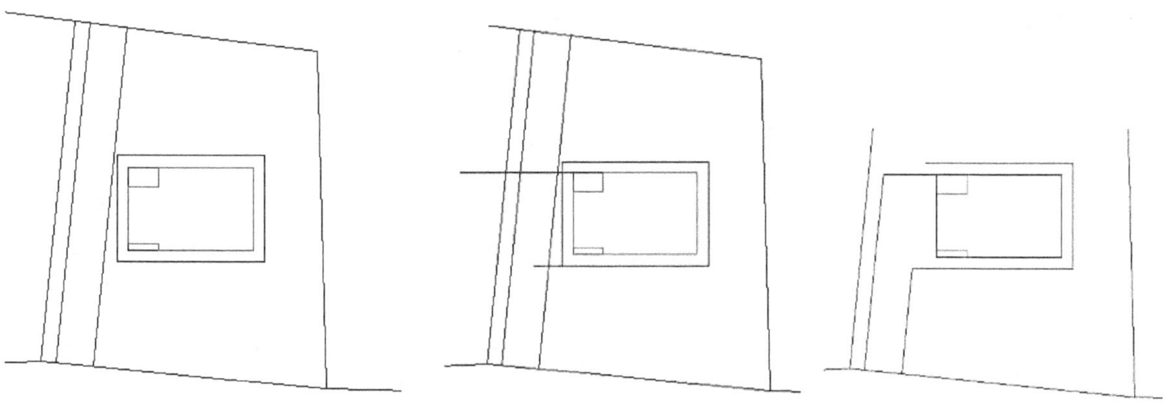

- Likewise, create other lines and trim the unwanted portions, as shown. Also, delete the unwanted lines.

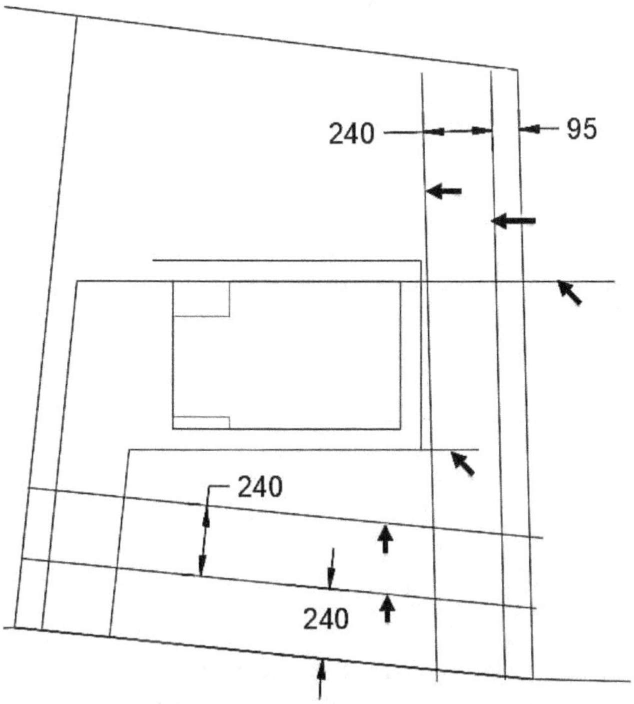

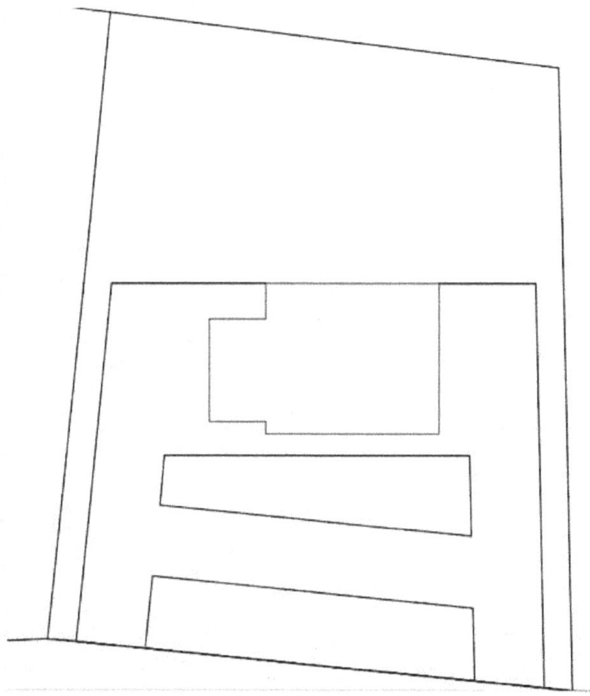

- Create a vertical line from the bottom right corner point, as shown. Move the vertical line by 281.5 inches toward left.

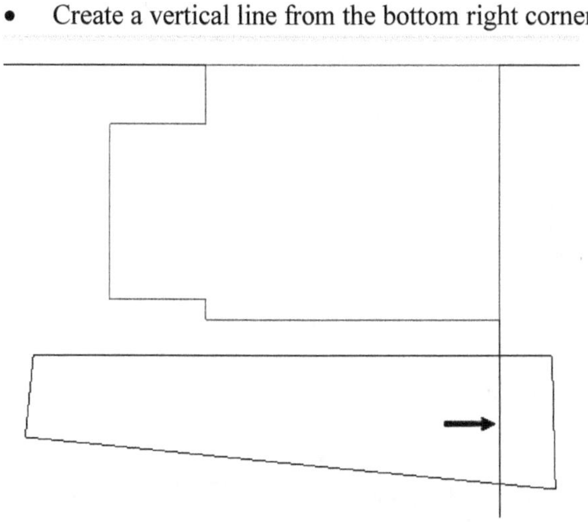

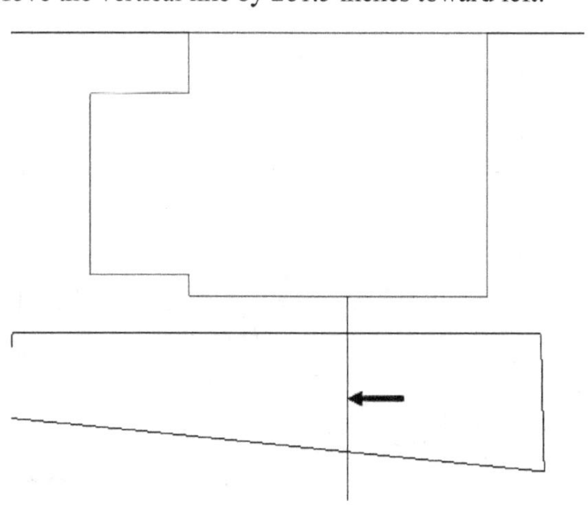

- Offset the vertical line by 47.25 inches on both sides. Trim the unwanted portions of the lines, as shown.

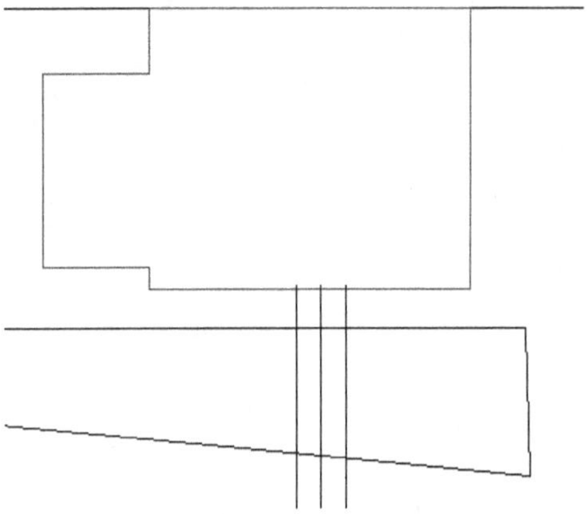

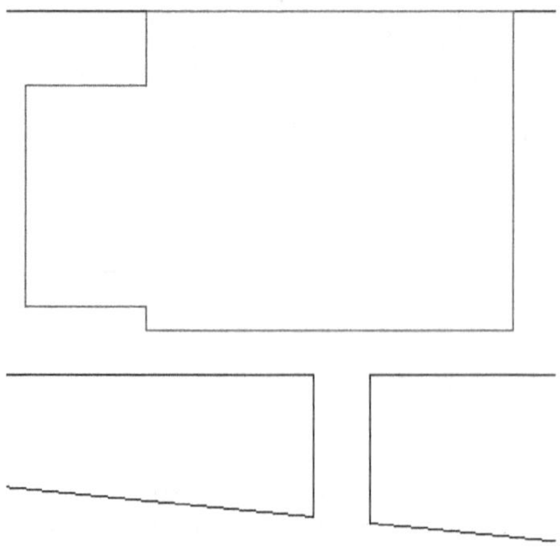

- Fillet the corners, as shown.

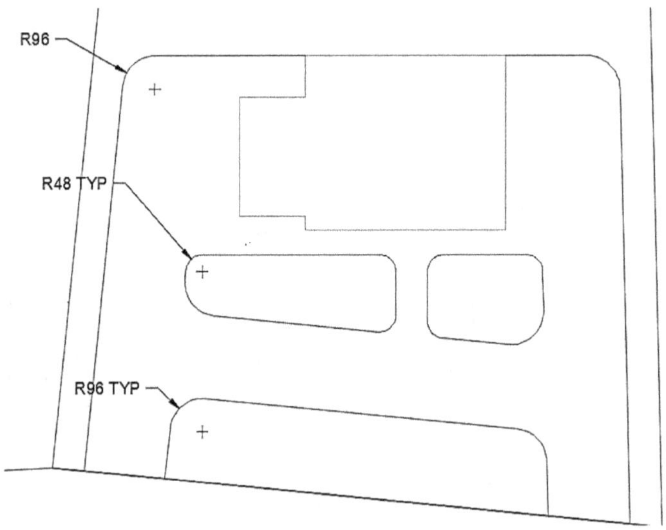

- Type F and press Enter. Select **Trim** from the command line, and then select **No Trim**. Select **Radius** from the command line, type 96, and press Enter. Create four fillets, as shown. Use the **Trim** tool to remove the unwanted portions, as shown.

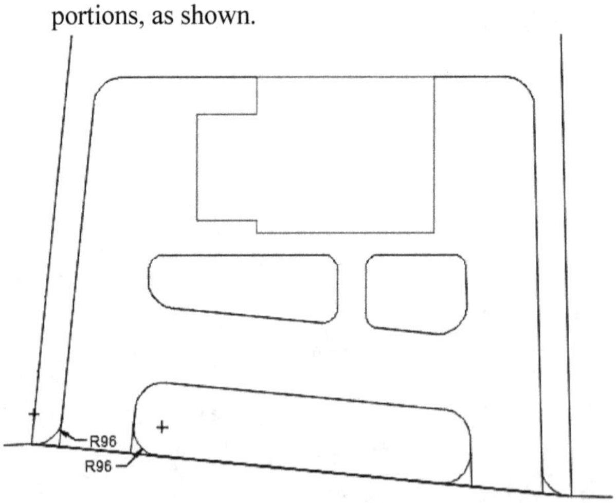

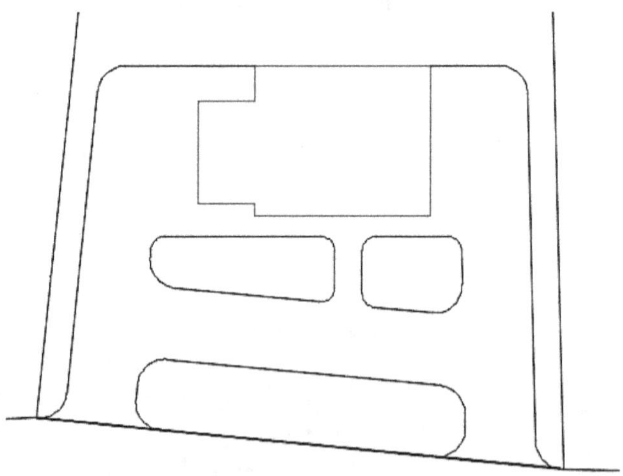

- On the ribbon, click **Home** tab > **Modify** panel > **Stretch**. Create a selection window from right to left, as shown. Press the Shift key and click on the unwanted entities from the selection set, as shown. Next, press Enter to accept the selection. Select the endpoint of the horizontal line and move the pointer upward. Type 40 and press Enter.

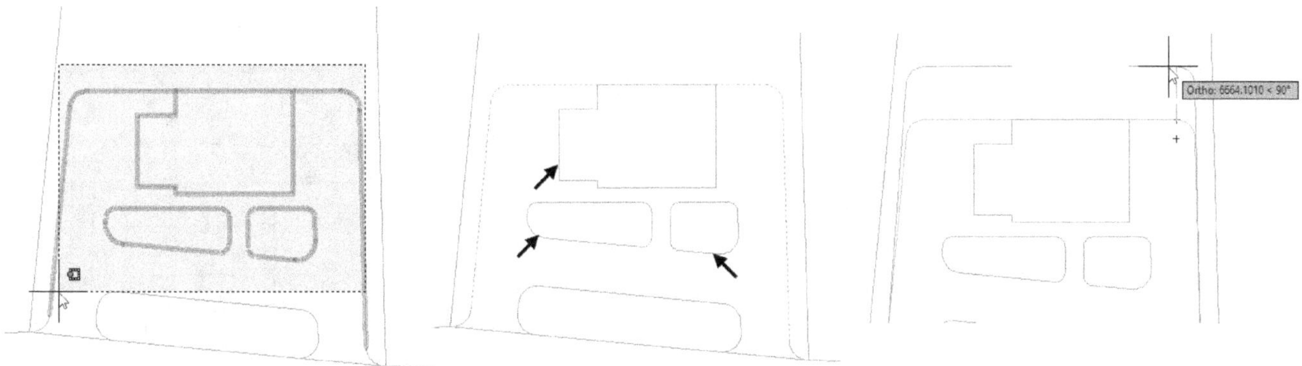

- Close the gap by connecting the two horizontal lines, as shown.

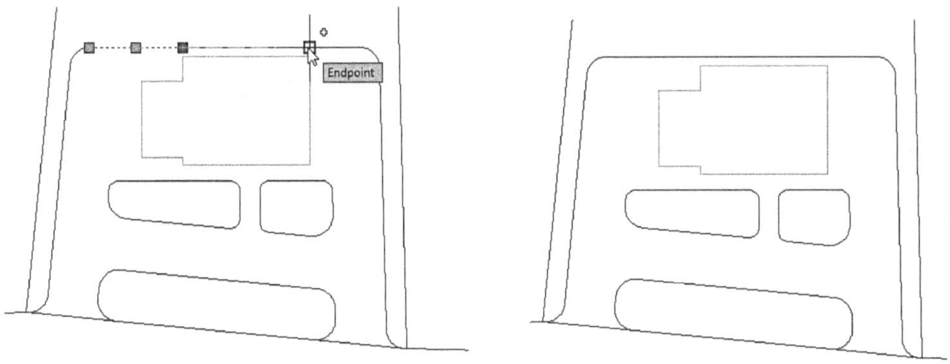

- On the **Surface** tab of the ribbon, expand the **Curves** panel, and click the **Join** tool.
- Select the four entities, as shown. Next, press Enter; the selected entities are converted into a polyline.

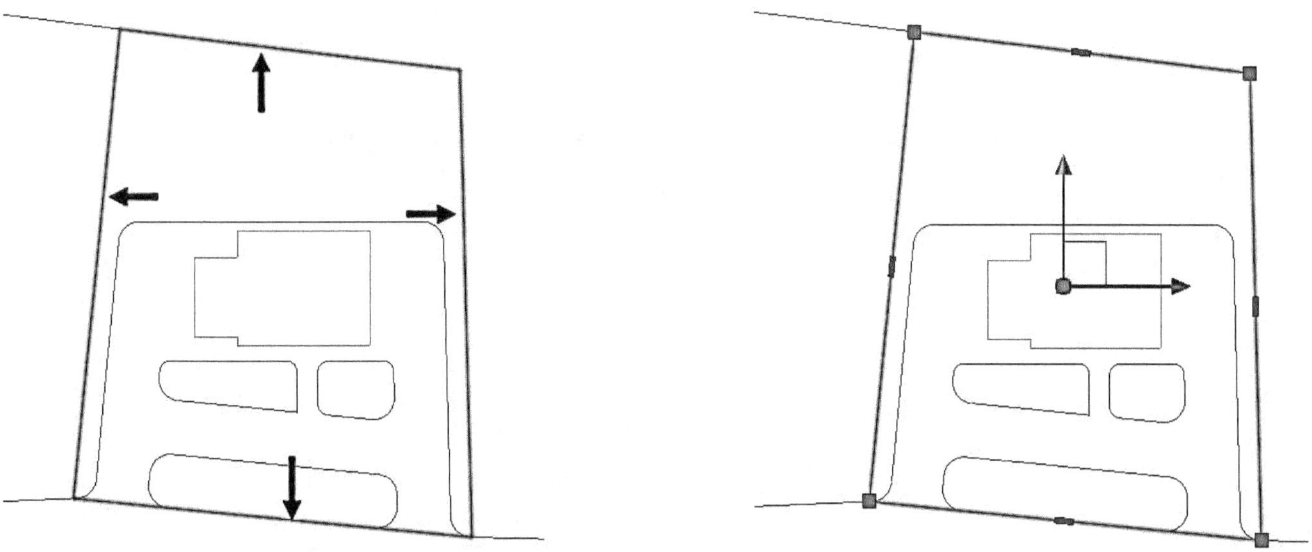

- Activate the **Join** command and select the entities, as shown. Next, press Enter to join the selected entities.

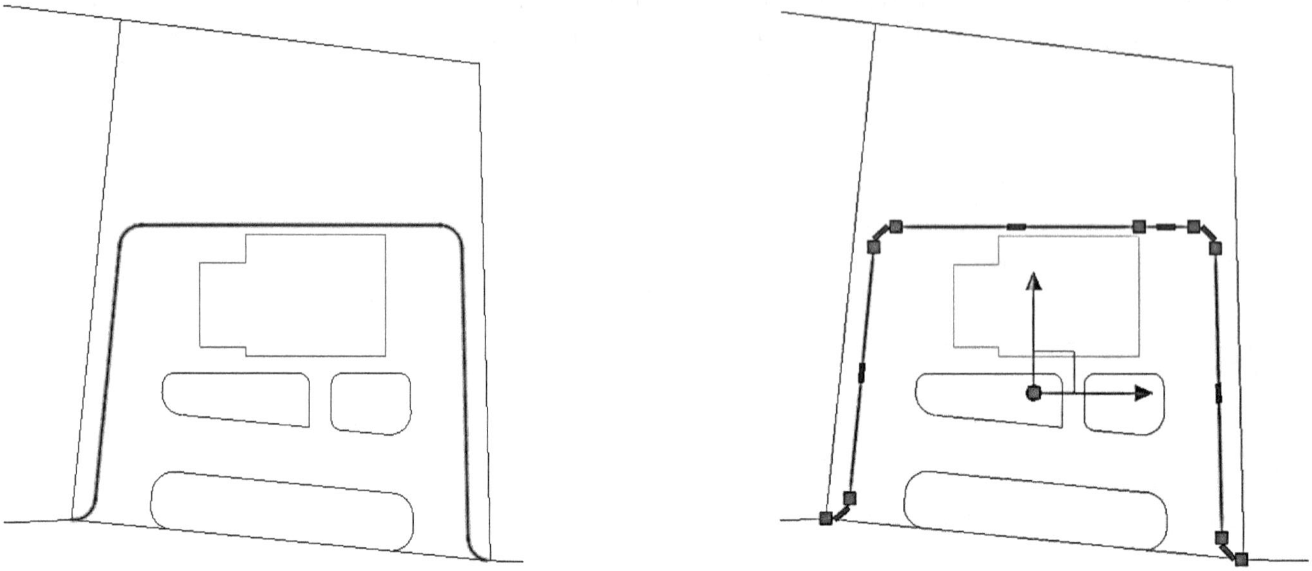

- Select the polyline, as shown. Click on the endpoint grip and select **Add Vertex**. Select the other endpoint of the polyline.

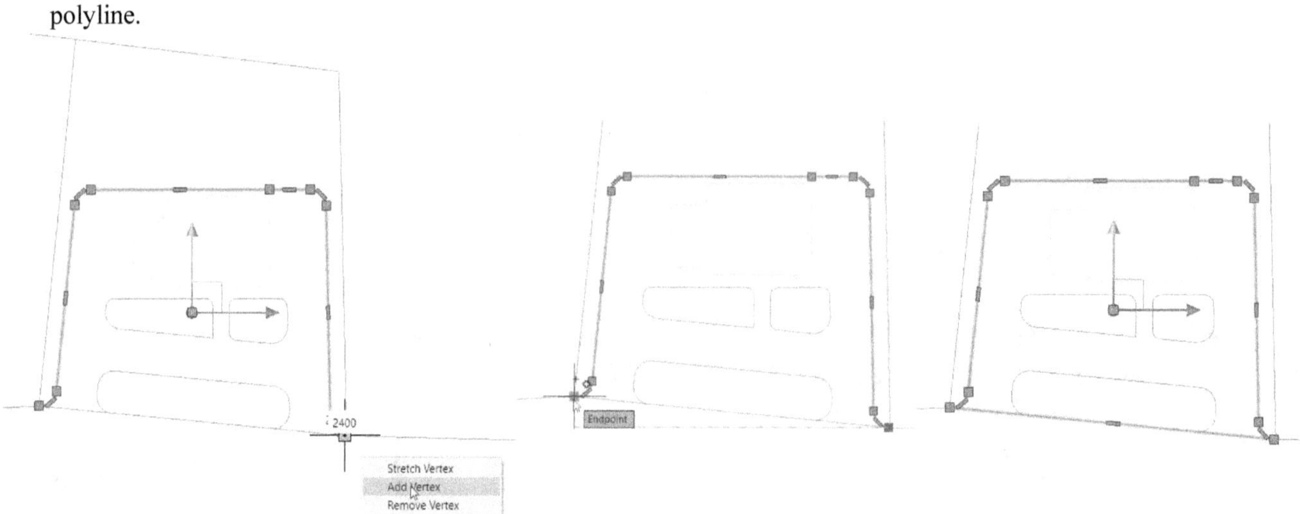

- Activate the **Join** command and drag a selection window across the entities, as shown. Press Enter to convert them into polylines.

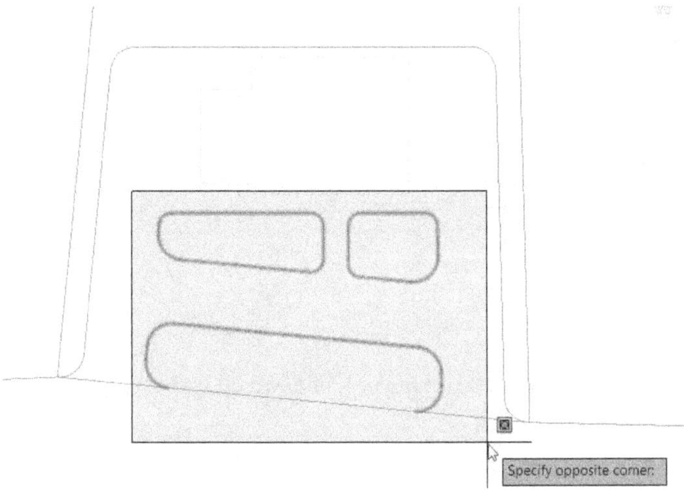

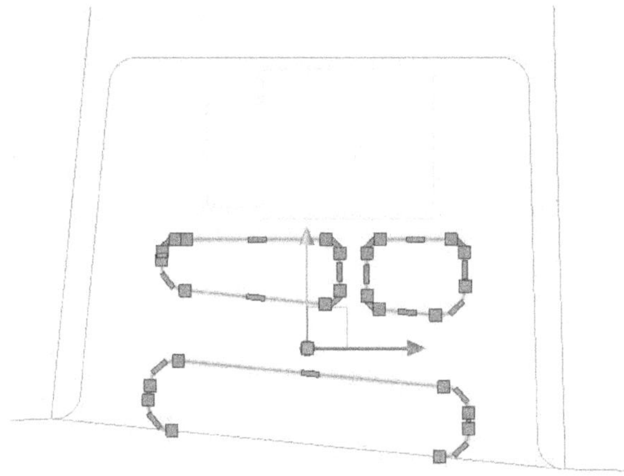

- On the **Home** tab of the ribbon, expand the **Modify** panel and click the **Edit Polyline** tool. Select the polyline, as shown. Select **Close** from the command line. Press Esc to deactivate the **Edit Polyline** tool.

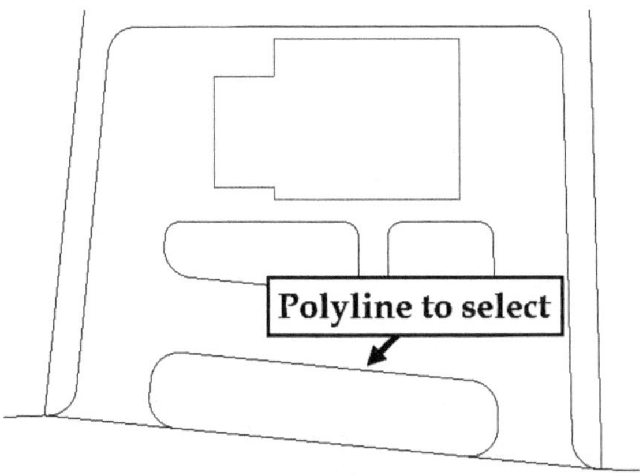

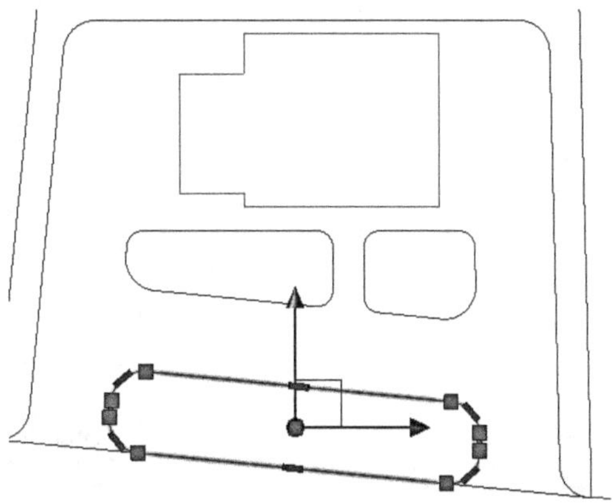

- On the ribbon, click **Surface** tab > **Create** panel > **Planar** . Select **Object** from the command line. Select the closed polyline, as shown. Next, press Enter.

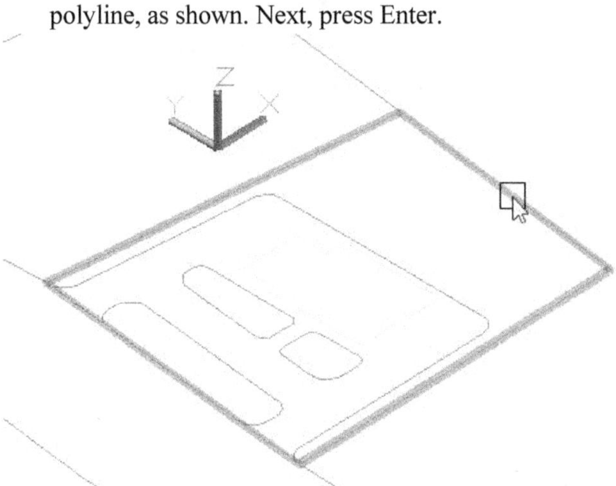

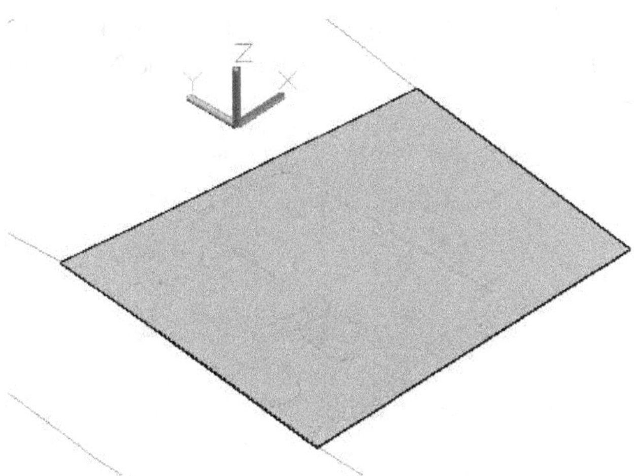

- On the ribbon, click **Surface** tab > **Edit** panel > **Trim** . Select the planar surface and press Enter. Select the polyline, as shown, and press Enter. Click in the area enclosed by the polyline; the planar surface is trimmed.

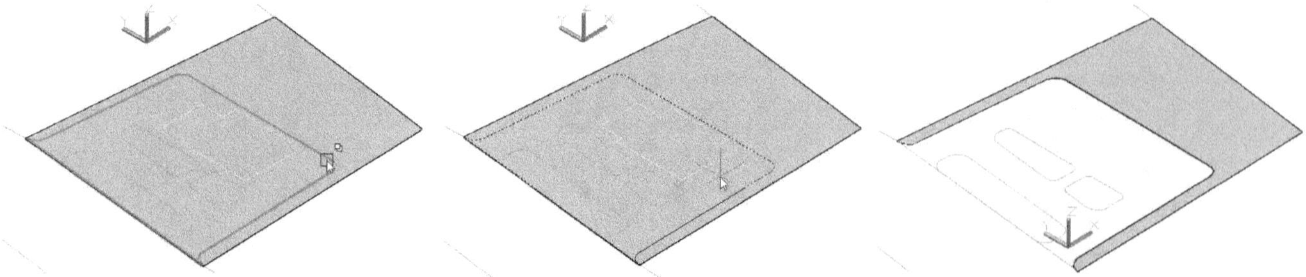

- Activate the **Planar** tool and select **Object** from the Command line. Next, select the polyline, which was used to trim the surface in the last step. Press Enter to create the planar surface.

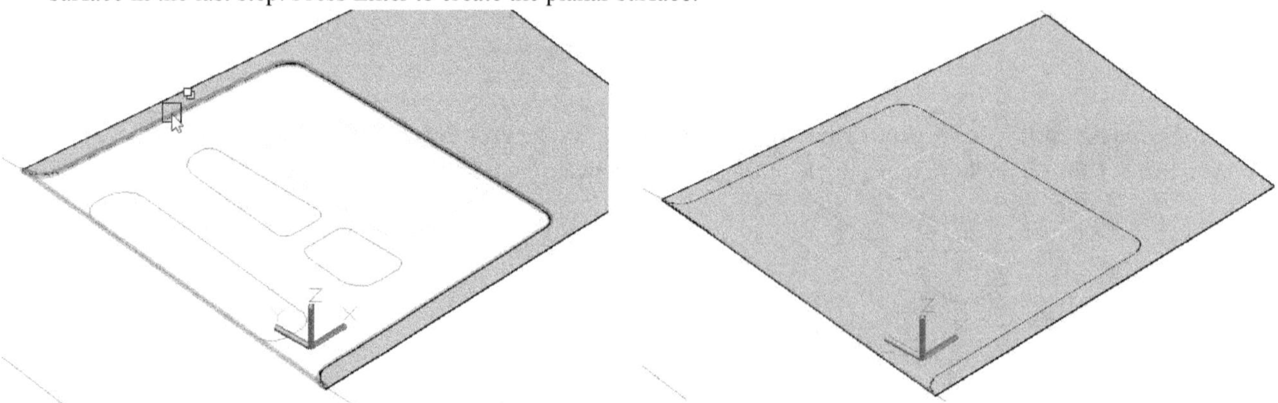

- Activate the **Trim**  tool and trim the planar surface created in the last step.

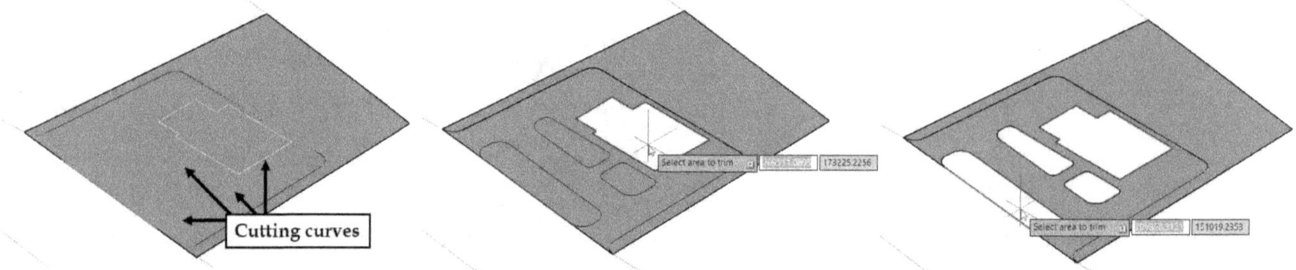

- Activate the **Planar** tool and select **Object** from the command line. Next, select the polylines which were used to trim the surface in the last step. Leave the top one. Next, press Enter to create the planar surface.

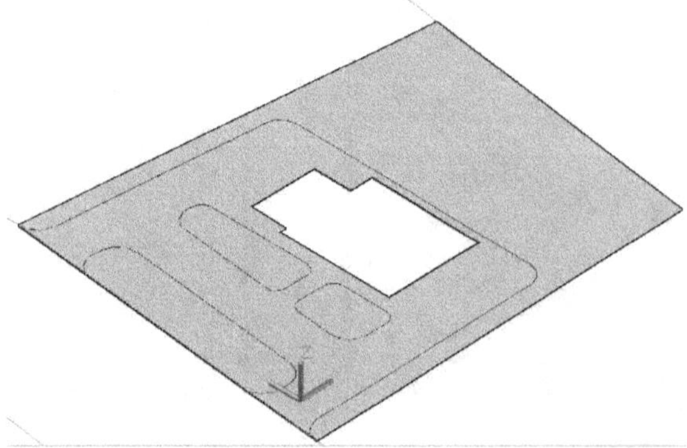

- Select all the planar surfaces, right click, and select **Group > Group**. All the planar surfaces are grouped.

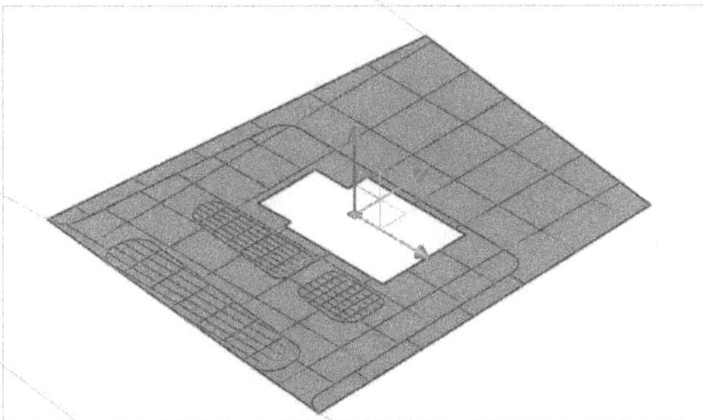

- Type **UCS** and press Enter twice. The UCS is restored to its default position.
- Type **COPYBASE** and press Enter. Select the corner of the subtracted region, as shown. Select the planar surface and press Enter.

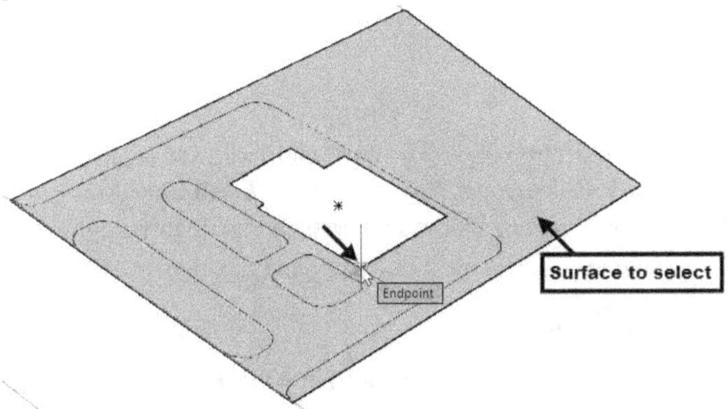

- Open the 3D-Modeling.dwg file.
- Press CTRL+V and select the corner point of the ground floor, as shown.

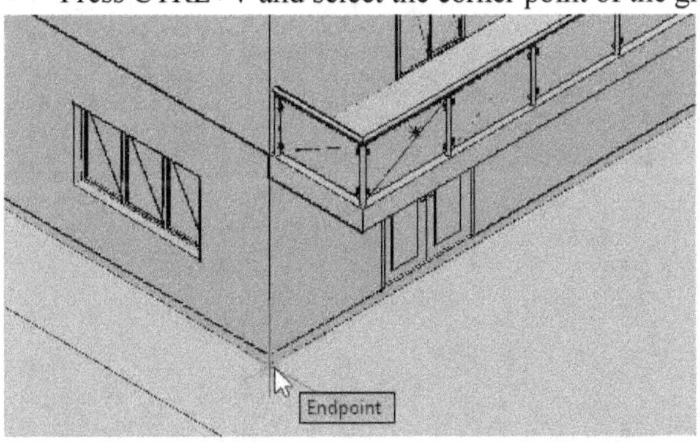

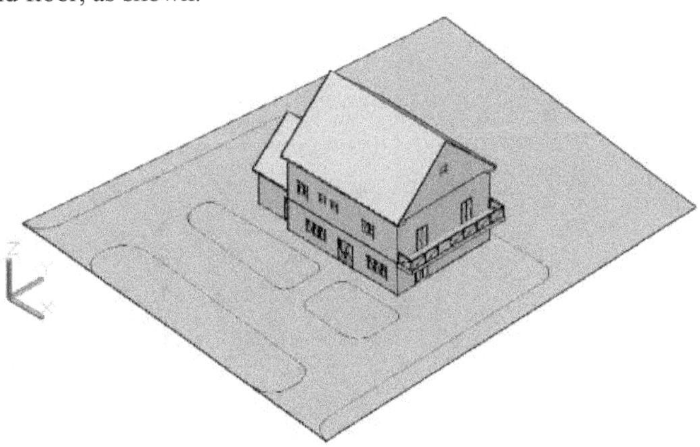

Part 3: Rendering

In this chapter, you learn to do the following:

- **Add Appearances and Textures to the model**
- **Apply Backgrounds and Scenes to the model**
- **Add Cameras and Lights**
- **Render Images**

Tutorial 1: Adding Materials

Adding materials is the first step in rendering a scene. Materials, when applied appropriately, give a realistic appearance to the model. In this tutorial, you add materials to the 3D model. Before starting this tutorial, you need to make sure that the Autodesk material library is installed on your computer.

- Open the 3D-Modeling.dwg file.
- Hide all the layers related to the Elevations and floor plans.
- On the ribbon, click **Visualize** tab > **Materials** panel > **Material Browser**. The **Material Browser** palette appears. It is divided into two portions: **Document Materials** and **Libraries**. The upper portion is called **Document Materials** and displays the materials used in the current document. The Libraries portion shows materials available in various libraries. By default, the **Favorites** and **Autodesk Library** are available in this portion. You can open existing libraries or create a new one using the drop-down available at the bottom of the palette.
- On the Material Browser, click the **Changes your views** drop-down in the **Document Materials** portion and select **Thumbnail View**. Likewise, change the view in the **Libraries** portion to **Thumbnail View**.

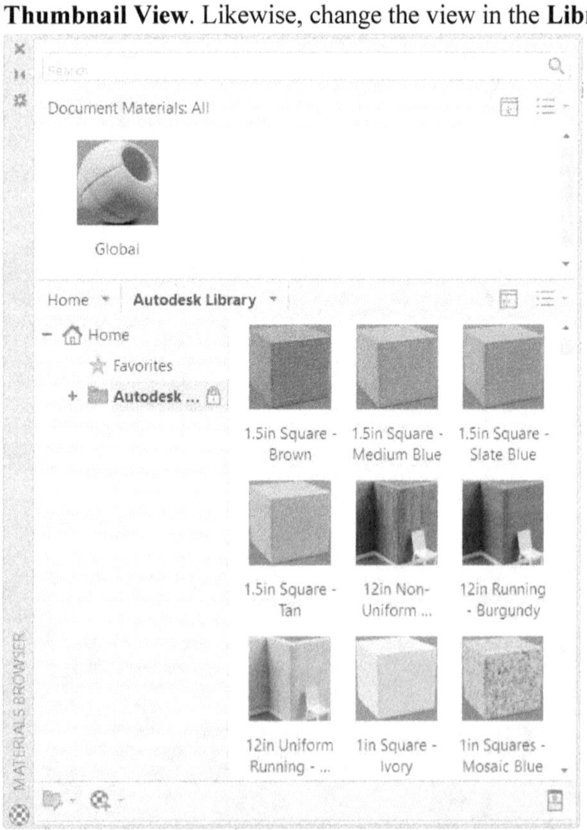

- On the Material Browser, in the **Libraries** portion, click **Autodesk Library > Wall Paint**. All the materials in the **Wall Paint** category appear. Place the pointer on the **Beige** material, and select **Adds material to document**; the material is added to the **Document Materials** portion. Likewise, add the White material to the **Document Materials** portion.

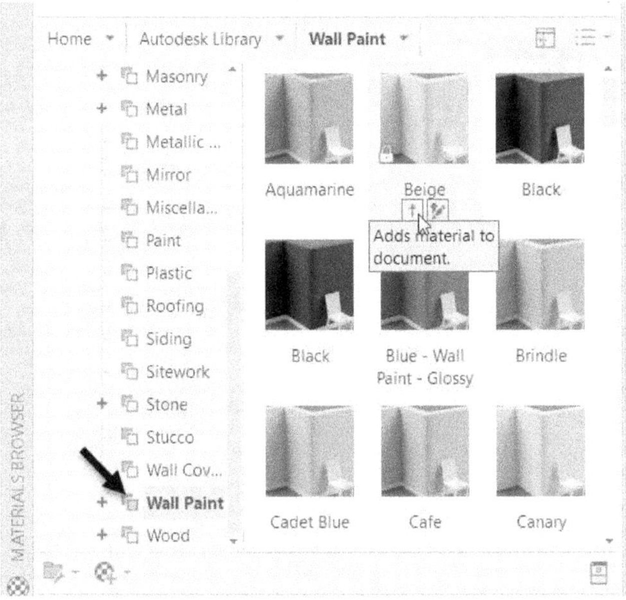

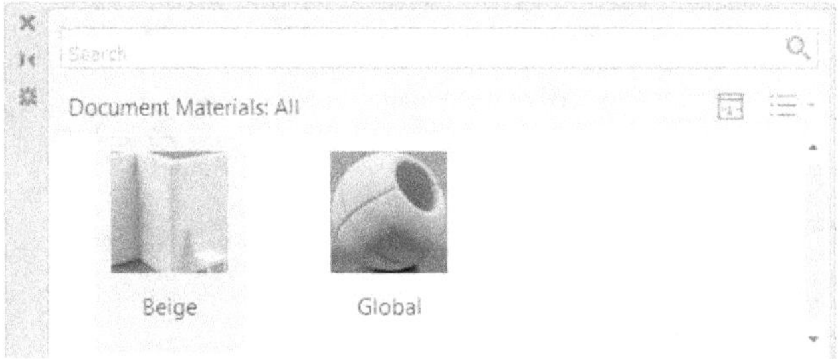

- Repeat the last step to add materials to the **Document Materials** portion. The materials and their categories are given next.

Category	Material
Sitework	Grass – Dark Bermuda
	Cobble Stone – Herringbone
Glass	Dark Blue – Reflective
Glass > Glazing	Clear
Siding	Horizontal 4in – White
Roofing	Shingles – Asphalt 3 – Tab Black
Paint	White
Metal > Steel	Stainless Steel -Bright
	Stainless Steel – Satin – Brushed Light
Wood	Teak

- On the **Visualize** tab of the ribbon, expand the **Materials** panel and click the **Attach By Layer** tool. The **Material Attachment Options** dialog appears.

  The dialog has two sections. The section on the left side has a list of materials available in the document, and the right side section displays the list of layers. You need to apply materials to the layers by dragging them from the material list and releasing them on the target layers.

- Scroll down in the material list such that the **Horizontal 4in –White** material is displayed. Also, scroll down the **Layer** list such that the 3D-Walls layer is displayed.
- Select the **Horizontal 4in-White** material, drag, and release it on the **3D-Walls** layer.

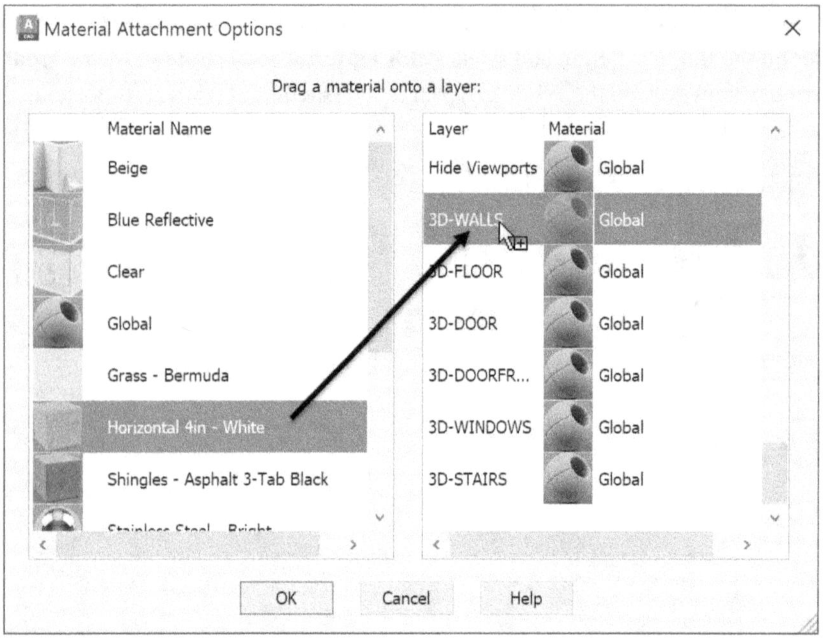

- Likewise, add materials to the other layers, as shown. Click **OK** on the dialog.

Material	Layer
Teak	3D-Doors
	3D-Doorframes
White (1)	3D-Windows
Stainless Steel - Bright	3D-Balcony
Shingles – Asphalt - 3 Tab Black	3D-Roof

- On the ribbon, click **Visualize** tab > **Visual Styles** panel > **Visual Styles** drop-down > **Shaded with edges**.

  The model is displayed with the materials.

- Select the planar surfaces of the sitework, as shown. On the **Material Browser** palette, in the **Document Materials** portion, right click on the **Grass- Dark Bermuda** material and select **Assign to Selection**.

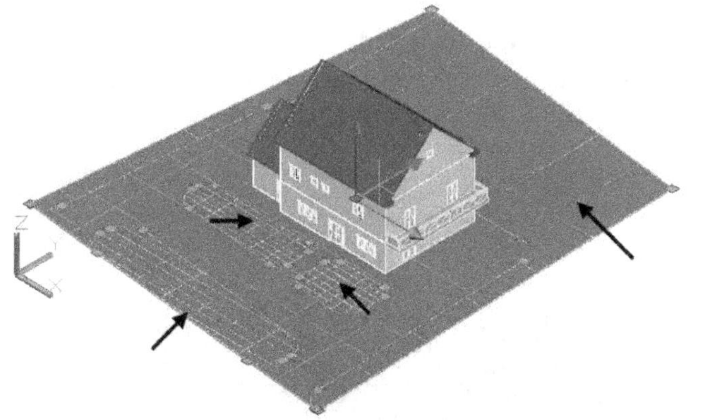

- On the **Material Browser** palette, in the **Document Materials** portion, select the **Cobble Stone - Herringbone** material, drag and place it on the remaining planar surface of the site work.

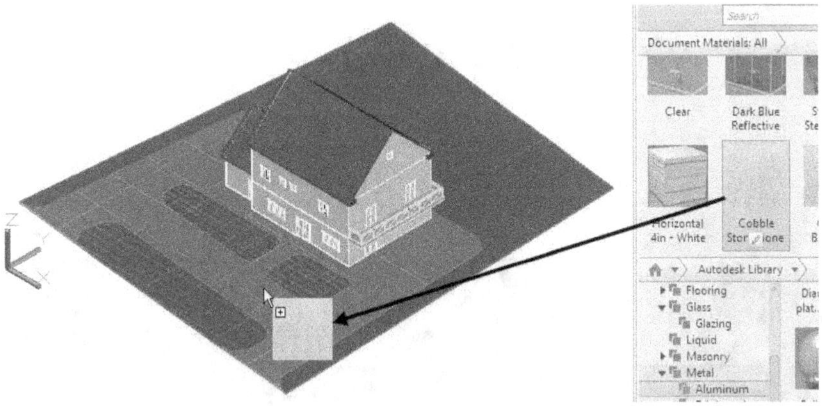

- Likewise, add materials to the other objects of the model, as shown. You need to explode the Rectangular pattern of the balcony glazing, and then apply the **Clear** material.

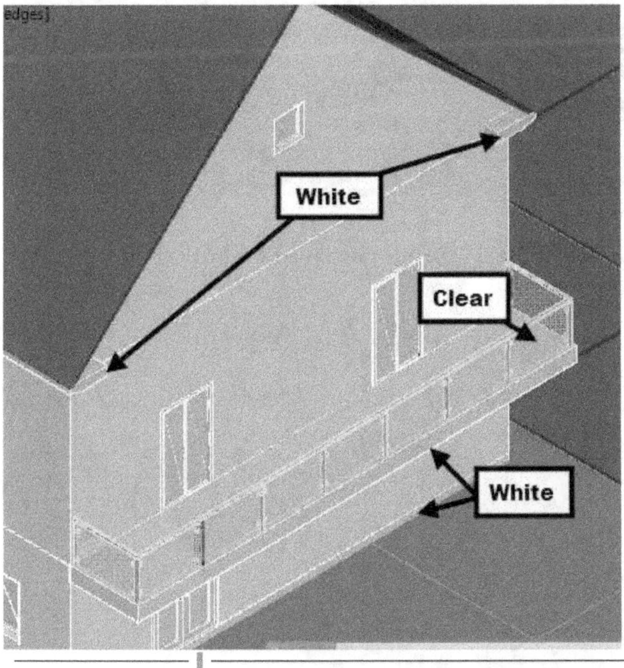

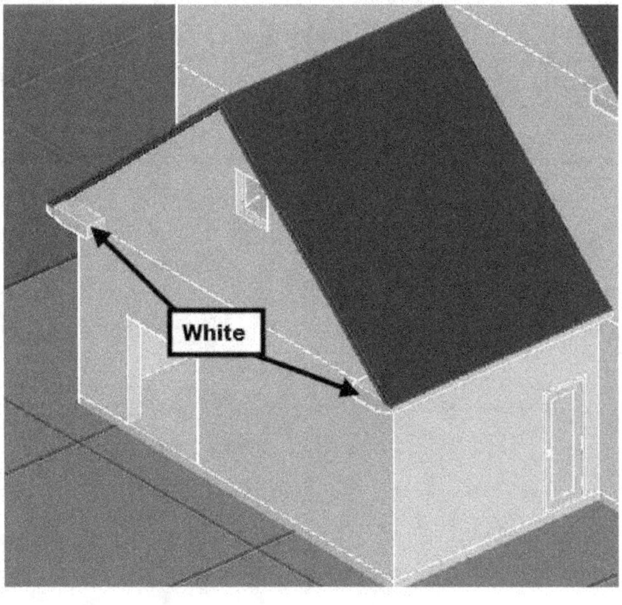

- On the ribbon, click **Home** tab > **Selection** panel > **Filter** drop-down > **Face**. Zoom to the windows and select the faces of the glazing. On the **Material Browser** palette, in the **Document Materials** portion, select the **Dark Blue Reflective** material. Ungroup the other windows sliding doors and add the **Dark Blue Reflective** material to the glazing.

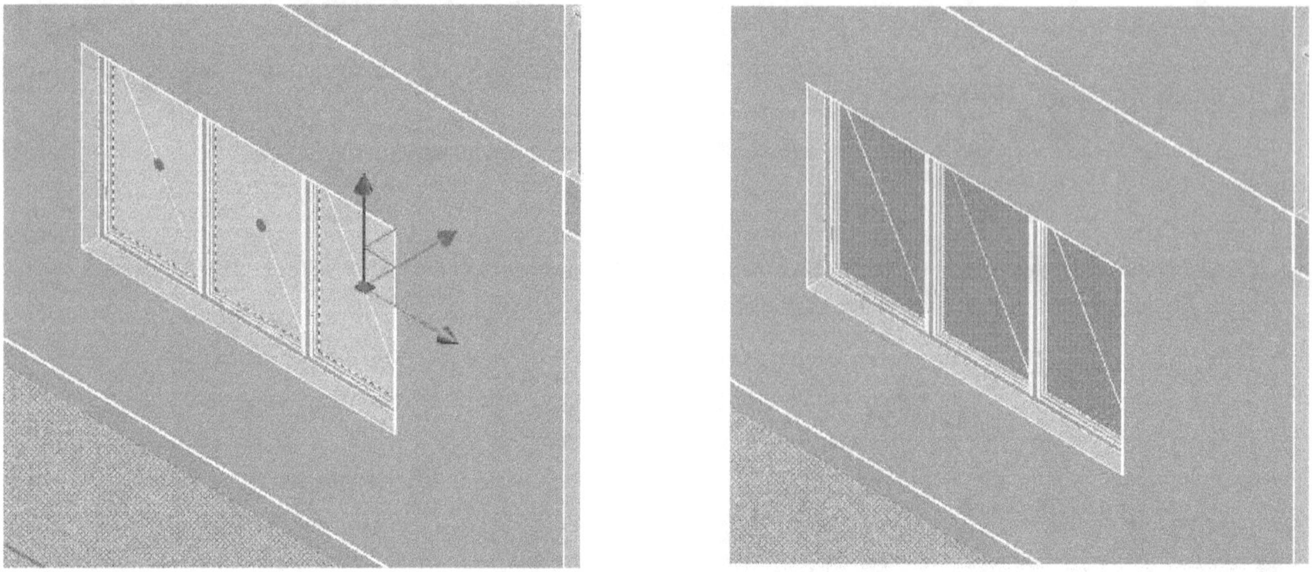

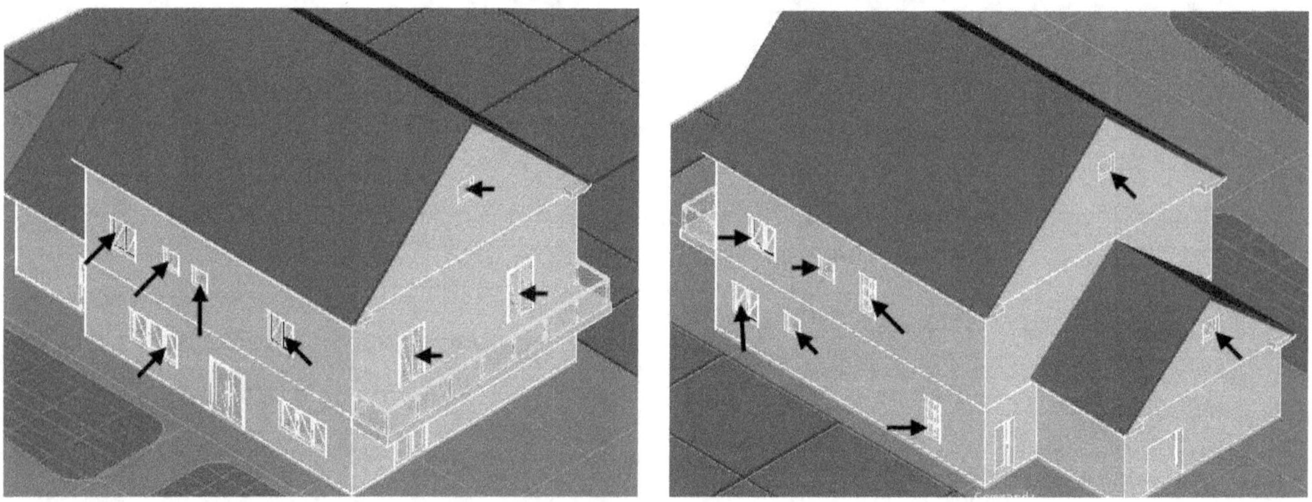

- Zoom to the double door and select the door handles. Select **Stainless Steel – Satin – Brushed Light** from the Material Browser.

- Likewise, add the **Stainless Steel – Satin – Brushed Light** material to other door handles.
- Save the model.

Tutorial 2: Adding Cameras

Cameras are used to define the viewpoint of a scene. You can add cameras in the graphics window and define its target point.

- On the ribbon, click **Visualize** tab > **Camera** panel > **Create Camera**.
- Select the corner point of the planar surface of the site plan, as shown; the camera is fixed at the specified point, and the target is attached to the pointer. Select the corner point of the window opening, as shown.

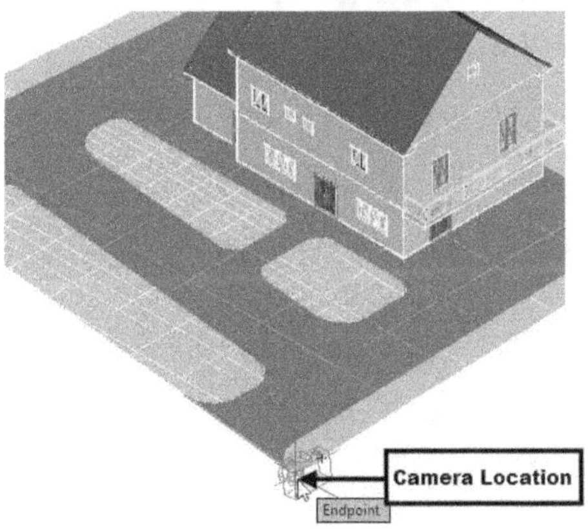

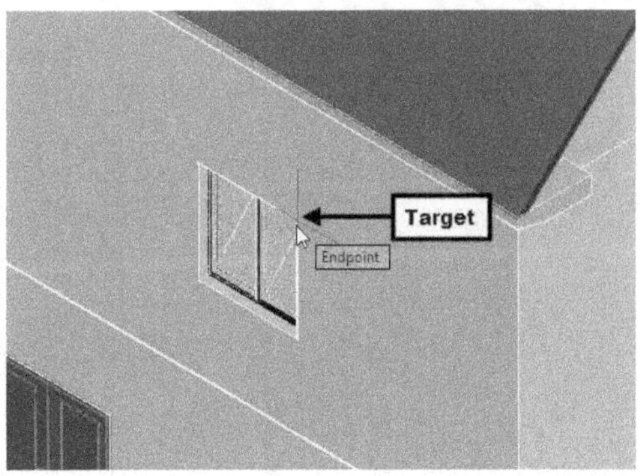

- Select **Name** from the command line. Type **Southeast camera** and press Enter.
- Select **Height** from the command line. Type 165 and press Enter. Select **eXit** from the command line.
- Select **View Controls > Custom Model Views > Southeast Camera** from the In-Canvas controls.

Notice that the camera does not cover the entire model. You need to edit its location and target to cover the complete model.

- Select **View Controls > SE Isometric** from the In-Canvas controls.
- Zoom to the model and select the camera; the **Camera Preview** dialog appears.
- Select the Lens Length/ FOV grip and move the pointer upwards; the preview in the **Camera Preview** dialog is updated.
- Type 20 and press Enter. Close the **Camera Preview** dialog.

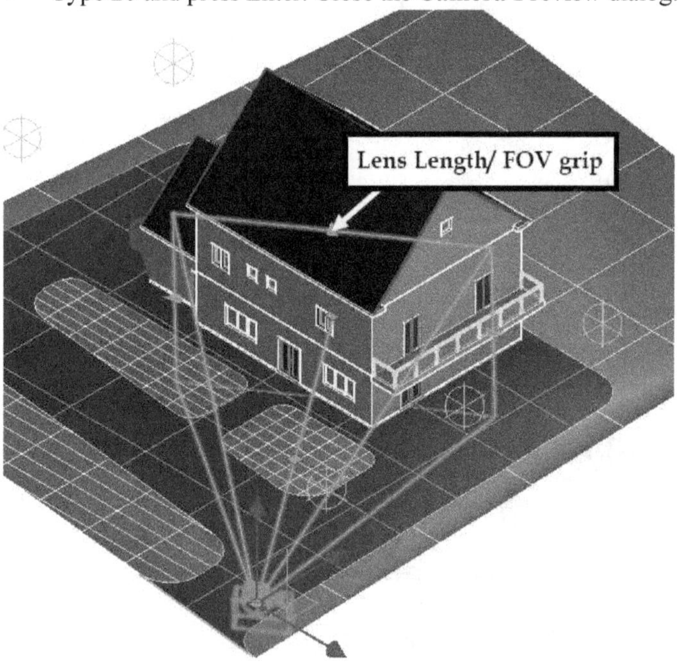

- Save the model.

Tutorial 3: Adding Lights

AutoCAD has a default lighting system in the model space. However, you can add new lights to the model. AutoCAD allows you to create four types of lights. Note that you need to turn off the default lighting to view the effect of the user-defined lights. To do so, expand the **Lights** panel and deactivate the **Default Lighting** icon. These lights are discussed next.

Point Light: The point light emits light in all directions from the location.

Spot light: Spotlights are similar to the directional lights. However, they create brighter and sharp lights targeting a specific area.

Distant Light: The distance light emits light rays that are parallel to each other.

Weblight: Weblight can be used to create lights based on the data from the light manufacturers. They give a precise output similar to the real-world lights. The data from the light manufacturers is provided in the IES format. The system computes the luminous intensity and direction of light using the data.

- Select **View Controls > Top** from the In-Canvas controls.
- On the **Visualize** tab of the ribbon, expand the **Lights** panel and deactivate the **Default Lighting** tool.
- On the **Visualize** tab of the ribbon, in the **Sun & Location** panel, click **Sun Properties** (Inclined arrow). On the **Sun Properties** palette, under the **Sun Angle Calculator** section, set the **Date** to 6/21/2022 and the **Time** to 11:00 AM.
- Under the **Sky Properties** section, change the **Intensity Factor** to 2.
- On the **Visualize** tab of the ribbon, expand the **Sun & Location** panel and select **Set Location > From Map** ; the **Geolocation – Online Map Data dialog** appears. Click **Yes** on the dialog; the **Autodesk – Sign In** dialog appears, if you are not logged into your Autodesk account. Sign in to your **Autodesk** account; the **Geographic location – Specify Location** dialog appears.
- Type 41.273656, -96.207061 in the **Address** box, and then press Enter. Click the **Drop Marker Here** button, and then click **Next**; the **Geographic location – Set Coordinate System** page appears. Type 32165 in the search box and select the **BLM - 15** coordinate system. Click **Next.**

Tip: You can find the coordinate system closest to the site location by visiting www.epsg.io and typing the location address in the search bar.

- Select the lower left corner point of the house to define the location. Turn off the Ortho Mode. Move the pointer upward and click to define the north, as shown.

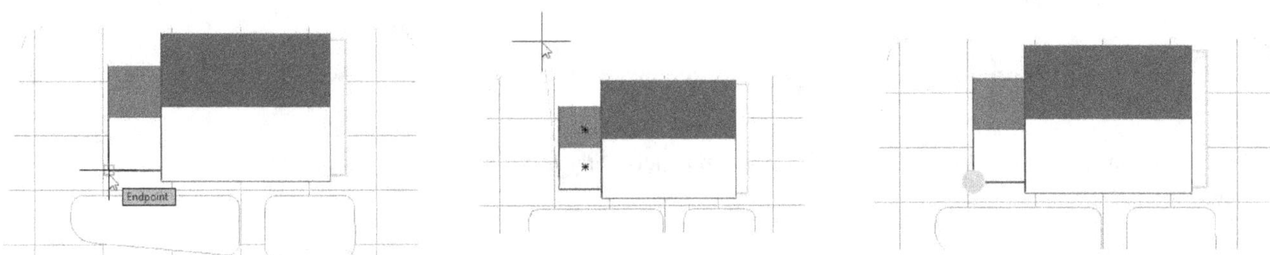

The **Geolocation** tab is added to the ribbon. You can use the tools on this tab to edit or remove the location, change its orientation, turn on/off the map, and so on.

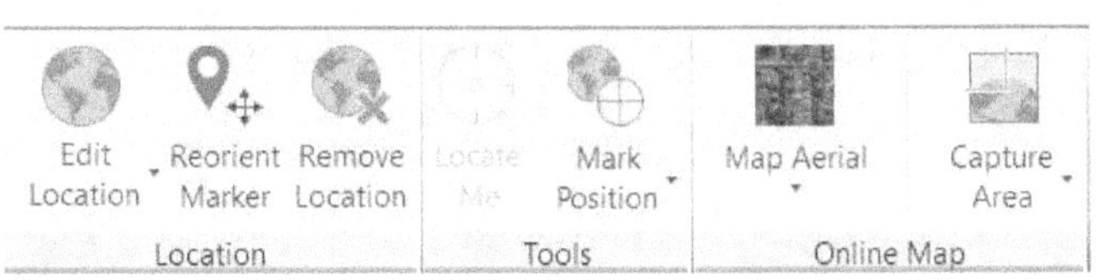

- Select **View Controls > Custom Model Views > Southeast Camera** from the In-Canvas controls.

- On the **Geolocation** tab of the ribbon, click the **Reorient Marker** tool. Select the corner point of the house, as shown. Press Enter to accept the earlier value of the North direction.

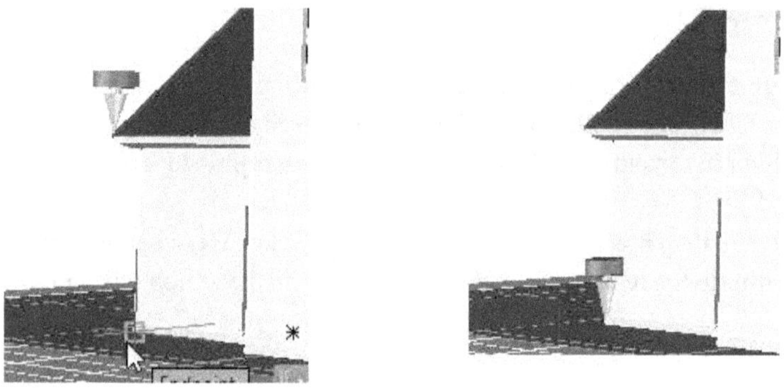

- On the ribbon, click **Visualize** tab > **Sun & Location** panel > **Sun Status** ; the **Lighting – Sunlight and Exposure** dialog appears. Select **Adjust exposure settings** from the dialog; the **Render Environment and Exposure** palette appears.
- On the **Render Environment and Exposure** palette, adjust the **Exposure** and **White Balance** values to 12 and 5500, respectively. Close the palette.
- On the ribbon, click **Visualize** tab > **Lights** panel > **Shadows** drop-down > **Full Shadows** .
- On the ribbon, click **Visualize** tab > **Sun & Location** panel > **Sky** drop-down > **Sky Background** .
- Save the model.

Tutorial 4: Rendering

Rendering is the process of generating Photorealistic images and videos.

- On the ribbon, click **Visualize** tab > **Render** panel > **Render to Size** . The **Render** Window appears, as shown. You can zoom in or zoom out of the image using the mouse. You can abort the rendering process by clicking the **Cancel rendering** icon.

- Close the **Render window** after completing the rendering.
- Select **View Controls > SE Isometric** from the In-Canvas controls.
- On the ribbon, click **Visualize** tab > **Lights** panel > **Create Light** drop-down > **Point** . Select the point of the planar surface, as shown. Select **Intensity factor** from the command line. Type 60 and press Enter. Select **eXit**.

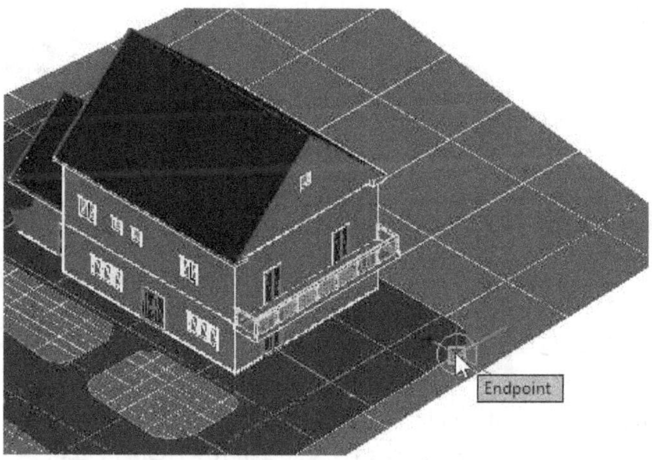

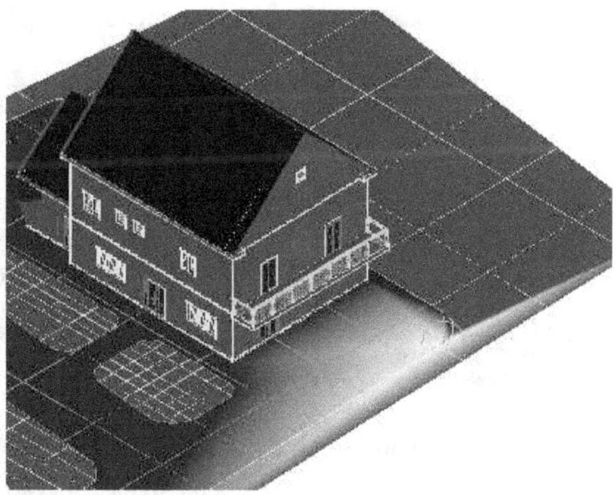

- Select the point light from the model space. On the ribbon, click **Home** tab > **Modify** panel > **Array** drop-down > **Rectangular Array**. On the **Array Creation** tab, change the **Columns** and **Rows** value to 1 and 3, respectively. Change the **Between** value on the **Rows** panel to -472. Click the **Associative** button on the **Properties** panel, and then click **Close Array**.

- Select the rectangular array, click on the Z-axis of the move gizmo, and move the pointer upward. Type 240 and press Enter.

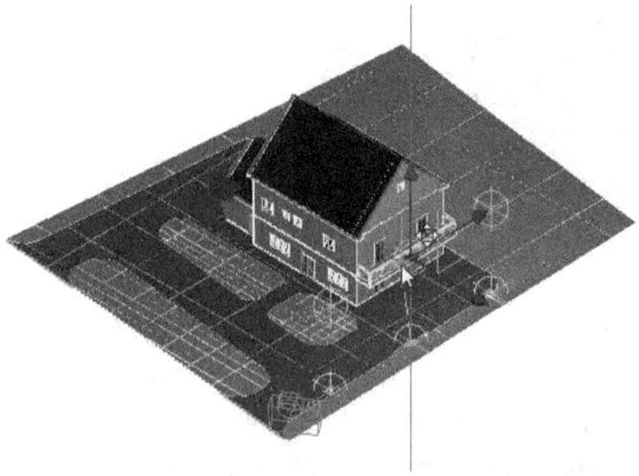 

- Create another point light on the other side of the house. Create a line on the planar edge, and then create the path array of point lights. Move the path array up to 240 inches upward.

- Select **View Controls > Custom Model Views > Southeast Camera** from the In-Canvas controls.
- On the **Visualize** tab of the ribbon, in the **Sun & Location** panel, click **Sun Properties** (Inclined arrow). On the **Sun Properties** palette, under the **Sun Angle Calculator** section, set the Date to 6/21/2021 and the **Time** to 21:00.
- On the ribbon, click **Visualize** tab > **Sun & Location** panel > **Sky** drop-down > **Sky Background and Illumination** .
- On the ribbon, click **Visualize** tab > **Render** panel > **Render to Size** drop-down > **3300 x 2550 px (11 x 8.5 @ 300 dpi)**.
- On the **Render** panel, click **Render Preset** drop-down > **High**. Also, select **Render in Window** from the **Render in** drop-down.

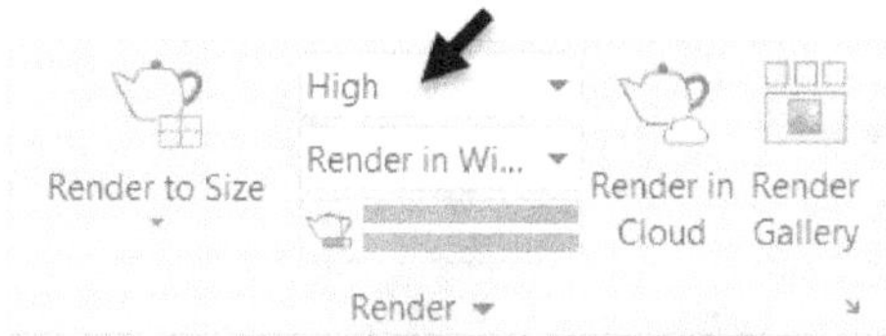

- On the **Render** panel, click **Render to Size** to start the rendering.
- Click **Saves the rendered image** to file on the Render window. Go to a location on the drive and select **JPEG (*.jpeg; *.jpg)** from the **Files of type** drop-down. Type the name of the file, and then click **Save.** On the **JPG Image Options** dialog, set the **Quality** value to 100, and then click **OK**.

- Save and close the drawing file.

Tutorial 5: Preparing Files for 3D Printing

In this tutorial, you prepare the 3D model for 3D printing.

- Download and open the 3D_Printing.dwg file.
- On the ribbon, click **Home > Coordinates > UCS, World** ; the XY Plane of the UCS is parallel to the ground plane.
- On the ribbon, click **Home** > **Layers** > **Freeze** , and then select roof and walls on the first floor. Press Esc to deactivate the command.

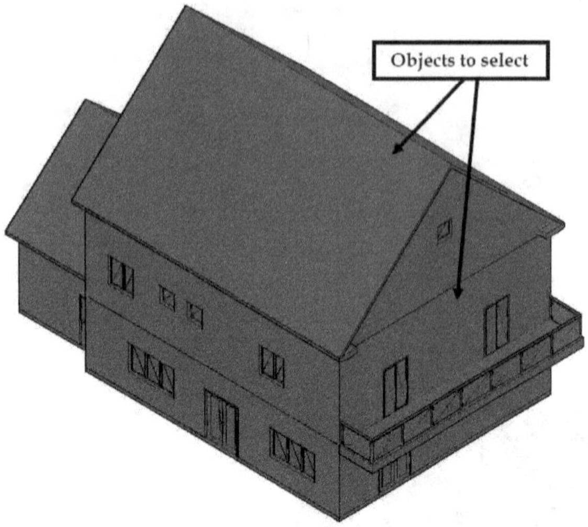

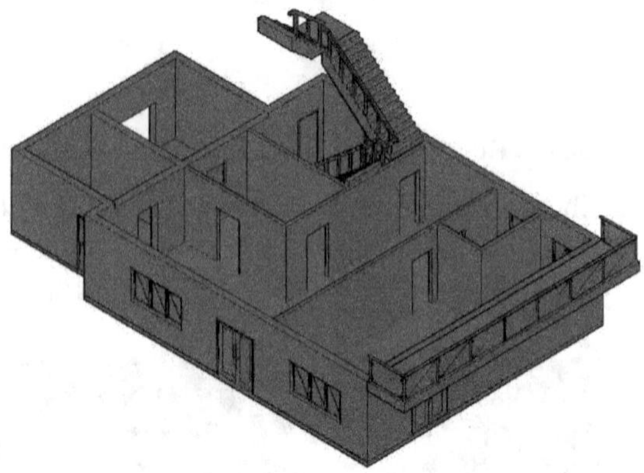

- On the Application Menu, click **Print > 3D Print** ; the **3D Printing – Prepare Model for Printing** message box appears. Click **Continue** on the message box.
- Draw a selection window across all the objects of the 3D model, and then press Enter; the **3D Print Options** dialog appears. Type **0.01** in the **Scale** box. Next, leave the default values on this dialog, and then click **OK**.

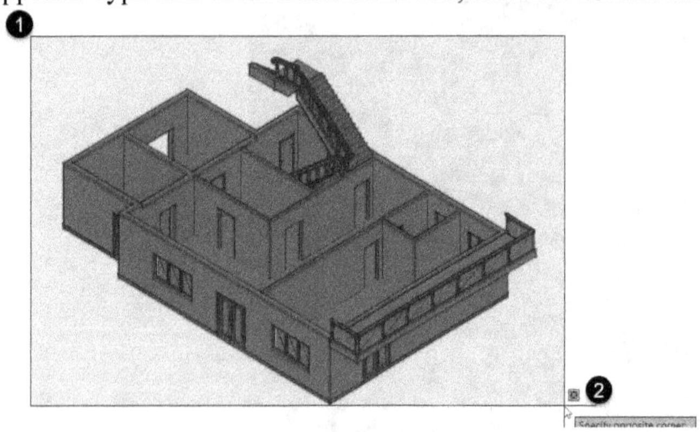

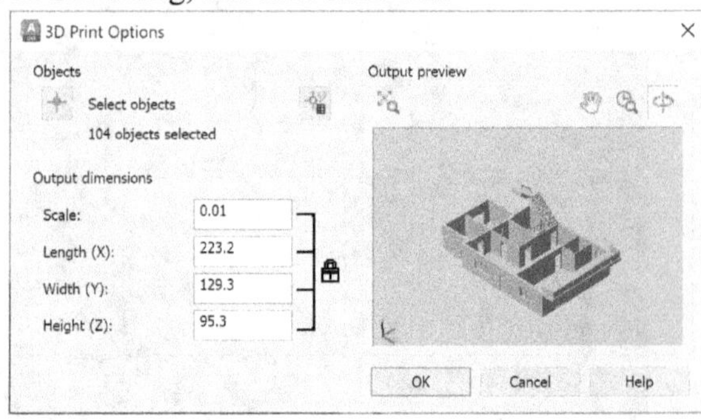

- Specify the location of the output file, type Ground_level in the **File name** box, and then click **Save**; the output is saved in the .stl format.

  Next, you need to print the first level.
- On the ribbon, click **Home > Layers > Layers** drop-down, and then click the **Freeze or thaw in All Viewports** icon next to the First Level layer. Next, freeze the Ground Level layer by clicking on the **Freeze or thaw in All Viewports** icon next to it.

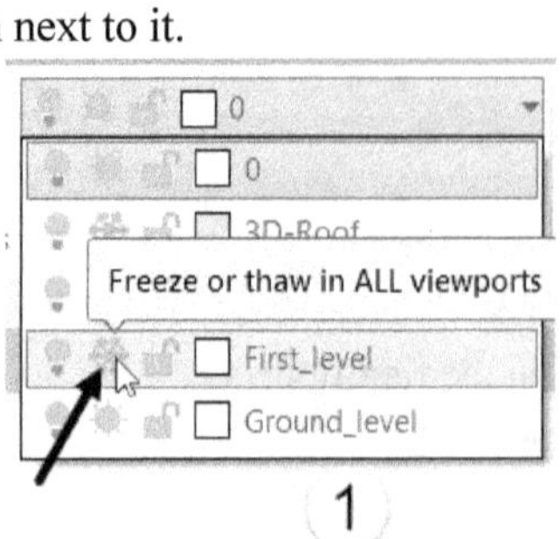

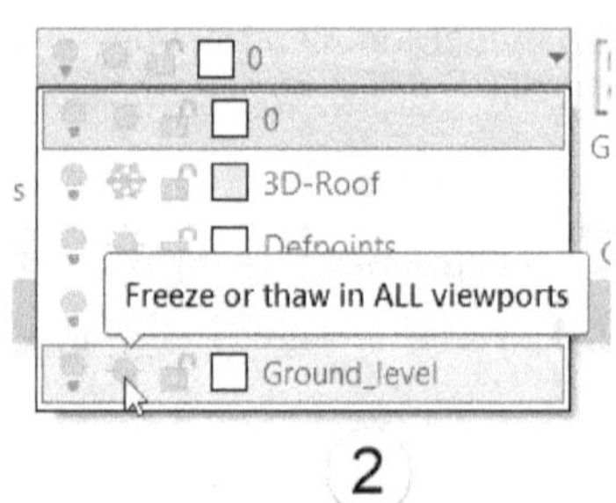

- On the Application Menu, click **Print > 3D Print** and then click **Continue** on the **3D Printing – PrepareModel for Printing** message box.

- Drag a selection window across all the objects of the first level, and then press Enter.

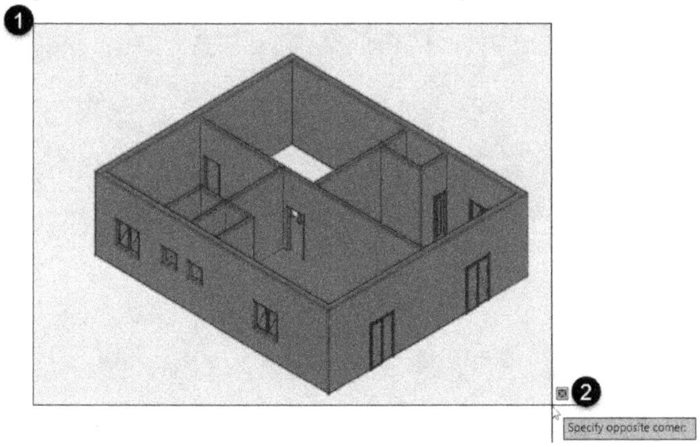

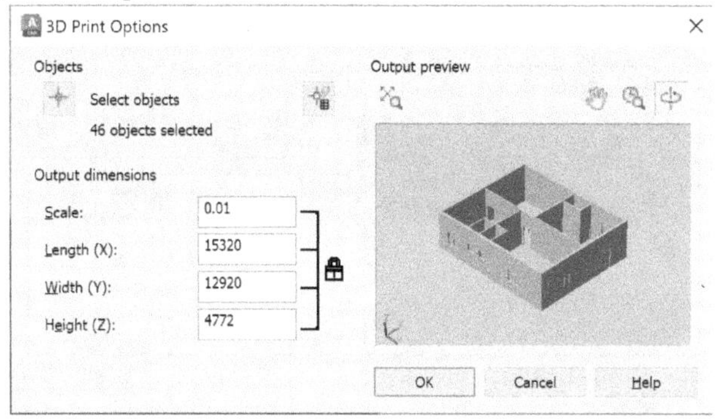

- Next, type 0.01 in the **Scale** box and then click **OK**.
- Type First_level in the **File name** box and click **Save**.
- Freeze the Ground_level and First_level layers, and then export the roof.

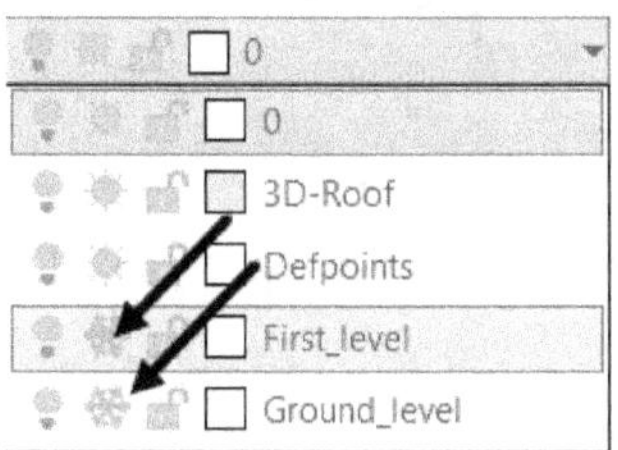

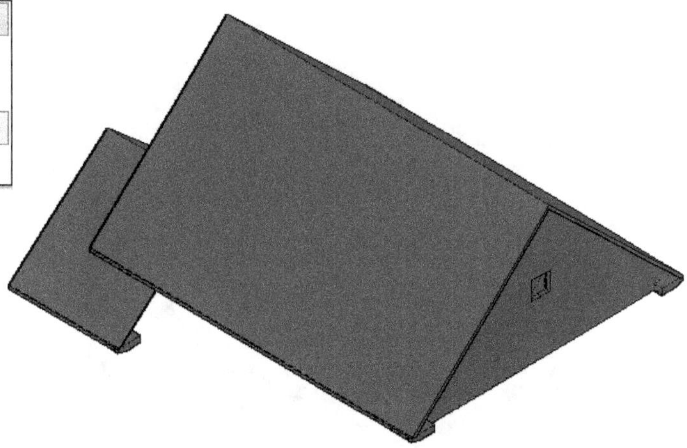

Now, the output files are ready to be opened in the 3D printer application provided by the 3D printer manufacturer.

www.ingramcontent.com/pod-product-compliance
Lightning Source LLC
LaVergne TN
LVHW080041210926
848481LV00011B/3253